Preface

The aim of this work is to offer intermediate and advanced English-speaking students, e.g. pre-university and university students, teachers, translators and self-taught students, a reasonably detailed account of the morphology and syntax of the Spanish of educated conversation and plain prose in Spain and Latin America in the late twentieth century.

Spanish is the main, usually the sole official language of no less than twenty countries, and it thus compares with English as one of the most widely spoken languages in the world. This fact raises severe problems for lexicographers and grammarians. It is relatively easy to lay down the law in a grammar or dictionary of French or German, both comparatively standardized languages in the sense that over the centuries powerful élites have imposed their own linguistic habits as the criteria of 'correct' usage and so ensured that the boundaries between standard and substandard or dialectal usage are pretty clearly drawn. English is less standardized, but most of the English-speaking world defers to received ('BBC') British or standard American practice on most questions, and the essential unity of the language is guaranteed partly by the wealth and prestige of British and American literature, but above all by the flood of films from the United States which continues to Americanize the vocabulary and structures (much less the pronunciation) of English everywhere to a greater extent than most speakers realize.

Spanish is a good deal less unified than these languages. There was an age – it seems to have ended some time in the 1960s – when the criteria of internationally 'correct' Spanish were dictated by the *Real Academia Española*, but the prestige of this institution has now sunk so low that its most solemn decrees are either ignored or only fitfully applied – witness the fate of the spelling reforms expounded in the *Nuevas normas de prosodia y ortografía* which were made prescriptive in 1959 and are still in 1987 only selectively observed in print and are ignored or misunderstood by literate persons everywhere. The fact is that in Spanish 'correctness' is nowadays determined – as in most languages – by majority educated usage and taste, but consensus about educated usage is obviously elusive in a language spoken in twenty independent, widely scattered and sometimes mutually hostile countries.

Peninsular Spanish itself is to some extent in flux. Recent years have seen a democratization of grammar and vocabulary as well as of politics: the Latinate literary language of the old Establishment has yielded to a standard loosely based on the speech of the new urban middle classes of the Madrid region, but this evolution is resisted by purists and disputes about what constitutes 'good' Spanish are numerous and acrimonious. But it is above all the variety, vigour and rising prestige of Latin-American Spanish that complicates the task of compilers of dictionaries or grammars. Spanish is still obviously one language in the sense that anyone who knows it well can travel the Spanish-speaking world without excessive problems of intelligibility as far as written and educated spoken language is concerned. But *at the level of detail*, i.e. at the level at which advanced textbooks must work, Spanish is characterized by regional and national variations of vocabulary and to a much lesser extent syntax that can be very disconcerting, especially when it comes to trying to define for a foreign student what constitutes 'correct' Spanish. The day is (or ought to be) long past when one could claim or imply that the only type of Spanish worthy of formal description and study is the dialect of Northern and Central Spain ('standard' Castilian), which is after all the language of only about eight per cent of the Spanish-speaking world. Spain is no longer in any sense the literary, cultural or linguistic centre of the Hispanic world and its modern literature attracts little attention in Latin America. But no other Spanish-speaking country has taken over the place Spain once held, and there is now no single identifiable Hispanic cultural or linguistic centre but rather a number of competing, equally powerful and widely separated centres. Nor is it conceivable that any one Spanish-speaking country or region will, in the foreseeable future, emerge to impose linguistic standards in Spanish in the way that the USA will continue to do in the case of English.

This problem of diversity need not trouble the beginner who is struggling with the basic grammar and vocabulary of the language, but it grows more acute as one advances beyond the intermediate level. It disheartens a foreign student to find that *Collins Spanish-English English-Spanish* dictionary gives twelve different national Latin-American meanings for the word *chiva* including 'goat', 'sheep', 'goatee', 'bus', 'car', 'blanket', 'naughty girl', 'immoral woman' and 'knapsack'. The dimensions of the problem become clearer when one reads such headlines in a popular Peruvian daily as *Choros chupan tres palos a Cristal* ('thieves steal three million *soles* from Crystal Brewery') or *Lorchos datean que los afilaron tres años* ('Peruvians claim they were trained for three years'), language that mystifies Argentines and Mexicans as much as Spaniards. And the problem of variety must frequently perplex the fair-minded grammarian who can no more denounce as 'incorrect' a typical Latin-American sentence like *es con ella que quiero hablar* ('it's her that I want to talk to': Spaniards usually insist on *es con ella con la que quiero hablar*), than assert that *dentro de* is the 'correct' Spanish for 'inside' when a writer as famous as Borges uses the (for Spaniards) unacceptable *adentro de*.

Such in themselves minor but cumulatively daunting problems lengthen the task of anyone aspiring to write an objective account of informal, living Spanish. The problem is commonly glossed over in textbooks either by tacitly ignoring the existence of Latin-American Spanish (the solution of not a few British textbooks of Spanish) or by confining one's discussion to a sort of colourless international *lingua franca* such as one finds in *Selecciones del Reader's Digest*, a version of Spanish which, though recognizably Latin-American, is carefully stripped of the colloquialisms and regionalisms that give everyday Spanish its immense vigour and charm.

Neither stratagem will serve in works which, like this one, try to describe Spanish as a living spoken language and also to do justice to its international variety. The approach we have adopted has been to supply many examples from European Spanish, the native language of one of the authors, checked against the reactions of other Peninsular speakers and compared with – though not always judged by – the reactions of as many Latin-American speakers as we could find. In order to counteract the Peninsular bias of this corpus, we have illustrated as many important points as possible with additional examples from well-known Latin-American authors; examples which, except where stated, seem to us also to be good European Spanish and therefore indicative of what one may assume is international Spanish usage. We hope that this method will give readers both a sense of authentic Spanish speech and also a picture of the diversity – and the underlying unity – of a language spoken from the Rio Grande to Patagonia as well as in Spain. Despite this, it is certain that some of our everyday Peninsular examples will amuse or even exasperate readers from the Americas, especially in view of the fact that linguistic relations between Spain and her ex-colonies are not always cordial . . . We apologize for the quaintly European flavour of some of our examples, and we hope that the spirit of this grammar is as international as it can be in the face of the sometimes irreconcilable claims of Argentine, Chilean, Colombian, Cuban, Mexican, Peruvian, European and all the other subtly flavoured national varieties of the language.

These international problems apart, it is clear that Spanish usage is often intrinsically curiously fluid: an example is the *le/lo* controversy that divides the Spanish-speaking world in general and Spain in particular, so that one cannot confidently say without lengthy qualifications what is the correct third-person masculine direct object pronoun (and purists from Spain should recall that the Academy now recommends Latin-American practice on this point). In this and a few other cases we have used a statistical approach based on questionnaires designed simply to give a brief and no doubt quite unscientific indication of the uncertainties of usage even within a fairly clearly defined dialect area.

In the case of quotations in Latin-American Spanish we mention the country of origin of the author. This does not indicate, unless otherwise stated, that the text is local in flavour, but merely shows that the feature under discussion is also current across the Atlantic. Quotations from spoken passages in novels and plays are marked 'dialogue' as a reminder that the language is not the author's but the characters'. The fact that fictional characters may be illiterate does not mean that their utterances are always ill-formed: the dialogue that we quote is, in our judgement and except where described otherwise, typical conversational usage worthy of imitation by foreigners. As far as possible, we indicate whether usage is formal, colloquial, familiar or popular, and it is no doubt the case that foreign students, pending real fluency in the language, should use familiar and, above all, 'popular' forms with caution. It is well known that in any language some things that pass unnoticed in relaxed native speech sound shocking when said with a foreign accent.

Although the language described is usually informal written and spoken Spanish, the approach and terminology of the grammar are conservative and points are often clarified by example rather than by theoretical argument, which is kept to a minimum. The fact that we use traditional terms like 'subject', 'object', 'indirect object', 'demonstratives', etc. does not imply complete ignorance of the unscientific and often arbitrary basis of such labels; but to speak of 'nominals', 'disjuncts', 'deictics' and so on would have frightened off the type of reader we had in mind. Words and constructions are therefore discussed under those headings by which ordinary readers unfamiliar with modern linguistic terms will most easily recognize them.

Examples of written language come from texts published since the 1960s, many of them from the 1980s. There is almost no mention of older forms of Spanish: problems of space have been so severe that historical explanations have – with regret – been omitted. This grammar also concentrates on syntactic and morphological questions, for which reason, and because of problems of space, lexical issues such as word formation and diminutive and other affective suffixes are given very summary treatment and pronunciation rules relegated to a brief appendix. It is assumed that readers have a native knowledge of English and explanations have been drastically shortened by reference to English wherever the languages seem to coincide. Since interference from French, and occasionally Italian and Portuguese, is a perennial problem for teachers of Spanish, sporadic mention of these languages is made in order to emphasize some peculiarity of Spanish.

Acknowledgments

Like everyone who works in the field we are indebted to the labours of Andrés Bello, María Moliner, Manuel Seco, Ramsey and Spaulding and other eminent grammarians and lexicographers. The chapter on personal pronouns owes much to E. García's interesting *The Role of Theory in*

Linguistic Analysis: the Spanish Pronoun System (Amsterdam/Oxford 1975), and we often quote from C.E. Kany's invaluable *Spanish-American Syntax* (Chicago 1945, reprinted and translated into Spanish). Three other works often supplied information, explanations and insights: *A Grammar of Contemporary English* by R. Quirk, S. Greenbaum, G. Leech and J. Svartvik (London 1972), *A Reference Grammar of Modern French* by A. Judge and F.G. Healey (London 1983), and especially *German Grammar and Usage* by A.E. Hammer (London 1971), perusal of which originally inspired the present work.

A very large number of Spanish speakers from many countries have helped us and we cannot name them all. Our sincere thanks go to every one: without them we could not have finished. We are, however, heavily indebted to Antonia Moreira Ahmed and María Álvarez for their thoughtful opinions on Peninsular usage; to Sheila Hague for her valuable criticisms of the proofs; to Lynn Ingamells of Queen Mary College London who generously read and commented on the manuscript; to Steve Jones, whose knowledge of Spanish and several other languages and quick grasp of linguistic arguments have constantly illuminated difficult points; to his Colombian wife Candy whose protests often reminded us that Peninsular Spanish is but one variety among many, and to Professor Alan Paterson of the University of St Andrews whose kind words of encouragement raised morale at critical moments more, perhaps, than he realized.

Despite all this invaluable assistance we are acutely aware that a book of this nature must contain mistakes, omissions and inaccuracies for which we alone assume entire responsibility.

John Butt
Carmen Benjamin

King's College,
London

Conventions, spelling and abbreviations

Tú fuistes, *habían muchos*: an asterisk denotes a form rejected by educated speakers and to be avoided by learners.

?*Se puso detrás mío*, ?*daros la mano*: an initial uninverted question mark shows that the form is not accepted by all speakers.

'Colloquial' describes forms which are accepted in spontaneous educated speech, but usually avoided in writing or formal speech, e.g. *si tuviera dinero, me compraba un piso* for *me compraría un piso*.

'Familiar' describes forms common in very informal speech, but to be used cautiously by a foreign student of the language.

'Popular' describes forms which are commonly heard but may be stigmatized as uneducated by some speakers.

Forms separated by / are alternatives, e.g. *sin que yo viera/viese*. Alternatives are shown to remind the reader of possibilities which are often neglected, but by no means all alternative forms are systematically marked.

Words in round brackets may be optionally deleted with no or only slight effect on the meaning or style of the original, e.g. *con tal (de) que* 'provided that'.

Obvious Europeanisms, e.g. *fontanero* for *plomero* 'plumber', *acera* for *vereda* 'pavement' are occasionally noted with their Spanish-American equivalent, but in general no attempt has been made to Americanize the vocabulary of unattributed examples.

In the case of quotations from Spanish-American writers the author's country of origin is noted. This indicates that a form is also current in that country or region as well as in Spain, but it must not be taken to imply – except where noted – that the language of the quotation is local in flavour. Spanish-American quotations have usually been chosen as examples of more or less universal usage, and they may indeed have been 'normalized' by editors or publishers, especially if the text was published in Spain.

Where an extract is taken from conversation in a novel it is marked as 'dialogue'. Except where indicated, this means that the quotation is in our judgement typical educated spoken Spanish worthy of imitation by a foreign learner. The fact that the novel may be popular in tone or the character illiterate does not mean that the particular quotation is ill-formed.

The spelling of Spanish words follows the Academy's *Nuevas normas*, which came into force in 1959 and are now usually followed by editors in all Hispanic countries. In the case of the word *sólo* and of the demonstrative pronouns (*éste, ése, aquél*) we have however followed what seems to be the current practice of good editors, i.e. we generally retain the accent where it was used before 1959, though in a few doubtful cases we omit it. In its wisdom, the Academy made the use of the accent on these words obligatory only where real ambiguity arises, with the result that most people seem more confused than ever on the subject.

The English used throughout is British in spelling and idiom. The translations of the Spanish quotations are sometimes deliberately literal, and have no literary pretensions.

Grammar books systematically falsify language by being obliged to quote brief sentences out of context. Even the most ambiguous sentences, e.g. 'flying planes can be dangerous', 'she saw her looking at her' are virtually never ambiguous when uttered in a context established by previous conversation, intonation, gesture, facial expression, the identity of the speaker and hearer, etc., but printed in isolation many apparently clear sentences become a rich source of philosophical and linguistic conundrums. This problem is especially acute in a language like Spanish which does not systematically mark sex, number or person in its pronouns and verbs. Thus *viene*, in the absence of further clues, means 'he's coming', 'it's coming', 'she's coming', 'you're coming'; *se lo daba* may mean 'I gave it to him', 'I gave it to her', 'I gave it to you', 'I gave it to them' (masc. or fem.) or 'I gave it to you' (*ustedes*), 'he gave it to him', 'he gave it to her', 'she gave it to you', 'you gave it to them', and all the other combinations. To translate such sentences always by the third-person masculine is arbitrary, misleading and possibly shows sexual bias; but to indicate systematically every possibility would be tedious. The masculine singular has generally been preferred in this work, but from time to time alternatives are shown, or the feminine form has been used in English if only to recall that a native speaker does not automatically form a mental picture of a male subject on hearing the word *tosió* 'she/you/he/it coughed', and that, out of context, there is no special reason for translating *habla ruso* as 'he speaks Russian' rather than 'you speak Russian' or 'she speaks Russian'.

The following abbreviations are used:

Arg.	Argentina, Argentine
Col.	Colombia(n)
dial.	dialogue
Esbozo	Real Academia Española, *Esbozo de una nueva gramática de la lengua española* (1973)
Fr.	French
Ger.	German
It.	Italian

lit.	literally, literal translation
Mex.	Mexico, Mexican
Nuevas normas	Real Academia Española, *Nuevas normas de prosodia y ortografía. Nuevo texto definitivo* (1959)
Port.	Portuguese
SA	Spanish America(n)
S. Cone	Southern Cone, i.e. Argentina, Chile, Uruguay, Paraguay
Var.	L. Ingamells & P. Standish, *Variedades del español actual* (1975)

We follow the practice of some Spanish publishers in acknowledging the Italian descent of the Argentine novelist Ernesto Sabato by printing his surname with no accent, but it is pronounced and often written Sábato.

The spellings *México, mexicano* are used for the older *Méjico, mejicano* on the grounds that they are encouraged by the Mexicans themselves and are increasingly used in all Spanish-speaking countries.

Spanish-speaking Latin Americans take understandable exception to the terms 'Hispanic' and 'Spanish America(n)', just as citizens of the USA would no doubt object to being called 'British Americans'. 'Latin America(n)' is, however, grossly inaccurate as a linguistic description since it includes Brazil and, presumably, Haiti and other French-speaking countries of the Americas. The terms Spanish America(n) and Hispanic are used in the present work in a purely linguistic sense, without cultural or political overtones.

Select bibliography

(Includes only works cited in the text and books, not articles, likely to be of use to advanced students. A number of rather technical works have been omitted.)

ABAD NEBOT, F. 1977: *El artículo: sistema y usos*

ALARCOS LLORACH, E. 1970: *Estudios de gramática funcional del español*

ALCINA FRANCH, J. and BLECUA, J.M. 1975: *Gramática española*

ALONSO, A. and UREÑA, P. 1957: *Gramática castellana*

ALONSO, M. 1962: *Evolución sintáctica del español*

BEINHAUER, W. 1973: *El español coloquial*, 2nd revised Spanish ed.

BELLO, A. and CUERVO, R. 1960: *Gramática de la lengua castellana*, 6th ed.

BOSQUE, I. 1980: *Sobre la negación*

CANO AGUILAR, R. 1981: *Estructuras sintácticas transitivas en el español actual*

CARNICER, R. 1969: *Sobre el lenguaje de hoy*

—— 1972: *Nuevas reflexiones sobre el lenguaje*

—— 1977: *Tradición y evolución en el lenguaje actual*

CARRATALÁ, E. 1980: *Morfosintaxis del castellano actual*

CRIADO de VAL, M. 1958: *Gramática española*

FENTE GÓMEZ, R. 1971: *Estilística del verbo en inglés y español*

—— with FERNÁNDEZ, J. & FEIJOO, J. 1972: *Perífrasis verbales*

—— 1976: *El subjuntivo*, 3rd ed.

FERNÁNDEZ, S. 1951: *Gramática española* vol. I. (Phonology, Nouns & Pronouns).

GARCÍA, E. 1975: *The Role of Theory in Linguistic Analysis: The Spanish Pronoun System*

GILI y GAYA, S. 1972: *Estudios de lenguaje infantil*

—— 1979: *Curso superior de sintaxis española*, 12th ed.

HARMER, L.C. and NORTON, F.J. 1957: *A Manual of Modern Spanish*, 2nd edition. (This is basically the 1935 edition with updates, including modernized spelling. Silent on many points, as befits what is essentially a basic course in Spanish)

IANNUCCI, J.E. 1952: *Lexical Number in Spanish Nouns with Reference to their English Equivalents*

KANY, C.E. 1951: *American Spanish Syntax*, 2nd ed. (Provides copious examples, but does not reliably indicate register: many of the examples may be substandard. There is a Spanish translation).

LAMÍQUIZ, V. 1982: *El sistema verbal español*

LINCOLN CANFIELD, D. 1981: *Spanish Pronunciation in the Americas*

LORENZO, E. 1971: *El español de hoy, lengua en ebullición*, 2nd ed.

LUJÁN, M. 1980: *Sintaxis y semántica del adjetivo*

LUQUE DURÁN, J.D. 1976: *Las preposiciones*, 2nd ed. 2 vols.

—— 1977: *Ser y estar*

LUZ GUTIÉRREZ, M. 1978: *Estructuras sintácticas del español actual*

MACPHERSON, I.R. 1975: *Spanish Phonology: Descriptive and Historical*

MANTECA ALONSO CORTÉS, A. 1981: *Gramática del subjuntivo*

MARCOS MARÍN, F. 1978: *Estudios sobre el pronombre*

MARSÁ, F. 1984: *Cuestiones de sintaxis española*

—— 1986: *Diccionario normativo y guía práctica de la lengua española*

MARTÍN ZORRAQUINO, M.A. 1979: *Las construcciones pronominales en español*

MARTÍNEZ AMADOR, E.M. 1982: *Diccionario gramatical y de dudas del idioma*

MARTÍNEZ de SOUSA, J. 1977: *Dudas y errores de lenguaje* 2nd ed.

MOLINA REDONDO, J. 1974: *Usos de 'se'*. An excellent brief survey of this thorny problem.

MOLINER, M. 1966: *Diccionario de uso del español*. 2 vols. An invaluable albeit unwieldy reference manual. Few Latin-American examples.

NASH, R., ed. 1973—: *Readings in Spanish-English Contrastive Linguistics*

NAVAS RUIZ, R. 1963: *Ser y estar*

RAMSEY, M. and SPAULDING, J.K. 1965: *A Textbook of Modern Spanish* Originally composed by Ramsey in the early 1890s and extensively revised by Spaulding in the 1940s. Remarkably thorough but the examples are now dated.

REAL ACADEMIA ESPAÑOLA, 1931: *Gramática de la lengua española*

—— 1952: *Nuevas normas de prosodia y ortografía* (made prescriptive in 1959)

—— 1973: *Esbozo de una nueva gramática de la lengua española* (a sketch for a new Academy grammar that is still awaited)

ROCA PONS, J. 1958: *Estudios sobre perífrasis verbales del español*

ROSENBLAT, A. 1971: *Nuestra lengua entre dos mundos*

SAGUES SUBIJANA, M. 1983: *Manual de gramática española*

SECO, M. 1986: *Diccionario de dudas y dificultades de la lengua española*, 9th revised edition. Seco is the Spanish Fowler: he may be reliably consulted on most syntactical and lexical questions. Progressive and comprehensive; sensitive to Latin-American usage.

SECO, R. 1967: *Manual de gramática española*. Revised and expanded by M. Seco. 9th ed.

SMITH, C. ed. 1971: *Collins Spanish-English English-Spanish Dictionary*. Rich in examples and Latin-American usage. An expanded edition is expected in 1988.

STEEL, B. 1976: *Manual of Colloquial Spanish*

STOCKWELL, R., BOWEN, J. and MARTIN, J. 1965: *The Grammatical Structures of English and Spanish*

VIGARA TAUSTE, M. 1980: *Aspectos del español hablado*

Main sources

Many of the unattributed examples in the text are simplified, abbreviated or otherwise modified phrases and sentences from a wide range of modern texts, both fiction and non-fiction. The following works in particular have supplied a number of attributed examples, chiefly on the grounds that they provided instances of usage that avoided extremes of colloquialism, archaicism or literary sophistication or because they contained examples of conversational usage typical of both continents:

ABC (daily newspaper, Seville)

ALDECOA, I. (Spain) *Cuentos completos*

BORGES, J.L. (Argentina) *Obras completas*

BUERO VALLEJO, A. (Spain) *Irene o el tesoro*
  En la ardiente oscuridad
  Hoy es fiesta
  Historia de una escalera

Cambio16 (weekly magazine, Madrid)

CORTÁZAR, J. (Argentina) *Bestiario*
  Final de juego
  Las armas secretas
  Rayuela
  Argentina

CABRERA INFANTE, G. (Cuba) *Tres tristes tigres*

DONOSO, J. (Chile) *Casa de campo*
FUENTES, C. (Mexico) *La muerte de Artemio Cruz*
   Aura
   La cabeza de la hidra
GARCÍA MÁRQUEZ, G. (Colombia) *El coronel no tiene quien le escriba*
   Cien años de soledad
   Crónica de una muerte anunciada
   El amor en los tiempos del cólera
GOYTISOLO, L. (Spain) *Recuento*
INGAMELLS, L. and STANDISH, P. 1975: *Variedades del español actual.* A useful anthology of Spanish texts from all the major Spanish-speaking countries.
MARSÉ, J. (Spain) *Si te dicen que caí*
   La muchacha de las bragas de oro
La Nación (daily newspaper, Buenos Aires)
El País (daily newspaper, Madrid)
PUIG, M. (Argentina) *La traición de Rita Hayworth*
   El beso de la mujer araña
   Pubis angelical
SABATO, E. (Argentina) *El túnel*
   Sobre héroes y tumbas
SASTRE, A. (Spain) *Teatro político*
El Tiempo (daily newspaper, Bogota)
Triunfo (weekly magazine, Madrid, now defunct)
La Vanguardia (daily newspaper, Barcelona)
VARGAS LLOSA, M. (Peru) *La casa verde*
   Conversación en la catedral
   La tía Julia y el escribidor
   La guerra del fin del mundo
   Historia de Mayta
   ¿Quién mató a Palomino Molero?
   Contra viento y marea

1 Gender of nouns

It is useful, in discussing the gender of Spanish nouns, to distinguish between nouns which refer to human beings and higher animals, and nouns referring to inanimate things or lower animals.

1.1 Nouns referring to human beings and higher animals

Nouns referring to male human beings or to the male of the higher animals – lions, tigers, horses, cows, dogs, etc. – are almost always masculine, and females are feminine.

This remark is not as obvious as it seems: the gender of animate nouns is more biological in Spanish than in French where *le professeur* or *le docteur* can be a woman and *la recrue* may be a man (Spanish *el/la recluta*), or in Italian where a policeman may be *la guardia* (forms like *la recluta, la centinela* used of men are found in Golden-Age Spanish). However, a few Spanish nouns of single fixed gender, e.g. *la víctima, la celebridad* may refer to males or females: see 1.1.11 for a selection.

1.1.1 Special forms for male and female

Some nouns have special forms for the male and female which must be learned separately. The following list is not exhaustive:

el abad	*la abadesa*	abbot/abbess
el actor	*la actriz*	actor/actress
el barón	*la baronesa*	baron/baroness
el caballo	*la yegua*	stallion/mare
el carnero	*la oveja*†	ram/ewe
el conde	*la condesa*	count/countess
el duque	*la duquesa*	duke/duchess
el emperador	*la emperatriz*	emperor/empress
el gallo	*la gallina*†	cockerel/hen
el héroe	*la heroína*	hero/heroine (or heroin)
el marido	*la mujer*	husband/wife (or woman)
el padre	*la madre*	father/mother
el príncipe	*la princesa*	prince/princess
el rey	*la reina*	king/queen
el toro	*la vaca*	bull/cow
el yerno	*la nuera*	son-in-law/ daughter-in-law

el varón	la hembra	male/female
(el macho)		
el zar	la zarina	tsar/tsarina

Note Daggers (†) mark a feminine form which is also used for the species in general. Usually the masculine is the generic form: *los caballos* = 'horses' as well as 'stallions'.

1.1.2 Feminine of nouns ending in -*o*
The great majority make their feminine in -*a*:

el abuelo	la abuela	grandfather/grandmother
el amigo	la amiga	friend
el gato	la gata	cat
el hermano	la hermana	brother/sister
el tío	la tía	uncle/aunt
etc.		

Some words denoting professions or activities are invariable:

el/la piloto	pilot/racing driver
el/la modelo	model
el/la reo	accused (in court)
el/la soprano	soprano
el/la testigo	witness

Others, like *el médico* or *el catedrático* are controversial. See 1.1.7 for a discussion.

1.1.3 Feminine of nouns ending in -*or*, -*ón*, -*ín*, -*és*
All those ending in -*or*, -*ón*, *ín* and -*és* make their feminine in -*a*:

el asesor	la asesora	adviser/consultant
el doctor	la doctora	doctor
el profesor	la profesora	teacher
el anfitrión	la anfitriona	host/hostess
el campeón	la campeona	champion
el león	la leona	lion/lioness
el bailarín	la bailarina	dancer
el burgués	la burguesa	bourgeois/bourgeoise
etc.		

Note Adjectives (which in Spanish can almost always double as nouns) ending in -*és* make their feminine in -*a*: *el francés/la francesa* 'Frenchman/Frenchwoman'. The only important adjective in -*és* which does not change in the feminine seems to be *cortés/descortés* 'polite'/'impolite'.

1.1.4 Nouns ending in -*a*
These are invariable:

el/la artista	artist	el/la espía	spy
el/la astronauta	astronaut	el/la guía	guide (la guía also
el/la atleta	athlete		'guide book')
el/la camarada	comrade	el/la nómada	nomad
etc.			

Occasional uneducated masculine forms in -*isto* are heard. *El modisto* 'fashion designer' is accepted in everyday Peninsular usage.

1.1.5 Feminine of nouns ending in *-nte*

The majority are invariable:

el/la adolescente	adolescent	*el/la creyente*	believer
el/la agente	police officer/agent	*el/la descendiente*	descendant
el/la cantante	singer	*el/la representante*	representative

etc.

But some feminine forms in *-nta* are in standard use (at least in Spain: they may be unacceptable in parts of the Americas):

el acompañante/la acompañanta	companion/escort
el asistente/la asistenta	batman/valet/daily help
el comediante/la comedianta	comic actor/actress
el dependiente/la dependienta	shop assistant
el gigante/la giganta	giant
el infante/la infanta	royal prince/princess
el pariente/la parienta	relative ,
el principiante/la principianta	beginner

Note The following also occur, the invariable form being more formal:

el/la asistente social	social worker (also *la asistenta social*)
el/la cliente	customer (familiarly *la clienta*)
el/la presidente	president (also *la presidenta*)

In general, the tendency to form the feminine in *-nta* may spread, although forms like **la estudianta* for *la estudiante* are considered substandard.

1.1.6 Feminine of nouns ending in *-e* or a consonant

Apart from those already mentioned, these are mostly invariable:

el/la alférez	subaltern
el/la enlace	shop steward/union representative
el/la intérprete	interpreter
el/la líder	(political) leader
el/la joven	young man/woman
el/la rehén	hostage
el/la mártir	martyr
el/la médium	(spiritualist) medium
el/la tigre (la tigresa is heard)	tiger

etc.

But *el monje/la monja* 'monk'/'nun', *el sastre/la sastra* 'tailor'. For *la jefa* see 1.1.7.

1.1.7 Feminine of nouns referring to professions

The improving status of women in the Hispanic world has produced linguistic problems since some feminine forms of the professions originally had pejorative or comic overtones or denoted the wife of the male, cf. *el bachiller* (someone who has passed the equivalent of the baccalaureat), *la bachillera* 'blue stocking', *el sargento/la sargenta* 'sergeant'/'battle-axe' (i.e. a fierce woman), *el general/la generala* 'general'/'the general's wife'. Consequently formal language tends to make nouns ending in *-o* which denote professions invariable: *el/la abogado* 'lawyer' (counsel) (*la*

abogada, originally 'intercessionary saint', is widespread in SA); *el/la catedrático* 'professor' (*la catedrática* is gaining ground); *el/la médico* doctor (*la médica* is spreading, but may sound comical); *el/la miembro* 'member' (of clubs: *el socio* is said of men and sometimes even of women, but *la socia* may mean 'prostitute').

El/la ministro 'minister' is common, but *la ministra* is increasingly acceptable. Both *la primer ministro* and *la primera ministra* are used for the feminine of *el primer ministro* 'prime minister'. The former is more common, though *El País* writes *la primera ministra*, which logically ought to mean 'the first of the women ministers'.

In some circles in SA *la jefa* is an accepted feminine of *el/la jefe* 'boss', but it may sound comical in Spain though its use is increasing.

Other nouns in *-o* may be regular: *el arquitecto/la arquitecta* 'architect', *el biólogo/la bióloga* 'biologist', *el filósofo/la filósofa* 'philosopher', *el político/la política* 'politician', *el sociólogo/la socióloga* 'sociologist', etc.

However, forms like *la arquitecto*, *la filósofo* may be preferred and are common in respectful language.

1.1.8 Nouns referring to mixed groups of males and females

With rare exceptions (some noted at 1.1.1), the masculine plural denotes either a group of males, or of males and females:

los ingleses	English men or the English
los niños	little boys or children
los profesores	men teachers, teachers in general
los reyes	kings, or the king(s) and queen(s)
los padres	fathers or parents
los perros	male dogs, or dogs in general

etc.

1.1.9 Gender of inanimate nouns when applied to humans

Feminine nouns applied to male humans may acquire masculine gender:

la cámara	camera	*el cámara*	camera man
la piel	skin	*el piel roja*	redskin
la primera clase	first class	*un primera clase*	someone first-class
la superventa	top sale	*el superventa*	top seller (male)
la trompeta	trumpet	*el trompeta*	trumpet-player

etc.

The reverse case is better avoided: *la que toca la trompeta* 'the woman playing the trumpet', not *la trompeta*, which is the instrument.

1.1.10 Gender of names applied across sex boundaries

A female name applied to a male acquires masculine gender: *tú eres un Margaret Thatcher* 'you're a Margaret Thatcher' (said to a man of his political ideas); but the reverse seems less certain: *María, tú eres otro Ronald Reagan* 'Maria, you're another Ronald Reagan' (but *otra Reagan* is accepted by some).

1.1.11 Nouns of invariable gender applied to either sex

Common examples are:

el ángel	angel
el bebé	baby
la celebridad	celebrity
el desastre	'disaster'
el esperpento	'fright', 'weird-looking person'
la estrella	star (TV, etc.)
el genio	genius
el ligue	'date', casual boy or girlfriend
la persona	person
el personaje	character (in novels, etc.)
la víctima	victim

and a few other words, most involving sexual innuendo or comparisons with objects, cf. *el pendón* 'trollop' (lit. 'pennant'), *el marimacho* 'tomboy', etc.

Note The titles *Alteza, Excelencia, Ilustrísima* (Grace, title of bishops) and *Majestad* are feminine, but the person addressed keeps his/her gender: *Su Majestad estará cansado* (to king), 'Your Majesty must be tired'.

1.2 Gender of nouns referring to lower or less familiar animals

Nouns denoting the lower or less familiar animals are treated as though they referred to inanimates, i.e. the noun is of fixed, arbitrary gender:

el sapo	toad	*el puma*	puma
la araña	spider	*la marsopa*	porpoise
la ardilla	squirrel	*el panda*	panda
la ballena	whale	*la rana*	frog

etc.

If sex must be distinguished, the male is denoted by adding *macho* and the female by adding *hembra*: *la ardilla macho* 'male squirrel', *el cangrejo hembra* 'female crab', etc.

Agreement of adjectives in good Spanish is with the noun, not the animal:

La rana macho está muerta	the male frog is dead
El ratón hembra es blanco	the female mouse is white

Neither *macho* nor *hembra* agrees in gender or number: *las cebras macho* 'male zebras'; *los gavilanes hembra* 'female sparrowhawks'.

Note There is a tendency in familiar language and popular journalism to give such nouns biological gender: *el/la gorila* 'he-gorilla' and 'she-gorilla' (properly invariably *el gorila*), *el/la jirafa* 'giraffe' (*la jirafa* is properly invariably feminine).

1.3 Gender of nouns referring to inanimates (including plants)

The gender must be learned for each noun. The gender of inanimate nouns is arbitrary, usually unpredictable, has no sexual implications and occasionally changes from place to place or century to century. There are few infallible rules, and only those are quoted which in our view do not encourage false generalizations.

Students of other Romance languages should not borrow genders indiscriminately: cf. French *une oasis*, Sp. *un oasis*; Fr. *la fin*, Ital. *la fine*, Sp. *el fin* 'end'; Portuguese *a viagem* (fem.), Sp. *el viaje* 'journey', and countless others.

1.3.1   Masculine by meaning

Many nouns acquire the gender of an underlying or implied noun (metonymic gender). The following are typical:

(a)   Rivers (*el río*): *el Amazonas*, *el Jarama*, *el Manzanares*, *el Plata*, *el Sena*, *el Támesis*, *el Volga*.

Locally some rivers may be feminine, but outsiders rarely know this and the masculine is always correct. Some writers have been known to give foreign rivers the gender of their language of origin, e.g. *la Sena* (*la Seine*), but this sounds affected.

(b)   Mountains, oceans, seas and lakes (*el monte*, *el océano*, *el mar*, *el lago*): *el Etna*, *el Everest*, *el Himalaya* (singular), *el Pacífico*, *el Caribe*, *el Windermere*.

(c)   The names of cars, boats and aircraft (*el coche*, *el barco*, *el avión*): *un Fiesta*, *un Mercedes*, *un haiga* (colloquial Sp., 'flashy car'), *el Queen Elisabeth*, *el Marie Celeste*, *un DC10*, *un Mig 21*. Also *el caza* 'fighter aircraft'. Light aircraft are usually feminine because of the underlying noun *la avioneta*: *una Cessna*.

(d)   Months and days of the week (*los meses y los días de la semana*): *enero/abril pasado*, *el lunes*, *el viernes*.

(e)   Wines (*el vino*): *el Borgoña* 'Burgundy', *el champaña/el champán* 'champagne', *el Chianti*, *un Rioja*.

(f)   Pictures (*el cuadro*) by named artists: *un Constable*, *un Leonardo*, *un Rembrandt*, *un Riley*.

(g)   Sports teams (*el equipo*): *el Barça* 'Barcelona', *el Betis* 'Seville FC'; *el España* 'Spain', *el Bilbao*, etc.

(h)   All infinitives and all words referred to for grammatical or typographical purposes: *el fumar* 'smoking', *el escupir* 'spitting',

quita el «de» y pon un «del»	take out the 'of' and put an 'of the'
(printer talking)	
el «cama» no se lee	you can't read the word 'bed'

(i)   Any adverb, interjection or other genderless word used as a noun: *un algo* 'a "something"', *un no sé qué*, 'a *je ne sais quoi*' (i.e. 'indefinable quality'), *ella está siempre con un «ay»* 'she's always sighing'/'always got troubles'.

(j)   Numbers (*el número*): *un seis*, *un 5*, *la Generación ·del 98* 'Generation of 98', *el dos por ciento* 'two per cent'.

(k)   Musical notes: *el fa*, *el la* (underlying noun unclear).

(l)   Colours (*el color*): *el azul* 'blue', *el rosa* 'pink', *el ocre* 'ochre.'

(m)   Certain trees (*el árbol*) whose fruit is feminine, e.g.

el almendro	*la almendra*	almond
el avellano	*la avellana*	hazel
el castaño	*la castaña*	chestnut
el cerezo	*la cereza*	cherry
el ciruelo	*la ciruela*	plum
el granado	*la granada*	pomegranate
el guindo	*la guinda*	morello cherry
el mandarino	*la mandarina*	tangerine
el manzano	*la manzana*	apple
el naranjo	*la naranja*	orange
el nogal	*la nuez*	walnut
el papayo	*la papaya*	papaya
el peral	*la pera*	pear

1.3.2   Masculine by form

(a)   Nouns ending in *-o*: *el eco* 'echo', *el tiro* 'shot'.
There are about ten exceptions:

la dinamo	dynamo	*la mano*	hand
(also *dínamo*)		(diminutive *manita, manecilla*)	
la foto	photo	*la moto*	motorbike
la Gestapo	the Gestapo	*la nao*	ship (archaic)
la libido	libido	*la polio*	polio
la magneto	magneto		

La radio 'radio' is feminine in Spain, but in Mexico and Central America, and sporadically elsewhere in SA, *el radio* is the set and *la radio* is 'radio station'. *El radio* also means 'radius', 'radium' and 'radiogram'.

(b)   Words ending in *-aje*, *-or*, *-án*, *-ambre*, or a stressed vowel:

el equipaje	luggage	*el refrán*	proverb
el paisaje	landscape	*el enjambre*	swarm
el amor	love	*el rubí*	ruby
el valor	value	*el champú*	shampoo
el mazapán	marzipan		

etc.

But: *la labor* 'labour', *la flor*, 'flower'.

El hambre 'hunger' is feminine: see 3.1.1 for explanation of the masculine article.

1.3.3   Common masculine nouns ending in *-a*

Many errors are caused by the assumption that nouns ending in *-a* are feminine. Many nouns ending in *-ma*, and several other nouns in *-a* are masculine:

(a)   Common masculine nouns in *-ma*

el anagrama	anagram	*el fantasma*	ghost
el anatema	anathema	*el fonema*	phoneme
el aroma	aroma	*el holograma*	hologram
el cisma	schism	*el lema*	slogan/watchword

el clima	climate	*el panorama*	panorama
el coma	coma	*el pijama*	pyjamas
(*la coma* = 'comma')		(*la piyama* in parts of Spanish America)	
el crisma	holy oil	*el plasma*	plasma
(but *te rompo la crisma* 'I'll knock		*el poema*	poem
your block off')		*el prisma*	prism
el crucigrama	crossword puzzle	*el problema*	problem
el diagrama	diagram	*el programa*	programme
el dilema	dilemma	*el radiograma*	radiogram
el diploma	diploma	*el reúma*	rheumatism
el dogma	dogma	(also *el reuma*)	
el drama	drama	*el síntoma*	symptom
el emblema	emblem	*el sistema*	system
el enigma	enigma	*el telegrama*	telegram
el esquema	scheme	*el tema*	theme/topic/
el estigma	stigma		subject
		el trauma	trauma

and most other scientific or technical words ending in -*ma*. For a list of feminine words in -*ma* see 1.3.6.

Notes (i) A few of these words are feminine in dialects and pre-nineteenth-century texts, especially *problema*, *clima* and *fantasma*, cf. *pobre fantasma soñadora* in Lorca's *El maleficio de la mariposa*.

    (ii) Also masculine are

el aleluya	halleluya	*el mapa*	map
(*la aleluya* is 'doggerel'/jingling rhyme)		*el mediodía*	noon
el alerta	alert	*el mañana*	the morrow/
(*el alerta rojo*	'red alert'		tomorrow
la alerta is spreading)		(*la mañana* = 'morning')	
el caza	fighter plane	*el nirvana*	Nirvana
el cometa	comet	*el planeta*	planet
(*la cometa* = 'kite', the toy)		*el telesilla*	ski-lift
el día	day	*el tranvía*	tram
el extra	extra, extra	*el visa*	visa
	payment	(SA *la visa*, traditionally *el visado*)	
el guardarropa	wardrobe (all such	*el vodka*	vodka
	compounds are	*el yoga*	yoga
	masc.)		
el insecticida	insecticide		
(and thus all chemicals in -*icida*)			

1.3.4 Feminine by meaning

The following are feminine, usually because of an underlying noun:

    (a) Companies (*la compañía*, *la firma*): *la Westinghouse*, *la ICI*, *la Seat*, *la Hertz*, *la Volkswagen*, *la Ford*.

    (b) Letters of the alphabet (*la letra*): *una b*, *una c*, *una h*, *la omega*. *El delta* 'river delta' is masculine.

    (c) Islands (*la isla*): *las Azores*, *las Baleares*, *las Antillas* 'West Indies', *las Canarias*, etc.

    (d) Roads (*la carretera* 'road' or *la autopista* 'motorway' being the underlying noun): *la N11*, *la M4*.

1.3.5 Feminine by form

Nouns ending in *-eza, -ción, -sión, -dad, -tad, -tud, -umbre, -ie, -nza, -cia, -sis, -itis*

la pereza	laziness	*la superficie*	surface
la acción	action	*la esperanza*	hope
la versión	version	*la presencia*	presence
la verdad	truth	*la crisis*	crisis
la libertad	freedom	*la tesis*	thesis
la virtud	virtue	*la diagnosis*	diagnosis
la servidumbre	servitude	*la bronquitis*	bronchitis
la serie	series		

etc.

Note But the following are masculine: *el análisis, el apocalípsis, el paréntesis* 'parenthesis'/'bracket', *el énfasis* 'emphasis', *el éxtasis* 'ecstasy'.

1.3.6 Common feminine nouns ending in *-ma*

The majority of nouns ending in *-ma* are masculine (see 1.3.3), but many are feminine. The following are common examples (asterisked forms require the masculine article for reasons explained at 3.1.1):

la alarma	alarm	*la flema*	phlegm
el alma*	soul	*la forma*	shape
la amalgama	amalgam	*la gama*	selection/range
el arma*	weapon	*la goma*	rubber
el asma*	asthma	*la lágrima*	tear (i.e. teardrop)
la broma	joke	*la lima*	(wood, nail) file/
la calma	calm		lime (fruit)
la cama	bed	*la llama*	flame/llama
la cima	summit	*la loma*	hillock
la crema	cream	*la máxima*	maxim
la Cuaresma	Lent	*la merma*	decrease
la chusma	rabble	*la norma*	norm
la diadema	diadem/tiara	*la palma*	palm
la doma	breaking-in/taming	*la paloma*	dove
(= *domadura*)		*la pantomima*	pantomime
la dracma	drachma	*la prima*	bonus/prize/
la enzima	enzyme		female cousin
la escama	scale (fish)	*la quema*	burning
la/el esperma	sperm	*la rama*	branch
la esgrima	fencing (with	*la rima*	rhyme
	swords)	*la sima*	chasm/abyss
la estima	esteem	*la suma*	sum
la estratagema	stratagem	*la toma*	taking
la firma	firm/signature	*la yema*	egg yolk/fingertip

1.3.7 Gender of countries, provinces, regions

Countries, provinces or regions ending in unstressed *-a* are feminine

la España/Francia/Argentina de hoy Spain/France/Argentina today
la conservadora Gran Bretaña conservative Britain

etc.

The rest are masculine:

(*el*) *Perú*, (*el*) *Paraguay*, (*el*) *Canadá*;
Aragón, *Devon*, *Tennessee* (all masculine).
The above rule should be followed, although natives do not always observe it.

Some place names include the definite article and may exceptionally be feminine, cf. *las Hurdes* (near Salamanca, Spain).

For use of the article with countries and place names, see 3.2.11.

Note Such constructions as *todo Colombia lo sabe* 'all Colombia knows it' are nevertheless normal, especially with the adjectives *todo*, *medio*, *mismo*, etc., probably because the underlying noun is felt to be *pueblo* 'people'. Cf. *Todo Piura está muerta* 'the whole of Piura is dead' (Vargas Llosa, Peruvian dialogue).

1.3.8   Gender of cities, towns and villages
Cities ending in unstressed -*a* are normally feminine, the rest are masculine:

la Barcelona de ayer	the Barcelona of yesterday
la Roma de Horacio	Horace's Rome
el Londres de Dickens	Dickens's London
el Moscú turístico	the tourist's Moscow

But there are exceptions like *Nueva York*, *la antigua Cartago*, and popular language tends to make cities feminine:

Bogotá, antes de ser remodelada . . .	Bogota, before it was refashioned . . .
(Colombian press, in *Variedades*, 20)	

Villages are usually masculine even when they end in -*a*, because of underlying *el pueblo* 'village'.

1.3.9   Gender of compound nouns
Compound nouns consisting of a verb plus a noun (frequent) are masculine:

el cazamariposas	butterfly net	*el paraguas*	umbrella
el cuentarrevo-	tachometer/rev	*el sacacorchos*	corkscrew
luciones	counter	*el saltamontes*	grasshopper
el lanzallamas	flamethrower	*el tragaperras*	fruit machine

etc.

The gender of other compound nouns should be learned separately.

1.3.10   Gender of foreign words
These are usually masculine regardless of their gender in the source language, unless they clearly replace or are closely associated with a native feminine word. Examples taken from various printed sources:

el affaire	affair (love or political)
el after-shave	
el best-seller	
los boxes	pits (in motor racing)
el boom	financial boom
el campus	
el/la cassette	(some say *el* for the player, *la* for the tape)

el chalet	detached house
la chance	chance (Spanish America only)
el Christmas	Christmas card
el déficit	economic deficit
el dumping	commercial dumping
el echarpe	(light) scarf (fem. in French)
	(pronounced as a Spanish word)
la élite	(pronounced as in French)
el footing	jogging (from French)
la gillette	safety razor
el hardware	
la hi-fi	
el jazz	
el long play	L-P (record)
el marketing	
la opus	in music. *El Opus* = Opus Dei
el poster	
el pub	(in Spain, a fashionable bar)
el ranking	
el recordman	record-holder (from French?)
el reprise	pick-up (i.e. acceleration of a car)
la roulotte	caravan
el slogan	(publicity) slogan
el software	
el (e)spray	aerosol

There is wide variation between the various Hispanic countries as to the source and number of recent loanwords, so no universally valid list can be drawn up.

1.3.11 Gender of abbreviations

This is determined by the gender of the main noun:

la ONU	UN
la OTAN	NATO
la CEE	EEC
las FF.AA.	Armed Forces
(*Fuerzas Armadas*)	
la UVI	Intensive Care Unit
(*Unidad de Vigilancia Intensiva*)	
el PCE	*Partido Comunista Español*
el FBI	
el BOE	*Boletín Oficial del Estado*
	(where Spanish laws are published)
la CIA	
la EGB	*Educación General Básica*, the basic
	course in Spanish schools
el OVNI	UFO
(*objeto volante no identificado*)	

If the gender of the underlying noun is unknown the abbreviation is masculine unless there is a good reason otherwise: *el (*or *la) KGB*, *el IRA* 'the IRA' (*la ira* = 'anger'), *el Comecon*, but *la RAF*, *la USAF* (because of *las fuerzas aéreas* 'air force'), etc.

1.3.12   Gender acquired from underlying noun (metonymic gender)

Many of the examples in previous sections illustrate instances where one noun has acquired the gender of another which has been suppressed. This accounts for many apparent gender anomalies, cf. *el Psicosis = el Bar Psicosis* (*la (p)sicosis* = 'psychosis'), *el Avenida = el Cine Avenida* (*la avenida* = 'avenue'), *una EBRO = una camioneta EBRO* 'an EBRO light truck', *la Modelo = la Cárcel Modelo* 'Model Jail', *la setenta y tres = la habitación número setenta y tres* 'room 73'.

1.3.13   Doubtful genders

There are a few words of doubtful gender. The following list gives the gender preferred in the modern language:

el azúcar	sugar, though curiously a following adjective may be feminine, e.g. *el azúcar moreno/a* 'brown sugar'
la dote	dowry/gifts (in plural – *tiene dotes* 'he's gifted')
la tilde	the sign over an *ñ*
el/la linde	parish boundary
el calor	heat (*la calor* is rustic)
el color	colour (*la color* is rustic)
la sartén	frying pan (masc. in Bilbao and locally in Spain, and throughout SA)
el hojaldre	puff pastry (SA *la hojaldra*)
el/la pringue	fat/grease/sticky dirt (*esto está pringoso* 'this is sticky')

Pre-twentieth century texts may contain now extinct anomalous genders, e.g. *la puente* 'bridge', *la fin* 'end', *la análisis* 'analysis', etc.

1.3.14   Gender of *mar*, 'sea'

Masculine, except in poetry, the speech of sailors and fishermen, in nautical terms (*la pleamar/la bajamar* 'high/low tide', *la mar llana* 'dead calm') and whenever the word is used as a colloquial intensifier: *la mar de tonto* 'absolutely stupid'; *la mar de gente* '"tons" of people'.

1.3.15   Some Spanish-American genders

Some words are given different genders in provincial Spain and/or some parts of Latin America. Examples current in educated usage and writing in some (but not all) Spanish-American countries are:

el bombillo	(Sp. *la bombilla*)	light bulb
el llamado	(*la llamada*)	call
el vuelto	(*la vuelta*)	change (money)
el protesto	(*la protesta*)	protest

There are surely many other examples, locally more or less accepted in educated speech.

1.3.16 Words with two genders

A number of common words have meanings differentiated solely by their gender. Well-known examples are:

	Masc.	Fem.
cometa	comet	kite (toy)
coma	coma	comma
consonante	rhyming word	consonant
cólera	cholera	wrath/anger
corte	cut	the Court/'Madrid'
capital	capital (money)	capital (city)
cura	priest	cure
delta	river delta	delta (Greek letter)
doblez	fold/crease	duplicity
editorial	editorial	publishing house
frente	front (military, weather)·	forehead
guardia	policeman	custody/guard
génesis	genesis (= birth)	Genesis (Bible)
mañana	tomorrow/morrow	morning
margen	margin	riverbank
moral	mulberry tree	morals/morale
orden	order (opposite of disorder)	order (= command or religious order)
ordenanza	messenger/orderly	decree/ordinance
parte	official bulletin	part
pendiente	earring	slope
pez	fish	pitch (i.e. tar)
policía	policeman	police force
radio	radio	radius/radium/spoke
terminal	terminal (computers)	terminus
vocal	member of a board	vowel

Note *Arte* 'art' is masculine in the singular, but feminine in the plural: *el arte español* 'Spanish art', *las bellas artes* 'fine arts'. But note set phrase *el arte poética* 'Ars Poetica'/'treatise on poetry'.

2 Plural of nouns

2.1 Formation of the plural of nouns

(a) There are three ways of forming the plural: (1) add *-s*; (2) add *-es*; (3) no change (zero plural).

(b) If *-es* is added to a final *z*, the *z* becomes *c*: *la paz/las paces*; *la voz/las voces*.

Words ending in *-g* (rare) or *-c* should properly be spelt *-gues*, *-ques* if *-es* is added, but in practice only *-s* is added nowadays, e.g. *el frac/los fraques* 'dress coat/tails', usually *los fracs*.

(c) If, after adding *-es*, the stress naturally falls on the last syllable but one, an accent written in the singular disappears:

el alacrán	*los alacranes*	scorpion
el irlandés	*los irlandeses*	Irishman
la nación	*las naciones*	nation
el/la rehén	*los/las rehenes*	hostage

etc.

This does not apply to words which end in *-í* or *-ú*: *el pakistaní/los pakistaníes* 'Pakistani', *el tabú/los tabúes* 'taboo'.

2.1.1 Plural in *-s*
(a) Nouns ending in an unstressed vowel or in stressed *e* (including one-syllable words ending in *e*):

el huevo	*los huevos*	egg
el peso	*los pesos*	peso/weight
la serie	*las series*	series
el clisé	*los clisés*	cliché/photo negative
el café	*los cafés*	coffee/café
el pie	*los pies*	foot/feet

(b) Nouns of more than one syllable ending in *-ó* (rare):

el dominó	*los dominós*	domino(es)

(c) Many foreign words ending in a consonant. See 2.1.4.

2.1.2 Plural in *-es*
(a) Native (or nativized) nouns ending in a consonant other than *-s*:

el color	*los colores*	colour
el/la chófer	*los/las chóferes*	driver

(*el chofer* in some American republics)

el origen	los orígenes	origin
la nación	las naciones	nation
el rey	los reyes	king

(b) Nouns ending in a stressed vowel plus -*s*, and all words of one syllable not ending in -*e*:

el anís	los anises	anis drink
el autobús	los autobuses	bus
el país	los países	country
	los síes y los noes	the 'yesses' and 'noes' usually *sís y nos* in speech
el mes	los meses	month
la tos	las toses	cough
el dios	los dioses	god

(c) Nouns ending in -*í*, -*ú* or -*á* (the latter are rare):

el rubí	los rubíes	ruby
el tabú	los tabúes	taboo
el bajá	los bajaes	pasha
el jacarandá	los jacarandaes	jacaranda tree

Exceptions: *papá/papás*; *mamá/mamás*; *sofá/sofás* (illiterate *sofases), *el menú/los menús* 'menu'.

Note to (c): these are written forms, and are appropriate for rare words or formal language, but plural in -*s* alone is normal with familiar words even in educated speech: *los jabalís* (properly *jabalíes*) 'wild boars', *los rubís, los tabús, los zahorís* 'clairvoyants'/'water diviners', and always *el tisú/los tisús* 'paper tissues' and *el menú/los menus* 'menus'. A literary plural form of a truly popular word, e.g. *la gachí/las gachís* 'woman' (Spanish slang) would sound ridiculous.

The Spanish-American words *el ají* 'chili, chili sauce', and *el maní* 'peanut' often form the plurals *los ajises, los manises* in speech.

2.1.3 No change in the plural (zero plural)

(a) Words of more than one syllable ending in an unstressed vowel plus *s*:

el/los lunes	Monday(s) (similarly all weekdays)
el/los atlas	atlas(es)
la/las crisis	crisis/crises
el/los paréntesis	bracket(s)

Similarly: *el campus, el detritus, el mecenas* 'patron of the arts', *la tesis* 'thesis', *el virus*, etc.

(b) Words ending in -*x*, e.g. *el/los fénix*

(c) Latin words – at least in careful language:

los altos déficit presupuestarios (*El País*)   high budgetary deficits

So, *los superávit* 'budgetary surpluses', *los accésit* 'second prizes' etc., but usually however *los memorándums, los referéndums*. In speech these may be treated like other foreign words (see 2.1.4). Spanish speakers do not try to impress by using Latin plurals, cf. our 'cacti' and 'memoranda'.

(d) Words ending in a consonant plus -*s*: *los bíceps, los fórceps*.

2.1.4 Plural of foreign words ending in a consonant

The universal tendency is to treat them all as English words and add -*s*, whatever their origin, although grammarians grumble about this 'English plural' which Manuel Seco calls *una plaga de nuestra lengua de hoy*.

As a rule, if a word ends in *b*, *c*, *f*, *g*, *k*, *m*, *p*, *t*, *v*, or *w*, or in any two or more consonants, it is almost certainly a foreign word and will make its plural in -*s* unless it ends with a *s*, *sh* or *ch* sound, cf. such words as *kibbutz*, *flash*, *lunch*, *sketch*, in which case it will probably be invariable – almost certainly so in speech:

el álbum	*los álbums*	(formal style *los álbumes*)
el boicot	*los boicots*	boycott
el complot	*los complots*	(political) plot
el coñac	*los coñacs*	cognac
el córner	*los córners*	corner (in soccer)
el hit	*los hits*	hit parade
el penalty	*los penaltys*	(in soccer)

etc.

Notes (i) *Sandwich*, different from a *bocadillo*, should make the plural *sandwiches*, but *los sandwich* is sometimes heard.

(ii) Some words are nativized, e.g. *el bar/los bares*, *el gol/los goles* 'goal', *el hotel/los hoteles*, *el dólar/los dólares*, *el máuser/los máuseres*, *el neutron/los neutrones*, *el quasar/los quasares*, etc.

(iii) Academy plurals like *gong/gongues*, *póquer/póqueres* ('poker' – the game), *zigzag/zigzagues*, etc. are felt to be ponderous: -*s* alone is added. However *el film(e)/los filmes* is not uncommon, and *el club/los clubes* is normal in Spanish America for the common Peninsular *los clubs* (*El País* prefers *clubes*). *El frac* 'dress coat'/'tails' makes its plural as *fracs* or *fraques* (the latter is uncommon).

El cóctel 'cocktail' has a theoretical written plural *los cócteles* but *los cóctels* is always said (at least in Spain).

(iv) Some writers and editors occasionally treat foreign words ending in a consonant like Latin words (see 2.1.3c), so forms like *los hit*, *los laser* are sometimes seen. Zero plural forms are very often given to foreign words in everyday speech.

2.1.5 Proper names

If a proper name is felt to indicate a collective entity (e.g. a family), it has no plural form: *los Franco*, *los Mallol*, *los Pérez*. A group of individuals who merely happen to have the same name will be pluralized according to the usual rules (though names in -*z* are almost always invariable):

Este pueblo está lleno de Morenos, *Blancos y Péreces/Pérez*	this village is full of Morenos, Blancos and Perezes
No todos los Juan Pérez del mundo (J. Donoso, Chile)	not all the Juan Perezes in the world
los Góngoras del siglo dieciocho	the Gongoras of the eighteenth century

Notes (i) The same principle also applies to named objects which form families: *los Ford* 'Ford cars', *los Chevrolet*, *los Simca*.

(ii) Royal houses are considered to be successive individuals: *los Borbones* 'the Bourbons'; *los Habsburgos*.

2.1.6   Compound nouns

(a)   Those (the most common) consisting of a verb plus a plural noun do not change in the plural:

el/los abrelatas	tin-opener	*el/los portaviones*	aircraft carrier
el/los limpiabotas	shoe-shine	*el/los lanzamisiles*	missile-launcher

(b)   There is a growing class of compounds consisting of two juxtaposed nouns. Normally only the first noun is pluralized. The following forms have been noted from various written sources:

arco iris	*los arcos iris*	rainbow
cárcel modelo	*las cárceles modelo*	model prison
coche cama	*los coches cama*	sleeping car
hombre rana	*los hombres rana*	frogman
hora cero	*las horas cero*	zero hour
niño prodigio	*los niños prodigio*	child prodigy
perro policía	*los perros policía*	police dog
sistema antimisil	*los sistemas antimisil*	antimissile system

But always:

país miembro	*los países miembros*	member country
tierra virgen	*las tierras vírgenes*	virgin land

Pluralization of the second noun robs it of its adjectival force: *los hombres ranas* sounds like 'men who are frogs', cf.

las ediciones pirata	pirate editions	*los editores piratas* pirate publishers

(c)   Other compound nouns are treated as single words with regular plurals:

altavoz	*los altavoces*	loudspeaker
(SA *el altoparlante*)		
bocacalle	*las bocacalles*	side street
correveidile	*los correveidiles*	tell-tale
sordomudo	*los sordomudos*	deaf-mute
hidalgo	*los hidalgos*	nobleman

(The old plural was *hijosdalgo*.)

2.1.7   Irregular plurals

(a)   Three common nouns shift their stress in the plural:

el carácter	*los caracteres*
el espécimen	*los especímenes*
el régimen	*los regímenes*

(b)   *El lord*, plural *los lores* (British) 'lord': *la Cámara de los Lores* 'The House of Lords'.

Los media 'the media', but usually *los medios*: *los medios masivos* 'mass media'.

El hipérbaton 'hyperbaton' usually makes *los hipérbatos*.

2.2   Syntax and semantics of plural nouns

2.2.1   Mass nouns and count nouns in Spanish and English
The range of count and mass nouns in Spanish differs from English. A

count noun refers to countable items, 'egg'/'two eggs'; mass nouns denote non-countable items ('justice', 'bread', but not *two justices, two breads).

In both languages mass nouns can often be pluralized to mean different varieties of the thing in question, cf. 'her fear'/'her fears', 'my love'/'my loves', 'I love French wine'/'I love French wines', 'the water of Finland'/'the waters of Finland'.

This device is far more frequent in Spanish than in English, and idiomatic translation of the resulting plural noun may require thought, e.g.:

Si aparece por tu casa, lo echas sin contemplaciones (J. Marsé, dialogue)	if he turns up at your house, throw him out on the spot/without second thoughts
Para nosotros existen dos urgencias (interview in *Cambio16*)	for us there are two urgent issues (lit. 'urgencies')

Examples (some taken from Iannucci (1952) and Stockwell *et al.* (1965)):

la amistad	friendship	*las amistades*	friends
la atención	attention	*las atenciones*	acts of kindness
la bondad	goodness	*las bondades*	good acts
la carne	meat	*las carnes*	fleshy parts
la crueldad	cruelty	*las crueldades*	cruel acts
la gente	people	*las gentes*	peoples/various peoples
la información	information	*las informaciones*	news items
el negocio	business	*los negocios*	business affairs
el pan	bread	*los panes*	loaves of bread
el progreso	progress	*los progresos*	advances
la tostada	toast	*las tostadas*	slices of toast
la tristeza	sadness	*las tristezas*	sorrows
el trueno	thunder	*los truenos*	thunderclaps

etc.

2.2.2   Nouns denoting symmetrical objects

As in English, these nouns are usually invariably plural:

los auriculares	earphones
las gafas (SA *los anteojos*)	glasses
los gemelos	binoculars/cuff-links/twins
las tijeras	scissors

but usage is uncertain in some cases, with a colloquial tendency towards the singular. The more usual form (in Spain) comes first:

los alicates/el alicate	pliers/pincer
las bragas/la braga	knickers/panties
los calzoncillos/un calzoncillo	underpants
la nariz/las narices	nose (the plural is colloquial)
las pinzas/la pinza	peg/pincers/tweezers/dart (sewing)
el pantalón/los pantalones	trousers (equally common)
las tenazas/la tenaza	tongs/pliers

Note   *las escaleras/la escalera* 'stairs' (plural more common), but singular if it means 'a ladder'.

2.2.3   Nouns always plural in Spanish

As in English, some nouns or phrases are normally always plural, e.g.:

las afueras	outskirts	*las cosquillas*	tickling
los alrededores	surroundings	*los enseres*	goods and chattels
los altos (SA)	upstairs flat	*las ganas*	urge/desire
los bajos (SA)	downstairs flat	*las nupcias* (archaic)	wedding rites
los bienes	goods	*las tinieblas*	darkness
buenos días	good morning	*los víveres*	provisions
buenas tardes	good afternoon	*los ultramarinos*	groceries
buenas noches	good night	*las vacaciones*	holiday
	(greeting or goodbye)		

etc.

2.2.4 Number agreement with collective nouns

Collective nouns, often or always treated as plural in English (especially in colloquial British), are normally singular in Spanish:

El gobierno considera . . .	the government consider(s)
El comité debate . . .	the committee is/are discussing
El 31% de los ciudadanos se muestra partidario de permanecer en la OTAN (*El País*)	31% of citizens are in favour of remaining in NATO
La gente dice . . .	people say . . .
La tripulación está a su disposición	the crew is/are at your disposal
Un sinnúmero de personas observaba el famoso Big Ben (*El Comercio*, Lima)	a vast crowd of people was/were watching the famous Big Ben
La masa de los creyentes no era menos compleja que sus creencias (O. Paz, Mex.)	the mass of believers were no less complex than their beliefs

Notes (i) If an adjective or verb governed by a collective noun is separated from the noun by a pause or intervening words, it is usually plural:

Una minoría presentó una petición al rey, convencidos de que . . .	a minority presented a petition to the king, convinced that . . .
La muchedumbre entró en el palacio, pero al enfrentarse con las tropas se dispersaron pacíficamente	the crowd entered the palace but on encountering the troops they dispersed peacefully

    (ii) Sometimes an intervening plural noun may invoke plural agreement, although the singular is generally preferred:

El común de los mortales no teme(n) a la muerte	most mortals do not fear death
La gama de los pequeños Seat recibe(n) cada vez mayor atención	the small Seat range is attracting increasing attention

2.2.5 Agreement with *mayoría, minoría, parte, resto, mitad* and similar words

The singular is common (but the plural is found), unless some phrase follows, typically a plural adjective or participle, which refers to the members of the group individually.

La mayoría de los internos realizó una huelga de brazos caídos (*El País*)	the majority of inmates went on a sit-down strike
La mayoría duermen, hechos ovillos (Vargas Llosa, Peru)	the majority are curled up asleep

Algunos pudieron salvarse, pero el resto desaparecieron (better *desapareció*)	some managed to save themselves but the rest disappeared
Un mínimo de 13 presos habían sido asistidos de heridas (*El País*)	a minimum of 13 prisoners had been treated for injuries
Una treintena de presos de la Modelo se autolesiona (*El País*)	some 30 prisoners in the Model Jail inflict wounds on themselves
La mitad de ellos no llegaron (better *llegó*)	half of them didn't arrive

But *ser* is peculiar in that it usually agrees with a plural predicate, not with a singular subject:

Todo son ventajas	it's all advantages
Esto son lentejas y eso son guisantes	this is lentils and that's peas
El escrito eran sus 'condiciones' para que las Fuerzas Armadas aceptaran el sistema establecido (*Cambio16*)	the document was his 'conditions' for the Armed Forces accepting the established system
Su morada más común son las ruinas . . . (Borges, Arg.)	their most usual dwelling-place is (in) ruins
El gobierno no son más que cuatro desgraciados	the government are just a pack of worthless wretches

See 9.16d for further discussion of these examples.

2.2.6   Plural noun after *tipo de*, etc.
After *tipo de* and similar phrases, count nouns are often made plural:

Ya que ese tipo de rostros es frecuente en los países sudamericanos (E. Sabato, Arg.)	since that type of face is frequent in South American countries

2.2.7   Singular for objects of which a person has only one
The English sentence 'they cut their knees' is ambiguous: one knee or both? Spanish normally clarifies the issue by using the singular if only one each is implied or if only one thing is possessed:

Les cortaron la cabeza	they cut off their heads
Se quitaron el sombrero	they took off their hats
Compraron coche	they bought cars (one each or one car)
Todos tenían novia	all had girlfriends (one each)
Tres israelíes con pasaporte alemán (*Cambio16*)	three Israelis with German passports

This rule is sometimes ignored in Spanish-American speech: *nos hemos mojado las cabezas* (Bolivia, quoted Kany, 26) 'we've wet our heads'. It is quite often ignored in Peninsular speech with articles of clothing or other objects.

2.2.8   Singular for plural
Singular nouns (often denoting people) may sometimes be used to represent large numbers after words like *mucho*, *tanto*, etc., often, but not exclusively, with an ironic tone:

Hay tanto niño repipi en ese colegio	there are a load of 'clever-clever' children in that school
En verano viene mucho inglés . . .	in summer you get a lot of English . . .
Con tanto anglófilo como anda por ahí	with all those Anglophiles about . . .

3 Articles

3.1 Forms of the articles

| | Definite article (the) | | Indefinite article (a, an) | |
	masc.	fem.	masc.	fem.
Singular	*el*	*la*	*un*	*una*
Plural	*los*	*las*	*unos*	*unas*

Note For the so-called 'Neuter Article', *lo*, see 7.2.

3.1.1 *El* and *un* before feminine nouns

El and *un* are always used before feminine nouns beginning with a stressed *a*- or *ha*-, but the gender remains feminine. This important rule must not be broken though it is not always observed in pre-nineteenth-century texts and in some dialects:

el África *contemporánea*	contemporary Africa	*un/el área* *el habla*	an/the area language/speech
el/un águila	the/an eagle	*el hampa madrileña*	the Madrid under-
el alma humana	the human soul		world

etc.

Other examples are *el abra* (SA only) 'mountain pass' (Sp. *el puerto*), *el alba* 'dawn' (poetic), *el alza* 'rise'/'increase', *el ancla* 'anchor', *el arma* 'weapon', *el arpa* 'harp', *el aula* 'lecture room', *el haba* 'bean', *el hacha* 'axe', *el hada* 'fairy', *el hambre* 'hunger', *el haya*, 'beech tree', etc.

The plural is always with *las/unas: las águilas, las hachas*, etc.

Compare *la/una asociación, la/una apertura* 'opening', *la/una armonía* 'harmony', where the first vowel is not stressed.

Exceptions: *La a, la hache* a, h (letters of the alphabet).

La Ángela, la Ana, and other women's names (see 3.2.11g for the rare use of the article with personal names).

La Haya 'the Hague'; *la/una haz* (archaic) 'surface'/'face' (*el haz*, masc. = 'bundle'/'sheaf'); *la árabe* 'Arab woman'; *la ácrata* 'anarchist woman'.

Notes (i) This rule should apply to those rare feminine compound nouns whose first element would have begun with a stressed *a* had it stood alone: *el aguamarina* 'aquamarine'; *un avemaría* 'an Ave Maria'.

(ii) The rule applies only to nouns:

la/una ardua lucha	arduous struggle
. . . *una amplia estancia con libros y cuadros* (F. Umbral)	a wide room with books and paintings
la árida Libia	arid Libya
la/una ancha puerta	wide door
Suele asumir la forma de una alta mujer silenciosa (Borges, Arg.)	she usually takes the form of a tall silent woman

(iii) It is a bad error (common in spontaneous speech, at least with the less common nouns) to treat such words as masculine in the singular, in other words one must say: *un aula oscura* 'a dark lecture hall', *el habla popular hispanoamericana* 'popular Spanish-American speech' etc., not **un aula oscuro*, etc.

(iv) *Algún*, *ningún* are usual in everyday language before such nouns; *este*, *ese* and *aquel* are common in speech but feminine forms are written – *esta área* 'this area'; *esa agua* 'that water'.

3.1.2 *Del* and *al*
De plus *el* is shortened to *del* ('of the'); *a* plus *el* is shortened to *al* ('to the'). *De* + *él* ('he') and *a* + *él* are not abbreviated.

The abbreviated forms are not used (at least in writing) if the article is part of a proper name:

La primera página de El Comercio	page one of *El Comercio*
Viajaron a El Cairo	they journeyed to Cairo
Fuimos a El Escorial	we went to El Escorial

3.2 Uses and omission of the definite article

Article usage is especially elusive, and usage of the definite article notoriously so: why *does* one say *en la práctica* but *en teoría*, *Ministerio de Justicia* but *Ministerio del Trabajo*? The following remarks must be supplemented by careful study of good writing and educated speech.

Perhaps the most striking difference between Spanish and English is the use of the definite article with generic nouns: *la naturaleza* 'nature', *la pronunciación española* 'Spanish pronunciation', although this rule is by no means hard and fast. Careful study of the following pages should make it clear to students of French that although use of the definite article in Spanish resembles French usage, the definite article in Spanish is in fact less used than its modern French counterpart, and is apparently less used than fifty years ago, possibly as a result of the influence of English.

3.2.1 A useful rule for the use of the definite article
With two important exceptions, where the definite article is used in English it is also used in Spanish:

La caída del gobierno	the fall of the government
Es difícil definir el uso del artículo definido	it is difficult to define the use of the definite article

Exceptions: **(a)** Ordinal numbers with kings, popes, etc.: *Fernando séptimo* 'Ferdinand *the* Seventh', *Carlos quinto* 'Charles *the* Fifth'.

(b) A number of set adverbial phrases in Spanish take no article whereas their English equivalent usually does. They must be learned separately:

en nombre de	in the name of	*en alta mar*	on the high seas
a título de	in the capacity of	*de plantilla*	on the payroll/staff
a voluntad de	at the discretion of	*cuesta abajo*	down (the) hill
a gusto de	to the liking of	*cuesta arriba*	up (the) hill
a corto/largo plazo	in the short/long run	*hacia oriente*	towards the east
		(hacia el este)	
en camino	on the way		

etc.

3.2.2 Definite article with more than one noun

If two or more nouns are listed, each has its own article if they are individually particularized or are felt to indicate dissimilar things:

el padre y la madre	the father and mother
entre el hotel y la playa	between the hotel and (the) beach
El coche y la bicicleta están en el garaje	the car and the bicycle are in the garage
el agua y la leche	the water and (the) milk
Por el contrario, ello ayuda a mantener el país en el subdesarrollo, es decir la pobreza, la desigualdad y la dependencia (Vargas Llosa, Peru)	on the contrary, it helps to keep the country in a state of underdevelopment — i.e. poverty, inequality and dependence

But very often, if the nouns are felt to form a single complex idea, or are felt to mean the same thing (often the case after *o* 'or'), all but the first article may be omitted, especially in writing:

el misterio o enigma del origen . . . (O. Paz, Mex.)	the mystery or enigma of the origin . . .
El procedimiento y consecuencias son semejantes (Vargas Llosa, Peru)	the procedure and consequences are similar
Si una universidad debe pagar el precio de la enseñanza gratuita renunciando a contar con los laboratorios, equipos, bibliotecas, aulas, sistemas audiovisuales indispensables para cumplir con su trabajo {. . .} aquella solución es una falsa solución (Vargas Llosa, Peru)	if a university has to pay the price of free education by giving up the laboratories, equipment, libraries, lecture rooms, audiovisual systems indispensable for it to do its work {. . .} that solution is a false solution

Notes (i) If the first noun in a list is feminine and the second masculine, the article should appear before both: one could say *las aulas y los equipos*, but not **las/los aulas y equipos*.

(ii) Pairs of animate nouns of different sex both require the article: *el hermano y la hermana* 'the brother and sister', *el toro y la vaca* 'the bull and (the) cow', not **el toro y vaca*.

(iii) In doubtful cases retention of the articles is safer: *tráeme los tenedores y las cucharas* 'bring me the forks and spoons'.

3.2.3 Definite article with generic nouns

With the exceptions noted at 3.2.6, the definite article is required before generic nouns, i.e.

(a) mass (i.e. uncountable) nouns which refer to an idea or substance in general:

la informalidad	informality/unreliability

el catolicismo español	Spanish catholicism
El salvado es bueno para la digestión	bran is good for the digestion
El acero inoxidable es carísimo	stainless steel is extremely expensive
La sangre no tiene precio	blood has no price

etc.

Colour nouns require the article in the same way as abstract nouns: *el azul* 'blue'; *el negro* 'black': *el amarillo es un color que no me gusta* 'yellow is a colour I don't like'.

(b) Count nouns which denote all the members of their class:

Los belgas beben mucha cerveza	(the) Belgians drink a lot of beer
Los ordenadores hacen imposibles los problemas difíciles	computers make difficult problems impossible
Reivindicaban los derechos de la mujer moderna	they were campaigning for the rights of (the) modern woman/of modern women
El tigre es un animal peligroso	the tiger is a dangerous animal

Notes (i) These rules are especially binding when the noun is the subject of a verb:

El amor es ciego	love is blind
No me gusta la manzanilla	I don't like camomile
El murciélago es un animal fascinante	the bat is a fascinating animal
El azúcar es malo para los dientes	sugar is bad for the teeth

When the generic noun is the object of a verb or is preceded by a preposition, the definite article may be omitted. See 3.2.6 for examples.

See 3.2.4 for discussion of sentences like *expertos americanos dicen* . . . 'American experts say' in which the noun may in fact be partitive, i.e. does not really apply to every member of the class it denotes.

(ii) Sentences like *me gusta el vino, me gustan las cerezas* are therefore ambiguous out of context: 'I like the wine/the cherries' or 'I like wine/cherries'. In practice context or intonation makes the meaning clear, or a demonstrative – *este vino, estas cerezas* – can be used for the first meaning.

3.2.4 Omission of article before partitive nouns

The definite article is omitted before nouns which do not refer to the whole of their class, but only to some or part of it ('partitive nouns'):

(a) partitive mass nouns:

Tiene paciencia	he's got patience
Eso necesita valor	that needs courage
Me has pagado con desprecio	you've rewarded me with contempt
Las rosas piden agua	the roses want water
Los ingredientes con que se amasa el ser humano: amor, terror, fracaso, destino, libertad, fe, esperanza, risa, y llanto (Última Hora, Bolivia)	the ingredients that go to make up the human being: love, terror, failure, fate, freedom, faith, hope, laughter and tears

As the last of the above examples shows, the difference between generic and non-generic mass nouns is not always obvious. See 3.2.6 for further comments on the subject.

(b) Partitive count nouns:

No se te olvide traer clavos	don't forget to bring (some) nails
Incluso nos dieron flores	they even gave us (some) flowers
Llevan armas	they're carrying weapons

Unqualified partitive nouns rarely appear in front of the verb of which they are the subject:

Caían bombas por todas partes	bombs were falling everywhere
(Not **bombas caían por todas partes*)	

See 31.8b for further remarks on this topic.

Two or more nouns together do, however, sometimes appear in this position without the article in literary styles:

Ingleses y alemanes, en cuyos idiomas	Englishmen and Germans, in whose
no existe la ñ, encuentran cierta	languages ñ does not exist, find it
dificultad en pronunciarla	somewhat difficult to pronounce

Nouns qualified by an adjective or some other word or phrase may appear without the article at the head of a sentence, especially in newspaper style:

Expertos americanos dicen que . . .	American experts say that . . .
Cosas como ésas sólo te pasan a ti	things like that only happen to you
(from Moliner, normal construction)	

3.2.5   Definite article required before nouns restricted by a qualifier

As in English, a noun qualified or restricted by a following word or phrase usually becomes specific and requires the article. Compare

Estamos hablando de religión	we're talking (about) religion
Compro oro	I buy gold

and

Estamos hablando de la religión de los antiguos persas	we're talking about the religion of the ancient Persians
Está hecho del oro que trajeron de las Indias	it's made from the gold they brought from the Indies
Admiramos al Cervantes humanista	we admire the humanist (in) Cervantes

This rule must be understood to override any of the rules of article omission which follow. But a qualifier does not always make a noun specific; the qualified noun may still constitute a generic entity in its own right:

Una estatua de oro macizo	a statue of solid gold
Unas lecciones de democracia práctica	a few lessons in practical democracy
No hablo con traidores de su patria	I don't talk to traitors to their own country

3.2.6   Apparent exceptions to the rules outlined in 3.2.3

The general rule given above – that generic nouns require the definite article – creates problems. In the sentence *yo como carne* 'I eat meat', *carne* seems to be generic: it refers to all meat and so might seem to require the definite article.

Such apparent exceptions usually arise because the noun does not really refer to the whole of its class, but only to a part, although this may not be obvious. This is especially true of nouns which (a) follow prepositions or (b) are the object of certain kinds of verb:

   (a)   Omission after prepositions

Nouns following prepositions very often really only denote a part or an aspect of the thing they refer to and not the totality of it, and therefore take no definite article:

Le gusta salir con ingleses	she/he likes going out with English people

(one or a few at a time, not the whole species at once)

El Ministerio de Justicia	The Ministry of Justice

(local, not universal justice – but note *el Ministerio del Trabajo*)

una fábrica de transistores	a transistor factory
Sólo una minoría cuenta con electricidad	only a minority have electricity
Dio una conferencia sobre poesía árabe	he gave a lecture on Arabic poetry

(i.e. aspects of it, not the whole thing)

Me suena a mentira	it sounds like a lie
Entre puritanismo, democracia y liberalismo no había oposición sino afinidad (O. Paz, Mex)	between puritanism, democracy and liberalism there was no opposition but an affinity

(b)   After certain verbs, e.g. of consumption, desire, production, nouns which are at first sight generic may on further examination be seen to be basically partitive, for which reason they do not take the definite article:

Los lagartos comen moscas	lizards eat flies

(one or two flies at a time, but not the whole species at once)

Escribo novelas de ciencia ficción	I write science-fiction novels
Claro que uso jabón	of course I use soap
Queremos paz	we want peace

But if the verb really affects the whole of its object in general – usually the case with verbs of human emotion like 'love', 'hate', 'admire', 'criticize', 'censure', 'reject', etc. – then the article is required:

Odio las novelas de ciencia ficción	I hate science-fiction novels
Adoro el helado de vainilla	I love vanilla ice cream
Hay que combatir el terrorismo	terrorism must be fought

Notes (i)   As noted in 3.2.3 n. ii, use of the definite article may involve an ambiguity in Spanish: *no me gustan las cerezas* can mean either 'I don't like cherries' or 'I don't like the cherries', i.e. the ones here. As a result, a sentence like *no queremos guerra* 'we don't want (any) war' may be more universal in meaning than *no queremos la guerra* 'we don't want the war', i.e. this particular war.

   (ii)   Omission or retention of the article with abstract and mass nouns after a preposition often depends on the point of view of the speaker. One can say either *publicó tres artículos sobre poesía* 'he published three articles on poetry' or . . . *sobre la poesía* 'on Poetry'. The latter implies the universal abstraction, 'Poetry'; the former implies 'aspects of poetry'. The difference is slight, and the strong modern tendency is to omit the article, cf. *Hay que distinguir entre revolución, revuelta y rebelión* (O. Paz, Mexico) 'one must distinguish between revolution, revolt and rebellion'.

(c)   Omission in adverbial phrases

The article is omitted in many adverbial phrases consisting of a preposition plus a noun:

la confusión por antonomasia	confusion personified/par excellence
a cántaros	in pitcherfuls
en balde	pointlessly/in vain

a quemarropa	point-blank
por avión	by plane
en tren/coche	by train/car
Estamos aquí de observadores	we're here as observers
De niña yo sólo hablaba catalán	as a little girl I only spoke Catalan

See chapter 28 for detailed examples of prepositional usage.

3.2.7 The definite article after *de*
When two nouns are joined by *de* to form what is effectively a compound noun, the article is omitted before the second noun. Compare *la rueda del coche* 'the wheel of/from the car', and *una rueda de coche* 'a car wheel':

la carne de la vaca	the meat from the cow
la carne de vaca	beef
los sombreros de las mujeres	the women's hats
sombreros de mujer	women's hats
el dolor de muelas	toothache
un crimen de pasión	a crime of passion
lecciones de contabilidad	lessons in accountancy

Such combinations are often denoted in English by compound nouns: *la noche de la fiesta* 'the night of the party'; *noche de fiesta* 'party night'.

3.2.8 Use of the definite article after *haber* ('there is'/'there are')
Spanish does not normally allow the definite article to appear after *haber* (French *il y a*), except when it means 'exist' as opposed to 'is there'; e.g. one says *hay agua* 'there's water', *hay gente* 'there are people', but:

Estaba también el cartero	the postman was there too
Ha venido el médico/ahí está el médico	there's the doctor (i.e. the doctor's come)

and

Para los pecadores hay el infierno	there's Hell for sinners (i.e. Hell exists)
Por un lado hay las grandes fiestas, y por el otro, las distracciones institucionales (Cambio16)	on the one hand there are the major fiestas, and on the other hand, institutionalized amusements

Note **Hay el cartero*, **hay el médico* are typical Catalanisms.

3.2.9 Omission of the definite articles in book, film and other titles
At the beginning of titles of works of literature or art the definite article is often suppressed before nouns which are not felt to be unique entities:

Política y estado bajo el régimen de Franco	*Politics and the State under the Franco Régime*
Casa de campo, de José Donoso	*The Country House*, by J. Donoso
Selección de poemas	*Selected Poems*

But with specific nouns:

La casa verde, de M. Vargas Llosa	*The Green House*, by . . .
La Iglesia en España ayer y mañana	*The Church in Spain yesterday and tomorrow*

3.2.10 Omission in headlines
In Spain the grammar of headline language is fairly normal, and article

omission follows the general rules. In Latin America a type of headline jargon has emerged which follows English in omitting articles:

Ingleses toman Islas Georgias luego de combate de 2 horas (*La Prensa*, Lima)	British take Georgias after two-hour battle
Causa de deslizamiento verán expertos (*idem*)	Experts to investigate cause of landslide
Afirma divorcios producen temblor (*Última Hora*, Dom. Republic, *Var*. 20)	'Divorces cause Earthquakes' Claim

For the word order of these SA headlines see 31.7.

3.2.11   The definite article with proper nouns

(a)   With unique entities

Usage is the same as in English, except that the definite article is used with mountains, volcanoes, Heaven and Hell: *El Taj Mahal, el Atlántico, el infierno* 'Hell', *el cielo/el paraíso* 'Heaven'/'Paradise', *el Diablo* 'the Devil', *la Virgen* 'the Virgin', *el Everest, el Mont Blanc.*

As in English, it is not used with personal names as opposed to epithets or titles: *Dios* 'God'; *Cristo* 'Christ' (very rarely *el Cristo*); *Jesucristo* 'Jesus Christ'; *Satanás* 'Satan'.

For the article before ordinary personal names see **(g)** below.

(b)   With names of languages

Usage is capricious and departures from the following rules may occur:

(i) no article after *en*, or, usually, after *saber, aprender, hablar*:

en español, en inglés	in Spanish, in English
Sé quechua	I know Quechua
Aprendo alemán, habla griego	I'm learning German, he speaks Greek

(ii) Optional article after *entender* 'understand', *escribir* 'write', *estudiar* 'study':

Entiendo (el) inglés	I understand English
Escribe (el) italiano	he writes Italian

(iii) After *de* meaning 'from' and after other prepositions, the article is used:

traducir del español al francés	to translate from Spanish to French
una palabra del griego	a word from Greek
Comparado con el ruso, el español parece poco complicado	compared with Russian, Spanish seems uncomplicated

(iv) After *de* meaning 'of' the article is used only if the whole language is meant: *curso de español* 'Spanish course' (really aspects of Spanish); *dificultades del español* 'difficulties of Spanish' (in general); *las sutilezas del japonés* 'the subtleties of Japanese'.

(v) After *traducir* 'translate', *dominar* 'master', *chapurrear* 'speak badly', *destrozar* 'murder' and other verbs and prepositions the article is retained: *domina perfectamente el portugués* 'he's a complete master of Portuguese'; *chapurrea el inglés* 'he speaks broken English'.

(vi) If the language is the subject of a verb it requires the article: *el francés es difícil* 'French is difficult'; *el español es una lengua hermosa* 'Spanish is a beautiful language';

(vii) If the language is qualified by a following word or phrase, the article is required: *el español de Colombia*; *el inglés que se habla en Tennessee* 'the English spoken in Tennessee'.

(c) Definite article with names of countries

Newspaper style nowadays tends to omit the definite article with countries. *El País* (Spain) writes *Beirut, capital de Líbano*, and one even sees *en Reino Unido, en URSS* in advertisements.

Ordinary language is subject to disagreements, but current usage in Spain seems to be:

(i) Optional: *(la) Alemania Occidental/Oriental* 'West/East Germany', *(la) Arabia Saudí*, *(la) Argentina* (article normal in Argentina itself), *(el) Brasil, (el) Canadá, (el) Ecuador, (las) Filipinas* 'Philippines', *(el) Irán, (el) Irak, (el) Japón, (el) Pakistán, (el) Paraguay, (el) Perú, (el) Uruguay, (el) Vietnam*. (*El País* drops the article with all of these, but it seems more common than not in speech.)

(ii) Usual: *el Camerún* 'Cameroon', *el Congo, el Líbano* 'Lebanon', *El Oriente Medio* 'Middle East', *el Senegal, el Sudán, la Somalia, el Yemen*. (But *El País* tends to omit the article with these.)

(iii) Obligatory: *la India, El Salvador, la Unión Soviética*.

Other countries do not take the article: *tres años en Bulgaria/Egipto/Noruega/Europa Oriental/África del Sur* 'three years in Bulgaria/Egypt/Norway/Eastern Europe/South Africa'.

Notes (i) The United States is normally *los Estados Unidos* (plural) but *Estados Unidos* (singular) appears in journalism and in SA. *Gran Bretaña* 'Great Britain' does not normally take the article, but *el Reino Unido* 'the United Kingdom' does.

(ii) In older texts, particularly in solemn style, names of countries occasionally appear with the article: *la Francia, la Inglaterra*, etc.

(iii) All place names require the article when they are qualified or restricted by an adjective or following phrase or clause:

la España contemporánea contemporary Spain
La Suecia que yo conocía the Sweden I knew

(d) With provinces, regions, cities and towns

Some place names include the article as an inseparable feature: *los Ángeles, el Cairo*; *la Coruña*; *la Habana* 'Havana'; *el Havre*; *la Haya* 'the Hague'; *la Mancha*; *la Paz*; *la Plata*; *la Rioja*, etc.

Otherwise the article is not used – unless 3.2.5 applies, as in *el Buenos Aires de hoy, la Soria de Antonio Machado*.

(e) With streets, roads, squares

The definite article is used before nouns denoting roads, squares, avenues, lanes, alleys and similar places:

Vive en la plaza/calle de la Independencia he lives in Independence square/street
la panadería de la avenida Fleming the baker's in Fleming Avenue

(f) With days of the week

The definite article appears with days of the week where in English we use 'on':

Llegan el martes	they're arriving on Tuesday
Cerrado los viernes	closed on Friday(s)

but

Trabajo de lunes a jueves	I work from Monday to Thursday

(g) With names and titles

(i) With personal names

Women's names may take the definite article if they are very famous: *la Loren*; *la Garbo*.

If a woman is referred to by surname alone, the article is used to show that she and not her husband is meant: *la González, la Pardo Bazán*.

The use of the definite article before names of ordinary men and women may sound uneducated, rustic or insinuating: *la María, la Josefa, el Mario*. (In some places, e.g. Chile, Catalonia, this usage is common even in educated speech.)

(ii) With sports teams

The masculine article is always used before sports teams: *el Granada* 'Granada FC'; *el Manchester United*; *el Argentina*.

(iii) Article before nouns of family relationship

Abuelo/abuela take the article: *entré a dar un beso a la abuela* 'I went in to give grandmother a kiss'; *el abuelo comía en silencio* 'grandfather was eating in silence'.

Tío/tía 'uncle/aunt' also take the article *di un beso a la tía* 'I gave auntie a kiss'. But if the person is named the article is omitted – at least in educated language: *le di un beso a tía Julia* 'I kissed aunt Julia'.

In rural areas *tío/tía* may be used before the christian names of local worthies: *el tío José/la tía Paca* 'old José'/'old Paca'.

With *papá, mamá* use of the article may also sound uneducated to some speakers if the noun stands alone: *dale un beso a papá* 'give daddy a kiss'.

(iv) With titles

The definite article is used before the title of a person being talked about: *el señor Moreira, el profesor Smith, el general Rodríguez, el presidente Belaúnde, el doctor Fleming, el padre Blanco* 'Father Blanco'. But it is not used before *don, doña, fray, san, santa, sor* and foreign titles like *míster, monsieur, Herr*: *don Miguel, don José, fray Bentos, santa Teresa, sor Juana, míster Smith*.

It is not used if the person is directly addressed: *pase usted, señor Sender/señor Presidente/padre Blanco* 'come in Mr Sender/Mr President/ Father Blanco'.

Note: In military circles the formulas *mi general, mi capitán*, etc. are required when addressing officers.

Don/doña are used before the given names of older persons of respected social status, and on envelopes (less now than formerly): *señor don Ángel Ramírez, doña Josefa, don Miguel*.

3.2.12   Definite article in apposition
The definite article is normally omitted in apposition:

Madrid, capital de España	Madrid, capital of Spain
Simón Bolívar, libertador de América	S. Bolívar, the liberator of (South) America

But it is retained:

(a)   if the following phrase is used to remove a possible confusion of identity: *Miró, el autor* 'Miró the author' (i.e. not the painter); *Córdoba, la ciudad argentina* 'Cordoba, the Argentine city' (and not the one in Spain);

(b)   if the following phrase is a comparative or superlative: *Cervantes, el mayor novelista español* 'Cervantes, the greatest Spanish novelist'; *Joaquín, el más listo de los dos* 'Joaquín, the cleverer of the two'.

(c)   if the phrase is qualified by a following word or phrase:

Javier Marcos, el arquitecto que diseñó las dos fuentes	J. M., the architect who designed the two fountains

3.2.13   Colloquial use of *la de*
In familiar language, *la de* may mean 'loads of', 'tons of':

Con la de números de abogado que vienen en la guía . . .	with all the dozens of lawyers' numbers there are in the directory . . .
. . . la de veces que han dicho eso	. . . the number of times they've said that!

3.2.14   With numbered nouns
Unlike English, nouns identified by a number take the article:

Vivo en el piso 38	I live in flat 38
una disposición del artículo 277 de la Constitución	a provision in Art. 277 of the Constitution

3.2.15   Phrases denoting place
The following require the article in Spanish:

a/en/de la cama (*en cama* is also possible)	to/in/from bed
a/en/de la iglesia	to/in/from church
al/en el/del cielo/infierno	to/in/from Heaven/Hell
al/en el/del hospital	to/in/from hospital/
en la cárcel/en la escuela/en el trabajo	in prison/at school/ at work
en el escenario	on stage
en la televisión	on television
en el espacio	in space
en el mar	at sea, on/in the sea
debajo de la tierra (but *bajo tierra*)	underground
a/en/de casa (Often *a/en/de la casa* in SA)	at/in/from home

3.2.16   After the verb *jugar*
The verb *jugar* requires the article: *jugar a la pelota* 'to play ball/with a

ball', *jugar al ajedrez* 'to play chess', *jugar a las cartas* 'to play cards'; *jugar al escondite* 'to play hide and seek'.

3.2.17   After pronouns
The article is required after first and second-person plural pronouns in phrases like the following: *ustedes los uruguayos* 'you Uruguayans', *nosotros los pobres* 'we poor people', *vosotras las españolas* 'you Spanish women . . .'

It is also used when the pronoun is deleted:

Las mujeres de los mineros siempre estamos en vilo pensando en los hombres	we miners' wives are always on tenterhooks thinking about the men
(A. López Salinas, dialogue)	
Los ingleses siempre ocultáis vuestras emociones	you English always hide your emotions

3.3   Uses and omissions of the indefinite article

Use of the indefinite article in Spanish generally corresponds to the use of 'a'/'an' in English, but its syntax differs from English in two respects:

(a)   it is omitted before singular count nouns in certain contexts (described below): *tengo coche* 'I've got a car', *Mario es ingeniero* 'Mario's an engineer', *lo abrió sin llave* 'he opened it without a key', *es mentira* 'it's a lie';

(b)   it can appear in the plural: *unos pantalones* 'a pair of trousers', *han organizado unas manifestaciones* 'they've organized demonstrations', *son unos genios incomprendidos* 'they're misunderstood geniuses'.

Note: for *uno/una* as an impersonal pronoun see 24.3.1.

3.3.1   Indefinite article before more than one noun
The indefinite article is usually required before each noun in a list of nouns – more so than in English:

Entraron un hombre y una mujer	a man and (a) woman entered
Compré una máquina de escribir y una papelera para mi despacho	I bought a typewriter and (a) wastepaper basket for my office

However, omission is necessary when the nouns refer to the same thing:

una actriz y cantante	an actress and singer (one woman)
Este libro está escrito con una maestría y delicadeza insólitas	this novel is written with unusual skill and delicacy
un cuchillo y abrelatas	a combined knife and tin-opener

3.3.2   Omission before singular count nouns: general
The indefinite article is very often omitted before singular count nouns in circumstances difficult to define, whenever the non-specific, generic nature of the following noun is stressed. Omission is more common in writing than in speech:

Nigeria estrenó ayer nuevo presidente civil después de trece años de régimen militar (*El País*)	Yesterday Nigeria received a new civilian president after thirteen years of military rule
O nos ponemos de acuerdo y se va a referéndum . . .	either we agree and a referendum is held . . .
Voy a pedir hora	I'm going to ask for an appointment
(*una hora* = one hour or a specific time)	
Hay examen de final de curso	there is an end-of-term examination
(*un examen* is more specific as to the number of examinations.)	

3.3.3 Omission before nouns denoting profession, status, sex

The indefinite article is omitted before professions, occupations, social status and, often, sex:

Soy piloto/son buzos	I'm a pilot/they're divers
Mi mujer es enfermera	my wife's a nurse
Es soltero	he's a bachelor
Eran ladrones	they were (full-time) thieves
Se hizo detective	he became a detective
. . . *y aunque Alejandra era mujer* . . . (E. Sabato, Arg.)	and although Alejandra was a woman . . .

But nouns denoting personal qualities require the article: cf. *es negrero* 'he is a trader in black slaves' (profession); *es un negrero* 'he's a "slave driver"' (i.e. makes you work too hard); *eres un genio* 'you're a genius'; *es un ladrón* 'he's a thief' (i.e. not professionally).

Notes (i) If a noun denoting a profession is qualified or restricted by a phrase or adjective, it requires the article:

Es un poeta fracasado	he's a failed poet
Es un actor que nunca encuentra trabajo	he's an actor who never finds work

But if the resulting noun phrase is still a profession or is generic, no article is used: *soy profesor de español*. See 3.3.4.

(ii) The article is retained if it means 'one of . . .':

¿Quién es ese que ha saludado? (Es) un profesor	who was that who said hullo? (He's) one of the teachers

3.3.4 Retention of indefinite article before qualified nouns

As soon as nouns are qualified (restricted) by a clause, phrase or adjective they become specific and the article is obligatory: *tengo padre* 'I've got a father', *tengo un padre que es inaguantable* 'I've got an unbearable father'. But if the resulting noun phrase is still generic the article may still be omitted: *tú eres hombre respetable* 'you're a respectable man', *es pastor protestante* 'he's a protestant vicar'.

Note This rule also applies in the plural: *es un conservador arrepentido/son unos conservadores arrepentidos* 'he's a repentant conservative'/'they're repentant conservatives':

Es un ejemplo/son unos ejemplos que hemos encontrado en tu novela	it's an example/they're examples we found in your novel

El tipo había estudiado su carrera en   the fellow/guy had studied for his degree
   Inglaterra y en seguida me llené de   in England, and I was immediately filled
   unos celos juveniles hacia él   with juvenile jealousy towards him
   . (F. Umbral)

3.3.5 Indefinite article in appositive phrases
The indefinite article is normally omitted in apposition in written language:

El Español de hoy, lengua en ebullición   Spanish today, a Language in Ferment
    (book title)

Estuvimos quince días en Acapulco,   we spent a fortnight in Acapulco, a place
   lugar que nunca olvidaré   I'll never forget
a orillas del Huisne, arroyo de apariencia   on the banks of the Huisne, a seemingly
   tranquila . . . (Borges, Arg.)   tranquil stream

But in informal language, or if the noun in apposition is qualified by an adjective or clause, the article may optionally be retained:

. . . *el Coronel Gaddafi de Libia, un*   Colonel Gaddafi of Libya, a fervent
   ardiente admirador del ayatollah   admirer of Ayatollah Khomeini
   Jomeini . . . (*Cambio16*)

3.3.6 Indefinite article to distinguish nouns from adjectives
Many Spanish nouns are indistinguishable in form from adjectives: use of *un/una* indicates that the noun is meant:

Juan es cobarde   John is cowardly
Juan es un cobarde   John is a coward
Papá es (un) fascista   father is a fascist
Soy (un) extranjero   I'm foreign/a foreigner

The noun is usually more emphatic than the adjective. The indefinite article is also used in the plural so as to retain the distinction: *son desgraciados* 'they're unhappy', *son unos desgraciados* 'they're wretches'.

3.3.7 Omission after *ser*
Omission of the indefinite article after *ser* is frequent (a) in certain common phrases, (b) in literary style. (A rare English counterpart is the optional omission of 'a' with 'part', cf. 'this is (a) part of our heritage' *esto es (una) parte de nuestro patrimonio*.)

Omission is much more common in negative sentences and apparently more frequent in Peninsular Spanish than in Latin-American.

   (a)   In the following phrases omission seems to be optional:

Es (una) coincidencia   it's a coincidence
Es (una) cuestión de dinero   it's a question of money
Es (una) víctima de las circunstancias   he/she's a victim of circumstances

No clear rule can be formulated since the article is retained in other common phrases of a similar type:

Es una lata (colloquial)   it's a nuisance
Es una pena   it's a pity
Es un problema   it's a problem
Es un desastre   it's/he's a disaster
Ha sido un éxito   it was a success

Omission often occurs after the negative verb even though it is not usual after the positive verb:

No es molestia/problema	it's no bother/problem
No es exageración	it's no exaggeration
No es desventaja	it's not a disadvantage

(b) Elsewhere, omission generally produces a literary effect:

La codorniz es ave tiernísima (M. Delibes)	the quail is an extremely tender bird (to eat)
Es ley de nuestra lengua la debilitación de la 'd' intervocal (Carnicer)	weakening of intervocalic 'd' is a law of our language
Es privilegio peculiar de ciertos linajes de pura sangre celta (Borges, Arg.)	it is a special privilege of certain thoroughbred Celtic families

In these examples the article would be normal in speech.

Notes (i)   If the following noun is not generic, the article is retained. Thus *es mar de veras* (Vargas Llosa, Peruvian dialogue) 'it's (a) real sea', but *el hombre es un lobo para el hombre* 'man is a wolf to man' (but not a member of the wolf species).

   (ii)   Omission of the indefinite article before a qualified noun tends to produce an archaic or heavily literary effect, as in *entra una señora con sombrero verde con plumas de avestruz* 'a lady with a green hat with ostrich feathers enters', where *un sombrero verde* would nowadays be much more normal. Similarly, where Unamuno wrote *era un viejecillo {. . .} con levitón de largos bolsillos* 'he was a little old man . . . with a large frock-coat with deep pockets', a modern writer might prefer *un levitón*. Purists occasionally complain about this increasing use of the indefinite article which they attribute to English or French influence.

3.3.8   Omission after *tener*, *llevar*, *usar* and similar verbs

Spanish omits the indefinite article after a number of verbs such as *tener*, *comprar*, *sacar* 'take' or 'draw out' (with cinema tickets, etc. = 'buy' or 'book'), *buscar*, *llevar* 'wear', before a certain type of noun. These nouns usually represent things of which one would normally expect to have only one at a time: umbrella, pen, spoon, nanny, valet, cook, hat etc., and omission of the article focuses attention on the verb rather than the noun, e.g. in the case of *tener*, on the fact one has it rather than on what one has. Often the noun denotes some object or person – wife, garden, video recorder, telephone, freezer – which in some way defines the social status of the speaker:

Pepe ya tiene secretaria	P.'s got a secretary now
Ya he sacado entrada	I've already got a ticket
Vamos a buscarle novia	let's look for a girlfriend for him
Siempre lleva anillo	he always wears a ring
Hubo quien se ofendió y sacó pistola (Vargas Llosa, Peru)	there was one person who took offence and pulled a gun
Barcelona tiene puerto y parque y tranvía y metro y autobús y cine (L. Goytisolo)	B. has a port, park, tramway, metro, buses and cinema(s)
Los gatos suelen tener cola	cats usually have tails

The indefinite article reappears if the particular identity of the object is relevant:

Llevaba una falda blanca	she was wearing a white skirt

| *Tenía* {. . .} *una carita de chico pecoso . . .* (F. Umbral) | she had a cute face like a freckled boy's |

Use of the indefinite article with unqualified nouns may therefore hint at some suppressed comment: *tiene una mujer . . .* 'he's got a wife' . . . (and is she . . .), *tiene un coche . . .* 'you should see his car' . . . This may sound insinuating.

Note   If it would be normal to have more than one of the things denoted, or if the idea of 'one' is relevant, the article must be used: *¿tienes un hermano?* do you have a brother? – not **¿tienes hermano?*:

¿Tienes un dólar?	have you got a dollar?
¿Has comprado una novela?	have you bought a novel?
Tiene un novio en Burgos y otro en Huelva	she's got one boyfriend in Burgos and another in Huelva

3.3.9   Omission after *como, a modo/manera de, por, sin, con*

(a)   The indefinite article is omitted after *a manera de, a modo de* and after *como* when it means 'in the capacity of' or 'by way of':

a manera de prólogo	by way of a prologue
a modo de bastón	as/like a walking stick
como ejemplo	as an example
Utilicé mi zapato como martillo	I used my shoe as a hammer
Vino como ayudante	he came as an assistant

(b)   It is omitted after *por* when it means 'instead of', 'in place of' or 'for' in phrases like: *por respuesta le dio un beso* 'she gave him a kiss as a reply'; *por toda comida me dieron un plato de arroz* 'for a meal they gave me a plate of rice' (i.e. 'all I got for a meal was . . .').

(c)   It is usually omitted after *sin* without:

No lo vas a poder cortar sin cuchillo/ no vas a poder cortarlo sin cuchillo	you won't be able to cut it without a knife
Ha venido sin camisa	he's come without a shirt on
un gato sin cola	a cat without a tail

But if the idea of 'one' is stressed, the article is required:

| *sin una peseta* | without a (single) peseta |
| *sin un amigo a quien contar sus problemas* | without a friend to tell his problems to |

(d)   It is omitted after *con* when it means 'wearing', 'equipped with' and in many other adverbial phrases:

Siempre va con abrigo	he always wears an overcoat
una casa con jardín	a house with a garden
La Esfinge {. . .} *es un león echado en la tierra y con cabeza de hombre* (Borges, Arg.)	the Sphinx is a lion stretched out on the ground, with a man's head
Lo escribí con lápiz	I wrote it with a pencil
con ganas/violencia	enthusiastically/violently

etc.

3.3.10   Omission after *qué*, and before *tal*, *medio*, *cierto*, *otro*

The following constructions differ from English:

¡qué cantidad!/¡qué ruido!	what a quantity!/noise!
¿Cómo ha podido hacer tal/semejante cosa? (colloquially *una cosa así*)?	how could he have done such a thing!?
(*un tal* = 'a certain')	
media pinta/medio kilo	half a pint/kilo
cierta mujer/otra cerveza	a certain woman/another beer

See 9.7 for *cierto* and 9.12 for *otro*.

3.3.11   Uses of *unos/unas*

The Spanish indefinite article appears in the plural with various meanings, some of them elusive:

(a)   before numbers, 'approximately':

unos trescientos mil pesos	about 300,000 pesos
Se calculó que el terremoto duró unos 25 segundos	it was calculated that the earthquake lasted some twenty-five seconds

(b)   'A few':

Le dieron unas monedas	they gave him a few coins
Tomamos unas cervezas	we had a few beers
Todavía tenía unos restos de fe	he still had a few vestiges of faith

Very often the meaning is merely 'a number of', i.e. a limited but vague quantity. When used thus, it may merely moderate the force of a following noun. It can therefore add a modest note, and may sometimes be the equivalent of 'some' or the colloquial 'just a couple of':

El gobierno ha organizado unas elecciones (*Cambio16*)	the government has organized elections

(Omission of *unas* would imply something grander, e.g. general elections.)

Mira estas fotos – son unas vistas tomadas en Guadalajara	look at these photos – they're just a few shots taken in Guadalajara

But sometimes use of *unos* makes little difference –

El pacifismo debería traducirse en unos comportamientos políticos que no tuviesen ninguna indulgencia con los violentos (*La Vanguardia, unos* deletable)	pacifism ought to be translated into (a set of) patterns of political behaviour which show no indulgence towards the violent

(c)   'A pair of' before plural nouns denoting symmetrical objects (see 2.2.2 for a list), or objects occurring as pairs:

Llevaba unos pantalones a rayas	he was wearing striped trousers
Se había puesto unas gafas que no intelectualizaban su rostro (F. Umbral)	she had put on a pair of glasses which did not give her face an intellectual air
. . . sacándose las medias con unos absurdos guantes de lana (*idem*)	taking off her stockings with a pair of absurd woollen gloves
He comprado unas cortinas de seda	I've bought a pair of silk curtains

(d)   Use of *unos/unas* may, in some contexts, show that the noun following is not used generically:

Son niñas	they're little girls
Son unas niñas	they're (acting like) little girls
Son payasos	they're (circus) clowns
Son unos payasos	they're (acting like) clowns

(e)   *Unos/unas* may be needed to show that the following noun is a noun and not an adjective or noun used as an adjective. See 3.3.6 for examples.

Note: *Unos/unas* is required before nouns which usually only appear in the plural, to show that only one is meant: *me he caído por unas escaleras* 'I've fallen down some/a flight of stairs'; *voy a tomarme unas vacaciones* 'I'm going to have a holiday'.

4 Adjectives

(a)   It is useful to distinguish 'descriptive' and 'attributive'* adjectives. Compare *un libro aburrido* 'a boring book', which is the same as *un libro que es aburrido* 'a book which is boring' (descriptive) and *la presión sanguínea* 'blood pressure', which is the same as *la presión de la sangre* (attributive). Attributive adjectives, a growing class in modern Spanish, have the property that they never precede the noun, whereas most other adjectives may do so – the difference between *un difícil problema* and *un problema difícil* being one of the more subtle problems facing the student of Spanish. For further discussion of attributive adjectives see 4.6.

(b)   Almost all Spanish adjectives function as nouns if an article or demonstrative is added: *rojo/los rojos* 'red'/'the reds', *enfermo/estos enfermos* 'ill'/'these ill people', *reptil/los reptiles* 'reptilian'/'reptiles', etc. However the converse is not true: adjectives are formed in unpredictable ways from nouns: *automóvil* > *automovilístico*, *legislación* > *legislativo*, *montaña* > *montañoso*, *fango* > *fangoso* 'mud'/'muddy', *leche* > *lácteo* 'milk', etc., although a few, e.g. *miembro*, *virgen* may function as adjectives, cf. *los países miembros* 'member countries', *las tierras vírgenes* 'virgin territories', etc.

(c)   Spanish adjectives are marked for number and, where possible, for gender. However a small group of rather anomalous adjectives, e.g. *macho*, *violeta*, are usually invariable in form.

(d)   Some adjectives can be used with object pronouns and the verb *ser*: *me es importante, nos es indispensable, estas materias primas le son muy necesarias* 'these raw materials are very necessary for him/you', etc. But most cannot. See 11.8 for discussion.

(f)   Adjectives and participles in *-ante*, *-iente* are discussed under participles at 18.4.

(e)   The gerund in *-ndo* may not be used as an adjective: *una muñeca que anda* 'a walking doll', not *una muñeca andando* – ' a doll walking'. There are two exceptions, *hirviendo* 'boiling' and *ardiendo* 'burning':

Tráeme agua hirviendo	bring me some boiling water
Tienes la frente ardiendo	your forehead is burning

*This is the term used in *Collins Spanish-English/English-Spanish Dictionary* (1971). Judge and Healey use the term 'relational' in their *Reference Grammar of Modern French* (1983).

Yo más bien soy un carbón ardiendo   I feel more like a burning coal
  (i.e. sexually excited. Peruv. dialogue in
  Vargas Llosa)

Chorreando 'dripping wet' may be an exception in *llevo la ropa chorreando* 'my clothes are dripping wet'.

Hirviendo, ardiendo and similar words are invariable in form, take no suffixes and cannot appear before a noun. See chapter 19 for further details on the use of the gerund.

4.1 Morphology of adjectives

Spanish adjectives are of three types:

Type 1: Those which agree in number and gender with the noun.
Type 2: Those which show agreement for number but not gender.
Type 3: Those which are invariable (few and mostly colours).

4.1.1 Type 1 adjectives (marked for number and gender)
These include adjectives whose masculine singular ends in:

  -o, with the rare exceptions noted at 4.1.3
  -án
  -és, except *cortés* 'courteous' and *descortés* 'discourteous', which are type 2.
  -ín, usually a diminutive suffix (but see note iii)
  -ón, usually an augmentative suffix (but see note iii)
  -or, with the dozen or so exceptions listed in note (i)
  -ote and *-ete*

and adjectives of place of origin or nationality, not ending in *-a, -í, -e, -al* or *-ar*, e.g. *celta, iraní, londinense, provenzal, balear*, which are type 2.

The feminine is formed by changing any final vowel into *-a* or, if the masculine singular ends in a consonant, by adding *-a*. The plural is formed by adding *-s* to a vowel, *-es* to a consonant. *z* is changed to *c* before *e*:

	Singular	Plural	
Masc.	*bueno*	*buenos*	good
Fem.	*buena*	*buenas*	
Masc.	*musulmán*	*musulmanes*	Muslim
Fem.	*musulmana*	*musulmanas*	
Masc.	*aragonés*	*aragoneses*	Aragonese
Fem.	*aragonesa*	*aragonesas*	
Masc.	*saltarín*	*saltarines*	restless/
Fem.	*saltarina*	*saltarinas*	fidgety
Masc.	*mandón*	*mandones*	bossy
Fem.	*mandona*	*mandonas*	
Masc.	*hablador*	*habladores*	talkative
Fem.	*habladora*	*habladoras*	
Masc.	*regordete*	*regordetes*	plump
Fem.	*regordeta*	*regordetas*	
Masc.	*español*	*españoles*	Spanish
Fem.	*española*	*españolas*	

Masc.	*andaluz*	*andaluces*	Andalusian
Fem.	*andaluza*	*andaluzas*	

Notes (i) Adjectives in *-or* which have a comparative meaning are all type 2 (i.e. have no separate feminine form):

anterior·	previous	*menor*	minor/smaller/
exterior	outer		younger
inferior	lower/inferior	*peor*	worse
interior	inner/interior	*posterior*	later/subsequent
mayor	greater/older	*superior**	upper/superior
mejor	better	*ulterior*	later/further

*But: *la madre superiora* 'mother superior'

(ii) *Montés* 'wild' (i.e. not domesticated) is usually invariable: *gato montés* 'wild/untamed cat', *cabra montés* 'wild goat'.

(iii) Two or three adjectives ending in *-ín* or *-ón* are type 2 (have no feminine form): *marrón* 'brown', *afín* 'related'/'similar': *una camisa marrón*, 'a brown shirt', *ideas afines* 'related ideas'.

4.1.2 Type 2 adjectives (marked only for number)

No difference between masculine and feminine. This class includes (with the exceptions noted above) all adjectives whose masculine singular ends in a consonant or in *-a, -e, -ú, -í*. The plural is formed by adding *-s* to a final vowel other than stressed *-í* or *ú* which add *-es*, and *-es* to a final consonant. *z* is written as *c* before *e*:

Singular	**Plural**	
azteca	*aztecas*	Aztec
suicida	*suicidas*	suicidal
grande	*grandes*	big/great
iraní	*iraníes*	Iranian
hindú	*hindúes*	Hindu/Indian
cortés	*corteses*	courteous
gris	*grises*	grey
feliz	*felices*	happy

Notes (i) Adjectives ending in *-í* may make their plural in *-ís* in spontaneous speech, and some, e.g. *maorí/maoríes* or *maorís* 'Maori' are uncertain.

(ii) If a diminutive or augmentative suffix is added to one of these adjectives, it then becomes type one: *mayorcito/mayorcita* 'grown up', *grandote/grandota* 'extremely large'.

(iii) *Dominante* forms a popular feminine *dominanta* 'bossy'/'domineering'. A few other popular forms in *-nta* may occur, but in general adjectives ending in *-nte* are not marked for gender, whereas some nouns ending in *-nte* are.

4.1.3 Type 3 adjectives (marked for neither number nor gender)

Members of this group, which includes a number of colour adjectives, are invariable in form, presumably because they are felt to be nouns rather than adjectives. They are not numerous:

singular	**plural**
un pantalón beige	*unos pantalones beige*
una camisa beige	*camisas beige*

(a)   Common members of this class are: *alerta** 'alerta' (*estamos alerta* 'we're alert'); *extra**; *hembra* 'female' (*los ratones hembra* 'female mice'); *macho* 'male'; *ultra** 'extreme right-wing'; *sport* (*coches sport* 'sports cars'); *modelo* (*las granjas modelo* 'model farms'); *clave** 'key' (*el punto clave* 'the key issue'); *monstruo* ' monster' (*una casa monstruo*).

Notes (i)   This group is unstable, and the words asterisked often agree in the plural: *problemas claves, pagos extras* –

Nuestra obligación es vivir	our obligation is to live constantly
constantemente alertas	alert . . .
(Vargas Llosa, Peru)	

(ii)   Although they look like nouns, *maestro*, *virgen* and *perro* agree like normal adjectives: *llaves maestras* 'master keys', *tierras vírgenes* 'virgin territories', *¡qué vida más perra!* 'what a rotten life!'

(iii)   *Varón* 'male' (of humans) is type 2: *niños varones* 'male children'.

(iv)   Pluralization of the adjectival word restores its function as a noun. Compare *niños modelo* 'model children' and *niños modelos* 'child models'.

(b)   Any suitable noun, preceded by *color*, *de color* or *color de*, can describe a colour: *ojos color (de) humo* 'smoke-coloured eyes'; *color barquillo* 'wafer-coloured'.

The phrase with *color* is sometimes dropped, and the noun is then used like a type 3 adjective (i.e. it does not agree): *tres botones naranja/ rosa/beige/malva/violeta/esmeralda* 'three orange/pink/beige/mauve/ violet/emerald buttons'; *corbatas salmón* 'salmon ties'; *cintas fresa* 'strawberry colour ribbons'.

Other nouns so used are: *añil* 'indigo'; *azafrán* 'saffron'; *azur* 'azure'; *café* 'coffee'; *carmesí* 'crimson'; *cereza* 'cherry'; *chocolate*; *crema* 'cream'; *escarlata* 'scarlet'; *grana* 'scarlet'; *granate* 'garnet'/'dark red'; *lila* 'lilac'; *oro* 'gold' (*dorado* = 'golden'); *paja* 'straw'; *sepia*; *turquesa* 'turquoise', etc.

Notes (i)   Colloquially, and in some writers, *naranja, rosa, malva, violeta* and a few others may be pluralized – *flores malvas* 'mauve flowers', *los jacarandaes se pusieron violetas* (E. Sabato, Arg.) 'the jacarandas turned violet', *las uñas violetas* (C. Barral, Spain, quoted Carnicer) – but this seems to be avoided in careful language:

. . . *sus ojos violeta parpadean*	her violet eyes are blinking
(J. Marsé)	
pliegos de papel llegados de Europa,	folds of paper from Europe, blue, mauve,
azules, malva, rosa, verdes	pink, green
(F. Umbral)	

(ii)   It is unusual to find such adjectives before a noun, except by poetic licence: *como sonreía la rosa mañana* (A. Machado) 'as pink dawn was smiling'.

(iii)   *Color* or *de color* is, in practice, usually inserted before such words in everyday language: *una bicicleta color naranja* 'an orange bicycle', *zapatos color mostaza* 'mustard-colour shoes'.

(c)   Modified colour adjectives are invariable:

hojas verde oscuro	dark green leaves

calcetines azul claro	pale/light blue socks
pantalones azul marino	navy-blue trousers
una masa gris castaño	a grey-brown mass

There are special words for some common mixed colours: *verdirrojo* 'red-green'; *verdiblanco* 'greenish white'; *verdinegro* 'very dark green'; *blanquiazul* 'bluish white'; *blanquinegro* 'black and white'; *blanquirrojo* 'red and white'. These agree like normal adjectives.

4.1.4 Compound adjectives
Some compound adjectives are single words and behave like any adjective: *muchachas pelirrojas* 'red-haired girls', *cuernos puntiagudos* 'sharp-pointed horns'.

In hyphenated compounds only the second element agrees:

movimientos político-militares	political-military movements
teorías histórico-críticas	historical-critical theories

4.1.5 Shortened form of some adjectives
A number of common adjectives lose their final syllable in certain circumstances.

(a) The singular of *grande* is shortened to *gran* before any noun: *un gran momento* 'a great moment', *una gran comida* 'a great meal'. The *-de* is infrequently retained in literary styles for purposes of emphasis or before words beginning with a vowel: *este grande héroe nacional* 'this great national hero'.

Grande is not shortened if *más* or *menos* precede: *el más grande éxito* 'the greatest success' (better *el mayor éxito*).

(b) The following lose their final vowel when placed before a singular *masculine* noun or combination of adjective and masculine noun:

alguno	*algún remoto día*	some remote day
bueno	*un buen cocinero*	a good cook
malo	*un mal ingeniero*	a bad engineer
ninguno	*en ningún momento*	at no moment
postrero	*tu postrer día*	your last day (archaic)
primero	*mi primer gran amor*	my first great love
tercero	*el tercer candidato*	the third candidate

Notes (i) The full form must be used if a conjunction or similar word separates the adjective from the noun:

esta grande pero costosa victoria	this great but costly victory
un bueno aunque agrio vino	a good though sour wine

(ii) Popular speech (especially Spanish-American) sometimes uses short forms before feminine nouns, but this should be avoided: *la primera mujer* 'the first woman', not **la primer mujer*; *ninguna española* 'no Spanish woman'; *buena parte de* 'a good part of'.

(iii) *Algún* and *ningún* are also found before feminine nouns beginning with a stressed *a-* or *ha-*. See 9.4 and 21.4.5 for details.

(iv) For details on *cualquiera* see 9.8.

(v) *Santo* 'saint' is shortened to *San* before the names of all male saints except those beginning with *Do-* or *To-*: *san Juan, san Blas, santo Tomás*. It is not shortened when it means 'holy': *el Santo Padre* 'the Holy Father', *todo el santo día* 'the whole day through', *el*

Santo Oficio 'the Holy Office' (the Inquisition).
   (vi)   For the short forms of *tanto* and *cuanto* (*tan* and *cuan*) see 9.15 and 22.5b.

4.2   Agreement of adjectives

4.2.1   Agreement of post-posed adjectives
(a)   One or more masculine nouns require a masculine adjective: *un elefante asiático, mil pesos mexicanos, mi padre es inglés.*
   One or more feminine nouns require a feminine adjective: *la Grecia antigua, mil pesetas españolas, mi madre es inglesa.*
   Two or more nouns of different gender require a masculine plural adjective:

Profesores y profesoras ingleses	English men and women teachers
Puentes y casas decrépitos	derelict bridges and houses
Novelas y cuentos italianos	Italian novels and short stories

   (b)   If several adjectives follow a plural noun, and each adjective refers to only one individual item, the adjective will be singular: *los presidentes venezolano y peruano* 'the Peruvian president and the Venezuelan president'. *Los presidentes venezolanos y peruanos* means 'the presidents of Venezuela and the presidents of Peru'.

4.2.2   Agreement of pre-posed adjectives
A plural adjective followed by a singular noun sounds unnatural: the adjective usually agrees with the first noun only:

con exagerada cortesía y deferencia	with exaggerated courtesy and deference
Aquella dulzura y encanto de su hermana	that gentleness and charm of his sister

   The plural may be used to avoid severe ambiguities: *sus amados hijo y nieto* 'his beloved son and grandson' (both beloved).

4.2.3   'Neuter' agreement
An adjective that refers to no noun in particular is masculine singular in form:

Es absurdo hacerlo sin ayuda	it's absurd to do it without help
Es peligroso, pero lo haré	it's dangerous, but I'll do it
Fantástico . . . la cantidad de dinero que gasta en tabaco	fantastic . . . the amount of money he spends on tobacco
La miseria no tiene nada de sano y placentero (Vargas Llosa, Peru)	extreme poverty has nothing healthy or agreeable about it

Notes (i)   In *tampoco es bueno demasiada natación* (L. Goytisolo, dialogue) 'too much swimming isn't good either' the adjective does not modify the noun *natación* but the idea *demasiada natación. Buena* would also be correct.
   (ii)   For adjectives with the article *lo* (*lo bueno, lo grande*, etc.) see 7.2.

4.3   Formation of adjectives of place

4.3.1   Adjectives from countries and regions
The following are noteworthy:

Alemania	*alemán*	*Gales*	*galés*
América	*americano*		(Wales/Welsh)
(often = Latin-American. See note (i))		*Galicia*	*gallego*
Argelia	*argelino*	*Gibraltar*	*gibraltareño*
(Algeria)		*Grecia*	*griego*
(la) Argentina	*argentino*	*Guatemala*	*guatemalteco*
Austria	*austriaco*	*Holanda*	*holandés*
Bélgica	*belga*	*Honduras*	*hondureño*
Bolivia	*boliviano*	*Hungría*	*húngaro*
(el) Brasil	*brasileño*	*la India*	*indio,*
(el) Canadá	*canadiense*		also *hindú,*
Canarias	*canario*		plur. *hindúes*

indio is often taken to mean Amerindian,
especially in Spanish America

Castilla	*castellano*	*Inglaterra*	*inglés*
(Castile/Castilian.		(often used for	
See note (ii))		'British')	
Cataluña	*catalán*	*Irlanda*	*irlandés*
Chile	*chileno*	*(el) Japón*	*japonés*
China	*chino*	*Marruecos*	*marroquí*
Colombia	*colombiano*	*Méjico*	*mejicano*

(spelt *México/mexicano* by Mexicans,
and increasingly elsewhere, but
pronounced *-ji-*)

Costa Rica	*costarriqueño*	*Nicaragua*	*nicaragüense*
	or *costarricense*	*Panamá*	*panameño*
Dinamarca	*danés* (Danish)	*(el) Paraguay*	*paraguayo*
Ecuador	*ecuatoriano*	*(el) Perú*	*peruano*
Egipto	*egipcio*	*Polonia*	*polaco* (Polish)
	(not *egipciano*)	*Portugal*	*portugués*
Escocia	*escocés*	*Puerto Rico*	*portorriqueño*
	(Scottish)	*el Salvador*	*salvadoreño*
Estados Unidos	*estadounidense*	*Suecia*	*sueco*
	(rare in speech.		(Swedish)
	See note (i))	*Suiza*	*suizo*
Europa	*europeo*	*Uruguay*	*uruguayo*
Francia	*francés*	*Vascongadas*	*vasco*
		País Vasco	
		Venezuela	*venezolano*

Notes (i)   The adjective from *América Latina* or *Latinoamérica* is *latinoamericano* or *americano*. *Norteamericano* is in practice always taken to mean our 'American' and is more common than *estadounidense*. The adjective from *América del sur* 'South America' – which does not include Central America, Mexico or the Caribbean – is *sudamericano*. *Suramericano* is considered wrong, but is often heard in Spanish America.

   (ii)   *Castellano* is the Castilian language, strictly speaking the dialect of Castile, which came to be the dominant literary language of Spain, although *castellano* everywhere may mean simply 'Spanish'. Catalans, Basques and Galicians sometimes object to Spanish being called *el español*.

(iii) *Indiano* used to denote a 'colonial' who had made his money in Latin America.

(iv) *Árabe* means 'Arab' or 'Arabic'.

4.3.2 Adjectives from towns

There is no general rule for deriving adjectives from the names of towns, and some localities pride themselves on adjectives of obscure derivation, e.g. *Huelva – onubense.*

Some of the more common are:

Álava	*alavés*	*Nápoles*	*napolitano*
Alcalá	*complutense*	*Nueva York*	*neoyorquino*
(used of the old university of Alcalá, now			
sited in Madrid)			
Ávila	*abulense*	*Oviedo*	*ovetense*
Badajoz	*pacense*	*Pamplona*	*pamplonés/*
Barcelona	*barcelonés*		*pamplonica*
Bilbao	*bilbaíno*		(invariable)
Bogotá	*bogotano*	*París*	*parisiense,*
Buenos Aires	*porteño/bonaerense*		also *parisién*
Burgos	*burgalés*		'Paris-style' (also
Cádiz	*gaditano*		*parisino*)
Caracas	*caraqueño*	*la Paz*	*paceño/pacense*
Córdoba	*cordobés*	*Quito*	*quiteño*
la Coruña	*coruñés*	*Río de Janeiro*	*carioca*
Cuenca	*conquense*	*Roma*	*romano*
Florencia	*florentino*	*Salamanca*	*salmantino/*
Granada	*granadino*		*salamanqués*
la Habana	*habanero*	*San Sebastián*	*donostiarra*
Lima	*limeño*		(a Basque word)
Londres	*londinense*	*Santander*	*santanderino*
	(note spelling)	*Santiago*	*santiaguino* (Chile)
Lugo	*lucense*		*santiagués* (Spain)
Madrid	*madrileño*	*Sevilla*	*sevillano*
Málaga	*malagueño*	*Toledo*	*toledano*
Murcia	*murciano*	*Valencia*	*valenciano*
Moscú	*moscovita*	*Valladolid*	*vallisoletano*
		Zaragoza	*zaragozano*

4.4   Intensive forms of the adjective

4.4.1   The suffix -*ísimo*: meaning and formation

The suffix -*ísimo* can be added to many adjectives. It intensifies the original meaning: *Ana es riquísima* 'Ana is extremely rich'. It should be used sparingly. It cannot be added to all adjectives, and there are irregularities.

This suffix is sometimes misnamed a 'superlative' suffix, but it cannot be used in comparisons and is best thought of as an intensifier. -*ísimo* is added after removing any final vowel: *grande/grandísimo, guapa/guapísima.*

(a) Adjectives ending *co/ca* and *go/ga* require spelling changes to keep the hard sound of the *c* or *g*: *rico/riquísimo* 'rich'; *vago/vaguísimo* 'vague'/'lazy';

(b) adjectives ending in -*z* change the *z* to *c*: *feliz/felicísimo* 'happy'; *feroz/ferocísimo* 'ferocious';

(c) for adjectives ending in two vowels, see 4.4.2;

(d) adjectives ending in -*ble* change this ending to -*bil*: *amable/amabilísimo* 'friendly'; *posible/posibilísimo*. *Endeble/endeblísimo* 'feeble' is a rare exception.

4.4.2 Adjectives which do not take -*ísimo*
The following adjectives do not take the suffix -*ísimo*:

(a) Those ending in *í, uo, io,* or *eo* if not stressed on the *e*: e.g. *baladí* 'trivial', *arduo* 'arduous', *espontáneo* 'spontaneous', *rubio* 'blond', *tardío* 'late'.

Exceptions: *agrio/agrísimo* 'sour', *amplio/amplísimo* 'wide'/'extensive', *frío/friísimo* 'cold', *limpio/limpísimo* 'clean', *ordinario/ordinarísimo* 'ordinary'/'rude', *pío/piísimo* 'pious', *sucio/sucísimo* 'dirty'.

(b) Words stressed on the antepenultimate syllable (*esdrújulas*) ending in -*ico,* -*fero,* -*geno,* -*voro*: *político, mamífero* 'mammal(ian)', *homogéneo, carnívoro.*

(c) Augmentatives, diminutives and comparatives: *preguntón* 'inquisitive', *bonito* 'pretty', *grandote* 'enormous', *mayor, menor. Es mayorcísimo* 'he's very old' is very colloquial.

(d) Compound adjectives, e.g. *patizambo* 'knock-kneed', *ojituerto* 'one-eyed'.

(e) Many adjectives of more than three syllables ending in -*ble*: *inexplicable*; *incontestable* 'unquestionable', *desmontable* 'collapsible'.

Exceptions: there are exceptions, though some are uncommon: *agradable/agradabilísimo* 'agreeable', *apacible/apacibilísimo*, 'mild', *miserable/miserabilísimo, venerable/venerabilísimo.*

(f) Those whose meaning cannot be further intensified: *estupendo, ideal, infinito, inmortal, total,* etc.

Exceptions: *mismo/mismísimo* 'very' (*la mismísima persona* 'the very same person'), *singular/singularísimo.*

(g) Time and number adjectives: *anual, diario* 'daily', *nocturno, semanal* 'weekly', *quinto* 'fifth', *último* 'last', *vigésimo* 'twentieth', etc.

Exception: *primer/primerísimo* 'first'/'very first of all'.

(h) *Hirviendo* 'boiling' and *ardiendo* 'burning'.

(i) Technical and scientific adjectives and most adjectives ending in -*ista*, e.g. *decimal, termonuclear, transformacional, comunista, nacionalista,* etc.

4.4.3   Irregular intensive forms

(a)   The following are best learnt as separate words:

óptimo	superb (literary)
pésimo	bad/dreadful
máximo	greatest/maximum/supreme
(*jefe máximo* – supreme leader)	
mínimo	slightest/least
supremo	superior/supreme
ínfimo	inferior/least/lowest (literary)
jovencísimo (from *joven*)	young
cursilísimo (from *cursi*)	affected/pseudo-refined
antiquísimo (from *antiguo*)	ancient

(b)   The following forms are occasionally found in older texts or very Latinate written language:

		Older form	Current form
áspero	harsh	*aspérrimo*	*asperísimo*
benévolo	charitable/benevolent	*benevolentísimo*	not used
célebre	famous	*celebérrimo*	not used
cruel	cruel	*crudelísimo*	*cruelísimo*
difícil	difficult	*dificílimo*	*dificilísimo*
fácil	easy	*facílimo*	*facilísimo*
fiel	faithful	*fidelísimo*	*fidelísimo*
frío	cold	*frigidísimo*	*friísimo*
libre	free	*libérrimo*	not used
magnífico	magnificent	*magnificentísimo*	not used
mísero (archaic)	wretched	*misérrimo*	not used?
munífico	munificent	*munificentísimo*	not used
pobre	poor	*paupérrimo*	*pobrísimo*
sabio	wise	*sapientísimo*	not used

(c)   The old rule whereby the diphthongs *ue* and *ie* were simplified to *o* or *e* when unstressed is now most often ignored, although *novísimo* 'very recent' is to be distinguished from *nuevísimo* 'very new':

fuerte	*fuertísimo*	(*fortísimo*)	strong
tierno	*tiernísimo*	(*ternísimo*)	tender
bueno	*buenísimo*	(*bonísimo*)	good
cierto	*ciertísimo*	(*certísimo*)	certain

Some words have never suffered modification: *viejo/viejísimo* 'old', *cuerdo/cuerdísimo* 'sane', etc.

4.5   Position of adjectives in relation to nouns

For the position of *alguno, ninguno, cualquiera, mismo*, possessive adjectives etc., consult these words in the index. For the position of ordinal numerals see 10.14.

It is hardly true to say that the adjective 'normally' follows the noun in Spanish. Adjective position is much more flexible than in English or French, but the underlying rules are difficult to formulate. Many factors of convention, sound and above all style and meaning combine to determine whether, for example, one says *un lejano ruido* or *un ruido lejano* 'a distant noise'. Moreover there seem to be as yet unresearched differences between Peninsular and American Spanish, the latter apparently allowing pre-nominal constructions unacceptable in Spain.

The basic rule seems to be:

(i) *Restrictive adjectives follow the noun.*
(ii) *Non-restrictive adjectives may precede or follow the noun. Some always precede the noun.*

Restrictive adjectives narrow the scope of the noun that precedes them: *vino espumoso* 'sparkling wine' denotes a restricted type of wine; *odio las novelas históricas* 'I hate historical novels' refers only to those novels which are historical.

Non-restrictive adjectives typically refer to the whole of the entity denoted by the noun: *las aburridas conferencias del decano* 'the dean's boring lectures', *la poco apetitosa cocina británica* 'unappetizing British cooking' are generalizations which attribute a quality to every member or aspect of the class of things denoted by the noun.

Unfortunately the distinction between restrictive and non-restrictive adjectives is elusive, and the decision about where to put the adjective often relies on a feel for the language rarely given to non-natives.

4.5.1 Restrictive adjectives
The following adjectives are restrictive, and therefore always follow the noun:

(a) those which create a new type or sub-set of the thing described by the noun:

el agua mineral	mineral water
el pan integral	wholemeal bread
el papel secante	blotting paper
los cazas computerizados	computerized fighter aircraft
las teorías freudianas	Freudian theories
tracción delantera	front-wheel drive
una central nuclear	a nuclear power station
pescado fresco	fresh fish

All the other examples in this section are in fact instances of this type of adjective which can be thought of as a transformed clause: *la poesía romántica* = *aquella poesía que es romántica, las manzanas verdes* = *aquellas manzanas que están verdes.*

(b) Those used for purposes of contrast, whether explicit or implied:

Tráigame una espumadera limpia, no una sucia	bring me a clean ladle, not a dirty one
Tengo un boli verde y otro azul	I have a green ball-point pen, and a blue one
Adoro los ojos azules	I adore blue eyes
No queremos agua salada	we don't want salty water

Note Luján (1980) and others note examples of contrastive pre-nominal adjectives –
? *estoy hablando de las hermosas casas, no de las feas* – but we have not found native
speakers who will accept such sentences.

(c)   Scientific or technical adjectives used to define or specify a noun (as
is almost always the case):

gramática transformativa	transformational grammar
crítica estructuralista	structuralist criticism
laboratorio lingüístico	language laboratory
mando remoto	remote control

Only the most far-fetched styles would use such adjectives poetically or
as epithets, though some, e.g. *unilateral, microscópico, (p)sicoanalítico,
materialista*, might conceivably be used as value judgements (see 4.5.2d).

(d)   Attributive adjectives. These express the origin, substance,
contents or purpose of a noun, e.g.

la nave espacial	space ship
túnel ferroviario	railway tunnel
la guerra nuclear	nuclear war
material bélico (= *material de guerra*)	war matériel

(e)   Adjectives of nationality, which are almost always restrictive:

el clima argentino	the Argentine climate
paella valenciana	paella Valencia-style
los monumentos aztecas	the Aztec monuments

Note: adjectives of nationality may occasionally be used as epithets (see 4.5.2a):

Mi española impulsividad me hace	my Spanish impulsiveness
escribir estas líneas	makes me write these lines
(reader's letter in *Cambio16*)	
su británica reserva	her British reserve

4.5.2   Non-restrictive adjectives

The following adjectives are typically non-restrictive, and may precede a
noun. They can be thought of not as transformations of a clause, but as
derived from a sentence based on *ser* plus an adjective: *la majestuosa
Cuarta Sinfonía de Sibelius* implies *la Cuarta Sinfonía de Sibelius es
majestuosa*, and not *aquella Cuarta Sinfonía de Sibelius que es majestuosa*.

The decision whether to put them in front of a noun depends on stylistic
and other subjective factors. Literary, solemn or poetic styles, journalism
and advertising language particularly favour pre-posed adjectives.

The following adjectives are pre-posed:

(a)   Epithets, i.e. adjectives used to describe qualities typically
associated with the noun. These are rare in ordinary speech or scientific or
technical language, but very common in literary, poetic or other types of
emotive or affective language:

mi distinguido colega	my distinguished colleague
el peligroso tigre asiático	the dangerous Asian tiger
el claro sol de estío (poetic)	the bright summer sun

las magníficas ruinas de Machu Picchu	the magnificent ruins at Machu Picchu
las devastadoras resacas del champaña barato (spoken lang. *champán*)	the devastating hangovers left by cheap champagne
el honroso uniforme del ejército	the honourable uniform of the army
los volubles dioses romanos	the fickle Roman gods

Epithets describe expected or typical qualities: one can say *un enorme elefante* but only *un elefante cojo* since lameness is not typical of elephants; *mi leal amigo* 'my loyal friend' but only *mi amigo vegetariano*; *un difícil problema* or *un problema difícil*, but only *un problema (p)sicológico*, since problems are not typically psychological; *mi española impulsividad* 'my Spanish impulsiveness' but probably not *?mi española timidez* since shyness is not supposed to be typical of Spaniards.

(b) Adjectives which refer to every member of a class whenever ambiguity must be avoided: *tuvo que parar en boxes para cambiar sus deterioradas ruedas* (*El País*) 'he had to stop in the pits to change his worn tyres' (*ruedas deterioradas* could imply that only some of his tyres were worn):

muchas gracias por las magníficas rosas	many thanks for the magnificent roses
Sus evasivas respuestas empezaban a irritarme	his evasive replies were starting to irritate me
las simpáticas peticiones de nuestros oyentes	our listeners' kind requests

For this reason, adjectives applied to unique entities are likely to be pre-posed, unless they apply only to an aspect or part of the thing:

Desde nuestro campamento se veía el imponente Everest	one could see imposing mount Everest from our camp
El izquierdista Frente Farabundo Martí	the left-wing F. Martí Front
Sólo veía la negra silueta de los pinos	he could see only the black silhouette of the pines

But

Existe un Unamuno político y comprometido, y otro contemplativo	there is a political, committed Unamuno, and another contemplative one
También visitamos la ciudad moderna	we also visited the modern (part of the) city

(c) Intensifiers, hyperboles and swearwords – which are extreme examples of adjectives used emotively and often stripped of all real meaning. If they are post-posed, they often recover their literal meaning.

mi negra suerte	my rotten luck
esta maldita máquina de escribir	this cursed typewriter . . .
Valiente soldado eres tú	a great soldier you are (I don't think . . .)
tu dichosa familia	your blessed family
estas condenadas hormigas	these damned ants
cien cochinas/piojosas pesetas (vulgar)	100 lousy pesetas

(d) In general, adjectives which describe the speaker's impression, assessment or evaluation of a thing, or its appearance to him. This can include a vast range of adjectives indicating shape, distance, size, colour, texture, age, passage of time, praise, blame, etc.

Sometimes the difference can be significant, as in *esta poética descripción de Lorca* 'this poetic description of Lorca's' (aesthetic judgement) and *el lenguaje poético de Lorca* 'the language of Lorca's poetry' (factual); or *las decimonónicas actitudes del ministro* 'the minister's nineteenth-century attitudes' (value judgement), and *la novela decimonónica* 'the nineteenth-century novel' (factual).

But very often the difference is merely stylistic, a pre-posed adjective being rather more literary, poetic or dramatic, a post-posed one more matter-of-fact. The following examples will help to train the ear. In every case the adjective could have followed the noun or noun-phrase:

en el remoto pasado	in the remote past
en un reciente discurso	in a recent speech . . .
una momentánea pausa	a moment's pause
un trágico accidente	a tragic accident
su increíble falta de tacto	his incredible lack of tact
un punzante olor	a pungent smell
esta irónica frase de Nietzsche	this ironic phrase of Nietzsche's
el casi olvidado nombre de James MacPherson (Borges, Arg.)	the almost forgotten name of J. M.
La revolución significó para mí una justa redistribución de la riqueza	the revolution meant for me a just redistribution of wealth
una guirnalda de blancas flores	a wreath of white flowers
La pera es de fácil digestión	pears are easily digested
otro de los estrambóticos personajes del autor	another of the author's outlandish characters
Esto obedece a una rigurosa lógica	this obeys a rigorous logic
el creciente costo de la tierra urbana	the rising cost of land within the cities
Además, en el mar hay barcos anclados en permanente contacto con los aviones nocturnos (García Márquez, Colombia, dialogue)	moreover, there are boats anchored at sea in permanent contact with the night aircraft
La ciudad donde, en el anterior siglo, se habían casado Bécquer y Casta Esteban (Popular press, Spain)	the city where, in the previous century, Becquer and Casta E. had married
Si usted me hace serenas preguntas, tendrá serenas respuestas (interview in *Gente*, Argentina)	if you ask me calm questions, you'll get calm answers
Por eso, para evitar la guerra, fuente de indecibles sufrimientos . . . (Vargas Llosa, Peru)	for this reason, to avoid war, the source of unspeakable suffering . . .

Notes (i)   Adjective position is arbitrarily fixed in many set phrases: *Alto Egipto* 'Upper Egypt', *el Sumo Pontífice* 'the Pope', *la Baja California* 'Lower California' (cf. *América Central*, *los Estados Unidos*, *la China Popular* 'People's China', etc.), *altos hornos* 'blast furnaces', *en alta mar* 'on the high seas', *Dios todopoderoso* 'almighty God', *sentido común* 'common sense', *gramática parda* 'smartness'/'cunning', etc.

   (ii)   If an adjective is qualified by an adverb it usually follows the noun: *esta noticia altamente reveladora* 'this highly revealing news item', *una chica frígidamente agresiva* 'a frigidly aggressive girl'; *con tres amigos igualmente roñosos* 'with three equally mean friends'. Compare:

Anuncian una útil linterna (not *linterna útil*)	they are advertising a useful torch

and
Anuncian una linterna muy útil   they are advertising a very useful torch
This is the safest option, although constructions like *la altamente reveladora noticia* 'the highly revealing news item', *la siempre inquieta juventud* 'ever restless youth', *las ya de por sí interesantes confesiones del autor* 'the in themselves interesting confessions of the author' are found in literary style, and can be explained in terms of the contrast between restrictive and non-restrictive adjectives.

(iii) Nouns with two or more adjectives: the restrictive adjective follows, the non-restrictive (i.e. least important) normally precedes: *los blancos ejércitos angélicos* 'the white armies of the angels'; *una elegante camisa blanca* 'an elegant white shirt'; *una siniestra cruz gamada* 'a sinister swastika'; *una enorme cúpula blanca* 'an enormous white dome'.

4.5.3   Adjectives with nouns joined by *de*
Choice of position here depends on whether the noun phrase is felt to be a compound word (i.e. a new idea) or merely a loose conjunction of words. Thus *las flores de España* is not a compound, so one says *las flores silvestres de España* 'the wild flowers of Spain' but not **las flores de España silvestres*. But *una casa de muñecas* 'a dolls' house' is a compound, so one says *una casa de muñecas barata* 'a cheap dolls' house' and not **una casa barata de muñecas*. Only long familiarity with the language will provide a certain guide as to what is or is not a compound noun. Some noun phrases are uncertain: one can say *una bicicleta amarilla de hombre* or *una bicicleta de hombre amarilla* 'a yellow man's bicycle' (the Spanish is unambiguous!). Further examples:

un cochecito de niño verde	a green pram
un médico de cabecera simpático	a nice family doctor
un libro lleno de curiosas referencias de	a book full of curious references of a
índole personal	personal nature

4.5.4   Position of *bueno, malo, grande, pequeño*
The general rule applies: when they are clearly restrictive, they follow the noun. When used restrictively they usually indicate objective qualities. When they precede the noun they usually express a subjective evaluation.

(a)   Objective qualities

Tengo un abrigo bueno para los fines de semana, y uno regular para los laborables	I've got a good coat for weekends, and a so-so one for weekdays
(Objective qualities)	
Deme un melón bueno	give me a good melon
(Objective, i.e. one that's not bad)	
{*Oscar Wilde*} *dijo que no hay libros buenos o malos sino libros bien o mal escritos* (Borges, Arg.)	O.W. said there are no good or bad books, only well or badly written books
Ponlo debajo del árbol grande	put it under the big tree
Trae la llave grande	bring the big key/spanner
Salía con un muchacho grande	she was going out with a big fellow
mi hermana mayor/menor	my elder/younger sister

(b)   Subjective qualities

un buen carpintero	a good carpenter

un buen vino tinto	a good red wine
un gran éxito	a great success
un gran ruido/poeta/embustero	a great noise/poet/liar
un pequeño problema	a slight problem
No hubo mayores problemas	there were no major problems
el mayor poeta mexicano	the greatest Mexican poet
ni la menor impresión de insinceridad	not even the slightest impression of insincerity

Notes (i)   With *hombre* and *mujer*, *bueno* tends to mean 'good' after the noun and 'harmless' before: *un buen hombre* means 'a harmless/simple man'. *Malo* is weaker before the noun. *Mala mujer* may be a euphemism for prostitute.

   (ii)   There are many set expressions: *lo hizo de buena gana* 'he did it willingly'; *oro de buena ley* 'pure gold'; *en buen lío te has metido* 'you're in a fine mess'; *a mí siempre me pone buena cara* 'he always makes an effort to be nice with me'; *¡qué mala pata!* 'what bad luck', etc.

   (iii)   *Grande* is usually pre-posed when it means 'great', but it may mean 'big' in either position.

4.5.5   Position of *nuevo* and *viejo*

The usual explanation is that these are pre-posed when they mean 'another' and 'previous/long-standing' respectively, but in practice it is doubtful whether the distinction is always clear-cut:

   Tenemos un nuevo presidente/un presidente nuevo 'we've got a new president'; *nuevos progresos técnicos* 'new (i.e. more) technological developments'; *un viejo amigo* 'an old friend' (i.e. long-standing, not aged).

   Nuevo is usually post-posed when it means 'brand-new' as is *viejo* when it means 'not new': *un coche nuevo* 'a brand-new car'; *un coche viejo* 'an old car'. *Viejo* may be pre-posed when it means 'not young': *un viejo americano* 'an old American'.

   This distinction is overridden for purposes of contrast: *prefiero el coche nuevo al viejo* 'I prefer our new (i.e. 'latest') car to the old one'.

4.5.6   Adjectives whose meaning varies according to position

The following are some common cases of changes of meaning determined by adjective position, but in many cases the distinction is not rigid, and a good dictionary should be consulted for further information.

	After noun	Before noun
antiguo	ancient	former or ancient
cierto	certain	certain
	(= beyond doubt)	(*en ciertos trenes* 'on certain trains')
medio	average	half
pobre	poor (= not rich)	miserable/wretched
puro	pure/clean	sheer
raro	strange/rare	rare
rico	rich	delicious
simple	simple-minded	simple (= mere)

valiente	courageous	'great' (ironic)
varios	assorted/various	several

Note For *mismo* see 9.10; *propio* 9.13; *solo* 9.14.

4.5.7 Adjectives which occur only in front of the noun

The following phrases contain adjectives which normally occur only in front of the noun:

Lo haré en ambos casos	I'll do it in both cases
Las llamadas democracias	the so-called 'democracies'
La mera mención del asunto	the mere mention of the topic
Llevaba mucho dinero	he was carrying a lot of money
Busquemos otro médico	let's look for another doctor
Me dejó en pleno centro	he left me right in the town centre
pocas veces	rarely
poca paciencia	little patience
el pretendido autor	the alleged/supposed author
un sedicente budista	a self-styled Buddhist
Trajeron sendos paquetes (literary)	they brought a parcel each
ante tamaña tontería	in the face of such a great act of stupidity
No puedo comer tanta cantidad	I can't eat such a quantity

4.6 Attributive adjectives

Spanish readily forms attributive adjectives from nouns cf. *mañana – matinal* (*la televisión matinal* 'breakfast TV'), *impuesto – impositivo* (*política impositiva* 'taxation policy'). These usually replace *de* + a noun in compound nouns of the type *la vida de familia* = *la vida familiar* 'family life'. Recent decades have seen many new coinages, perhaps because the result has a pleasing brevity or a satisfying technical ring. Some of these new formations are rejected as jargon or journalese by educated speakers, and many have not found their way into dictionaries or speech.

Very often Spanish-American coinages are different from Peninsular inventions. In a few cases (e.g. *viento* → *eólico*) the adjective is derived from a different root.

The following are taken from various printed sources, mostly journalistic:

de + noun	Attributive adjective	
problemas de presupuesto	*problemas prepuestarios* (SA *prepuestales*)	budget problems
estancia en la cárcel	*estancia carcelaria*	prison term
carestía de petróleo	*carestía petrolera*	high oil prices
programa de televisión	*programa televisivo*	television programme
medios de masas	*medios masivos*	mass media
política de energía	*política energética*	energy policy
programa de informaciones	*programa informativo*	information programme
proceso de autonomía	*proceso autonómico*	process of development towards autonomy

industria de automóviles	*industria automovilística*	car industry
energía del viento	*energía eólica*	wind energy
crisis de la banca	*crisis bancaria*	bank crisis
esfuerzo de defensa	*esfuerzo defensivo*	defence effort
defectos del oído	*defectos auditivos*	hearing defects
industria de hoteles	*industria hotelera*	hotel industry
sindicato de pilotos	*sindicato piloteril*	pilots' union
etc.		

Note Attributive adjectives present the English speaker with semantic difficulties as shown by these paired examples:

lenguaje shakespeariano	Shakespearean language
" "	the language of Shakespeare
una cantidad masiva	a massive quantity
los medios masivos	mass media
política defensiva	defence policy
actitud defensiva	defensive attitude
poesía amorosa	love poetry
una sonrisa amorosa	a loving smile

4.7 Translating the English prefix 'un-'

The Spanish prefix *in-* is much less common than the English 'un-', and English speakers should resist the temptation to invent imaginary words like **ineconómico* from 'uneconomical' (*poco económico*):

The languages coincide in many words:

inimaginable	unimaginable
insobornable	unbribable
intocable	untouchable
irreal	unreal
etc.	

But often a solution with *poco*, *no* or *sin* must be found:

poco profesional	unprofessional
poco caritativo	uncharitable
poco atractivo	unattractive
poco apetitoso	unappetizing
poco amistoso	unfriendly
poco favorable	unfavourable
poco práctico	impractical (not **impráctico*)
poco inteligente	unintelligent
no usado	unused
no autorizado/sin autorizar	unauthorized
sin principios	unprincipled
sin probar	untried
sin comprender	uncomprehending
sin convencer	unconvinced
etc.	

5 Comparison of adjectives and adverbs

Comparison in Spanish is not particularly complex, but the progress of English-speaking students is often hindered by interference from French, which encourages misuse of the article in the superlative, failure to use *tanto como* in comparisons of equality (Fr. *aussi . . . que*, etc.), misuse of *más de* and *más que* and failure to use *del que* or *de lo que* before clauses.

5.1 Regular comparison

(a) With the exception of six adjectives and adverbs listed at 5.2, all adjectives and adverbs form the comparative with *más* 'more' or *menos* 'less':

Éste es más amarillo que ése	this one is more yellow than that one
Los limones son más agrios que las cerezas	lemons are more bitter than cherries
Tú andas más despacio que yo	you walk slower than me
Desde aquí se ve más claramente	you can see it more (or 'most') clearly from here
En los libros de Virginia Woolf la trama es menos importante que los cambiantes estados de ánimo y los delicados paisajes (Borges, Arg.)	in Virginia Woolf's books plot is less important than the shifting states of mind and the delicate landscapes

Notes (i) For the difference between *más que/menos que* and *más de/menos de* see 5.5.1.

(ii) Before clauses, *más/menos del que* or *más menos de lo que* are usually required: *hay más de los que yo vi* 'there are more than I saw'. See 5.5.2.

(iii) The comparative of adverbs and, in some circumstances of adjectives, is not always distinguishable by form from the superlative. See 5.3 and 5.4.

(b) Omission of *más/menos*

Más and *menos* need not be repeated:

Es más inteligente y emprendedor que su hermano	he's more intelligent and enterprising than his brother
Es menos cómodo y limpio	it's less comfortable and clean

5.2 Irregular comparative forms

There are six adjectives and adverbs which have irregular comparative forms (comparative adjectives ending in *-r* are not marked for gender):

bueno/bien	good/well	*mejor*	better
malo/mal	bad/badly	*peor*	worse
pequeño	small	*menor* (or *más pequeño*)	smaller
grande	big	*mayor* (or *más grande*)	big/bigger/ great/greater
poco	little	*menos*	less
mucho	much	*más*	more

Notes (i)   *Mayor* and *menor* are discussed at 5.5.4 & 5.

(ii)   *Más bueno*, *más malo* are used of moral qualities though *mejor/peor* are more usual:

Pedro es mejor/más bueno que Ricardo	Pedro is better (i.e. a better person) than Ricardo
En el cielo tienes un padre mejor/más bueno que los tuyos de esta tierra	in Heaven you have a better father than your parents here on earth
Es más bueno que el pan (set phrase)	he has a heart of gold (lit. he is more good than bread)
Tú eres más malo que el Diablo	you're more wicked than the Devil

5.3   Superlative of adjectives

See 5.4 for the superlative of adverbs.

There are two ways of forming the superlative of adjectives: either with *el/la/los/las/más* 'the most' or *el/la/los/las menos* 'the least', or by using the comparative and relying on context to convey the superlative meaning.

(a)   Examples of superlative of adjectives with definite article:

el personaje más verosímil	the most lifelike character
el más complicado problema/el problema más complicado	the most complicated problem
Chesterton, el escritor más popular de su tiempo, es una de las figuras más simpáticas de la literatura (Borges, Arg.)	Chesterton, the most popular writer of his time, is one of the most likable figures in literature
Lo mejor/peor que te puede suceder . . .	the best/worst thing that can happen to you . . .

Note   Students of French must avoid repeating the article: *l'exemple le plus intéressant* = *el ejemplo más interesante* or *el más interesante ejemplo*. *El ejemplo el más interesante is not Spanish.

(b)   The definite article is not used in superlative constructions in the following four cases:

(i)   When a possessive adjective precedes *más* or *menos*

mi más leal amigo/mi amigo más leal	my most loyal friend
nuestro paciente más enfermo	our sickest patient
. . . pero mi capa más profunda se entristeció (E. Sabato, Arg.)	but the deepest layer in me (lit. 'my deepest layer') was saddened

(ii) After *estar*

Ella es la que está más alterada	she's the one who's most upset
Este caballo está más cansado	this horse is the most tired

Note Such sentences could also be understood as comparatives. The issue could be clarified by using *ser*: *ella es la más alterada, este caballo es el más cansado*.

(iii) After nominalizers – e.g. *el/la/los/las que, quien, aquel que*, etc. meaning 'the one(s) who/which:

La que es más abordable	the girl/woman who's most approachable
Los que son más laboriosos	the ones who are most hard-working
Quienes tienen mejores notas son . . .	the ones with the best marks are . . .

(iv) When the superlative does not involve comparison with another noun:

El idealismo siempre es más fácil cuando uno es joven	idealism is always easiest (or 'easier') when one's young
Es en su poemas largos donde es menos convincente	it is in his long poems that he is least (or 'less') convincing
Los domingos es cuando la lluvia es más deprimente	it's on Sundays that the rain is most depressing

Compare the following where true comparison with another noun is involved:

El amor sin celos es el más noble	love without jealousy is the noblest
Las pizzas con anchoas son las mejores	pizzas with anchovies are the best

Note Translation of sentences like 'the best restaurant in Argentina' usually require *de* not *en*: i.e. *el mejor restaurante de Argentina*. See 28.7.1b note (i) for discussion.

5.4 Superlative of adverbs

The definite article cannot be used – with the result that the superlative is not always clearly distinguishable from the comparative. Students of French must remember not to use the article: compare *c'est Richard qui danse le mieux* and *Ricardo es quien mejor baila*. Examples:

De las tres niñas la que canta mejor es Ana	of the three girls, the one who sings best is Ana
Él trabaja menos	he works least (or *less*)
Cuando más llueve es en verano	it's in summer that it rains most (or *more*)
Quien había llamado con más insistencia a la puerta	the person who had banged on the door most insistently
La que contesta menos frecuentemente/ con menos/con menor frecuencia . . .	the girl/woman who answers least/less frequently
Pero el caso de U . . . es el que más conmoción ha causado en los medios periodísticos (*El País: mayor* possible)	but the case of U . . . is the one which has caused most stir in journalistic circles

In the unlikely event of real ambiguity one of the following constructions can be used:

Él habla mejor que todos	he speaks better than everyone
Él habla mejor que ninguno	he speaks better than any of them
Él es quien habla mejor de todos	he is the one who speaks best of-all of them

Note   The difference between *el que más me gusta* and *el que me gusta más* 'the one I like more/most' is one of emphasis, the former being stronger and therefore more likely to carry a superlative meaning.

5.5   Use of *más/mayor* and *menos/menor*

5.5.1   *Más/menos que* or *más/menos de*?

The difference is crucial: *más de* is used before numbers or quantities:

Mi abuelo tiene más de cien años	my grandfather is more than 100 years old
Son más de las tres y media	it's past 3.30
Has traído más de lo necesario	you've brought more than necessary
Los hermanos Vicario les habían contado sus propósitos a más de doce personas (García Márquez, Colombia)	the Vicario brothers had told their intentions to more than twelve people
. . . en menos de diez minutos los ladrones lograron abrir una de las puertas del vehículo (*El Diario*, Bolivia, *Var.* 184)	in less than ten minutes the thieves managed to open one of the doors of the vehicle

Compare the following examples in which the expression following *más* or *menos* is not itself a quantity:

Este restaurante es más caro que antes	this restaurant is dearer than before
Cansa más el viaje que el empleo (Cortázar, Arg. dialogue)	the travelling is more tiring than the job
. . . ni siquiera sus padres sabían de él mucho más que nosotros (García Márquez, Colombia)	not even his parents knew much more about him than we did
Había hecho más que lo posible para que Ángela Vicario se muriera en vida (García Márquez, Colombia)	she had done more than was possible so that Angela Vicario would have no life at all (lit. 'die while alive')

Note   *No más . . . que* = *sólo*. Thus –

No he traído más que mil (i.e. *Sólo he traído mil*)	I've only brought 1000
No he traído más de mil	I haven't brought more than 1000
Aquí no hay más que cuatro gatos	the place is deserted/there's not a soul to be seen (lit. 'there are only four cats here')
Aquí no hay más de cuatro gatos (literal statement)	there are four cats here and no more
nada más que eso . . .	only that/that's all there is to it

5.5.2   Comparison with a clause (*más del que/de lo que*, etc.)

If a comparison of quantity (see preceding section) is made with a clause containing a noun or pronoun, the appropriate form of *más/menos del que* must be used:

Has traído menos aceite del que necesitábamos	you've brought less oil than we needed
Han venido más de las que se matricularon para el curso	more girls have come than registered for the course
Gasta más dinero del que gana (From Harmer & Norton, 250)	he spends more money than he earns

If comparison is made with a verb phrase, *de lo que* must be used:

Son más inteligentes de lo que parecen	they're more intelligent than they seem
El agua estaba menos caliente de lo que yo creía	the water was less hot than I thought
Lo hicieron menos bien de lo que esperábamos	they did it less well than we hoped
No se haga el estúpido más de lo que es (Vargas Llosa, Peru, dialogue)	don't try to be more stupid than you are

Notes (i)   This apparently unwieldy construction, i.e. *gasta más de lo que gana* 'he spends more than he earns', is necessary in Spanish since *gasta más que gana* usually means 'he spends more (i.e. 'rather') than earns'.

(ii)   Before a neuter participle or adjective denoting quantity, *más de lo/menos de lo* must be used:

más impresionante de lo esperado (= *de lo que se esperaba*)	more impressive than hoped
Has traído menos de lo convenido	you've brought less than agreed

(iii)   Care must be taken not to confuse this construction with *no . . . más que . . .* meaning 'only':

No hay más cera que la que arde	all that's left is what you can see (lit. 'the only wax there is that which is burning')
No hay más gasolina que la que necesitamos	there's only enough petrol as we'll need
No he traído más que lo que usted ha pedido	I've only brought what you asked for

(iv)   Constructions on the lines of **eres más inteligente que pareces* have been attested in good writers in the past, and a few informants thought they might occur in spontaneous speech. Most informants condemned them as badly formed.

5.5.3   *Más* as a colloquial intensifier

Más is used as an intensifier in familiar speech, without any comparative meaning:

Es que eres más tonto . . .	heavens you're stupid . . .
Está más borracho . . .	is he drunk!

5.5.4   Uses of *mayor*

(a)   *Mayor* is the same as *más grande* in comparisons involving physical objects, but is not normally used of small things like pins, insects, etc.

Esta aula es más grande/mayor que la otra	this lecture room is bigger than the other
Mallorca es la más grande/la mayor de las Baleares	Majorca is the biggest of the Balearic Islands

One cannot say **lo mayor*: *lo más grande lo ponemos abajo* 'let's put the biggest things underneath'.

(b)   Of persons it means 'older' or 'oldest':

Mi hermano es mayor que el tuyo	my brother is older than yours
mi hermano mayor	my elder brother
Tienes dieciséis años pero pareces mayor	you're sixteen but you look older

Mayor is also a euphemism for *viejo*: *una señora mayor* 'an elderly lady'.

(c)   *Mayor* is used to mean 'greater' or 'greatest': *su mayor éxito* 'his greatest success'; *el mayor criminal del mundo* 'the greatest criminal in the world'; *el mayor peligro* 'the greatest danger'; *su mayor preocupación/ alegría* 'his/her greatest worry/joy'.

(d)   Before nouns denoting sizes, intensity, frequency, power or quantity, *mayor* or *más* can be used, with *mayor* considered more elegant: *mayor/más anchura* 'greater width'; *mayor/más intensidad*; *mayor/más fuerza* 'greater strength'; *mayor/más potencia* 'more power'; *mayor/más frecuencia* 'greater frequency'; *mayor/más peso* 'more weight'. Further examples:

Más acentuado será el sabor del ajo, cuanta mayor cantidad lleve	the greater the quantity it contains, the more pronounced the garlic flavour will be
en mayor grado	to a greater degree
El rojo produce mayor efecto de sensualidad	the red produces a greater effect of sensuality
Deseo recibir mayor información	I would like to receive more information
Tiene mayor contenido vitamínico	it has a greater vitamin content
Para mayor elegancia, úsense sólo manteles blancos	for greater elegance, only white tablecloths should be used

In all these examples except *en mayor grado*, *más* is possible, though less elegant.

(e)   Before *número* or words and phrases indicating number, *mayor* is obligatory: *en mayor número de casos* 'in a greater number of cases'; *mayor índice de mortalidad infantil* 'a higher rate of infantile mortality'; *mayor incidencia de accidentes de tráfico* 'a higher rate of traffic accidents'.

(f)   Set phrases: *mayor de edad* 'of age'; *hacerse mayor* 'to become grown up/to grow up'; *ganado mayor* 'cattle' (horses, cows, mules only); *calle mayor* 'high street', etc.

5.5.5   Uses of *menor*
Menor differs from *mayor* in that it cannot refer to dimensions: *esta habitación es más pequeña que ésa*, not **menor que ésa*.

Note: *mi hermano menor* 'my younger brother' but *mi hermano es más joven que yo* 'my brother is younger than me', not **menor que yo . . .*

Menor is used in the same contexts as *mayor* in (c), (d) and (e). Examples:

Usted no tendrá la menor dificultad (or *mínima* or *más pequeña*)	you won't have the slightest difficulty

La menor provocación le hace explotar	the slightest provocation makes him explode
El riesgo de un enfrentamiento es cada vez menor	the risk of a confrontation is declining

Common set phrases: *menor de edad* 'under age'; *apto para menores* 'suitable for minors/young people'.

5.6 *mucho más, mucho menos, poco más*, etc.

(a) Before *más, menos, mayor* and *menor*, qualifying a noun, *mucho* or *poco* are adjectives, and must agree in number and gender – a fact which English-speakers are prone to forget:

Tienen muchos más hijos que tú	they have many more children than you
El proyecto era de mucha más envergadura que el anterior	the plan was much wider in scope than the previous one
Cincuenta personas eran muchas menos que en ocasiones anteriores	fifty people was much less than on previous occasions
Tenía pocas más ganas que antes	he was little keener (i.e. 'no keener') than before
Habían consumido mucha mayor cantidad de lo que se preveía	they had consumed a much greater quantity than was foreseen
mucha menor cantidad	a much smaller quantity

(b) Elsewhere, before adjectives and adverbs, *mucho* and *poco* are adverbs and invariable in form:

La diferencia era mucho mayor	the difference was much greater/less
Los alijos de hashish eran mucho más grandes de lo que se esperaba (*El País*)	the hauls of hashish were much greater than expected
Los problemas son mucho menos complejos de lo que se temía	the problems are much less complex than feared

5.7 'The more . . . the more . . .'/'the less . . . the less . . .'

Cuanto más . . . más . . ., cuanto menos . . . menos . . . are the standard formulas:

Cuanto más pensaba más me afligía . . . (Cortázar, Arg. dialogue)	the more I thought, the more upset I got . . .
Cuanto menos lo pienses de antemano, menos te va a doler	the less you think about it beforehand, the less it'll hurt
Cuantos más, mejor	the more the better

Colloquial speech may replace *cuanto* by *mientras* in this construction, a substitution which sounds popular or substandard in Spain but is considered normal by educated Latin Americans. (Use of *çontra* or even *entre* for *cuanto* is typical of everyday speech in many parts of Spanish America, but it is avoided in formal writing):

. . . mientras más pienses en ella, más tuya la harás (Fuentes, Mex. dialogue)	the more you think of her, the more you will make her yours

See 22.5n. for the spelling of *cuanto*.

5.8   Comparisons of equality

5.8.1   *tan como, tanto como*
The basic formula is *tan . . . como* or *tanto . . . como* 'as . . . as', not *tanto . . . que* which can only mean 'so much that': *se rió tanto que por poco revienta* 'he laughed so much he nearly burst'.

Tan is used before adjectives, adverbs and nouns; *tanto* is used before *como* itself, or when nothing follows:

No soy tan joven como tú	I'm not as young as you
Éstos no parecen tan grandes como los anteriores	these don't seem as big as the previous ones
Usted lo sabe tan bien como yo (Vargas Llosa, Peru, dialogue)	you know as well as I do
Contestó tan inteligentemente como quien más	she answered as intelligently as the best of them
No eres tan hombre como él	you're not as much of a man as him
No hablo tanto como tú	I don't talk as much as you
María no se esfuerza tanto	Maria doesn't make as much of an effort/ that much effort

Other non-comparative uses of *tan* and *tanto* are discussed at 9.15.

5.8.2   *Igual que, lo mismo que*
These are used to express equality:

Escribe igual que/lo mismo que tú (Not **igual como*, **lo mismo como*)	she writes the same way as you
Me trató igual que siempre (García Márquez, Colombia)	she treated me the same as always

Note   Comparison of equality with verb phrases can also be expressed by the formula *del mismo modo que/de la misma manera que/de igual modo que/ de igual manera que*:

Argüía de la misma manera que muchos filósofos de la época	he argued in the same way as many philosophers of the day

See 9.10 for further discussion of *mismo*.

5.8.3   *Igual* or *igualmente*?
Igualmente means 'equally', but *igual* (as well as being an adjective meaning 'equal') is an invariable adverb in its own right meaning 'the same'.

otros problemas igualmente difíciles	other equally difficult problems

but:

Una bata que le caía igual que hecha a medida (L. Goytisolo)	a housecoat which fitted her exactly as if it had been made to measure
¿Por qué no puedo yo hacerlo igual?	why can't I do it the same way/as well?
En eso ustedes son igual a las mujeres (M. Puig, Arg. dialogue) (also *igual que . . .*)	you're the same as women in that respect
Es igual que tú (also *igual a ti*)	she's the same as you

Tú eres igualmente delgado	you're equally slim
Tú eres igual de delgado	you're equally slim

Note *Igual* may function colloquially as an adverb meaning 'maybe':

Pues no sé, igual nos vamos mañana	well I don't know, maybe we'll leave tomorrow
Igual nos casamos	maybe we'll get married

This is popular style, rejected by some and probably confined to Spain. Spanish-Americans may interpret *igual* as meaning 'anyway', e.g. *igual nos vemos mañana* 'we're seeing one another tomorrow anyway'.

6 Demonstrative adjectives and pronouns

Spanish demonstrative adjectives and pronouns are identical in form, i.e. *este* means 'this' or 'this one' (masc.), *esas* and *aquellas* mean 'those' or 'those ones' (fem.). The ambiguities which occasionally arise from this may be resolved in writing by spelling the pronouns with an accent: see 6.3 for discussion.

Spanish differs from French, German and English in having two words for 'that', depending on the distance in time, space or, sometimes, emotion, between the speaker and the object referred to.

The demonstratives have neuter forms, *esto*, *eso*, *aquello*, which are discussed separately in chapter 7.

6.1 Forms of demonstratives

	this	that (near)	that (far)
masc.	*este*	*ese*	*aquel*
fem	*esta*	*esa*	*aquella*

	these	those (near)	those (far)
masc.	*estos*	*esos*	*aquellos*
fem.	*estas*	*esas*	*aquellas*

Neuter demonstrative pronoun (discussed in chapter 7)

	esto	*eso*	*aquello*

Notes (i) See 6.3 for when to write these with an accent.

(ii) The masculine singular forms do *not* end in -*o*!

(iii) *Esta*, *esa* and *aquella* should be used before feminine nouns beginning with stressed *a*- or *ha*-: *esta agua* 'this water', *esa aula* 'that lecture hall', *aquella haya* 'that beech tree over there', but forms like *este arma* are common in spontaneous speech.

6.2 Position of demonstrative adjectives

Normally before the noun: *esta miel* 'this honey'; *ese árbol* 'that tree', *aquellas regiones* 'those regions'.

Colloquially they may appear after the noun, usually to express an ironic or irritated attitude towards the objects named: *esa mujer* 'that woman', *la mujer esa* 'that dashed woman'; *¡ay, las cintas estas!* 'oh, these ribbons!' –

Pero con la agencia esa que ha montado, se está forrando el riñón (Buero Vallejo, dialogue)	but with that agency he's set up, he's simply raking it in
En seguida dejé de tener importancia para la gente aquella (F. Umbral, dialogue)	I immediately ceased to have any importance for those people

The definite article is obligatory if a demonstrative adjective follows the noun. The demonstrative in this case remains an adjective even though it follows the noun, so it is not written with an accent.

6.3 Demonstratives as pronouns

The demonstratives also serve as pronouns meaning 'this (one)'/'that one', Fr. *celui-ci, celle-là*, etc. The old rule required that these should always be distinguished from the adjectives by a written accent, but even in carefully edited texts printed before 1959 many inconsistencies are found. The *Nuevas normas* of the Academy now state that the accent may be omitted unless ambiguity arises, as in *esta protesta* 'this protest' and *ésta protesta* 'this woman is protesting'; *este español* 'this Spaniard' and *éste español* 'this Spanish *one*'. Strict application of the Academy's rules would mean that one would virtually never write the accent since real ambiguities are very rare, and both the Academy and the reliable grammarian Manuel Seco now consider sentences like *esta es mía* 'this one's mine', *un libro como ese* 'a book like that one' to be correct. But most publishing houses, newspaper editors, the more cautious grammarians and ordinary citizens everywhere still write – or try to write – the accent on the pronouns even when there is no ambiguity. The foreign student is therefore faced with an embarrassing choice between following the Academy and offending the eye of educated persons, or trying systematically to distinguish demonstrative adjectives from pronouns, which is not always easy.

The present book tries to follow educated usage, so the accent usually appears on demonstrative pronouns, although we omit it in a few cases in which we cannot decide whether the demonstrative is an adjective or a pronoun.

There is one important inconsistency in educated usage. It has always been the practice in modern times, even before 1959, to omit the accent from demonstrative pronouns which are the antecedent of a relative clause or act as nominalizers (*aquel de, este de,* etc.). For this reason we print *esta novela es mejor que aquella en que* . . . 'this novel is better than that in which', *este/ese que* . . . 'this/that one that . . .', *aquel de* . . . 'the one of/from . . .' etc. Even conservative grammarians omit the accent from the demonstrative pronouns in this case, although the reason is not entirely clear.

The upshot of all this is that if the Academy's *Nuevas normas* mean anything, the accent could in fact be correctly omitted in every single example of demonstrative pronouns quoted in this book – the two examples *ésta protesta* and *éste español* excepted.

Examples of demonstrative pronouns:

Con un catarro como ése no debías salir	with a cold like that (one) you shouldn't go out
Dame otro cuchillo – éste no corta	give me another knife – this one doesn't cut
Ése sí que es inteligente	now that one – he really is intelligent
Antonio salía cada vez más de casa, circunstancia ésta que a su madre no le pasaba inadvertida (Note position of dem. pronoun in apposition)	Antonio left the house more and more, this being a circumstance which did not pass unnoticed by his mother
Aquéllas eran las condiciones en que teníamos que trabajar	those were the conditions in which we had to work
. . . su proximidad o lejanía respecto de la persona que habla o de aquella a quien se habla (Academy Grammar, 1928 edition, p. 39: accent omitted from *aquella* followed by relative pronoun)	. . . one's closeness to or distance from the person speaking or to whom one is speaking

Note Use of demonstratives to refer to someone present is humorous or insulting: *pregúntaselo a éste* 'ask this one here' (e.g. pointing to her husband); *¡éstos fuera!* 'get this lot out!'

6.4   Use of *este, ese* and *aquel*

(a)   *Este* refers to things near to or associated with the speaker, and is usually equivalent to 'this': *este libro, estos arbustos* 'these bushes', *esta catástrofe, estas circunstancias*.

(b)   *Ese* means 'that near you' (i.e. near, or associated with the hearer or reader): *ese libro* 'that book (by you)', *en esas circunstancias* 'in those circumstances (that you mention)'.

(c)   *Aquel* resembles the old English 'yonder' and points to things distant in time or space from both speaker and hearer or reader; *aquella montaña* 'that mountain (over there)', *en aquella época* 'at that (distant) time'. It is discussed in detail at 6.4.1.

Alcánzame ese libro rojo	Pass me that red book
Prefiero ese que tú tienes	I prefer that one (masc.) that you've got
¿Cómo se llama aquella estrella?	what's that star (up there) called?
¿Quién se acuerda ya de aquellas tardes sin televisión?	who can still remember those evenings without television?

6.4.1   *Aquel* or *ese*?

Aquel may be yielding ground to *ese* in some dialects, and some grammarians complain about a tendency to use *ese* where *aquel* is more elegant. But the distinction is a real one for the immense majority of speakers on both continents, and must be respected by the foreign student. *Aquel* is used:

(a) to indicate the most distant of a set of things:

¿Quién plantó ese árbol?	who planted that tree?
¿Ése? No, aquél de detrás	That one? No, the one behind
No esa torre sino aquélla	not that tower but that one further on

(b) to indicate the remote past:

Once an event has been located in the past, *ese* may be used in subsequent references to it:

Recuerdo que aquel día hubo tormenta y que en aquella/esa ocasión yo había salido sin paraguas	I remember that that day there was a storm and on that occasion I'd gone out without an umbrella
¿Te acuerdas del 39? Pues en aquella (or esa) época yo vivía en Bilbao	do you remember '39? Well, at that time I was living in Bilbao

(*Esa* is possible here because the year is specified)

In some phrases *aquel* is obligatory:

¡Qué noche aquélla!	what a night that was!
¡Qué tiempos aquéllos!	what times they were!

(c) Further examples of *ese* and *aquel*

¿Te acuerdas de aquella chica con la que se casó mi primo?	do you remember that girl my cousin married?
Era como uno de esos payasos de circo que dan miedo a los niños	he was like one of those circus clowns who frighten the children

(*Aquellos* would only be possible here if such circus clowns no longer existed.)

Usted nació en marzo de 1943. ¡Qué concidencia! Yo también nací en ese mes	you were born in March 1943? What a coincidence! I was born in that month too!

(*Ese*, because the month is intimately associated with the hearer.)

¿Te acuerdas de aquel escritorio que el abuelo quemó cuando tenías cinco años?	do you remember that desk that grandfather burnt when you were five?

(*Aquel* appropriate for something no longer in existence).

. . . la luna ya como de invierno, con su halo violeta de medusa y aquellas estrellas como un hielo hecho añicos (L. Goytisolo)	the moon like a winter moon now, with its violet halo like a jellyfish's, and those stars like shattered ice

(*Aquellas* appropriate for a childhood memory)

Yo dormí en esa habitación aquella noche	I slept in that room that night

(*Aquella habitación* would sound wrong by dissociating the room from the night.)

Notes (i) In writing, *aquel que* (no written accent) replaces *el que* if the latter is followed by a relative pronoun. In speech the noun may be repeated:

Estos fósiles son más reveladores que aquellos en (los) que la estructura de los huesos está borrada	these fossils are more revealing than the ones in which the bone structure is blurred

(Not **los en que . . .*)

See 6.5c for another example.

(ii) *Aquel* should not be used in conjunction with a historic present because of the absurdity of simultaneously stressing the remoteness and the immediacy of an action; i.e. not **en aquel año Cervantes escribe Don Quijote* 'in that year Cervantes wrote

Don Quixote': *en este año C. escribe Don Quijote*, or *en aquel año C. escribió Don Quijote*.

6.4.2 'The former, the latter'

Since *aquél* denotes something remote, and *éste* something close, they conveniently translate 'former' and 'latter':

Ramírez ha publicado dos novelas, Dos vidas y Tormenta de primavera, aquélla concebida dentro de la tradición realista, ésta de un tono más modernista	R. has published two novels, *Two Lives* and *Spring Storm*, the former conceived within the realist tradition, the latter more modernist in tone

6.5   Translation problems involving demonstratives

(a)   'The . . . which/who', 'those . . . who', etc.
El que or *quien* are the usual equivalents; *aquel que* (usually written without an accent) is used in formal language: *la que ha dicho eso, que se ponga de pie* 'stand up the girl who said that', etc. See chapter 30 (nominalizers) for full discussion.

(b)   'Those of them', 'those of you', etc.
Aquellos de is frowned on, except perhaps before *ustedes* or *vosotros*:

Los que vivimos en Gibraltar	those of us who live in Gibraltar
Los que aplaudieron ayer	those of them who applauded yesterday
Los nicaragüenses que sabemos la verdad	those of us Nicaraguans who know the truth
Aquellos de (entre) ustedes que afirman eso	those of you who claim that
Los que no hayan firmado el formulario	those (of them/you) who haven't signed the form

(**los de ellos* or **aquellos de ellos* in this context are not Spanish.)

(c)   'The one in which', 'those where', etc.
Aquel, customarily written without an accent in this construction, is a literary replacement for *el que* when a preposition governs a relative pronoun: i.e. one writes *la habitacion era más cómoda que aquella en que había dormido antes* 'the room was more comfortable than the one in which he has slept before'. The spoken language usually prefers to repeat the noun: *la habitación era más cómoda que la habitación en la que había dormido antes. *La en que* is not possible.

(d)   'That's why . . .', 'that's where', 'that's who', 'that was when' etc.
Translation of these phrases may involve the problem of 'cleft' sentences, e.g.:

Fue por eso por lo que pagó demasiado (SA *fue por eso que pagó demasiado*)	that was why he paid too much
Fue con ésa con la que se casó	it was that girl whom he married
Fue en ese momento cuando se rió	it was at that moment that he laughed

See 30.2 for a detailed discussion of cleft sentences.

7 Neuter article and pronouns

7.1 Neuter gender

Nouns in Classical Latin could have one of three genders, masculine, feminine or neuter. Most neuter nouns came to be confused with masculine in Vulgar Latin, and nowadays all the Romance languages are effectively two-gender languages. In Spanish a few neuter pronouns and an article have survived and remain as important features of the modern language. These forms are the 'neuter article' *lo*, the neuter demonstrative pronouns *esto*, *eso* and *aquello*, the neuter third-person pronoun *ello*, the neuter relative pronouns *lo que* and *lo cual*, and the neuter nominalizer *lo que*.

They are necessary in Spanish because masculine or feminine articles and pronouns must refer to a noun (present or implied) and must therefore take the gender of that noun. But if no noun is present or implied, the article or pronoun can be neither masculine nor feminine and it must appear in the neuter form. Examples should make this clear:

No quiero hablar de aquél	I don't want to talk about that one (i.e. car, book or some other masculine noun)
No quiero hablar de aquello	I don't want to talk about that
No me gusta ése	I don't like that one (*celui-là*)
No me gusta eso	I don't like that (*cela*)
los nuevos/las nuevas	the new ones (masc.)/the new ones (fem.)
lo nuevo	what is new

7.2 The 'neuter article' *lo*

For the pronouns *lo que*, *lo de*, see 30.1.5 and 30.1.3. For the pronoun *lo* ('him', 'it') see chapter 11. For SA *en lo de* meaning 'at the house of', see 30.1.3b.)

The neuter relative pronoun is *lo que* or *lo cual*. They are discussed at 29.11.

For the colloquial construction *la que te espera cuando llegues a casa . . .* 'are you in for it when you get home . . .' see 30.1.5n.

7.2.1   *Lo* plus masculine singular adjective

A masculine singular adjective preceded by *lo* may become a sort of abstract noun. Translation sometimes requires ingenuity:

Lo importante es que diga la verdad	the important thing is that he should tell the truth
Eso es lo increíble de todo eso	that's the incredible thing about all that
Lo bueno sería que tú volvieras a perder el dinero	what would be great (ironic) is if you lost the money again
¿Estoy en lo correcto?	am I on the right lines?
Lo mío es confundir (Unamuno)	my style is to confuse
Ninguna mujer compra lo primero que ve	no woman buys the first thing she sees
Papá se ha enterado de lo nuestro	father has found out about us
A la impresión de enorme antigüedad se agregaron otras: la de lo interminable, la de lo atroz, la de lo completamente insensato (Borges, Arg.)	to the impression of enormous antiquity were added others: the impression of endlessness, of horror, of utter irrationality
En su caso lo tonto no quita lo valiente	in his case stupidity doesn't stop him being brave
Lo energético es un registro esencial de nuestra seguridad económica (*ABC*)	the energy issue is an essential item in our economic security
a pesar de lo antes dicho	despite what was said earlier
Entre los coches nuevos, lo más interesante ha sido el Renault (*el más interesante* = 'the most interesting one')	among the new cars, what was most interesting was the Renault
en lo alto de la colina	on the top of the hill

Note   Other Romance languages lack this device: *le plus tragique* can mean both 'the most tragic thing' and 'the most tragic one'.

7.2.2   *Lo* plus adjectives or adverbs meaning 'how'

Lo with an adjective or adverb often translates the English 'how'. It commonly occurs after verbs of perception ('see', 'realize', 'understand', 'know'). When used thus the adjective must agree with the noun:

   (a)   With adjectives

No me había dado cuenta de lo guapa que era	I hadn't realized how attractive she was
Ahora que comprendo lo sensibles que son . . .	now that I understand how sensitive they are . . .
¿No se ha fijado en lo delgada que se ha quedado	haven't you noticed how thin she's become?
Cuando la voz, que casi no oía por lo queda, cesa, tarda en descubrirlo, por lo atrasado que está en el dictado (Vargas Llosa, Peru)	When the voice, which he could scarcely hear because it was so soft, ceased, he took time to realise it, because he was so behind with the dictation (lit. 'because of how behind he is . . .')

   (b)   With adverbs and adverbial phrases

Yo llegué confiando en lo bien que lo iba a pasar	I arrived sure of what a good time I was going to have
¿Has oído lo bien que habla?	did you hear how well he talks?

Tienes que hacerlo lo antes posible	you have to do it as soon as possible
Cuélgalo lo más arriba que puedas	hang it as high/as far up as you can
Lo más atrás posible	as far back as possible
Lo más a la derecha posible	as far to the right as possible
Lo antes que puedo salir de casa es a las seis	the earliest I can leave home is at six

Notes (i)   A common colloquial construction is *con lo* + adjective. Translation varies with context:

Pobre Ángel, con lo enfermo que está . . .	poor Angel, and being so ill
Tú, con lo inteligente que eres, a ver si lo puedes abrir	you're so intelligent, let's see if you can open it

(ii)   *De* + *lo* is also found in familiar speech as an intensifying phrase:

Viene de lo más arregladita	she's coming all dressed up
Es de lo más religioso	he's incredibly religious
Tomaban su cerveza de lo más tranquilos (Vargas Llosa, Peru, dialogue)	they were drinking their beer really quietly

(iii)   *Lo* is rarely found before nouns.

7.3   Neuter demonstrative pronouns

These take the invariable forms *esto, eso* and *aquello*. Since they cannot be confused with demonstrative adjectives they *never* take the written accent – a fact which learners and natives constantly forget.

They refer to no noun in particular (cf. Fr. *ceci, cela*).

The difference between *esto* 'this', *eso* 'that' and *aquello* 'that' (distant) reflects the difference between *este, ese* and *aquel*, discussed at 6.4. *Aquello* has specialized uses, discussed below at 7.3.1.

¿Quién ha hecho esto?	who did this?
Quisiera llamar a cobro revertido. De eso nada	I'd like to make a transfer charge call. No way/out of the question
Dios sabe cómo salió de aquello	Heaven knows how he got out of that

Notes (i)   The choice between a neuter or non-neuter demonstrative may cause problems: compare *esto es un soneto* 'this is a sonnet' and *éste es un soneto – los demás sólo tienen trece versos* 'this (one) is a sonnet – the rest have only thirteen lines'. If the speaker has in mind a specific noun, the masculine or feminine pronoun must be used as appropriate:

Ésa no es una razón para hacerlo	that's no reason for doing it
Ésa es otra de las invenciones de ustedes (Vargas Llosa, Peru, dialogue)	that's another of your inventions
¿Qué es esto?	what's this?
¿Quién es éste?	who's this (man or boy)
Éste es el problema	this is the problem
Esto es un problema	this is a problem
Esto no es una limosna sino un derecho	this isn't charity (lit. 'alms') but a right
Éste es un pueblo desgraciado	this is a wretched village
Si a esto se puede llamar marido, que venga Dios y lo vea	if you can call this (thing) a husband, then I'm a Dutchman (lit. 'then let God come and see it')

(Neuter pronoun appropriate, given the tone of the remark.)

(ii)   *La verdad* often takes a feminine pronoun – perhaps oddly to English speakers: *no tengo ni talento, ni fuerza. Ésa es la verdad* (Sabato, Arg., dialogue). 'I have neither talent nor strength. That's the truth'.

7.3.1   *Aquello*: special uses

(a)   *Aquello* may allude to some inauspicious or suspect thing from which the speaker wishes to distance himself:

Prefiero no pensar en todo aquello	I'd rather not think about all that . . .
¿Qué hay de aquello de los billetes falsos?	what's happening about that business of the forged notes?
¿Cómo podía yo pensar que aquello que parecía tan mentira era verdadero? (Cortázar, Arg. dialogue)	how could I think that that thing which seemed such a lie was true?
Con la OPEP se acabó aquello de usar gasolina como agua (*Cambio16*)	with OPEC (all) that business of using petrol like water came to an end

(b)   *Aquello* often corresponds to 'the saying that', though *eso* may also be used:

En realidad todo se reduce a aquello de que ojos que no ven . . . (Cortázar, Arg. dialogue)	really it all boils down to 'what the eye doesn't see . . .'
Spengler dijo aquello de que 'la civilización en última instancia siempre es salvada por un puñado de soldados' (*Cambio16*)	Spengler made that remark that 'in the final instance, civilization is always saved by a handful of soldiers'

7.4   Ello

This is a neuter third-person pronoun. It is invariable in form and must be used to translate 'it' when this pronoun does not refer to any specific noun. Compare *en cuanto al régimen militar, prefiero no hablar de él* 'as for the military regime, I prefer not to talk about it' and *todo fue tremendamente violento, y prefiero no hablar de ello* 'it was all tremendously embarrassing, and I prefer not to talk about it'. When it is used as the subject of a verb, it normally requires translation by 'this'. This latter usage is rather literary; *esto* comes more readily in speech:

Si algo me impresionó durante aquella entrevista, ello fue que el presidente tenía un tic nervioso	if anything impressed me during that interview, this was that the President had a nervous tic
Habitó un siglo en la Ciudad de los Inmortales. Cuando la derribaron, aconsejó la fundación de otra. Ello no debe sorprendernos . . . (Borges, Arg.)	he dwelt for a century in the City of the Immortals. When they demolished it, he recommended the foundation of another. This (fact) should not surprise us . . .

etc.

Note   As the first example shows, the pronoun *algo*, 'something' is itself of neuter gender and is subsequently pronominalized by *ello or esto*.

8 Possessive adjectives and pronouns

8.1 Forms of possessive adjectives and pronouns

Spanish possessives have two forms. The short forms, *mi, tu, su,* etc. are the normal, unstressed possessive adjectives and appear in front of a noun or noun phrase; they correspond to the English 'my', 'your', 'his', 'her', etc. The full forms *mío, tuyo, suyo,* etc. roughly correspond to the English 'mine', 'yours', 'hers', etc. and can only follow the noun or stand in isolation.

Number and gender agreement is determined by the number and gender of the noun possessed. All forms agree in number, but only those whose masculine singular ends in *-o* agree in gender.

(a)   The short forms are:

Personal pronoun	masculine	feminine	
yo	*mi/mis*		my
tú/vos	*tu/tus*		your (familiar)
él/ella/usted	*su/sus*		his/her/its/your
nosotros/nosotras	*nuestro/nuestros*	*nuestra/nuestras*	our
vosotros/vosotras	*vuestro/vuestros*	*vuestra/vuestras*	your
ellos/ellas/ustedes	*su/sus*		their/your

(b)   The full forms are:

yo	*mío/míos*	*mía/mías*	mine
tú/vos	*tuyo/tuyos*	*tuya/tuyas*	yours
él/ella/usted	*suyo/suyos*	*suya/suyas*	his/hers/yours
nosotros/nosotras	*nuestro/nuestros*	*nuestra/nuestras*	ours
vosotros/vosotras	*vuestro/vuestros*	*vuestra/vuestras*	yours
ellos/ellas/ustedes	*suyo/suyos*	*suya/suyas*	theirs/yours

Notes (i)   *Vosotros/vosotras* is not used in Spanish-American language and is replaced by *ustedes. Su/suyo* are therefore used for both familiar and polite address.

(ii)   *Tu/tuyo* are the forms corresponding to *vos* in *voseo* areas of Spanish America: cf. *vos tenés tu birome* (Arg.) 'you've got your ballpoint pen', Spain *tú tienes tu bolígrafo.*

8.2   Use of the short form of possessives

This is straightforward provided the rules of agreement are mastered:

mi padre/mis padres	my father/my parents
mi madre/mis flores	my mother/my flowers
¿Dónde está tu coche?	where's your car?
No me fío de su informalidad	I don't trust his unreliability
En nuestro tiempo esas cosas no sucedían	those things didn't happen in our time
vuestra casa/vuestras casas	your house/your houses
Si ustedes quieren dejar sus cosas aquí . . .	if you want to leave your/his/her/their things here . . .
Si ellos no quieren dejarnos su cortacésped	if *they* don't want to lend us their lawnmower

Notes (i)   Unlike English, the possessives are normally only deleted if the following nouns are felt to refer to the same or aspects of the same thing. Thus one says *mi padre y mi madre* 'my father and mother' (different people) but *mi amigo y colega* 'my friend and colleague' (same person); *su paciencia y valor* 'his patience and courage' (aspects of a single virtue), *nuestros cuentos y novelas* 'our short stories and novels' (aspects of a single œuvre).

(ii)   *De nosotros* for *nuestro* is common in popular speech in Spanish America.

(iii)   The third-person *su/suyo* can have six meanings: 'his', 'her', 'its', 'your' (*usted*), 'their', 'your' (*ustedes*). Context nearly always makes the meaning clear, but ownership may be stressed or ambiguities removed by using *de él/ella, de usted, de ellos/ellas, de ustedes* as appropriate: *los paraguas de ustedes* 'your (plural) umbrellas', *la camisa de él* 'his shirt'.

Kany, 68ff. remarks that in Spanish America *su*, out of context, is assumed to mean *de usted/de ustedes*, so that *de él, de ella, de ellos* are often used to mean 'his'/'her'/'their': *el libro de él, la casa de ella*, etc. In Spain *su* is assumed out of context to be third-person, so that *de usted/ustedes* may need to be added to emphasize the meaning 'your'.

The possibility of ambiguity is illustrated by the question 'is this handkerchief yours or hers?' which one would probably say *¿este pañuelo es de usted o de ella?*, whereas *¿este pañuelo es suyo?* 'is this handkerchief yours?' is clear if no one else is present.

8.3   Definite article instead of possessives

Often an object pronoun suffices to show who is the possessor: *Ricardo se aflojó la corbata* 'R. loosened his (own) tie', *me quité los calcetines* 'I took off my socks', *voy a bajarle los humos* 'I'm going to take him down a peg or two', *me ha aparcado mal el coche* 'he's parked my car badly', *a que te quito la novia* 'I'll take your girlfriend away from you for sure'.

This construction is usual with parts of the body and for clothing or other personal effects. In the case of clothing, the possessive adjective can normally only be used when the article is not being worn, in which case either construction is possible:

He dejado tu camisa en el otro cuarto/ te he dejado la camisa en el otro cuarto	I've left your shirt in the other room
Que el Pelícano se abre el pecho y alimenta con su propia sangre a los hijos es la versión común de la fábula (Borges, Arg.)	that the pelican tears open its breast and feeds its children with its own blood is the common version of the fable

Le extendió la mano lateralmente a
    Martín, que estaba petrificado
    (Sabato, Arg.)
	she stretched out her hand sideways to
	    Martín, who was petrified

Vio que ella se ponía las manos sobre
    la cara como si le dolieran las sienes
    (*ibid.*)
	he saw her putting her hands over her
	    face as though she had a pain in her
	    temples

Wong se puso a mirarle la mano
    (Cortázar, Arg.)
	Wong started to look at his (someone
	    else's) hand

Bébete el café	drink up your coffee
Arréglate el pelo	tidy your hair
Les robaron el coche	they stole their/your car

But when the thing possessed is emphasized or particularized by context, an adjective or by other words, or ambiguity must be avoided, the possessive adjective may reappear:

. . . alimenta con su propia sangre a los *hijos . . .*	(in the second example)
Usted póngase su camisa, no la mía	you put on your shirt, not mine

Alejandra se acercó y apretándole el
    brazo le dijo que se verían pronto.
    Martín inclinó su cabeza.
    (Sabato, Arg., *la cabeza* possible)
	A. came closer, and squeezing his arm
	    told him they would meet soon. Martin
	    bowed his head.

Vi sus ojos grandes, fatigados, sonrientes
    y como lacrimosos (F. Umbral)
	I saw her eyes, big, tired, smiling and
	    seemingly tearful

X deja sus manos suaves y perfumadas (or *le deja las manos . . .*)	X leaves your hands soft and perfumed
toco tus labios . . . (popular song)	I touch your lips . . .

Note As the last two examples show, advertisers and lovers like to particularize the object of their attentions. *Te toco los labios* sounds accidental or matter-of-fact: a mother says *dame la mano, que vamos a cruzar la calle* 'hold my hand, we're going to cross the road'; an ardent suitor might say *dame tu mano*.

8.4   Use of the strong or pronominal forms of the possessive

(a)   To translate English '. . . of mine/yours/his/ours', etc.:

un amigo mío	a friend of mine
un conocido tuyo	an acquaintance of yours
un pariente vuestro	a relation of yours
Ha vuelto a. hacer una de las suyas	(s)he's up to his/her usual tricks again (lit. 'a trick of hers' or 'his'/'yours')
una actitud muy suya	a very typical attitude of his/hers/ yours/theirs
algo mío/nada nuestro	something of mine/nothing of ours
estos zapatos míos	these shoes of mine
esa tendencia suya	that tendency of hers/his/yours/theirs

(b)   As a literary, rather stilted variation on the usual possessive:

en mi novela/en la novela mía	in my novel/in this novel of mine
nuestro pan/el pan nuestro de cada día	our daily bread

(c)   In Spain, in formulas of address:

Bueno, hijo mío, me voy	well, dear, I'm off

(lit. 'my son', a term of endearment used by women to men)

Te aconsejo que no, amigo mío	I advise you not to, my friend

(Spanish America prefers *mi hijo*, *mi hija*, *mi amigo*, etc.)

(d)   To translate the pronouns 'mine', 'yours':

¿De quién es este bloc? Mío	whose note-pad is this? Mine
Este garabato es tuyo	this scrawl is yours
Éste es vuestro, ¿verdad?	this one is yours, isn't it?

Note   The pronominal form is used in a number of set phrases:

en casa vuestra/en vuestra casa	in your home
de nuestra parte/de parte nuestra	for our part
a pesar mío/suyo	despite me/him
a costa mía	at my cost
en torno suyo	around him/her/them/you
a propuesta suya	at his suggestion
muy señor mío	Dear Sir (in letters)

8.5   Use of the article with possessives

8.5.1   The article with *mío*, *tuyo*, etc. is obligatory

(a)   After prepositions. Compare:

¿De quién es el coche? Mío	whose car is it? Mine

and

¿En qué coche vamos? En el mío	which car are we going in? In mine

Further examples:

No hablo del tuyo sino del nuestro	I'm not talking about yours but mine
A tu primo sí le/lo conozco, pero no al suyo	I know your cousin, but not his/hers

(b)   When the pronoun is the subject or object of a verb (even though the verb may be deleted):

Coge el mío	take mine
Tu padre te deja salir, el mío no	your father lets you go out, mine doesn't
Los dos vídeos son buenos, pero el nuestro es mejor	the two video recorders are good but ours is better
Qué vida tan triste la suya	what a sad life his/hers/yours/theirs is

(c)   Elsewhere, to stress the notion of possession, cf. the difference between 'mine' and 'my one': *no puedes dormir en esta cama: es la mía* 'you can't sleep in this bed: it's mine' (i.e. exclusively for me); *ese cepillo no, es el mío* 'not that brush – it's mine'.

8.5.2   The neuter article with *lo mío*, *lo suyo*, etc.

The neuter form of the possessive has various meanings:

Mi marido sabe lo nuestro	my husband knows about us
Ahora estás en lo tuyo	now you're in your element
Lo vuestro es alucinante	what happened to you is mind-boggling

8.6 Possessives after prepositions and adverbs

A common construction in colloquial American Spanish, also found in popular speech in Spain, is the use of possessive pronoun forms after prepositions and some adverbs, in place of *de* + the prepositional pronoun: ?*detrás mío* = *detrás de mí* 'behind me', and even, in substandard speech, **entró antes mío* (from Carnicer), 'he went in before me':

Adentro mío yo soy igual que todos los reaccionarios (M. Puig, Arg., dialogue: Spain *dentro de mí* or *por dentro*)	Inside (me) I'm the same as all the reactionaries
Quiero estar cerca tuyo (*ibid.*, Spain *cerca de ti*)	I want to be near you

Foreign students should avoid this construction. However, the following are considered correct: *alrededor mío* (or *a mi alrededor*) 'around me', *en torno nuestro* (literary) 'around us', *en contra suya* (*en contra de él*), 'against him'.

9 Miscellaneous adjectives and pronouns

Many of the words discussed in this chapter are of problematic classification and have multiple uses as adjectives, pronouns or adverbs. For easy reference they are, where possible, discussed under a single heading.

9.1 *Ajeno*: adjective, marked for number and gender

A rather literary word meaning 'someone else's': *el dolor ajeno* (*el dolor de otros*) 'other people's sorrow'; *en casa ajena* (*en casa de otro*) 'in another person's house'.

Se preocupa demasiado por lo ajeno	he concerns himself too much with other people's business

It is not used in this meaning after *ser:*

esta agenda es de otro	'this is someone else's diary'

Note *Ajeno* often translates 'a stranger to', 'remote from':

Un joven ajeno a todo lo que es sentido común	a young man who is a stranger to all common sense
Éstos son problemas ajenos a mi responsabilidad	these are problems outside my responsibility
Está ajeno a todo lo que no sean sus propios problemas	he is oblivious to everything but his own problems

9.2 *Algo*: invariable pronoun/adverb

The usual equivalent of 'something' or, in interrogative or 'pseudo-negative' sentences, 'anything' (Fr. *quelquechose*):

Aquí hay algo que no me suena	there's something here that doesn't sound right to me
Detrás se veía algo grande, negro	behind one could see something big, black
¿Ves algo?	can you see anything?
Le vi algo en la cara que me hizo pensar que haría carrera	I saw something in his face which made me think he'd make a good career
Serán pocos los que hayan traído algo	there probably won't be many who have brought anything

Adverbially it means 'rather', 'somewhat', though *un poco*, *un tanto* or *más bien* are equally common in speech:

Estamos algo inquietos	we're rather worried
Es algo complicado explicarlo	it's rather complicated to explain
Te has apartado algo del asunto	you've rather wandered off the subject

Notes (i)   *Algo así, algo así como* are translations of 'something like . . .': *pesa algo así como siete kilos* 'it weighs around 7 kilos'; *se llama Nicanora, o algo así* 'she's called Nicanora, or something like that'.

   (ii)   In negative sentences *nada* translates 'anything': *no sabe nada* 'he doesn't know anything'; *yo no sé dónde está nada en esta casa* 'I don't know where anything is in this house'.

   (iii)   The English question opener 'do you know something . . .?' must be translated *¿sabes una cosa? ¿Sabes algo?* means 'do you know anything?'

9.3   *Alguien*: invariable pronoun

'Someone'/'somebody'. It also translates 'anyone'/'anybody' in questions and certain other types of sentence. It is not marked for gender.

Ha venido alguien a cobrar el recibo de la luz	someone's come to take the money for the electricity bill
¿Conoces a alguien que pueda darme un presupuesto para reparar el coche?	do you know anyone who could give me an estimate for mending my car?

Notes (i)   **Alguien de los estudiantes, *alguien de ellos* are rejected by grammarians and must be replaced by *alguno de los estudiantes, alguno de (entre) ellos*, although *alguien de entre ustedes* is accepted by some authorities:

Si alguien de entre ustedes/alguno de ustedes lo sabe, que lo diga	if someone amongst you/any of you knows, say so

But occasionally *alguien de* is necessary since unlike *alguno* it does not indicate gender:

Yo creo que alude a alguien de esta casa	I think he's alluding to someone in this house

   (ii)   Moliner notes that *?darle una cosa a alguien que él no desea* offends the ear since *alguien* is too vague for a specifically masculine pronoun: *darle una cosa a alguien que no lo desea*.

   (iii)   'Give it to someone else' *dáselo a algún otro/a alguna otra persona*. (**Alguien otro* is not Spanish.)

   (iv)   *Uno* is sometimes colloquially used for 'someone' when gender is an important part of the message:

Se ha peleado con uno en la calle	he's had a fight with someone (male) in the street
Se casó con una de Valencia	he married some girl from Valencia

9.4   *Algún, alguno, algunos; alguna, algunas*: adjective/pronoun marked for number and gender

These may be used either as adjectives or (except for the short form *algún*) pronouns.

   (a)   As adjectives:

The usual translation is 'some' (Fr. *quelque*). *Algún* is used before a singular masculine noun or noun phrase: *algún día* 'some day'; *algún remoto rincón de Extremadura* 'some remote corner of Extremadura'.

Algún is common immediately before feminine nouns beginning with a stressed *a-* or *ha-*: *algún alma perdida* 'some lost soul', *algún arma defensiva* 'some defensive weapon', but *alguna* should be used in writing.

In the singular, *alguno* and *uno* are often interchangeable, but *alguno* strictly means 'one or maybe more' and has no exact English equivalent, cf. 'one or another', 'some or other'.

En algún momento de la historia de nuestra lengua vos estuvo en boga como pronombre personal	at one time or another in the history of our language, *vos* was fashionable as a personal pronoun
Tienes que prometerme que si algún día te cansas me lo dirás en seguida	you must promise me that if some day you get tired, you'll tell me straight away
Sólo se veía por las desiertas playas algún turista extranjero	all one could see along the deserted beaches was the occasional foreign tourist
Era la única forma de hacerlo con alguna garantía de éxito	it was the only way of doing it with any guarantee of success
¿Tiene usted algún manual de programación? Sí, alguno hay	do you have any programming manuals? Yes, there may be one . . .
Nadie cree que la gravedad de la crisis actual sea equiparable a la de 1929, y pocos se permiten establecer algún paralelismo (Cambio16)	no one thinks the severity of the present crisis is comparable to that of 1929, and few are prepared to draw any kind of parallel

(and not **ningún paralelismo* because *pocos* is not a negative word.)

En algunos casos la diferencia es muy marcada	in some cases the difference is very marked
Algunos sí, otros no	some are, and some aren't

Note In formal style *alguno* may follow a noun, in which case it is an emphatic equivalent of *ninguno*, 'none', 'no . . . at all':

No cultivaba forma alguna de contacto con el pueblo (J. Marsé)	he cultivated absolutely no kind of contact with the common people
En modo alguno entraba en mis propósitos ingresar en el ejército	in no way at all was it part of my plans to join the army
. . . o mejor una lista de palabras que no tuviera orden alguno (Cabrera Infante, Cuba, dialogue)	or better a list of words with no order at all

(b) As pronouns:

Se había puesto de acuerdo con alguno de sus compañeros	he'd made an agreement with one or other of his workmates
Se lo habrá llevado alguna de las vendedoras	one of the salesgirls must have taken it away
¿Sabes si viene alguna a la fiesta?	do you know if any of the girls is coming to the party?
¿Has recibido cartas de tu familia? Bueno, alguna, sí	have you had any letters from your family? Well, one or two, yes

In the plural 'some' or 'a few' are the usual translations:

Con algunos de tercero vas a tener que hacer ejercicios de verbos irregulares	you're going to have to do irregular verb exercises with some of the third year
Algunos ya están deseando marcharse	some already want to go

Notes (i) When *alguno* is combined with a second-person pronoun agreement of the verb seems to be optional, although third-person agreement came more naturally to our informants: *si alguno de vosotros lo sabéis/si alguno de vosotros lo sabe* 'if any of you know(s) it'.

(ii) *Algún* does not translate 'some' or 'any' in front of a non-count noun, e.g. 'give me some water' *dame agua*, 'you haven't bought any milk' *no has comprado leche*.

In some cases *un poco* or *ninguno* may be appropriate translations: 'any' in the sense of 'it doesn't matter which' is *cualquiera*. See 9.8.

¿Tiene usted pan integral?	have you got any wholemeal bread?
Yo también quiero un poco	I want some (a little) too
¿Chuletas de ternera? No tenemos	Veal chops? We haven't got any
No tenemos ninguno	we haven't got a single one (masc.)
No queda apenas ninguno	there are hardly any (masc.) left
Comidas a cualquier hora	meals at any time

(iii) When *alguno* is the object, direct or indirect, and is placed before the verb for purposes of focus, agreement is governed by the number of an accompanying noun or pronoun:

A alguno de vosotros os quisiera ver yo en un lío como éste	I'd like to see one of you in a mess like this
A alguno de ellos les quiere dar el premio	it's one of them that he wants to give the prize to

9.5 *Ambos*: adjective marked for number and gender

'Both', though it is rather literary and *los/las dos* usually replaces it in speech.

En ambos casos	in both cases
¿Cuál de los dos es correcto?	which of the two is correct? Both
Ambos/Los dos	

9.6 *Cada*: invariable

'Each', 'every'. *Cada* always precedes the noun:

Cada loco con su tema	every madman has his obsession
Un libro por cada tres alumnos	one book for every three students
No puedes estar molestando a la gente cada dos por tres	you can't keep bothering people every two minutes
Me llama a cada momento	he's constantly on the phone to me
Cada vez que te miro	every time I look at you

Notes (i) *Cada vez más/menos* usually translate 'more and more' and 'less and less': *es cada vez más complicado* 'it gets more and more complicated'; *era cada vez menos generosa* 'she was less and less generous'.

(ii) *Cada* is often heard in familiar speech to mean something like 'all sorts of . . .': *dice cada tontería* 'the nonsense he talks . . .'; *hay cada ladrón por ahí* 'the thieves there are around there . . .'.

(iii) 'Each one', 'each person':

Que cada uno (or cada cual/cada quien) haga la lectura que le parezca conveniente	let each person read it as it suits him

(iv) *?Me baño cada día* or *?voy cada mañana* for . . . *todos los días*, . . . *todas las mañanas* are said to be spreading, but are rejected by careful speakers.

9.7   *Cierto*: adjective, marked for number and gender

'Certain' i.e. 'specific'. Used thus it precedes the noun:

en ciertos casos	in certain cases
cierto alemán	a certain German
en cierta novela suya	in a certain novel of his

Determinado is a more formal synonym: *en determinados trenes existe un servicio de camareros* 'on certain trains waiter service is provided'.

Notes (i)   *Un cierto/una cierta* for 'a certain' are sometimes condemned as Gallicisms or Anglicisms, but are very common in all styles. *Un cierto* is found before partitive nouns – *yo era consciente de (una) cierta tendencia suya a exagerar* 'I was aware of a certain tendency of his to exaggerate' – and as a colloquial alternative to *un tal*: *se casó con un cierto Dionisio de México* 'she married a certain Dionisio from Mexico'.

(ii)   Placed after the noun *cierto* means 'fixed', 'accurate': *hemos tenido noticias ciertas de otro enfrentamiento en la frontera* 'we have received accurate reports of another frontier clash'.

9.8   *Cualquier, cualquiera, cualesquiera*: adjective/pronoun, marked for number

As an adjective 'any'; as a pronoun 'anybody'/'any one' (Fr. *n'importe quel*).

(a)   As an adjective

Before any noun or noun phrase, the final *a* of *cualquiera* (but not, usually, of *cualesquiera*) is. dropped: *en cualquier momento* 'at any moment'; *cualquier mujer* 'any woman', *en cualquier triste pueblo andino* 'in any wretched village of the Andes'; *inventan cualquier motivo para justificarse* 'they invent any motive to justify themselves'.

The plural adjective *cualesquiera* is nowadays normally expressed by the singular since the meaning is almost the same, e.g.

Cualquier mujer que no simpatice con el feminismo . . .	any woman/any women who doesn't/don't sympathize with feminism . . .

Cualquier(a) normally precedes the noun: *duerme a cualquier hora del día* 'he sleeps at any hour of the day', *se puede pagar con cualquier moneda* 'one can pay in any currency'. The idea of random choice is strengthened if it follows the noun, cf. English 'any at all'. When used thus of people the effect is often pejorative, as is the English 'any old':

Tráeme un libro cualquiera	bring me any (old) book
Vamos a pasear por una calle cualquiera	let's just walk down any street
Su esposa no es una mujer cualquiera	his wife isn't just any woman (i.e. she is rather special)

Notes (i)   *Cualquiera* before a feminine noun is an occasional and doubtful colloquial variant, cf. ?*de cualquiera manera* (dial. in Carlos Fuentes, Mexico). It is, however, attested in Ortega y Gasset, Valera and a few other pre-mid 20th-century stylists.

(ii)   *Una cualquiera* is heard colloquially with the meaning 'trollop', 'slut'.

(b) As a pronoun:

The final *-a* is always retained. The plural *cualesquiera* is hardly used in speech, and is disappearing even in writing.

Puede usted elegir cualquiera de estos tres modelos	you can choose any one of these three models
Cualquiera diría que eres un millonario	anybody would think you're a millionaire
Eso lo sabe cualquiera	anyone knows that
Cualquiera que sea el resultado	whatever the result is
Cualesquiera (or cualquiera) que sean tus motivos	whatever your motives are
Se les garantiza plaza escolar a sus hijos cualquiera que sean sus estudios (*El País* – singular for plural)	their children are guaranteed schoolplaces, whatever their studies (i.e. whatever they have studied)

9.9 *Demasiado*: adjective marked for number and gender, or invariable adverb

As an adjective 'too many'/'too much'; as an adverb 'too', 'too well'.

(a) Used as an adjective, it must agree in number and gender:

Has comido demasiadas uvas	you've eaten too many grapes
No (le) conviene al trigo que caiga demasiada lluvia	it isn't good for the wheat for too much rain to fall
Esto ha sucedido en demasiados casos	this has happened in too many cases
Llévate un poco de carne – has traído demasiada	take away a bit of meat – you've brought too much
Has traído demasiados pocos tornillos	you've brought too few screws

(*Demasiado* is treated as an adjective before *poco*.)

Nowadays *demasiado* is always placed before the noun.

(b) As an adverb (invariable in form)

Tú hablas demasiado	you talk too much
A ése me lo conozco demasiado	I know him only too well
No cuentes demasiado conmigo	don't count on me too much

9.10 *Mismo* (and Spanish-American variants): adjective, marked for gender and number

(a) 'The same':

When it means 'the same' it is always placed before any noun or noun phrase that it qualifies.

Lleváis la misma blusa	you're wearing the same blouse
Una gripe y un catarro no son la misma enfermedad	a bout of flu and a cold aren't the same illness
Estos dos casos son el mismo	these two cases are the same (i.e. identical)
Estos dos son los mismos	these two are the same (i.e. as before)
¿Es usted don Francisco? El mismo	are you Don F.? I am indeed (lit. 'the same')

Notes (i) *Lo mismo* may mean *la misma cosa*, or it may be adverbial. *Lo mismo* is heard in familiar European Spanish with the meaning 'perhaps':

Como me vuelvan a decir lo mismo/la misma cosa . . .	if they say the same thing to me again . . .
Lo mismo hace imitaciones de políticos que juegos de manos	he just as easily does imitations of politicians as conjuring tricks
Lo mismo te da una propina	maybe he'll give you a tip
No nos divertimos lo mismo que si hubieras estado tú	we didn't have such a good time as we would have if you'd been there

*Lo mismo como is substandard for *lo mismo que.*

(ii)   The following should be noted:

Esa casa es lo mismo que (igual que) aquélla	that house is the same as that other one (i.e. the same is true of it)
Esa casa es la misma que compró Agustín	that house is the same one that A. bought

(b)   Placed either before or after a noun, but always after a pronoun, *mismo* means 'selfsame'/'very'/'right', or emphasizes a pronoun, e.g. *yo mismo* 'I myself', *ella misma* 'she . . . herself':

Vivo en Madrid mismo/en el mismo Madrid	I live in Madrid itself
Aparca el helicóptero en su mismo jardín/su jardín mismo	he parks the helicopter right in his garden
¿Quién construyó tu chalet? Yo mismo (fem. *yo misma*)	who built your house/bungalow? I did myself
Yo creo que obran por sí mismos	I think they're acting on their own behalf

If there is danger of ambiguity, *mismo* must be placed after the noun if it means 'very', 'selfsame': *el mismo Papa* 'the Pope himself' or 'the same Pope'; *el Papa mismo* 'the Pope himself'.

Propio (see 9.13b) means the same as *mismo* in this sense, but it is not used with pronouns.

(c)   Placed after an adverb or adverbial phrase, *mismo* is itself an adverb and is therefore invariable:

por eso mismo	for that very reason
ahora mismo/ya mismo	right now/right away
aquí mismo	right here

But if the adverbial phrase contains a noun not accompanied by the definite article, *mismo* may or may not agree with it.

esta noche mismo/misma	this very night
vino esta mañana mismo	it came this very morning
en España mismo/misma no se pudo evitar la llegada del bikini	in Spain itself it was impossible to prevent the arrival of the bikini

However if the definite article is present *mismo* agrees:

Lo descubrieron en la chimenea misma	they found it in the chimney itself

Notes (i)   *Mismísimo* is a colloquial emphatic form of *mismo* in sense **(b)**: *el mismísimo presidente le felicitó* 'the president himself congratulated him.'

(ii)   Mexican and Central-American speech (not writing) often uses *mero* in contexts under **(b)**: *en la mera (misma) esquina* 'right on the corner'; *lo hizo él mero (él mismo)* 'he did it himself'; *ya mero (ahora mismo).*

In various parts of Latin America, from Chile to Mexico, *puro* may be used in the same way: *en la pura cabeza (en la misma cabeza)* 'right on the head', etc. (from Kany, 57ff).

(iii)   *Mismamente* (= *igual*) is rustic or jocular.

9.11 *Mucho* and *poco*: adjectives, marked for number and gender, or invariable adverbs

'Much', 'little'. Used as adjectives they agree in number and gender. Used as adverbs they are invariable.

(a)   Adjectival uses:

Mis hijos no me hacen mucho caso	my children don't pay much attention to me
En el patio hay muchos limoneros	there are a lot of lemon trees in the patio
Pon poca pimienta	don't put much pepper on/in it
Somos muchos/pocos	there are a lot/not many of us
Su poca paciencia	his scant patience
¿Cuánta harina has comprado? Poca	how much flour have you bought? Not much
Lo poco gusta, lo mucho cansa	brevity is the soul of wit (lit. 'little pleases, much tires')
Muchas se quejan de las nuevas horas de apertura	many women complain about the new opening hours

Note   In the following sentences *mucho* and *poco* do not agree with the preceding noun, but refer to the general idea underlying the sentence:

¿Trescientos mil dólares? Es mucho	300,000 dollars? It's a lot
¿Mil cajas de ciruelas? Es poco	1000 boxes of plums? That's not much
Compare	
Mil cajas para cien días son pocas	1000 boxes for 100 days isn't/aren't a lot
Setenta libros por estante son muchos	seventy books to a shelf is/are a lot

(b)   Adverbial uses:

Estoy añorando mucho a mi patria	I'm missing my home country a lot
Sale poco últimamente	he hasn't been out much lately
Por mucho que te quejes . . .	however much you complain . . .
Por poco que lo quieras	however little you want it
No sabes lo poco que me gusta ese hombre	you don't know how little I like that man

Notes (i)   Before *más*, *menos*, *mayor* and *menor*, when these are followed by a noun (present or implied), *mucho* or *poco* are adjectives, and must agree in number and gender – a fact which English-speakers are prone to forget:

Tienen muchos más hijos que tú/tienen muchos más que tú	they have many more children than you/ they have many more than you

But before adjectives and adverbs, *mucho* and *poco* are adverbs and invariable in form:

La diferencia era mucho mayor	the difference was much greater/less

For further examples see 5.6 (Comparison).

(ii)   *Muy* 'very' can be thought of as a shortened form of *mucho*, used before adjectives and adverbs. The full form therefore reappears when it is used alone: *¿es laborioso? Mucho.* 'Is he hard-working? Very'.

(iii)   *Poco* negates an adjective: *poco frecuente* = *no frecuente*:

Estoy poco acostumbrado al trabajo manual	I'm not used to manual labour
El argumento es poco convincente	the argument is unconvincing
Es poco más honrado de lo que tú dices	he is no more honest than you say

Compare *es un poco más honrado de lo que tú dices* 'he's a bit more honest than you say'.

(iv)   'Very much' = *muchísimo. Muy mucho* is archaic or jocular.

(v)   *Un poco de* is invariable, but phrases like *?una poca de sal* 'a bit of salt' are heard in very popular or jocular speech.

9.12   *Otro*: adjective/pronoun, marked for number and gender

Adjectivally 'other'/'another'; pronominally 'another one'/'others':

Otra persona no te creería	another person wouldn't believe you
Ponle otro sello (SA *estampilla*)	put another stamp on it
Por otra parte . . .	on the other hand . . .
En circunstancias otras que aquellas en que . . .	in circumstances other than those in which . . .
El que lo hizo fue otro	the one who did it was someone else
Hay quienes ven la vida lógica y ordenada, otros la sabemos absurda y confusa (Cabrera Infante, Cuba, dialogue)	there are some who see life as logical and ordered, others of us know it's absurd and confused
Se lanzaban la pelota unos a otros	they were throwing the ball to one another

Notes (i)   **Un otro* 'another' (Fr. *un autre*, Catalan *un altre*) is not Spanish: *dame otro* – 'give me another'.

(ii)   The possessives *mi, tu, su, nuestro, vuestro* precede *otro*, but other adjectives follow it, although *mucho* may appear in either position:

tu otro pantalón	your other trousers
otros grandes acontecimientos	other great events
Sé que estoy manipulada como otra mucha gente (interview in *Cambio16*, also *mucha otra . . .*)	I know I'm being manipulated like a lot of other people
en otros pocos casos	in a few other cases
otras dos Coca Colas	two more Coca Colas
Pero agravó la condición de otros varios millones de campesinos (Vargas Llosa, Peru)	but it worsened the condition of several million other peasants

(iii)   *Los/las demás* may be a synonym of *los otros/las otras* if the latter means 'the rest'/'the remaining':

Inglaterra siguió utilizando el sistema no decimal cuando los otros/los demás/ el resto de los países europeos lo habían abandonado hace mucho tiempo	England continued to use the non-decimal system when the other European countries had abandoned it long ago

9.13   *Propio*: adjective, marked for number and gender

(a)   Usually it means 'own', as in:

mi propio taxi	my own taxi
tus propias convicciones	your own convictions
Tiene chófer propio	he has his own driver
Es suyo propio	it's his own

(b)   'Selfsame', 'very', etc. (same as *mismo* at 9.10b.):

Las tachaduras son del propio autor	the crossing out is by the author himself

Nos dio audiencia el propio obispo	the Bishop himself granted us an audience

(c) 'Appropriate', 'right', 'peculiar', 'characteristic';

Ese olor es propio del butano	that smell is characteristic of butane
Ese lenguaje no es propio de un diplomático	that language is not suitable for a diplomat
Es propio de ella llegar tres horas tarde	it's like her to arrive three hours late

9.14 *Solo*: adjective, marked for number and gender; *sólo*: invariable adverb

The adjective means 'alone', the adverb means 'only'. The adverb used always to be distinguished by the written accent, but the Academy's *Nuevas normas* of 1959 decree that an accent is now necessary only to avoid ambiguity, so one may legitimately now write *solo tres* or *sólo tres* for 'only three'. Nearly thirty years later most editors still follow the old rules, but there is much inconsistency. In this book the accent always appears on the adverb.

Ambiguity is only possible with the masculine singular adjective, e.g.

un hombre solo/un hombre sólo	a man alone/only one man
solo en casa/sólo en casa	alone in the house/only at home

Solamente is an unambiguous equivalent of *sólo*.

(a) Adjectival uses:

No renunciaré, aunque todos ustedes dimitan y yo me quede solo	I won't give up, even if all of you resign and I am left alone
Usted sola no podrá hacerlo	you (fem.) alone won't be able to manage it
El solo anuncio de su llegada ha despertado una avalancha de protestas	the mere announcement of his arrival has aroused an avalanche of protests
Dos cafés solos	two black coffees
(cf. *dos cafés sólo*	only two coffees)

(b) Adverbial examples:

Los socialistas sólo cuentan con un tercio del electorado	the socialists only count on a third of the electorate
Millones de personas disfrutan de la luz eléctrica con sólo accionar un simple conmutador	millions of people enjoy electric light merely at the press of a switch
Sólo así se solucionarán estos problemas	only in this way will these problems be solved

Notes (i) A negative + *más . . . que* is a common way of translating 'only' (cf. French *ne . . . que . . .*):

No hizo más que reírse	all he did was laugh
No piensa más que en sí misma	she only thinks of herself

Más que must not be confused with *más de*. The latter is used with numerical values and means 'more than': *no había más de cincuenta* 'there were not more than fifty'; *no había más que cincuenta* 'there were only fifty'.

(ii) *A solas* strictly means 'alone' (i.e. unaccompanied), and is occasionally required for the sake of clarity, e.g. in:

Lo solucionó a solas	he solved it alone (no one else present)

Lo solucionó solo   he solved it alone (without help)

A solas cannot be used of inanimate things. In sentences like *estuvo a solas con sus pensamientos* 'he was alone with his thoughts' it is an elegant, rather poetic alternative to *solo*.

(iii)   Translating 'the only . . .', 'the only one . . .', 'his only', etc. *Único* is required if no noun follows:

Él es el único que sabe conducir   he's the only one who can drive
Lo único es que no sé nadar   the only thing is I can't swim
Es hijo único   he's an only child
But
El único/solo ser por quien deseo vivir   the only person I want to live for
Son el único/solo sustento del gobierno   they're the government's only support

9.15   *Tanto*: adjective, marked for number and gender; invariable adverb

For the use of *tanto* and *tan* in comparisons see 5.8.1.

(a)   So much/so many:

As an adjective it must agree in number and gender. As an adverb it is invariable:

(i)   Adjectival (or nominal) uses

Se quedó calvo de tantas preocupaciones   he went bald with so many worries
Se me fue el santo al cielo de tanto hablar   I clean forgot from so much talking (lit.
(adverbially, *de hablar tanto*)   my Saint went up to Heaven with so
                                               much talking)

Te he advertido tantas veces   I've warned you so many times
No creí que se atrevería a tanto   I didn't think he would be that daring
Es un tanto místico   he's a bit of a mystic (or 'he lives in the
                                            clouds')

Cobran un tanto por ciento de comisión   they take a certain percent as commission

(ii)   Adverbial uses

Hay más de tres kilos. ¡No tanto!   there are more than three kilos. Not
                                            that much!

Corrió tanto que no podía hablar   he ran so much that he couldn't speak
Tanto era así que . . .   so much was it so that . . .
(see note (ii) for ?*tan era así . . .*)

(b)   Other common uses of *tanto*:

Tanto mejor/tanto peor para ellos   all the better/so much the worse for them
La rana es tanto un plato favorito de los   the frog is as much a favourite dish of the
  franceses como buena presa para las   French as it is a good prey for snakes
  serpientes
El fenómeno es tanto menos explicable   the phenomenon is even less explicable
  cuanto que cientos de astrónomos   in that hundreds of astronomers claim
  afirman haberlo observado   to have seen it

Notes (i)   Before adjectives or adverbs, *tan* is required: *usted ha sido tan acogedor* 'you've been so welcoming'; *se levanta tan de mañana que nadie le ve salir* 'he gets up so early in the morning that no one sees him leave'; *lo hizo tan de pronto* 'he did it so suddenly'; *tan a propósito* 'so much on purpose, so relevantly', *tan inteligentemente*, etc.

Mejor, *peor*, *mayor* and *menor* are exceptions: *tanto mejor/peor para usted* 'so much the better/worse for you'; *el peligro era tanto mayor debido a la radiactividad* 'the danger was so much greater due to radioactivity'.

(ii) ?*Tan es así*, ?*tan se conocían*, for *tanto es así* or *tanto se conocían*, are considered substandard but are common in Spanish-American speech.

(iii) *Tanto* plus a singular noun is a colloquial expression for 'lots of', 'so many': *hay tanto ricacho por aquí* 'there are loads of stinking rich people round here'.

(iv) *Tanto que* for 'as much as' is not Spanish: *no viaja tanto como tú* 'he doesn't travel as much as you'. *Tanto cuanto* in this context is archaic. *Tanto que* means 'so much that': *comió tanto que reventó* 'he ate so much that he burst'.

For detailed discussion of comparison see chapter 5.

9.16 *Todo*: adjective/pronoun, marked for number and gender

'All', 'every', 'the whole of', 'any':

(a) Not followed by *un* or *el*:

Usually 'every' or 'any':

Todo producto alimenticio que contenga colorantes artificiales . . .	any food product containing artificial colouring . . .
Todo español sabe que . . .	every Spaniard knows that . . .
en todo caso	in any case

In all these cases *cualquier* could replace *todo*.

(b) With definite article, possessives or demonstratives, or before proper names.

Usual translation 'the whole of'/'all':

toda la noche	all night
todos los griegos	all (the) Greeks
todos los cinco	all five of them
Incluso Ricardo, con toda su paciencia, se salió del seminario	even Ricardo, with all his patience, walked out of the seminar
Todo aquel febrero no paró de llover	all that February it didn't stop raining
Todo Barcelona habla de ello	all Barcelona's talking about it
(See 1.3.7n. for discussion of gender of *todo* in this example)	

(c) With definite article and periods of time, 'every':

El fontanero (SA *plomero*) *viene todos los meses*	the plumber comes every/once a month
todos los viernes/años	every Friday/year

Notes (i) *Cada* must be used if the actions are new ones rather than repetitions, or when the period of time is preceded by a number:

Cada día sale con una chica nueva	every day he goes out with a new girl
Cada diez minutos sale con alguna nueva burrada	every ten minutes he comes out with some new nonsense
Tres gotas cada cuatro horas	three drops every four hours

(ii) Moliner, 1930, notes that *al* . . . is more elegant than *todos los* . . . when describing rate or quantity per period of time: *se fuma cuatro paquetes al día*, *lee un par de novelas a la semana*, etc.

(d) Pronominally, the singular means 'everything', the plural 'everyone'/'everybody'/'all of them':

Se enfada por todo	he gets cross about everything
Es todo propaganda	it's all propaganda
¿Dónde están las fresas? Me las he comido todas	Where are the strawberries? I've eaten them all
Pago por todos	I'm paying for everyone

Note   After a neuter *todo* – as after all singular nominals – Spanish often makes the verb agree with a following plural noun (cf. *ce sont des mensonges*, Ger. *es sind alles Lügen*):

Todo son mentiras	it's all lies
Con nuestro nuevo plan de ahorros, todo son ventajas	with our new savings plan it's all advantages
Pero todo eso, el canto de Bessie, el arrullo de Coleman Hawkins, ¿no eran ilusiones, y no eran algo todavía peor? (Cortázar, Arg.)	but wasn't all that – Bessie's singing, C.H.'s soothing voice – illusions, and wasn't it something still worse?
Al perro flaco todo se le vuelven pulgas	everything turns to fleas for a skinny dog (i.e. one misfortune follows another)

See 30.2.3 note (ii) for further discussion.

(e) Agreement of *todo* should be noted in the following examples:

Su cara era toda pecas	her face was all freckles
El cielo era todo nubes	the sky was all clouds
Esa niña es toda ojos (from Moliner, II, 1930)	that girl's all eyes

But the adverbial *todo* is not uncommon in this construction:

Estas chuletas son todo hueso	these chops are all bone
Tu amiga es todo sonrisas esta mañana	your friend's all smiles this morning

(f) Relative clauses involving *todo*

The following sentences, many inspired by Hammer (1971), 189, illustrate some translation problems:

Todos los que dicen eso	all who say that
Todo el que diga eso	anyone who says that
Todo aquel que diga eso (literary)	anyone who says that
Todo lo que escribe es bueno	everything he writes is good
Cuanto/todo cuanto escribe es bueno (literary)	everything he writes is good
Este poeta, cuyas palabras todas quedarán grabadas en nuestro corazón	this poet, whose every word will remain engraved on our hearts
El césped, por toda cuya superficie crecían malas hierbas	the lawn, over all of whose surface weeds were growing
Esta ciudad, de la que conozco todas las iglesias	this city, all of whose churches I know
Estas novelas, todas las cuales he leído	these novels, all of which I have read
Estos niños, los padres de todos los cuales yo conozco	these children, all of whose parents I know
Estas páginas, escritas todas ellas en japonés	these pages, all of which are written in Japanese
El palacio, del que no hay habitación que yo no haya visitado	the palace, all of whose rooms I have visited

Notes (i) *Todo* occasionally follows the noun in flowery style: *el cielo todo estaba sembrado de estrellas* 'the whole sky was strewn with stars'; *el mundo todo le parecía un jardín encantado* 'the whole world seemed to him an enchanted garden'.

(ii) *Todo el mundo* is a set phrase meaning 'everybody'.

(iii) *Todo* followed by the indefinite article usually translates 'a whole . . .':

Se comió toda una tarta de melocotones	he ate a whole peach tart
Hubo toda una serie de malentendidos	there was a whole series of misunderstandings

9.17 *varios*: adjective, marked for number and gender

(a) 'Several', in which case it normally – but not invariably – precedes the noun:

en varias partes del país	in several parts of the country
Mis motivos son varios	my motives are several
los aspectos varios de la cuestión	the several aspects of the question
(literary: from Moliner, II, 1442)	

(b) 'Various', 'varied' (usually follows the noun):

flores de colores varios	flowers of various colours
La fauna de esta zona es muy varia/ variada	the fauna of this zone is very varied

Note Translating 'various':

en diversas ocasiones	on various occasions
en diferentes puntos de los Andes	in various places in the Andes
enfocar un problema desde diversos ángulos	to approach a problem from various angles

10 Numerals

The Spanish numeral system is neither particularly complex nor plagued with irregularities, though this overall predictability makes such unexpected forms as *quinientos* 500 (for the non-existent **cinco cientos*), *setecientos* 700, *novecientos* 900, easier to forget.

Spanish cardinal numerals are invariable in form, with the important exceptions of *uno* 'one' and *cientos* 'hundreds' which both agree in gender with the noun counted.

The ordinal numbers above tenth are avoided in informal language and are usually replaced by the corresponding cardinal numbers.

10.1 Cardinal numbers

0 *cero*	11 *once*	22 *veintidós*	40 *cuarenta*
1 *uno/una*	12 *doce*	23 *veintitrés*	50 *cincuenta*
2 *dos*	13 *trece*	24 *veinticuatro*	60 *sesenta*
3 *tres*	14 *catorce*	25 *veinticinco*	70 *setenta*
4 *cuatro*	15 *quince*	26 *veintiséis*	80 *ochenta*
5 *cinco*	16 *dieciséis*	27 *veintisiete*	90 *noventa*
6 *seis*	17 *diecisiete*	28 *veintiocho*	100 *cien/ciento*
7 *siete*	18 *dieciocho*	29 *veintinueve*	101 *ciento uno/*
8 *ocho*	19 *diecinueve*	30 *treinta*	*una*
9 *nueve*	20 *veinte*	31 *treinta y*	102 *ciento dos*
10 *diez*	21 *veintiuno/a*	*uno/una*	185 *ciento ochenta*
		32 *treinta y dos* etc.	*y cinco*

200 *doscientos/doscientas*
300 *trescientos/trescientas*
400 *cuatrocientos/cuatrocientas*
500 *quinientos/quinientas* (n.b.)

600 *seiscientos/seiscientas*
700 *setecientos/setecientas* (n.b.)
800 *ochocientos/ochocientas*
900 *novecientos/novecientas* (n.b.)

1000 *mil*
1001 *mil un/uno/una*
but note *mil y una pesetas* 1001 ptas
1006 *mil seis*
1107 *mil ciento siete*
1993 *mil novecientos/as noventa y tres*

2001 *dos mil un/uno/una*
but note *dos mil y una pesetas* 2001 ptas
2022 *dos mil veintidós*
5000 *cinco mil*
10.000 *diez mil*
500.014 *quinientos/as mil catorce*

936.257 *novecientos/as treinta y seis mil doscientos/as cincuenta y siete*
1.000.000 *un millón*; 100.000.000 *cien millones*
$1.000.000 *un millón de dólares*

7.678.456 ptas *siete millones seiscientas setenta y ocho mil cuatrocientas cincuenta
y seis pesetas*
1.000.000.000.000 *un billón* (the American billion is still translated *mil millones*,
although US usage may be influencing some parts of the Hispanic world).

Notes (i)   16–29 inclusive are rather arbitrarily written as one word, as are 200, 300, 400,
500, 600, 700, 800, 900. Forms like *diez y seis* for *dieciséis* are old-fashioned.
   (ii)   *Uno* is not used before *ciento* and *mil* except in rare cases of ambiguity:
Una pareja de ratas es capaz de procrear   a pair of rats is capable of producing
   más de ciento veinte crías por año   more than 120 offspring per year
más de mil colegios equipados con   more than one thousand schools equipped
   televisores en color   with colour television
But compare
trescientos/as un/una mil ochenta y cuatro 301,084
trescientos/as mil ochenta y cuatro   300,084
   (iii)   A point is used in Spain and South America to separate thousands, but a comma is
found in Central America: *fechada el 3 de mayo de 1.976/1976* 'letter dated 3 May, 1976';
19.000 libras esterlinas £19,000.

10.2   Gender of numbers

Numbers (unlike letters of the alphabet) are masculine:
Yo puse un siete, no un nueve   I put a 7, not a 9
un cinco de bastos   a five of clubs
Tú eres el cinco   you're number five
This is also true of *cientos* and *miles* when they are used as nouns (i.e. when
they are followed by *de*):

los miles de víctimas de los tifones   the thousands of victims of the typhoons
Los escasos cientos de personas que   the few hundred persons present at the
   asistían a la manifestación   demonstration

10.3   Agreement of *uno* and the hundreds

Uno and *cientos* must agree in gender – a rule constantly overlooked by
foreign students. The singular, *ciento/cien*, is not marked for gender:
un peso/una peseta   one peso/one peseta
veintiuna pesetas   twenty-one pesetas
quinientos dólares   five hundred dollars
setecientas libras   seven hundred pounds
en la página quinientas catorce   on page 514
Yo duermo en la cuatrocientas   I'm sleeping in (room) 400
(*habitación* omitted)

10.4   Millions

Millón is a masculine noun and is connected by *de* to the noun or noun
phrase it qualifies:

Este plan prevé una inversión global de más de 6.000 millones de pesetas, de los que mil millones se invertirán el próximo año (El País)	this plan provides for an overall investment of more than 6,000 million ptas of which 1,000 million will be invested next year

Un millón is a singular noun, so a following verb or noun must agree accordingly:

El millón y medio restante fue invertido . . .	the remaining million and a half were/ was invested . . .

10.5   *Un* or *uno*?

Uno loses its final vowel before a masculine noun or noun phrase, as does *una* before nouns beginning with stressed *a-* or *ha-*.

Veintiuno is shortened to *veintiún* in the same contexts.

un tigre, dos tigres, tres tigres	one tiger, two tigers, three tigers (a tongue-twister)
veintiún mil hombres	21,000 men
No hay más que veintiuno	there are only 21 (masc.)
párrafo ciento uno	paragraph 101
Inglaterra, país tradicional de los fantasmas, ve uno nuevo por sus calles (Cambio16)	England, the traditional land of ghosts, is witnessing a new one in its streets
Llévese este vaso y traiga uno nuevo	take this glass away and bring a new one
un águila, veintiún armas	one eagle, 21 weapons

10.6   *Cien* or *ciento*?

Ciento is shortened to *cien* before another numeral which it multiplies, or before a noun or noun phrase:

cien mil bolívares	100,000 bolivares
cien millones	100 million
cien marcos	100 marks
cien buenas razones	100 good reasons

but

ciento once	one hundred and eleven
en la página ciento dieciocho	on page one hundred and eighteen

In theory *ciento* should be used when the number stands alone:

¿Cuántos son? Ciento	How many are there? A hundred
Vendimos más de ciento	we sold over a hundred

But this rule is obsolete in Spanish America and moribund in Spain:

Yo vivo en el cien	I live in number 100
Hemos comprado cien	we bought a hundred

etc.

although it is observed in the expression of percentages: see next section.

10.7 Expression of percentages

Ciento is used with all numbers, although the phrase *cien por cien* 'one hundred per cent' is also found for *ciento por ciento*:

cincuenta por ciento	fifty per cent
tanto por ciento	so much per cent
El PCE sólo obtuvo el 8 y pico por ciento de los votos (*El País*)	the Spanish Communist Party only obtained slightly more than 8 per cent of the votes
Ni uno solo de sus afiliados aceptará tripular el buque si no existe la seguridad, cien por cien, de que los vertidos son inocuos (*El País*)	not one of its {the National Union of Seamen's} members will agree to man the boat without a hundred-per-cent guarantee that the material to be dumped is harmless

10.8 Collective numerals

There is a series of collective numerals, cf. our 'score', sometimes used to express approximate quantities:

un par de veces	a couple of times
una decena	ten (little used)
una docena	a dozen (often approximate, used less in Spanish)
la cuarentena	quarantine, forty
un centenar	a hundred
un millar	a thousand

Notes (i) *Cuatro* is sometimes used colloquially in Spain (and perhaps elsewhere) to mean 'a couple'/'a handful': *no hay más que cuatro gatos* 'there's not a soul about'; *no son más que cuatro desgraciados los que ponen los pegatines fascistas* 'it's only a handful of wretches who put up fascist stickers'.

  (ii) *Centenar* and *millar* are used for expressing rate: *mil dólares el centenar/millar* '1000 dollars the hundred/the thousand' (or more colloquially . . . *cada cien/por cada cien, cada mil*).

10.9 Mathematical expressions

Dos y tres son cinco	two plus three equals five
Dos por tres son seis	two times three equals six
Ocho dividido por dos son cuatro (sometimes *ocho entre dos* . . .)	eight divided by two equals four
Once menos nueve son dos	eleven minus nine equals two
Tres es la raíz cuadrada de nueve	three is the square root of nine
Nueve es el cuadrado de tres	nine is three squared
Forma un cuadrado de diez metros	it's 10 metres square
dos metros cuadrados	2 square metres

The division sign is written with a colon, e.g. $3:6 = 0,5$ *(tres dividido por seis son cero coma cinco)*.

10.10 Fractions, decimals

1/2 *una mitad*; 1/3 *un tercio*; 2/3 *dos tercios*; 1/4 *un cuarto*; 1/5 *un quinto*; 3/7 *tres séptimos*; 7/10 *siete décimos*.

    La tercera parte, la quinta parte, la décima parte etc. are normally used in non-mathematical contexts: *la tercera parte de los accidentes de tráfico* 'a third of traffic accidents'. See also 10.13 for other fractions.

10.11 Articles with numbers

Certain common numerical expressions, especially percentages, usually appear with the article. This is especially true when the numerical value is preceded by a preposition:

Vivo en el cinco	I live in number 5
La inflación ha subido en un tres por ciento	inflation has risen by 3 per cent
El 20 por ciento de los mexicanos dice(n) que . . .	20 per cent of Mexicans say that . . .
El porcentaje de éxito llega al 70 por ciento.	the success rate reaches 70%.

But

Ha costado entre tres mil y cinco mil ptas	it cost between 3,000 and 5,000 ptas

10.12 Ordinals: first to tenth

These must agree in number and gender: *el quinto libro/la quinta casa* 'the fifth book'/'the fifth house'. Ordinals 1st–10th are in everyday use, but the cardinals encroach even on them in phrases like *el siglo nueve/noveno*, *Alfonso diez/décimo*, the ordinal being considered more correct.

primer(o)	first	*sexto*	sixth
segundo	second	*séptimo/sétimo*	seventh
tercer(o)	third	*octavo*	eighth
cuarto	fourth	*noveno*	ninth
quinto	fifth	*décimo*	tenth

Examples:

el tercer hombre	the third man	*Carlos III (tercero)*	Charles III
la tercera vez	the third time	*Fernando VII séptimo*	Ferdinand VII
		el siglo décimo/ diez	tenth century

etc.

Notes (i) *Primero* and *tercero* lose their final vowel before a masculine singular noun or noun phrase: *el primer récord mundial* 'the first world record', *el tercer gran éxito* 'the third great success'.

    (ii) *Séptimo* is commonly pronounced *sétimo* and the Academy approves of this as an alternative spelling. Most Spanish speakers do not.

    (iii) *Nono* is used for *noveno* when referring to Popes: *Pío nono* Pope Pius IX.

(iv) Modern usage says *el siete de agosto* 'the seventh of August', *el tres de mayo* 'the third of May' and even *el uno de enero* 'the first of January' etc., although some authorities prefer *el primero de* for the first of the month.

10.13 Ordinal numbers above tenth

The use of special ordinal forms for these numbers is declining, and they are now mainly used only in official or formal language.

Forms in the rightmost column are used for fractions in technical language: *tres doceavos* 'three-twelfths'. They are heard used as ordinals in Spanish America and occasionally in Spain, but this is rejected by grammarians (but *doceavo* 'twelfth' is widely accepted).

undécimo	eleventh	*onceavo*
duodécimo	twelfth	*doceavo*
decimotercero	thirteenth	*treceavo*
(*d-tercer* before sing. masc. nouns)		
decimocuarto	fourteenth	*catorceavo*
decimoquinto	fifteenth	*quinceavo*
decimosexto	sixteenth	*dieciseisavo*
decimoséptimo	seventeenth	*diecisieteavo*
decimoctavo	eighteenth	*dieciochavo*
decimonoveno/decimonono	nineteenth	*diecinueveavo*
vigésimo	twentieth	*veinteavo*
vigésimo/a primero/a	twenty-first	
(*vigésimo primer* before sing. masc. nouns)		
vigésimo/a quinto/a etc.	twenty-fifth	*veinticincavo*
trigésimo	thirtieth	*treintavo*
trigésimo/a sexto/a	thirty-sixth	
cuadragésimo	fortieth	*cuarentavo*
quincuagésimo	fiftieth	*cincuentavo*
sexagésimo	sixtieth	*sesentavo*
septuagésimo	seventieth	*setentavo*
octogésimo	eightieth	*ochentavo*
nonagésimo	ninetieth	*noventavo*
centésimo (in common use)	hundredth	*centavo*
ducentésimo	two hundredth	
tricentésimo	three hundredth	
cuadringentésimo	four hundredth	
quingentésimo	five hundredth	
sexcentésimo	six hundredth	
septingentésimo	seven hundredth	
octingentésimo	eight hundredth	
noningentésimo	nine hundredth	
milésimo (in common use)	thousandth	
dosmilésimo	two thousandth	
cuatrocientosmilésimo	four hundred thousandth	
millonésimo	millionth	

Notes (i) In informal styles – written and spoken – ordinal forms over tenth are either avoided, e.g. *mañana cumple treinta años* 'tomorrow's his thirtieth birthday', *¿en qué capítulo viene? En el trece* 'What chapter's it in? Thirteen', or the ordinary ordinal number is used instead, e.g. *el veinticinco aniversario* 'the twenty-fifth anniversary', *la trescientas cincuenta reunión del comité* 'the 350th meeting of the committee'.

(ii) **Decimoprimero*, **decimosegundo*, for *undécimo*, *duodécimo*, are common mistakes in spoken Spanish.

(iii) Forms like *décimo tercero*, *décimo cuarto*, in which both words agree in number and gender, are nowadays old-fashioned. *Vigesimoquinto/a*, *vigesimoséptimo/a*, etc. are also increasingly common for 21st to 29th.

10.14　Position of ordinals

Like most adjectives, they may follow or precede a noun, occasionally with changes of meaning. They usually precede, but used emphatically or contrastively, or with titles, they follow the noun:

en el tercer capítulo	in the third chapter
en el capítulo tercero (unusual)	
los tres primeros párrafos	the first three paragraphs (i.e. pars 1, 2 & 3)
los tres párrafos primeros	the three first paragraphs (i.e. par. 1 of 3 different chapters)
Isabel segunda (Isabel II)	Elizabeth the Second
por la enésima vez	for the umpteenth time

10.15　Distribution

Di cien mil pesos a cada uno	I gave 100,000 pesos to each of them
Traían sendos ramilletes de flores	each bore a bouquet of flowers
(literary style: *cada uno traía un ramillete*	each one was carrying a bouquet)
Cada uno paga lo suyo	each will pay his share
cada cinco meses	every five months

10.16　Single, twofold, double, treble, etc.

un billete de ida	a single ticket
una habitación individual	a single room
todos y cada uno de los problemas	every single problem
con una sola excepción	with a single exception
con una excepción única	
ni uno solo	not a single one
Mi sueldo es el doble del suyo	my salary is double his
el doble acristalamiento	double glazing
una cama de matrimonio	double bed
Duplicaron la suma	they doubled the sum
Esta cantidad es el triple de ésa	this quantity is triple that

10.17　Dimensions and other numerical expressions

Este cuarto mide 2,5 (dos coma cinco) por 3,75 (tres coma setenta y cinco) metros	this room measures 2.5 metres by 3.75

El área es de tres metros cuadrados	the area is 3 square metres
Forma un cuadrado de dos metros	it's two metres square
mil centímetros cúbicos	1000 cc
El cable tiene cien metros de largo	the cable's 100m long
Tiene cinco metros de hondo/ancho	it's five metres deep/wide
un motor de ocho caballos	an 8 horsepower engine
un motor de dos tiempos	a two-stroke engine
un ángulo de treinta grados	a 30-degree angle
Forma un ángulo recto	it makes a right-angle
Debe haber cinco bajo cero	it must be five degrees below zero
números pares/impares/primos	even/odd/prime numbers
dos nueveavos dividido por tres sieteavos	two ninths divided by three sevenths

10.18 Numerals: rules for writing

Figures are used:

(a)   in timetables: *salida a las 20.30, llegada a las 09.15*;

(b)   dates: *el 23 de marzo de 1971* (occasionally 1.971);

(c)   for exact figures: *2,38 kilómetros, 58 por ciento, 419 páginas, 63 grados bajo cero, 223 habitantes*.

Words are used:

(a)   for time elapsed: *veinticinco años, han pasado quince segundos*;

(b)   for approximate figures: *hubo más de quinientos heridos*;

(c)   for numbers which are quoted as spoken by someone: *me dijo que quería comprar quince* 'he said he wanted to buy fifteen'.

(d)   for telling the time (in literary works): *llegó a las diez y media/a las cuatro cuarenta y cinco*.

(Source: J. Martínez de Sousa, *Dudas y errores de lenguaje*, 294–5.)

10.19 Writing the date

15 de marzo de 1989; *2 de mayo de 1932*; *1* (or *1°*) *de abril de 1998* (pronounced *primero de abril*, although *uno de abril* is heard), *5-VII-1992* or *5-7-1992*, etc.; the hundreds should not be omitted.

Typists often use a point in years, *1.990*, but this is not usual in printed texts.

10.20 Telephone numbers

The foreign student's mastery of the higher numbers is constantly tested by the custom, common throughout the Hispanic world, of pronouncing phone numbers by a combination of tens or hundreds and tens:

542 6722 = *quinientos cuarenta y dos sesenta y siete veintidós* or *cinco cuarenta y dos sesenta y siete veintidós*.

11 Personal pronouns

For possessive adjectives and pronouns, see chapter 8.

11.1 Classification and forms

'Subject' pronouns may be optionally used to emphasize the subject of a verb: *yo hablo*, 'I'm talking', *él duerme* 'he's sleeping'. 'Object' pronouns (other than third-person) may be used *either* as the direct object *or* the indirect object of the verb, *te quiero* 'I love you', *te hablo* 'I'm talking to you', *nos vio* 'he saw us', *nos dio* 'he gave (to) us'. As far as forms are concerned, there is no need to distinguish between 'direct' and 'indirect' object pronouns in Spanish, since there is only one set for all persons but the third, where the difference between the 'direct' object forms (*lo/la/los/las*) and the 'indirect' forms (*le/les*) only vaguely coincides with the traditional distinction between direct and indirect objects.

Spanish has a partial set of prepositional personal pronouns (*mí, ti, sí*) which must be used after prepositions. The ordinary subject pronouns are used for the other persons.

Se is traditionally called a 'reflexive' third-person object pronoun, but this ubiquitous word is usually not 'reflexive' and it sometimes apparently functions as a verbal subject. It is discussed at length in chapters 12 and 24.

Table 11.1 Spanish personal pronoun forms
This contains all the personal pronoun forms currently in use. *Ello* is discussed separately in chapter 7 (neuter gender). The uses of *se*, traditionally called a 'reflexive' pronoun, are discussed in chapters 12 (pronominal verbs) and 24 (passive and impersonal sentences).

Person	Emphatic subject	Object	Prepositional	
Singular				
1	yo	me	mí	I
2	tú	te	ti	you (familiar)
	vos	te	vos	'' (familiar)[1]
	usted	lo/la/le	usted	'' (polite)
3	él	lo/la/le	él	he, it
	ella	la/le	ella	she, it
	ello	lo/le	ello	it (neuter)
	se		sí	'reflexive'

102

Table 11.1 *continued*

Person	Emphatic subject	Object	Prepositional	
Plural				
1	nosotros	nos	nosotros	we (masc.)
	nosotras	nos	nosotras	'' (fem.)
2	vosotros	os	vosotros	you (familiar masc. Spain)
	vosotras	os	vosotras	'' ('' fem. '')
	ustedes	los/las/les	ustedes	'' (polite, also familiar in Spanish America)
3	ellos	los/les	ellos	they (masc.)
	ellas	las/les	ellas	'' (fem.)
		se	sí	'reflexive'

[1] In parts of Spanish America only; acceptability dependent on country and style.

11.2 Use of subject pronouns

11.2.1 Emphasis

The ordinary subject pronoun is expressed by the verb ending: *hablo* 'I speak', *habló* 'he/she/you spoke', *vendió* 'he/she/you sold'; *salieron* 'they/you went out', etc. The forms *yo/tú/él/ella/ ustedes/ellos/ellas* are therefore usually only required for emphasis:

Estuve enfermo	I was ill
Yo estuve enfermo	*I* was ill
Hablas mucho	you talk a lot
Tú hablas mucho	*you* talk a lot
Es contable	he/she is an accountant, or you (i.e. *usted*) are an accountant
Él es contable, pero ella es ama de casa	*he* is an accountant, but *she* is a housewife

etc.

It is a bad error, rife among English speakers, to use subject pronouns when no emphasis is intended. To do so draws confusing attention to the subject of the verb, as in an English sentence pronounced with unnecessary stress on the pronoun, e.g. '*I* got up at eight, *I* showered, *I* had coffee, *I* went to work . . .' etc.

The subject pronouns are used:

(a) When the pronoun stands alone:

¿Quién ha venido? Ellos	who's come? They have
¿Quién lo ha hecho? Nosotros	who did it? We did
¿Quién es? Yo	who is it? Me

(b) In contrast:

Tú eres listo, pero ella es genial	you are clever, but she's a genius
Yo no, pero ustedes sí	I don't (or 'not me'), but you do (or 'you')

(c)   *Usted/ustedes* are used more frequently, either to avoid ambiguity or to stress the polite tone of an utterance:

¿Adónde van ustedes?	where are you going?
Si (usted) quiere, iré con usted	if you wish, I'll go with you

(d)   Third-person pronouns may be required for clarity, since a sentence like *viene mañana* is ambiguous out of context: *ella viene mañana* 'she's coming tomorrow', *usted viene mañana*; *él habla inglés* 'he speaks English'. Other subject pronouns may occasionally be used to clarify ambiguous verb endings: *yo tenía/él tenía* 'I had/he had'; *que yo fuese/que él fuese* 'that I should go (or 'be')'/'that he should go (or 'be')'.

11.2.2   Subject pronouns for inanimate nouns

Although *él/ella/ellos/ellas* may translate 'it' or 'them' when applied to inanimate things, in practice they are usually taken to stand for human beings when they are used as the subject of a verb, i.e. one does not pronominalize *el viento sopla* 'the wind's blowing' as **él sopla*, which is understood as 'he's blowing': *sopla* = 'it's blowing'.

But subject pronouns are sometimes used in Spanish America to replace an inanimate subject where Peninsular speakers would use either no pronoun at all, or *éste*:

La 'oposición' ha desaparecido de la radio, de la televisión y de la prensa diaria en el Perú. Ella subsiste, mínima, hostigada, desde las columnas de todos los periódicos (Vargas Llosa, Peru)	the 'opposition' has vanished from radio, television and daily press in Peru. It continues to operate, minimal, harassed, from the columns of all the newspapers
. . . si algún 'interés' tengo que defender como autor, él está mucho más cerca de los países socialistas que de los capitalistas (Vargas Llosa; his views have since changed.)	if I have any 'interest' to defend as an author, it is much closer to the socialist countries than the capitalist

11.3   Formal and informal modes of address

11.3.1   *Voseo*

Vos replaces *tú* in many parts of Latin America, but it may be too intimate for casual use by foreigners. It is everywhere stylistically informal, and is replaced by *tú* in prayers and other solemn language.

It is used in the spoken language of most social circles in Argentina, Uruguay, Paraguay, and in Central America except (most of) Mexico. In Colombia, Chile, Ecuador and Venezuela it is often heard, is possibly spreading, but may be considered as 'lower-class' or provincial, though usage varies between countries and regions.

It is not usual in Bolivia, Peru, Panama, Cuba, Mexico and Puerto Rico, but there are local pockets of *voseo*.

Even where *voseo* is current in speech, *tú* is often written, even in intimate letters.

The possessive adjective for *vos* is *tu/tus*, the object pronoun is *te*, and the prepositional form is *vos*: *¿te das cuenta de que estoy hablando de vos?* 'do you realize I'm talking about you?'.

The verb forms used with *vos* fluctuate according to region and are best learned locally. Argentine usage may be studied in the dialogue of novels by Julio Cortázar (e.g. *Rayuela*), Manuel Puig and Ernesto Sabato.

Note   *Voseo* descends from the Golden Age use of *vos* a a polite second-person singular pronoun. *Vos* was still heard in early nineteenth-century Spain (to judge from Larra's *Artículos de costumbres* of the 1830s), and survives in Spain in ritual language in official documents, and in pseudo-archaic style – e.g. Buero Vallejo's *Las meninas*. In Spain the archaic *vos* takes the normal verb endings for *vosotros*, and the possessive adjective/pronoun is *vuestro/a/os/as*.

11.3.2   *Tú* (*vos*) or *usted*?

Tú (or, where it is used, *vos*) is used between friends, members of family, to children, and generally between strangers under the age of about thirty, to animals, in insults and in prayers or invocations.

It is used more readily than French *tu* or German *Du* (at least in Spain), and almost always between persons who are on Christian-name terms. Its use is more common than thirty years ago, and is sometimes considered a mark of a democratic outlook.

Tú/vos should not be used to older strangers, persons in authority or to elderly persons unless they invite its use.

Note   Generalization on this subject is hazardous. In some parts of SA *tú/vos* is not used so readily, and one finds dialects (e.g. Colombia) where all three pronouns, *usted*, *tú* and *vos* may be used in the course of a single conversation depending on the degree of intimacy reached at any moment. *Usted* is informal in Colombia.

11.3.3   *Vosotros/as* or *ustedes*?

Vosotros (*vosotras* to two or more females) is the plural of *tú* and is used to two or more persons with whom the speaker is on relaxed or Christian-name terms. It is standard in Spain, but in Spanish America it is replaced by *ustedes* in all but archaic styles – a phenomenon also found in popular speech in Southern Spain and the Canaries. A mother in Spanish America addresses her child as *tú* or *vos*, her children as *ustedes*.

11.3.4   Use of *usted, ustedes*

These are polite forms corresponding to Fr. *vous*, German *Sie* (but see preceding section on Spanish-American usage). They require third-person verb forms: *usted habla* 'you speak'; *ustedes hablan* 'you (plural) speak'.

In writing, *usted/ustedes* may be abbreviated to *V./Vs.*, *Vd./Vds.*, or *Ud./Uds.*

Object forms of *usted/ustedes* are discussed under third-person pronouns.

Note As subject pronouns, *usted/ustedes* need only appear once at the beginning of a text or utterance, and then occasionally thereafter to recall the politeness of tone.

Whereas total omission of *usted/ustedes* may sound too informal, constant repetition may sound obsequious.

11.4 *Nosotros/as, nos*

Women referring to themselves and the rest of a group of women should use *nosotras*.

The first person plural is often used in books and articles when the author is modestly referring to himself. It is less pompous than the English 'royal We': *En este trabajo hemos procurado enfocar el problema de la inflación desde* . . . 'In this work I ('we') have tried to approach the problem of inflation from . . .'

Nos for *nosotros* is obsolete, but is used by popes and bishops in official documents or ritual utterances.

11.5 Prepositional forms

11.5.1 Use after prepositions

Only *yo*, *tú* and *se* have separate prepositional forms: *mí*, *ti* and *sí*. (*sí* is discussed at 11.5.3.) Otherwise the normal subject forms are used after prepositions (with the exceptions noted below).

No sabe nada de mí	he knows nothing about me
No tengo nada contra ti	I've nothing against you
Creo en vos (Argentina, etc.)	I believe in you
no delante de usted	not in front of you
Me refiero a él/ella	I'm referring to him/her
Confiamos en ustedes	we trust in you
Corrió tras ellos	he ran after them
aparte de ellas	except for them (fem.)

Six prepositions or preposition-like words require the ordinary form of the subject pronouns (but not of the pronoun *se* – see 11.5.3 note (i)): *entre* 'between'/'among'; *excepto* 'except'; *incluso* 'including'/'even'; *menos* 'except'; *salvo* 'except'; *según* 'according to':

Todos lo hicieron menos/excepto/salvo tú	they all did it except/save you
Que se quede entre tú y yo	let's keep it between you and me
Según tú y él	according to you and him

Note For constructions like ?*detrás tuyo* for *detrás de ti* 'behind you', or ?*delante mío* for *delante de mí* 'in front of me' (common in Spanish America, substandard or popular in Spain), see 8.6.

11.5.2 *Conmigo, contigo*

These special forms replace *con* + *yo*, *con* + *tú*: *¿vienes conmigo?* 'are you coming with me?'; *no quiero discutir contigo* 'I don't want to argue with you'.

In areas of *voseo*, *contigo* is rarely heard: *no quiero discutir con vos* 'I don't want to argue with you'.

11.5.3 *Sí, consigo*

These are special prepositional forms of the pronoun *se*. *Sí* is used after prepositions and *consigo* is a special form which replaces *con* + *se* and means 'with him/her/it/yourself' or 'with your/themselves'.

Sí is often combined with *mismo* when it is used reflexively:

Están muy contentos de sí mismos	they're very pleased with themselves
No se refiere a sí misma	she's not referring to herself
Este fenómeno ya es muy interesante de por sí	this phenomenon is in itself very interesting
Un brillante que para sí lo quisieran muchos (advertisement)	a diamond many would like for themselves
Volvió en sí	(s)he came round (regained consciousness)
No puede dar más de sí	he's doing the best he can
Está disgustada consigo misma	she's cross with herself

Notes (i) *Se* is unique in being the only pronoun requiring a prepositional form after *entre* and *según*: *entre tú y yo*, but *entre sí* 'among themselves'.

Entre sí may also mean 'to himself': *dijo entre sí* 'he said to himself'/'he murmured under his breath'.

(ii) *Sí* is not always really 'reflexive' as the following example shows:

El acento sirve para distinguir a los ingleses entre sí	accent serves to distinguish one Englishman from another

(iii) There is a curious colloquial tendency to reject other persons of *volver en sí* 'to regain consciousness' and *dar de sí* 'to give of oneself'. One hears *recobré el conocimiento* (correct) or even *volví en sí, but the expected *volví en mí* is often avoided, even by many educated speakers.

(iv) There is a good deal of disagreement about *sí* and *consigo* in the modern language. When *sí* refers to a specific person, the modern tendency is to prefer a non-reflexive prepositional pronoun.

In answer to a questionnaire, the great majority of informants (professional people and students, Spanish) rejected *sí* in the following sentences:

Hablan francés entre ellos (?*entre sí*)	they speak French among themselves
Yo sé que usted toca para usted misma (?*para sí misma*)	I know you play (music) for yourself
Lo mantuvo contra ella con uno de sus brazos (E. Sabato, Arg.)	she held him against herself with one arm
Tenía las manos apoyadas en la barra, delante de él (*ante sí*)	his hands were resting on the bar, in front of him(self)

(*Ante sí* is tolerable, since *ante* is itself literary. But *delante de él* is normal in speech, though some speakers respect the difference between 'in front of him(self)' and 'in front of him' (someone else).

Cerró la puerta tras él (?*tras sí*)	he shut the door after him(self)
El policía los vio venir hacia él (?*hacia sí*)	the policeman saw them coming towards him(self)
Guárdeselo para usted	keep it for yourself

11.6   Object pronouns

The term 'object pronouns' is used in this book to refer to the forms *me/te/lo/la/le/ nos/os/los/las/les* and *se* (although the latter is sometimes a grammatical subject). Traditional grammars often divide these into two lists, 'accusative' or 'object' pronouns and 'dative' or 'indirect object' pronouns, but only the third-person set has two forms (*le/les* as opposed to *lo/la/los/las*). The third-person pronouns are discussed separately under 11.6–7.

For 'pronominal' verbs (also called 'reflexive verbs'), see chapter 12.

11.6.1   Forms of 1st and 2nd-person object pronouns

	singular	*plural*
1st person	*me*	*nos*
2nd person	*te*	*os* (see note **iii**)

Notes (i)   *Usted/ustedes* take third-person object pronouns.

(ii)   *Te* is the object form of *tú* or *vos* (where *vos* is used): *vos sabés que te vi ayer* (Arg.) 'you know I saw you yesterday'; *vos te arrepentirás* (Arg.) 'you'll be sorry'.

(iii)   *Os* corresponds to *vosotros* and is therefore rare in SA where *ustedes* is used for both polite and familiar address:

Spain (familiar):	*sabéis que os vi ayer*	you know I saw you yesterday
Spain (polite):	*saben que los vi ayer*	
Spanish America (fam. or polite):	*saben que los vi ayer*	

11.6.2   Use of 1st and 2nd-person object pronouns

The main problem raised for the English-speaking learner by these (and the third-person) pronouns is the variety of translations possible for each form. Basically the object pronouns merely indicate the person 'affected' by a verb phrase. They do not, however, indicate *how* the object is affected and this must be worked out from the meaning of the verb, from context or by common sense. Thus *me* can be translated at least thirteen ways in the following examples:

Me han visto	they've seen me
Me dejó una finca	he left an estate *to* me
Me ha aparcado el coche	he's parked the car *for* me
Entró en mi tienda y me compró una agenda	he came into my shop and bought a diary *off/from* me
Me sacaron tres balas	they took three bullets *out of* me
Me han quitado a mis hijos	they've taken my children *from* me (or 'they have taken me away from my children')
Me tiene envidia	he's envious *of* me
Me tiró una bola de nieve	he threw a snowball *at* me
Me encontraron mil pesetas	they found 1000 ptas *on* me
Me echaron una manta	they threw a blanket *over* me
Voy a comprarme un helado	I'm going to buy *myself* an ice cream

Siempre me pone pegas	he always finds fault *with* me
Me rompió el brazo	he broke *my* arm

It is not clear whether the terms 'object' and 'indirect object' are useful descriptions of these various uses. 'Indirect object' may encourage students to limit their use of object pronouns to dative constructions and to neglect such sentences as *me quitó el libro* 'he took the book off me'.

Lists A and B (11.6.4 and 11.6.6) provide examples of sentences in which *me/te/os/nos* could be substituted for *le/les* or *lo/la/los* – provided the result makes sense.

A special case arises when the object pronoun and the subject pronoun (usually indicated by the verb ending) refer to the same person or thing, e.g. *me lavo* 'I'm washing (myself)', *te equivocaste* 'you were mistaken', *Miguel se va* 'Miguel's leaving', *nos caímos* 'we fell over'. We call such verbs 'pronominal verbs', and discuss them in chapter 12.

11.6.3 Use of 3rd-person object pronouns

These overworked pronouns correspond to *usted/ustedes* 'you' as well as to the third person:

Doctora Smith, le aseguro que la llamé ayer	Dr Smith (fem.), I assure you I rang you/her yesterday
Lo vi ayer	I saw him/it/you yesterday
Los vi ayer	I saw them/you yesterday

Correct choice between *lo/los* and *le/les* in the masculine, and between *la/las* and *le/les* in the feminine is notoriously controversial.

The chief controversy bears on the choice of the correct pronoun to indicate a human male direct object: Spanish-Americans and many Spaniards from Andalusia and other non-Central regions usually translate 'I saw him' as *lo vi*, but Castilian, i.e. Central Spanish and standard European literary language overwhelmingly favours *le vi*. The Academy is itself *loísta* but, in the face of massive resistance in Spain, 'tolerates' *le vi*. The following table and sentences illustrate the Academy's current preferences, expressed in *Esbozo* 3.10.5c:

	'direct object'	'indirect object'
Singular		
masculine	*lo* (*le* 'tolerated' for human males)	*le*
feminine	*la*	*le*
Plural		
masculine	*los* (not *les*)	*les*
feminine	*las*	*les*

Ángela vio a Antonio	*lo vio* or *le vio* ('tolerated')
Angela saw Antonio	she saw him
Antonio vio a Ángela	*la vio*
Antonio saw Angela	he saw her

Vio el libro	*lo vio*
(S)he saw the book	(s)he saw it
Vio la casa	*la vio*
(S)he saw the house	(s)he saw it
María dijo 'hola' a Juan	*le dijo 'hola'*
Maria said hallo to Juan (and vice-versa)	she said hallo to him/her
Vio a los hombres	*los vio*
(S)he saw the men	(s)he saw them
Vio a las mujeres	*las vio*
(S)he saw the women	(s)he saw them
Vio los libros	*los vio*
(S)he saw the books	(s)he saw them
Vio las casas	*las vio*
(S)he saw the houses	(s)he saw them
Dijo 'hola' a María y a José	*les dijo 'hola'*
(S)he said hallo to María and José	(s)he said hallo to them
Dijo 'hola' a María y a Ángela	*les dijo 'hola'*
(S)he said hallo to Maria and Angela	(s)he said hallo to them

There is great uncertainty about these rules, and the Academy has itself changed its mind about them several times in the last 150 years. Nor is its current hesitant preference for *lo* as the third-person direct object pronoun for human beings – a bias which reflects the Academy's partiality for Classical Latin – likely to impress those millions of educated Spaniards for whom *lo vi* means 'I saw it' and not (usually) 'I saw him'.

The Academy ruling, based as it is on a problematic distinction between 'direct' and 'indirect' objects, does not do justice to the subtlety of the language. The following pages attempt to provide a succinct account of the complexities of the problem. (For a full discussion see E. García, 1975.)

11.6.4 Use of *le/les*

The principle underlying the use of *le/les* seems to be the following: They replace any person or thing actively interested in or by the meaning of the verb phrase; 'interested by' here broadly meaning either 'gaining from' or 'losing by' an event.

The nature of this interest must be inferred from the meaning of the verb phrase or from clues provided by context. It can include the following types of involvement and, of course, their negative equivalents. Whatever departures from these examples he/she may hear, the foreign student is advised to use *le/les* in the following contexts:

List A: Typical uses of *le/les*
Le can be translated 'him', 'her', 'it', 'you', *les* as 'you' or 'them'. The choice in translation may be dictated by context, but in some of these examples is arbitrary.
    (i)   Receiving or acquiring any thing, impression or sensation

Le di la carta	I gave her/him/you the letter
Voy a darle una mano de pintura	I'll give it a coat of paint
Les dio vergüenza	it made them ashamed (lit. 'gave shame to them')

No le dije la verdad	I didn't tell you the truth
Les suministramos acero y petróleo	we supply them steel and (crude) oil
Ángel le alcanzó un cigarrillo	Angel handed him a cigarette
Le tirábamos bolas de nieve	we were throwing snowballs at her
Les llegaba un olor de hojas nuevas	a smell of new leaves reached them
Le pusieron una inyección	they gave you an injection
Le echaron una sábana	they threw a sheet over him
Se le agrega queso rallado	grated cheese is added to it
Se le pegó una brizna de hierba	a blade of grass stuck to her
Le valió una sonrisa	it earned him a smile
Su padre le contagió sus locuras	his father infected him with his mad ways
Les enseñé el camino	I showed them the way
Le tocó el premio gordo	she got first prize
Les corresponde la mitad	they're/you're entitled to half
Les interesa callarlo	it's in their interest to keep it quiet
Le convenía que fuera así	it suited him that way
No les es ventajoso	it's not advantageous to them
Esa chaqueta no le va	that jacket doesn't suit him/her
Las cosas le iban mal	things were going badly for her
Le hemos lavado tres camisas	we've washed three shirts for him
Enciéndele un cigarrillo	light a cigarette for her
Le prometió que haría un esfuerzo	he promised her he'd make an effort
No le pasó nada	nothing happened to him
Le sobrevino una tremenda tragedia	a great tragedy happened to him
Cuando se le sube el whisky	when the whisky goes to her head
Se le ocurrió llamar a la policía	he had the idea of phoning the police
No le parece mucho	it doesn't seem much to him
Le constaba que . . .	it was a fact to him that . . .
Le suena mal	it sounds wrong to her
Le da igual	it's all the same to him
La secretaria le cayó bien	he took a liking to the secretary
Le gusta la miel	she/he/it likes honey
Le agradó la respuesta	the reply pleased her
Les dolía que sus padres no contestasen/ contestaran	it pained them that their parents didn't reply
Cuánto les pesaba haber hablado	how sorry they were for having talked

(ii)   Loss or removal from

Les han robado un millón de soles	they've stolen a million soles from them/ you
Esto le ha quitado un peso de encima	this has taken a weight off her mind
Mario le ha quitado a Ana	Mario's taken Ana away from him (n.b. construction)
Le he comprado un cuadro	I've bought a picture from him
Le están sacando una muela	they're taking one of his teeth out
Le costó un dineral	it cost her a fortune
Se le cae el pelo	his hair's falling out
Se le ha muerto un hijo	a son of his has died
Se le pasa pronto	she gets over it quickly
Le arrancaron la pistola	they seized the pistol off him

(iii)   Sufficiency, insufficiency, lack, excess

Les basta decir que sí	all they have to do is say 'yes'
Le faltan mil pesos	he's 1000 pesos short

Le faltaba un dedo meñique	one of his little fingers was missing
Mil pesetas al día le alcanzaban para vivir	she could manage on 1000 ptas a day
Le sobraba (la) razón	he was only too right
El traje le está grande	her suit is too big for her

(iv)   Requesting, requiring, ordering

Le hicieron varias preguntas	they asked him several questions
Le pidieron sus señas	they asked him his name and address
Les rogaron que se sentasen/sentaran	they requested them to sit down
Les ordenaron rendirse	they ordered them to surrender
Les exigía un esfuerzo continuo	it required continuous effort from them
Les llamó la atención	he/it attracted their attention (or 'he told them off')

Note   Compare *le mandó que comprara/comprase pan* 'he ordered her/him to buy bread' and *la mandó a comprar pan* 'he sent her to buy bread'.

(v)   Numerous phrases involving *tener* plus an emotion (although the equivalent verbs, *respetar*, *temer*, etc. may take *la/las/los* and in SA *lo*):

Le tiene miedo	he fears him/her/you
Su madre le tenía poco cariño	his mother felt little fondness for him
Le tiene ojeriza	she has it in for him
Le tenías una envidia tremenda	you were enormously envious of him

(vi)   Numerous set phrases consisting of *hacer* plus a noun:

El frío les hacía mucho daño	the cold did them a lot of harm
El chico le hizo una mueca	the boy pulled a face at him
Mi nieto nunca les hacía caso	my grandson never heeded them
Tienes que hacerle frente a la realidad	you have to face up to reality
Le hacía falta reflexionar	she/he needed to reflect

(vii)   To indicate persons or things affected by something done to a part of their body or to some intimate possession (for further details on this construction, and for the omission of the possessive adjective with parts of the body and intimate possessions, see 8.3):

¡Le estás pisando los pies!	you're treading on his feet
Los fríos le hielan los dedos	the cold weather freezes his fingers
A esa edad se les ablanda el cerebro	their brains go soft at that age
Don Juan le acariciaba las mejillas	Don Juan was stroking her cheeks
Los nervios le jugaban malas partidas	his nerves were playing tricks on him
Se le ha hundido la moral	her morale has collapsed
No le veo la gracia	I don't see what's funny in it
Los labriegos se amotinaron porque les volvieron a gravar el aceite	the peasants revolted because they taxed their olive oil again
Le he roto la camisa	I've torn his shirt
Le dejaron las gafas hechas añicos	they shattered her glasses

(viii)   In a number of less easily classified cases which may all be perceived to convey ideas of 'giving', 'removing', 'benefiting', involving', 'affecting intimately':

¿Qué le vamos a hacer?	what can be done about it?
No le hace (S. Cone; Spain: *no tiene que ver*)	that's irrelevant
¡Dale!	hit him! Go on! Get moving!
Le agradezco	I thank you

El cura les (also *los*) *aconsejaba que no lo hicieran/hiciesen*	the priest advised them not to do it
Le encontraron mil pesos	they found 1000 pesos on her
La respuesta de su hija le afectó mucho (*lo* possible in SA)	his daughter's reply affected him a lot
etc.	

Note   This multiplicity of meanings can give rise to ambiguities of the type already noted:

Le compré un vestido	I bought a dress off her/for her
Cómprame algo	buy something for/off me
Ángel me robó una manzana	Angel stole an apple from me/for me/on my behalf

Context nearly always makes the sense plain, or the sentence can be recast: *compró una calculadora para mí* 'he/she bought a calculator for me', etc.

11.6.5   Dialect differences in the use of *le/les*
(a)   *La/las* for *le/les* ('*laísmo*'):
Students of Peninsular, particularly Madrid Spanish will often encounter the use of *la* for *le* in many of the above contexts to indicate the feminine gender:

?*La dije la verdad*	I told her the truth
?*La quitaron mil pesetas*	they took 1000 ptas off her
?*A una de estas bujías se la exige un rendimiento cinco veces superior* (*Cambio16*)	one of these spark plugs is expected to yield five times higher output
?*Yo la alabo el gusto* (Delibes, dialogue)	I praise her taste

Laísmo is nowadays condemned by most educated Spaniards (who may still use it themselves), and students are advised always to use *le/les* for the feminine in the above contexts. *Laísmo* is very rare (but not unknown) in Spanish America, but very common in pre-twentieth century Peninsular literature.

(b)   The use of *lo/los* for *le/les* in the contexts given in List A, heard in some parts of Spanish America, must be avoided.

11.6.6   *Lo/la/los/las*
(a)   Introductory:
There are two main reasons why it is not easy to define the relationship between the two sets of third-person object pronouns, *lo/la/los/las* and *le/les*.

The first is dialect differences, not only within Spain and between Spain and Spanish-speaking America, but also between the various regions of Spanish America itself. These differences seem to be in constant flux so that in texts written only fifty years ago rules may operate which are different from those now in favour.

The second is the fact that the distinction between *le/les* and *lo/la/los/las* is not governed by choice of verb alone, but also, in many cases, by the speaker's subjective assessment of the status of the person or thing affected by the verb, or by other considerations of context. Since a grammar book cannot easily account for context, abstract rules about these pronouns are of limited value.

One can easily challenge the traditional rule that *lo/la* is the pronoun of the 'direct object', and *le* the pronoun of the 'indirect object'. In both of the following sentences 'her' is the direct object of 'flattered': (a) 'he flattered her', (b) 'the joke flattered her'. Consequently we expect the Spanish translation to be *él la halagó* and *la broma la halagó* – and this indeed is what many native speakers accept. However, most seem to prefer *la broma le halagó*.[1]

The picture is complicated by the fact that schools in the Hispanic world normally use Latin grammatical terms and teach that *le* is the pronoun of the *objeto indirecto*. As a result, educated native speakers are often uncertain about their own usage and condemn constructions which are instinctively produced by good speakers and writers everywhere. For example, many who normally say *le halagó* will apologize for speaking 'badly' since they are taught that *la* is the only possible pronoun for a feminine direct object.

As a result, although the rules for the use of *le/les* already given in 11.6.4, and the rules for *lo/la/los/las* to be given below will enable foreign learners to form sentences which are acceptable to the majority of native speakers, they do not always explain the actual use of these pronouns in writing or educated speech. Some of the factors explaining this unpredictability are discussed at 11.6.8ff.

(b)   Uses of *lo/la/los/las*:

Lo/la/los/las are the third-person direct object pronouns, 'direct' object understood here as the person or thing affected by a verb phrase but not 'involved' or 'interested' in the ways described in List A. In the following list of examples it will be seen that even when dramatically affected by the verb phrase (as in 'they killed her') the person or thing denoted by the pronoun is not actively involved as a participant in the action or as an interested party. In fact the condition of the pronoun is very often literally that of an object which merely has the action of the verb 'done to it'.

---

[1]In an attempt to reduplicate García's (1975) experiments on natives of Buenos Aires, we issued a questionnaire to 28 educated speakers (mostly university students or professionals, 80% from Madrid) asking them to insert *la* or *le* in the following sentences:

(i) *A María todo el mundo . . . halaga*   everyone flatters Maria
(ii) *María comprendió que fue una*   Maria understood it was a joke, but it
     broma, pero . . . halagó que esa   flattered her that the joke was possible
     broma fuera posible

In (i) 87% put *la*, in (ii), 90% put *le*. When the sample was increased by adding 20 Spanish-Americans from five different countries, the picture did not alter. The distinction between *lo/la* and *le* is therefore clearly not simply the traditional difference between 'direct' and 'indirect' object.

List B: Contexts normally requiring *lo/la/los/las* (direct object)
The first item in the pair *lo/le* reflects standard Spanish-American usage and the Academy's current recommendation. The second item is standard literary and Northern and Central usage in Spain. See 11.6.7 for discussion.

(i)   Direct physical actions

Lo/le interrogaron	they interrogated him
La operaron	they operated on her
El perro lo/le mordió	the dog bit him
Coge estos papeles y quémalos	take these papers and burn them
¡Detengan a los contrabandistas y llévenlos a la cárcel!	arrest the smugglers and take them to jail!
A usted lo durmieron con algún mejunje en la sidra (Borges, Arg. dialogue)	they put you to sleep with some potion in the cider
Perdone, no quería molestarlo/le	sorry, I didn't mean to bother you (to a male)
Saca el carburador y límpialo	take out the carburettor and clean it
¿Y tu cámara? La he perdido	what about your camera? I've lost it
Vimos la casa y la compramos en el acto	we saw the house and bought it on the spot

Note   For *su marido le pega mucho* 'her husband beats her a lot' (for the non-existent **la pega mucho*) see 11.6.13.

Similarly *tirar* takes *le* when it means 'to pull (someone)'; *tirarlo* = 'to throw it away'. Some speakers also prefer *le* with *besar* 'to kiss'.

(ii)   Verbs denoting perception – 'seeing', 'hearing', 'knowing', etc.

Al director no lo/le conozco personalmente	I don't know the director personally
Lo/le vi ayer en el mercado	I saw him/you yesterday in the market
Sabía que el ladrón estaba en la habitación porque lo/le oí	I knew the thief was in the room because I heard him
Todos las contemplaron con asombro	they all gazed at them (fem.) in amazement
El agente lo/le miraba	the policeman was looking at him

(iii)   Praise, blame, admiration, love, hatred and other actions denoting attitudes towards a person or thing:

Sus profesores lo/le alaban	his teachers praise him/you
A las monjas las envidio mucho	I envy nuns a lot
Lo/le admiro profundamente	I admire him deeply
Su marido la adora	her/your husband adores her
(For some Spanish Americans *lo quieren* = 'they want him', *le quieren* = 'they love him'.)	
La considero una amiga	I consider her/you a friend

(iv)   'Naming', 'nominating', 'describing' (but see 11.6.13 for the verb *llamar*):

Los denominaron 'los decadentes'	they named them 'the decadents'
Lo/le nombraron alcalde	they nominated him mayor
Las describió en términos despectivos	he described them (fem.) in pejorative terms
Lo calificó de tragedia	he described it as a tragedy

(v)   Many other actions done to things or persons but not 'involving' them in the ways described in List A:

La crisis energética no la podrá solucionar ningún gobierno elegido	the energy crisis won't be solved by any elected government

El Canciller los recibirá a las siete y cuarto	the Chancellor will receive you/them at 7.15
Este país no hay quien sepa gobernarlo	there's no one who knows how to govern this country
Habrá que defenderlos	we'll have to defend them
No pude convencerla	I couldn't convince her
Intentaba evitarlos	I was trying to avoid them
etc.	

Notes (i)   *Lo/la/los/las* agree in gender with the noun they replace. If they do not replace a specific noun, *lo* is used: *dijo que llegaría a las siete, pero no lo creo* 'he said he'd arrive at seven, but I don't believe it'; *esto no lo aguanta nadie* 'no one can stand this'.

(ii)   *Me/te/nos/os* could be used in any of the above sentences in place of the third-person pronoun, provided the result makes sense.

11.6.7   Dialect differences in the use of *lo/la/los/las*
(a)   *Le/les* for *lo/los* in standard Peninsular Spanish
In Madrid and generally in Castilian or standard Peninsular language, *le* is used in the above contexts when the pronoun refers to a male human: *no le conozco* 'I don't know him', *no le he visto* 'I haven't seen him', *a usted sí que le vi ayer* 'I did see you yesterday'. Many educated Spaniards describe *no lo he visto* – out of context – as American or provincial when the *lo* refers to a human male.

In the plural, *los* is more usual than *les* in the same contexts and the Academy in fact rejects the use of *les* for human direct objects (but the Academy is apparently unaware of the complexities described in sections 11.6.8ff, complexities which may justify the use of *les* in some circumstances):

Con estos jóvenes cabe hacer una de dos cosas: o fusilarlos, o tratar de comprenderlos (Ortega y Gasset)	there is one of two things to be done with these young people: either shoot them, or try to understand them

Les for human direct objects sounds old-fashioned to many Spaniards, but it is quite common among *leísta* speakers:

Les llevaron a una casa donde estuvieron mucho rato esperando (Juan Benet)	they took them to a house where they waited for a long time
Les sorprendo y mueven las manos en ademanes de bienvenida (I. Aldecoa, monologue)	I surprise them, and they wave their hands in welcome

Everyday speech and racy prose in Spain, e.g. popular journalism or colloquial narrative prose, is showing increasing signs of *loísmo*, and students may find great inconsistency in the use of *le* or *lo* with reference to human males.[1]

---

[1]Sometimes no discernible principle seems to dictate the choice between *lo* and *le* in the speech of some Peninsular speakers: some 20 examples of the verb *mirar* associated with a human male, taken from descriptive passages in D. Sueiro's novel *La noche más caliente* (1965) – Sueiro was born in Galicia but worked as a journalist and novelist in Madrid – showed *le* for 'him' in 56% of the cases and *lo* in the other 44%.

The use of *lo* for male humans is standard in Spanish America and must be adopted by students of American Spanish. However, use of *le/les* where *lo/la/los/las* might have been expected is not unknown in the Americas, especially in some regions and styles, cf. 11.6.9.

(b) *Le* for inanimate nouns
In Spain, in popular speech in Madrid and elsewhere, and in pre-twentieth century texts, one finds *le* used as the direct object pronoun for inanimate nouns: **no le he leído todavia* 'I haven't read it {*el libro*} yet'; *unos niegan el hecho, otros le afirman* 'some deny the fact, others assert it' (P. Feijoo, mid-eighteenth century). This usage, approved by the Academy until the 1850s, is nowadays considered sub-standard or dialectal, unless it is a rare instance of genuine personification.

(c) *Le* for *la* applied to human females
One locally finds *le* for *la* when the direct object is a human female, e.g. in Paraguay and regionally in Spain, e.g. Navarre or the Basque Country – cf. the prose of Unamuno: *yo le admiraba* for *yo la admiraba*. This should not be imitated – unless it is an instance of the nuances described under 11.6.8ff.

11.6.8 The *leísmo/loísmo* controversy: general

One interesting theory about the difference between *le/les* and *lo/la/los/las* (developed at length in García [1975]) is that *le* denotes a higher level of involvement by the entity denoted by the pronoun, whereas *lo* denotes a low level of active involvement or response. Thus in the sentence *le dimos algo de comer* 'we gave him/her something to eat' there is no doubt that *le* is more active than *algo*, since receiving implies active participation. Similarly the human object of a verb like *obedecer* 'to obey' seems to be more active than the object of a verb like 'to see': being seen requires no response, participation or activity. As a result *le obedecía* for 'I was obeying him/her' is required, whereas **le vi* for 'I saw *her*' (or 'him' in *loísta* dialects) sounds wrong to most speakers.

This distinction involves the speaker's assessment of the degree of activity or participation of the object, and opinions will differ. Some speakers will translate 'her husband never helps her in the house' as *su marido nunca la ayuda en casa*, others as . . . *nunca le ayuda en casa* (García, 1975). It is a matter of debate whether help 'involves' its recipient actively or not and it is impossible to decide out of context which form is correct. Moreover, since *la/las/los* (and in SA *lo*) imply less participation or less activity than *le/les*, some speakers discern a polite nuance in the use of *le/les* which acknowledge the relevance of the reaction or attitude of the person denoted by them.

The following paragraphs attempt to explain some of this variation, but it must be remembered that many native speakers do not exploit all the potential of the system, and they will often disagree about the correct pronoun to use in any one context.

11.6.9 *Le/les* preferred when subject is inanimate

Le/le are often the preferred object pronouns when they denote a human being and the subject of the verb is inanimate.[1]

Examples (all Spanish-American except the second):

Él se miraba la sangre que le había salpicado (Vargas Llosa, Peru)	he looked at the blood that had spattered him
La abuela no vendrá porque ya le fatiga el andar mucho (Linares Rivas, quoted Ramsey & Spaulding)	grandmother won't come because walking tires her a lot now
Sin embargo, le molestaba encararse con Parodi (Borges, Arg.)	yet it troubled him to come face to face with Parodi
Si [la muela] le molesta mucho, lo puedo atender hoy mismo (Peruvian dentist to male patient, in *Var.* 238)	if it [the tooth] is troubling you a lot, I can attend to you today
Durante mucho tiempo le angustió esa novedad (E. Sabato, Arg.)	for a long while that turn of events filled him with anguish

A number of verbs often (but not invariably) take *le/les* when their subject is inanimate. The following examples illustrate this tendency:

Le acometió una duda	a doubt assailed him/her
La angustia le acompañaba siempre	anguish went with her always
Yo la acompañaba siempre	I always went with her
A Consuelo le admiró que no contestase	it surprised Consuelo that he did not reply
A Consuelo la admiro mucho	I admire Consuelo a great deal
El dolor que le afligía . . .	the pain that afflicted him/her . . .
No sabe la suerte que le aguarda	he/she doesn't know the fate that's waiting for him/her
Yo la aguardé (likewise *esperar*)	I awaited her
Le alcanzan mil pesetas para vivir	1000 ptas are enough for him/her to live on
No pude alcanzarla	I couldn't catch up with her
El gas les hace reír	the gas makes them laugh
Yo los haré reír	I'll make them laugh

etc.

And similarly such verbs as the following: *asistir*, *asustar*, *ayudar*, *calmar*, *coger*, *complacer*, *convencer*, *distraer*, *encantar*, *estorbar*, *fascinar*, *fatigar*, *indignar*, *inquietar*, *interesar*, *molestar*, *preocupar*, *sorprender*, *seducir*, *tocar*, *tranquilizar*, etc.

---

[1]García notes of Buenos Aires speakers that whereas only 14% of a sample would translate 'he convinced him' as *él le convenció* (the rest say *él lo convenció*), 54% say *este color no le convence* 'this colour doesn't convince him'. We found that of 23 educated Spaniards, mostly from Madrid, only 20% used *le* in *yo la convencí* 'I convinced her', but 70% preferred *le* in *si a tu suegra este color no le convence, qué elija otro* 'if this colour doesn't convince your mother-in-law, let her choose another'.

One explanation for this phenomenon is that the verb changes its meaning when the subject is inanimate: thus *la convence* means 'he convinces her' but *le convence* in the above example means 'she likes it'. In other words, use of *le* highlights the 'object' as *reacting* to the subject.

11.6.10   Inconsistency in use of *lo/le* in Spain as direct object pronouns

In Spain, it is possible that for some speakers use of *lo* denotes contempt, a low estimate of the person's rationality (e.g. infants), or helplessness, but in general choice of *le* or *lo* seems to be dictated by region. The following examples may show *lo* used with the nuance described, but the choice often seems arbitrary with the preference for *le*:

Le he amenazado con causa criminal y se ha desinflado. Mañana lo tienes aquí con el vil metal (Buero Vallejo, dialogue)	I threatened him with criminal proceedings, and that took the wind out of him. Tomorrow you'll have him here with the filthy lucre
Lo agarramos por los sobacos y por las piernas y lo subimos . . . dejándole tendido en la puerta de aquel pisito (J. Marsé, dialogue about a drunkard: inconsistent use of *le/lo*)	we grabbed hold of him under the arms and by the legs, and carried him up and left him lying in the doorway to that little flat
Después lo hemos traído aquí (Buero Vallejo: refers to the dead Ignacio in *En la ardiente oscuridad*)	then we brought him here

Note   García *op. cit.* reports that some Argentine speakers detect a difference between *le llevaron al hospital* and *lo llevaron al hospital*, 'they took him to the hospital', the former implying the patient is walking or cooperative, the latter that he is helpless or unconscious, and it seems that some Spaniards also accept the distinction. For Colombian informants only *lo llevaron* was possible.

Some Peninsular speakers likewise report that the difference between *lo vi* and *le vi* 'I saw him' is that *lo* suggests that the person was unaware that he had been seen, whereas *le* suggests that some greeting or response was exchanged. But comparison of examples (b) and (f) in the footnote suggests that in central Castile this distinction does not operate.

As far as Peninsular usage is concerned, however, it would be inaccurate to say that *lo* is used systematically to denote passivity or helplessness. Questionnaires[1] elicited a very slight increase in preference for *lo* for very ill, drunk or dead human masculine singular direct objects, but *le* is clearly preferred to *lo* by most speakers in all cases.

11.6.11   *Le/les* preferred with *usted/ustedes*

Some speakers prefer *le/les* as the object pronoun for *usted/ustedes* and reserve *lo/la*, etc. for third-person use:

¡Buenas tardes, hijitos! Les encuentro muy alegres (Buero Vallejo, dialogue)	Good afternoon, my dears! I find you very cheerful

[1]Circulated among 55 Spaniards (most of them under 25) living in Madrid, Segovia and Valladolid, the traditional homeland of Castilian *leísmo*:

	Percentage	
	lo	le
(a) *El abuelo está muy malo . . . recogieron ayer medio muerto en la calle*	27	73
(b) *. . . vi ayer en la calle, y me dijo que su mujer está mucho mejor*	15	85
(c) *Cuando . . . recogieron ya estaba muerto*	44	56
(d) *A Pepe . . . recogeré más tarde para ir al teatro*	38	62
(e) *Él estaba completamente borracho cuando yo . . . vi*	29	71
(f) *Yo sé que él es el ladrón, porque . . . vi salir de piso*	16	84
(g) *Si no quiere venir, . . . traes a la fuerza*	23	77

Si le molesta el humo, señora, lo apago	if the smoke troubles you, Señora, I'll put it out

But

Lo apagué porque la molestaba el humo	I put it out because the smoke was bothering her

Note Argentine informants were convinced that they would say *no quería molestarle* 'I didn't mean to bother you', speaking to their boss, but *molestarlo* when speaking about him. Colombian informants said *molestarlo* in both cases.

11.6.12 Preference for *le/les* after impersonal or reflexive *se*

If impersonal or reflexive *se* precedes a third-person pronoun there is a tendency to prefer *le/les*, especially when the latter refer to a person:[1]

Se le notaba tímida y cortada (L. Goytisolo)	one could see she was timid and embarrassed
Se le notaba alegre (Vargas Llosa, Peru, *lo* expected)	one could see he was cheerful
Entonces se le leerá como se le debió leer siempre . . . (Vargas Llosa, Peru, essay on Camus)	then he will be read as he always should have been read . . .
A los esperpentos de Valle-Inclán siempre se les ha considerado ejemplos de expresionismo español (Buero Vallejo, essay)	V.-Inclán's *esperpentos* have always been considered examples of Spanish expressionism
Hola doctor, ¡qué bien se le ve! (Peruvian speaker, *Var.* 238, *lo* expected)	hullo doctor, you're looking well!
Licha se le prendió de la solapa (Fuentes, Mex.)	Licha pulled him to her by his lapels
Licha se le volvió a abrazar (*ibid.*)	Licha put her arms round him again

Use of *le/les* for the direct object is here a device for removing some of the ambiguities that arise in Spanish from the scarcity of object pronoun forms. Use of *lo/la* after *se* invites the interpretation of the latter as some other manifestation of the ubiquitous pronoun *se*, particularly as a standard substitute for *le* by the rule that two object pronouns in *l* cannot occur side-by-side (see section 11.11.2 for discussion). Thus *le cortó la cabeza* 'he cut his head off' is pronominalized *se la cortó* 'he cut it off' (for the expected **le la cortó*). For this reason *se la notaba pálida* suggests 'he noticed that his/her hand, face (or some other grammatically feminine noun) was pale'. Compare the following examples in which *se* replaces *le*:

[1]In the following sentences, however, distributed to 55 Spaniards from Madrid, Segovia and Valladolid, the immense majority preferred *lo* to *le*, despite the fact that the area is heavily *leísta*:

	Percentages	
	lo	*le*
Se rompió una pierna y se . . . llevaron al hospital en ambulancia	75	25
A mi padre me . . . voy a llevar a pasar las vacaciones conmigo	62	38

This is presumably a peculiarity of the verb *llevar*: *le* is reserved for the meaning 'carry *to* him/her', and *lo* for the meaning 'take' or 'wear'.

Se lo cobró	he took it off him/her/you
Se la vendió a ella	he sold it (fem.) to her
Se lo leyó a su padre	(s)he/ read it to his/her father
etc.	

11.6.13   *Le/les*: some problem verbs
The following verbs everywhere prefer *le/les* if their object is human:

Entender 'understand': *no le entiendo* 'I don't understand him/her/ you'.

Obedecer 'obey': *a las madres siempres les obedezco en todo* 'I always obey the nuns in everything'.

Discutir 'argue'/'discuss', when used in the meaning 'to answer back': *¿Desde cuándo le discutía?* 'since when had she been answering him back?' (Vargas Llosa, Peruvian dialogue).

Pegar 'to beat': *{Lalita} te contó que le pegué* (dialogue in Vargas Llosa, Peru) 'Lalita told you I hit her'; *dicen que le pega mucho* 'they say he hits him/her/you a lot';

Pegarlo/pegarla etc. is assumed to mean 'to stick (i.e. glue) it'.

Creer 'to believe': *Yo no le creo, señora*, 'Madam, I do not believe you', but *sí que lo creo*, 'I *do* believe it'.

Llamar. Many speakers prefer *le/les* when the verb means 'to give a name': *se llama María, pero todo el mundo le llama «Chelo»; se nos informó en un «briefing», que le llaman* (Cuban TV interview) 'we were told in a "briefing", as they call it'.

(For christening, educated usage says *le pusieron María de nombre* 'they called her "Maria" '.)

La/lo/(le)/los/las are the usual forms when the verb means 'phone' or 'call to': *yo la llamaré apenas haya alguna novedad* 'I'll call you as soon as there's news'.

11.6.14   *Le/les* in double accusative constructions
In *Juan la oyó* 'John heard her' *la* is normal since 'she' is not 'actively participant' in any of the ways described in 11.6.4, List A.

In 'John heard her sing an aria', there are two objects, one ('aria') less active than the other, 'her', who is singing. Spanish speakers normally use *le* to denote the more active object:[1] *Juan le oyó cantar un aria* (*la* occurs,

---

[1]Questionnaires, based on examples from García, elicited the following replies from 20 educated *madrileños*, which confirmed García's finding with Spanish-American speakers:

	Percentage	
	la	*le*
María no quería venir, pero . . . obligamos a venir		
Maria didn't want to come, but we obliged her to come	70	30
Pobre María, su padre siempre . . . obliga a decir la verdad		
poor Maria, her father always obliges her to tell the truth	35	65
A María nunca . . . dejan salir de casa		
they never let Maria leave the house	33	57

particularly in Spain, but may be rejected by educated speakers). Similarly in *loísta* regions *le oí decirlo* 'I heard him say it'.

Notes **(i)** *Ver* normally takes *lo* (in Spain *le*)/*la*/*los*/*las*: *yo me quedé con ella porque quería verla firmar el contrato* 'I stayed with her because I wanted to see her sign the contract'.

(ii) *Dejar* 'to let' may elicit *la* (and in SA *lo*) – *la dejaron hacerlo* 'they let her do it'. *Permitir* takes *le*: *le permitieron hacerlo*.

11.7   Pronouns with verbs of motion

The object pronouns cannot replace the preposition *a* plus a noun if mere physical arrival or approach is involved: *voy a la reunión – voy allí* (not **le voy*) 'I'm going to the meeting'/'I'm going to it'; *acude a ella* 'he goes to her':

Cuando tiene problemas siempre va a ella	when he has problems he always goes to her
Me dirijo a ustedes	I'm turning to you/addressing you/writing to you
Todo el occidente que vino a nosotros (Vargas Llosa, Peru)	the whole of the west (i.e. western world) which came to us
Suele recurrir a él cuando no le queda más remedio	he usually turns to him when he has no alternative

However, object pronouns are often used colloquially with the following verbs, particularly if the verb is third-person:

Se me acercó/se acercó a mí	he approached me
Él se le acercó por la espalda (J. Marsé)	he approached her from behind
Ella se le reunió al doblar la esquina (L. Goytisolo)	she caught up with him as she was turning the corner
No sólo los sollozos de los niños y de los nativos se alzaron entonces, sino que se les unieron los de los sirvientes (José Donoso, Chile)	not only did sobbing from the children and natives break out then, but the servants' (sobs) were added to it

Notes (i) This construction is rare in the first and second persons: *se le opuso* 'he opposed him', but *te opusiste a él* 'you opposed him'. Forms with other persons may occur in SA: a Mexican informant claims that *?me le arrodillé a la Virgen* 'I kneeled before/to the Virgin' is heard in his country, but the sentence was rejected by Spaniards and Argentines.

(ii) *Se le puso delante*, *se me puso delante* 'he stood in front of him', 'he stood in front of me' also occur colloquially for *se puso delante de él/se puso delante de mí*, and are more emotional in tone. See 11.10 for further discussion.

(iii) The example from José Donoso is an exception to the rule that object pronouns are

---

*Un mensaje de la Superiora . . . dejó comprender a María que tenía que
    abandonar el convento*
a message from Mother Superior made Maria understand that she must
    leave the convent
(two objects and a non-human subject: *dejó* for *hizo* is American)

not used with such verbs when the sentence refers to a non-human entity: the normal construction would be *se acercó al puente > se acercó a él* not **se le acercó*.

(iv) Object pronouns are used to denote a person affected by *venirse* (if its subject is inanimate), *venir con* and *llegar* (if its subject is inanimate):

El armario se le vino encima	the cupboard collapsed on him/her/you
Siempre me viene con pejigueras	he's always coming to me with irritating details
Cuando me llegó la noticia de su triunfo	when news of his triumph reached me

(v) In *le viene a decir que . . .* 'he's coming to tell him that . . .' the *le* belongs to the *decir*: *viene a decirle que . . .* In *le viene bien* 'it suits him' advantage, not motion, is involved.

11.8   Pronouns with *ser* and *resultar*

(a)   With adjectives:

The choice is between *me es necesario* and *es necesario para mí*. The former is possible with *ser* only if the adjective expresses a meaning included in list A, 11.6.4. *Resultar* allows the construction with a wider range of adjectives, and may be thought of as the 'involving' counterpart of *ser*:

Les es/resulta necesario	it's necessary for them
Me es/resulta importante	it's important to me
Nos era imprescindible contactar a sus padres	it was absolutely necessary for us to contact his parents

But

La casa era demasiado blanca para mí/ me resultaba demasiado blanca	the house was too white for me
Era muy feo para ella	it was very ugly for her
Le resultaba muy feo	he seemed very ugly to her

The following list will give an idea of the kind of adjective which can take object pronouns with *ser*:

agradable/desagradable	agreeable/disagreeable
conocido/desconocido	known/unknown
conveniente/inconveniente	suitable/unsuitable
fácil/difícil	easy/difficult
grato/ingrato	pleasing/displeasing
indiferente	indifferent
leal	loyal
molesto	bothersome
necesario/innecesario	necessary/unnecessary
permitido/prohibido	allowed/prohibited
posible/imposible	possible/impossible
simpático/antipático	nice/nasty (persons)
sincero, franco	sincere, frank
suficiente/insuficiente	sufficient/insufficient
urgente	urgent
útil/inútil	useful/useless
etc.	

Notes (i)   Many of these adjectives could also be constructed with *para* or *con*: *es conveniente para ellos/les es conveniente* 'it's suitable for/to them'; *voy a ser franco con* *usted/le voy a ser franco* 'I'll be frank with you'. The object pronouns convey a higher level of personal involvement.

(ii)   *Grande, pequeño, ancho* 'wide' take *le/les* if they mean 'too big', 'too small', 'too narrow': *ese puesto le está grande* 'that job's too big for him'; *le está ancho* 'it's too narrow for him'. Otherwise *resultar* must be used, or *para*: *es grande para él* 'it's big to/for him', etc.

(b)   *Ser* plus personal pronouns with nouns:
This occurs only with a few nouns, most derived from or close in sense to the adjectives listed above.

Si le es molestia, dígamelo	if it's a nuisance for you, tell me
Me/le era un gran placer/era un gran placer para mí/él	it was a great pleasure for/to me/him, etc.
Nos es de interés . . .	it's of interest to us . . .

Notes (i)   Spanish does not allow a pronominal construction like the English 'I was always a good mother to him', which is translated: *siempre fui una buena madre para él.*
(ii)   *Resultar* has limited use with nouns:

Mi temporada aquí me está resultando un verdadero viaje de estudios (Borges, letter style)	my stay here is turning out to be a real study trip for me
Si le resulta un problema	if it turns out to be a problem to you

11.9   *Lo* with *ser* and *estar*

The predicate of *ser* and *estar* is 'echoed' by *lo*:

Parece buena la tierra desde aquí. Lo es.	the land looks good from here. It is
Usted no es don Roberto. Y si lo fuera . . .	You aren't Don Roberto. And (what) if I were?
La Luna está muerta y lo ha estado siempre	the Moon is dead and always has been
¿Tolera usted estar solo, o tolera la necesidad que tenga su cónyuge de estarlo? (quiz on marriage in *ABC*: *cónyuge* is the correct form, but *cónyugue* is common in speech)	can you stand being alone, or can you stand your partner's need to be (alone)?
Estoy cansada. Pero tú lo estás más	I'm tired. But you're more tired still

11.10   Object pronouns used to denote personal involvement

Object pronouns may be inserted in a verb phrase to show that a person is intensely affected. Compare the indignant Frenchman's *regardez-moi ça!* 'just look at that for me!', 'just look at that, will you!'.

The effect can sometimes hardly be translated into standard English, although popular speech sometimes uses 'on me', 'on you', etc. in order to include the person affected. Compare *se me han ido de casa* 'they've left home "on me"'; *se le murió el padre* 'his father died'; *se le ha averiado el coche* 'his car's broken down "on him"'.

This device is more typical of familiar speech, or when there is a strong emotional involvement on the speaker's part, e.g. a parent speaking to a child:

Mi marido se me está quedando delgadísimo	my husband's getting terribly thin
Me le has estropeado tres camisas	you've spoilt three of his shirts for me
Péiname al niño	do the child's hair for me
Sírvamele un café a la señorita (Argentina, quoted García 1975, not accepted in Spain)	serve a coffee to the young lady for me
Cuídamele (or *cuídamelo*) *bien*	look after him well for me

This device of including mention of an interested party is more favoured in parts of Spanish America than in Spain. *Me le pintaste la mesa* 'you painted the table for him for me' is apparently acceptable for some Spanish-American speakers. Peninsular Spanish tends to avoid clusters of two object pronouns when neither is a direct object.

11.11 Order of object pronouns

11.11.1 Order of consecutive object pronouns

The invariable order of object pronouns when two or more appear together is:

se	*te/os*	*me/nos*	*le/lo/la/les/los/las*

i.e., *se*, if it occurs, comes first, second person precedes first, and third-person pronouns come last.

María te lo dijo	Maria told it to you
Me lo habré dejado en casa	I must have left it at home
Te lo llevé al tinte	I took it to the cleaner's for you
No querían comunicárnoslo	they didn't want to tell it to us
¿Por qué no se lo prueba?	why don't you try it on?
Se te ha caído la tinta	you've dropped the ink
Se le ha muerto un hijo	a son of his/hers has died
Nos los vamos a comprar	we're going to buy them for ourselves
Se nos ha vuelto listísimo	he's turned into a genius 'on us'
Yo me le fui encima, pero ella chilló (Cortázar, Arg., Spain *yo me le eché encima*)	I lunged at her, but she screamed

Note Reversal of the correct order, e.g. **me se ha caído*, etc., is a classic howler of uneducated speech.

11.11.2 *Se* for *le/les* when they are followed by *lo/la/los/las*

If *le* or *les* are immediately followed by *lo*, *la*, *los* or *las*, the *le* or *les* is replaced by *se*: *le doy* 'I give to him/her/you' + *lo* 'it' = *se lo doy* 'I give it to him/her/you' – never **le lo doy*:

Quiero dárselo	I want to give it to him
Se lo dije a ella	I told her
Se lo dije a ellos	I told them (masc.)
El guiso está a punto, pero no se lo	the stew's ready but I'm not going to
voy a servir todavía	serve it to you yet
¿Quiere usted que se lo envuelva?	do you want me to wrap it for you?

Notes (i)   This phenomenon is traditionally explained by the cacophony of too many *l*'s. Whether this is the reason or not, it is useful to remember that in Spanish two object pronouns beginning with *l* cannot stand side by side.

   (ii)   *Se lo dije* may thus mean 'I told it to him, her, you (*usted*)', 'them' (*ellos* or *ellas*) or 'you (plural *ustedes*)'. *A él/ella/usted/ellos/ellas/ustedes* may be added if context does not make the issue clear.

   There is a tendency in Spanish-American speech, very common even in quite educated language, to mark a plural indirect object by pluralizing the direct object pronoun, i.e. **se los dije*, **se los di*, for *se lo dije/di (a ellos/ellas/ustedes)*, cf. *a un policía le había gustado más bien poco la gracia y se los había dicho* (Cortázar, *Rayuela*, dialogue) 'one policeman didn't really like the joke and told them so' (for *se lo había dicho*). This should not be imitated by foreign students.

11.12   Position of object pronouns

The position of object pronouns in relation to a verb depends on the form of the verb.

11.12.1   Pronouns with verbs in finite tenses

Pronouns come immediately before the verb in the order given at 11.11.1. In compound tenses the pronouns are placed before the auxiliary:

Se los entregamos	we gave them to him/her/it/them/you
Te los enviaré luego	I'll send you them later
Os las guardaré (Spain)	I'll keep them (fem.) for you
La he visto	I've seen her/it/you
Se me ha roto el cinturón	my belt's broken

Notes (i)   In literary style, commonly until the twentieth century, object pronouns were often joined to verbs in finite tenses: *contestóles así* 'he answered them thus' (= *les contestó así*); *encontrábase exiliado* 'he found himself exiled' (= *se encontraba exiliado*); *ocurriósele* 'it occurred to him/her' (= *se le ocurrió*).

   Rules for this construction are omitted here since it is now extinct for practical purposes, except in a few set phrases (e.g. *habráse visto* . . . 'well, did you ever . . .', *diríase* 'one might say', *dícese* 'it is said', etc.), and in burlesque or Spanish-American journalistic styles (e.g. in formal style in Argentine newspapers).

   (ii)   No word may come between the object pronouns and a verb. In pronunciation these pronouns are unstressed and spoken as though they formed part of the verb: *'telodijo'*, *'osladaré'* etc.

11.12.2   Position with imperatives

(a)   If the imperative is negative, position is the same as in 11.12.1: *no me lo digas* 'don't tell me it'; *no lo hagas* 'don't do it'; *no os lo creáis* 'don't get the idea'; *no se lo envíen* 'don't send it to him/her/them'.

(b) If the imperative is positive, the pronouns are joined to the verb as suffixes in the usual order: *dámelo* 'give me it'; *hazlo* 'do it'; *váyanse* 'go away' (plural); *¡déjame!* 'leave me!'; *dígannoslo* 'tell it to us'; *dádselo* 'give it to him' (*vosotros* form); *pregúntenselo* 'ask (plur.) them it'.

Note If the pronoun *-os* is added to a second-person plural imperative, the *-d* is dropped: *callad + os* = *callaos* 'be quiet'; *levantaos* 'get up'; *quedaos* 'stay'. (Exception: *idos* 'go away', in speech usually *iros*.)

Everyday speech in Spain (*vosotros* is not used in Spanish America) tends to avoid these forms in favour of the infinitive: *callaros, quedaros, iros*, etc. This construction is censured by purists and avoided in careful speech, but since the *vosotros* imperative is typical of familiar speech, the popular forms can be expected to spread.

(c) Subjunctive used as an imperative:
The first and third persons have no specific imperative forms: the subjunctive is used instead. (*Usted/ustedes* also require the present subjunctive).

If the verb is not preceded by *que* the pronouns are suffixed to it: *tráiganlo* 'bring him/it'; *díganselo* 'tell it to him'; *veámoslo* 'let us see it' (formal).

If the verb follows *que* or is negated, the pronouns precede the verb: *que lo diga* 'let him say it'; *no se lo crean* 'do not believe it'.

Notes (i) If *nos* is added to a first-person plural subjunctive, the final *-s* of the verb is dropped: *levantemos + nos* = *levantémonos* 'let's get up'; *asegurémonos* 'let us assure ourselves'.

Spoken language normally avoids this construction by using a verbal periphrasis: *vamos a sentarnos* 'let's sit down'; *bueno, a levantarse* 'well, let's get up'; *vamos a verlo* 'let's have a look'.

(ii) *Ir* forms its first-person plural imperative irregularly: *vamos, vámonos* 'let's go'. The expected form *vayámonos* is nowadays virtually extinct, and *vayamos* is used only as a subjunctive.

(iii) 'Impersonal *se*' often appears in an impersonal imperative form much used in official documents, notices, textbooks, etc.: *rellénense los espacios en blanco* 'fill in the blanks'; *colóquese una forma adecuada del verbo en las siguientes frases* 'insert an appropriate form of the verb in the following sentences'; *hágase tu voluntad* 'Thy will be done'; *véase la página treinta* 'see page thirty'; *contéstese a las siguientes preguntas* 'answer the following questions'.

11.12.3 Position with infinitives
If the infinitive is used as a noun or follows an adjective or participle plus a preposition, pronouns are suffixed to it in the usual order:

Sería una locura decírselo	it would be madness to tell it to him
mejor enviárselo ahora	best send it to him/her/them now
Rechazaron el proyecto por considerarlo demasiado caro	they rejected the project on the grounds it was too expensive
Estamos hartos de oírtelo	we're fed up with hearing it from you

But if the infinitive depends on a previous verb, there are two possibilities:
   (a) Join the pronouns to the infinitive as in the previous examples:

Quiero hacerlo	I want to do it
Pudieron salvarla	they managed to save her
Intentaron robárnoslo	they tried to steal it from us
Propusieron alquilárnoslos	they suggested renting them to us
Acabo de dártelo	I've just given it to you

This is the safest, and in the view of some strict purists, the only 'correct' option.

(b)   Place the pronouns before the finite verb: *lo quiero hacer*, etc. See the following section for discussion.

11.12.4   Mobile object pronouns

There is a very strong tendency in spoken Spanish to shift clitic object pronouns leftwards in constructions involving infinitives: *quiero verlo > lo quiero ver*, etc. This construction, which has a long history, is possible with a large number of common verbs, but it is subject to controversy and apparently arbitrary constraints. The following are everyday examples current on both continents; the enclitic forms are more formal:

querer

Te la quiero enseñar/quiero enseñártela	I want to show it to you
Por mucho que yo os lo quiera dar/ quiera dároslo, no puedo	however much I want to give it to you, I can't

poder

No puedo atenderle/no le puedo atender en este momento	I can't attend to you at this moment

deber

Deberías explicárnoslo/nos lo deberías explicar	you ought to explain it to us

tener que/haber que

Tiene que devolvértelo/te lo tiene que devolver/hay que hacerlo/lo hay que hacer	he has to give it back to you/ you have to do it

acabar de

Pero si acabo de verlo/lo acabo de ver	but I've just seen him! (contradicting *si*)

llegar a

Incluso llegué a caerme/me llegué a caer por unas escaleras	I even managed to fall down a flight of stairs

haber de

He de consultarlo/lo he de consultar con la almohada	I'd better sleep on it (lit. 'consult my pillow')

dejar de

No dejes de llamarla/no la dejes de llamar	don't forget to phone her

ir a

Me temía que Roberto fuera a contárselo/se lo fuera a contar a mamá	I was worried that Roberto would go and tell it to mother

volver a

Como vuelvas a decírmelo/como me lo vuelvas a decir, me voy	if you say it to me again, I'm going

hacer

Me hizo abrirlo/me lo hizo abrir	he made me open it

The list at 17.1 indicates those common verbs which allow this shifting of clitic pronouns, although some verbs, e.g. *fingir*, are controversial.

Notes (i)   Pronouns cannot be shifted in this way if:
(a) The earlier verb is a 'pronominal' verb (see chapter 12 for a definition), cf. *volverse* 'to turn around', *se volvió a mirarla* 'he turned to look at her' but not **se la volvió a mirar*, which is only possible if we take the *se* to mean *le*, as in *el médico volvió a mirarle la lengua* 'the doctor looked at his tongue again'.
Compare the following examples in which *ver* and *dejar* are not 'pronominal' verbs:

Nos ha visto hacerlo	he saw us do it
Nos lo ha visto hacer	
Os dejaron llamarla	they let you ring her
Os la dejaron llamar	

(b) If any other word intervenes between the verb phrase and the following infinitive: *trató varias veces de hacerlo* 'he tried several times to do it' but not **lo trató varias veces de hacer*; *puedes empezar ahora mismo a hacerlo* 'you can start doing it now', but not ?*lo puedes empezar ahora mismo a hacer*; *quisiera no hacerlo* but not **lo quisiera no hacer*, or **la quiero mucho ver*, etc.
This rule is not always respected in familiar speech, cf. *no le tengo nada que envidiar*, familiar for *no tengo nada que envidiarle* 'I've got nothing to envy him/her/you for'.
The difference between a phrase like *tratar de* which allows clitic pronoun shifting, and *tardar en* which does not, is presumably that the preposition *de* has become so intimately fused to *tratar* that the two words are processed by the speaker as a single word. Only long familiarity with the language can resolve this problem of when clitic pronoun shifting is possible.
(c) If the main verb is a positive imperative: *procura hacerlo* 'try to do it'.
(ii)   In *voy a verla* either motion or futurity is meant. Normally, *la voy a ver* can only be interpreted as a future form of the verb: 'I shall see her', although familiar speech may allow shifting with both meanings:

Ellos me fueron a comprar el billete	they went and bought my ticket for me
(Interview in *Triunfo*, Spain)	

(iii)   If more than one infinitive is involved, several solutions become possible, the first being safest for foreigners:

No quiero volver a decírtelo	I don't want to tell you it again
No quiero volvértelo a decir	" "
No te lo quiero volver a decir	
Puedes empezar a hacerlo	you can start to do it
Puedes empezarlo a hacer	" "
Lo puedes empezar a hacer	
Debes tratar de hacerlo	you must try to do it
Debes tratarlo de hacer	" "
Lo debes tratar de hacer	

However, if two pronouns are joined as clitics they must stay together if they are shifted. In other words, starting from *tienes que vérselo hacer* which, for Peninsular speakers at least, is the correct way of saying 'you have to see him doing it', the only permitted colloquial shift is *se lo tienes que ver hacer*. ?*Le tienes que ver hacerlo* and **le tienes que verlo hacer* are not permitted, although we found that Spanish-American informants rejected *se lo tienes que ver hacer* in favour of *le tienes que ver hacerlo*.

11.12.5   Position of pronouns with the gerund:
(a)   In combination with *estar* (continuous verb forms) and a few other auxiliary verbs, the pronouns are either attached or pre-posed:

Te lo estoy contando	I'm telling you it
Estoy contándotelo	" "
Nos estuvieron esperando	they waited for us
Estuvieron esperándonos	" "
Os lo estoy diciendo	I'm saying it to you
Estoy diciéndooslo	(*vosotros*)
Se lo va contando/va contándoselo	he goes around telling it to them
Se me quedó mirando/se quedó	he remained gazing at me
mirándome	
(the *se* belongs to *quedarse*)	

The second construction is rather more formal and is probably safer for foreign students.

(b)   In other cases, the pronouns are attached to the gerund: *disfruta mirándolo* 'he enjoys himself looking at it'; *se divierte quemándolos* 'he amuses himself by burning them'; *contesta insultándolos* 'he replies by insulting them', etc.

Notes (i)   *Seguir* allows both constructions, but some native speakers did not accept pronoun shifting with *continuar*: *se seguían viendo/seguían viéndose* 'they went on seeing one another'; *me sigue dando la lata/sigue dándome la lata* 'he's still pestering me'. But *continuaban viéndose, continúa dándome la lata*.

(ii)   In case (a), if the auxiliary verb is an infinitive preceded by one of the verbs listed at 17.1 which allow 'pronoun shifting', several solutions are possible: *debe estar recordándolo/debe estarlo recordando/lo debe estar recordando*; *tenía que quedarse mirándola/tenía que quedársela mirando/ se la tenía que quedar mirando*.

11.12.6   Position with past participles
Pronouns come before the auxiliary verb:

Se ha equivocado	he's made a mistake
Se lo ha traído de China	he's brought it from China
Te lo hemos mandado ya	we've already sent it to you

Notes (i)   In phrases in which pronoun shifting is possible, there are two options:

Se lo hemos tenido que vender/	we had to sell it to him
hemos tenido que vendérselo	
La he vuelto a ver/he vuelto a verla	I've seen her again
No he podido abrirlo/no lo he podido	I couldn't open it
abrir	
Ha debido hablarle/Le ha debido hablar	he must have spoken to him

(ii)   Personal pronouns are no longer suffixed to past participles. The example given in Ramsey & Spaulding, 4.15, *Era un proprietario rico de Cáceres, donde había nacido y criádose* 'He was a rich landowner of Cáceres where he was born and brought up' would nowadays be recast as . . . *donde había nacido y se había criado*.

11.13   Emphasis of object pronouns

(a)   Object pronouns may be emphasized by adding *a* and the prepositional form of the pronoun:

Te lo darán a ti, pero no a él	they'll give it to you, but not to him

No te los doy a ti sino que me los guardo para mí mismo	I'm not giving them to you but keeping them for myself
La vieron a ella, pero no a mí	they saw her, but not me
Nos criticaron a nosotros, pero a nadie más	they criticized us, but no one else

(b) Reflexive verb phrases may be emphasized by the appropriate number and gender of *mismo* added to a prepositional pronoun. Reciprocal sentences can be emphasized by the appropriate form of *el uno* and *el otro*:

Se lavaron	they washed (themselves)/ they were washed
Se lavaron a sí mismos	they washed themselves
Es difícil vivir con quien no se estima a sí mismo (ABC)	it's difficult to live with someone who does not value himself ('herself' is undoubtedly intended as well)
Se quieren el uno al otro	they love one another
Se quieren la una a la otra	(two females)
Se envidian los unos a los otros	they envy one another (more than two involved)

Note If a male and female are involved in a reciprocal sentence, the logical form might be thought to be *el uno a la otra*, but usage makes both pronouns masculine:

Antonio y María se quieren el uno al otro	Antonio and Maria love one another

11.14   Redundant object pronouns

Spanish makes constant, apparently superfluous use of pronouns even when the thing they refer to is named by a noun: cf. *le di un anillo a María* 'I gave Maria a ring'; *los demás los tienes que dejar aquí* 'the rest you'll have to leave here'.

Some of these redundant pronouns are virtually obligatory, others are more typical of informal styles.

11.14.1   Redundancy when object precedes verb

If, for purposes of emphasis or focus, the direct or indirect object of a verb precedes the verb, a redundant pronoun is usually obligatory.

Compare *compré esta casa hace cinco años* and *esta casa la compré hace cinco años* 'I bought this house five years ago'.

Examples:

Lo que dice en público jamás lo consentiría nadie de los dirigentes de la pequeña pantalla (Cambio16)	what he says in public would never be tolerated by the people in charge of the 'small screen' (TV)
A alguno de vosotros os quisiera ver yo en un buen fregado (D. Sueiro, familiar Spanish dialogue)	I'd like to see one of you in a real mess
Eso no me lo negarás	you won't deny me that
Al profesor Berlin no le parece tan importante que Maquiavelo propusiera esa disyuntiva (Vargas Llosa, Peru)	it does not seem so important to Professor Berlin that Machiavelli suggested this dilemma

Notes (i)   The pronoun is omitted after *eso* in such phrases as *eso creo yo, eso digo yo* 'that's what I think' (but compare *eso lo digo yo* 'that's what I say'). Omission in other cases is very rare, but not unknown.

(ii)   For a discussion of the effect of putting the object before the verb see chapter 31.

(iii)   Undefined nouns, e.g. nouns not preceded by an article or demonstrative adjective, do not invoke a redundant pronoun: *mucha prisa ha debido tener* 'he *must* have been in a hurry'.

11.14.2   Redundant pronouns and 'indirect objects'

A redundant pronoun is normally inserted to show that a noun is 'involved', by the verb in one of the ways listed in List A, 11.6.4 (i.e. 'receiving', 'losing', 'advantage', 'involvement', etc.):

Esta solución le pareció a doña	this solution seemed to be the best one
Matilde la más acertada	to Doña Matilde
(J.M. Guelbenzu)	
Se le notan cada vez más los años	you can tell Martínez's age more and
a Martínez	more
Lo que a usted le conviene . . .	what would suit you . . .
¿Qué has hecho con las chuletas? Se	what have you done with the chops? I
las di al cocinero	gave them to the cook
Bueno, si no le dicen a uno cómo hay	well, if they don't tell one how to do it . . .
que hacerlo . . .	
Les tenía mucho miedo a los truenos	he was very frightened of thunder
A vos te la tienen jurada (Arg.)	they've got it in for you
Le puso un nuevo conmutador a la radio	he put a new knob on the radio

Note   Omission of the redundant pronoun depersonalizes the indirect object, and would be appropriate in formal writing, official documents or business letters where a distant tone is required:

Escriba una carta al Ministerio de	write a letter to the Ministry of Finance
Hacienda	
Comunique los detalles al señor presidente	inform the president of the details
Esto no corresponde a Odradek	this is not a trait of Odradek's
(Borges: Odradek is a non-human	
creature)	
Es necesario dar cera a este tipo de suelo	this type of floor must be waxed every
todas las semanas	week

In most cases the redundant pronoun is used, more so than fifty years ago, and almost always with proper names: *dáselo a Mario* 'give it to Mario'; *se lo robaron a Mariluz* 'they stole it from Mariluz'.

11.14.3   *Le* for *les*

There is a strong tendency in spoken language everywhere to use the singular *le* in this construction for the plural *les*, especially if the pronoun refers to a non-human entity:

Cualquiera le da vuelta a las razones	anyone might ponder on the reasons why
por las que te viniste conmigo	you came to me
(J.M. Guelbenzu, dial.)	
No darle importancia a los detalles	not to ascribe importance to details
¿Quieres devolverle la isla de Manhattan	Do you want to give Manhattan Island
a los Algonquins?	back to the Algonquins?
(C. Fuentes, Mex. dialogue)	

Sus ácidas diatribas contra la Argentina son precisamente consecuencia de su pasión nacional, como le ha pasado a tantos españoles ilustres (E. Sabato, Arg., on Borges, in *El País*)	his vitriolic diatribes against Argentina are precisely a consequence of his passion for the nation, as has happened to so many famous Spaniards
Y ese pequeño elemento ya justificaría que yo le pusiera la firma a sus papeles (M. Puig, Arg. dialogue)	and that little detail would be enough to justify my signing your papers
Le viene natural a los niños (educated Spaniard, overheard)	it comes naturally to children
Bayardo San Román le puso término a tantas conjeturas con un recurso simple (García Márquez, Colombia)	Bayardo San Román put an end to so much conjecture by a simple stratagem

This tendency is so deep-rooted even in educated speech, that *él les* (for *le*) *da mucha importancia a las apariencias* sounds frankly odd to many speakers. But it is technically 'wrong', and should be avoided in formal writing – e.g. in this case by omitting the redundant pronoun altogether.

11.14.4 Redundant direct object pronouns
Use of a redundant direct object pronoun is common with *todo* and is required where a pronoun is emphasized (see 11.13a). In other cases it is less acceptable in Spain where it is avoided in writing and careful speech. It is common in Spanish America, where it is also found in informal writing, especially with proper names:

Ahora me lo tienes que contar todo (normal)	now you have to tell me everything
Morgan . . . también lo mandó llamar a Abdulmalik (Borges, Arg. dialogue)	Morgan . . . also had Abdulmalik sent for
Ella lo amaba a Andrés (Colombian speech, quoted Kany, 149)	she loved Andres
Le quiere mucho a ese hijo (Spain, familiar)	she loves that son a lot
Lo veía a Bruno fumando, esperando, mirando (E. Sabato, Arg.)	he could see Bruno smoking, waiting, watching

11.14.5 Redundancy in relative constructions
Redundant pronouns occur in spoken Spanish in relative clauses, especially in non-restrictive clauses, and may appear in writing, particularly if several words separate the *que* and the verb which affects it:

Te voy a hacer una confesión que nunca me animé a hacerla a nadie (SA, quoted Kany, 150)	I'm going to make you a confession I never had the courage to make to anybody
Los gramáticos aconsejan muchas cosas que nadie las dice (Spain, informant)	grammarians recommend lots of things that no one says
Sólo por ti dejaría a don Memo a quien tanto le debo (C. Fuentes, Mex. dialogue)	only for you would I leave Don Memo, whom I owe so much

This construction may sound uneducated, especially in restrictive clauses (the first two examples), and is best left to native speakers.

12 Pronominal verbs

12.1 General

Pronominal verbs are those which are accompanied by an object pronoun (i.e. *me*, *te*, *se*, *nos*, *os*, *se*) which is of the same person as the subject of the verb, for example *yo me lavo* 'I'm washing (myself)', *vais a cansaros* 'you're going to tire yourselves/get tired', *(él) se ha marchado* 'he's gone/left'. The usual object pronouns are used with such verbs, except in the third person (*usted*, *ustedes* included) which uses the invariable 'reflexive pronoun' *se* for both singular and plural.

A very large number of Spanish verbs can be thus pronominalized, even intransitive verbs like 'to be' and 'to die'. Older grammars sometimes call such forms as *me voy*, *se cayó*, *se lava* 'reflexive verbs' but this name is very misleading. 'Reflexive' verbs are those in which the subject performs an action on him/herself, 'I'm washing myself', 'he praises himself', but only a small percentage of pronominal verbs are actually reflexive. The range of meanings associated with pronominalized verbs is illustrated in the following list, which is not exhaustive:

(a) 'Reflexive'

Se está afeitando/está afeitándose	he's shaving (himself)
No te conoces (a ti mismo/a)	you don't know yourself

(b) 'Reciprocal' (plural verbs only)

Ustedes se insultan mucho	you insult one another a lot
Se querían tanto	they loved one another so much

(c) To denote accidental or unplanned actions

Me caí en la calle	I fell down in the street
El agua se sale por aquí	the water's leaking here

(d) To emphasize the point of departure of a movement

Se salió de la reunión	he walked out of the meeting
Se han ido de casa	they've left home

(e) To show that an action concerns or interests the subject alone:

Yo sé lo que me hago (Spain only?)	(don't worry) I know what I'm doing

(f) To make a transitive verb intransitive

La puerta se abrió	the door opened
No te enfades	don't get angry

(g) To stress the 'totality' of an action

Se fumó un paquete entero	he smoked a whole packet

Se leyó el libro en una hora	he read the book in one hour

Other verbs that have pronominal counterparts, e.g. *reír/reírse*, *morir/morirse*, *ganar/ganarse*, *estar/estarse*, *esperar/esperarse*, *volver/volverse* (both in the meaning of 'to become' and 'to return'), *conocer/conocerse*, *escapar/escaparse*, etc. are best studied as separate lexical items. The most common are discussed in this chapter, and all of them should appear in good dictionaries of Spanish. Some pronominal verbs, e.g. *regresarse* 'to return', *enfermarse* 'to get ill' occur in Spanish America but are rejected in Spain: see 12.10.

Verbs which translate the English 'become', e.g. *ponerse*, *hacerse*, *volverse*, *convertirse en*, are usually pronominal verbs and are also discussed in this chapter at 12.5 and 12.6.

The pronoun *se* also appears in the following third-person construction:

Se sirven comidas	meals (are) served
Se ha dicho que . . .	it has been said that . . .
Se vive mejor en España	one lives better in Spain/life's better in Spain
Se le considera poco honrado	he's considered to be dishonest
Se detuvo a tres contrabandistas	three smugglers were detained

This passive or impersonal use of *se* is discussed separately in chapter 24.

Throughout the following discussion it must be remembered that very often the meaning of a pronominal verb is given by the context. Thus *se critican* means, in abstract, 'they criticize themselves', 'they criticize one another', or 'they are criticized'. Such ambiguities are almost always resolved by reference to the background of the sentence or by appealing to common sense.

12.2 Reflexive meaning of pronominal verbs

This use – not the most common – shows that an action is done by the subject to/for him/herself: *se está duchando* '(s)he's having a shower', *os alabáis mucho* 'you praise yourselves a lot', *me voy a comprar otro traje* 'I'm going to buy (myself) a new suit'. Four important features of this reflexive meaning are:

(i) The subject is usually animate (since a door doesn't usually wash or open itself).

(ii) The pronoun may stand for the direct or the indirect object: *me estoy afeitando* 'I'm shaving', *me estoy quitando la camisa* 'I'm taking my shirt off'.

(iii) The action can be voluntary or accidental.

(iv) The verb is always transitive:

Se está lavando	he/she's washing
Me corté con una lata	I cut myself with a tin
Se ha roto una pierna	he's broken a leg
¡Qué bien te peinas!	how well you do your hair!
¡Cuidado, que te vas a salpicar!	careful, you're going to get splashed!
Me estoy calzando	I'm putting my shoes on

Nos conocemos poco	we don't know ourselves very well (or one another)
Se daban crema para el sol	they were putting suncream on
Se mató en un accidente	he got killed in an accident

Notes (i)   The subject in these constructions may be emphasized by use of the subject pronoun, sometimes reinforced by the appropriate form of *solo* 'alone' or *mismo*:

Primero vistió a la niña y luego se vistió ella	first she dressed the child, then she dressed herself
No eches la culpa a nadie, te has manchado tú solo/mismo	don't blame anyone else, you stained yourself
La niña se pone los zapatos ella sola	the little girl puts on her shoes all by herself

   (ii)   If a preposition is used (including personal *a*) emphasis is obtained by using the appropriate prepositional form of the personal pronoun (*mí/ti/sí/nosotros/vosotros/ sí*) plus the correct number and gender of *mismo*:

Se decía a sí mismo que no servía para nada	he told himself he was good for nothing
Me odio a mí mismo	I hate myself
Nos mentimos a nosotros mismos con frecuencia	we lie to ourselves frequently

   (iii)   Verbs expressing hurt take either the prepositional or non-prepositional form:

Se hace daño él mismo/a sí mismo	he's hurting himself
Te perjudicas tú mismo/a ti mismo	you're damaging yourself

   (iv)   With a few common verbs the pronominal form may mean 'to get something done' as well as 'to do something for or to oneself':

Se va a hacer un traje rojo	she's going to make herself a red dress/ she's going to get a red dress made
Se ha construido un chalet	he built himself a house (either himself or to his specifications)
Me voy a cortar el pelo	I'm going to have my hair cut/I'm going to cut my hair

Ambiguity can be removed by the appropriate use of the personal pronoun followed by *mismo* or *solo*:

Se construyó la casa él mismo/solo	he built the house himself
Te puedes hacer una permanente tú misma/sola en casa	you can give yourself a perm at home

In some cases it is very unlikely that the action will actually be performed by the subject:

Me voy a operar de cataratas	I'm going to have an operation for cataracts
Si te duele esa muela, debías sacártela	if that tooth's aching you ought to have it out (or less likely, 'you ought to take it out')

   (v)   With a few verbs, the pronominal form may suggest that the action is the speaker's sole responsibility or concern:

(No te preocupes), yo sé lo que me hago	(don't worry), I know what I'm doing
Tú sabrás lo que te dices	*you* must know what you're saying

12.3   Reciprocal meaning of pronominal verbs

A plural pronominal verb may have a reciprocal meaning, i.e. show that an action is done to or for one another. In some cases *el uno al otro/los unos a los otros* can be added to make clear that the reciprocal meaning is intended: compare *se entristecen* 'they grow sad'/'they make themselves sad'/'they make one another sad', but *se entristecen los unos a los otros* 'they make one another sad'.

Se escriben periódicamente	they write to one another regularly
Hace años que no se hablan	they haven't been talking to one another for years
Pasó mucho tiempo sin que nos viésemos/viéramos	we didn't see one another for a long time
Se conocieron en Yucatán	they met in Yucatan
Se hacen la compra los unos a los otros	they do one another's shopping
Siempre se ponen pegas	they're always finding fault with one another

If one subject is feminine and the other masculine, masculine pronouns are used: *Pedro y María se quieren mucho el uno al otro.*

12.4   Pronominal verbs with inanimate subjects

This construction corresponds to the English intransitive form – *la ventana se rompió* 'the window broke' – or to the colloquial construction with 'got' – *se ha quemado el pastel* 'the cake got burnt'. For obvious reasons, inanimate subjects are usually third person:

La gripe se cura sola	flu gets better of its own accord
El barco se hundió	the boat sank
Se ha roto el cable	the cable broke
El motor se paró	the motor stopped
Las manzanas se están pudriendo	the apples are rotting/going rotten
El sol se encoge	the sun is shrinking
El líquido se extiende por la superficie	the liquid spreads over the surface
El agua se está helando	the water is freezing

Note   *Me/te/le/nos/os/les* is used after *se* to indicate ownership or to disclaim responsibility for an action:

Se me ha roto la jarra	my jug has got broken (the subject may or may have not contributed to the breaking)
Se me ha perdido la sortija	my ring has got lost (ditto)
Se me ha salido el zapato	I'm losing my shoe

12.5   Pronominalization and intransitivity

A large number of transitive verbs have pronominal intransitive counterparts. The pronominal form detransitivizes the transitive verb, or more accurately, blocks off the possibility of understanding a verb as transitive. Compare *preocupo* 'I worry (someone)', *me preocupo* 'I'm worried', *lo durmieron* 'they put him to sleep', *se durmieron* 'they went to sleep'. Many pronominal intransitive verbs have no transitive counterparts (at least in normal language), cf. *arrepentirse* 'repent , *abstenerse* 'abstain', which appear only in the pronominal form. Sometimes verbs change radically in meaning. Examples:

admirar	admire/surprise	*admirarse de*	be surprised at
brindar	toast	*brindarse a*	to offer
			to do something
cambiar	change (trans. & intrans.)	*cambiarse*	change clothes/ house, etc.
cansar	tire	*cansarse*	get tired
empeñar	pawn/pledge	*empeñarse en*	insist on
enamorar	to make someone fall in love	*enamorarse*	fall in love
irritar	irritate	*irritarse*	get irritated
ubicar (Spanish American)	locate/be located	*ubicarse*	be located

An important group under this heading denotes a change of mood or state with the meaning of 'to become, to get'. (For other ways of translating 'to become' see the following heading):

aburrir	to bore	*aburrirse*	to get bored
alegrar	to gladden	*alegrarse*	to become glad
asustar	to frighten	*asustarse*	to become frightened
divertir	to amuse	*divertirse*	to be amused
divorciar	to divorce	*divorciarse*	to get divorced
endurecer	to harden	*endurecerse*	to grow hard
enredar	to entangle	*enredarse*	to get entangled
entristecer	to sadden	*entristecerse*	to grow sad
extrañar	to find something odd/to miss	*extrañarse*	to be puzzled
fastidiar	to annoy	*fastidiarse*	to get annoyed
molestar	to bother	*molestarse*	to be bothered
vaciar	to empty	*vaciarse*	to become empty

etc.

Note Some common exceptional cases of non-pronominal verbs denoting 'to become, to get' are:

agonizar	to be dying
adelgazar (quedarse delgado)	to lose weight
amanecer	to dawn
anochecer:	
anochece	'night is falling'
aumentar	to increase
clarear	to grow bright
crecer	to grow
disminuir	to diminish
empeorar (SA *empeorarse*)	to get worse
enfermar (SA *enfermarse*)	to get ill
enflaquecer	to lose weight
engordar/ponerse gordo	to get fat
enloquecer/volverse loco	to go mad
enmudecer	to be silent
	to lose one's voice
enrojecer	to go red
ensordecer	to get deaf

envejecer	to grow old
but compare: *rejuvenecerse*	'to grow young again'
mejorar (*mejorarse* = 'recover')	to improve
nacer	to be born
oscurecer	to get dark
(but *el cielo se oscurece*	'the sky grows dark')
palidecer	to grow pale
resucitar	to come back to life

Amanecer and *anochecer* can also be used with animate subjects and objects: *amanecí de mal humor* 'I woke up bad tempered; *me anocheció en medio de la carretera* 'night found me on the road'.

12.6 Verbs of becoming

Spanish has no single word for the English 'become'. Apart from the use of the pronominal forms discussed in the previous section, the following verbs (most, but not all themselves pronominal) are also used with various shades of meaning:

(a) *Ponerse*, meaning 'to become, to get':
Ponerse is used to indicate change of mood, physical condition and appearance. The changes expressed by this verb are usually short-lived, with the exception of *ponerse viejo* 'to get old'. Thus there is a contrast between *se ha puesto muy pesado* 'he's become boring' and *se ha vuelto muy pesado* 'he's become a bore'. There is some overlapping with *quedarse* meaning 'to lose, to be left without' (e.g. *quedarse delgado* 'to become thin, to lose weight', see 12.6e). Often there are equivalent pronominal verbs, i.e. *alegrarse* for *ponerse alegre*, *entristecerse* for *ponerse triste*, or non-pronominal ones, i.e. *engordar* for *ponerse gordo*, *enfermar* for *ponerse enfermo*. *Ponerse* can be used of animate and inanimate nouns and situations:

Cuando se enteró se puso muy contenta/ triste/de mal humor/enfadada	when she heard about it she became very happy/sad/bad-tempered/cross
(*se entristeció/se enfadó* could be used)	
¡Qué pesado/tonto te estás poniendo!	you're becoming such a bore/a fool!
Se puso/quedó ronco de tanto hablar	he got hoarse from talking so much
Con tanto como comes te vas a poner gordo	you eat so much you're going to get fat
(for *delgado* see *quedarse*)	
Al verla se puso/quedó pálido/ palideció	when he saw her he went pale
Te pondrás fea de llorar	you'll get ugly from crying
En poco tiempo se ha puesto muy viejo/ se ha aviejado mucho	he's got very old in a short time
¡Qué sucio se ha puesto este mantel!	this table cloth has got very dirty!
La situación se ha puesto insoportable	the situation has got unbearable
El día se ha puesto gris	it's turned grey (i.e. the weather)
El tiempo se está poniendo frío	the weather is getting cold
El pescado se ha puesto malo	the fish has gone bad

Notes (i)   Colloquially it can also mean 'to make oneself, to get oneself up':

¡Qué guapa te has puesto!	you look very pretty!
	(lit. 'how well you've done yourself up')
Se puso muy elegante para ir a la boda	she dressed up to go to the wedding

It is often used with children to indicate that they are looking bigger or handsomer than ever:
¡Pero qué guapo/grande se ha puesto este niño! 'hasn't this child got handsome/big!'.

   (ii)   Idioms: *se puso de barro* . . . 'she got herself covered in mud'; *se puso de paella* . . .
'he made a pig of himself eating paella'; *se puso de contento* . . . 'he got so happy . . .'.

(b)   *Volverse*

Usually translates 'to become, to go' and implies involuntary mental or psychological change when applied to animate subjects. It can also be used of abstract inanimate nouns and circumstances. This change is felt to be more permanent than with *ponerse*:

Se volvió loco de tanto pensar	he went mad from thinking too much
Antes era muy sencilla pero ahora se ha vuelto muy orgullosa	she used to be very unaffected but now she's become very proud
Con la edad se ha vuelto muy de derechas	he's become very right-wing with age
Últimamente todo se vuelven complicaciones, dificultades y disgustos	recently everything has become complications, difficulties and upsets
. . . ¿donde se volvió asesino ese chico? (M. Puig, Arg., dialogue)	. . . where did that boy learn to be a murderer?

(c)   *Hacerse* 'to become'

Often implies voluntary effort. It is usual for religious, professional or political changes. It can also occasionally be used of circumstances:

Se hizo católico/se convirtió al catolicismo	he became a Catholic
Para hacerte arquitecto necesitas saber dibujo	you need to know how to draw to become an architect
De paso me hice amiga de todo el mundo	at the same time I became friendly with everybody

Notes (i)   There is little difference between sentences like *se está haciendo cada vez más vago* and *se está volviendo cada vez más vago* 'he's getting lazier and lazier' except that some wilfulness is implied in the first example.

   (ii)   Idioms: *hacerse tarde* 'to get late', *hacerse de miel* 'to become so soft that people can take advantage of one'.

   (iii)   *Llegar a ser* is used to indicate the result of a slow and sometimes difficult change. It implies 'to manage to become' or 'to become eventually':

Trabajó mucho y con el tiempo llegó a ser alguien/director general/una persona importante	he worked hard and in due time he became somebody/general manager/ an important person

   (iv)   'To become' with the meaning of 'to be appointed' is translated into Spanish as *nombrar* or *hacer*: *Le han nombrado/hecho ministro* 'he's become a Minister'.

(d)   *Convertirse en* 'to become/change/turn into'.

The verb precedes noun phrases but not adjectives. The change can be due to external circumstances:

Nada más tocarle el hada con la varita el príncipe se convirtió en rana	as soon as the fairy touched him with her wand, the prince turned into a frog
Se ha convertido en un drogadicto/un criminal	he's become a drug addict/a criminal
El transporte se ha convertido en un problema para todos	transport has become a problem for everybody
El turismo se ha convertido en una fuente de riqueza	tourism has become a source of riches
La silla se convierte fácilmente en una escalera	the chair turns easily into a step ladder

Note 'To change one's beliefs' is *convertirse a*. (See also *hacerse* 12.6c):

No todos los que se convierten a una religión se vuelven buenos	Not everybody who is converted to a religion becomes good

(e) *Quedarse* may be a verb of 'becoming' when it implies loss:

(i) Implying loss, incapacity:

Se quedó ciego/mudo/impedido	he became blind/dumb/disabled
Se quedó soltera/viuda	she never married/she became a widow
Se quedó/puso pálido/lívido	he lost his colour/turned purple
¡Qué delgado te has quedado!	haven't you got thin!
Me he quedado helado esperándote	I've got frozen waiting for you
Se quedó solo en el mundo	he was left alone in the world
Al morir su padre se quedó sin dinero	when her father died she was left without any money
A pesar del frío se quedó en cueros	in spite of the cold he took all his clothes off

(ii) Other meanings:

Se quitó el abrigo y se quedó con una falda gris y una blusa blanca	she took her coat off. She was wearing a grey skirt and a white blouse
Se quedó atrás	he was left behind
Me quedo con este sombrero	I'll take this hat
Quédese con la vuelta	keep the change
Me quedo en este hotel	I'll stay in this hotel
¿Te has quedado contento?	are you satisfied now?
Me quedé convencido de que era verdad	I was convinced that it was true
El gerente se quedó fastidiado (C. Fuentes, Mexico)	the manager was irritated

Notes (i) *Quedarse helado* can also apply to shock: *cuando se lo dijeron se quedó helado* 'he had a terrible shock when they told him'.

12.7 Pronominal verbs of motion

Many common verbs of motion acquire an extra nuance in the pronominal form.

The pronominal form may **(a)** draw attention to the point of departure as opposed to the destination, cf. *ir* 'to go somewhere', *irse* 'to go away (from somewhere)', French *aller/s'en aller*; or **(b)** denote that an action is untimely, accidental or unplanned, e.g. *caer* 'to fall', *caerse* 'to fall over/down'. Examples:

Vamos a casa de Pepe	we're going to Pepe's house
Me voy a casa de Pepe	I'm off to Pepe's house
El sol se fue ya	the sun's gone in
Ha venido de París a pasar unos días	she's come from Paris to spend a few days
Se ha venido de París porque no puede ver a los franceses	he's left Paris and come here because he cannot stand the French
Dijiste sus nombres cuando te viniste (J. Cortázar, Arg., dialogue)	you mentioned their names when you came here
El edificio se vino abajo	the building collapsed
No vuelvas tarde	don't come back too late
Salí con intención de ir a la fiesta, pero cuando llegué a la esquina me volví	I left to go to the party but when I reached the corner I turned back
Salimos del cine cuando terminó la película	we left the cinema when the film ended
Nos salimos del cine porque la película era muy violenta	we left the cinema because the film was very violent
Salió del convento a las cinco	he left the convent at 5 o'clock
Se salió del convento a los treinta años	she left the convent at the age of thirty
Espérame abajo/arriba que bajo/subo enseguida	wait for me downstairs/upstairs I'll be down/up in a minute
subirse a un autobús	to get on a bus
subirse a un árbol	to climb a tree
bajarse de un autobús/un árbol	to get out of a bus/down from a tree
Los prisioneros se escaparon	the prisoners escaped
Los ladrones escaparon a la justicia	the thieves escaped justice
Llegamos a Madrid	we arrived in Madrid
Llégate a la tienda de enfrente	pop over to the shop opposite
Unos periodistas alemanes se llegaron hasta el Palacio de la Zarzuela (*Cambio16*)	some German journalists got as far as the Zarzuela Palace
Se cayó de la mesa	it fell off the table (accidentally)
Me caí por unas escaleras	I fell down a flight of stairs
¡Que no se te caiga el paquete!	don't drop the parcel!
La bomba cayó en la fábrica	the bomb fell on the factory (intended)
El tigre cayó sobre su presa	the tiger fell on its prey
Cayó en la guerra	he fell (was killed) in the war
Esa calle cae lejos de aquí	that street lies far from here

Notes (i)   *Salirse* with an appropriate subject may mean 'to leak'. Compare

El agua sale por aquí	the water comes out here (where it should)

and

El grifo se sale	the tap's leaking

   (ii)   *Volverse* can mean 'to turn round', 'to turn back halfway', 'to return discontented' (unplanned return). *Volver* implies going, stopping, then returning or perhaps merely returning without having gone anywhere (the weather, happy days, etc.):

Me volví antes de llegar	I turned back before arriving
La primavera vuelve	Spring returns
Nunca volveré a aquella casa	I'll never return to that house
Se volvió hacia ella	he turned to (to face) her
Has vuelto muy moreno	you've come back very sun-tanned
Nos hemos vuelto porque no paraba de llover	we've come back (ahead of time) because it didn't stop raining

(iii) *Entrarse* emphasizes point of departure, but is not accepted by all speakers:

Salió al balcón pero volvió a entrar(se) porque hacía frío	she went out on to the balcony but came in again because it was cold

12.8 Pronominal verbs of consumption, perception or knowledge

A curious use of the pronominal form in these transitive verbs is to emphasize the totality of an act of consuming, perceiving or knowing. Thus we say *como pizza* (but not necessarily whole pizzas), but *me comí una pizza* 'I ate a (whole) pizza'.

Bebe mucho vino	he drinks a lot of wine
Se bebió un litro de vino	he drank a litre of wine
No deberías fumar	you shouldn't smoke
Se fuma tres paquetes al día	he smokes three packets a day
Ando mucho	I walk a lot
Me anduve cincuenta kilómetros	I walked 50 kilometres
Aprendo francés	I'm learning French
Me aprendí todo el capítulo en una hora	I learnt the whole chapter in an hour
Sabe mucho	she knows a lot
¿Te sabes los verbos irregulares?	do you know the irregular verbs?
Conozco Valencia	I know Valencia
Me conozco Valencia de cabo a rabo	I know Valencia inside out
Toma somníferos para dormir	he takes sleeping pills to sleep
Tómate un somnífero	take a sleeping pill
Pero aquella noche se sintió tan humillado que se tomó el brandy de un golpe (García Márquez, Col.)	but that night he felt so humiliated that he drank his brandy down in one go
Trago mal	I can't swallow properly
Se lo ha tragado	he's swallowed it
Vi a tu cuñada	I saw your sister-in-law
Se vio todo el museo en diez minutos	he saw the whole museum in ten minutes

Conocerse applied to people acquires a nuance: *conozco a Miguel/me conozco a Miguel* 'I know Miguel/I know Miguel (and his little tricks)'.

12.9 Other pronominal verbs with special nuances

A few pronominal verbs acquire various meanings in different contexts:

(a)   *Morir/se*

The pronominal form denotes natural death through illness. *Morir* is used for accidental or deliberate death: *(se) murió de un ataque al corazón* 'he died from a heart attack'; *murió en un accidente de avión* 'he died in a plane accident'. In formal written Spanish *morir* is more usual.

Ha muerto el primer ministro	the Primer Minister has died
La propia Tránsito Arias se murió convencida de que (García Márquez, Colombia)	Transito Arias herself died convinced that
Yo lloré al contarle que casi se nos había muerto esa noche (M. Puig, Argentina, dialogue)	I cried when I told him how he had nearly died that night

(b)   *Encontrar/se*

The transitive form means 'to find', the pronominal form 'to find something by chance' as in *encontré el libro que buscaba* 'I found the book I was searching for', *me encontré una moneda de oro* 'I found a gold coin', *me encontré a Pepe* 'I ran into Pepe (by chance)'.

(c)   *Ganar/se*

Ganar is used in the phrase *ganar mucho/poco dinero* 'to earn a lot/very little money', *¿cuánto ganas?* 'how much do you earn?' *Ganarse* highlights the object as exceptional or surprising:

Se gana un millón de ptas todos los meses	she earns 1,000,000 ptas every month
Se gana la vida bailando	she earns her living dancing
Se gana el cariño de todos	she wins everybody's affection

(d)   *Olvidar/se*

Olvidar usually implies intentional forgetting

No puedo olvidarla	I can't forget her

Olvidarse de implies accidental forgetting. It is not generally used before nouns:

Me he olvidado de lo que has dicho	I've forgotten what you said
Se han olvidado de que en la soledad la tentación es más grande (C. Fuentes, Mex.)	they've forgotten that temptation is greater in solitude

There is a third form, *olvidarse*, implying accidental forgetting, which can also be used before nouns. The verb agrees in number with the thing forgotten:

Aquel día se me habían olvidado las llaves	that day I had forgotten my keys
No se te olvide llamarme	don't forget to ring me

(e)   *Creerse*

The pronominal form usually implies unfounded belief:

Creo en ella	I believe in her
Ése se cree que habla francés	he thinks he speaks French
Se cree todo lo que le dicen	he believes everything they tell him
Yo (me) creía que él había llegado	I thought he had arrived

(f)   *Reírse*

Reírse is the more common form; *reír* is literary:

Se rió de su propia risa	she laughed at her own laughter
(G. García Márquez)	
Los dos se rieron	both laughed

(g) *Estarse*

The pronominal form *estarse* is used:

  (i) To form the imperative of *estar*:

¡Estate quieto!	sit still!
¡Estese tranquilo!	be calm/don't worry!

(ii) To express obligatory or deliberate being in a place. The translation is usually 'to stay':

Se tuvo que estar en casa porque vinieron	he had to stay at home because his aunt
sus tíos	and uncle came
Me estuve estudiando toda la noche	I stayed up all night studying
(from Moliner)	
He tenido que estar(me) a la cola todo	I had to queue all day
el día	

Quedarse would have been possible in all but the last example.

12.10   Spanish-American pronominal verbs

Most pronominal forms used in Spain are also current in Spanish America, but some pronominal verbs are found in Spanish America which sound quaint, rustic or plain wrong to Peninsular Spanish speakers. The following selection is not exhaustive, and not all are current in educated speech or in all countries:

  soñarse 'to dream', *devolverse* 'to return' (Spain *volver*), *regresarse* 'to return', *recordarse* 'to remember' (substandard in Spain), *prestarse* 'to borrow', *enfermarse* 'to get ill', *robarse* 'to steal', *crecerse* 'to be brought up', *aparecerse* 'to appear' (only used of ghosts and apparitions in Spain).

12.11   Interpretation of pronominal verbs with inanimate subjects

A third-person pronominal verb may also be interpreted as a passive: *se construyó en España* means the same as *fue construido en España* 'it was built in Spain' (see chapter 24 for more details).

  An occasional difficulty with pronominal verbs, for example *se abrió la puerta*, is therefore that of deciding whether they are to be interpreted as intransitive, i.e. 'the door opened', or passive 'the door was opened'. This problem only arises with certain verbs which have well-established pronominal intransitive forms, e.g. *abrir/abrirse* 'to open', *cerrar/cerrarse* 'to close', *encontrar/encontrarse* 'to find/to be located', *esconder/ esconderse* 'to hide', and many others which will be found listed in good dictionaries. Some verbs, e.g. *construir* 'to build', *derribar* 'to fell', *operar* 'to operate' do not have intransitive counterparts so confusion is hardly possible.

The general rule for clarifying which sense is intended is as follows:

If a pronominal verb has an established intransitive meaning, e.g. *abrirse*, *esconderse*, it will usually precede the subject if the passive meaning is intended, although this position does not preclude a pronominal interpretation. Thus *la puerta se abrió* usually means 'the door opened', but *se abrió la puerta* may mean either 'the door opened' or 'the door was opened'. Similarly:

Los libros se quemaron	the books burnt
Se quemaron los libros	the books burnt/were burnt
Las luces se encienden a las nueve	the lights come on at nine
Se encienden las luces a las nueve	the lights are lit/come on at nine
El hamster se esconde debajo de la cama	the hamster hides under the bed
Se esconde el hamster debajo de la cama	the hamster is hidden/hides under the bed
Tres ventanas se rompieron durante la tormenta	three windows broke in the storm
Se rompieron tres ventanas durante la manifestación	three windows were broken in the demonstration/?three windows broke during the demonstration
Tres barcos se hundieron	three boats sank
Se hundieron tres barcos	three boats sank/were sunk

In the second of each of these sentences the passive is the more likely meaning.

If the verb has no intransitive possibility, then only a passive meaning is possible:

Se derribaron tres árboles/tres árboles se derribaron	three trees were felled
Los motivos se ignoran/se ignoran los motivos	the motives are unknown

The foregoing points hardly constitute a hard and fast rule, and it must be remembered that complex word order rules, discussed in chapter 31, govern the choice between *los motivos se ignoran* and *se ignoran los motivos*.

12.12   Obligatory use of *uno* as impersonal pronoun with pronominal verbs

Uno/una must be used to give an impersonal meaning to a pronominal verb since two *ses* cannot occur side by side:

Se muere de frío en esta casa	he/she's dying from cold in this house
Se muere uno de frío en esta casa	one dies from cold in this house
Cuando está así, se irrita fácilmente por cualquier cosa	when he's like that, he gets easily irritated over anything
Cuando se está así, se irrita uno fácilmente por cualquier cosa	when one is like that, one gets easily irritated over anything
Con estas cosas se cansa mucho	he gets very tired with these things
Con estas cosas se cansa uno mucho	one gets very tired with these things

See 24.3.1. for more details.

13 Morphology of the verb

In this chapter translations have been omitted. So many verbs have multiple translations that a single English rendering would be misleading; readers should consult a good dictionary for the meanings of the verbs discussed.

Table 1, p. 183, gives an overview of a typical regular Spanish verb, with the simple, compound, continuous and passive forms included. Even this lengthy table is not exhaustive, but the remaining forms are mostly grammarians' inventions rather than examples of real language.

For ease of reference certain constantly required forms have been set out in separate tables:

Conjugation of regular verbs	Table 2	p. 185
Regular spelling changes	Table 3	p. 187
Conjugation of *ser*	Table 4	p. 189
Conjugation of *estar*	Table 5	p. 190
Conjugation of *haber*	Table 6	p. 191
Compound tenses	Table 7	p. 192

13.1 General remarks about the Spanish verb system

The following general remarks may show that the Spanish verb system is less complex in reality than in appearance.

(a) All Spanish verbs are divided into three conjugations distinguished by the vowel of the infinitive: 1: *-ar*, 2: *-er*, 3: *-ir*. The endings of regular verbs of the *-er* and *-ir* conjugations are identical except in the plural of the imperative, cf. *comed* and *vivid*, the plural of the first and second persons of the present indicative, cf. *comemos/vivimos*, *coméis/vivís*, and all forms based on the infinitive.

The full conjugation of three typical regular verbs in *-ar*, *-er* and *-ir* is shown in table 2, p. 185.

(b) There are certain predictable spelling changes which regularly affect all verbs. They are discussed at 13.2.2 and the most important are shown in table 3, p. 187.

(c) 'Radical changing verbs' have regular endings, but a vowel in the stem undergoes modification in some forms, cf. *contar*>*cuenta*, *perder*>*pierdo*, *jugar*>*juega*, *sentir*>*siente*>*sintió*. Such verbs are numerous and since there is no way of predicting from the infinitive whether a verb is of this type they are listed with the irregular verbs, p. 177.

(d)   The endings of the imperfect indicative are:

-ar verbs		*-er* and *-ir* verbs	
-aba	-ábamos	-ía	-íamos
-abas	-abais (no accent!)	-ías	-íais
-aba	-aban	-ía	-ían

These endings are added to the stem left after removing the infinitive ending. There are three exceptions: *ser* (*era, eras, era*, etc.), *ir* (*iba, ibas, iba*, etc.) and *ver* and its compounds (*veía, veías, veía*, etc, for the expected **vía*).

(e)   The endings of the future and conditional tenses are the same for all verbs:

Future		**Conditional**	
-é	-emos	-ía	-íamos
-ás	-éis	-ías	-íais
-á	-án	-ía	-ían

These endings are always added to the infinitive except in the cases of:

Infinitive	Future stem	Infinitive	Future stem
caber	cabr-	querer	querr-
decir	dir-	saber	sabr-
haber	habr-	salir	saldr-
hacer	har-	tener	tendr-
poder	podr-	valer	valdr-
poner	pondr-	venir	vendr-

(f)   The endings of the present subjunctive are always predictable: *-ar* verbs take the endings of the present indicative of regular *-er* verbs, and *-er* and *-ir* verbs take the endings of the present indicative of regular *-ar* verbs. With very few exceptions, the present subjunctive endings are added to the stem left after removing the *-o* of the first-person present indicative: e.g. *veng(o)-venga, conduzc(o)-conduzca, quep(o)-quepa*, etc.

The exceptions are radical changing verbs and:

Infinitive	1st-person present indicative	Present subjunctive
dar	doy	dé, des, dé, etc.
estar	estoy	esté, estés, esté, etc.
haber	he	haya, hayas, haya, etc.
ir	voy	vaya, vayas, vaya, etc.
saber	sé	sepa, sepas, sepa, etc.
ser	soy	sea, seas, sea, etc.

(g)   There are no exceptions to the rule that the past (i.e. imperfect) and future subjunctive endings are always added to the stem of the third-person singular of the preterite indicative. In the case of regular verbs this stem is found by removing the infinitive ending, e.g. *habl(ar)* > *habl-*. But in the case of irregular verbs the preterite stem is often irregular, e.g.

Infinitive	3rd-person pret. stem	Past & future subjunctives
herir	hir(ió)	hir-iera/hir-iese/hir-iere
ser	fu(e)	fu-era/fu-ese/fu-ere
producir	produj(o)	produj-era/produj-ese/ produj-ere

tener	tuv(o)	tuv-iera/tuv-iese/tuv-iere

etc.

(h) With two exceptions, compound verbs are conjugated like the simple verb, i.e. *descomponer* and *deshacer* are conjugated like *poner* and *hacer*. The only exceptions are *bendecir* and *maldecir*, conjugated at 13.3.26.

(i) The informal singular imperative is usually formed by removing the -*s* of the second-person singular of the present indicative: *llamas-llama*, *lees-lee*. There are nine exceptions:

Infinitive	Imperative (*tú* form)	Infinitive	Imperative (*tú* form)
decir	di	poner	pon
hacer	haz	salir	sal
haber	he (if it is ever used)	ser	sé
		tener	ten
ir	ve	venir	ven

The plural imperative (*vosotros*) form is always formed by replacing the -*r* of the infinitive by -*d*: *construir-construid*, *ser-sed*. This form is archaic in Spanish America, but is in everyday use in Spain. The -*d* is dropped in the pronominal form: *dad + os > daos*, *venid + os > veníos*. There is one exception, *idos* (from *irse*).

The imperative form corresponding to *vos* (Southern Cone, Central America) can usually be found by removing the -*d* from the *vosotros* form, which is not in everyday use in Spanish America. The final vowel is usually stressed: *tened > tené*, *contad > contá*, *decid > decí*. Pronominal verbs take the pronoun *te*, so the imperative of *lavarse* is *lavate*. *Vos* forms vary from country to country and are not listed in the verb tables.

The polite pronouns *usted* and *ustedes* have no independent imperative forms; they use the third-person singular and plural present subjunctive endings respectively: *dígame, tenga, oigan ustedes*, etc.

(j) The past participle is usually formed by replacing the -*ar* of the infinitive of -*ar* verbs by -*ado*, and the -*er* and -*ir* of the infinitive of the other two conjugations by -*ido*:

hablar	hablado	regir	regido
tener	tenido	ir	ido

etc.

There are a number of common exceptions listed at 18.2.

There are a few other common verbs which have a special adjectival participle, and there are some Spanish-American variants. These are discussed more fully in chapter 18.

(k) The perfect tenses, e.g. *he hablado, has visto, habían tenido, habrán hecho*, etc. are always predictable, provided one can conjugate *haber* (see p. 191) and knows the past participle of the verb. For this reason the perfect tenses are not listed in this chapter but the full perfect of *ver* 'to see' is shown in table 7, p. 192, by way of example.

(l)   The gerund is invariable and is usually formed by replacing the *-ar* of the infinitive by *-ando*, or the *-er* or *-ir* by *-iendo*. An unstressed intervocalic *i* is written *y*: *caer > cayendo* (not **caiendo*). There are some irregularities affecting radical changing verbs in *-ir* which follow the model of *sentir* and *pedir*: the stem vowel changes to *i*: *sintiendo, pidiendo*.

(m)   Spanish has a full range of 'continuous' forms, e.g. *estoy hablando, estuve esperando*, etc. These are all formed from the appropriate form of *estar* (see p. 190) and the invariable gerund. Use of the continuous is discussed in chapter 15.

(n)   There are several ways of expressing the passive, one of the most common being the use of *ser* (p. 189) with the past participle, which agrees in gender and number: *las órdenes fueron dadas* 'the orders were given . . .', *la carta fue recibida* 'the letter was received'. Use of the passive is discussed in chapter 24, and typical forms are shown on p. 184.

The continuous passive occurs occasionally: *pero yo no estoy siendo interrogado* 'but I'm not being interrogated'. It is predictably formed from the continuous of *ser* plus the participle.

13.2   Variants and spelling rules

13.2.1   Colloquial variants
The Spanish verb system is remarkably stable throughout the Hispanic world, despite the large number of forms and exceptions. Mistakes caused by attempted regularization of irregular forms, e.g. **cabo* for *quepo* or **produció* for *produjo*, **andé* for *anduve* are socially stigmatized. However regularized preterites of verbs in *-ducir*, e.g. **conducí, *produció* are common in popular Spanish-American speech and are sometimes heard in Spain.

Three popular spoken forms are very common, although they are stigmatized as uneducated – particularly the first two:

(1)   addition of *-s* to the second-person preterite singular, e.g. **distes* for *diste*, **hablastes* for *hablaste*;

(2)   pluralization of forms of *haber* (other than *hay*) when it means 'there is'/'there are', e.g. **habían muchos* for *había muchos*. This tendency is very common, especially in the imperfect, but it should not be imitated;

(3)   use of the infinitive for the *vosotros* form of the imperative: *dar* for *dad*, *callaros* for *callaos*, *iros* for *idos*, etc. This is discussed at 17.5c.

13.2.2   General spelling rules
Certain spelling changes are applied systematically throughout the verb system. The most common are shown in table 3, p. 187.

(a)   The sound of *g* as in *hago* is spelt *gu* before *e* or *i*: *pagar > pague, ruego > rogué*, etc.

The sounds *gwe* and *gwi* are written *güe*, *güi*: *averigüe, argüí*, etc.

(b) The sound /k/ is written *qu* before *e* and *i*, but *c* in all other cases: *sacar > saque*.

(c) Z, pronounced /θ/ (like *th* in 'think') in standard Peninsular Spanish, like *s* in 'sin' in Southern Spain and in Spanish America, is spelt *c* before *e, i*: *rezar > rece*, but the *z* must be restored before any other vowel *esparcir > esparza, vencer > venzo*, etc.

Speakers who use Spanish-American pronunciation will be unable to predict by sound alone the spelling of words like *cace/case, caza/casa*, etc.

(d) The sound /x/ (like the *ch* of 'loch') must be spelt *j* before *a, o, u*: *regir > rijo, coger > coja*, etc. The spelling of the syllables /xe/ and /xi/ must however be learnt separately, cf. *ruge* and *conduje* (which rhyme).

(e) The diphthong *ie* is written *ye-* at the beginning of a word. Thus *errar* makes its first-person singular present indicative *yerro* for the predicted **ierro*. See 13.3.20 for conjugation of *errar*.

(f) The diphthong *-ue-* is written *hue-* at the beginning of a word. Thus *oler* makes its first-person singular indicative *huelo* for the predicted **uelo*: see 13.3.29 for conjugation of *oler*.

Prefixes are ignored for this purpose, so the rare verb *desosar* 'to bone' (replaced nowadays by the regular *deshuesar*) shows such forms as *deshueso, deshuesa, desosamos*, etc.

13.2.3 Regular verbs in *-ar*
See p. 185 for the full conjugation of a typical regular verb in *-ar*. The spelling changes shown on p. 187 and discussed above (*z > c, g > gu* and *c > qu* before *e*) must be applied where required.

Verbs whose stem vowel is a diphthong, or whose infinitive ends in *-iar* or *-uar* present the complications described at 13.2.4 and 13.2.5.

13.2.4 Spelling of *aislar, reunir, prohibir* and similar verbs
When the penultimate syllable of an infinitive contains a diphthong whose second element is *i* or *u*, this diphthong may or may not be broken into two syllables when it is stressed: *prohibir > prohíbe* pronounced /proiβe/, *reunir – reúnes* pronounced /rreúnes/. Since 1959 this stressed vowel has been written with an accent. In the Academy's view the fact that *-h-* appears between the two vowels makes no difference. This ruling affects the following forms of the verb:

Present indicative

aíslo	reúne	prohíbe
aíslas	reúnes	prohíbes
aísla	reúne	prohíbe
aislamos	reunimos	prohibimos
aisláis	reunís	prohibís
aíslan	reúnen	prohíben

Present subjunctive

aísle	reúna	prohíba
aísles	reúnas	prohíbas

aísle	reúna	prohíba
aislemos	reunamos	prohibamos
aisléis	reunáis	prohibáis
aíslen	reúnan	prohíban

Singular imperative

aísla	reúne	prohíbe

Among verbs affected are:

ahijar	amohinar	desahitarse	maullar
ahilar	arcaizar	desraizar	prohijar
ahincar	aullar	enraizar	rehilar
ahitar	aunar	europeizar	sahumar
ahumar	aupar	hebraizar	sobrehilar
airar	cohibir	judaizar	

In other verbs the diphthong is not broken, i.e. when the diphthong is stressed the accent falls on its first vowel and no written accent appears, e.g. *arraigo*, *encausa*, etc. Similar are *amainar*, *causar*, *desahuciar* (variable, usually the diphthong is retained), *desenvainar*, *embaucar*, *embaular* (variable – the verb is hardly used anyway), *envainar*, *reinar*, *peinar*, *recauchar*, etc.

The new spelling is in general use in printed texts but nearly thirty years later most people still omit the accent in handwriting.

13.2.5 Verbs ending in *-iar*

There are two types of verb whose infinitive ends in *-iar*. The majority conjugate like *cambiar*, i.e. the *-ia* survives as a diphthong throughout, but about fifty conjugate like *liar*, i.e. the *i* may be stressed:

Infinitive cambiar *Gerund* cambiando
Past participle cambiado *Imperative* cambia cambiad

INDICATIVE

Present	Imperfect	Preterite	Future	Conditional
cambio	cambiaba	cambié	cambiaré	cambiaría
cambias	cambiabas	cambiaste	cambiarás	cambiarías
cambia	cambiaba	cambió	cambiará	cambiaría
cambiamos	cambiábamos	cambiamos	cambiaremos	cambiaríamos
cambiáis	cambiabais	cambiasteis	cambiaréis	cambiaríais
cambian	cambiaban	cambiaron	cambiarán	cambiarían

SUBJUNCTIVE

Present	Imperfect	(Future – almost obsolete)
cambie	cambiara/cambiase	cambiare
cambies	cambiaras/cambiases	etc.
cambie	cambiara/cambiase	
cambiemos	cambiáramos/cambiásemos	
cambiéis	cambiarais/cambiaseis	
cambien	cambiaran/cambiasen	

Infinitive liar *Gerund* liando
Past participle liado *Imperative* lía liad

INDICATIVE

Present	Imperfect	Preterite	Future	Conditional
lío	liaba	lié	liaré	liaría
lías	liabas	liaste	liarás	liarías
lía	liaba	lió	liará	liaría
liamos	liábamos	liamos	liaremos	liaríamos
liáis	liabais	liasteis	liaréis	liaríais
lían	liaban	liaron	liarán	liarían

SUBJUNCTIVE

Present	Imperfect	(*Future* – almost obsolete)
líe	liara/liase	liare
líes	liaras/liases	etc.
líe	liara/liase	
liemos	liáramos/liásemos	
liéis	liarais/liaseis	
líen	liaran/liasen	

The following list shows common verbs which conjugate like *liar* or about which the authorities are in disagreement:

agriar (disputed, usually like *cambiar*)
aliar
amnistiar
ampliar
ansiar
arriar
ataviar
autografiar
auxiliar (disputed, usually like *cambiar*)
averiar
aviar
biografiar
conciliar (disputed, usually like *cambiar*)
contrariar
criar
dactilografiar
desafiar
descarriar
descriarse
desliar
desvariar
desviar
enfriar
enviar
escalofriar
espiar

expatriar (disputed; also like *cambiar*)
expiar
extasiarse (disputed, usually like *liar*)
extraviar
fiar
filiar (but optionally like *cambiar*)
fotografiar
gloriar (se)
guiar
hastiar
historiar (disputed, like *cambiar*)
litografiar
malcriar
mecanografiar
paliar (usually like *cambiar*)
piar
porfiar
radiografiar
recriar
rociar
telegrafiar
vaciar
vanagloriarse (almost always like *cambiar*)
variar
vidriar (Academy recommends *cambiar*)

13.2.6 Verbs in *-uar*

All conjugate like *actuar*, except those ending in *-guar* and *-cuar*, which conjugate like *averiguar*, i.e. the *ua* forms an inseparable diphthong:

Infinitive actuar   *Gerund* actuando
Past participle actuado   *Imperative* actúa actuad

INDICATIVE

Present	Imperfect	Preterite	Future	Conditional
actúo	actuaba	actué	actuaré	actuaría
actúas	actuabas	actuaste	actuarás	actuarías
actúa	actuaba	actuó	actuará	actuaría
actuamos	actuábamos	actuamos	actuaremos	actuaríamos
actuáis	actuabais	actuasteis	actuaréis	actuaríais
actúan	actuaban	actuaron	actuarán	actuarían

SUBJUNCTIVE

Present	Imperfect	(*Future* – almost obsolete)
actúe	actuara/actuase	actuare
actúes	actuaras/actuases	etc.
actúe	actuara/actuase	
actuemos	actuáramos/actuásemos	
actuéis	actuarais/actuaseis	
actúen	actuaran/actuasen	

Verbs conjugated like *actuar* are:

acentuar	*evaluar*	*individuar*	*puntuar*
atenuar	*exceptuar*	*infatuar*	*redituar*
conceptuar	*extenuar*	*insinuar*	*situar*
continuar	*fluctuar*	*perpetuar*	*usufructuar*
desvirtuar	*graduar*	*preceptuar*	*valuar*
efectuar	*habituar*		

Infinitive averiguar   *Gerund* averiguando
Past participle averiguado   *Imperative* averigua averiguad

INDICATIVE

Present	Imperfect	Preterite	Future	Conditional
averiguo	averiguaba	averigüé	averiguaré	averiguaría
averiguas	averiguabas	averiguaste	averiguarás	averiguarías
averigua	averiguaba	averiguó	averiguará	averiguaría
averiguamos	averiguábamos	averiguamos	averiguaremos	averiguaríamos
averiguáis	averiguabais	averiguasteis	averiguaréis	averiguaríais
averiguan	averiguaban	averiguaron	averiguarán	averiguarían

SUBJUNCTIVE

Present	Imperfect	(*Future* – almost obsolete)
averigüe	averiguara/averiguase	averiguare
averigües	averiguaras/averiguases	etc.
averigüe	averiguara/averiguase	
averigüemos	averiguáramos/averiguásemos	
averigüéis	averiguarais/averiguaseis	
averigüen	averiguaran/averiguasen	

Note There are few verbs in *-cuar*, *evacuar* being the most common. It should be conjugated like *averiguar* – but without the dieresis – although conjugation like *actuar* is a common mistake in Spain and is apparently accepted usage in some countries.

13.2.7   Verbs ending in -*ear*
These are all regular. Two *e*s may occur side by side, as in *pasear*>*paseé*, *pasee, pasees, paseen*, etc.

13.2.8   Regular verbs in -*er*
See p. 185 for the full conjugation of a typical regular verb in -*er*.

If the infinitive ends in -*cer* or -*ger*, the spelling changes shown on p. 187 are applied (*g*>*j* and *c*>*z* before *a, o, u*). These affect the first-person singular of the present indicative, and all the present subjunctive.

The only verbs in -*cer* affected are *convencer, ejercer, mecer* and *vencer* (all regular) and *escocer, (re)cocer* and *(re)torcer*), for which see 13.3.12. The rest conjugate as at 13.3.10.

In verbs whose infinitive ends in -*eer*, e.g. *leer, poseer, creer, i* is written *y* if it is unstressed and falls between two vowels (i.e. a hypothetical form like **poseiendo* must be written *poseyendo*). *Poseer* is conjugated at 13.3.35.

13.2.9   Typical regular -*ir* verb
See p. 185 for the full conjugation of a typical verb in -*ir*. These verbs conjugate exactly like -*er* verbs except for the forms shown in bold type.

The spelling changes shown on p. 187 must be applied if the infinitive ends in -*cir* or -*gir*: *c*>*z* before *a, o, u*; *g*>*j* before *a, o, u*. However verbs in -*cir* are usually irregular and should be sought in the list at the end of the chapter (13.4).

13.3   Irregular verbs

13.3.1   General
Irregular verbs are listed in alphabetical order, though the very frequent verbs *ser, estar* and *haber* are shown in tables 4, 5 and 6, pp. 189–91.

Connoisseurs will not find such oddities as *abarse* (found only in the imperative singular) or *usucapir* (found only in the infinitive). These and similar verbs now obsolete in ordinary language should be sought in the Academy grammar or other specialized verb lists.

13.3.2   *Abolir*
Defective verb. Only those forms are used in which the verb ending begins with -*i*.

There are a few other verbs which share the same peculiarity, but none besides *abolir* and *agredir* is much used in the modern language:

aguerrir (only participle used in practice)
agredir see 13.3.4
arrecirse
aterirse (only infinitive and participle used?)

blandir
despavorir (only participle in use)
empedernir (participle only used?)
garantir (replaced in practice by garantizar)

Infinitive abolir   *Gerund* aboliendo
Past participle abolido   *Imperative* abolid. **Abole* is not used
INDICATIVE

Present	Imperfect	Preterite	Future	Conditional
not used	abolía	abolí	aboliré	aboliría
not used	etc.	etc.	etc.	etc.
not used				
abolimos				
abolís				
not used				

SUBJUNCTIVE

Present	Imperfect	Future (almost obsolete)
no forms	aboliera/aboliese	aboliere
in use	etc.	etc.

Unused forms must be replaced, e.g. **sin que se abola* by *sin que sea abolido* and so on.

13.3.3   *Adquirir*
The infinitive of this verb was once *adquerir*, which explains the appearance of *-ie-* when the stem vowel is stressed:

Infinitive adquirir   *Gerund* adquiriendo
Past participle adquirido   *Imperative* adquiere adquirid
INDICATIVE

Present	Imperfect	Preterite	Future	Conditional
adquiero	adquiría	adquirí	adquiriré	adquiriría
adquieres	etc.	etc.	etc.	etc.
adquiere				
adquirimos				
adquirís				
adquieren				

SUBJUNCTIVE

Present	Imperfect	Future (almost obsolete)
adquiera	adquiriera/adquiriese	adquiriere
adquieras	etc.	etc.
adquiera		
adquiramos		
adquiráis		
adquieran		

13.3.4   *Agredir*
This verb is classified by some as defective (like *abolir*), by others as a normal *-ir* verb, the former usage being the more conservative.

13.3.5   *Andar*
This verb is conjugated like a regular *-ar* verb throughout except for the preterite indicative and, consequently, the past and future subjunctive:

Preterite indic.	Imp. subjunctive	Future subjunctive (rare)
and**uve**	and**uve**ra/and**uve**iese	and**uve**iere
and**uve**iste	etc.	etc.
and**uve**o		
and**uve**imos		
and**uve**isteis		
and**uve**ieron		

13.3.6 *Asir*

In practice forms which contain a *g* are avoided, though other forms are occasionally heard, e.g. *me así a una rama para no caerme* 'I clutched hold of a branch so as not to fall', etc.

Infinitive asir   *Gerund* asiendo
Past participle asido   *Imperative* ase, asid
INDICATIVE

Present	Imperfect	Preterite	Future	Conditional
(asgo)	asía	así	asiré	asiría
ases	etc.	etc.	etc.	etc.
ase				
asimos				
asís				
asen				

SUBJUNCTIVE

Present	Imperfect	Future (almost obsolete)
(asga)	asiera/asiese	asiere
(asgas)	etc.	etc.
(asga)		
(asgamos)		
(asgáis)		
(asgan)		

13.3.7 *Balbucir*

This verb is nowadays replaced by the regular *balbucear*. *Balbucir* has, or had, the peculiarity that no form containing a *z* was used, so **balbuzo* and the present subjunctive are not found.

13.3.8 *Caber* (highly irregular)

Infinitive caber   *Gerund* cabiendo
Past participle cabido   *Imperative* cabe cabed
INDICATIVE

Present	Imperfect	Preterite	Future	Conditional
quepo	cabía	**cup**e	**cabr**é	**cabr**ía
cabes	etc.	**cup**iste	**cabr**ás	**cabr**ías
cabe		**cup**o	**cabr**á	**cabr**ía
cabemos		**cup**imos	**cabr**emos	**cabr**íamos
cabéis		**cup**isteis	**cabr**éis	**cabr**íamos
caben		**cup**ieron	**cabr**án	**cabr**ían

SUBJUNCTIVE

Present	Imperfect	Future (almost obsolete)
quepa	**cupi**era/**cupi**ese	**cupi**ere
quepas	**cupi**eras/**cupi**eses	
quepa	**cupi**era/**cupi**ese	
quepamos	**cupi**éramos/**cupi**ésemos	
quepáis	**cupi**erais/**cupi**eseis	
quepan	**cupi**eran/**cupi**esen	

13.3.9   *Caer*

Infinitive caer			*Gerund* cayendo	
Past participle caído			*Imperative* cae caed	

INDICATIVE

Present	Imperfect (regular)	Preterite (regular)	Future	Conditional
caigo	caía	caí	caeré	caerás
caes	caías	caíste	etc.	etc.
cae	caía	cayó		
caemos	caíamos	caímos		
caéis	caíais	caísteis		
caen	caían	cayeron		

SUBJUNCTIVE

Present	Imperfect (regular)	Future (almost obsolete)
caiga	cayera/cayese	cayere
caigas	cayeras/cayeses	etc.
caiga	cayera/cayese	
caigamos	cayéramos/cayésemos	
caigáis	cayerais/cayeseis	
caigan	cayeran/cayesen	

13.3.10   Verbs ending in *-cer*

All verbs ending in *-cer* conjugate as below except the regular *ejercer*, *(con)vencer* and *mecer*, and *escocer*, *(re)cocer* and *(re)torcer* (see 13.3.12).

Infinitive -cer			*Gerund* -ciendo	
Past participle -cido			*Imperative* -ce -ced	

INDICATIVE

Present	Imperfect (regular)	Preterite (regular)	Future	Conditional
-zco	-cía	-cí	-ceré	-cería
-ces	-cías	-ciste	etc.	etc.
-ce	-cía	-ció		
-cemos	-cíamos	-cimos		
-céis	-cíais	-cisteis		
-cen	-cían	-cieron		

SUBJUNCTIVE

Present	Imperfect (regular)	Future (almost obsolete) (regular)
-zca	-ciera/-ciese	-ciere
-zcas	-cieras/cieses	-cieres
-zca	-ciera/ciese	-ciere
-zcamos	-ciéramos/-ciésemos	-ciéremos
-zcáis	-cierais/cieseis	-ciereis
-zcan	-cieran/ciesen	-cieren

Further examples:

conocer	conozco, conoces; conozca, conozcas, conozca, etc.
merecer	merezco, mereces; merezca, merezcas, merezca, etc.
nacer	nazco, naces, nace; nazca, nazcas, nazca, etc.

13.3.11   Cerrar

A radical changing verb. The endings are those of regular -ar verbs, but the e of the stem changes to ie under stress. This is a very common type:

Infinitive cerrar   *Gerund* cerrando
Past participle cerrado   *Imperative* cierra cerrad

INDICATIVE

Present	Imperfect	Preterite	Future	Conditional
cierro	cerraba	cerré	cerraré	cerraría
cierras	etc.	etc.	etc.	etc.
cierra				
cerramos				
cerráis				
cierran				

SUBJUNCTIVE

Present	Imperfect	Future (almost obsolete)
cierre	cerrara/cerrase	cerrare
cierres	etc.	etc.
cierre		
cerremos		
cerréis		
cierren		

13.3.12   Cocer

This, and verbs like it, e.g. *torcer*, *retorcer*, conjugates exactly like *mover* save for the predictable spelling changes $c > z$ before a, o:

Infinitive cocer   *Gerund* cociendo
Past participle cocido   *Imperative* cuece coced

INDICATIVE

Present	Imperfect	Preterite	Future	Conditional
cuezo	cocía	cocí	coceré	cocería
cueces	etc.	etc.	etc.	etc.
cuece				
cocemos				
cocéis				
cuecen				

SUBJUNCTIVE

Present	Imperfect	Future (almost obsolete)
cueza	cociera/cociese	cociere
cuezas	etc.	etc.
cueza		
cozamos		
cozáis		
cuezan		

13.3.13   *Construir*

Verbs in *-uir* are not uncommon. An unstressed intervocalic *i* is spelt *y*, e.g. *construyó* for the expected *construió, and an unexpected *y* is inserted in a number of forms, e.g. *construyes* for expected *construes, etc.

Infinitive construir   *Gerund* construyendo
Past participle construido†   *Imperative* construye construid
†No written accent because *u* and *i* are both 'weak' vowels. Contrast *leído*, *creído*, etc. See chapter on spelling for explanation.

INDICATIVE

Present	Imperfect	Preterite	Future	Conditional
construyo	construía	construí	construiré	construiría
construyes	etc.	construiste	etc.	etc.
construye		construyó		
construimos		construimos		
construís		construisteis		
construyen		construyeron		

SUBJUNCTIVE

Present	Imperfect	Future (almost obsolete)
construya	construyera/construyese	construyere
construyas	etc.	etc.
construya		
construyamos		
construyáis		
construyan		

Note   *Argüir* is spelt with a dieresis whenever the *u* is followed by *i*. This preserves the pronunciation /gwi/: *arguyo*, *argüimos*, *argüí*, *arguya*, etc.

13.3.14   *Contar*

A radical changing verb. The endings are regular but the *o* of the stem changes to *ue* when stressed:

Infinitive contar   *Gerund* contando
Past participle contado   *Imperative* cuenta contad

INDICATIVE

Present	Imperfect	Preterite	Future	Conditional
cuento	contaba	conté	contaré	contaría
cuentas	etc.	etc.	etc.	etc.
cuenta				
contamos				
contáis				
cuentan				

SUBJUNCTIVE

Present	Imperfect	Future (almost obsolete)
cuente	contara/contase	contare
cuentes	etc.	etc.
cuente		
contemos		
contéis		
cuenten		

13.3.15 *Dar* (highly irregular)

Infinitive dar   *Gerund* dando
Past participle dado   *Imperative* da dad

INDICATIVE

Present	Imperfect	Preterite	Future	Conditional
doy	daba	di	daré	daría
das	dabas	diste	etc.	etc.
da	daba	dio†		
damos	dábamos	dimos		
dais	dabais	disteis		
dan	daban	dieron		

†No written accent since 1959

SUBJUNCTIVE

Present	Imperfect	Future (almost obsolete)
dé†	diera/diese	diere
des	dieras/dieses	etc.
dé†	diera/diese	
demos	diéramos/diésemos	
deis	dierais/dieseis	
den	dieran/diesen	

†The accent serves to distinguish the forms from the preposition *de*.

The imperative singular and third-person singular of the present indicative and subjunctive and the imperative singular of compounds of *dar* (little used) is stressed on the final vowel: *desdá*, *desdé*.

13.3.16 *Decir* (highly irregular)

Infinitive decir   *Gerund* diciendo
Past participle dicho   *Imperative* di decid

INDICATIVE

Present	Imperfect	Preterite	Future	Conditional
digo	decía	dije	diré	diría
dices	decías	dijiste	dirás	dirías
dice	decía	dijo	dirá	diría
decimos	decíamos	dijimos	diremos	diríamos
decís	decíais	dijisteis	diréis	diríais
dicen	decían	dijeron	dirán	dirían

SUBJUNCTIVE

Present	Imperfect	Future (almost obsolete)
diga	dijera/dijese	dijere
digas	dijeras/dijeses	etc.
diga	dijera/dijese	
digamos	dijéramos/dijésemos	
digáis	dijerais/dijeseis	
digan	dijeran/dijesen	

13.3.17   *Discernir*

This shows the common modification *e > ie*, but this type is very unusual in the *-ir* conjugation: only *cernir*, *concernir* (3rd person only) and the rare *hendir* conjugate like it:

Infinitive discernir
Past participle discernido

Gerund discerniendo
Imperative discierne discernid

INDICATIVE

Present	Imperfect	Preterite	Future	Conditional
discierno	discernía	discerní	discerniré	discerniría
disciernes	etc.	discerniste	etc.	etc.
discierne		discernió†		
discernimos		discernimos		
discernís		discernisteis		
disciernen		discernieron†		

SUBJUNCTIVE

Present	Imperfect	Future (almost obsolete)
discierna	discerniera/discerniese	discerniere
disciernas	etc.	etc.
discierna		
discernamos		
discernáis		
disciernan		

†not **discirnió*, **discirnieron*.

13.3.18   *Dormir, morir*

Dormir and *morir* are the only verbs of this kind.

Apart from the common change *o > ue*, the third-person preterite stem vowel is *u*. The *u* also appears in the 1st and 2nd plural of the present subjunctive and in the gerund.

Infinitive dormir
Past participle dormido (muerto)

Gerund durmiendo
Imperative duerme dormid

INDICATIVE

Present	Imperfect	Preterite	Future	Conditional
duermo	dormía	dormí	dormiré	dormiría
duermes	etc.	dormiste	etc.	etc.
duerme		durmió		
dormimos		dormimos		
dormís		dormisteis		
duermen		durmieron		

SUBJUNCTIVE

Present	Imperfect	Future (almost obsolete)
duerma	durmiera/durmiese	durmiere
duermas	durmieras/durmieses	etc.
duerma	durmiera/durmiese	
durmamos	durmiéramos/durmiésemos	
durmáis	durmierais/durmieseis	
duerman	durmieran/durmiesen	

13.3.19   *Erguir(se)*

This verb has alternative forms in some of its tenses, the forms with *y*- being more common. Examples: *no te agaches – ponte erguido* 'stop slouching – sit up', *se irguió como una serpiente* 'he rose up like a snake', *el perro irguió las orejas* 'the dog pricked up its ears', etc.

Infinitive erguir   *Gerund* irguiendo
Past participle erguido   *Imperative* yergue/irgue erguid

INDICATIVE

Present	Imperfect	Preterite	Future	Conditional
yergo/irgo	erguía	erguí	erguiré	erguiría
yergues/irgues	etc.	erguiste	etc.	etc.
yergue/irgue		irguió		
erguimos		erguimos		
erguís		erguisteis		
yerguen/irguen		irguieron		

SUBJUNCTIVE

Present	Imperfect	Future (almost obsolete)
yerga/irga	irguiera/irguiese	irguiere
yergas/irgas	etc.	etc.
yerga/irga		
yergamos/irgamos		
yergáis/irgáis		
yergan/irgan		

13.3.20   *Errar*

This verb conjugates like *cerrar*, i.e. *e>ie* when stressed, but the *ie* is written *ye*. In the Southern Cone and Colombia it is often made regular, i.e. *erro, erras, erra*, etc.

Infinitive errar   *Gerund* errando
Past participle errado   *Imperative* yerra errad

INDICATIVE

Present	Imperfect	Preterite	Future	Conditional
yerro	erraba	erré	erraré	erraría
yerras	etc.	etc.	etc.	etc.
yerra				
erramos				
erráis				
yerran				

SUBJUNCTIVE

Present	Imperfect	Future (almost obsolete)
yerre	errara/errase	errare
yerres	etc.	etc.
yerre		
erremos		
erréis		
yerren		

13.3.21   *Estar* and *Haber*
See Table 5, p. 190 and Table 6, p. 191.

13.3.22   *Hacer* (highly irregular)
There are several compounds, e.g. *deshacer, contrahacer*.

Infinitive hacer   *Gerund* haciendo
Past participle hecho   *Imperative* haz haced

INDICATIVE

Present	Imperfect	Preterite	Future	Conditional
hago	hacía	hice	haré	haría
haces	hacías	hiciste	harás	harías
hace	hacía	hizo	hará	haría
hacemos	hacíamos	hicimos	haremos	haríamos
hacéis	hacíais	hicisteis	haréis	haríais
hacen	hacían	hicieron	harán	harían

SUBJUNCTIVE

Present	Imperfect	Future (almost obsolete)
haga	hiciera/hiciese	hiciere
hagas	hicieras/hicieses	etc.
haga	hiciera/hiciese	
hagamos	hiciéramos/hiciésemos	
hagáis	hicierais/hicieseis	
hagan	hicieran/hiciesen	

13.3.23   *Ir* (highly irregular)

Infinitive ir   *Gerund* yendo
Past participle ido   *Imperative* ve id (see note)

INDICATIVE

Present	Imperfect	Preterite	Future	Conditional
voy	iba	fui†	iré	iría
vas	ibas	fuiste	irás	irías
va	iba	fue†	irá	iría
vamos	íbamos	fuimos	iremos	iríamos
vais	ibais	fuisteis	iréis	iríais
van	iban	fueron	irán	irían

†no written accent since 1959.

Note: the plural imperative of *irse* is irregularly *idos* (for the predicted **íos*).

SUBJUNCTIVE

Present	Imperfect	Future (almost obsolete)
vaya	fuera/fuese	fuere
vayas	fueras/fueses	etc.
vaya	fuera/fuese	
vayamos	fuéramos/fuésemos	
vayáis	fuerais/fueseis	
vayan	fueran/fuesen	

13.3.24 *Jugar*

This verb is unique in that *u > ue* when stressed. Note *g > gu* before *e*.

Infinitive jugar   *Gerund* jugando
Past participle jugado   *Imperative* ju**e**ga jugad

INDICATIVE

Present	Imperfect	Preterite	Future	Conditional
juego	jugaba	jugué	jugaré	jugaría
juegas	etc.	etc.	etc.	etc.
juega				
jugamos				
jugáis				
juegan				

SUBJUNCTIVE

Present	Imperfect	Future (almost obsolete)
juegue	jugara/jugase	jugare
juegues	etc.	etc.
juegue		
juguemos		
juguéis		
jueguen		

13.3.25 *Lucir*

Verbs in *-ducir* are conjugated like *producir*, see 13.3.36.

Infinitive lucir   *Gerund* luciendo
Past participle lucido   *Imperative* luce lucid

INDICATIVE

Present	Imperfect	Preterite	Future	Conditional
luzco	lucía	lucí	luciré	luciría
luces	etc.	etc.	etc.	etc.
luce				
lucimos				
lucís				
lucen				

SUBJUNCTIVE

Present	Imperfect	Future (almost obsolete)
luzca	luciera/luciese, etc.	luciere, etc.
luzcas		
luzca		
luzcamos		
luzcáis		
luzcan		

13.3.26   *Maldecir* (also *bendecir*)

Conjugated like *decir* in some tenses, and regularly in others. Forms which differ from *decir* are shown in bold type:

Infinitive maldecir   *Gerund* maldiciendo
Past participle mal**decido**   *Imperative* mal**dice** maldecid

INDICATIVE

Present	Imperfect	Preterite	Future	Conditional
maldigo	maldecía	maldije	mal**deciré**	mal**deciría**
maldices	etc.	maldijiste	mal**decirás**	mal**decirías**
maldice		maldijo	mal**decirá**	mal**deciría**
maldecimos		maldijimos	mal**deciremos**	mal**deciríamos**
maldecís		maldijisteis	mal**deciréis**	mal**deciríais**
maldicen		maldijeron	mal**decirán**	mal**decirían**

SUBJUNCTIVE

Present	Imperfect	Future (almost obsolete)
maldiga	maldijera/maldijese	maldijere
maldigas	maldijeras/maldijeses	etc.
maldiga	maldijera/maldijese	
maldigamos	maldijéramos/maldijésemos	
maldigáis	maldijerais/maldijeseis	
maldigan	maldijeran/maldijesen	

13.3.27   *Mover*

A radical changing verb. The endings are regular but the *o* of the stem changes to *ue* when stressed.

Infinitive mover   *Gerund* moviendo
Past participle movido   *Imperative* m**ue**ve, moved

INDICATIVE

Present	Imperfect	Preterite	Future	Conditional
m**ue**vo	movía	moví	moveré	movería
m**ue**ves	etc.	etc.	etc.	etc.
m**ue**ve				
movemos				
movéis				
m**ue**ven				

SUBJUNCTIVE

Present	Imperfect	Future (almost obsolete)
m**ue**va	moviera/moviese	moviere
m**ue**vas	etc.	etc.
m**ue**va		
movamos		
mováis		
m**ue**van		

13.3.28   *Oír* (also *desoír*)

Infinitive oír   *Gerund* oyendo
Past participle oído   *Imperative* oye oíd

INDICATIVE

Present	Imperfect	Preterite	Future	Conditional
oigo	oía	oí	oiré	oiría
oyes	oías	oíste	etc.	etc.
oye	oía	oyó		
oímos	oíamos	oímos		
oís	oíais	oísteis		
oyen	oían	oyeron		

SUBJUNCTIVE

Present	Imperfect	Future (almost obsolete)
oiga	oyera/oyese	oyere
oigas	oyeras/oyeses	etc.
oiga	oyera/oyese	
oigamos	oyéramos/oyésemos	
oigáis	oyerais/oyeseis	
oigan	oyeran/oyesen	

13.3.29 *Oler*

Oler is conjugated like *mover*, but shows the predictable spelling *hue* for *ue* when this diphthong is at the beginning of a word:

Infinitive oler
Past participle olido

Gerund oliendo
Imperative **hue**le oled

INDICATIVE

Present	Imperfect	Preterite	Future	Conditional
huelo	olía	olí	oleré	olería
hueles	etc.	etc.	etc.	etc.
huele				
olemos				
oléis				
huelen				

SUBJUNCTIVE

Present	Imperfect	Future (almost obsolete)
huela	oliera/oliese	oliere
huelas	etc.	etc.
huela		
olamos		
oláis		
huelan		

13.3.30 *Pedir*

The endings are regular, but the *e* of the stem changes to *i* when stressed, and in the gerund, 3rd-person preterite and past and future subjunctive:

Infinitive pedir
Past participle pedido

Gerund pidiendo
Imperative **pi**de pedid

INDICATIVE

Present	Imperfect	Preterite	Future	Conditional
pido	pedía	pedí	pediré	pediría
pides	etc.	pediste	etc.	etc.
pide		pidió		
pedimos		pedimos		
pedís		pedisteis		
piden		pidieron		

SUBJUNCTIVE

Present	Imperfect	Future (almost obsolete)
pida	pidiera/pidiese	pidiere
pidas	pidieras/pidieses	etc.
pida	pidiera/pidiese	
pidamos	pidiéramos/pidiésemos	
pidáis	pidierais/pidieseis	
pidan	pidieran/pidiesen	

13.3.31   *Perder*

A radical changing verb. The endings are regular, but the *e* of the stem changes to *ie* when stressed. This is a common type:

Infinitive perder   *Gerund* perdiendo
Past participle perdido   *Imperative* pierde perded

INDICATIVE

Present	Imperfect	Preterite	Future	Conditional
pierdo	perdía	perdí	perderé	perdería
pierdes	etc.	etc.	etc.	etc.
pierde				
perdemos				
perdéis				
pierden				

SUBJUNCTIVE

Present	Imperfect	Future (almost obsolete)
pierda	perdiera/perdiese	perdiere
pierdas	etc.	etc.
pierda		
perdamos		
perdáis		
pierdan		

13.3.32   *Placer*

This verb is rarely found except in the third person, and even then only in flowery literary language.

It is conjugated like *nacer* (see 13.3.10) except that alternative irregular forms (none of them nowadays in use) exist in the third person of three tenses:

Preterite	Present subjunctive	Imperfect subjunctive
sing. plugo	plega	pluguiera/pluguiese
plur. pluguieron		

13.3.33 *Poder* (highly irregular)

Infinitive poder   *Gerund* pudiendo
Past participle podido   *Imperative* not used

INDICATIVE

Present	Imperfect	Preterite	Future	Conditional
puedo	podía	pude	**pod**ré	**pod**ría
puedes	etc.	pudiste	**pod**rás	**pod**rías
puede		**pudo**	**pod**rá	**pod**ría
podemos		pudimos	**pod**remos	**pod**ríamos
podéis		pudisteis	**pod**réis	**pod**ríais
pueden		pudieron	**pod**rán	**pod**rían

SUBJUNCTIVE

Present	Imperfect	Future (almost obsolete)
pueda	pudiera/pudiese	pudiere
puedas	pudieras/pudieses	etc.
pueda	pudiera/pudiese	
podamos	pudiéramos/pudiésemos	
podáis	pudierais/pudieseis	
puedan	pudieran/pudiesen	

13.3.34 *Poner* (highly irregular)

And also compounds like *componer, imponer, proponer, descomponer, suponer*, etc.

Infinitive poner   *Gerund* poniendo
Past participle **puesto**   *Imperative* **pon**† poned

INDICATIVE

Present	Imperfect	Preterite	Future	Conditional
pongo	ponía	**puse**	**pond**ré	**pond**ría
pones	ponías	**pusiste**	**pond**rás	**pond**rías
pone	ponía	**puso**	**pond**rá	**pond**ría
ponemos	poníamos	**pusimos**	**pond**remos	**pond**ríamos
ponéis	poníais	**pusisteis**	**pond**réis	**pond**ríais
ponen	ponían	**pusieron**	**pond**rán	**pond**rían

†Accent on imperative of compounds, e.g. *componer – compón*.

SUBJUNCTIVE

Present	Imperfect	Future (almost obsolete)
ponga	pu**siera**/pu**siese**	pusiere
pongas	pu**sieras**/pu**sieses**	etc.
ponga	pu**siera**/pu**siese**	
pongamos	pu**siéramos**/pu**siésemos**	
pongáis	pu**sierais**/pu**sieseis**	
pongan	pu**sieran**/pu**siesen**	

13.3.35   *Poseer*

This verb and others like it, e.g. *leer*, *creer*, requires that an intervocalic *y* sound be written *y* and not *i*:

Infinitive poseer   *Gerund* poseyendo
Past participle poseído   *Imperative* posee, poseed

INDICATIVE

Present	Imperfect	Preterite	Future	Conditional
poseo	poseía	poseí	poseeré	poseería
posees	etc.	poseíste	etc.	etc.
posee		poseyó		
poseemos		poseímos		
poseéis		poseísteis		
poseen		poseyeron		

SUBJUNCTIVE

Present	Imperfect	Future (almost obsolete)
posea	poseyera/poseyese	poseyere
poseas	poseyeras/poseyeses	etc.
posea	poseyera/poseyese	
poseamos	poseyéramos/poseyésemos	
poseáis	poseyerais/poseyeseis	
posean	poseyeran/poseyesen	

13.3.36   *Producir*

Conjugated like *lucir* except for the preterite and for forms (past and future subjunctive) based on the preterite stem:

Infinitive producir   *Gerund* produciendo
Past participle producido   *Imperative* produce producid

INDICATIVE

Present	Imperfect	Preterite	Future	Conditional
produzco	producía	produje	produciré	produciría
produces	etc.	produjiste	etc.	etc.
produce		produjo		
producimos		produjimos		
producís		produjisteis		
producen		produjeron†		

†Note *ie*>*e* after *j*.

SUBJUNCTIVE

Present	Imperfect	Future (almost obsolete)
produzca	produjera/produjese	produjere
produzcas	produjeras/produjeses	
produzca	produjera/produjese	
produzcamos	produjéramos/produjésemos	
produzcáis	produjerais/produjeseis	
produzcan	produjeran/produjesen	

Note   Regularized forms of the preterite like **produció*, **conducí* are common mistakes of foreigners and even some natives, but they are stigmatized as illiterate.

13.3.37   *Querer* (highly irregular)

Infinitive querer   *Gerund* queriendo
Past participle querido   *Imperative* quiere quered
INDICATIVE

Present	Imperfect	Preterite	Future	Conditional
quiero	quería	**quise**	**querré**	**querría**
quieres	querías	**quisiste**	**querrás**	**querrías**
quiere	quería	**quiso**	**querrá**	**querría**
queremos	queríamos	**quisimos**	**querremos**	**querríamos**
queréis	queríais	**quisisteis**	**querréis**	**querríais**
quieren	querían	**quisieron**	**querrán**	**querrían**

SUBJUNCTIVE

Present	Imperfect	Future (almost obsolete)
quiera	**quisiera/quisiese**	**quisiere**
quieras	**quisieras/quisieses**	etc.
quiera	**quisiera/quisiese**	
queramos	**quisiéramos/quisiésemos**	
queráis	**quisierais/quisieseis**	
quieran	**quisieran/quisiesen**	

13.3.38   *Reír*

This verb is in fact conjugated in almost the same way as *pedir*, although the absence of an intervocalic consonant obscures the similarity:

Infinitive reír   *Gerund* riendo
Past participle reído   *Imperative* ríe reíd
INDICATIVE

Present	Imperfect	Preterite	Future	Conditional
río	reía	reí	reiré	reiría
ríes	reías	reíste	etc.	etc.
ríe	reía	**rió**†		
reímos	reíamos	reímos		
reís	reíais	reísteis		
ríen	reían	rieron		

†Note written accent. The only third-person singular preterites in *-io* which have no written accent are *dio* (from *dar*) and *vio* (from *ver*).

SUBJUNCTIVE

Present	Imperfect	Future (almost obsolete)
ría	riera/riese	riere
rías	rieras/rieses	etc.
ría	riera/riese	
riamos	riéramos/riésemos	
riais	rierais/rieseis	
rían	rieran/riesen	

13.3.39   *Reñir*

This and other verbs in *-eñir* are conjugated like *pedir*, except that, as usual, *ie* > *e* and *ió* > *ó* after *ñ*:

Infinitive reñir
Past participle reñido

Gerund riñendo
Imperative riñe reñid

INDICATIVE

Present	Imperfect	Preterite	Future	Conditional
riño	reñía	reñí	reñiré	reñiría
riñes	etc.	reñiste	etc.	etc.
riñe		riñó		
reñimos		reñimos		
reñís		reñisteis		
riñen		riñeron		

SUBJUNCTIVE

Present	Imperfect	Future (almost obsolete)
riña	riñera/riñese	riñere
riñas	riñeras/riñeses	etc.
riña	riñera/riñese	
riñamos	riñéramos/riñésemos	
riñáis	riñerais/riñeseis	
riñan	riñeran/riñesen	

13.3.40   *Roer*

The bracketed forms are less common alternatives. In practice the first-person singular indicative is avoided and may be expressed by *estoy royendo* 'I'm gnawing'.

Infinitive roer
Past participle roído

Gerund royendo
Imperative roe roed

INDICATIVE

Present	Imperfect	Preterite	Future	Conditional
roo (roigo, royo)	roía	roí	roeré	roería
roes	etc.	roíste	etc.	etc.
roe		royó		
roemos		roímos		
roéis		roísteis		
roen		royeron		

SUBJUNCTIVE

Present	Imperfect	Future (almost obsolete)
roa (roiga, roya)	royera/royese	royere
roas (roigas, royas)	royeras/royeses	etc.
roa (roiga, roya)	royera/royese	
roamos (roigamos, royamos)	royéramos/royésemos	
roáis (roigáis, royáis)	royerais/royeseis	
roan (roigan, royan)	royeran/royesen	

13.3.41   *Saber* (highly irregular)

Infinitive saber
Past participle sabido

Gerund sabiendo
Imperative sabe sabed

INDICATIVE

Present	Imperfect	Preterite	Future	Conditional
sé	sabía	supe	sabré	sabría
sabes	sabías	supiste	sabrás	sabrías
sabe	sabía	supo	sabrá	sabría
sabemos	sabíamos	supimos	sabremos	sabríamos
sabéis	sabíais	supisteis	sabréis	sabríais
saben	sabían	supieron	sabrán	sabrían

SUBJUNCTIVE

Present	Imperfect	Future (almost obsolete)
sepa	supiera/supiese	supiere
sepas	supieras/supieses	etc.
sepa	supiera/supiese	
sepamos	supiéramos/supiésemos	
sepáis	supierais/supieseis	
sepan	supieran/supiesen	

13.3.42   *Salir*

Infinitive salir
Past participle salido

Gerund saliendo
Imperative sal salid

INDICATIVE

Present	Imperfect	Preterite	Future	Conditional
salgo	salía	salí	saldré	saldría
sales	etc.	etc.	saldrás	saldrías
sale			saldrá	saldría
salimos			saldremos	saldríamos
salís			saldréis	saldríais
salen			saldrán	saldrían

SUBJUNCTIVE

Present	Imperfect	Future (almost obsolete)
salga	saliera/saliese	saliere
salgas	etc.	etc.
salga		
salgamos		
salgáis		
salgan		

13.3.43   *Sentir*

A common type of *-ir* verb. The endings are regular, but the stem vowel changes to *ie* or to *i* in certain forms:

Infinitive sentir   *Gerund* sintiendo
Past participle sentido   *Imperative* siente sentid
INDICATIVE

Present	Imperfect	Preterite	Future	Conditional
siento	sentía	sentí	sentiré	sentiría
sientes	sentías	sentiste	etc.	etc.
siente	sentía	sintió		
sentimos	sentíamos	sentimos		
sentís	sentíais	sentisteis		
sienten	sentían	sintieron		

SUBJUNCTIVE

Present	Imperfect	Future (almost obsolete)
sienta	sintiera/sintiese	sintiere
sientas	sintieras/sintieses	etc.
sienta	sintiera/sintiese	
sintamos	sintiéramos/sintiésemos	
sintáis	sintierais/sintieseis	
sientan	sintieran/sintiesen	

13.3.44   *Ser*
See table 4, p. 189.

13.3.45   *Tener* (highly irregular)
Infinitive tener   *Gerund* teniendo
Past participle tenido   *Imperative* **ten** tened
INDICATIVE

Present	Imperfect	Preterite	Future	Conditional
tengo	tenía	**tuve**	**tend**ré	**tend**ría
tienes	tenías	**tuviste**	**tend**rás	**tend**rías
tiene	tenía	**tuvo**	**tend**rá	**tend**ría
tenemos	teníamos	**tuvimos**	**tend**remos	**tend**ríamos
tenéis	teníais	**tuvisteis**	**tend**réis	**tend**ríais
tienen	tenían	**tuvieron**	**tend**rán	**tend**rían

Note imperative of *detener* = *detén, retener* = *retén*.

SUBJUNCTIVE

Present	Imperfect	Future (almost obsolete)
tenga	**tuviera/tuviese**	**tuviere**
tengas	**tuvieras/tuvieses**	etc.
tenga	**tuviera/tuviese**	
tengamos	**tuviéramos/tuviésemos**	
tengáis	**tuvierais/tuvieseis**	
tengan	**tuvieran/tuviesen**	

13.3.46   *Traer* (highly irregular)
Infinitive traer   *Gerund* trayendo
Past participle traído   *Imperative* trae traed

INDICATIVE

Present	Imperfect	Preterite	Future	Conditional
traigo	traía	**traje**†	traeré	traería
traes	traías	**traj**iste	etc.	etc.
trae	traía	**traj**o		
traemos	traíamos	**traj**imos		
traéis	traíais	**traj**isteis		
traen	traían	**traj**eron (not *trajieron)		

†*truje, trujiste* etc. is found in Golden-Age texts and survives sporadically in dialects.

SUBJUNCTIVE

Present	Imperfect	Future (almost obsolete)
traiga	**traj**era/**traj**ese	**traj**ere
traigas	**traj**eras/**traj**eses	etc.
traiga	**traj**era/**traj**ese	
traigamos	**traj**éramos/**traj**ésemos	
traigáis	**traj**erais/**traj**eseis	
traigan	**traj**eran/**traj**esen	

13.3.47   *Valer*

Infinitive valer   *Gerund* valiendo
Past participle valido   *Imperative* vale valed

INDICATIVE

Present	Imperfect	Preterite	Future	Conditional
valgo	valía	valí	**vald**ré	**vald**ría
vales	etc.	etc.	**vald**rás	**vald**rías
vale			**vald**rá	**vald**ría
valemos			**vald**remos	**vald**ríamos
valéis			**vald**réis	**vald**ríais
valen			**vald**rán	**vald**rían

SUBJUNCTIVE

Present	Imperfect	Future (almost obsolete)
valga	valiera/valiese	valiere
valgas	valieras/valieses	etc.
valga	valiera/valiese	
valgamos	valiéramos/valiésemos	
valgáis	valierais/valieseis	
valgan	valieran/valiesen	

13.3.48   *Venir* (highly irregular)

Infinitive venir   *Gerund* viniendo
Past participle venido   *Imperative* ven venid

INDICATIVE

Present	Imperfect	Preterite	Future	Conditional
vengo	venía	**vin**e	**vend**ré	**vend**ría
vienes	venías	**vin**iste	**vend**rás	**vend**rías
viene	venía	**vin**o	**vend**rá	**vend**ría
venimos	veníamos	**vin**imos	**vend**remos	**vend**ríamos
venís	veníais	**vin**isteis	**vend**réis	**vend**ríais
vienen	venían	**vin**ieron	**vend**rán	**vend**rían

SUBJUNCTIVE

Present	Imperfect	Future (almost obsolete)
venga	viniera/viniese	viniere
vengas	vinieras/vinieses	etc.
venga	viniera/viniese	
vengamos	viniéramos/viniésemos	
vengáis	vinierais/vinieseis	
vengan	vinieran/viniesen	

13.3.49   *Ver*

Note written accent in compounds forms: *prevés, prevé, prevén* (pres. indicative), *preví* (1st-pers. preterite), *prevé* (imperative).

Infinitive ver   *Gerund* viendo
Past participle **visto**   *Imperative* ve ved

INDICATIVE

Present	Imperfect	Preterite	Future	Conditional
veo	veía	vi	veré	vería
ves	veías	viste	etc.	etc.
ve	veía	vio†		
vemos	veíamos	vimos		
veis	veías	visteis		
ven	veían	vieron		

†No written accent since 1959

SUBJUNCTIVE

Present	Imperfect	Future (almost obsolete)
vea	viera/viese	viere
veas	etc.	etc.
vea		
veamos		
veáis		
vean		

13.3.50   *Yacer*

This verb is nowadays only used in the third person, and even then only in rather flowery literary style. It is conjugated like *nacer* but alternative forms are found:

Infinitive yacer   *Gerund* yaciendo
Past participle yacido   *Imperative* yace/yaz yaced

INDICATIVE

Present	Imperfect	Preterite	Future	Conditional
yazco†	yacía	yací	yaceré	yacería
yaces	etc.	etc.	etc.	etc.
yace				
yacemos				
yacéis				
yacen				

†Alternatively *yazgo, yago*

SUBJUNCTIVE

Present	Imperfect	Future (almost obsolete)
yazca†	yaciera/yaciese	yaciere
yazcas	etc.	etc.
yazca		
yazcamos		
yazcáis		
yazcan		

†The present subjunctive may be formed from the alternative first-person indicative bases, e.g. *yazga/yaga*, *yazgas/yagas*, etc.

13.4 List of irregular verbs

A number of excessively rare verbs have been omitted but this is no guarantee that verbs listed are in common use today. Bracketed forms indicate verbs which may be seen in the infinitive or past participle forms, which are often the only surviving remains of the verbs which are otherwise obsolete (cf. *aterirse*). For verbs in *re-* not listed here, see root verb.

Infinitive	model	Infinitive	model
abastecer	*-cer* 13.3.10	*andar*	see 13.3.5
abolir	see 13.3.2	*anochecer*	*-cer* 13.3.10
aborrecer	*-cer* 13.3.10	*anteponer*	*poner* 13.3.34
abrir		*apacentar*	*cerrar* 13.3.11
past participle *abierto*		*aparecer*	*-cer* 13.3.10
absolver	*mover* 13.3.27	*apetecer*	*-cer* 13.3.10
past participle *absuelto*		*apostar*	*contar* 13.3.14
abstenerse	*tener* 13.3.45	regular if it means 'to post a sentry'	
abstraer	*traer* 13.3.46	*apretar*	*cerrar* 13.3.11
acaecer	*-cer* 13.3.10	*aprobar*	*contar* 13.3.14
third-person only		*argüir*	*construir* 13.3.13
acertar	*cerrar* 13.3.11	*arrendar*	*cerrar* 13.3.11
acontecer	*-cer* 13.3.10	(*arrecirse*	*abolir* 13.3.2)
acordar	*contar* 13.3.14	*arrepentirse*	*sentir* 13.3.43
acostar (se)	*contar* 13.3.14	*ascender*	*perder* 13.3.31
acrecentar	*cerrar* 13.3.11	*asentar*	*cerrar* 13.3.11
adherir	*sentir* 13.3.43	*asentir*	*sentir* 13.3.43
adolecer	*-cer* 13.3.10	*asir*	see 13.3.6
adormecer	*-cer* 13.3.10	*asolar*	*contar* 13.3.14
adquirir	see 13.3.3	if it means 'to parch'. Usually regular	
aducir	*producir* 13.3.36	nowadays	
advertir	*sentir* 13.3.43	*atañer*	see table 3, p. 187, item 6
aferrar (se)	*cerrar* 13.3.11		
may be conjugated regularly		third-person sing. only	
agradecer	*-cer* 13.3.10	*atender*	*perder* 13.3.31
agredir	see 13.3.4	*atenerse*	*tener* 13.3.45
(*aguerrir*	*abolir* 13.3.2)	(*aterirse*	*abolir* 13.3.2)
alentar	*cerrar* 13.3.11	*atraer*	*traer* 13.3.46
almorzar	*contar* 13.3.14	*atravesar*	*cerrar* 13.3.11
z>c before *e*		*atribuir*	*construir* 13.3.13
amanecer	*-cer* 13.3.10	*avenir*	*venir* 13.3.48

Infinitive	model	Infinitive	model
aventar	*cerrar* 13.3.11	*consolar*	*contar* 13.3.14
avergonzar	*contar* 13.3.14	*consonar*	*contar* 13.3.14
z>c before *e*, and diphthong spelt *üe*,		*constituir*	*construir* 13.3.13
e.g. subjunctive *avergüence*		*constreñir*	*reñir* 13.3.39
balbucir	see 13.3.7	*construir*	see 13.3.13
bendecir	*maldecir* 13.3.26	*contar*	see 13.3.14
(*blandir*	*abolir* 13.3.2)	*contender*	*perder* 13.3.31
bruñir	*gruñir* see table	*contener*	*tener* 13.3.45
	3, p. 187 item 6	*contradecir*	*decir* 13.3.16
bullir	*zambullir* see table	*contraer*	*traer* 13.3.46
	3, p. 187 item 6	*contrahacer*	*hacer* 13.3.22
caber	see 13.3.8	*contraponer*	*poner* 13.3.34
caer	see 13.3.9	*contravenir*	*venir* 13.3.48
calentar	*cerrar* 13.3.11	*contribuir*	*construir* 13.3.13
carecer	*-cer* 13.3.10	*controvertir*	*sentir* 13.3.43
cegar	*cerrar* 13.3.11	*convalecer*	*-cer* 13.3.10
g>gu before *e*		*convenir*	*venir* 13.3.48
ceñir	*reñir* 13.3.39	*convertir*	*sentir* 13.3.43
cerner	*perder* 13.3.31	*corregir*	*pedir* 13.3.30
cernir	*discernir* 13.3.17	*g>j* before *a, o*	
cerrar	see 13.3.11	*costar*	*contar* 13.3.14
circunscribir		*crecer*	*-cer* 13.3.10
irreg. past participle *circunscrito*		*creer*	*poseer* 13.3.35
cocer	see 13.3.12	*cubrir*	
colar	*contar* 13.3.14	irreg. past participle *cubierto*	
colegir	*pedir* 13.3.30	*dar*	see 13.3.15
-g>j before *a, o*		*decaer*	*caer* 13.3.9
colgar	*contar* 13.3.14	*decir*	see 13.3.16
g>gu before *e*		*decrecer*	*-cer* 13.3.10
comenzar	*cerrar* 13.3.11	*deducir*	*producir* 13.3.36
z>c before *e*		*defender*	*perder* 13.3.31
compadecer	*-cer* 13.3.10	*deferir*	*sentir* 13.3.43
comparecer	*-cer* 13.3.10	*degollar*	*contar* 13.3.14
competir	*pedir* 13.3.30	diphthong spelt *üe*	
complacer	*-cer* 13.3.10	*demoler*	*mover* 13.3.27
componer	*poner* 13.3.34	*demostrar*	*contar* 13.3.14
comprobar	*contar* 13.3.14	*denegar*	*cerrar* 13.3.11
concebir	*pedir* 13.3.30	*g>gu* before *e*	
concernir	*discernir* 13.3.17	*denostar*	*contar* 13.3.14
concertar	*cerrar* 13.3.11	*dentar*	*cerrar* 13.3.11
concluir	*construir* 13.3.13	usually *dientar* nowadays	
concordar	*contar* 13.3.14	*deponer*	*poner* 13.3.34
condescender	*perder* 13.3.31	*derrengar*	*cerrar* 13.3.11
condolerse	*mover* 13.3.27	often regular nowadays; *g>gu* before *e*	
conducir	*producir* 13.3.36	*derretir*	*pedir* 13.3.30
conferir	*sentir* 13.3.43	*derrocar*	
confesar	*cerrar* 13.3.11	nowadays regular; *c>qu* before *e*	
confluir	*construir* 13.3.13	*desacertar*	*cerrar* 13.3.11
conmover	*mover* 13.3.27	*desacordar*	*contar* 13.3.14
conocer	*-cer* 13.3.10	*desagradecer*	*-cer* 13.3.10
conseguir	*pedir* 13.3.30	*desalentar*	*cerrar* 13.3.11
gu>g before *a, o*		*desandar*	*andar* 13.3.5
consentir	*sentir* 13.3.43	*desaparecer*	*-cer* 13.3.10

Infinitive	model
desapretar	*cerrar* 13.3.11
desaprobar	*contar* 13.3.14
desasosegar	*cerrar* 13.3.11
g > gu before *e*	
desatender	*perder* 13.3.31
desavenir	*venir* 13.3.48
descender	*perder* 13.3.31
desceñir	*reñir* 13.3.39
descolgar	*contar* 13.3.14
g > gu before *e*	
descollar	*contar* 13.3.14
descomedirse	*pedir* 13.3.30
descomponer	*poner* 13.3.34
desconcertar	*cerrar* 13.3.11
desconocer	*-cer* 13.3.10
desconsolar	*contar* 13.3.14
descontar	*contar* 13.3.14
desconvenir	*venir* 13.3.48
describir	
irreg. past participle *descrito*	
descubrir	
irreg. past participle *descubierto*	
desdecir	*decir* 13.3.16
desempedrar	*cerrar* 13.3.11
desengrosar	*contar* 13.3.14
desentenderse	*perder* 13.3.31
desenterrar	*cerrar* 13.3.11
desenvolver	*mover* 13.3.27
irreg. past participle *desenvuelto*	
desfallecer	*-cer* 13.3.10
desgobernar	*cerrar* 13.3.11
deshacer	*hacer* 13.3.22
deshelar	*cerrar* 13.3.11
desherrar	*cerrar* 13.3.11
desleír	*reír* 13.3.38
deslucir	*lucir* 13.3.25
desmembrar	*cerrar* 13.3.11
desmentir	*sentir* 13.3.43
desmerecer	*-cer* 13.3.10
desobedecer	*-cer* 13.3.10
desoír	*oír* 13.3.28
desollar	*contar* 13.3.14
desosar	see 13.2.2f
despedir	*pedir* 13.3.30
despedrar	*cerrar* 13.3.11
despertar	*cerrar* 13.3.11
despezar	*cerrar* 13.3.11
usually *despiezar*, regular; *z > c*	
before *e*	
desplacer	*-cer* 13.3.10
desplegar	*cerrar* 13.3.11
g > gu before *e*; now often regular	
despoblar	*contar* 13.3.14

Infinitive	model
desproveer	*poseer* 13.3.35
past participle *desprovisto/desproveído*	
desteñir	*reñir* 13.3.39
desterrar	*cerrar* 13.3.11
destituir	*construir* 13.3.13
destruir	*construir* 13.3.13
desvanecer	*-cer* 13.3.10
desvergonzarse	*contar* 13.3.14
z > c before *e*; diphthong spelt *üe*	
detener	*tener* 13.3.45
detraer	*traer* 13.3.46
devolver	*mover* 13.3.27
irreg. past participle *devuelto*	
diferir	*sentir* 13.3.43
digerir	*sentir* 13.3.43
diluir	*construir* 13.3.13
discernir	see 13.3.17
disentir	*sentir* 13.3.43
disminuir	*construir* 13.3.13
disolver	*mover* 13.3.27
irreg. past participle *disuelto*	
disponer	*poner* 13.3.34
distraer	*traer* 13.3.46
distender	*perder* 13.3.31
distribuir	*construir* 13.3.13
divertir	*sentir* 13.3.43
doler	*mover* 13.3.27
dormir	see 13.3.18
elegir	*pedir* 13.3.30
g > j before *a, o*	
embebecer	*-cer* 13.3.10
embellecer	*-cer* 13.3.10
embestir	*pedir* 13.3.30
embravecer	*-cer* 13.3.10
embrutecer	*-cer* 13.3.10
empedrar	*cerrar* 13.3.11
empequeñecer	*-cer* 13.3.10
empezar	*cerrar* 13.3.11
z > c before *e*	
empobrecer	*-cer* 13.3.10
enaltecer	*-cer* 13.3.10
enardecer	*-cer* 13.3.10
encanecer	*-cer* 13.3.10
encarecer	*-cer* 13.3.10
encender	*perder* 13.3.31
encerrar	*cerrar* 13.3.11
encomendar	*cerrar* 13.3.11
encontrar	*contar* 13.3.14
encubrir	
irreg. past participle *encubierto*	
endurecer	*-cer* 13.3.10
enflaquecer	*-cer* 13.3.10
enfurecer	*-cer* 13.3.10

Infinitive	model	Infinitive	model
engrandecer	*-cer* 13.3.10	*estreñir*	*reñir* 13.3.39
engreírse	*reír* 13.3.38	*excluir*	*construir* 13.3.13
engrosar	*contar* 13.3.14	*expedir*	*pedir* 13.3.30
now usually regular		*exponer*	*poner* 13.3.34
engullir	*zambullir* see	*extender*	*perder* 13.3.31
	table 3, p. 187	*extraer*	*traer* 13.3.46
	item 6	*fallecer*	*-cer* 13.3.10
enloquecer	*-cer* 13.3.10	*favorecer*	*-cer* 13.3.10
enmendar	*cerrar* 13.3.11	*florecer*	*-cer* 13.3.10
enmohecer	*-cer* 13.3.10	*fluir*	*construir* 13.3.13
enmudecer	*-cer* 13.3.10	*fortalecer*	*-cer* 13.3.10
ennegrecer	*-cer* 13.3.10	*forzar*	*contar* 13.3.14
ennoblecer	*-cer* 13.3.10	*z > c* before *e*	
enorgullecer	*-cer* 13.3.10	*fregar*	*cerrar* 13.3.11
enriquecer	*-cer* 13.3.10	*g > gu* before *e*	
enronquecer	*-cer* 13.3.10	*freír*	*reír* 13.3.38
ensangrentar	*cerrar* 13.3.11	past participle *frito*	
ensoberbecer(se)	*-cer* 13.3.10	*gemir*	*pedir* 13.3.30
ensordecer	*-cer* 13.3.10	*gobernar*	*cerrar* 13.3.11
entender	*perder* 13.3.31	*gruñir*	see table 3,
enternecer	*-cer* 13.3.10		p. 187 item 6
enterrar	*cerrar* 13.3.11	*guarecer*	*-cer* 13.3.10
entreabrir		*guarnecer*	*-cer* 13.3.10
irreg. past participle *entreabierto*		*haber*	see table 6, p. 191
entredecir	*decir* 13.3.16	*hacer*	see 13.3.22
entreoír	*oír* 13.3.28	*heder*	*perder* 13.3.31
entretener	*tener* 13.3.45	*helar*	*cerrar* 13.3.11
entrever	*ver* 13.3.49	*henchir*	*pedir* 13.3.30
3rd-person present singular *entrevé*		*hender*	*perder* 13.3.31
entristecer	*-cer* 13.3.10	*hendir*	*discernir* 13.3.17
entumecer(se)	*-cer* 13.3.10	*herir*	*sentir* 13.3.43
envanecer	*-cer* 13.3.10	*herrar*	*cerrar* 13.3.11
envejecer	*-cer* 13.3.10	*hervir*	*sentir* 13.3.43
envestir	*pedir* 13.3.30	*holgar*	*contar* 13.3.14
envilecer	*-cer* 13.3.10	*g > gu* before *e*	
envolver	*mover* 13.3.27	*hollar*	*contar* 13.3.14
irreg. past participle *envuelto*		*huir*	*construir* 13.3.13
equivaler	*valer* 13.3.47	*humedecer*	*-cer* 13.3.10
erguir	see 13.3.19	*impedir*	*pedir* 13.3.30
errar	see 13.3.20	*imponer*	*poner* 13.3.34
escabullirse	*zambullir* see	imperative singular *impón*	
	table 3, p. 187	*incluir*	*construir* 13.3.13
	item 6	*indisponer*	*poner* 13.3.34
escarmentar	*cerrar* 13.3.11	*inducir*	*producir* 13.3.36
escarnecer	*-cer* 13.3.10	*inferir*	*sentir* 13.3.43
escocer	*cocer* 13.3.12	*influir*	*construir* 13.3.13
escribir		*ingerir*	*sentir* 13.3.43
irreg. past. participle *escrito*		*inquirir*	*adquirir* 13.3.3
esforzar	*contar* 13.3.14	*instituir*	*construir* 13.3.13
z > c before *e*		*instruir*	*construir* 13.3.13
establecer	*-cer* 13.3.10	*interferir*	*sentir* 13.3.43
estar	see table 5, p. 190	*interponer*	*poner* 13.3.34
estremecer	*-cer* 13.3.10	*intervenir*	*venir* 13.3.48

Infinitive	model
introducir	*producir* 13.3.36
intuir	*construir* 13.3.13
invernar	*cerrar* 13.3.11
now usually regular	
invertir	*sentir* 13.3.43
investir	*pedir* 13.3.30
ir	see 13.3.23
jugar	see 13.3.24
languidecer	*-cer* 13.3.10
leer	*poseer* 13.3.35
llover	*mover* 13.3.27
lucir	see 13.3.25
maldecir	see 13.3.26
manifestar	*cerrar* 13.3.11
mantener	*tener* 13.3.45
medir	*pedir* 13.3.30
mentar	*cerrar* 13.3.11
mentir	*sentir* 13.3.43
merecer	*-cer* 13.3.10
merendar	*cerrar* 13.3.11
moler	*mover* 13.3.27
morder	*mover* 13.3.27
morir	see 13.3.18
mostrar	*contar* 13.3.14
mover	see 13.3.27
mullir	*zambullir* see table 3, p. 187
nacer	*-cer* 13.3.10
negar	*cerrar* 13.3.11
g > gu before *e*	
nevar	*cerrar* 13.3.11
obedecer	*-cer* 13.3.10
obscurecer	*-cer* 13.3.10
obstruir	*construir* 13.3.13
obtener	*tener* 13.3.45
ofrecer	*-cer* 13.3.10
oír	see 13.3.38
oler	see 13.3.29
oponer	*poner* 13.3.34
oscurecer	*-cer* 13.3.10
pacer	*-cer* 13.3.10
padecer	*-cer* 13.3.10
palidecer	*-cer* 13.3.10
parecer	*-cer* 13.3.10
pedir	see 13.3.30
pensar	*cerrar* 13.3.11
perecer	*-cer* 13.3.10
permanecer	*-cer* 13.3.10
perseguir	*pedir* 13.3.30
gu > g before *a, o*	
pertenecer	*-cer* 13.3.10
pervertir	*sentir* 13.3.43
placer	see 13.3.32

Infinitive	model
plegar	*cerrar* 13.3.11
g > gu before *e*	
poblar	*contar* 13.3.14
poder	see 13.3.33
podrir variant of *pudrir*: *-u-* used for all other forms save past part.	
podrido	
poner	see 13.3.34
poseer	see 13.3.35
posponer	*poner* 13.3.34
imperative singular *pospón*	
predecir	*decir* 13.3.16
predisponer	*poner* 13.3.34
preferir	*sentir* 13.3.43
prescribir	
irreg. past participle *prescrito*	
presuponer	*poner* 13.3.34
prevalecer	*-cer* 13.3.10
prevaler	*valer* 13.3.47
prevenir	*venir* 13.3.48
prever	*ver* 13.3.49
3rd-pers. present singular *prevé*	
probar	*contar* 13.3.14
producir	see 13.3.36
proferir	*sentir* 13.3.43
promover	*mover* 13.3.27
proponer	*poner* 13.3.34
proseguir	*pedir* 13.3.30
gu > g before *a*	
prostituir	*construir* 13.3.13
proveer	*poseer* 13.3.35
past. part. *provisto/proveído*	
provenir	*venir* 13.3.48
pudrir	regular
see also *podrir*	
quebrar	*cerrar* 13.3.11
querer	see 13.3.37
raer	*caer* 13.3.9
rayo is an alternative to *raigo*	
reaparecer	*-cer* 13.3.10
reblandecer	*-cer* 13.3.10
recaer	*caer* 13.3.9
recluir	*construir* 13.3.13
recocer	*cocer* 13.3.12
recomendar	*cerrar* 13.3.11
reconocer	*-cer* 13.3.10
reconvenir	*venir* 13.3.48
recordar	*contar* 13.3.14
recostar(se)	*contar* 13.3.14
reducir	*producir* 13.3.36
reelegir	*pedir* 13.3.30
g > j before *a, o*	
referir	*sentir* 13.3.43

Infinitive	model
reforzar	*contar* 13.3.14
z>c before *e*	
refregar	*cerrar* 13.3.11
g>gu before *e*	
regar	*cerrar* 13.3.11
g>gu before *e*	
regir	*pedir* 13.3.30
g>j before *a, o*	
rehacer	*hacer* 13.3.22
reír	see 13.3.38
rejuvenecer	*-cer* 13.3.10
remendar	*cerrar* 13.3.11
remorder	*mover* 13.3.27
remover	*mover* 13.3.27
rendir	*pedir* 13.3.30
renegar	*cerrar* 13.3.11
g>gu before *e*	
renovar	*contar* 13.3.14
reñir	see 13.3.38
repetir	*pedir* 13.3.30
replegar	*cerrar* 13.3.11
g>gu before *e*	
reponer	*poner* 13.3.34
reprobar	*contar* 13.3.14
reproducir	*producir* 13.3.36
requebrar	*cerrar* 13.3.11
requerir	*sentir* 13.3.43
resentirse	*sentir* 13.3.43
resolver	*mover* 13.3.27
past participle *resuelto*	
resollar	*contar* 13.3.14
resonar	*contar* 13.3.14
resplandecer	*-cer* 13.3.10
restablecer	*-cer* 13.3.10
restituir	*construir* 13.3.13
restregar	*cerrar* 13.3.11
g>gu before *e*	
retemblar	*cerrar* 13.3.11
retener	*tener* 13.3.45
reteñir	*reñir* 13.3.39
retorcer	*cocer* 13.3.12
c>z before *a, o*	
retraer	*traer* 13.3.46
retribuir	*construir* 13.3.13
retrotraer	*traer* 13.3.46
reventar	*cerrar* 13.3.11
reverdecer	*-cer* 13.3.10
reverter	*perder* 13.3.31
revestir	*pedir* 13.3.30
revolar	*contar* 13.3.14
revolcar(se)	*contar* 13.3.14
c>qu before *e*	
revolver	*mover* 13.3.27
past part. *revuelto*	

Infinitive	model
robustecer	*-cer* 13.3.10
rodar	*contar* 13.3.14
roer	see 13.3.40
rogar	*contar* 13.3.14
g>gu before *e*	
romper	
irreg. past participle *roto*	
saber	see 13.3.41
salir	see 13.3.42
satisfacer	*hacer* 13.3.22
seducir	*producir* 13.3.36
segar	*cerrar* 13.3.11
g>gu before *e*	
seguir	*pedir* 13.3.30
gu>g before *a* or *o*	
sembrar	*cerrar* 13.3.11
sentar	*cerrar* 13.3.11
sentir	see 13.3.43
ser	see table 4, p.189
serrar	*cerrar* 13.3.11
servir	*pedir* 13.3.30
sobrentender	*perder* 13.3.31
also *sobreentender*	
sobreponer	*poner* 13.3.34
sobresalir	*salir* 13.3.42
sobrevenir	*venir* 13.3.48
soldar	*contar* 13.3.14
soler	*mover* 13.3.27
future, conditional & past and future subjunctives not used	
soltar	*contar* 13.3.14
sonar	*contar* 13.3.14
sonreír	*reír* 13.3.38
soñar	*contar* 13.3.14
sosegar	*cerrar* 13.3.11
g>gu before *e*	
sostener	*tener* 13.3.45
soterrar	*cerrar* 13.3.11
subarrendar	*cerrar* 13.3.11
subscribir	see *suscribir*
subvenir	*venir* 13.3.48
subvertir	*sentir* 13.3.43
sugerir	*sentir* 13.3.43
suponer	*poner* 13.3.34
suscribir	
irreg. past participle *suscrito*	
sustituir	*construir* 13.3.13
sustraer	*traer* 13.3.46
tañer	see table 3, p. 187, item 6
temblar	*cerrar* 13.3.11
tender	*perder* 13.3.31
tener	see 13.3.45
tentar	*cerrar* 13.3.11

Infinitive	model	Infinitive	model
teñir	*reñir* 13.3.39	*tronar*	*contar* 13.3.14
torcer	*cocer* 13.3.12	*tropezar*	*cerrar* 13.3.11
c>z before *a, o*		*z>c* before *e*	
tostar	*contar* 13.3.14	*tullir*	*zambullir* see
traducir	*producir* 13.3.36		table 3, p. 187
traer	see 13.3.46		item 6
transcender	*perder* 13.3.31	*valer*	see 13.3.47
transferir	*sentir* 13.3.43	*venir*	see 13.3.48
transgredir	*abolir* 13.3.2	*ver*	see 13.3.49
also regular		*verter*	*perder* 13.3.31
transponer	*poner* 13.3.34	*vestir*	*pedir* 13.3.30
transcender	*perder* 13.3.31	*volar*	*contar* 13.3.14
trasegar	*cerrar* 13.3.11	*volcar*	*contar* 13.3.14
g>gu before *e*		*c>qu* before *e*	
trasferir	*sentir* 13.3.43	*volver*	*mover* 13.3.27
traslucir	*lucir* 13.3.25	past part. *vuelto*	
trasponer	*poner* 13.3.34	*yacer*	see 13.3.50
trastrocar	*contar* 13.3.14	*zaherir*	*sentir* 13.3.43
c>qu before *e*		*zambullir*	see table 3,
trocar	*contar* 13.3.14		p. 187, item 6
c>qu before *e*			

Table 1: Overview of the Spanish verb

Spanish verbs may appear in the following forms:

infinitive	*hablar*	discussed in chapter 17
gerund	*hablando*	discussed in chapter 19
past participle	*hablado*	discussed in chapter 18
imperative	*habla* (*tú*)	
	hablad (*vosotros/vosotras*)[1]	
	hable (*usted*)	
	hablen (*ustedes*)	

ACTIVE VOICE
INDICATIVE

Simple tenses   discussed in chapter 14.1

present[2]	*yo hablo*, etc.	I speak
imperfect	*yo hablaba*, etc.	I was speaking
preterite	*yo hablé*, etc.	I spoke
future	*yo hablaré*, etc.	I shall/will speak
conditional	*yo hablaría*, etc.	I would speak

Perfect tenses   discussed at 14.6–8

All formed with the auxiliary *haber* (see p. 191) and the past participle, which does *not* agree in number or gender in these tenses.

present	*yo he hablado*, etc.	I have spoken
pluperfect[3]	*yo había hablado*, etc.	I had spoken
future	*yo habré hablado*, etc.	I will have spoken
conditional[4]	*yo habría hablado*, etc.	I would have spoken
	yo hubiera hablado, etc.	
pretérito anterior[5]	*yo hube hablado*, etc.	I had spoken

Table 1: Continued

Continuous   discussed in chapter 15
The continuous forms misleadingly resemble the English progressive, e.g. 'I'm talking/, he's going'.

Simple tenses

present	*yo estoy hablando*, etc.	I'm speaking
imperfect	*yo estaba hablando*, etc.	I was speaking
preterite	*yo estuve hablando*, etc.	I spoke/had a talk[6]
future	*yo estaré hablando*, etc.	I'll be speaking
conditional	*yo estaría hablando*, etc.	I'd be speaking

Perfect tenses

present	*yo he estado hablando*, etc.	I have been speaking
pluperfect	*yo había estado hablando*, etc.	I had been speaking
future	*yo habré estado hablando*, etc.	I shall/will have been speaking
conditional	*yo habría estado hablando*, etc.	I would have been speaking

SUBJUNCTIVE[7]   discussed in chapter 16

Simple tenses

present	*(que) yo hable*, etc.
imperfect[8]	*(que) yo hablara*, etc.
	(que) yo hablase, etc.
future[9]	*(que) yo hablare*, etc.

Perfect tenses (all formed with *haber*)

present	*(que) yo haya hablado*, etc.
pluperfect	*(que) yo hubiera/hubiese hablado*, etc.
future[9]	*(que) yo hubiere hablado*, etc.

Continuous

Simple tenses

present	*(que) yo esté hablando*, etc.
imperfect[8]	*(que) yo estuviera/estuviese hablando*, etc.
future[9]	*(que) yo estuviere hablando*, etc.

Perfect tenses

present	*(que) yo haya estado hablando*, etc.
pluperfect[8]	*(que) yo hubiera/hubiese estado hablando*, etc.
future	not used

PASSIVE VOICE

There are a number of ways of translating the English passive, the most common being the passive with *ser*, e.g. *esta novela fue publicada en México* or the third-person pronominal form, e.g. *esta novela se publicó en México*. These forms, not always interchangeable, are discussed in chapter 24, but a selection of the chief tenses are shown here by way of illustration. The participle in the *ser* form must agree in number and gender:

INDICATIVE

Simple tenses

present	*es publicado/se publica*	it is published
imperfect	*era publicado/se publicaba*	it used to be published
preterite	*fue publicado/se publicó*	it was published
future	*será publicado/se publicará*	it will be published
conditional	*sería publicado/se publicaría*	it would be published

Perfect tenses

present	*ha sido publicado/se ha publicado*	it has been published
pluperfect	*había sido publicado/se había publicado*	it had been published

Table 1: Continued

future	*habrá sido publicado/se habrá publicado*	it will have been published
conditional	*habría sido publicado/se habría publicado*	it would have been published

Continuous
The passive continuous with *ser* is not very common. It is discussed in particular at 15.3. The perfect continuous passive (*ha estado siendo publicado*, etc.) is not common enough to warrant separate treatment.

present	*está siendo publicado/está publicándose*[10]	it is being published
imperfect	*estaba siendo publicado/estaba publicándose*	it was being published
future	*estará siendo publicado/estará publicándose*	it will be being published

SUBJUNCTIVE
present	*(que) sea publicado/(que) se publique*
imperfect[8]	*(que) fuera publicado/(que) se publicara*
	(que) fuese publicado/(que) se publicase
future[9]	*(que) fuere publicado/(que) se publicare*

Continuous
The subjunctive continuous passive is also extremely rare in practice.
present	*(que) esté siendo publicado/(que) se esté publicando*

[1]Replaced by *ustedes* form in Spanish America.
[2]May be used for future or past in some circumstances.
[3]The *-ra* subjunctive often functions as an indicative pluperfect in subordinate clauses in literary styles, especially in Spanish America. See 14.8.1.
[4]The *-ra* form of *hubiera* is an optional alternative for the conditional *habría* in this tense.
[5]Uncommon. See 14.9 for discussion.
[6]i.e. 'I was speaking for a certain length of time'. See 15.2 note (ii) for discussion.
[7]Translation of the subjunctive depends on context.
[8]The *-ra* and *-se* forms are interchangeable except in the cases mentioned at 16.1.1.
[9]Almost obsolete except in set phrases, legal documents and the flowery journalese of some American republics, e.g. Argentina. See 16.9.
[10]The variant *se está publicando*, *se estaba publicando*, etc. is discussed at 11.12.5a.

Table 2: Conjugation of regular verbs

The three verbs *hablar* 'to speak', *comer* 'to eat' and *vivir* 'to live' conjugate regularly throughout and are unaffected by spelling changes.

infinitive	hablar	comer	vivir
(stem	habl-	com-	viv-)
gerund	hablando	comiendo	viviendo
past part.	hablado	comido	vivido
imperative			
(tú)	habla	come	vive
(vosotros/as)[1]	hablad	comed	vivid
(usted)	hable	coma	viva
(ustedes)	hablen	coman	vivan

INDICATIVE
Present
hablo	hablamos	como	comemos	vivo	vivimos
hablas	habláis	comes	coméis	vives	vivís
habla	hablan	come	comen	vive	viven

Table 2:　Continued

Present perfect

he hablado, etc.	he comido, etc.	he vivido, etc.

Imperfect

hablaba	hablábamos	comía	comíamos	vivía	vivíamos
hablabas	hablabais	comías	comíais	vivías	vivíais
hablaba	hablaban	comía	comían	vivía	vivían

Preterite

hablé	hablamos	comí	comimos	viví	vivimos
hablaste	hablasteis	comiste	comisteis	viviste	vivisteis
habló	hablaron	comió	comieron	vivió	vivieron

Pluperfect[2]

había hablado, etc.	había comido, etc.	había vivido, etc.

Pretérito anterior[3]

hube hablado, etc.	hube comido, etc.	hube vivido, etc.

Future

hablaré	hablaremos	comeré	comeremos	viviré	viviremos
hablarás	hablaréis	comerás	comeréis	vivirás	viviréis
hablará	hablarán	comerá	comerán	vivirá	vivirán

Future perfect

habré hablado, etc.	habré comido, etc.	habré vivido, etc.

Conditional

hablaría	hablaríamos	comería	comeríamos	viviría	viviríamos
hablarías	hablaríais	comerías	comeríais	vivirías	viviríais
hablaría	hablarían	comería	comerían	viviría	vivirían

Perfect conditional[4]

habría hablado, etc.	habría comido, etc.	habría vivido, etc.
hubiera hablado, etc.	hubiera comido, etc.	hubiera vivido, etc.

SUBJUNCTIVE

Present

hable	hablemos	coma	comamos	viva	vivamos
hables	habléis	comas	comáis	vivas	viváis
hable	hablen	coma	coman	viva	vivan

Present perfect

haya hablado, etc.	haya comido, etc.	haya vivido, etc.

Imperfect[5]

(a)　-ra form

hablara	habláramos	comiera	comiéramos	viviera	viviéramos
hablaras	hablarais	comieras	comierais	vivieras	vivierais
hablara	hablaran	comiera	comieran	viviera	vivieran

(b)　-se form

hablase	hablásemos	comiese	comiésemos	viviese	viviésemos
hablases	hablaseis	comieses	comieseis	vivieses	vivieseis
hablase	hablasen	comiese	comiesen	viviese	viviesen

Pluperfect[6]

hubiera hablado, etc.	hubiera comido, etc.	hubiera vivido, etc.
hubiese hablado, etc.	hubiese comido, etc.	hubiese vivido, etc.

Table 2: Continued

Future[7]

hablare	habláremos	comiere	comiéremos	viviere	viviéremos
hablares	hablareis	comieres	comiereis	vivieres	viviereis
hablare	hablaren	comiere	comieren	viviere	vivieren

[1] The *ustedes* form is used in Spanish America for familiar address as well as polite.
[2] The *-ra* form is often used for the pluperfect in subordinate clauses in literary styles, especially in Spanish America. See 14.8.1.
[3] Uncommon. It is discussed at 14.9.
[4] The *-ra* form of *haber*, e.g. *hubiera*, is an alternative in this tense.
[5] The two forms are interchangeable except in the circumstances noted at 16.1.1.
[6] The two forms are usually interchangeable, but both forms, particular *hubiera hablado*, may also be a variant form of the future perfect conditional indicative *habría hablado*.
[7] Obsolete in normal styles. See 16.9.

Table 3: Spelling changes

The following spelling rules apply to all Spanish verbs, regular and irregular:

(1)   Infinitives ending in *-zar, -cer* and *-cir*:[1]
z is spelt *c* before *i* or *e*.
c is spelt *z* before *a, o, u*.
EXAMPLES:

	rezar		*vencer*		*esparcir*	
Present indicative	rezo	rezamos	venzo	vencemos	esparzo	esparcimos
	(z throughout)		vences	vencéis	esparces	esparcís
			vence	vencen	esparce	esparcen
Preterite	recé	rezamos	vencí	vencimos	esparcí	esparcimos
	rezaste	rezasteis	(c throughout)		(c throughout)	
	rezó	rezaron				
Present subjunctive	rece	recemos	venza	venzamos	esparza	esparzamos
	reces	recéis	venzas	venzáis	esparzas	esparzáis
	rece	recen	venza	venzan	esparza	esparzan

No other forms affected.

(2)   Infinitives ending in *-car, -quir*[2]
c is spelt *qu* before *e* and *i*.
qu is spelt *c* before *a, o, u*.
EXAMPLES:

	sacar		*delinquir*	
Present indicative	saco	sacamos	delinco	delinquimos
	(c throughout)		delinques	delinquís
			delinque	delinquen
Preterite	saqué	sacamos	delinquí	delinquimos
	sacaste	sacasteis	(qu throughout)	
	sacó	sacaron		
Present subjunctive	saque	saquemos	delinca	delincamos
	saques	saquéis	delincas	delincáis
	saque	saquen	delinca	delincan

No other forms affected.

Table 3: Continued

---

(3) Infinitives ending in -*gar* -*guir*.
g is spelt *gu* before *i* and *e*.
gu is spelt *g* before *a*, *o*, *u*.
EXAMPLES:

	llegar		*seguir* (irregular)	
Present indicative	llego	llegamos	sigo	seguimos
	(*g* throughout)		sigues	seguís
			sigue	siguen
Preterite	llegué	llegamos	seguí	seguimos
	llegaste	llegasteis	(*gu* throughout)	
	llegó	llegaron		
Present subjunctive	llegue	lleguemos	siga	sigamos
	llegues	lleguéis	sigas	sigáis
	llegue	lleguen	siga	sigan

No other forms affected.

---

(4) Infinitives ending in -*guar*.
The u is written ü before *e*. See 13.2.6 for examples.

---

(5) Infinitives ending in -*ger*, *gir*[3]
g is spelt *j* before *a*, *o*, *u*.
EXAMPLES:

	proteger		*fingir*	
Present indicative	protejo	protegemos	finjo	fingimos
	proteges	protegéis	finges	fingís
	protege	protegen	finge	fingen
Present subjunctive	proteja	protejamos	finja	finjamos
	protejas	protejáis	finjas	finjáis
	proteja	protejan	finja	finjan

No other forms affected.

---

(6) Infinitive in -*ñer*, *ñir*, -*llir*.
ie is spelt *e*.
ió is spelt *ó*.
EXAMPLES:

	tañer		*gruñir*		*zambullir*	
Gerund	tañendo		gruñendo		zambullendo	
Preterite	tañí	tañimos	gruñí	gruñimos	zambullí	zambullimos
	tañiste	tañisteis	gruñiste	gruñisteis	zambulliste	zambullisteis
	tañó	tañeron	gruñó	gruñeron	zambulló	zambulleron
Imperfect	tañera	tañéramos	gruñera	gruñéramos	zambullera	zambulléramos
subjunctive	tañeras	tañerais	gruñeras	gruñerais	zambulleras	zambullerais
	tañera	tañeran	gruñera	gruñeran	zambullera	zambulleran
	tañese	tañésemos	gruñese	gruñésemos	zambullese	zambullésemos
	tañeses	tañeseis	gruñeses	gruñeseis	zambulleses	zambulleseis
	tañese	tañesen	gruñese	gruñesen	zambullese	zambullesen
(Fut. subj.	tañere, etc.		gruñere, etc.		zambullere, etc.)	

---

(7) Verbs in -*eer*: all conjugated like *poseer* at 13.3.35.

Table 3: Continued

(8)   Verbs in -*uir*: all conjugated like *construir* at 13.3.13.

[1]But nearly all verbs in -*cer* and -*cir* are irregular and should be consulted in the list of irregular verbs.
[2]*Delinquir* seems to be the only example in -*quir* and is itself rarely used.
[3]Verbs in -*jar*, e.g. *amortajar*, and -*jer*, e.g. *tejer*, retain the *j* throughout.

Table 4:   Conjugation of *ser* 'to be'

infinitive	ser
gerund	siendo
past participle	sido
imperative	sé (tú) [1], sed (vosotros/as)
	sea (usted), sean (ustedes)

SIMPLE TENSES
INDICATIVE

Present 'I am', etc.		**Imperfect** 'I used to be/was', etc.		**preterite** 'I was', etc.	
soy	somos	era	éramos	fui[3]	fuimos
eres[2]	sois	eras	erais	fuiste	fuisteis
es	son	era	eran	fue[3]	fueron

Future 'I will be', etc.		**Conditional** 'I would be', etc.	
seré	seremos	sería	seríamos
serás	seréis	serías	seríais
será	serán	sería	serían

SUBJUNCTIVE

Present		**Imperfect**[4]				**Future**[5]	
sea	seamos	fuera	fuéramos	fuese	fuésemos	fuere	fuéremos
seas	seáis	fueras	fuerais	fueses	fueseis	fueres	fuereis
sea	sean	fuera	fueran	fuese	fuesen	fuere	fueren

PERFECT TENSES (all forms conjugated with *haber* and the past participle *sido*.)
INDICATIVE

Present	he sido, etc.	'I have been'
Pluperfect	había sido, etc.	'I had been'
Future	habré sido, etc.	'I will have been'
Conditional	habría sido, etc.	'I would have been'

SUBJUNCTIVE

Present	haya sido, etc.
Pluperfect	hubiera/hubiese sido, etc.
Future	hubiere sido, etc. (obsolete)

CONTINUOUS[6]
INDICATIVE

Present	estoy siendo, etc. 'I'm being'
Imperfect	estaba siendo, etc. 'I was being'
Preterite	not used
Future	estaré siendo, etc. 'I will be being'
Conditional	estaría siendo 'I would be being'

Table 4:   Continued

SUBJUNCTIVE[7]
Present   (que) esté siendo, etc.
Imperfect   (que) estuviera/estuviese siendo

[1]The accent distinguishes it from the pronoun *se*.
[2]The Argentine *vos* form is *sos*.
[3]No written accent since 1959.
[4]The *-ra* and *-se* forms are usually interchangeable. See 16.1.1.
[5]The third-person of the future subjunctive of *ser* is occasionally seen in set phrases like *sea lo que fuere* (less formally *sea lo que sea*) 'come what may'.
[6]Continuous forms of *ser* are increasingly common in the modern language, but are viewed with suspicion by some purists. See 15.3.
[7]Continuous subjunctive forms are more theoretical than real.

Table 5:   Conjugation of *estar* 'to be'

The difference between *ser* and *estar* is discussed in chapter 25.
Infinitive   estar
Gerund   estando
Past participle   estado
Imperative[1]   está (tú), estad (vosotros/as)
                        esté (usted), estén (ustedes)

SIMPLE TENSES
INDICATIVE

Present 'I am', etc.		**imperfect** 'I used to be/was', etc.		**preterite** 'I was', etc.	
estoy	estamos	estaba	estábamos	estuve	estuvimos
estás	estáis	estabas	estabais	estuviste	estuvisteis
está	están	estaba	estaban	estuvo	estuvieron

Future 'I will be', etc.		**conditional** 'I would be', etc.	
estaré	estaremos	estaría	estaríamos
estarás	estaréis	estarías	estaríais
estará	estarán	estaría	estarían

SUBJUNCTIVE

Present		**Imperfect**[2]			
esté	estemos	estuviera	estuviéramos	estuviese	estuviésemos
estés	estéis	estuvieras	estuvierais	estuvieses	estuvieseis
esté	estén	estuviera	estuvieran	estuviese	estuviesen

Future[3]

estuviere	estuviéremos
estuvieres	estuviereis
estuviere	estuvieren

PERFECT TENSES (all forms conjugated with *haber* and the past participle *estado*.)
INDICATIVE

Present	he estado, etc.	'I have been'
Pluperfect	había estado, etc.	'I had been'
Future	habré estado, etc.	'I will have been'
Conditional	habría estado, etc.	'I would have been'

Table 5: Continued

SUBJUNCTIVE	
Present	haya estado, etc.
Pluperfect	hubiera/hubiese estado, etc.
Future	hubiere estado, etc. (obsolete)

CONTINUOUS
Estar is not used in the continuous, i.e. *está estando* is not Spanish.

[1]The pronominal forms, *estate*, *estaos* (colloquially *estaros*), *estese*, *estense* are used in the imperative.
[2]The *-ra* and *-se* forms are usually interchangeable. See 16.1.1.
[3]Virtually obsolete.

Table 6: Conjugation of auxiliary verb *haber*

This verb is used to form the perfect tenses of all regular and irregular verbs. (For discussion of compound tenses see 14.6–8). Compound forms of *haber* are not used to form perfect tenses: there is nothing corresponding to the French *il a eu dit*. The verb 'to be' is not used as an auxiliary in Spanish (cf. French *je suis allé(e)*, Italian *sono andato/sono andata*, etc.).

Haber is also used in the third person only as the main 'existential' verb, cf. *había muchos* 'there were a lot', *habrá menos de cinco* 'there will be less than five' (compare French *il y avait beaucoup*, *il y aura moins de cinq*). The third-person present indicative is *hay*. The plural forms are not used, though sentences like *habían muchos*, *habrán tres* are so common in spontaneous speech that some grammarians now reluctantly admit them as colloquialisms. Foreign students should avoid them.

Infinitive	haber
Gerund	habiendo
Past participle	habido
Imperative	(not used)

INDICATIVE

Present		**Present Perfect**[1]	**Imperfect**		**Preterite**	
he	hemos[2]	ha habido	había	habíamos	hube	hubimos
has	habéis		habías	habíais	hubiste	hubisteis
ha (hay)	han		había	habían	hubo	hubieron

Pluperfect[1]	**Pretérito anterior**	**Future**	
había habido	(not used)	habré	habremos
		habrás	habréis
		habrá	habrán

Future perfect[1]	**Conditional**[3]		**Perfect conditional**[1]
habrá habido	habría	habríamos	habría habido
	habrías	habríais	hubiera habido
	habría	habrían	

SUBJUNCTIVE

Present		**Present perfect**[1]
haya	hayamos	haya habido
hayas	hayáis	
haya	hayan	

Table 6: Continued

Imperfect[4]

(a) -ra form

hubiera	hubiéramos
hubieras	hubierais
hubiera	hubieran

(b) -se form

hubiese	hubiésemos
hubieses	hubieseis
hubiese	hubiesen

Pluperfect[1]

hubiera habido

hubiese habido

Future (obsolete in normal styles)

hubiere	hubiéremos
hubieres	hubiereis
hubiere	hubieren

[1]Used only as compound forms of *hay*.

[2]*Habemos* is used in the phrase *nos las habemos* 'we're dealing with', e.g. *En don Luis nos las habemos nuevamente con el Hombre y la Mujer* (Montesinos, quoted by M. Seco, *Diccionario de dudas*, 9th ed., p. 109) 'in Don Luis we are dealing once again with Man and Woman'.

[3]The *-ra* subjunctive form is a common alternative for the conditional, i.e. *te hubiera llamado* for *te habría llamado* 'I would have phoned you'. See 14.5.2 for discussion)

[4]The two forms are usually interchangeable. See 16.1.1.

Table 7: Full conjugation of the compound tenses of *ver*, using *haber* as auxiliary

Note the irregular past participle, *visto*.

INDICATIVE

Present perfect 'I have seen', etc.

he visto	hemos visto
has visto	habéis visto
ha visto	han visto

Future perfect 'I shall have seen'

habré visto	habremos visto
habrás visto	habréis visto
habrá visto	habrán visto

Pretérito anterior 'I had seen'[2]

hube visto	hubimos visto
hubiste visto	hubisteis visto
hubo visto	hubieron visto

Pluperfect 'I had seen', etc.

había visto	habíamos visto
habías visto	habíais visto
había visto	habían visto

Conditional[1] 'I would have seen', etc.

habría visto	habríamos visto
habrías visto	habríais visto
habría visto	habrían visto

SUBJUNCTIVE

(Translation of the Spanish subjunctive depends on context)

Present

haya visto	hayamos visto
hayas visto	hayáis visto
haya visto	hayan visto

Pluperfect (the -ra and se forms are usually interchangeable)

hubiera visto	hubiéramos visto	hubiese visto	hubiésemos visto
hubieras visto	hubierais visto	hubieses visto	hubieseis visto
hubiera visto	hubieran visto	hubiese visto	hubiesen visto

Table 7: Continued

Future (almost obsolete)

hubiere visto	hubiéremos visto
hubieres visto	hubiereis visto
hubiere visto	hubieren visto

Continuous forms
INDICATIVE

Present ('I have been seeing')

he estado viendo	hemos estado viendo
has estado viendo	habéis estado viendo
ha estado viendo	han estado viendo

Pluperfect ('I had been seeing')

había estado viendo	habíamos estado viendo
habías estado viendo	habíais estado viendo
había estado viendo	habían estado viendo

Future perfect ('I will have been seeing')

habré estado viendo	habremos estado viendo
habrás estado viendo	habréis estado viendo
habrá estado viendo	habrán estado viendo

Conditional perfect ('I would have been seeing', etc.)

habría estado viendo	habríamos estado viendo
habrías estado viendo	habríais estado viendo
habría estado viendo	habrían estado viendo

SUBJUNCTIVE

Present

haya estado viendo	hayamos estado viendo
hayas estado viendo	hayáis estado viendo
haya estado viendo	hayan estado viendo

Pluperfect (the -ra and -se forms are usually interchangeable)

hubiera estado viendo	hubiéramos estado viendo
hubieras estado viendo	hubierais estado viendo
hubiera estado viendo	hubieran estado viendo

hubiese estado viendo	hubiésemos estado viendo
hubieses estado viendo	hubieseis estado viendo
hubiese estado viendo	hubiesen estado viendo

Future (almost obsolete)

hubiere estado viendo	hubiéremos estado viendo
hubieres estado viendo	hubiereis estado viendo
hubiere estado viendo	hubieren estado viendo

---

[1]Or *hubiera visto, hubieras visto*, etc.
[2]Uncommon. See 14.9 for discussion.

14 Use of indicative (non-continuous) verb forms

This chapter discusses the use of the indicative, non-continuous verb forms. The continuous is discussed in chapter 15; the subjunctive in chapter 16.

The full range of possible forms of a typical regular verb are shown in table 1, p. 183. The traditional names of the tenses are misleading because, like the word 'tense' itself, they too strongly suggest that the main function of the 'tenses' is to indicate time. But these names are so entrenched that to use a more scientific terminology would be unhelpful.

Any attempt at a brief overview of the role of tense and aspect in the Spanish verb system would be confusing, but the following points deserve emphasis:

(a) There is no 'present' tense in Spanish, if by 'present' is meant a tense form whose sole function is to express present time. The uses of the simple 'present' *hablo*, *fumas*, *van*, are several and varied.

(b) There is no 'future tense' in Spanish, in the sense that there is no verb form whose exclusive function is to indicate future time, as can be seen from the following three sentences:

Te llamo esta noche	I'll call you tonight
Te llamaré esta noche	" " "
Te voy a llamar esta noche	" " "

These three sentences express different nuances, but all are 'future'. See 14.4 for further discussion.

(c) The difference between the preterite and imperfect tenses, e.g. *quise/quería* and to some extent between the pluperfect and *pretérito anterior*, e.g. *había terminado/hube terminado*, involves the distinction between perfective and imperfective 'aspect', i.e. between actions which were or were not complete in the past. English does not systematically indicate aspect differences, so that without further information one cannot tell whether the preterite or the imperfect is the correct translation of the English simple past; compare *yo los veía (todos los días)* (imperfective) 'I saw them (every day)' and *yo los vi (ayer)* (presumably perfective/completed) 'I saw them (yesterday)'.

The difference between perfective and imperfective Spanish verbs can be quite elusive for Anglophones, who may have problems in differentiating sentences like *era un problema difícil* and *fue un problema difícil*, which can really only be translated 'it was a difficult problem'. See 14.3.2 for further discussion.

(d)   Unlike French and German, Spanish has a full range of continuous forms which misleadingly resemble the English progressive: *está lloviendo* 'it's raining', *estabas pensando* 'you were thinking', *he estado comiendo* 'I've been eating'. The main problem here is the present tense, since the distinction between *lee* and *está leyendo* is neither the same nor as clear-cut as the difference between 'he reads' and 'he's reading'. Nor is the distinction between the past imperfective continuous *estaba hablando* 'I was speaking' and the perfective continuous *estuve hablando* 'I had a talk'/'I spoke' (for a specific length of time) immediately obvious to Anglophones. See chapter 15 for the continuous form.

(e)   The difference between the preterite *hablé* and the present perfect *he hablado* is maintained in spoken as well as written Spanish, whereas it is blurred in French, German and Italian. However, this difference only partly coincides with the distinction between 'I spoke' and 'I've spoken'. The difference between the perfect and preterite is governed by slightly different rules in most of Spanish America.

See 14.7 for more details.

14.1   The 'present' tense: general

'Present' is a severe misnomer since this form may be used for timeless, future and even past events. The chief difficulty of this form for English speakers is to distinguish it from the present continuous, i.e. between *habla* and *está hablando*: Anglophones habitually identify the latter form with the English progressive 'he's singing', but the relationship between the two forms is different in Spanish.

14.1.1   Uses of the 'present' tense form
(a)   As a timeless or habitual present:

Llueve mucho en Irlanda	it rains a lot in Ireland
Fumo más de sesenta al día	I smoke more than sixty a day
María es venezolana	Maria's Venezuelan
Los sonetos tienen catorce versos	sonnets have 14 lines
Las gaviotas comen peces	gulls eat fish
No tengo tarjeta de crédito	I don't have a credit card

This is probably the commonest use of this verb form.

(b)   To denote events occurring in the present
The chief problem here is how to distinguish it from the present continuous. With some verbs and contexts, there is often only a slight difference between the simple present and the continuous:

Escribe una novela	he's writing a novel
Está escribiendo una novela	" " "
Llueve	it's raining
Está lloviendo	" "

¿Qué haces?	what are you doing?
¿Qué estás haciendo?	" " "

The following remarks should be read in conjunction with the discussion of the continuous form in chapter 15.

The non-continuous present is used with verbs which denote states rather than actions, or for events which may be thought of either as having just finished or as about to occur, but not necessarily actually in progress *now*, e.g.:

(i)   States:

¿Por qué estás tan triste?	why are you so sad?
Hace frío	it's cold
Parece cansada	she seems tired
¡Cómo brilla la luna!	isn't the moon bright!
Hoy lleva traje de chaqueta	she's wearing a suit today

(ii)   Events which are present but not necessarily actually in progress:

Acusamos recibo de su carta del 3 de enero	we acknowledge receipt of your letter of January 3
A mí me suena poco natural	it sounds unnatural to me
La oposición considera una maniobra el aperturismo anunciado por el régimen	the opposition considers the liberalization policy announced by the regime to be a manoeuvre
¿Por qué te metes en ese asunto?	why are you getting involved in that business?
¿Qué dices?	what did you say (just then)? or 'what do you say'?
¿No oyes los perros?	can't you hear the dogs?
¡Que me ahogo!	I'm drowning!
¡Ya voy!	I'm coming!
Espérate que meto esto en el horno	wait while I put this in the oven
Yo disiento	I disagree

None of the sentences under **(ii)** refers to an event which is strictly speaking in progress *now*, but to events which have either just happened (*¿qué dices?*), are about to happen (*¡que me ahogo!*), or which are present but temporally vague or possibly habitual or timeless, e.g. *yo disiento*.

Nevertheless, the present and continuous forms sometime overlap in meaning (see 15.1 for further examples).

(c)   Certain actions in the future

For the use of the present tense form with a future meaning, see 14.4.3.

(d)   For completed past actions

This use of the present tense form (the 'historic present') is much favoured as a way of dramatizing descriptive passages in literature, but it also occurs in colloquial language, more commonly than the equivalent in popular English ('Mrs Brown comes up to me and says . . .').

Literary use of the historic present is very common. Translation by an English present often produces an unfortunate effect:

En los primeros matorrales del bosquecillo, frena a la mula y sus ojos claros, ávidos, buscan en una y otra dirección. Por fin, distingue a unos pasos,	He stopped his mule at the first thickets of the copse and his bright, eager eyes sought in both directions. Eventually he spotted, a few paces away, a man in

acuclillado, explorando una trampa,	leather sandals and hat, crouching and
a un hombre con sandalias y sombrero	inspecting a trap, with a machete in his
de cuero, machete a la cintura y	belt and trousers and shirt of fine
pantalón y blusa de brin. Galileo Gall	canvas. Galileo Gall dismounted and
desmonta y va hacia él tirando a la	went towards him pulling the mule by
mula de la rienda.	the reins.
–¿Rufino? –pregunta–. ¿El guía	'Rufino?' he asked. 'Rufino, the guide
Rufino de Queimadas?	from Queimadas?'
(Vargas Llosa, Peru)	

Note   The historic present is used in ordinary speech after *por poco* 'all but' and *casi* 'nearly':

Me caí por unas escaleras y por poco/	I fell down a flight of stairs and nearly
casi me rompo el tobillo	broke my ankle

(e)   As a familiar, rather curt imperative:

Tú te callas	you just keep quiet
–Mamá, ¿yo qué hago?	'What shall I do, mother?'
–Desayuna, y te pones a estudiar	'Have breakfast, and do some studying.'
(Aldecoa, dialogue)	

14.2   The preterite

The Spanish preterite is past in time and perfective, less commonly inchoative (inceptive), in aspect: i.e. it normally describes events which are both past and completed, or describes them as beginning in the past. *Yo fui* thus differs from the English form 'I was' in being marked for time and aspect, whereas the English is only marked for time. Compare *yo fui jefe de departamento* 'I was head of department' (and then stopped) and *yo era jefe de departamento* 'I was head of department' (at the time, etc.).

Similarly, 'he got cross with his dog' means either *se enfadó con su perro* or *se enfadaba con su perro*. Correct translation of the English simple past thus requires a decision about which verbal aspect is implied by the English form.

Some English past verb forms are unambiguously imperfective, e.g. 'he was getting angry', 'he used to get angry', 'he would usually get up at ten-thirty'. Such forms normally call for the imperfect tense form in Spanish.

14.2.1   Use of the preterite
The preterite is used:

(a)   To indicate an event which is past and complete. The difference between the preterite and imperfect often expresses an idea which is not easily translated into English. Compare

Tuvimos que atravesar dos desiertos para	we had to cross two deserts to get to the
llegar al oasis	oasis (and we did)

and

Teníamos que atravesar dos desiertos	we had (still) to cross two deserts to get to
para llegar al oasis	the oasis

The first (completed or perfective aspect) looks back on the crossing as accomplished, the second (incomplete or imperfective aspect) envisages the crossing as yet to be made.

Further examples:

Ayer anduve más de quince kilómetros	yesterday I walked more than fifteen kilometers
Fue un error no devolverle el dinero	it was a mistake not to return the money to him
La fiesta fue un éxito	the party was a success
Primero fui carpintero, después fui taxista, y después fui domador de leones	first I was a carpenter, then I was a taxi driver and then I was a lion tamer
El viernes tuve asma	I had an attack of asthma on Friday

Notes (i)   The imperfect is used for characteristics as opposed to actions or states, cf. *mi tía era soltera. Nunca estuvo casada* 'my aunt was a spinster. She was never married'. Compare also *Miguel era poeta* 'Miguel was a poet' and *Miguel fue director gerente* 'Miguel was (i.e. occupied the post of) managing director'.

Use of the preterite for a characteristic is highly idiosyncratic, cf.

Sir Thomas Browne (1605–82) supo el griego, el latín, el francés, el italiano y el español, y fue uno de los primeros hombres de letras que estudiaron anglosajón (Borges, Arg., more usually *sabía griego . . .*)	Sir Thomas Browne (1605–82) knew Greek, Latin, French, Italian and Spanish, and was one of the first men of letters to study Anglo-Saxon

For a further comparison of preterite and imperfect see 14.3.2.

(ii)   In cleft sentences (discussed in chapter 30), the tense of *ser* is dictated by the tense of the other verb(s):

Fue usted quien lo hizo	it was you who did it (once)
Era usted quien lo hacía	it was you who used to do it

   (b)   The preterite is occasionally used to indicate the beginning of a state or action. Compare

Mi hija habló a los once meses (i.e. *empezó a hablar*)	my daughter started talking at eleven months

and

Mi hija hablaba a los once meses	my daughter was talking by eleven months
Cuando el café estuvo listo le alcanzó una tacita (Sabato, Arg., dialogue)	when the coffee was ready she handed him a small cup
Una vez el dinero estuvo en mis manos, compré la casa	as soon as the money came into my hands, I bought the house
La chica avanzó hacia él, y cuando estuvo a su lado le dijo . . . (Sabato, Arg.)	the girl advanced towards him, and when she reached his side, said to him . . .
La conversación se fue espaciando	the conversation started to peter out

14.2.2   Preterite for finite periods of time

If a finite period of time in the past is mentioned, the preterite tense must be used for an event which went on for the duration of the period and then ended. By 'finite' period is meant a period of time of a specific length, i.e. whose beginning and end are known:

Estuve destinado en Bilbao dos años	I was posted in Bilbao for two years
Te olvidas del tiempo que estuviste casado	you're forgetting the time you were married
Por un instante pensé que me caía	for a moment I thought that I was falling
Los dinosaurios reinaron sobre la tierra durante millones de años	the dinosaurs reigned on Earth for millions of years
La ETA tuvo menos actividad durante el régimen de Franco que al instalarse la democracia (Vargas Llosa, Peru)	ETA (Basque terrorists) was less active during the Franco régime than when democracy was introduced
Durante años no pudimos hablar de otra cosa (García Márquez, Col.)	For years we could talk of nothing else
Mientras el poeta fue/era un narrador, sólo pudo contar con la tradición oral	as long as the poet was a narrator, he could only count on oral tradition
Al verte me acordé de lo compenetrados que estuvimos entonces (Buero Vallejo, dialogue)	when I saw you I remembered how close we were then (i.e. throughout that period)

Notes (i) The period of time is often implied rather than explicit. Use of the preterite may, for example, denote a lifetime envisaged as a finite period concluded by the person's death:

Siempre dormía como durmió su padre, con el arma escondida dentro de la funda de la almohada (García Márquez, Col.)	he always used to sleep as his father (*had*) slept, with his gun hidden in his pillowcase
Siempre quiso ser marinero	he always wanted to be a sailor (i.e. throughout his life)

(ii) In sentences involving phrases like *todos los días*, *todos los años*, the beginning and end of the period are not specified so the imperfect must be used:

Todos los veranos veraneaban en San Sebastián	every summer they spent their holidays in San Sebastian
Todas las mañanas regaba el jardín	he watered the garden every morning
Cuando yo era pequeño yo le/lo veía pasar casi todos los días	when I was little I saw him pass nearly every day

(iii) If the period is specified, but the action consists of a series of repeated (discontinuous) events, either form is possible, the imperfect apparently being commoner:

Aquella semana se levantaba/levantó a las siete, y desayunaba/desayunó a las ocho	that week he rose at seven, and breakfasted at eight
El verano pasado salía/salió todos los días con él	last summer she went out with him every day
Aquel año trabajaba/trabajó mucho	he worked hard that year

14.2.3 Special uses of the preterite

Some verbs undergo a change of meaning according to aspect. This is particularly true of *poder*, *saber*, *tener*, *querer*, *conocer*:

(a) Poder

The preterite of *poder* either means 'to manage to' (as opposed to 'be able to'), or it implies that something which might have happened did not in fact occur:

Pudo hacerlo	he managed to do it/could have done it
Podía hacerlo	he was able to do it (and may or may not have done it)
El día que pudo estallar la Tercera Guerra Mundial	the day World War III could have broken out

Pensando en lo que pudo haber sido, y no fue (J. Marsé)	thinking of what might have been and wasn't

(b)   The preterite of *saber* means 'to find out', 'realize':

Supe que no era cierto	I found out it wasn't true
Cuando supe la noticia . . .	when I heard the news . . .
Sabía que no era cierto	I knew it wasn't true

(c)   *Tener* and *querer*:

Tuve la impresión de que . . .	I got the impression that . . .
Tuve una carta	I got/received a letter
Tenía la impresión de que . . .	I had the impression that . . .
Cuando tuvo ocasión de estudiar consiguió con la universidad a distancia el título de ingeniero (*Cambio16*)	when he got the chance to study, he graduated as an engineer from the Open University
Quiso hacerlo	he *tried* to do it
Quería hacerlo	he wanted to do it
No quiso hacerlo	he refused to do it
No quería hacerlo	he didn't want to do it (but may have done it)

(d)   *Conocer*

Conocí a Antonia	I met Antonia (for the first time)
Conocía a Antonia	I knew Antonia

For further comparison of the preterite and imperfect, see 14.3.2.

14.3   The imperfect

The Spanish imperfect form expresses past time and incomplete (imperfective) aspect. The English simple past is marked only for time, so that 'I drank two glasses of wine with my lunch' is strictly speaking untranslatable into Spanish unless the context supplies clues about the aspect of the event: 'when I was young, I drank two glasses every day . . .' (imperfective – . . . *bebía dos vasos*) and 'last night I drank two glasses . . .' (perfective – *anoche bebí . . .*).

English forms like 'I used to drink', 'I was drinking', 'I would (habitually) drink' are unambiguously imperfective and almost always require translation by the Spanish imperfect.

In colloquial language the Spanish imperfect may be a substitute for the conditional. See 14.3.1d and 23.6 for examples.

14.3.1   Uses of the imperfect

The imperfect form is used for past events which were incomplete at the time of the utterance. It commonly indicates that an event was in the process of happening in the past, without reference to its beginning or end.

The imperfect is used:

(a)   To indicate any state or action which was already in progress when some other event occurred. It is thus the correct tense for background descriptions:

Me levanté y descorrí las cortinas. *Hacía un día espléndido*	I got up and drew the curtains. It was a splendid day
Como el cielo estaba despejado fuimos a la playa	since the sky was clear we went to the beach
Yo volvía del cine cuando vi a Niso	I was coming back from the cinema when I saw Niso
Cuando entré en el cuarto noté que olía a quemado	when I entered the room I noticed there was a smell of burning
Reagan reconoció que tenía noticia de algunas bajas entre las fuerzas invasoras	Reagan admitted that he had news of some casualties among the invading forces

(b) To indicate states or actions which continued in the past for an unspecified period. It is thus much used for characteristics, situations and habitual actions.

Matías era un hombre alto, calvo y un poco cargado de hombros	Matías was a tall, bald, slightly round-shouldered man
Me enfadé porque Pepe me había dicho que yo era tonto	I got angry because Pepe had told me that I was stupid
En el siglo dieciséis hacía más frío que ahora	it was colder in the sixteenth century than now
. . . Le exasperaban estas comidas mexicanas de cuatro o cinco horas de duración (C. Fuentes, Mex.)	. . . These Mexican meals lasting four or five hours exasperated him
Doña Amalia, por otra parte, era obesa, y se negaba a reconocer que la gula era peor pecado y más insalubre vicio que la dipsomanía (C. Barral)	Doña Amalia, on the other hand, was overweight, and refused to recognize that greed was a worse sin and more unhealthy vice than dipsomania

If the time period is specified, see 14.2.2.

(c) To express an event which is felt already to have begun at the time of some completed event:

Me di cuenta de que debían volver pronto	I realized they must be returning soon
Me marchaba ya cuando has llamado	I was just leaving when you rang

(d) The imperfect is commonly used as a colloquial alternative to the conditional to indicate an immediate future:

Prometió que venía/vendría	he promised he would come
Juró que lo hacía/haría	he swore he'd do it

But this is not possible with *ser* or if the future is not immediate:

Creía que sería posible	I thought it would be possible
Juró que me amaría siempre	he promised he would love me always
(not *amaba . . .*)	

See 23.3.1 for further uses of the imperfect for the conditional.

(e) As an alternative to the imperfect continuous

If the event is truly past (e.g. 'I was leaving the next day' is in fact a type of future) and non-habitual, the difference between the continuous and non-continuous imperfect is usually neutralized, i.e. *yo fumaba* and *yo estaba fumando* mean the same thing, e.g.

Yo hablaba/estaba hablando con los vecinos cuando llegaron los bomberos	I was talking to the neighbours when the firemen came

(f) In children's language

One interesting use of the imperfect is found in children's language:

Vamos a jugar a que yo era un vaquero *y tú eras un indio*	let's pretend I'm a cowboy and you're an Indian

(g)   As a way of showing courtesy in requests and enquiries

¿Qué deseaba?	what would you like?
Perdone, quería hablar con el director	excuse me, I'd like a word with the manager

(h)   In newspaper styles, as an alternative for the preterite in order to produce a dramatically drawn-out effect:

La historia de cómo . . . un hombre de cincuenta años mataba en la Noche Vieja de 1977 a su amante, una niña de 14 años, es de nuevo actualidad (*Cambio16*)	the story of how a man of fifty killed his lover, a girl of 14, on New Year's Eve 1977, is in the news again
Un cuarto de hora después . . . dos grapos asesinaban a un policía armado (*El País*)	a quarter of an hour later two members of GRAPO[1] murdered an armed policeman

[1] A left-wing terrorist group active in Spain in the 1980s.

14.3.2   Imperfect or preterite? Translation problems

Out of context, it is impossible to know whether the English sentence 'I went to work by car' means *fui al trabajo en coche* or *iba al trabajo en coche*. The English original must be examined closely for clues in the form of phrases like 'when the weather was bad', 'every day' which show that an imperfect tense is required.

The English continuous 'he was working' may be translated three ways, according to context: *trabajaba, estaba trabajando, estuvo trabajando*. See 15.2 notes i and ii for discussion of the differences.

The English 'used to . . .' is almost always translated by a Spanish imperfect: 'I used to smoke a lot, but I've given it up now' *antes fumaba mucho, pero lo he dejado ya*.

The difference between perfective and imperfective aspect is often elusive for Anglophones. The following examples may clarify the issue:

Fue un error decírselo	it was a mistake to tell him (we committed it)
Era un error decírselo	it was a mistake to tell him (we may or may not have committed it)
El problema fue difícil	the problem was difficult (but we solved it)
El problema era difícil	the problem was difficult (no information about whether we solved it or not)
Tuve que hablar con ella	I had to talk to her (and did)
Tenía que hablar con ella	I had to talk to her (and may or may not have done)
Estuve enfermo	I was ill (and got better)
Estaba enfermo	I was ill (at the time)
No pude ver lo que me rodeaba	I was unable to see what was around me (and didn't see it)
No podía ver lo que me rodeaba	I couldn't see what was around me (at the time, but may have later)
Fui a preguntar	I went to ask

Iba a preguntar . . .	I was going to ask . . .
No le gustó la comida	he didn't enjoy his meal (but he ate it)
No le gustaba la comida	he didn't like his meal (and may or may not have eaten it)
Se le doblaron las piernas	his legs gave way under him
Se le doblaban las piernas	his legs were giving way
Estuve hablando con ella	I had a talk with her
Estaba hablando con ella	I was (in the process of) talking to her
Cuando estuve en Cuba . . .	when I visited Cuba . . .
Cuando yo estaba en Cuba . . .	when I was in Cuba . . .
Creí que hablabas en serio	I thought you were talking seriously
Creía que hablabas en serio	I used to think you talked seriously
(Can also mean more or less the same as *creí que* . . .)	
Debió hacerlo Juan	John ought to have done it (on that occasion) or John must have done it (on that occasion)
Debía hacerlo Juan	John used to have to do it, John must have done it (i.e. habitually) or John ought to do it
Debía (de) saber mucho (*debía* may be an alternative for *debería*.)	he must/ought to have known a lot
Debiste (de) llegar tarde	you must have arrived late
Quise hablar con José	I wanted to talk to José (but failed)
Quería hablar con José	I wanted to talk to José (and may or may not have suceeded)

14.4 Future tense

Spanish has several ways of expressing the future and the so-called 'future tense' (*hablaré, vendrás*) is not the most common in everyday speech (from which it is said to be disappearing except in its 'suppositional' role described at 14.4.2):

(a) *Esta noche vamos al cine*	tonight we're going to the cinema
(b) *Esta noche vamos a ir al cine*	tonight we're going to go to the cinema
(c) *Esta noche iremos al cine*	tonight we'll go to the cinema
(d) *Esta noche hemos de ir al cine*	tonight we're to go to the cinema

(a) is typically a description of an event which is pre-arranged or a fixture due to happen in the immediate future. (b) is a foreseen or 'intentional' future, and it is often an informal substitute for the future tense proper *iremos, seré,* etc. (c) is less common in colloquial language, and very often excludes the idea of pre-arrangement. Consequently it may sound rather uncertain or, depending on tone and context, may sound like an order or promise. (d) is sometimes heard in Spanish America with a future meaning, but in the Peninsula implies obligation, and is not very common.

14.4.1 Uses of the future tense form
Sometimes, particularly in informal speech, the present and future forms

are interchangeable. However, the future is used:

(a) For provisional or less certain statements about the future, or for statements about the future where no other word makes it clear that the future is meant:

– *Nos veremos mañana en Palacio para el premio al profesor Bernstein, ¿no es cierto?* (C. Fuentes, Mex. dialogue)	we'll see one another tomorrow at the Palace for the prize-giving to Prof. Bernstein, won't we?'
Si llueve se aplazará el partido	if it rains the match will be postponed
Tienes razón. Mira: las cosas se reanudan . . . Vuelve la esperanza . . . Ahora bajaremos y como un pobre hombre más, tomaré tu cuaderno y te confesaré mi maldad . . . Y si tus ojos me condenan . . . aceptaré mi dolor y procuraré recobrarte (Buero Vallejo, dialogue)	you're right. Look: things are renewed. Hope comes back . . . Now we'll go downstairs, and like one more wretched fellow I'll take your notebook and confess my wickedness . . . And if your eyes condemn me I'll accept my suffering and try to get you back.

(The emotional tone makes the future appropriate. The future is also appropriate for promises. See below)

Me ha dado diez mil pesetas. Con esto tiraré hasta la semana próxima, y luego veremos (*luego vemos* is impossible here)	He gave me 10,000 ptas. I'll manage with that till next week, and then we'll see
En cuanto pasemos el túnel ya verás cómo cambia el tiempo. Hará más frío (Aldecoa, dialogue)	when we get through the tunnel you'll see how the weather changes. It'll be colder
En un remoto futuro el sol se apagará	in the remote future the sun will go out
Por la noche nos iremos al cine Juan y yo (Buero Vallejo, dialogue, *nos vamos* possible)	this evening Juan and I will go/are going to the cinema
Para entonces todos estaremos calvos	we'll all be bald by then (said of something which will take a long time)

Notes (i)   Nevertheless, the difference between utterances like *te veo mañana* and *te veré mañana* is elusive. The former is informal and indicates something so firmly pre-arranged as to be felt to be a present reality. The latter is slightly less certain. Thus *esta noche vamos al teatro* is usual, but if uttered in the morning, with the prospect of many other chores intervening, one might say *esta noche, cuando lo tengamos todo hecho, iremos al teatro.* However, in educated speech there is a great deal of overlap between the present and future, cf. *te llamo a las seis* and *te llamaré a las seis* (almost indistinguishable).

(ii)   Words meaning 'perhaps', which by nature indicate uncertainty – *acaso, tal vez, quizá, a lo mejor* – may, when they refer to some future event, appear either with the future form or (except *a lo mejor*) with the present subjunctive, but *not* with the present indicative: *quizá/tal vez venga/vendrá mañana.* See 16.7.3 for details.

(b) For promises (which by nature are not pre-arrangements):

Ten confianza en mí. No te decepcionaré	have confidence in me. I won't disappoint you
¡No pasarán!	they shall not pass!
Hoy eres la Cenicienta, pero mañana serás una princesa	today you're Cinderella, but tomorrow you'll be a princess
Pero también debo decir que estoy con Suárez, y estaré con él como	but I should also say that I back (lit. 'am with') Suarez, and I will back him as

presidente nacional del partido mientras dure su mandato (Joaquín Garrigues, quoted *Cambio16*)	national chairman of the party as long as his mandate lasts

(c)   For suppositions or approximations: see next section.

14.4.2   Suppositional future

An important function of the future tense in ordinary Spanish (especially in the Peninsula) is to express suppositions or approximations. This is apparently the first use of the future form learnt by Spanish children, who tend to discover its function as a pure future from their schoolteachers (S. Gili y Gaya, *Estudios de lenguaje infantil*, 59).

Idiomatic use of the future in approximations often produces much more authentic Spanish than clumsy sentences involving *aproximadamente* or *alrededor de*.

In questions, the future expresses wonder, incredulity or conjecture:

Habrá más de cien personas en la fiesta	there must be more than a hundred people at the party
María tendrá unos veinte años	Maria's about 20 years old
Un par de años hará . . . Gannon me escribió de Gualeguaychu (Borges, Arg.)	it must be a couple of years ago Gannon wrote to me from Gualeguaychu
¡Habráse visto semejante tontería!	did anyone ever see such nonsense?!
¿Qué será esto?	I wonder what this is
¿Qué hora será?	I wonder what the time is
(Spanish-American: *¿Qué horas serán?*)	
Tendrá unos veinte metros de largo	it's about 20 metres long
¿Dónde está tu monedero? Me lo habré dejado en casa	where's your purse? I must have left it at home
¿Qué estará tramando ella?	I wonder what she's up to
No dirás que no te cuido	you're not going to say that I don't look after you (are you?)

Note   Kany, 190, notes that this use of the future is more common in Spain than in parts of Spanish America, where *deber (de) . . .* often replaces it: *deben de ser las cinco* = *serán las cinco* (or *deben (de) ser las cinco*).

14.4.3   Present tense with future meaning

The present is much used in informal language to refer to the immediate future. If the subject is human, it conveys an idea of certainty and is therefore especially used for fixtures or appointments, cf. English 'I'm going to Spain next year', 'we attack tomorrow'. If the subject is inanimate, the action is foreseen as a certainty or fixture.

The fact that the verb refers to the future is normally shown by some time phrase like *mañana, esta noche, el año que viene*:

Vamos a España el año que viene	we're going to Spain next year
¿Quién paga mañana?	who's paying tomorrow?
En seguida bajo	I'll be down right away
Te llamo esta noche	I'll ring you tonight
Dentro de un cuarto de hora estoy en tu casa (García Márquez, dialogue, Col.)	I'll be at your house in a quarter of an hour

Si viene por aquí, ¿qué digo?	if he comes round here, what shall I say?
La semana que viene hay corrida	there's a bullfight next week
El tren sale mañana a las seis	the train leaves tomorrow at six
Esta noche hay tormenta, verás	tonight there'll be a storm, you'll see
Nos vemos	goodbye/'see you again'
mañana es imposible	tomorrow is impossible

Notes (i)   This use of the present tense is particularly common with verbs of motion (*ir*, *venir*, *salir*, *llegar*). With other verbs it is best thought of as an informal alternative for the future tense, although there is often a difference of nuance.

(ii)   Events in an unspecified future are by nature less certain, so the present tense should not be used: *si las cosas continúan así, ya no habrá árboles* 'if things go on like this, there will be no more trees left'.

(iii)   If there is no contextual clue which clearly shows that the statement refers to the future, the present tense is assumed to be a true present and the future must be shown by some unambiguously future form, e.g. *ir a* + infinitive or the future tense proper. Compare *me parece que no hay sitio* 'I think there's no room' and *me parece que no habrá/va a haber sitio* 'I think there won't be room'.

(iv)   *Ser* is commonly used this way for calendar statements: *mañana es jueves* 'tomorrow is Thursday', but *mañana el discurso será pronunciado por el presidente* 'tomorrow the speech will be delivered by the president'.

14.5   The conditional: general

The conditional is formed by adding the endings of the imperfect of *-er* or *-ir* verbs to the infinitive or, in the case of a few irregular verbs (listed at 13.1e), to the future stem: *yo hablaría, tú tendrías, él sabría*, etc.

The name 'conditional' is apt only insofar as it describes a common use of the form, viz. the expression of the idea that an event is dependent on some other factor, as in *podríamos ir mañana* 'we could go tomorrow (if the weather's nice, if we're free, etc.)'. But it has other functions which have nothing to do with the idea of conditionality, e.g. the expression of suppositions or approximations in the past and the expression of the future in the past.

For the purpose of agreement the conditional counts as a past tense, so the subjunctive in a subordinate clause governed by the conditional must be in the past; compare *es absurdo que vengas mañana* 'it's absurd for you to come tomorrow' and *sería absurdo que vinieras/vinieses mañana* 'it would be absurd for you to come tomorrow'.

Colloquial language shows a marked tendency to replace the conditional by the imperfect, especially in conditional sentences (see 23.3.1).

Replacement of the imperfect subjunctive by the conditional, e.g. **si yo tendría dinero* for *si yo tuviera dinero* 'if I had some money' is very common in popular speech in Navarre and neighbouring regions, in Argentina and perhaps locally elsewhere, but foreigners should shun this tendency.

One important use of the conditional, neglected by Anglophones, is its ability to express suppositions or approximations in the past. It is thus the past form of the much-used suppositional future described at 14.4.2: cf. *tendrá diez años* 'he must be ten years old' and *tendría diez años* 'he must have been ten years old'.

14.5.1 Uses of the conditional
The conditional is used:

   (a)   In implied conditions:

¿Quieres ir a la manifestación? Sería interesante	do you want to go to the demonstration? It would be interesting
Sería una locura ponerlo en marcha sin aceite	it would be crazy to start it up with no oil
De nada serviría un nuevo golpe porque sólo perjudicaría al país (Headline, Bolivian press)	another coup d'état would be pointless, because it would only damage the country

   (b)   For suppositions or approximations about the past:

Aquel día andaríamos más de cincuenta kilómetros	that day we must have walked more than 50 km
Tendría (or *tenía/debía de tener*) *unos treinta años*	he must have been about thirty
Llevaba un saco sport que en algún tiempo habría sido azul marino (E. Sabato, Arg. *Saco = americana* or *chaqueta* in Spain)	he was wearing a sports jacket which must once have been navy blue

In some styles, especially journalism and more so in Spanish America, the conditional is used for rumours or unsubstantiated reports. This construction is generally condemned by grammarians as a Gallicism:

Gregorius habría nacido en Glasgow . . . (Cortázar, Arg.)	Gregorius was apparently born in Glasgow
Según nuestro enviado especial en Bayona, la desaparición de los etarras estaría motivada por cuestiones de seguridad (*ABC*, Spain)	according to our special correspondent in Bayonne, security reasons are said to be the motive for the disappearance of the ETA members

   (c)   To express the future in the past (i.e. as a close equivalent of *iba a. . . + an* infinitive). This device is much abused in Spanish journalism:

Yo sabía que papá bajaría/bajaba/ iba a bajar a las once	I knew father would come down at 11 o'clock
Dijo que lo haría/hacía luego	he said he'd do it later
Cerró la puerta con cuidado; su mujer dormía profundamente. Dormiría hasta que el sol hiciera su primera presencia en la ventana (Aldecoa)	he shut the door carefully; his wife was fast asleep. She would sleep until the sun first showed at the window
Entonces tuvo una aventura que se desarrollaría en tres estapas diferentes	he then had an adventure that was to develop in three different stages
Finalmente, en diciembre de 1980, el globo 'Tramontana' se elevaría sobre los cielos de Zanzíbar y emprendería su viaje hacia Tanzania (*Cambio16*)	finally, in December 1980, the balloon 'Tramontana' was to rise over the Zanzibar sky and set out on its journey to Tanzania

   (d)   In rhetorical questions:

¿Alguien se atrevería a decir que la 'socialización' ha hecho más libres a los diarios? (Vargas Llosa, Peru)	would anyone dare to say that 'socialization' has made newspapers more free?

14.5.2   Replacement of the conditional by the *-ra* subjunctive

The *-ra* subjunctive may be a stylistic variant for the conditional when this is used as a true conditional (and not, for example, as a suppositional tense or future in the past).

This is normal in all styles with the auxiliary *haber*: *habría sido mejor/ hubiera sido mejor* 'it would have been better'.

It is also common with *querer* and *deber*: *yo querría/quisiera hacerlo* 'I'd like to do it'; *deberías/debieras haberlo hecho* 'you should have done it'.

With *poder* it is rather literary: *podría haber sido/pudiera haber sido*.

With other verbs it is nowadays uncommon and very poetic:

Abril, sin tu asistencia clara, fuera invierno de caídos esplendores . . . (Juan Ramón Jiménez)	'April, without thy bright presence, would be (i.e. *sería*) a winter of fallen splendours'

Note   Use of the *-se* subjunctive for the conditional is not favoured by the grammarians, but is found in spontaneous speech:

. . . y hubiese sido muy sospechoso que yo me negase (M. Puig, Arg. dialogue)	and it would have been very suspicious if I'd refused

14.6   Compound tenses: general

The compound tenses, e.g. the present perfect, pluperfect, *pretérito anterior*, and the perfect subjunctive forms, all use the auxiliary *haber* or, much less commonly and the *pretérito anterior* excepted, *tener*. No Spanish verbs form the perfect with *ser* as an auxiliary. (*Llegar, ir, venir* are very rare archaic or journalistic exceptions, cf. *el verano es ido* 'summer is gone').

Unlike French and Italian, the past participle is invariable and does not agree in number and gender with the object of the verb (unless *tener* is used instead of *haber*: see 14.6.3).

The participle may be deleted in English, but not in Spanish: 'have you tried the sausages? Yes, I have' – *¿has probado las salchichas? Sí* or *Sí, las he probado*. However, deletion occasionally occurs with the pluperfect tense, to judge by *¿Se había reído? Sí, se había. Pero esta vez sin sarcasmo* (dialogue in Vargas Llosa, *¿Quién mató a Palomino Molero?*). Spanish informants thought that this might be a sporadic feature of informal speech.

14.6.1   Compound tenses: word order

Learners should respect the rule that no words may come between the auxiliary and the participle, cf. French *j'ai toujours dit . . . = siempre he dicho*. However it is often broken, especially in literary style:

Se habrá tal vez olvidado	you may have forgotten
Se ha más que duplicado la cifra (From *Hoja del lunes*)	the figure has more than doubled
Habrá probablemente ya muerto (i.e. *probablemente habrá muerto ya*)	he must already be dead

Lorenzo, 205 sees no objection to the insertion of words like *ni siquiera*, *incluso*, *apenas*, *ya*, *siempre*, *nunca*, *jamás*, *aún* between auxiliary and participle.

14.6.2   Suppression of *haber* in compound tenses
The auxiliary may optionally be suppressed to avoid repetition:

No sólo había tocado la mano y mirado los ojos de la mujer que más le gustaba tocar y mirar del mundo (C. Fuentes, Mex.)	not only had he touched the hand and looked at the eyes of the woman he most liked to touch and look at in the world
. . . yo también he pasado por baches y conocido la duda (L. Goytisolo, dialogue)	I've been through rough patches as well and known doubt

14.6.3   *Tengo hecho, tengo comprado, etc.*
Tener is occasionally used as an auxiliary to denote the successful acquisition of some object or the fulfilment of some task, cf. 'I've painted the windows' and 'I have got all the windows painted', 'I've got all my homework done'. The participle agrees in number and gender with the object of the verb. The verb must be transitive and have a direct object (**tengo sido*, cf. Portuguese *tenho sido*, is not Spanish):

Ya tengo compradas las entradas	I've already bought the tickets
Después de las vacaciones tendré hechos todos mis deberes	after the holidays I'll have all my homework done
Yo tenía concertada hora con el jefe	I had arranged an appointment with the boss
Me parece que ese jueves de diciembre tenía pensado cruzar a la orilla derecha y beber vino en el cafecito de la rue des Lombards (Cortázar, Arg., dialogue)	I think that that Friday in December I had planned to cross to the right bank and drink wine in the little café in the rue des Lombards

14.7   Present perfect tense

Spanish differs from French, German and Italian, and broadly resembles English, in that the difference in meaning between the preterite – *hablé* 'I spoke' – and the present perfect – *he hablado* 'I've spoken' – is maintained in both written and spoken language.

Students of languages in which the distinction is blurred or lost in the spoken language must avoid translating sentences like *je l'ai vu hier, ich habe ihn gestern gesehen, l'ho veduto ieri* as **le/lo he visto ayer* (correctly *le/lo vi ayer*). Such misuse of the present perfect is sometimes heard in popular Madrid speech.

Spanish usually uses the present perfect wherever English does, but the reverse is not true: the Spanish present perfect often requires translation by the English simple past. Moreover, in the majority of the Spanish-speaking world (Galicia, Asturias and all of Spanish America) the preterite is in fact more common than the present perfect, cf. *no vino todavía* (SA) and *no ha venido todavía* (Spain), 'he hasn't come yet'.

14.7.1 Uses of the present perfect

The present perfect is used:

(a) For events which have happened in a period of time which includes the present – e.g. today, this afternoon, this week, this month, this year, this century, always, already, never, still, yet. In this respect, English and Spanish coincide (as far as Peninsular usage is concerned):

No he visto a tu madre esta semana	I haven't seen your mother this week
En sólo dos generaciones se ha desertizado un 43% de la superficie terrestre (Advert. in *ABC*)	in only two generations 43% of the earth's surface has been reduced to desert
Hemos ido dos veces este mes	we've been twice this month
Ya han llegado	they've already arrived
Siempre he pensado que . . .	I have always thought that . . .
Aún/todavía no han llegado	they haven't arrived yet

Notes (i) The preterite may be used with the effect of severing the link between the event and the present moment. Compare *vi a tu suegra esta mañana* and *he visto a tu suegra esta mañana* 'I saw/have seen your mother-in-law this morning'.

(ii) Words like *siempre, nunca* may or may not include the present: compare *yo siempre he sido un problema para mis padres* 'I've always been a problem for my parents' and *yo siempre fui un problema para mis padres* 'I always was a problem for my parents' (e.g. when I was young. But some speakers do not systematically respect the difference of meaning in either language).

(iii) American Spanish shows a preference for the preterite in the above contexts. (Compare American English 'did they arrive yet?', 'did you sell your apartment yet?'):

¿Todavía no llegó tu padre?	hasn't your father come yet?
Aún no salieron del cine	they haven't come out of the cinema yet
¿Qué hubo?	how're things?
(Colombia, Venezuela, etc. Spain *¿Qué hay?*)	
Ya nos llegó la moderna solución (Advert. in *El tiempo*, Colombia)	Now we've got the modern answer!
En el curso de los últimos años se lograron (Spain *se han logrado . . .*) *notables progresos en el conocimiento de la función de los riñones* (Chilean press, *Var.* 220)	in recent years notable progress has been made in (our) knowledge of the function of the kidneys

(b) For any very recent event (in practice, any event which has happened since midnight). Very recent events (e.g. seconds ago) almost always take the perfect tenses:

Esta mañana me he levantado/me levanté a las seis	I got up at six this morning
¿Has oído la explosión?	did you hear the explosion?
¿Quién ha dicho eso?	who said that (just now)?
No he sido yo. Ha sido él	It wasn't me. It was him
La he visto hace un momento	I saw her a moment ago
No he podido hacerlo	I couldn't do it

No he querido venir antes por no querer molestar	I didn't want to come earlier so as not to cause bother
No he entendido lo que ha dicho	I didn't understand what he said
Ha muerto Franco (Headline)	Franco is dead

Notes (i)   American and North-Western Peninsular Spanish may require the preterite in these examples, but for speakers of standard European Spanish *?la vi hace un momento* sounds wrong because the event is very recent.

(ii)   The above examples are chosen to show how Spanish freely uses the present perfect of recency with verbs like *querer, ser,* where English allows only the simple past: *no he querido hacerlo* 'I didn't want to do it', *¿quién ha sido el gracioso que se ha llevado las llaves?* 'who's the clown who took the keys away with him (just now)?').

(iii)   Spanish thus differs from English in that the present perfect is used of any very recent event, completed or not. English allows 'have you heard the news?' since the news can still be heard, but not *'have you heard that explosion?'. Cf. *¿habéis visto el relámpago?* 'did you see the flash?'.

(c)   For any past event which is relevant to the present, or whose effects still bear on the present (English and Spanish coincide in this respect):

¿Por qué estás tan cansado? Porque he andado más de trece kilómetros	why are you so tired? Because I've walked more than thirteen kilometres
¿Quién ha roto esta ventana?	who's broken this window?
Todo el mundo habla de Fulano porque ha publicado otra novela	everyone's talking about so-and-so because he's published a new novel
Pero aunque es evidente que Simone de Beauvoir ha leído con detenimiento a estos autores y aprovechado sus técnicas . . . (Vargas Llosa, Peru)	but although it is obvious that Simone de Beauvoir has read these authors closely and (has) taken advantage of their techniques . . .

Note   One occasionally finds the present perfect in conjunction with some word or phrase which denotes the non-recent past, e.g. 'yesterday', 'two months ago'. However, unless the event happened in the course of the present day, the preterite is safer. Some native speakers strongly preferred the preterite in the following sentences:

Ayer, a la caída de la tarde, cuando el gran acantilado es de cinabrio, he vuelto a la isla (I. Aldecoa)	yesterday, at nightfall, when the big cliff is the colour of cinnabar, I returned to the island
Se trata de un ejercicio que ha perdido la iniciativa hace meses (*Cambio16*)	it involves an exercise which lost its initiative months ago
A mí todo lo que me ha sucedido me ha sucedido ayer, anoche a más tardar (Cortázar, Arg. dialogue)	everything that has happened to me happened yesterday, last night at the latest
Hace pocos días, un pacifista danés ha sido acusado de espionaje a favor de Moscú (*La Vanguardia*, Spain)	a few days ago a Danish pacifist was accused of spying for Moscow

(d)   Usually, in negative time phrases of the sort –

Hace años que no te he visto (or *no te veo*) .	I haven't seen you for years

Positive sentences of this type usually require the present tense: *hace años que le veo todos los días* 'I've been seeing him every day for years'.

(e)   The present perfect is sometimes used of famous quotations, e.g.

Aristóteles ha dicho que . . . 'Aristotles said . . .', though Carnicer, *Nuevas reflexiones*, 176, questions this usage. The present, preterite or imperfect is safer.

14.8 Pluperfect

This corresponds quite closely to the English pluperfect, and is used for events or states which preceded some past event and are felt to be relevant to it. The preterite or imperfect are used for the subsequent event, not the perfect:

Yo ya me había dado cuenta de que ustedes no estaban	I had already realized that you weren't there
Sabíamos que ya había vendido el coche	we knew that he had already sold the car

In some circumstances the English pluperfect may be translated by the Spanish preterite. See 14.9 for examples.

14.8.1 Pluperfect in *-ra*

Imperfect subjunctive forms in *-ra* (*hablara*, *tuviera*, *fuera*) are frequently found in literature and journalism as a supposedly elegant alternative for the pluperfect, especially in American Spanish but also and increasingly in Spain among those who think of themselves as stylists. This construction is apparently only found in subordinate, chiefly relative clauses. When used thus, the verb has no subjunctive meaning at all. Lorenzo, 160, remarks of the construction *evidentemente la sentimos como afectada, pero hay muchas gentes que lo son*. This relic of the Latin pluperfect is not heard in speech (but see note ii):

Fue el único rastro que dejó en el que fuera su hogar de casada por cinco horas (García Márquez, Colombia)	it was the only trace she left in what had been her marital home for five hours
Y en la propia Nicaragua, la dinastía de Somoza, que fuera directamente colocada en el poder por Estados Unidos . . . (M. Benedetti in *El País*)	and in Nicaragua itself, the Somoza dynasty, which had been directly installed in power by the United States . . .

Notes (i)   One even finds examples of the imperfect subjunctive in *-se* used as an indicative pluperfect in the same contexts as the *-ra* form described above:

Así había dado con el hombre capaz, muy versado en asuntos económicos, que conociese en la Logia (A. Carpentier, Cuba)	he had thus come across the able man, well versed in economic matters, whom he had met in the (Masonic) Lodge

But this is very rare and rather forced.

(ii)   The *-ra* pluperfect is often heard in Castilian as spoken by Galicians. It survives in standard Peninsular speech in a few constructions, e.g. after *a los* . . . *años de que* . . ., *a los* . . . *días de que* . . ., etc.

A los cinco años de que ganara la lotería ya no tenía dinero	five years after winning the lottery he had no money left

14.8.2   -ra and -se pluperfect after después de que

The rule for the choice of verb form after *después de que* should logically be subjunctive for as yet unfulfilled events, and indicative for fulfilled events, i.e. *comeremos después de que lleguen los demás* 'we'll eat after the rest arrive' (unfulfilled), *decidimos comer después de que llegasen/llegaran los demás* 'we decided we would eat after the rest arrived' (unfulfilled), *comimos después de que llegaron los demás* 'we ate after the rest had arrived' (fulfilled). Cf.

. . . *después de que las hijas mayores la ayudaron a poner un poco de orden en los estragos de la boda* (García Márquez, Colombia)	after the elder daughters (had) helped her to put a bit of order in the devastation left by the wedding

However, written and formal spoken language, for no obvious reason, frequently uses the *-ra* or *-se* form even for fulfilled events in the past.

If the subject of both verbs is the same, *después de que* is replaced by *después de* + infinitive: *nos fuimos después de haber hecho todo* 'we left after we had done everything'. Even if the subjects are different colloquial language may still use the infinitive construction, e.g. *después de llegar Pepe* for *después de que llegó Pepe*, but learners should probably avoid this. Examples:

. . . *después de que Nigeria hiciese pública su decisión de firmar el acta* (*El País*)	after Nigeria made public its decision to sign the communiqué/minutes
. . . *dos años después de que Batista tomara el poder* (*Cambio16*)	two years after Batista took power

Colloquial forms:

Comimos después de llegar los demás (*después de que llegaron/llegaran*)	we ate after the rest arrived
?*Nos fuimos después de haber terminado los albañiles las ventanas* (Popular Spanish. Better *después de que terminaron/terminaran/terminasen*)	we left after the bricklayers had finished the windows

See 16.4.6 note (i) for more details on the subjunctive after *después de que*, and 17.3 for discussion of the infinitive after subordinators.

14.9   Anterior preterite: *hube hablado, hube acabado*

This tense, called *pretérito anterior*, is a perfective pluperfect, and expresses an event completed just before a following past event. It is normally confined to literature and is uncommon in speech except, perhaps, after *apenas*:

Cuando hubieron terminado de reírse, examinaron mi situación personal (A. Cancela, quoted *Esbozo*, 3.14.6)	when they'd finished laughing they examined my personal situation
Se marchó apenas hubo comido	he left as soon as he had eaten
Le escribió el mismo día, no bien se hubo marchado (L. Goytisolo)	he wrote to her the same day, when she had only just left

... *así que, una vez que me hube*   so as soon as I had taken my blouse
   quitado la blusa ...   off ...
   (E. Sabato, Arg., dialogue)

Notes (i) This tense is only used after *después (de) que, luego que, así que, cuando, no bien, enseguida que, en cuanto, tan pronto como, apenas,* and other phrases which emphasize the immediate anteriority of the preceding event. In ordinary language it may be replaced by the preterite:

Cuando terminaron de reírse	when they'd stopped laughing
Tan pronto como llegamos, pasamos al comedor	as soon as we arrived, we went through to the dining room
En cuanto amaneció, partimos	as soon as day had broken, we left

or by the pluperfect:

Apenas había ordenado el señor juez el levantamiento del cadáver para llevarlo al depósito judicial, rompieron el silencio unos gritos de mujer (García Pavón)	the judge had scarcely ordered the removal of the body to the official morgue when the silence was broken by women shouting

(ii) The *pretérito anterior* refers to a single completed event. After the same time phrases, repeated or habitual events are expressed by the ordinary pluperfect: *en cuanto habíamos terminado el trabajo, volvíamos a casa* 'as soon as we had finished work, we used to return home'.

15 Continuous forms of the verb

15.1 General

Spanish has a full range of continuous or durative verb forms compounded from the appropriate tense of *estar* and the gerund: *estoy hablando*, *estuve cenando*, *estaré escribiendo*, etc.

These resemble English progressive forms, e.g. 'I'm talking', 'I was having supper', 'I'll be writing', but the similarity is misleading. The Spanish continuous form differs from its English analogue in two important respects:

(a) It can only refer to an action which is actually in progress at the time of the sentence, whereas the English progressive doubles as a future tense and also, occasionally, as a habitual form:

Estoy comiendo	I'm (actually) eating
Estaré durmiendo	I'll be sleeping/asleep (at that time)
Estaba hablando	I was (in the process of) talking

But:

Llegamos mañana	we're arriving tomorrow (future)
Si te pones así, me voy	if you get like that, I'm going (future)
Mi hijo va a un colegio mixto	my son is going to a mixed (i.e. co-educational) school (habitual)
Te envío ésta para decirte que . . .	I'm sending you this to tell you that . . . (either really means 'I have sent' or 'I shall send')
Yo salía a la mañana siguiente para París	I was leaving the following morning for Paris (future in the past)

The rule about simultaneous action must be strictly applied. One shouts *¡que me caigo!* 'I'm falling' if one is slipping from a branch, but *¡me estoy cayendo!* makes sense only if one is actually in mid-air. Similarly 'I'm drowning' really means 'I'm about to drown', so Spanish speakers shout *¡que me ahogo!*.

(b) The Spanish continuous extends, but does not substantially alter the meaning of the non-continuous verb form, so that the continuous and non-continuous are sometimes virtually interchangeable:

¡Que se queman las salchichas!	the sausages are burning!
¡Que se están quemando las salchichas!	" " " "
Yo hablaba con Mario	I was talking to Mario
Yo estaba hablando con Mario	" " "

The difference is in fact rather elusive, particularly in the present tense. The present tense in Spanish, e.g. *escribo*, *hago*, etc., is temporally imprecise, and may indicate present, future, timeless or even past events (see 14.1.1 and 14.4.3). Continuous forms are much more specific: compare *fuma* 'he smokes' or 'he's smoking' and *está fumando* 'he's (actually) smoking'. It seems that a continuous action must be perceived to be in progress: Peninsular informants said *está lloviendo* on seeing rain through a window, and thought that *llueve* might sound poetic or archaic. But most said *asómate a ver si llueve* 'look out and see if it's raining', or *¿llueve o no llueve?* 'is it raining or not?', the reason apparently being that someone who asks whether it is raining has obviously not perceived rain actually falling. If the questioner had heard the patter of rain, *¿está lloviendo?* would be more appropriate since the phenomenon is perceived.

With some verbs (e.g. *leer* 'to read', *charlar* 'to chat'), or where the duration of an action is emphasized, the continuous is more appropriate than the simple form: *estuve leyendo toda la mañana* is better Spanish than *leí toda la mañana* (example and argument from Moliner, II, 1393).

The continuous form is apparently more common than fifty years ago, and some of its current uses seem to reflect the influence of English, cf. this extract from a commercial circular from Spain: *Su dirección nos ha sido facilitada por nuestra Embajada en su país y nos estamos permitiendo distraer un instante su atención para poner nuestros servicios a su disposición* . . . where *nos permitimos distraer* . . . seems more plausible.

15.2   Uses of the continuous forms

The continuous is used:

(a)   To make clear that an event is, was or will be actually in progress at the time:

Ahora no se puede poner – está haciendo sus cuentas	he can't come to the phone now, he's doing his accounts
No quería molestarla, porque estaba trabajando	I didn't want to bother her/you because she was/you were working
¿Me estarán viendo desde esa ventana?	are they watching me from that window?
Arriba golpearon dos veces, sin mucha fuerza. – Está matando las cucarachas – propuso Gregorius (Cortázar, Arg., dialogue)	there were two knocks from upstairs, not very loud. 'He's killing the cockroaches', Gregorius suggested
Pero ¡si te estoy escuchando!	but I *am* listening to you!

Notes (i)   In the case of the imperfect tense, the continuous and non-continuous are often interchangeable if they really refer to the past, i.e. *pensaba* and *estaba pensando* both mean 'I/he was thinking', but the continuous cannot be used to translate sentences like 'I was giving a lecture the following morning' (*yo daba una conferencia a la mañana siguiente*).

(ii)   The preterite continuous is different in meaning from the non-continuous preterite. *Hablé con él* means 'I spoke to him', *estuve hablando con él* means 'I talked to him for a time', i.e. 'I had a talk with him'. Often the preterite continuous merely emphasizes the fact that an action continued over a period of time, cf. *esperamos dos horas* 'we waited two hours' and *estuvimos esperando dos horas* 'we waited for (all of) two hours'.

(b)   To show that an action is temporary or in some way unexpected:

Vive en París, pero últimamente está viviendo en Madrid	he lives in Paris, but at the moment he's living in Madrid
¿Dónde estás trabajando estos días?	where are you working these days?
Me estoy sintiendo mal	I'm (suddenly) feeling ill

(c)   To express surprise, indignation or lively interest:

Pero ¿qué estás haciendo?	but what *are* you doing?
¿Qué me estás contando?	what *are* you telling me!?
¿En qué estábamos pensando tú y yo cuando engendramos a estos seres, me quieres explicar? – le pregunta la madre al padre	'do you mind explaining to me what you and I were thinking of when we conceived these creatures?', the mother asks the father
(Carmen Rico-Godoy in *Cambio16*)	

(d)   To show that an action is prolonged over a period of time:

Estuve hablando dos horas con tu hermano	I was talking with your brother for two hours
He estado pensando que tú no siempre dices la verdad	I've been thinking that you don't always tell the truth
Pero, ¿vas a estar esperándola todo el día?	but are you going to keep on waiting for her all day?!
El rostro de María sonreía. Es decir, ya no sonreía, pero había estado sonriendo un décimo de segundo antes	Maria's face was smiling. I mean, it wasn't smiling now, but it had been smiling a tenth of a second before
(E. Sabato, Arg.)	

(e)   For accumulative, repetitive events:

Está yendo mucho al cine estos días	he's going to the cinema a lot these days
Está viniendo a casa mucho estos días	he comes to the house a lot these days
La estás viendo demasiado, hijo	you're seeing too much of her, son
Estaba fumando tres paquetes al día cuando yo lo conocí	he was smoking sixty a day when I met him
Lleva años que se está yendo pero nunca acaba de irse	he's been leaving for years but never gets round to going

Venir, ir, may appear in the continuous form in this sense, but not usually in other contexts.

(f)   With the future of *estar*, to denote events felt already to be happening in the present, or to conjecture about what is actually in progress:

Mañana a estas horas estaremos volando sobre el Pacífico	tomorrow at this time we'll be flying over the Pacific
Estarán comiendo a estas horas	they'll probably be eating at this time of day

Note   *Llevar* is used in the continuous only with the sense of 'to carry':

Lleva camisa	he's wearing a shirt
Está llevando una camisa a su madre	he's taking a shirt to his mother

15.2.1   Restrictions on the use of the continuous
Continuous forms are not normally used:

(a)   With certain verbs which refer to emotional states, e.g. *odiar, amar, aborrecer, saber,* e.g. *odio tener que quedarme en casa* 'I hate having to stay at home'. In this respect Spanish and English coincide, but some verbs which denote inner states or 'invisible' actions may appear in the continuous in Spanish but not in English, e.g.

Me estoy creyendo todo lo que dices	?I'm believing everything you say
Estoy viendo que vamos a acabar mal	I can see we're going to end badly
Te estás mereciendo una bofetada	you deserve (i.e. 'are asking for') a slap
Estoy temiendo que va a llegar tarde	I'm afraid he's going to arrive late

Note   *Doler* 'to hurt' may appear in either form, much as in English: *me duele/me está doliendo la barriga* 'my stomach aches/is aching'.

(b)   For verbs that describe states rather than actions (English often allows the progressive form for states):

Normalmente lleva corbata azul, pero hoy lleva una corbata roja	normally he wears a blue tie, but today he's wearing a red tie
Tres arañas de luces colgaban del techo	three chandeliers were hanging from the roof
Lo que falta es . . .	what's lacking is . . .
La luna brillaba sobre las olas	the moon was shining on the waves
Parece cansada	she's looking tired
¡Qué bien huele la madreselva hoy!	isn't the honeysuckle smelling good today!

Notes (i)   Verbs denoting physical posture or position can refer only to an action, not to a state. English speakers are often misled by forms like 'he's sitting down' which almost always means *estaba sentado. Estaba sentándose* = 'he was in the process of sitting down.'

Estaban tumbados	they were lying down
Estaba agachado	he was bending down
(Compare *estaba agachándose*	he was in the process of bending down)

   (ii)   *Tener* 'to have' is rare in the continuous, except in the frequentative sense described earlier: *me dijo que estaba teniendo problemas con su vecino* 'he told me he was having problems with his neighbour'.

(c)   The continuous is not used with *estar* (*estar estando is not Spanish), or usually with *ir, venir, regresar, volver, andar*, except in the frequentative sense (15.2e):

¿Adónde vas?	where are you going?
Viene ahora	he's coming now
Cuando volvíamos del cine me subí un momento a ver a la abuela	when we were coming back from the cinema I went up to see grandmother for a moment
Estás estúpido hoy	you're being stupid today

15.3   Continuous forms of *ser*

Some grammarians frown on continuous forms of *ser* as Anglicisms, but they are not uncommon, especially in Latin America, and occur in speech as well as writing to judge by the dialogue of some novels.

   It seems unreasonable to deny the language the nuance provided by a continuous form of *ser*, e.g.:

Por un instante pensó que de algún modo él, Martín, estaba de verdad siendo necesario a aquel ser atormentado (E. Sabato, Arg.)

for an instant he thought that he, Martin, was really necessary to that tormented creature (lit. 'being necessary')

La convocatoria a las distintas manifestaciones está siendo variada (*La Vanguardia*, Spain)

(lit.) the calling to the various demonstrations is varied (i.e. the people attending come from various sources)

-Todos tenemos varias existencias - volvió a interrumpir Maldonado . . . -, ¿usted no? -Licenciado - dijo glacialmente el peinado a la bross -, yo no estoy siendo juzgado (C. Fuentes, Mex. dialogue)

'We all have several lives', Maldonado interrupted again. 'Don't you?' '*Licenciado*[1]' - the man with the brush haircut said glacially, 'I'm not being judged.'

Estás siendo muy bueno hoy

you're being very good today

But unless passive with *ser* must be used it seems wise to observe Carnicer's rejection (*Nuevas reflexiones*, 43ff) of sentences like *la fachada está siendo reparada* 'the front of the building is being repaired' in favour of *se está reparando la fachada*.

---

[1]Mexican respect title for lawyers

16 The subjunctive

16.1 General

The subjunctive is a very important feature of Spanish and there is no conclusive evidence that it is disappearing from the language, as some have claimed, although it is true that spontaneous speech, especially Spanish-American, sometimes uses the indicative where formal language requires the subjunctive.

There seems to be a single principle underlying nearly all uses of the Spanish subjunctive, although there are some cases which defy easy classification. The subjunctive is closely associated with subordinate clauses, especially clauses introduced by *que*, and with relative clauses. Examination of the clauses in which the subjunctive appears shows that the great majority share a common feature: the meaning of the main clause makes the event described in the subordinate clause 'unreal', i.e. not known to be a reality at the time of the sentence. Such 'unreality' may arise from the fact that:

(a) The event has or had not yet happened:

Llegamos antes de que saliera/saliese el tren	we arrived before the train left
Cenaremos cuando lleguen los demás	we'll have supper when the rest arrive
Te lo dejo con tal de que me lo devuelvas	I'll lend it you provided you return it to me

(This principle governs many cases of the use of the subjunctive after subordinators meaning 'when', 'after', 'before', 'as', 'in order to', 'as soon as', etc.)

(b) It never happened or is not known to have happened:

Entré sin que me viera/viese nadie	I entered without anyone seeing me
No creo que sea verdad	I don't think it's true

(c) The subject wants, orders, hopes, fears, intends or causes the event to happen or not to happen (although these are probably instances of case **(a)**, i.e. the event was not yet a reality at the time of the main clause):

Quiero que me lo digas	I want you to tell me it
Me dijo que lo hiciera/hiciese	she told me to do it
Espero que no venga	I hope he doesn't come
Me temo que se haya perdido	I'm afraid it's got lost
Era su intención que nadie se diera/ diese cuenta	it was his intention that no one should find out

(d) The event is merely a possibility:

Es posible que venga	it's possible that he'll come
Tal vez te llame mañana	perhaps (s)he'll ring you tomorrow
. . . la idea de que el hombre viaje a las estrellas	the idea of Man travelling to the stars

(e) The subject of the verb is not known to exist or has not been identified:

No hay nadie que le entienda	there's no one who can understand him
Cásate con alguien que sepa cocinar	marry someone who can cook

(f) The speaker is not stating that the event is a fact so much as expressing a reaction to it (this is a more complex instance of the 'unreality' principle[1]):

Sería mejor que te callaras/callases	it would be better if you kept quiet
Es increíble que nadie lo haya encontrado	it's incredible that no one found it
Me molesta que hables así	it upsets me that you should talk like that
¡Qué pena que no hayas venido antes!	what a shame you didn't come earlier!

One lingering misconception about the Spanish subjunctive is that it expresses 'doubt', but the sentence *me acostaré cuando se ponga el sol* 'I'll go to bed when the sun sets' does not doubt that the sun will set; the subjunctive is required after *cuando* because the sunset is still in the future.[2] Likewise in *el hecho de que España no tenga petróleo explica en parte las dificultades económicas del país* 'the fact that Spain has no oil explains in part the country's economic difficulties' there is no doubt about Spain's having no oil; it is merely a rule that phrases meaning 'the fact that' usually require the subjunctive. This latter rule does not clearly fit the 'unreality' principle, and is probably best learnt as an exception.

As was stated earlier, the subjunctive is intimately associated with subordinate clauses, especially with those introduced by *que*. It is much less common in main clauses, but it occurs (a) as the normal imperative form corresponding to *usted/ustedes*, e.g. *siéntese por favor* 'please sit down', and (b) usually after most words meaning 'perhaps' (see 16.7.3 for details). See 16.7 for discussion of the use of the subjunctive in main clauses.

---

[1]This does not of course mean that the event is 'unreal'; merely that its reality is not the issue. The effect of the subjunctive in differentiating reactions from objective assertions is occasionally clearly visible, cf. the two sentences *es una tragedia que haya sucedido* 'it's a tragedy that it happened' and *es una tragedia que ha sucedido* (indicative) 'it's a tragedy that has happened'; the latter is matter-of-fact, the former is a value judgement. Compare also the two sentences *es una mentira que haya dicho «María»* (reaction) 'it's a lie that he said "María" ' and *es una mentira que ha dicho María* 'it's a lie Maria told' (i.e. 'it's one of Maria's lies': factual). One reason for the survival of the Spanish subjunctive is the need to clarify the function of the overworked *que*, which in the first example of each pair is a subordinating conjunction, and in the second a relative pronoun.

[2]Spanish here differs from French and Italian, which use the future indicative in clauses with future reference introduced by a time subordinator, cf. *on y ira quand il fera beau temps*, *ci andremo quando farà bel tempo* (both verbs future) and *iremos allí cuando haga buen tiempo* (second verb subjunctive).

Only two simple (non-compound) tenses of the subjunctive are in use, the present, formed as explained at 13.1f, and the imperfect, formed as explained at 13.1g. Except in the cases mentioned in the next section, the *-ra* and *-se* forms of the imperfect subjunctive are freely interchangeable. The future subjunctive, discussed at 16.9 is virtually obsolete and has now been replaced by the present subjunctive.

In general the syntax of the subjunctive is quite stable throughout the Hispanic world, at least in written language and educated speech; its replacement in some constructions in the speech of Navarre and Northern Spain, Argentina and elsewhere by the conditional or future is confined to popular speech and is rejected by educated speakers. Although the following chapter sets out rules for the use of the subjunctive, it must be remembered that its use often depends on the speaker's point of view, which is itself determined by context. As a result native speakers will occasionally deviate from the rules for reasons which cannot be stated in the abstract.

16.1.1   The *-ra and -se* imperfect subjunctive
There are two imperfect subjunctives, one in *-ra* and one in *-se*: their forms are set out at 13.1g and table 2, p. 185.

When they are used as subjunctive forms they seem to be entirely interchangeable, and the two forms are shown side by side in most of the following examples. The *-ra* form is statistically more frequent and in some parts of Spanish America has all but ousted the *-se* form, though not in Argentina to judge by the popular dialogue in Manuel Puig's novels.

The *-ra* form has a few other functions as an indicative form which it does not share with the *-se* form, at least in normal styles:

(a)   It may be a supposedly elegant literary variant for the indicative pluperfect, especially in Spanish-American literary texts. See 14.8.1 for examples.

(b)   It regularly replaces the conditional of *haber*, e.g. *habría sido mejor/hubiera sido mejor* 'it would have been better', and less commonly of a few other verbs. See 14.5.2 for discussion.

(c)   It is used in a few set phrases: e.g. *acabáramos* 'now I see what you're getting at', *otro gallo nos cantara* 'that would be another story'.

Historically the *-ra* form descends from the Latin pluperfect indicative, and Portuguese and some dialects of North-Western Spain preserve this pluperfect function.

16.2   Subjunctive after 'subjective' statements

16.2.1   Subjunctive after statements of 'influence' followed by *que*
The subjunctive is obligatory if the meaning of the main clause implies 'influencing' the outcome of the subordinate clause. 'Influence' typically involves wanting, ordering, advising, prohibiting, allowing, causing or

avoiding. It is arguable that this use of the subjunctive is the same as the one described in the following section: i.e. the meaning of the statement in the main clause can be reduced to wanting or not wanting something to happen, which implies a value judgement.

Quiero que estudies más	I want you to study harder
Mandaron que te siguiéramos/ siguiésemos	they ordered us to follow you
Aconseja a tu yerno que lo haga	advise your son-in-law to do it
Soy partidario de que lo publiquen	I'm in favour of them publishing it
Esto dio como resultado que no le hicieran/hiciesen caso	the upshot of this was that they ignored him/her
Dice que vengas	he says you must come
Estamos deseando que llueva	we're hoping for rain
Procuraremos evitar que nadie mencione el asunto	we'll try to avoid anyone mentioning the matter
Me salvé de puro milagro de que los ladrones me mataran/matasen	by a sheer miracle I avoided being killed by the thieves
La idea era que las chicas ayudasen/ ayudaran a los chicos	the idea was that the girls should help the boys
Cierta impaciencia generosa no ha consentido que yo aprendiera a leer (Borges, Arg.)	a certain generous impatience did not allow me to learn to read
El primer paso, le dijo, era lograr que ella se diera cuenta de su interés (García Márquez, Colombia)	the first thing to do, she said to him, was to get her to notice his interest
Carvalho instó a Biscuter a que se llevase el bocadillo (M. Vázquez Montalbán)	Carvalho asked Biscuter to take away the sandwich
Nadie impidió que Hemingway escribiera y publicase sus libros (G. Cabrera Infante, Cuba)	nobody prevented Hemingway from writing and publishing his books

and similarly after *permitir que* 'permit', *prohibir que* 'prohibit', etc.

Notes (i)   A noun phrase like *la decisión de que, la orden de que, el deseo de que*, etc. can replace the main verb:

La orden de que se apagaran/apagasen las luces fue el coronel quien la dio	it was the colonel who ordered the lights to be turned off
El anhelo de que Dios exista	the longing for God to exist
La ambición de que su hija llegara/ llegase a ser primer ministro	the ambition that his daughter should become Prime Minister
La petición de que se la indultara/ indultase no llegó a tiempo	the petition for her reprieve didn't arrive in time

    (ii)   *Explicar que* 'to explain that' is discussed at 16.2.6c.

    (iii)   When the main clause contains the verbs *prohibir, permitir, mandar* 'to order', *obligar* or some other verb of similar meaning, either a subjunctive or an infinitive construction is possible:

Te prohíbo cantar	I forbid you to sing
Te prohíbo que cantes	
Le obligan a llegar pronto	they make him come early
Le obligan a que llegue pronto	
Me mandan a recoger el correo	they send me to collect the post
Me mandan a que recoja el correo	

Permitió a su hija bailar	he allowed his daughter to dance
Permitió a su hija que bailara/bailase	

16.2.2   Subjunctive after emotional reactions and value judgements followed by *que*

The subjunctive is obligatory in such sentences. 'Emotional reaction' covers a vast range of possibilities including regret, pleasure, displeasure, surprise. It also includes value judgements like *¡qué pena que!*, *¡qué lástima que!*, *es terrible que*, *es lógico que*, *es natural que*, *sería mejor que*, *es necesario que*, *es imprescindible que*. It is important to differentiate between value judgements and statements of fact like *es verdad que* 'it's true', *es obvio que* 'it's obvious that', etc. which require the indicative although the distinction may appear arbitrary to an English speaker. For the latter see 16.2.6. For statements of fearing and hoping see 16.2.3; for statements of doubt, possibility and plausibility see 16.2.4–5.

Me molesta que te quejes tanto	it annoys me that you complain so much
Les sorprendió que no lo supiera/supiese	they were surprised she didn't know
Lamentan que no lo recuerdes	they're sorry you can't remember it
Me alegra que te guste	I'm happy you like it
Me importa un bledo que se celebre o no se celebre	I couldn't care less whether it takes place or doesn't
Le irritó que María permaneciese callada	he/she was irritated at Maria's remaining silent
Es natural que le riña	it's only natural that she tells him off
¡Qué pena que no lo encuentres!	what a pity you can't find it!
Es lógico que lo niegue	it's logical for him to deny it
Es una vergüenza que dejen que pasen estas cosas	it's a disgrace that they allow these things to happen
Sería mejor que le reconociese el médico	it would be better if the doctor examined him
Es necesario que consigas las entradas	it's necessary that you should get the tickets
Basta que les des la mitad ahora	it's enough for you to give them half now
Fue una lástima que no me lo dijeras/dijeses	it was a pity you didn't tell me
Fue una casualidad que yo me encontrara/encontrase allí	it was pure chance that I was there
¡Qué rabia que no nos suban el sueldo!	what a nuisance that we won't get a salary rise!
Ya era hora (de) que alguien le quitara/quitase el trabajo al ama de casa	it was time somebody lightened the housewife's load
El catedrático de portugués se sorprendió mucho de que yo me sorprendiera cuando me contó (. . .) que este año sólo tenía un estudiante (Vargas Llosa, Peru)	the professor of Portuguese was very surprised that I was surprised when he told me (. . .) that he only had one student this year
Quizá le parezca mal que hable así de ella, porque es usted su amigo (G. Torrente Ballester, Spain)	perhaps you will disapprove of my talking about her like that, because you are her friend

Notes (i)   After expressions denoting emotional reactions which are followed by *de que* the subjunctive is more normal in formal language and safer for non-natives, although the indicative tenses are sometimes found in informal speech when the verb is in the present or past:

Me alegré de que (pensaban)/pensaran/ pensasen hacerlo	I was glad that they intended to do it
Se indignaba de que sus suegros (creían)/ creyeran/creyesen en la pena de muerte	he/she was outraged that his/her in-laws believed in the death penalty
Se horrorizaba de que la (trataban)/ trataran/tratasen así	he was shocked at their treating her this way
Se queja de que Berta la hace quedarse a dormir la siesta (indic. normal) (M. Puig, Arg., dialogue)	she complains about Berta making her stay in to sleep in the afternoon
El arzobispo se había escandalizado de que un católico militante y culto se hubiera atrevido a pensar en la santidad de un suicida (García Márquez, Colombia)	the archbishop was shocked that a practising and educated Catholic could have dared to think in terms of the saintliness of a man who had committed suicide

(ii)   *Menos mal que* 'thank heavens that' takes the indicative, as does *mejor* when it is a colloquial abbreviation of *es mejor que*:

Menos mal que no se ha roto	thank heavens it's not broken
Menos mal que hice un cursillo de maquillaje	it's a good job I did a make-up course
Es mejor que lo dejemos para más tarde	we'd better leave it until later
Mejor lo dejamos para más tarde	better that we leave it for later

(iii)   In American Spanish a value judgement about a past event may sometimes apparently be expressed by the indicative. This is especially true if *ser* is not used:

El innegable genio de Joyce era puramente verbal; lástima que lo gastó en la novela (Borges, Arg.)	Joyce's undeniable genius was purely verbal; a pity that he used it on the novel
Era curioso que Morelli abrazaba con entusiasmo las últimas hipótesis de trabajo de la ciencia física (J. Cortázar, Arg.)	it was curious that Morelli enthusiastically embraced the latest working hypotheses of physical science

(iv)   In sentences constructed with *lo* + adjective + *ser* + *que* the subjunctive is required if the verb in the main clause points to the future:

Lo peor será que no venga nadie	the worst thing will be if no one comes
Lo malo sería que no terminaran/ terminasen el trabajo a tiempo	the trouble would be if they didn't finish the work on time

If the main verb is timeless, habitual or in the past, the verb is usually in the indicative:

Lo peor es que él nunca se pone al teléfono	the worst thing is that he never answers the phone
Lo molesto era que él fumaba demasiado	the nuisance was that he smoked too much
Lo terrible fue que no vino	the terrible thing was that he did not come

In some cases use of the subjunctive depends on the meaning:

Lo increíble era que Pedro no lo sabía	the incredible thing was that Pedro didn't know about it
Lo increíble era que Pedro no lo supiera/supiese	the incredible thing was that Pedro didn't know about it

In the foregoing two examples there is a slight difference between moods. The indicative assumes that Pedro did not know, whereas the subjunctive leaves open the question whether he knew or not. The choice depends on whether the action denoted by the subordinate verb is a reality to the speaker. Compare:

Lo peor es que mi padre nunca dice nada	the worst thing is that my father never says anything

and a possible reply to this –

Sí, lo peor es que no diga nada	yes, the worst thing is that he doesn't say anything (i.e. *if* that is the case)

In the second example the speaker does not claim actual knowledge of the facts described by the first speaker. This subtle distinction will be found to operate in many examples of subjunctive use.

16.2.3 Statements of fear and hope

Temer(se)/tener miedo de que 'to fear', *esperar que* 'to hope' and other statements of similar meaning are classified as emotional reactions and require the subjunctive:

Temo que le moleste	I'm afraid it may upset him
Por eso me da recelo que te metas en política (Usigli, Mex., dialogue)	that's why I get nervous about you getting into politics
El temor de que dijera que sí	the fear that he would say yes
Espero que le convenzas	I hope you convince him
La esperanza de que todo acabe bien	the hope that everything will end well

But the conditional or future indicative is found with *temer* and with *esperar* when it means 'to expect' rather than 'to hope':

Temo que no pagarán tanto	I fear they won't pay that much
Espero que te concederán el premio	I expect they'll give you the prize
Esperaba que te concederían el premio	I expected they'd give you the prize

The indicative is also used with *ir a* 'to go to':

Temo que me va a oír	I'm afraid he's going to hear me
Espero que me vas a pagar	I hope you're going to pay me

But the subjunctive is required if the above construction is negated:

No temía que me fuera a atacar	I wasn't afraid he was going to attack me
No esperaba que le fuera a escribir	I didn't expect she was going to write to him

Note Redundant *no* (see 21.1.3 Negation) instead of *que* after *temer* changes the meaning. The subjunctive is obligatory:

Temo que no te va a gustar	I'm afraid you're not going to like it
Temo no te vaya a gustar demasiado	I'm afraid in case/lest you're going to like it too much
Temo no te vayas a enfadar	I'm afraid in case/lest you get cross

16.2.4 Statements of doubt

Dudar que takes the subjunctive, but when it is used in the negative is often followed by an indicative when it really means 'to be sure':

Dudo que sea verdad	I doubt whether it's true
No dudo que sea verdad lo que dices	I don't doubt whether what you say is true
No dudo que es verdad lo que dices	I don't doubt that what you say is true
No dudo que vendrá/venga	I don't doubt he'll come
El no dudaba que vendría/viniera/ viniese	he/she didn't doubt he would come

No hay duda (de) que ella puede ser discutida (Vargas Llosa, Peru)	there is no doubt that it can be debated

16.2.5 Statements of possibility and plausibility

These always require the subjunctive:

Es posible que haya tormenta	there may be a storm
Era probable que sucediera así	it was probable that it would happen that way
Es previsible que para el año 2500 tengamos ordenadores superinteligentes que les darán ciento y raya a sus inventores humanos	it's foreseeable that by the year 2500 we will have superintelligent computers which leave their human inventors standing
Puede ser que este auge se prolongue y enriquezca con escritores más originales y propios (Vargas Llosa, Peru)	this boom may last and be enriched by more original and more native authors
La sola posibilidad de que aquella muchacha no lo viese más lo desesperaba (E. Sabato, Arg.)	the mere possibility that that girl wouldn't see him again filled him with despair
Es fácil que no te paguen	it's likely that they won't pay you

Notes (i) *Pueda que* is a common Spanish-American alternative for *puede que/puede ser que*:

Pueda que algo te den y te mejores (M. Puig, Arg., dialogue)	maybe they'll give you something and you'll get better

(ii) Use of the subjunctive after words meaning 'perhaps' is governed by different rules. See 16.7.3.

(iii) For *posiblemente*, *probablemente* see 16.7.3d.

16.2.6 Subjunctive after negated verbs of knowing, perceiving, stating or communicating

(a) If the main clause denotes knowledge, perception, stating, communicating, the subordinate verb is in the indicative unless the main clause contains a negative. This also applies to statements of fact like *es verdad/cierto/evidente/indudable/seguro que*, etc.

However the subjunctive is often optional after such negations, depending on the degree of uncertainty involved. In some cases the subjunctive causes a slight change of meaning:

Digo que es así	I say that it is so
No digo que sea así	I don't say that it is so
Creo que él lo conoce	I think he knows him
No creo que él lo conozca	I don't think he knows him
Recuerdo que tu madre era esbelta	I remember your mother was slim
No recuerdo que tu madre fuera/fuese esbelta	I don't remember your mother being slim
Veo que te has cortado el pelo	I see you've had your hair cut
No veo que te hayas cortado el pelo	I can't see (i.e. don't believe) you've had your hair cut

Yo sabía que él estaba ahí	I knew he was there
Yo no sabía que él estaba ahí	I didn't know he was there
Yo no sabía que él estuviera/estuviese ahí (almost no difference)	I didn't know he was there
No es seguro que el gobierno reduzca/ reducirá los impuestos fiscales	it's not certain that the Government will lower income taxes
Esto no significa que haya que esperar un cambio radical de actitud (J. Cortázar, Arg.)	this doesn't mean that one must expect a radical change of attitude
No creo que sea para ponerse así don Baldomero (G. Torrente Ballester, Spain)	I don't think it's worth getting like that over it, Don Baldomero
Claro que aparte de fumar y beber no veía que se pudiera hacer otra cosa (Vargas Llosa, Peru)	obviously, apart from smoking and drinking he didn't see that there was anything else to do

Notes (i)   The verb *negar* 'to deny' requires a subjunctive:

Niego que haya venido	I deny she's come

But the indicative is apparently sometimes found in Spanish America, cf. *niego que hubo bronca* 'I deny there was a row' (*Proceso*, Mexico).

(ii)   Note that a negative question does not amount to a negation, so the indicative is used:

¿No es verdad que ha dicho eso?	isn't it true that he said that?

(iii)   Compare the different translations of *decir* in the following examples:

Ha dicho que venía	he/she said he/she was coming
No he dicho que venía	I didn't say I was coming
No he dicho que viniera/viniese	I didn't tell him to come
El chofer dijo que él se ganaba la vida como podía, y al que no le gustara que bajase y tomase un taxi para él solito (Carlos Fuentes, Mex., *chofer = chófer* in Spain)	the taxi driver said he earned his living as well as he could and anybody who didn't like it, could get off and take a taxi for himself

(iv)   If the verb in the main clause is in the imperative form, the verb in the subordinate clause remains in the indicative:

No digas que es verdad	don't say it's true
No crea usted que es tonto	don't imagine that he's stupid

(v)   *No ser que* is normally followed by the subjunctive, but not in questions:

No es que yo diga que es mentira	it's not that I'm saying that it's a lie
No era que yo no la quisiera/quisiese	it wasn't that I didn't love her
¿No será que no quiere hacerlo?	isn't the case that he doesn't want to do it?
¿No sería que no quedaban más?	wouldn't it be that there were none left?

But the following example must speak for itself:

No era que tomaba posesión del mundo (Unamuno, Spain)	it wasn't that he was taking possession of the world

(b)   Subjunctive after *creer, parecer, suponer* and *sospechar*

The subjunctive occasionally appears after these verbs even when they are positive. The meaning is then more hypothetical or hesitant:

A veces parece que estás soñando	sometimes it seems you're dreaming
A veces parece que estés soñando	sometimes it seems as if you were dreaming

Sospecho que es mentira	I suspect it is a lie
Sospecho que sea mentira	I suspect it may be a lie
Como si la Historia fuera una especie de saltamontes; y parece que lo sea pero en otro sentido (A. Sastre, dialogue)	as if History were a sort of grasshopper; and it seems that it is but in a different sense
¿Usted cree que esto ayude? (Manuel Puig, Arg., dialogue)	do you really think that this helps?

(c)   Subjunctive after *comprender, explicar*

Comprender takes the subjunctive when it means 'to sympathize':

Comprendo que no quieras pedir dinero prestado	I understand your not wanting to borrow money
Yo comprendo que los concejales defendieran sus posiciones dentro del partido (Santiago Carrillo in *Cambio16*)	I understand the councillors defending their positions inside the party

Explicar usually takes the subjunctive except when it really means 'to state' or 'to say':

Esto explica que las mutaciones de la literatura estén estrechamente ligadas a las innovaciones técnicas	this explains how changes in literature are intimately linked to technical innovations

But:

Manuel explicó que había estado enfermo	Manuel explained that he had been ill

16.3   Noun phrases as subordinators

When a noun phrase replaces a verb phrase it is normally connected to a following subordinate clause by *de que*: compare *esperamos que llueva* 'we hope it will rain' and *la esperanza de que llueva* 'the hope that it will rain', and see 27.4.2 for further discussion.

In general the mood of the subordinate verb after such noun phrases is governed by the rules that would affect verb phrases of the same meaning as the noun phrase, i.e. *la posibilidad de que* . . . requires the subjunctive because *es posible que* does.

There are, however, a number of complications with phrases meaning 'the fact that', and with a number of other noun phrases.

(a)   With *el hecho de que/el que/que* 'the fact that' the subjunctive is normally used with statements of influence and reaction and with value judgements, especially if the phrase is at the head of the sentence:

El que en semanas se haya conseguido cabrear a la vez a todos . . . es todo un síntoma que se debería convertir en preocupación (*Cambio16*)	the fact that it has been possible to annoy everybody simultaneously in a matter of weeks is a symptom which should become a matter of concern
Que los valores estéticos sean los predominantes y definitorios es demoledor (*El País*: E. Tierno Galván)	the fact that aesthetic values are the principal and definitive ones is overwhelming
Que tres aviones se destrocen, se desplome un tren, . . . arda una discoteca, y todo en menos de un mes quizá sea simplemente casualidad (*Cambio16*)	the fact that three aeroplanes are destroyed, a train plunges into a ravine, a discotheque catches fire, and all in less than a month, is perhaps pure chance

Lo que me hace insoportable tu vanidad es el hecho de que hiera la mía (Cartoon by J. Ballesta in *Cambio16*)	what makes your vanity unbearable is the fact that it wounds mine
No hay duda de que el hecho de que me hayan dado el Nobel va a dar mayor resonancia a todo lo que diga y haga (García Márquez, Colombia)	there is no doubt that the fact that they've given me the Nobel prize will give more weight to everything I say and do
Que las Malvinas pertenezcan a la República Argentina es un hecho indiscutible (J. Cortázar, Arg., some speakers prefer *pertenecen*)	(the fact) that the Falkland Islands belong to the Republic of Argentina is an unquestionable fact

However the indicative is the rule when the main verb is a verb of knowing, perceiving, stating or communicating, or, apparently, when *el hecho de que* is preceded by a preposition:

Se ha dado cuenta del hecho de que tiene que trabajar para vivir	he/she has realized he has to work in order to live
No lo hace por el hecho de que no le gusta	she doesn't do it because she doesn't like it
Le disgustaría que no viniera sólo por el hecho de que viene él	she would be upset if you didn't come only because he was coming
Que a las autoridades francesas les gusta tratar amistosamente con terroristas es algo demostrado (*Cambio16*)	the fact that French authorities like to have friendly dealings with terrorists is demonstrably true
. . . quizá tenga ello también algo que ver con el hecho de que la actividad artística misma (. . .) está moviéndose ahora hacia la recuperación de esa funcionalidad (*Cambio16*)	. . . perhaps it may also have something to do with the fact that artistic activity itself (. . .) is moving now towards recovering that function

Nevertheless there are numerous cases in which the mood of the verb introduced by *el hecho de que* seems to be dictated by stylistic factors. In these cases the subjunctive seems to be the safe option. The following examples must speak for themselves:

Le molesta el hecho de que no venga/ viene a verle	the fact that she doesn't come to see him annoys him
No le daba importancia al hecho de que él no le hacía/hiciera/hiciese caso	she didn't mind the fact that he paid her no attention
No quiero que el hecho de que te conozco/ conozca sea un obstáculo	I don't want the fact that I know you to be an obstacle
El hecho de que no me veía/viera/ viese me hacía sentirme seguro	the fact that she couldn't see me made me feel safe

   (b)   There is a series of miscellaneous noun phrases after which choice between the subjunctive and indicative is determined by meaning. Two factors may combine or operate independently to invoke the subjunctive: (a) the type of verb in the main clause, (b) the reality or non-reality of the event expressed by the subordinate clause.

   In the following examples the verb in the main clause is of a type (emotional reaction, possibility, etc.) which would itself require the subjunctive, so the subjunctive is normal:

Le contrarió la casualidad de que encontrase/encontrara ahí a su primo	he was annoyed by happening to find his cousin there
Podría dar la casualidad de que hubiera/ hubiese huelga	there might possibly be a strike
No podía soportar la idea de que no le dieran/diesen el puesto	he couldn't stand the idea of not getting the job

In the following sentences the indicative is used because the subordinate verb indicates an established fact or reality:

Siempre daba la casualidad de que no llegaban a tiempo	it always happened that they never arrived on time (habitual fact)
Se tenían que enfrentar con el problema de que no tenían dinero	they had to face up to the problem of not having any money (fact)
Consiguió que aceptara la idea de que no le darían el puesto	she managed to get him to accept the idea that they wouldn't give him/her the job (i.e. accepting a fact)
Tengo la convicción de que no hace nada	I'm convinced he does nothing (knowledge)
Se encontró con la sorpresa de que estaba de mal humor	he was surprised to find that she was in a bad mood (factual)
Le atormentaba la obsesión de que su mujer le engañaba	he was tormented by the obsession that his wife was being unfaithful to him (factual as far as the speaker knows)

(c) There remains a grey area in which the choice between subjunctive and indicative is either more or less optional, or is dictated by some principle so elusive that it defies our ingenuity to explain it. The following examples must speak for themselves:

Tuve la suerte de que no me viera/vio	I was lucky in that he didn't see me (on that occasion) (factual, subjunctive more usual)

But:

Tenía la suerte de que no me veía	I was lucky in that he didn't see me (on one or several occasions. Indicative only)
Tenía siempre la preocupación de que le iba/fuera a pasar algo	he always worried that something might happen to him
Vivía con la pesadilla de que perdería su dinero	he lived with the nightmare of losing his money (indicative only)
Le animaba la ilusión de que lo conseguiría	he was encouraged by the dream of getting it (same subject for both verbs)
Le animaba la ilusión de que ella lo conseguiría/consiguiera	he was encouraged by the dream that she would get it

16.4 Subjunctive after other subordinators

16.4.1 Introductory

Words and phrases discussed here are *cuando, antes de que, sin que, mientras, para que, como si, aunque, a condición de que,* etc. Some of these always require a subjunctive (e.g. *antes de que, para que, sin que*), but most take either mood according to their meaning. The subordinate verb is in the subjunctive only if it refers to some event which has or had not yet happened, or is or was not known to have happened (e.g. *le animo cuando viene* 'I encourage him when he comes', *le animaré cuando venga* 'I'll encourage him when he comes').

The subordinate clause may precede or follow the main clause.

The underlying principle is that the subjunctive is used for events which are *not yet* realities at the time of the main clause. Thus sentences like 'I arrived before the train left', 'I'll wait until you do it', 'I got in without him seeing' require the subjunctive because in every case the second verb denotes an event which is, or was, still unrealized at the time of the main verb.

Only subordinators which may take the subjunctive are discussed here. For subordinators which take only the indicative see chapter 27.

For replacement of the subjunctive by the infinitive see 17.3.

16.4.2 Subjunctive with subordinators of purpose

A que, a fin de que, para que/porque, con el objeto de que, con el propósito de que, con la intención de que, no fuera que, etc. When they mean 'so that', 'in order to' they are always followed by a subjunctive because they obviously precede an action which has not yet happened:

Vengo a que/para que me dejes un poco de azúcar	I've come to borrow some sugar
Me callé porque/para que no me acusaran/acusasen de metomentodo	I kept silent so that they wouldn't accuse me of interfering
He escrito una circular a fin de que se enteren todos	I've written a circular so that everybody knows about it
Volvió la cara al pasar no fuera que le reconocieran	he turned his face when he passed by to avoid being recognized

Note   For the difference between *por* and *para* when both refer to purpose, see 28.14.7.

16.4.3 Subjunctive with subordinators of cause and consequence

(a)   *Puesto que, ya que, como* 'since' etc. are followed by the indicative. (See 27.5.2). *Como* in conditional sentences is discussed at 23.5.2.

Invítame ya que/puesto que tienes tanto dinero	since you have so much money you can pay for me
Como tienes tanto dinero me puedes invitar	since you have so much money you can pay for me
(*Como* must appear at the head of the sentence)	
Como estaba sordo, no lo oyó	since he was deaf he didn't hear it

(b)   *Porque* is usually followed by an indicative but requires the subjunctive when it means 'just because/only because' and the main verb is negated. Sometimes it can be precede by *sólo*:

Porque tú lo digas, no voy a callarme	I'm not going to shut up just because you say so

No lo hago porque tú lo digas	I'm not doing it just because you say so

But:

No lo hago porque tú lo dices	I won't do it because you say so
No lo hago sólo porque tú lo dices	the reason I'm doing it is not only because you tell me to
No salgo contigo sólo porque tienes un Ferrari	the fact that you have a Ferrari is not the only reason I go out with you

Compare:

Sólo porque tengas un Ferrari no voy a salir contigo	the fact that you have a Ferrari is not a good enough reason for me to go out with you

The subjunctive is used after *bien porque . . . o/ya porque . . . o* meaning 'whether . . . or':

Bien/ya porque tuviera algo que hacer o porque estuviera cansado, el caso es que no estuvo muy amable con nosotros	whether he had something to do or whether he was tired, the fact is that he wasn't very kind to us

(c) *De ahí que* is normally followed by a subjunctive:

Su padre murió de una borrachera, de ahí que no beba	his father died from a drunken fit, that's why he doesn't drink
De ahí que entre la codorniz agosteña y la septembrina haya una distancia (M. Delibes)	hence the fact that there is a difference (lit. 'distance') between the August quail and the September quail
De ahí que el Papa haya incluso presionado al nuevo Gobierno (El País)	this is why the Pope has even put pressure on the new Government

16.4.4 Subjunctive with subordinators of result, aim and manner

The basic rule is that these take the indicative when they imply result and the subjunctive when they refer to an aim or intention.

(a) *Así que, conque/de modo que/de manera que* when they indicate result always call for the indicative (unless they are followed by an imperative in the negative):

Tú sólo tienes la culpa, de modo que no te puedes quejar	you've got only yourself to blame so you' can't complain
Tú sólo tienes la culpa, de modo que no te quejes	you've got only yourself to blame so don't complain
Llegaré tarde, de modo que no tienes que preparar nada	I'll be late so you don't have to prepare anything
Lo hicieron en silencio de modo que no se enteró el portero	they did it in silence so (as a result) the doorman didn't find out

Así que, de manera que or *conque* would have been equally correct in the above examples.

The problem with *de modo que/de manera que/de forma que* is that they may indicate either aim or result and in the former case take the subjunctive. Unfortunately English no longer systematically clarifies the difference so that the sentences *lo hizo de modo que nadie se enteró* and *lo hizo de modo que nadie se enterase* may both be translated 'he did it so no one realized' despite the fact that they mean entirely different things in Spanish. Strictly speaking the first means 'he did it and no one realized' and

the second means 'he did it in such a way that no one should realize'.
Translating from English into Spanish often poses the dilemma that there is
no way of knowing whether the English original implies result or aim.
Compare:

Salió de modo/manera que nadie lo notara/notase	he left so no one would notice
Salió de modo/manera que nadie lo notó	she left so/and nobody noticed
Compórtate de modo/manera que no sospeche	behave so as to avoid him suspecting
Entró silenciosamente de modo/manera que yo no la oyera/oyese	she came in quietly so that I wouldn't hear her
Entró silenciosamente de modo/manera que no la oí	she came in quietly so I didn't hear her

   (b)   *Como* requires the subjunctive when it refers to an action which is
or was still in the future:

Hazlo como quieras	do it however you like
Lo hizo como quiso	he did it the way he wanted
Te dije que podías venir como quisieras	I told you you could come any way you
(For *como* + subjunctive meaning 'if' see 23.5.2)	liked

   (c)   *Como si* 'as if' and *sin que* 'without' always take the subjunctive:

Debes hacerlo sin que tenga que decírtelo	you must do it without my having to tell you
Me miró como si no me viera	she looked at me as if she couldn't see me
Éste las trató con gran familiaridad, como si las viera todos los días (C. Fuentes, Mexico)	he treated them very familiarly just as if he saw them every day

16.4.5   Subjunctive with subordinators of possibility

En caso de que, no sea que/no vaya a ser que call for the subjunctive:

Ponte el impermeable no sea que/no vaya a ser que llueva	put your raincoat on in case it rains
En caso de que no esté, llámame	if she's not in give me a ring
Las pondré en la maleta en caso de que las necesites	I'll put them in the suitcase in case you need them
Las puse en la maleta en caso de que las necesitaras/necesitases	I put them in the suitcase in case you need them

But *por si* takes the indicative (though *por si acaso* may take either mood):

Llévate el paraguas por si (acaso) llueve	take the umbrella in case it rains
Aquí tienes su teléfono por si (acaso) te hace falta	here's her phone number in case you need it
Por si fuera poco (set phrase)	as if this wasn't enough

16.4.6   Subjunctive with subordinators of time:

antes de que	before,	*luego que*	when/as soon as
apenas/así que/	as soon as	*mientras*	while/as long as
no bien/nada		*siempre que*	as long as
más que/		*tan pronto como*	as soon as

en cuanto	as soon as	*cada vez que*	every time that
a poco de que/al poco rato de que	soon after	*a la vez que*	at the same time as
cuando	when	*una vez que*	once/as soon as
después de que	after	*a medida que/ según/conforme*	as
hasta que	until		

etc.

The subordinate verb is in the subjunctive when its action is or was still in the future. Students of French and Italian must resist the temptation to use the future tense after these subordinators. Compare *je lui donnerai son livre quand il arrivera*, *gli darò il suo livro quando arriverà* and *le daré su libro cuando **llegue*** 'I'll give him his book when he arrives':

Me saludará cuando llegue	she'll greet me when I arrive/she arrives
Me saluda cuando llega	she greets me when she arrives (habitual)
Íbamos a cenar cuando llegaran/ llegasen los demás	we were going to have supper when the rest arrived (i.e. they had not yet arrived)
A medida que/según/conforme vayan entrando se lo diré	I'll tell them as they come in
A medida que/según/conforme iban entrando se lo decía	I told them as they came in
Tan pronto como acabe la huelga, las cosas marcharán mejor	things will get better as soon as the strike is over
Tan pronto como acabó la huelga todo se arregló	as soon as the strike was over everything was all right
Hasta que no llegue a ser ministro no se quedará contento	he won't be satisfied until be becomes a Minister
Hasta que no llegó a ser ministro no se quedó contento	he wasn't satisfied until he became a Minister
En cuanto se estrene la obra, se agotarán las entradas	all the tickets will be sold after the first night
Siempre que la vea se lo diré	I'll tell her every time I see her
Tienes que estar en la terminal antes de que cierren la consigna	you must be at the terminal before the left-luggage closes
. . . las ideas se irán haciendo más y más claras en la medida en que nos aventuremos más y más por la senda que iremos construyendo (C. Almeyda in *El País*)	the ideas will get increasingly clear as we venture further along the path we will be building
. . . Papi no apaga la luz hasta que yo no termine de rezar (M. Puig, Arg., dialogue)	daddy doesn't turn the light off until I finish saying my prayers

Notes (i) *Después (de) que* 'after' and similar phrases – *a los pocos días de que*, 'a few days after, *desde que* 'since', etc – always take the subjunctive when they refer to an as yet future action. If they refer to a past action they should logically take the indicative, but in written Spanish the *-ra* and *-se* forms are quite common. (For a more detailed discussion see 14.8.2):

Desde que entrara en prisión, el 23 de agosto de 1969 . . . (*Cambio16*)	since he was confined to prison on 23 August 1969
Han pasado 38 años desde que Rafael Alberti abandonara España (*El País*)	38 years have passed since Rafael Alberti left Spain
El enriquecimiento del agua con flúor se puso de moda a mediados de los años	addition of fluoride to water became fashionable in the mid forties after a

cuarenta, después de que un grupo de científicos observara que . . . (Cambio16)	group of scientists observed that . . .

(ii) *Mientras (que)* 'as long as, while'. When it means 'as long as/provided' the subjunctive is obligatory but when it refers to the future and cannot be translated by 'as long as', either mood is possible.

Mañana puedes hacer la comida mientras (que) yo arreglo la casa/mientras (que) yo arregle la casa	tomorrow you can do the cooking while I tidy the house
Mientras (que) yo tenga dinero, no te faltará	you won't want for money as long as/ while I have it
Mientras (que) sigas así, no conseguirás nada	you won't get anywhere while/as long as you go on like that
Mientras (que) vivió conmigo le fue bien	so long as/while he/she lived with me things were all right for her
Le dije que no conseguiría nada mientras no trabajara más	I told her she'd achieve nothing while she didn't work harder

N.b. *Mientras que* can also be a coordinator: *yo trabajo todo el día mientras que tú no haces nada* 'I work all day while you do nothing'. The *que* is normal here.

16.4.7   Subjunctive with subordinators of condition and exception
They all call for the subjunctive. (For *si* and *como* see 23.5).

(a)   Condition: *con tal (de) que/siempre que/siempre y cuando* (more emphatic) 'provided that', *a condición de que* 'on condition that', *bajo (la) condición de que* 'on condition that', *a cambio de que* 'in exchange for':

El Gobierno está preparado a negociar siempre que/siempre y cuando/ con tal (de) que/a condición de que sean razonables	the Government is ready to negotiate provided they are reasonable
Siempre que no haya daño o riesgo para otros, debe ser cada persona la que decida libremente sobre lo que crea que es bueno para sí	provided there is no danger or risk to others, every individual must decide freely what they consider good for themselves
Te convido a cenar con tal (de) que me dejes escoger el restaurante	I'll buy you dinner provided you let me choose the restaurant
Estaba dispuesto a colaborar siempre que pudiera llevar la voz cantante	he was ready to cooperate provided he could call the tune
Cuando yo le informé sobre la conducta de usted añadió cincuenta mil pesetas a la minuta a cambio de que yo hiciera esta llamada telefónica (M. Vázquez Montalbán)	when I told him about your behaviour he added fifty thousand pesetas to my bill† in return for my making this telephone call †lawyers' bill of costs

(b)   Exception: *a no ser que / salvo que/excepto que, a menos que* when they mean 'unless', *fuera de que* (less common), *como no sea que, como no fuera que*:

Me casaré contigo a no ser que/salvo que hayas cambiado de idea	I'll marry you unless you've changed your mind
Íbamos de vacaciones en agosto salvo/ a no ser que/como no fuera que yo estuviera muy ocupado	we took our holidays in August unless I was very busy
No sé qué sugerir. Como no (sea que) vayamos al teatro	I don't know what to suggest unless we go to the theatre

16.4.8 Subjunctive with subordinators of concession

Así, aunque/aun cuando (more emphatic) 'although', *a pesar de que* (more common than *a despecho de que* and *pese a que*) 'despite the fact that' require the subjunctive if they point to an event which is or was still in the future. *Suponiendo que* 'supposing' always takes subjunctive:

Es un valiente, no lo confesará así/ aunque le maten	he's a brave man, he won't admit it even if they kill him
No lo confesó aunque le ofrecieron dinero	he didn't confess although he was offered money
No lo confesaría aunque le mataran/ matasen	he wouldn't confess it even if they killed him
Suponiendo que venga, ¿le vas a dejar entrar?	supposing he comes, are you going to let him in?
Vendieron la finca, a pesar de que el abuelo se oponía	they sold the estate, despite the fact that grandfather opposed it
Venderán la finca, a pesar de que el abuelo se oponga	they'll sell the estate, despite the fact that grandfather will/may oppose it
Dijeron que iban a vender la finca, a pesar de que el abuelo se opusiera/ opusiese	they said they would sell the estate despite the fact that grandfather would oppose it

Notes (i) A subjunctive is normally used after *aunque* when a statement is discounted:

Aunque no te gusten las películas ésta te va a gustar	even if you don't like films you'll like this one
Aunque sea español no me gustan los toros	even though I'm Spanish I don't like bullfights
Las generalidades de esa magnitud, aunque se formulen con brillantez, no sirven de gran cosa (Vargas Llosa, Peru)	generalizations of that magnitude, even when brilliantly formulated, aren't much use

(ii) The difference between *aunque* with the subjunctive or indicative is often minimal:

Los partidos (. . .) pueden contar con un buen número de intelectuales, artistas y líderes en distintos ámbitos que se sienten integrados en el partido, aunque nunca hayan rellenado una ficha del mismo y no lleven su carné (A. Muñoz Alonso, *Cambio16*)	the parties can count on a good number of intellectuals, artists and leaders in various fields who feel themselves to belong to the party even though they have never filled out an application for it and don't carry its membership card

16.5 Translating 'whether . . . or', 'however', 'whatever', 'whoever', 'whichever' and 'the more . . .'

Such phrases are often translated by the *forma reduplicativa*, i.e. such constructions as *digan lo que digan, pase lo que pase*. In general the subordinate verb is in the subjunctive if it refers to some event which has or had not yet happened, or is or was not known to have happened.

(a)   **Whether . . . or:** *'forma reduplicativa'*
The verb accompanying this construction must be in the subjunctive:

Quieras o no quieras, lo tienes que hacer	Whether you want to or not you have to do it
Estaré de tu parte, tengas razón o no la tengas	I'll be on your side, whether you're right or wrong
Estuviese o no enfermo, lo cierto es que no vino al trabajo	whether he was ill or not, the fact is he didn't come to work

(b)   **However:** *por mucho que/por más que* + verb, *por mucho* + noun + verb, *por muy* + adjective + verb.
Use of the subjunctive follows the usual rule: if the event referred to is or was a reality, the indicative is used:

Por mucho que/más que se lo dijo, no lo hizo	he didn't do it however much she asked him
Por mucho que se lo digas, no lo hará	he won't do it however much you ask him
Por mucho calor que haga, no abrirá la ventana	however hot it gets he won't open the window
Por más consejos que le dio, no cambió de parecer	he didn't change his/her mind despite all the advice he/she gave him (lit. however much advice she gave him)
Por muy listo que sea no lo conseguirá	however clever he is he won't succeed
Contra la autocompasión es preferible sostener, por demencial que parezca, que los verdaderos exilados son los regímenes fascistas de nuestro continente (J. Cortázar, Arg.)	to combat self-pity it is preferable to maintain, however crazy it seems, that the real exiles are the fascist régimes on our continent
Por más que llueva no se le van a resucitar los novillos muertos (M. Puig, Arg.)	however much it rains, his steers won't come back to life
Por modesta que fuera su familia, no era el más pobre del colegio (Vargas Llosa, Peru)	however humble his family may have been he wasn't the poorest one in the school

Notes (i)   With verbs meaning 'say', 'order' etc., the subjunctive may appear even though the action is apparently a reality:

Por mucho que/más que se lo dijera, no lo hacía	however often she told him, he didn't do it

The imperfect indicative *decía/hacía* and the preterite *dijo/hizo* are also possible. The difference is one of nuance, the subjunctive being rather more emphatic or insistent.

(ii)   *Por poco que* requires the subjunctive:

Por poco dinero que tenga, siempre vive a lo grande	however little money he has, he always lives in style
Por poco dinero que tuviera, siempre vivía a lo grande	however little money he had, he always lived in style

(c)   **The more . . . the more:** *cuanto/a/os/as más . . . más*
The general rule is applied: if the event is a reality the indicative is used:

Cuanto más/mientras más coma más querrá	the more he eats the more he'll want
Cuanto más/mientras más comía, más quería	the more he ate the more he wanted

Cuanta más/mientras más leche eches, más espesará	the more milk you add, the thicker it'll get
Yo sabía que cuanto más bebiera/ bebiese más me emborracharía	I knew that the more I drank, the drunker I would get

For *mientras* in these sentences see 5.7.

(d) Whatever

Cualquiera que, and *comoquiera que* are often felt to be stilted and are replaced in the written and spoken language by the *forma reduplicativa*. (For *cualquiera* see 9.8)

Las camelias cualquiera que/sea cual sea su color son bonitas	camelias are lovely whatever their colour
No me quiere vender el cuadro le pague lo que le pague	he/she doesn't want to sell me the painting whatever I offer him/her
Cómpralo sea como sea	'buy it whatever it looks like' or 'buy it whatever the cost'

Note *Como quiera que sea* could be used in the last example but is less common.

(e) Whichever: relative pronoun + subjunctive

Escoge la maceta que más te guste	choose whichever flower pot you like most
¿Cuál me llevo? El que usted quiera	which should I take? Whichever (one) you like

(f) Whenever: *cuando*

The verb may take the subjunctive or indicative depending on whether the event referred to is a reality:

Vienen cuando quieren	they come whenever they want
Vendrán cuando quieran	they'll come whenever they want

Cuando quiera que is old fashioned for *cuando. Cuando quiera que* is an occasional literary alternative for *siempre que*:

Cuando quiera que en la vida española se ponen tensos los ánimos . . . (Pérez de Ayala, quoted by M. Seco)	whenever passions are stirred in Spanish life . . .

(g) Anyone who . . ., whoever . . .

Cualquiera que 'anyone who . . .' is not replaceable by the *forma reduplicativa*:

Cualquiera que te vea pensará que vas a una fiesta	anyone who sees you will think you're going to a party

If 'anyone who . . .' means 'those who . . .', 'people who . . .', a nominalizer plus the subjunctive is used, i.e. *quien* or *el que*:

El que/quien se crea eso está loco	anyone who believes that is mad

Quienquiera is also found in the same contexts but it is not as common:

Quienquiera se crea eso está loco (G. Cabrera Infante, Cuban dialogue)	anyone who thinks that is mad

For translation of 'whoever it is . . .', *quienquiera que . . .* seems to be in free variation with the *forma reduplicativa*:

No abras la puerta, sea quien sea/ quienquiera que sea	don't open the door whoever it is

(h) **Wherever** *dondequiera* or *forma reduplicativa*

Dondequiera que voy/vaya donde vaya me le encuentro	wherever I go I meet him
Dondequiera que vaya/vaya donde vaya me le encontraré	wherever I may go I'll meet him
Dondequiera que fuese/fuese donde fuese, me le encontraba (or *fuera . . .*)	wherever I went I met him

16.6 Subjunctive in relative clauses

In this section nominalizers such as *el que* 'the one that', *quien* 'the one who', *aquellos que* 'those who' etc., are treated as relative pronouns. (See chapter 30 for nominalizers and 16.5 for *cualquiera que, quienquiera que, cuandoquiera que, dondequiera*).

16.6.1 Subjunctive in relative clauses when the antecedent is not yet known or experienced

Spanish uses the subjunctive in such cases to express a nuance which English usually ignores. Compare *los que digan eso* 'those who say that' (if anyone does) and *los que dicen eso* 'the people who say that' (and they exist). The difference in Spanish is striking. Contrast:

Prefiero un coche que tenga cuatro puertas	I prefer a car with four doors (i.e. any car)
Prefiero ese coche que tiene cuatro puertas	I prefer that car with four doors
Busco un médico que sepa acupuntura	I'm looking for a doctor (i.e. 'any') who knows acupuncture
Conozco a un médico que sabe acupuntura	I know a doctor who knows acupuncture
No leo novelas que tengan más de doscientas páginas	I don't read novels which have more than two hundred pages
Tengo muchas novelas que tienen más de doscientas páginas	I've got many novels with more than two hundred pages

Further examples:

¿Cuál quiere usted? El que usted recomiende	which one do you want? Any one you recommend
Me voy a casar con el primero que me lo pida	I'm going to marry the first man who asks me
Haz lo que quieras	do whatever you like
¿Sabes de alguien que tenga apellido en este país? (E. Sabato, Arg.)	do you know anyone in this country who has a surname (i.e. an illustrious name)?
El poeta aspira a una imagen única que resuelva en su unidad y singularidad la riqueza plural del mundo (Octavio Paz, Mex.)	the poet strives for a unique image which will resolve in its unity and singularity the plural richness of the world
. . . quien haya seguido la elaboración de esta novela (Vargas Llosa, Peru)	. . . anyone who has followed the preparation of this novel

16.6.2 Subjunctive in relative clauses when the existence of the antecedent is denied

If the antecedent does not exist, the verb in the relative cause is in the subjunctive:

No hay nadie que sepa tocar más de un violín a la vez	there is no one who can play more than one violin at once
No había mendigo a quien él no diera/ diese limosna	there was no beggar to whom he wouldn't give alms
No hay quien le entienda	there's no one who can understand him
En realidad no existen culturas 'dependientes' y emancipadas ni nada que se les parezca (Vargas Llosa, Peru)	in reality there are no 'dependent' and emancipated cultures or anything like them
Nada hay en él que pueda ofender directamente a la Junta argentina (J. Cortázar, Arg.)	there's nothing in it that could directly offend the Argentine Junta

16.6.3 Subjunctive after the relatives *donde* and *cuanto*

(For *dondequiera que* see 16.5h).
The subjunctive is used if the reference is to a yet unknown or non-existent entity:

Comeré en el pueblo donde me pare	I'll eat in whichever village I stop in
Comí en el pueblo donde me paré	I ate in the village I stopped in
Buscó una zona donde el mar llegara debilitado (M. Vázquez Montalbán)	he looked for an area where the sea was coming in with less force
Te daré cuanto me pidas	I'll give you anything you ask
Le di (todo) cuanto me pidió	I gave her everything she asked

16.6.4 Subjunctive after superlative expressions

The subjunctive may follow superlative statements in literary Spanish, but it is unusual in everyday written or spoken language:

El mayor incendio que jamás se ha/ haya visto	the greatest fire ever seen
La mayor transacción con divisas fuertes que se haya hecho en el Río de la Plata (E. Sabato, Arg.)	the largest hard-currency transaction ever made in the River Plate region

Compare these less literary examples:

El político más carismático que he visto en mi vida	the most charismatic politician I've seen in my life
Eres la chica más simpática que he conocido	you're the most likeable girl I've ever met
Dijo que era la mayor barbaridad que a nadie se le había ocurrido	he said it was the greatest stupidity anybody had ever thought of

16.7 Subjunctive in main clauses

The subjunctive is primarily a feature of subordinate clauses but it may appear in a main clause in certain circumstances.

16.7.1   Subjunctive with the imperative
(a)   All negative imperatives in Spanish require the subjunctive:

No vengas mañana	don't come tomorrow
No traigáis la maleta	don't bring (plural) the suitcase
No digan nada	don't say anything

Note   In Spain forms like *no decid nada may be heard in popular speech for *no digáis nada*. They should be avoided.

(b)   The subjunctive is also used in positive imperative statements with the pronouns *usted, ustedes* and *nosotros*:

Guarden silencio	please be quiet
¡Váyase usted de aquí!	go away!
Analicemos los motivos de esta acción	let's analyse the reason for this action
Pasemos ahora a hablar del tema principal de esta reunión	let's go on to discuss the main subject of this meeting

Note   Use of the first-person plural imperative is confined to formal style. In colloquial language the phrase *vamos a* followed by an infinitive is usual:

Vamos a sentarnos	let's sit down/we're going to sit down
(Not *sentémonos*)	
Vamos a quejarnos de su proceder	let's complain about his behaviour/we're
(Rather than *quejémonos*)	going to complain . . .
(Vamos) a ver si es verdad	let's see if it's true

16.7.2   Subjunctive in reiterated orders and in wishes
(a)   Preceded by *que*:

¡Que te diviertas!	have a good time!
Que no se te olvide echar la carta	don't forget to post the letter
Que no te retrases para la cena esta noche	don't be late for dinner tonight
Que no dejes de hacer lo que te encargué	don't forget to do what I asked you
Nosotros los sandinistas vamos a resolver la situación. Que no se meta el imperialismo norteamericano en esto, que no se metan los soviéticos porque esto lo resolveremos nosotros, los revolucionarios (El País, interview)	we Sandinistas will solve the situation. Let American imperialism keep out of this business, let the Soviets keep out, because we revolutionaries will solve this

(b)   Preceded by *ojalá* and *quién. Así,* used jokingly, parodies a typical gipsy curse:

¡Ojalá nos toquen las quinielas!	let's only hope we win the pools!
¡Quién fuera millonario!	if only I were a millionaire!
¡Dios se lo pague!	may God repay you!
¡Ojalá no llueva!	if only it doesn't rain!
¡Así se te pegue mi catarro!	I hope you get my cold!
Ojalá cunda tu ejemplo entre los españoles responsables: ojalá se entable entre nosotros un amplio debate (El País)	let's hope your example spreads among responsible Spaniards; let's hope a wide-ranging debate is set up between us

There is also a less common expression with the same meaning as *ojalá*:

Fueran como tú todas las mujeres	if only all women were like you

16.7.3 Subjunctive after words meaning 'perhaps', 'possibly'
There are several commonly used words meaning 'perhaps': *acaso, tal vez, quizá(s)*[1], *a lo mejor, posiblemente*.

(a) *Tal vez* and *quizá(s)* mean the same. Use of the subjunctive is sometimes optional with them although the subjunctive is always correct[2]. It is important to remember that if the event is still in the future only the future indicative or the present subjunctive may be used, not the present indicative:

Quizá/tal vez venga/vendrá mañana   perhaps she'll come tomorrow
(not **viene mañana*)

and if the event *was* still in the future, only the imperfect subjunctive or the conditional should be used:

Quizá/tal vez vinieran/viniesen/   perhaps they would come the following
vendrían al día siguiente   day
(not **venían*)

The subjunctive may only be used if *quizá(s)* or *tal vez* precede the verb they modify. Examples:

Tal vez fuese una discusión auténtica.   maybe it was a real argument. Maybe
Tal vez representaban una comedia en   they were putting on an act for my
mi honor (interview, Madrid press)   benefit
Por un segundo se le ocurrió a Petrone   for a second it occurred to Petrone that
que tal vez esa noche estuviera cuidando   perhaps that night she was looking after
al niño de alguna parienta o amiga   some female relative's or friend's child
(Cortázar, Arg.)
Quizá haya sido tu madre la que ha   perhaps it was your mother who rang
llamado
Quizá fue demasiado obsequioso con   perhaps he was too obsequious towards
los poderosos (O. Paz, Mex.)   the powerful
(*obsequioso* usually = 'attentive' without overtones in the Peninsula)

(b) *Acaso* is rather literary in the meaning 'perhaps': *acaso sea verdad que* 'perhaps it is true that . . .', *acaso sus padres la estén ayudando a escondidas* 'perhaps her parents are helping her secretly' (the subjunctive is required). It is very common however in all styles followed by the indicative as a device for adding a sarcastic note to questions:

¿Acaso no saben los críticos que esta   don't the critics know that I wrote this
novela la escribí cuando tenía   novel when I was sixteen?
dieciséis años?
¿Acaso has visto alguna vez que no llueva   have *you* ever seen that it didn't rain in
en verano?   Summer?

(c) *A lo mejor* does not take the subjunctive.[3] It is ubiquitous on both continents, but it is largely confined to spoken language:

---

[1]*Quizá* is the preferred form in writing.
[2]Use of the indicative is spreading, but it may still sound incorrect to some speakers.
[3]We have seen it with the subjunctive in the Colombian press, but doubt that this is accepted usage.

Ni siquiera la nombró. A lo mejor se ha olvidado de ella (Vargas Llosa, Peru, dialogue)	he didn't even mention her. Maybe he's forgotten her
No es fácil, a lo mejor por culpa de la camisa que se adhiere a la lana del pulóver (Cortázar, Arg.)	it isn't easy, perhaps because of the shirt sticking to the wool of the pullover

In Spain *igual* and *lo mismo* are also used in informal or popular speech in the meaning 'perhaps': . . . *si te viera todos los días, igual acabaría despreciándote* (Zunzunegui, quoted B. Steel, 134) 'if I saw you every day I might end up despising you'; *llama a la puerta. Lo mismo te da una propina* 'knock on the door. Maybe he'll give you a tip'.

(d)   *Posiblemente* 'possibly' is usually followed by the subjunctive:

Posiblemente quedara algo de alcohol etílico en nuestras venas humorísticas (García Márquez, Colombia)	perhaps there was still some ethyl alcohol left in the veins of our humour

However, *posiblemente* also occurs with the indicative. As a direct verbal modifier it is not particularly colloquial; *es posible que*, *quizá* or *tal vez* are more common.

Probablemente is usually found with the indicative:

. . . *alguna oscura sensación de incertidumbre, que probablemente será tan incierta como el resto* (Cortázar, Arg.)	some obscure sensation of uncertainty which will probably be as uncertain as the rest
Probablemente en ningún momento te fuiste del cuarto . . . *(idem)*	probably you never left the room for a moment

16.7.4   Subjunctive in common phrases

(a)   *O sea que* 'in other words':

Ha dicho que tiene que trabajar, o sea que no quiere venir	he said he had to work, in other words he doesn't want to come

(b)   In the phrases *que yo sepa/que yo recuerde*:

Que yo recuerde es la primera vez que le he visto	as far as I remember it's the first time I've seen him
¿Ha llegado Pepe? No que yo sepa/por lo que yo sé	has Pepe arrived? Not as far as I know
Que se sepa nadie lo ha hecho antes	as far as anybody knows, it hasn't been done before

(c)   In a few phrases:

Acabáramos	now I see what you're getting at
Otro gallo nos cantara si le hubiéramos/ hubiésemos hecho caso	it would have been another story if we had listened to him
¡Cómo tiras el dinero! Ni que fueras millonario . . .	the way you throw money about anyone would think you're a millionaire

16.8   Tense agreement: subjunctive

There is no rigidly fixed pattern of tense agreement between main and subordinate clauses, but the following are the most usual combinations:

(a)   Main clause in present indicative:
(i) Present subjunctive:

Me gusta que hable	I like her to talk
Quiero que dejes de fumar	I want you to stop smoking

(ii) Perfect subjunctive:

Me encanta que hayas venido	I'm delighted you've come

(iii) Imperfect subjunctive (see note(i)):

Es imposible que lo dijera/dijese	it's impossible that he said it

(b)   Main clause in future:
Present subjunctive:

Nos contentaremos con que terminen *para finales del mes*	we'll be content with them finishing by the end of the month

(c)   Main clause in conditional or conditional perfect:
Imperfect subjunctive:

Nos contentaríamos con que terminaran/ *terminasen para finales del mes*	we'd be content with them finishing by the end of the month
Yo habría preferido que se pintara/ *pintase de negro*	I'd have preferred it to be painted black

(d)   Main clause in present perfect (see note (ii)):
Present perfect or past subjunctives:

Te he dicho que te estés quieto	I told you to be still
Ha sido un milagro que no te hayan *reconocido/reconocieran/reconociesen*	it was a miracle that they didn't recognize you

(e)   Main clause in imperfect, preterite or pluperfect (see notes (iii) and (iv)):
(i) Imperfect subjunctive:

La idea era que cobrarais/cobraseis *los viernes*	the idea was that you'd get paid on Fridays
Me sorprendió que fuera/fuese tan alto	it surprised me that he was so tall
Yo te había pedido que me prestaras/ *prestases cien dólares*	I'd asked you to lend me 100 dollars

(ii) Pluperfect subjunctive:

Me sorprendía que hubiera/hubiese *protestado*	I was surprised that he had protested

(f)   Main clause in imperative:
Present subjunctive

Díganles que se den prisa	tell them to hurry

Notes (i)   The combination present + imperfect subjunctive occurs when a comment is being made about a past event:

No es cierto que él nos devolviera/ *devolviese/haya devuelto el dinero*	it isn't true that he gave us back the money

There seems to be little difference here between the perfect and imperfect subjunctive, and occasionally the present subjunctive can also be used:

Algunos niegan que Cristóbal Colón *fuera/fuese/haya sido/sea el primer* *descubridor de América*	some deny that Christopher Columbus was the first discoverer of America

(ii)   The present perfect (*ha dicho, ha ordenado*, etc.) is strictly speaking classified as a present tense for the purposes of agreement, but it is not uncommon to find the imperfect subjunctive used when the event in the subordinate clause is also past. Compare

Ha dado órdenes de que nos rindamos   he's given orders for us to surrender

and

El clima que se está creando ha llevado   the climate that is being created has
a que se hablara de intervención del   led to talk of Army intervention
Ejército (*Cambio16*; also *hable*)

(iii) The combination past indicative + present subjunctive is optionally possible when the subordinate clause refers to a timeless or perpetual event:

Dios decretó que las serpientes no   God decreed that snakes should have no
tengan/tuvieran/tuviesen patas   legs

(*las piernas* is used only of human legs)

(iv) When the subordinate event is in the future and the time of the main verb is the recent past, the present subjunctive is sometimes found in the subordinate clause:

El Gobierno vasco reclamó ayer que se le   the Basque Government demanded
transfiera el mando efectivo de las   yesterday that effective control over
fuerzas de seguridad del Estado en el   the State security forces in the Basque
País Vasco (*El País*)   Country should be transferred to itself

Use of the present when both verbs refer to the past is common in popular Spanish-American speech, but is unacceptable to Peninsular speakers:

El inspector aduanero le pidió a la   the Customs inspector asked the girl to
muchacha que le muestre su casaca   show him her coat
(*La Prensa*, Peru. Spain *mostrara/*
mostrase. In Spain *la casaca* = 'dress
coat')

16.9   Future subjunctive

This is nowadays obsolete in ordinary language, except in a few literary variants of set phrases such as *sea lo que fuere/sea lo que sea* 'whatever it may be', *venga lo que viniere/venga lo que venga* 'come what may'. It is much used in legal documents, official regulations, charters and similar texts, and may occasionally appear in ordinary language to indicate a very remote possibility:

. . . *lo cual ofrece amplísimas ventajas*   . . . which offers very wide advantages
en la extracción del motor o en   when removing the engine or in repair
reparaciones, caso de que las hubiere   work – if such a thing should ever arise
(Advertisement. *hubiera/hubiese* more
normal)

It is more common in Spanish-American newspaper style, at least in Argentina:

. . . *sólo la aplicación de un plan de*   . . . only the application of a plan of
estrictas medidas, aun cuando éstas   strict measures, even if these were
resultaren antipopulares, permitirá salir   unpopular, would permit us to get out
de la actual situación   of the present situation
(*La Nación*, Buenos Aires)

17   The infinitive

The Spanish infinitive characteristically ends in -ar, -er or -ir; in a few infinitives, such as *freír, reír, sonreír*, the vowel bears an accent. The Spanish infinitive cannot in itself express number, mood, time or person (this latter fact should be remembered by students of Portuguese). It is also sometimes ambiguous as to voice, i.e. it can sometimes apparently be passive in meaning, e.g. *¿Es para llevarse o comer aquí?* 'is this to take away or eat here?'.

The infinitive may act as a verb or noun, and in the latter case it is masculine singular – *fumar es malo para la salud*.

Like the gerund, the infinitive often takes clitic personal pronouns, e.g. *antes de hacerlo* 'before doing it', cf. French *avant de le faire*. When the infinitive is governed by a verb, position of the pronouns may in some cases be optional – with stylistic consequences, as in *quiero verlo* and *lo quiero ver*. This topic is discussed at 11.12.4 (Personal pronouns) and below at 17.1b.

17.1   Infinitive governed by verb

This section refers to constructions like *sabe nadar* 'he can swim', *te desafío a hacerlo* 'I challenge you to do it', etc. These constructions have many parallels in English, although there are some surprises and Spanish is of course free of the complication raised by the rather unpredictable choice between the infinitive and the -ing form, cf. 'he claimed to have done it' = *pretendía haberlo hecho* and 'he remembered having done it' = *se acordaba de haberlo hecho*.

There are two main types of construction in Spanish in which an infinitive is governed by a verb:

(a)   Co-referential constructions

If the subject of a main clause and of a subordinate clause are co-referential, i.e. refer to the same person or thing, the verb in the subordinate clause may be replaced by an infinitive.

This may be obligatory, as can be seen from the following pairs:

Él quiere que lo haga   he wants him (someone else) to do it (not co-referential

Quiere hacerlo   he wants to do it (co-referential)

Prefiero que tú lo abras	I prefer you to open it
Prefiero abrirlo yo mismo	I prefer to open it myself

etc.

Constantly recurring verbs which require the infinitive in co-referential constructions are *poder*, *saber*, *querer* (and all verbs of wanting), *pedir* (and verbs of requesting).

The meaning of some verbs is such that only a co-referential construction is possible: *acabo de hacerlo* 'I've just done it', *me abstendré de criticaros* 'I'll refrain from criticizing you', *tiene que irse* 'he's got to go', and thus also *deber*, *soler* 'to be accustomed to', *acostumbrar a* 'to be accustomed to', *acercarse a*, e.g. *me acerqué a hablarle* 'I went up to him to speak to him', *alcanzar a* 'to manage to', *aparentar* 'to seem to', *atreverse a* 'to dare to', *empezar a/comenzar a* 'to begin to', *dejar de* 'to give up', *echarse a* 'to begin (suddenly)', *llegar a* 'to manage to', *ofrecer* 'to offer' (e.g. *ofreció acompañarla*, 'he offered to accompany her'), etc.

In some cases both languages optionally allow replacement of the finite verb, and the non-finite construction has the advantage of being unambiguously co-referential in the third person:

Desmintieron que hubieran/hubiesen lanzado el misil	they denied that they'd launched the missile
Desmintieron haber lanzado el misil	they denied having launched the missile
Reconozco que lo hice	I recognize I did it
Reconozco haberlo hecho	I recognize having done it
Afirmaba que él lo hizo	he claimed he did it
Afirmaba haberlo hecho	he claimed to have done it
Recuerdo que lo compré	I remember I bought it
Recuerdo haberlo comprado	I remember having bought it

In a few cases Spanish optionally allows an infinitive construction where English does not. The Spanish infinitive construction is unambiguously co-referential:

Dice estar enfermo	he says he (himself) is ill
Dice que está enfermo	he says he (himself or someone else) is ill
Creíamos que la habíamos visto antes	we thought we'd seen her before
Creíamos haberla visto antes	" " " "

(b) Infinitive in non-co-referential sentences

With some verbs an infinitive may be used even though the subjects are not co-referential, i.e. refer to different persons or things, cf. *les ordenó rendirse* 'he ordered them to surrender', *la vi hacerlo* 'I saw her do it'. This construction is much less common in Spanish than in English, which says 'I want him *to do* it', 'I prefer them *to come* early' etc., where Spanish must use the subjunctive. In the case of verbs of permitting and prohibiting either an infinitive or a subjunctive construction may be used in Spanish: *te prohíbo cantar/te prohíbo que cantes* 'I forbid you to sing'. See 16.2.1 note (iii) for further examples.

One problem common to all sentences in which an infinitive is the complement of another verb is that of 'clitic shifting', i.e. the fact that suffixed personal pronouns may be optionally inserted before the main verb. Compare *yo no puedo hacerlo* and *yo no lo puedo hacer* 'I can't do it'. This is regularly done in informal styles with certain common verbs, discussed at 11.12.4, but it seems to be possible in relaxed speech with a large number of verbs, although the construction is avoided in formal language and may seem doubtful on reflexion to some speakers. Thus *lo quiero ver* is simply a colloquial variant of *quiero verlo*; *la espero ver* is rather more colloquial for *espero verla* 'I hope to see her'; most informants rejected ?*lo fingió hacer* for *fingió hacerlo* 'he pretended to do it'; and **lo fue condenado a hacer* is not possible for *fue condenado a hacerlo* 'he was condemned to do it'.

The following list shows some of the more common verbs which are followed by an infinitive. French equivalents are supplied as a reminder to students of that language to avoid all-too-frequent blunders like **se acercó de él* for *se acercó a él* 'he approached him (*il s'approcha de lui*). Verbs which are preceded by a dagger may allow clitic shifting in colloquial speech although foreign students should probably confine this construction to the verbs listed at 11.12.4.

List 17.1   Verbs (+ prepositions) followed by infinitive

abstenerse de	refrain from	†*aparentar*	seem to
†*acabar de*:		†*aprender a*	learn to
acabo de verla	I've just seen her	*arrepentirse de*	regret/repent
		†*asegurar*	assure
†*aconsejar*	advise	*atreverse a*	dare to
	(Fr. *conseiller de*)	*autorizar a*	authorize to
acordarse de	remember	*avergonzarse de*	be ashamed of
	(cf. *recordar*)	†*ayudar a*	help to
acercarse a	approach	*bajar a*	go down to
	(Fr. *s'approcher de*)	†*buscar*	seek to
			(Fr. *chercher à*)
†*acertar a*	manage to/succeed in	*cansarse de*	tire of
		†*cesar de*	cease from
†*acostumbrar a*	be accustomed to	†*comenzar a*	begin to
†*acordar*	agree to	*comprometerse a*	undertake to
acusar de	accuse of	*comunicar*	announce/
afirmar	claim/state		communicate
†*alcanzar a*	manage to:		(more usually
es todo lo que alcancé a ver	'it's all I managed to see'		with *que . . .*)
		conceder	concede to
amenazar	threaten to	*condenar a*	condemn to
amenazó matarle or	(Fr. *menacer de*)	*conducir a*	lead to
		†*confesar*	confess
le amenazó con matarle		†*conseguir*	succeed in
		consentir en	consent to
†*anhelar*	long to	*consistir en*	consist of
animar a	encourage to	*contribuir a*	contribute to
†*ansiar*	long to	*convenir en*	agree to

convidar a	invite to	*incitar a*	incite to
†*creer*	believe	*inclinar a*	incline to
cuidar de	take care of	*insistir en*	insist on
†*decidir*	decide to	†*intentar*	try to
	(Fr. *décider de*)	*interesarse en*	interest in
decir	say	(or *por*)	(Fr. *s'intéresser*
declarar	declare		*à*)
†*dejar*	let/allow:	*invitar a*	invite to
le dejó hacerlo or	'he let her do it'	*jactarse de*	boast of
se lo dejó hacer		†*jurar*	swear to
†*dejar de*	leave off	*juzgar*	judge
†*demostrar*	demonstrate		(but usu. with
desafiar a	challenge to		*que . . .*)
	(Fr. *défier de*)	*limitarse a*	limit oneself to
†*desear*	desire/wish to	†*lograr*	succeed in
desesperar de	despair of	†*llegar a*	
dignarse	deign to	e.g. *incluso*	'he even went so
disponerse a	get ready to	*llegó a robar*	far as to steal
disuadir de	dissuade from	*dinero*	money'
divertirse en	amuse oneself by	*llevar a*	lead to
	(usually with	†*mandar*	order to
	gerund; Fr.		(Fr. *ordonner de*)
	s'amuser à)	*mandar a*	send to
dudar en	hesitate over	(*le mandó a*	'he sent him to do
	(Fr. *hésiter à*)	*hacerlo*	it')
echar(se) a	begin to	*manifestar*	state/declare
empeñarse en	insist on	*maravillarse de*	marvel at
†*empezar a*	begin to	*meterse a*	start to
encargarse de	take charge of	*mover a*	move to
†*enseñar a*	show how to/teach	*merecer*	deserve to
	to	†*necesitar*	need to
†*esperar*	hope/expect/wait	*negar*	deny
†*evitar*	avoid	(*negarse a*	refuse to)
	(Fr. *éviter de*)	†*obligar a*	oblige to
excitar a	excite to		(Fr. *obliger de*)
figurarse	imagine	*obstinarse en*	insist obstinately on
†*forzar a*	force to	*ofrecer*	offer
fingir	pretend to	†*oír*	hear
guardarse de	take care not to	*olvidar*	forget
gustar de	like to	*olvidarse de* and	*olvidar* alone is
	(but usually *le*	*olvidársele* +	uncommon with
	gusta fumar,	infinitive	the infinitive
	etc.)	*optar* (usually	opt to/for
habituarse a	get used to	*optar por*)	
†*hacer*	make	†*ordenar*	order to
	(*la hizo callar*,		(Fr. *ordonner de*)
	etc.)	†*parar de*	stop
hartarse de	tire of/have	†*parecer*	seem to
	enough of	†*pasar a*	go on to
imaginar	imagine	*pasar de*	'to be uninterested
†*impedir*	prevent from		in'
	(Fr. *défendre*	*pedir*	ask to
	de)		(Fr. *demander à*,
impulsar a	urge on to		*demander de*)

†*pensar*:
　pienso hacerlo 'I plan to do it'
　pensaban en hacerlo they were thinking about doing it
†*permitir* allow to (Fr. *permettre de*)
persistir en persist in
persuadir a persuade to (Fr. *persuader de*)
†*poder* be able to
precipitarse a rush to
prepararse a get ready to
†*preferir* prefer to
presumir de (approx.) boast about . . .
†*pretender* (see 17.2 note ii)
†*procurar* try hard to
†*prohibir* prohibit from (Fr. *défendre de*)
†*prometer* promise to (Fr. *promettre de*)
quedar en agree to
†*querer* want to

†*recordar* remember to
rehusar refuse to (Fr. *refuser de*)
†*renunciar a* renounce
resignarse a resign oneself to
resistirse a resist
†*resolver* resolve to (Fr. *résoudre de*)
†*saber* know how to
sentir regret/be sorry for
†*soler*:
　solía hacerlo 'he habitually did it'
†*solicitar* apply to
tardar en be late in/be a long time in (Fr. *tarder à*)
†*temer* fear to
†*tender a* tend to
†*terminar de* finish
†*tratar de* try to
vacilar en hesitate over
venir de come from . . .
†*ver* see (see 17.2.2)
†*volver a* to . . . again

Notes (i) Verbs preceded by a dagger allow clitic pronoun shifting (at least in Peninsular Spanish and, we believe, elsewhere), i.e. one can say *acabo de hacerlo* or *lo acabo de hacer*, *pienso mudarme mañana* 'I'm thinking of moving tomorrow' or *me pienso mudar mañana*. Doubtful verbs, e.g. *fingir*, *afirmar*, are not marked. Clitic pronoun shifting is discussed at 11.12.4.

　(ii) Verbs of motion, e.g. *salir*, *bajar*, *ir*, *volver*, *entrar*, *acercar(se)* always take *a* before an infinitive: *bajó a hablar con ella* 'he went down to talk to her', *entraron a saludar al profesor* 'they went in to say hallo to the teacher', etc.

17.2　Infinitive construction with certain verbs

Spanish allows the direct infinitive construction with a number of verbs of saying, believing, etc., a construction which may seem bizarre to English speakers (one cannot say *'he says to be ill' for 'he says he's ill').

　The infinitive construction has the advantage of (normally) being co-referential, i.e. it eliminates the ambiguity of *dice que lo sabe* which may refer to a fourth person. Nevertheless, the ambiguous construction with *que* is much more common in informal language.

Dice estar enfermo he says he (i.e. himself) is ill
Dice que está enfermo he says that he is ill (either himself or someone else)

Creo tener razón I think I'm right
Creo que tengo razón 　"　　　　"

Había creído volverse loco, pensado en matarse (Vargas Llosa, Peru)	he had imagined he was going mad, thought about killing himself
La maniobra con que el régimen creyó engañar al mundo	the manoeuvre by which the regime thought it would deceive the world
Teherán informa haber conquistado una decena de pueblos (*El País*) (Better *informa que?*)	Tehran declares that it has conquered some ten villages
Esta tesis ha demostrado ser falsa (*Cambio16*)	this thesis (i.e. theory) has turned out to be false
Seat estudia reducir bruscamente sus modelos (*Cambio16*: . . . *cómo reducir/el modo de reducir* are better)	Seat is studying a sharp reduction in its (range of) models

Notes (i)   In written language, an infinitive may appear with non-co-referential subjects with verbs of saying or believing in relative clauses, presumably as a way of avoiding two *que*s:

Las tres muchachas, que él creía ser hijas de don Mateo	the three girls, whom he believed to be the daughters of Don Mateo

   (ii)   *Pretender* suffers a change of meaning:

Pretende ser marxista	he tries to be a Marxist
Pretende que es marxista	he claims he's a Marxist

   (iii)   After verbs of ordering, obliging, and sometimes after verbs of perception, a passive may be required in the English translation:

Mandó ejecutar a tres de los guerrilleros	he ordered three of the guerrillas to be executed
Hizo traer una silla	he had a chair brought
Nunca la oí nombrar	I've never heard her mentioned

A subjunctive construction with *que* . . . could be used in the first two examples.

17.2.1   Verbs of permitting, forbidding, etc.

These are discussed under the subjunctive 16.2.1, but it is worth noting that they can appear without an object or with only one object in Spanish, but not in English: *esto prohíbe pensar que* . . . 'this prohibits *us* from thinking . . .':

Todavía siguen inéditas las cifras que permitirían conocer el grado de ejecución y cumplimiento de los Presupuestos del Estado (*El País*)	figures are not yet published which would show (lit. 'allow to know') the extent to which State budget allocations have been paid and observed
. . . *lo que obligó a evacuar a numerosos habitantes de la vecina República* . . . (*ibid.*)	which required the evacuation of numerous inhabitants from the neighbouring Republic

17.2.2   Infinitive after verbs of perception

The infinitive is used after verbs like *ver*, *oír*, to denote a completed action. An incomplete action is indicated by the gerund. See 19.2.4 for more examples. Compare 'I saw him smoke a cigar' and 'I saw him smoking a cigar':

Te vi entrar	I saw you come in
La oí hacerlo/se lo oí hacer	I heard her do it
Te vi firmarlo/te lo vi firmar	I saw you sign it
Vimos llegar el avión	we saw the plane arrive
(n.b. word order)	

17.3   Infinitive after subordinators

An infinitive construction is possible after many subordinators, e.g. *hasta, con tal de, en caso de, a pesar de, para, con el objeto de* and other subordinators of possibility, *nada más* 'as soon as', *por, sin, antes de, después de*.

Foreign students should apply the rule of co-referentiality: the infinitive should be used only if the subject of the subordinate verb is the same as the main verb's. If the subjects are not co-referential, the subjunctive or indicative must be used, as explained in 16.4. Compare *lo haré nada más acabar esto* 'I'll do it as soon as I've finished this' and *lo haré nada más que acabe esto* 'I'll do it as soon as he/she has finished this'. The latter sentence could also mean 'as soon as I finish', but a third-person interpretation comes most readily to mind. Further examples:

Lo haré después de comer	I'll do it after I've had lunch
Lo haré después de que hayáis comido	I'll do it after you've had lunch
Entré sin verte	I entered without seeing you
Entré sin que tú me vieras/vieses	I entered without you seeing me
Se fue antes de contestar	he left before he answered
Se fue antes de que yo contestase/ contestara	he left before I answered
Enfermó (SA se enfermó) por no comer	he fell ill from not eating
Se enfadó al enterarse	he got angry when he found out
Se hace camino al andar (Antonio Machado)	one makes one's path as one goes along

However, spontaneous language sometimes uses an infinitive construction with these subordinators even when the subjects are not co-referential; this also occurs with the construction *al* + infinitive 'on . . . ing': *me di cuenta al llegar* (co-referential) 'I realized on arriving' is correct, ?*me di cuenta al llegar Juan* (not co-referential) is a frequent but dubious way of saying *me di cuenta cuando llegó Juan*. This tendency is best avoided by foreigners, since native speakers often on reflection reject such utterances as badly formed:

Le miraba sin él darse cuenta (J. Marsé, dialogue: *que diese/diera cuenta*)	he watched him without him realizing
?*Me fui después de llegar tú* (. . . *de que tú llegases/llegaras*)	I left after you arrived
?*Llegamos antes de empezar la película* (. . . *de que empezara/empezase*)	we arrived before the film started
?*Tuvimos que hacerlo por ser la única solución (porque era . . .)*	we had to do it because it was the only solution
?*Al comprar uno de nuestros productos, te obsequiamos con un magnífico regalo* (Advertisement: better *cuando compras . . .*)	when you buy one of our products we will give you a magnificent present
?*Fracasó en el intento de suicidarse al estar las pastillas en malas condiciones* (*porque las pastillas estaban en malas condiciones*)	he failed in his attempt at suicide because the pills were in bad condition

17.3.1   Infinitive: passive or active?
The Spanish infinitive sometimes acquires a passive force especially after *sin*, *por*, *a* and *para*:

Esto aún está por ver	this is still to be seen
una cerveza sin abrir	an unopened beer
casas a medio construir	half-built houses
un movimiento sin organizar	an unorganized movement
Estas cartas están sin contestar	these letters are unanswered

17.4   Infinitive as noun

The infinitive may function as a noun, in which case it is sometimes translated by an English *-ing* form. Used as a noun, an infinitive is always masculine singular:

Mañana me toca lavar el coche	it's my turn to wash the car tomorrow
Votar Comunista es votar contra el paro	to vote Communist is to vote against unemployment
Mejor no hacerlo	best not do it . . .
Odio ordenar	I hate sorting/tidying
un atolondrado ir y venir	a mad coming and going

17.4.1   Article before infinitive
The definite article is nowadays not often used with the infinitive except:

    (a)   In the common construction *al* + infinitive:

Al entrar, se dio cuenta de que no había nadie	on entering, he realized no one was there
Tómese una pastilla al acostarse	take a pill on going to bed

    (b)   When the infinitive is qualified by an adjective or noun phrase:

Oyó el agitado girar de una cucharilla contra un vaso (L. Goytisolo)	he heard the agitated grating of a teaspoon against a glass
con el andar de los años	as the years passed by

    (c)   In other cases, use of the definite article often seems to be optional though it is much less common in informal styles.

    In all the following examples, the definite article, where it appears before the infinitive, could have been omitted. The style would have been slightly less literary:

Paula no pudo evitar el reírse (J.J. Plans)	Paula couldn't help laughing
Odiaban el vivir en casa de sus abuelos	they hated living in their grandparents' house
En 1604 Jaime I de Inglaterra decía que el fumar era 'abominable para el ojo, odioso para la nariz, dañino para el cerebro y peligroso para los pulmones' (Cambio16)	in 1604 James I of England said that smoking was 'abominable to the eye, hateful to the nose, damaging to the brain and dangerous to the lungs'
El hacer esto le costó mucho trabajo	doing this cost him a great deal of effort
Esto permite a los robots el ser reprogramados para . . .	this allows robots to be re-programmed to . . .

But the article is retained in some constructions involving *en*:

La moda en el vestir influye en la moda del maquillaje	fashion in dressing influences fashion in make-up,
Algunos españoles son un poco enfáticos en el hablar	some Spaniards are rather ponderous in their manner of speaking
Le conocí en el andar	I recognized him from his way of walking

But not in others:

Hice mal en venir. aquí	I did wrong in coming here
Tardaron horas en hacerlo	they took hours to do it

(d) The indefinite article occurs before a qualified infinitive

En un abrir y cerrar de ojos	in the wink of an eye
Después de dos años de un agitado avanzar por el camino de la libertad	after two years of agitated progress along the road to liberty

17.5 Infinitive as an imperative

The infinitive may appear as an imperative

(a) In abbreviated written style, e.g. in notices, instructions or advertisements. The effect is rather telegraphic:

Rellenar en mayúsculas	fill in using block letters
Interesados, escribir Apartado Correo 1284	persons interested write Post Box no. 1284
Ver página siguiente	see following page

(b) To make a rather withering past imperative:

Me arrepiento de haberla llamado. No haberlo hecho, entonces	I regret having phoned her. You shouldn't have done it then
Haber pensado antes, ¿eh? . . .	we should have thought first, shouldn't we . . .

(c) In Spain, as a colloquial variant of the second-person familiar imperative in *-d* (*vosotros* is replaced by *ustedes* in Spanish America). This form is not accepted by some speakers, but is increasingly common:

Callaros = callaos	be quiet
Venir = venid	come on
Despertaros = despertaos	wake up
Venga, daros la mano (daos)	come on, shake hands
etc.	

(d) As a colloquial exhortation:

Bueno, a dormir	okay, let's get some sleep

17.6 'Rhetorical' infinitive

The infinitive may also be used in rhetorical questions or to express incredulity or bewilderment:

¡Pagar yo cien mil por eso! . .	what! Me pay 100,000 for that!
¡Enamorarme yo a mis años!	me fall in love at my age!
Pero ¿cómo abrirlo sin llave?	but how (on earth) does one open it without a key?

17.7   Adjective + *de* + infinitive

Students of French must learn the difference between sentences like

Es difícil aprender español	it's difficult to learn Spanish

and

El español es difícil de aprender	Spanish is difficult to learn

The first type does not use the preposition *de*; i.e. *de* is not used when the infinitive of a transitive verb is followed by an object or clause:

No es fácil creerlo	it isn't easy to believe it
Es increíble pensar que el hombre	it's incredible to think that man has
ha pisado la luna	walked on the moon

But the *de* appears when no object follows:

Eso es difícil de averiguar	that's difficult to check
Es imposible de comprobar	it's impossible to prove

17.8   Infinitive preceded by *que*

The following construction must be noted – particularly by students of French (cf. *j'ai beaucoup à faire, rien à faire*, etc.)

Tengo mucho que hacer	I've got a lot to do
Voy a comprar algo que leer	I'm going to buy something to read
Dame algo que/para hacer	give me something to do
Eso nos ha dado bastante que hacer	this has given us enough to do
Te queda mucho que sufrir en este mundo	you've a lot left to suffer in this world

But this *que* construction cannot be used with verbs of needing, requesting, searching:

Necesito algo para comer	I need something to eat
Quiero algo para beber	I want something to drink
Pidió algo para calmar su dolor de	he asked for something to soothe his
muelas	toothache
Busco algo para . . .	I'm looking for something to . . .

18 Participles

This chapter discusses the past participle and the present participle in *-ante*, *-(i)ente*.

18.1 Past participle: general

For the morphology of the past participle see next section.

The past participle has two main uses:

(a) In combination with *haber*, and more rarely *tener*, to form the perfect tenses. The perfect tenses of all verbs are formed with *haber* and in this case the participle is invariable in its masculine singular form. If *tener* is used (optionally possible only with transitive verbs, and not common) the participle agrees in number and gender with the object: *ya tengo compradas las entradas/ya he comprado las entradas* 'I've bought the tickets'. For detailed discussion of the uses of the perfect tenses see 14.6–7.

(b) It may function adjectivally, in which case it agrees in number and gender like any adjective: *una exagerada reacción* 'an exaggerated reaction', *un argumento improvisado* 'an improvised argument', *una desesperada tentativa* 'a desperate attempt', etc.

Adjectival participles may, like ordinary adjectives, be converted into nouns by use of an article or demonstrative: *los desaparecidos* 'those who disappeared', *un muerto* 'a dead body', *ese herido* 'that wounded person', *¿Qué dirán por su parte los censurados?* 'what will those who have been censured have to say for themselves?'. Such nominalization often neatly replaces an English relative clause.

Many words ending in *-ado*, *-ido* are used only as adjectives, e.g. *adecuado* 'appropriate/adequate', *desgraciado* 'unhappy', *desmesurado* 'disproportionate', *indiscriminado* 'indiscriminate', *descarado*, 'shameless'.

Some past participles have become true adjectives, i.e. they may in appropriate circumstances appear before a noun: *una arriesgada aventura* 'a risky venture', *la controvertida propuesta* 'the controversial proposal', etc. Other past participles remain verbal, and they may not precede a noun: *un árbol talado* 'a felled tree', *un periódico quemado* 'a burnt newspaper', *una reunión pospuesta/aplazada* 'a postponed meeting', *un libro impreso* 'a printed book'.

Further examples of participles which may also function as true adjectives are:

alabado	praised	*elevado*	elevated
alarmado	alarmed	*emocionado*	excited/moved
alejado	remote	*justificado*	justified
debido	due	*marcado*	marked
dedicado	dedicated	*resignado*	resigned
desconocido	unknown	*supuesto*	alleged/supposed

and many others.

Such adjectival participles have the peculiarity that they may appear with *ser* without creating a passive sentence. Thus *su reacción era exagerada* 'his reaction was exaggerated', *mi llanto era desesperado* 'my weeping was desperate', *su cara me era desconocida*, 'her/his face was unknown to me', but *Miguel fue entrevistado* 'Miguel was interviewed'. In other words, if a participle cannot be used adjectivally use of *ser* usually forms a passive sentence: *la puerta era abierta* can only mean 'the door used to be opened' (by someone). In such cases it may be possible to give the participle an adjectival meaning by using *estar*: *la puerta estaba abierta* 'the door was open', *la ciudad estaba destruida* 'the city was in a state of destruction'. The difference between *estaba destruido* and the passive with *ser*, *fue destruido* is discussed at 24.1.4.

18.2   Past participles: forms

The past participle is formed in most cases by replacing the *-ar* of an infinitive by *ado*, or *-er* and *-ir* by *-ido*: *hablar/hablado*, *tener/tenido*, *construir/construido*, *ir/ido*, *ser/sido*, etc.

There are a few common irregular past participles:

Infinitive	Past participle
absolver (and all verbs in *-solver*)	*absuelto*
cubrir (and compounds)	*cubierto*
decir " "	*dicho*
escribir " " , e.g. *describir*, etc.	*escrito*
hacer " "	*hecho*
imprimir " "	*impreso*
morir " "	*muerto*
poner " "	*puesto*
romper	*roto*
ver " "	*visto*
volver " "	*vuelto*

A few have separate adjectival and verbal participles, cf. *está despierto porque le he despertado* 'he's awake because I've woken him'. Bracketed forms are attested but virtually never encountered, the irregular form being more common:

	Adjectival	Verbal	
bendecir	*bendito*	*bendecido*	bless
confundir	*confuso*	*confundido*	confuse
despertar	*despierto*	*despertado*	awake

elegir	electo	elegido	elect
freír	frito	(freído)	fry
imprimir	impreso	imprimido	print
maldecir	maldito	maldecido	curse
prender	preso	prendido	pin on (but consult dictionary)
proveer	provisto	proveído	equip with
soltar	suelto	soltado	release
suspender	suspenso	suspendido	fail (exams)

18.2.1 'Latin' past participles in Spanish America

A number of verbs have both normal participles and adjectival participles which are learned forms based on Latin participles. The learned forms are very rare in the Peninsula except in set phrases, e.g. *el presidente electo*, but some of them are common in Spanish America, especially the Southern Cone, e.g. *salió electo* 'he was elected' for *salió elegido*:

	Usual form	Learned form	
convencer	convencido	convicto	convinced
corromper	corrompido	corrupto	corrupt
describir	descrito	descripto	describe
dividir	dividido	diviso	divide
elegir	elegido	electo	elect
inscribir	inscrito	inscripto	enter (a written item)
prescribir	prescrito	prescripto	prescribe

etc.

Examples:

Ocurre en las regiones antárticas descriptas con extraordinaria vividez (Borges, Arg., Spain *descritas*)	it happens in the Antarctic regions described with extraordinary vividness . . .
Incluye todos los shampoos prescriptos por médicos (*Gente*, Arg., Spain *recetados*)	it includes all the shampoos prescribed by doctors
su apoyo irrestricto (*ibid.* Spain *incondicional*)	his unlimited support
. . . escritores que fueron conservadores convictos (Vargas Llosa, Peru: in Spain *convicto* = 'convicted')	writers who were convinced conservatives

Spanish Americans may reject the regular participles in such sentences, but the learned forms are repudiated as 'affected' by most Peninsular speakers.

Note *Muerto* is normally used as the passive participle of *matar* when applied to human beings: *su padre fue muerto durante la guerra* 'his father was killed in the war' but *unos bandidos habían matado a su padre* 'some bandits had killed his father'. This usage is rejected by some Spanish Americans.

18.3 Participle clauses

Participle clauses are common in Spanish. Such clauses are often the same as in English, but slight differences occur (and see also 26.2.4):

Me fui, convencido de que él no sabía nada	I left, convinced he knew nothing
El alcalde de Barcelona, acompañado del alcalde de Madrid	the mayor of Barcelona accompanied by the mayor of Madrid
(acompañado por = 'escorted by')	
José González, nacido el 23 de marzo	José González, born on 23 March
Aceptó irritada	she accepted irritably
¿Dónde vas? preguntó alarmado	where are you going, he asked in alarm
Su padre, muerto en 1956 . . .	his father, who died in 1956 . . .

'Absolute' participle clauses are quite common, especially in literary styles. Some absolute participle constructions are stylistically normal, others are rather literary. They can rarely be translated literally:

Llegados a Madrid, se alojaron en el mejor hotel (see note)	having arrived in Madrid, they stayed at the best hotel
Concluidas las primeras investigaciones, la policía abandonó el lugar de autos	the initial investigations having been concluded, the police left the scene of the crime
Por fin, trascurridos siete años desde la publicación de su primera novela . . .	At last, seven years having passed since the publication of his first novel . . .
Terminada la guerra, muchos ex-combatientes prefirieron no volver a su patria	once the war was over, many ex-combatants preferred not to return to their own country
Después de vendida la casa, nos arrepentimos (from Seco, 246)	once the house was sold, we regretted it
Arrasado el jardín, profanados los cálices y las aras, entraron a caballo los hunos en la biblioteca monástica (Borges, Arg., very literary)	having demolished the garden and profaned chalices and altars, the Huns rode into the monastery library
Cortados el teléfono y el telégrafo e inutilizada la radio, la única manera es que alguien vaya a Huancayo a dar aviso (Vargas Llosa, Peru, dialogue. Spanish-American? Spain . . . *con el teléfono cortado* etc.)	with the phone and telegraph cut and the radio out of action, the only way is for someone to go to Huancayo with a message

Note *Llegar* seems to be the only verb of motion which allows this construction. One cannot say **entrada en el agua se puso a nadar* 'having entered the water she began to swim' – *cuando entró en el agua se puso a nadar*.

18.4   Participles in *-ante, -iente* or *-ente*

Adjectival present participles may be formed from many verbs. Verbs with infinitive in *-ar* form them by replacing the *r* of the infinitive by *nte*, e.g. *alarmar > alarmante*, 'alarming' *inquietar > inquietante* 'worrying'. Verbs in *-er* or *-ir* replace the infinitive ending by *-iente* or *-ente*, the choice being unpredictable, cf. *convincente* 'convincing', *procedente* 'proceeding', *sorprendente* 'surprising', *conducente* 'leading (to)', but *creciente* 'growing', *hiriente* 'wounding', *concerniente* 'concerning', etc.

Forms in *-nte* cannot be coined from all verbs and must be learned separately from the dictionary, especially in view of the remark in note (ii).

Some forms in *-nte* are quite recent and may seem strange to older speakers, e.g. *preocupante* 'worrying', now well-established.

They are often used in written, mainly journalistic style to replace relative clauses in the same way as English participles in *-ing*:

una situación cambiante	a changing situation
el ministro saliente	the outgoing minister
condiciones vinculantes (El País)	binding conditions
resultados sobresalientes	outstanding results
un éxito fulminante	a fulminating success
En 1984 todavía 157.000 personas,	in 1984, 157,000 people belonging to
pertenecientes a diferentes clases sociales	various social classes and coming from
y procedentes de lugares muy distintos	widely different places, voted . . . etc.
de nacimiento, votaron . . . (El País)	
En fin, todo conducente a la violencia	in short, anything leading to simple-
obtusa . . . (Triunfo)	minded violence . . .
el millón y medio restante	the remaining 1.5 million

Notes (i)   The gerund in *-ando* or *-iendo* cannot replace the *-nte* form in any of these examples. English speakers, especially those who know French (cf. *un jeune homme parlant arabe* 'a young man speaking Arabic') may be tempted by some of these examples to use both the gerund and participles in *-nte* where only a relative clause is possible in Spanish. See 19.1 for discussion.

(ii)   English speakers are tempted to create non-existent words along the lines of 'moving' – **moviente* (*piezas móviles* 'moving parts', *espectáculo conmovedor* 'moving spectacle'). Compare also *plegable* 'folding', *agua potable* 'drinking water', *confiado/crédulo* = 'confiding', *planta trepadora* = 'climbing plant', and many others.

(iii)   Many forms in *-nte* are not strictly speaking participles but non-verbal adjectives, e.g. *brillante, corriente, aparente, reciente*, etc.

A few popular formations excepted, e.g. *dominanta* 'bossy' (of a woman), neither participles nor adjectives ending in *-nte* have a separate feminine form. However, some nouns in *-nte* form a feminine in *-nta*. See 1.1.5.

(iv)   Note irregular forms *hiriente, convincente*.

19 The gerund

19.1 General

The gerund of -*ar* verbs ends in -*ando*, of -*er* and -*ir* verbs in -*iendo*. It is invariable in form. Pronouns may be attached to it: *estaba esperándolos* (or *los estaba esperando*). See 11.12.5 for discussion of pronoun attachment with the gerund.

The Spanish gerund is quite dissimilar to the English -*ing* form, which serves as gerund, present participle, verbal noun and adjective, and also unlike the French form in -*ant* which covers the functions of both the Spanish gerund and the participle forms in -*ante*, -*(i)ente*. The Spanish gerund functions as a verbal modifier, and can therefore properly only modify verbs (actually present or implied), but not nouns. **Una caja conteniendo libros* 'a box containing books' is therefore bad Spanish since there is no verb. Such misuse of the gerund is, however, common even among natives, cf. *una Ley decretando* . . . 'a Law decreeing' (correctly *una Ley por la que se decreta*), and it is probably not always 'incorrect' if we find it in the prose of an excellent grammarian like Manuel Seco:

El propósito de [Probo], el hombre solo afrontando a la multitud, no se pudo realizar (*Diccionario*, xiii)	it was not possible to realize the goal of Probus, the man alone facing the multitude

although this example is almost certainly a type of caption, in which case the construction is correct (see 19.2.3b). English-speakers, especially if they know French, tend to misuse the gerund as a participle, cf. 'a young man speaking Arabic', *un jeune homme parlant arabe*, but *un joven que habla/hablaba árabe*.

19.2 Basic uses of the gerund

19.2.1 To modify the main verb in a sentence
In this case it functions rather like an adverb. The gerund may be used:

(a) To indicate simultaneous actions:
The action denoted by the gerund must be happening at the same time as or almost simultaneously with that of the main verb: **el ladrón huyó volviendo horas más tarde* *'the thief fled, returning hours later' is bad

Spanish; *abriendo la puerta entró en la casa* (= *abrió la puerta y entró en la casa*) is less acceptable than 'opening the door, he entered the house':

Se fue gritando	he went off shouting
Nos recibió bañándose	he received us while he was bathing
Se levantó dando por terminada la entrevista	he got up, judging the interview to be at an end
Metió la carta en el sobre, cerrándolo a continuación	he put the letter in the envelope, sealing it afterwards

Note With the verbs *ser* and *estar* it can translate 'when' or 'while', a construction strange to English-speakers:

Estando en París, me enteré de que su padre había muerto	while I was in Paris, I found out his father had died
Le conocí siendo yo bombero	I met him while I was a fireman
Te lo diré, pero no estando aquí esta señora	I'll tell you, but not while this lady is here

(b) To indicate the method by which an action is performed:

Hizo su fortuna comprando acciones a tiempo	he made his fortune buying shares at the right time
Te puedes poner en contacto conmigo llamando a este número	you can contact me by ringing this number
He perdido mucha salud trabajando bajo tierra	I've done a lot of harm to my health (lit. 'lost a lot of health') by working underground

Note This use is often equivalent to a condition:

Apretando/si aprietas de ese modo lo vas a romper	you'll break it if you squeeze like that/ by squeezing like that
Poniéndose/si se pone así conmigo usted no conseguirá nada	you'll get nowhere if you get like that with me

(c) To express purpose (= *para* + infinitive):
This construction occurs with verbs of communication:

Me escribió diciéndome/para decirme que fuera/fuese a verle	he wrote telling me to come and see him
Nos llamó pidiendo/para pedir dinero	he rang us asking for money

(d) To indicate cause (= *ya que . . ., puesto que . . .* + finite verb):
The gerund can indicate the immediate cause of a subsequent action:

Siendo estudiante, tendrás derecho a una beca	since you're a student, you'll have the right to a grant
Tratándose de usted, no faltaba más	since it's you, there's no need to mention it . . .
Dándose cuenta de que no le escuchaba, se calló	realising she/he wasn't listening, (s)he stopped talking

(e) To express concession (= *aunque* + finite verb):
The Spanish gerund occasionally signifies 'although', often in combination with *aun* 'even'. In this it differs from the English *-ing* form:

Siendo inteligente, parece tonto	although intelligent, he seems like a fool
Aun estando enfermo nos resulta útil	he's useful to us, even though he's ill
Llegando tarde y todo, nos ayudó mucho	although he arrived late, he helped us a lot

(f)   Preceded by *como* to replace *como si*:

Me miró como riéndose (= como si se estuviera/estuviese riendo)	he looked at me as though he were laughing

19.2.2   *En* + gerund

In older language and in some dialects this is an equivalent to *al* + infinitive: *en llegando al bosque* = *al llegar al bosque* 'on arriving at the woods' (cf. French *en arrivant à* . . .). The construction seems to be virtually extinct in modern educated usage.

19.2.3   Gerund used to qualify the object of a verb

Like the English *-ing* form, the gerund can also denote actions performed by the object of certain kinds of verb:

(a)   With verbs like *coger* 'catch', *pillar* 'catch', *arrestar* 'arrest', *dejar* 'leave', *encontrar* 'find':

La cogió robando	he caught her stealing
La dejé llorando	I left her crying
Encontré a mis hermanos discutiendo	I found my brothers (or brothers and sisters) quarrelling

(b)   With verbs of representation like 'paint', 'draw', 'photograph', 'show', 'describe', 'imagine', 'represent', etc.:

La pintó tocando el clavicémbalo	he painted her playing the harpsichord
Esta fotografía muestra al rey bajando del avión	this photo shows the king getting out of the plane
Me los imagino emborrachándose	I can imagine them getting drunk
Me los describió cazando leones	he described them to me hunting lions

Note   Captions, e.g. under pictures, fall into this category. In captions the gerund very often appears with no accompanying finite verb. This is considered correct, but should be avoided in other contexts:

Dos 747 siendo preparados para el despegue	two 747s being prepared for take-off
El Presidente de la República bailando la rumba	the President of the Republic dancing the rumba

19.2.4   Gerund after verbs of perception

Commonly after the verb *ver* 'to see', and occasionally after *oír* 'to hear', and a few other verbs of perception, the gerund may be used to qualify the object of the main verb. Usually the infinitive is also possible in this construction, the difference being one of aspect: the infinitive normally denotes a completed action and the gerund an action perceived while still in process. Compare

La vi fumando un cigarrillo	I saw her (while she was) smoking a cigarette
La vi fumar un cigarrillo	I saw her smoke a cigarette

There is usually an optional alternative with a finite verb:

La vi que fumaba un cigarrillo	I saw her smoking a cigarette

With verbs of motion it seems that the gerund is not usually possible: 'I saw him coming towards me' is *le/lo vi venir hacia mí* or *le/lo vi que venía hacia mí*, but not **le/lo vi viniendo hacia mí*.

Oír 'hear' and *sentir* 'feel'/'hear' may take a gerund, but prefer either the infinitive or the construction with *que* and a finite verb. The infinitive is the safest option for foreigners:

La oí toser/que tosía	I heard her coughing
Oí entrar a alguien/que alguien entraba	I heard someone coming in

But the gerund is possible if its subject is an inanimate noun:

Cuando el sargento . . . oye la corneta ordenando la retirada (Vargas Llosa, Peru)	when the sergeant hears the trumpet sounding the retreat

19.3   Other uses of the gerund

19.3.1   Gerund with *andar*
This translates the English 'to go around doing something', with the same faintly pejorative implication of pointless activity:

Siempre anda buscando camorra	he's always going round looking for a fight
un payaso de esos que andan contando chistes	one of those clowns who go around telling jokes

Note   *Ir* could replace *andar* here.

19.3.2   Gerund with *ir*
(a)   Expresses slow or gradual action:

Nos vamos haciendo viejos	we're getting older
Cada vez voy teniendo menos memoria	my memory's getting worse and worse
La situación va mejorando	the situation's on the mend
Ella se fue doblando hasta caer al suelo (*Cambio16*)	she slowly doubled up and fell to the ground
La conversación se fue espaciando	the conversation became desultory/ drawn-out

(b)   By extension, to express careful, painstaking or laborious actions:

Ya puedes ir preparando todo para cuando llegue	you can set about getting everything ready for his arrival
Gano lo necesario para ir tirando	I earn enough to get by
Ve escribiendo todo lo que te dicte	write down everything as I dictate it to you

19.3.3   Gerund with *llevar*
This provides a neat translation of 'for' in time expressions:

Llevo dos meses pintando esta casa	I've been painting this house for two months
Llevo años diciéndolo	I've been saying it for years

19.3.4   Gerund with *quedarse*
This translates the idea of 'remain doing something':

Cuando llegué se quedaron cenando	when I arrived they went on having supper
Me quedé ayudándolos un rato	I stayed on for a while to help them
Se quedó mirándome	she stood staring at me

19.3.5   Gerund with *salir*
Usually translates English phrases involving 'come out'/'go out':

Salió ganando	he came out the winner
Salieron corriendo	they ran out

19.3.6   Gerund with *seguir* and *continuar*
Seguir often translates 'still' or 'to go on':

Sigue buscando un empleo	he's still looking for a job
Seguimos viéndonos de vez en cuando	we went on seeing one another from time to time

Continuar also takes the gerund:

Continuó hablando en persa	he continued to speak in Persian

Note   **continuar a hablar* (French *continuer à parler*) is not Spanish!

19.3.7   Gerund with *venir*
To express an action which steadily accumulates or increases with time. It often conveys mounting exasperation:

Hace años que viene diciendo lo mismo	he's been saying the same thing for years
Dice que hace mucho que la viene viendo	he says he's been seeing her for a long time
El endeudamiento viene convirtiéndose en la mayor pesadilla de los años ochenta	indebtedness is becoming the biggest nightmare of the eighties
La sensación de aislamiento en la Moncloa viene siendo progresiva (*Cambio16*)	the sensation of isolation at the Moncloa (Spanish Downing Street) is steadily growing

19.3.8   Gerund with *acabar*
Means 'end by':

Siempre acaba enfadándose	he always ends by getting mad
Acabarás haciendo lo que ella diga	you'll end up doing what she says

Acabar por + infinitive is an equivalent, and is the more common construction in negative statements:

Acabarás por no salir nunca de casa	you'll end up never going out of the house

19.4   Translating the English *-ing* form

The following consists mainly of cases where the English *-ing* form may *not* be translated by the Spanish gerund.

19.4.1   When the *-ing* form is the subject of a verb

This is normally translated by an infinitive or by a suitable noun:

Learning a language is fun	*aprender un idioma es divertido*
Eating too much butter is bad for the heart	*comer demasiada mantequilla es malo para el corazón*
No smoking	*prohibido fumar*
Skiing is expensive	*esquiar/el esquí cuesta mucho*
Salmon fishing is an art	*la pesca de salmón es un arte*

19.4.2   When the *-ing* form is the object of a verb

In this case there are two possibilities:

   (a)   When the same subject performs both actions, use an infinitive or a noun:

He dreads having to start	*teme tener que empezar*
I like swimming	*me gusta nadar/me gusta la natación*
He gave up gambling	*dejó de jugar/dejó el juego*
Try ringing him	*intenta llamarle*
There's nothing I like better than working in the garden	*no hay nada que me guste más que trabajar en el jardín*

   (b)   When the actions are performed by different subjects, use a clause or noun – the subjunctive must be used where required by the rules laid out in chapter 16:

I can't stand Pedro singing	*no puedo ver que Pedro cante*
I didn't mind him/his living here	*no me importaba que viviera/viviese aquí*
I recommended promoting him	*recomendé su ascenso/que le ascendiesen/ascendieran*
I approve of you(r) getting up early	*me parece bien que te levantes temprano*

Note   Some verbs allow the gerund. See 19.2.3.

19.4.3   The *-ing* form used in a passive sense

Care is needed when the English *-ing* form replaces a passive infinitive, cf. 'your hair needs cutting' (= 'your hair needs to be cut'). The Spanish translation should be made non-passive and an infinitive or a clause used:

Your hair needs cutting	*(te) hace falta que te corten el pelo* or *que te cortes el pelo*
This needs attending to	*hace falta cuidarse de esto/ hay que atender a esto*
You're not worth listening to	*no vale la pena escucharte*
It wants polishing	*hace falta sacarle brillo*

19.4.4   The *-ing* form preceded by prepositions

Unless the preposition is 'by' (see 19.2b) an infinitive or clause must be used:

I'm looking forward to seeing you	*tengo ganas de verte*
I prefer swimming to running	*prefiero nadar a correr*
He was punished for being late	*le castigaron por llegar tarde*
This is a good opportunity for showing what you mean	*ésta es una buena oportunidad para demostrar lo que quieres decir*
He's thinking of starting a business	*piensa empezar un negocio*
You get nothing in life without working	*no se consigue nada en esta vida sin trabajo/sin trabajar*
He was furious at being mistaken for his brother	*le enfureció que le confundieran/ confundiesen con su hermano*

19.4.5   The *-ing* form before nouns

(a)   If the *-ing* form is itself a noun, translation is usually by an infinitive or a noun:

driving licence	*carnet de conducir*
dancing shoes	*zapatos de baile*
fishing rod	*caña de pescar*

(b)   If the *-ing* form is a participle (adjective) then a relative clause may be used, unless a participle in *-ante, -(i)ente* exists (see 18.4):

a walking doll	*un muñeco andante*
the chiming bells	*las campanas que tañen/tañían*
a worrying problem	*un problema inquietante*
a convincing reply	*una respuesta convincente*

But often an idiomatic solution must be sought in either case:

flying planes	*aviones en vuelo*
turning point	*el punto decisivo*
	la vuelta de la marea, etc.
steering wheel	*el volante*
dining room	*el comedor*

Note   For the use of *hirviendo* 'boiling' and *ardiendo* 'burning' as adjectives, see 4e.

20 Personal *a*

20.1 Personal *a*: general

The use of *a* before certain types of grammatical object is a feature of Spanish so important as to warrant a separate chapter.

In the sentence *Pepe vio a su tío* 'Pepe saw his uncle', omission of the *a* would be a crass error. In *Pepe ha roto un plato* 'Pepe's broken a plate', *a* before *un* is impossible. Between these two clear-cut cases there is a series of situations in which use of the personal *a* is a complex choice which may be determined by questions of style or emotional context.

The logic underlying the use of personal *a* is that Spanish, in common with a number of languages (e.g. Romanian, Hindi), tends to differentiate between types of direct object, and to mark human direct objects. In the case of Spanish, *identified* or *particularized* human direct objects are marked by a preceding *a*. However, 'personal' *a* is a misnomer since it also sometimes appears with inanimate direct objects, particularly, but not only whenever there might be doubt about which is the subject and which the object, as sometimes happens in Spanish where word order is quite flexible.

20.2 Personal *a* before nouns denoting human beings

Personal *a* is required before a direct object which denotes a known or identified human being, or a 'personified' animal.

Before a direct object which is a personal name or title – *Pedro*, *el jefe*, *mamá* – personal *a* is never omitted.

As far as the distinction between identified and non-identified human beings is concerned, *a* is used if the object is particularized in some way: cf. *vi tres ingleses en la playa* 'I saw three Englishmen on the beach' but *vi a tres ingleses que llevaban pantalones a cuadros* 'I saw three Englishmen wearing check trousers' (and therefore particularized Englishmen).

With animals, use of personal *a* depends on the extent to which the creature is humanized. Pets virtually always take personal *a*, but in other cases use of *a* depends on factors of emotion or context: the more familiar the language, the more likely the use of *a*. At the zoo one is likely to say *vamos a ver a los monos* 'let's go and see the monkeys' but, probably, *vamos a ver los insectos* 'let's go and see the insects', monkeys being more

269

lovable than cockroaches. Clinical or scientific language would naturally use personal *a* much more sparingly.

No conozco a Feliciano	I don't know Feliciano
Acompañé a mi madre a la clínica	I accompanied my mother to the clinic
Llevó a las niñas al zoo	he took the girls to the zoo
¡Mira a los turistas!	look at the (i.e. those) tourists!
La policía busca a un individuo con una cicatriz en el labio inferior	the police are seeking an individual with a scar on his lower lip
Admiran mucho al cámara (cf. *admiran la cámara* 'they admire the camera')	they admire the cameraman a great deal
¿Quieres pasear al perro?	do you want to take the dog for a walk?
Dejad de atormentar al gato	stop tormenting the cat

Compare the following sentences in which the object of the verb is not individually particularized:

Busco un marido que me ayude en la casa	I'm looking for a husband who will help me in the house
Vi un periodista en el jardín	I saw a journalist in the garden
Veía un chico que jugaba en silencio (E. Sabato, Arg.)	I saw a child playing in silence
Amenazaron con no dejar un terrorista vivo en todo el país	they threatened not to leave a single terrorist alive in the whole country
El idioma inglés distingue la Sirena clásica de las que tienen cola de pez (Borges, Arg.)	the English language distinguishes the classical Siren from those which have fishes' tails (mermaids)
Este DC-10 ha traído pasajeros desde Berlín	this DC-10 has brought passengers from Berlin
El macho es el hombre terrible {. . .} el padre que se ha ido, que ha abandonado mujer e hijos (O. Paz, Mex.)	the macho is the terrible man {. . .} the father who has gone off and left wife and children
Utilizaron un perro lobo para el experimento	they used an Alsatian dog for the experiment
Mira los turistas, siempre gastando dinero	look at tourists (for example), always spending money

Notes (i)   A noun linked by *como* to a previous noun which itself has a personal *a* (or to a pronoun standing for such a noun) must also take personal *a* (though it may be omitted colloquially if there is no ambiguity):

Tuve que recoger a mi hermana como a un fardo	I had to pick my sister up as though she were a bundle
Su reacción fue de las primeras cosas que delató a Adriano Gómez como a un ser peligroso (J. Donoso, Chile)	his reaction was one of the first things to expose A. Gomez as a dangerous person
Tuve que tratarle como a un niño de seis años	I had to treat him like a six-year old

(ii)   A proper name may occasionally denote inanimate objects, in which case personal *a* cannot be used:

Dice conocer todo Shakespeare	he says he knows the whole of Shakespeare (i.e. the works)
Van a subastar un Turner	they're going to auction a Turner (painting)
Procura tomar la reina	try to take the queen (chess)

20.3   Personal *a* before pronouns

Pronouns which stand for a person take personal *a*; these include *alguien*, *alguno*, *uno*, *ambos*, *cualquiera*, *nadie*, *otro*, *ninguno*, *quien*, *todo*, *él*, *ella*, *usted* and other personal pronouns, and relative pronouns (*el que*, *el cual*, *quien* but not the pronoun *que* when it is used alone – see 29.3 note (iii) for discussion):

He visto a alguien en el pasillo	I've seen someone in the corridor
No conozco a nadie	I don't know anyone
Era capaz de insultar a cualquiera	he was capable of insulting anybody
¿A quién has visto?	who(m) did you see?
La persona a quien yo más echaba de menos	the person I missed most
A ella es a quien quiere, no a ti	it's her he loves, not you

But:

La persona que yo había visto	the person I had seen

etc.

20.4   Personal *a* before personified nouns

A personified noun usually requires personal *a*. The decision as to whether a noun is personified or not is, however, dependent on complex factors of context:

Tú temes al éxito tanto como al fracaso	you fear success as much as failure
Los cazas llevan bengalas de magnesio para confundir a un misil dirigido (*Cambio16*)	the fighters carry magnesium flares to confuse a guided missile

The last example shows how certain verbs, e.g. *confundir*, *criticar*, *satirizar*, *insultar*, etc. tend, by their meaning, to personify their object. This explains – though does not justify – the occurrence of sentences like *?criticaba a las novelas de fulano* 'he criticized so-and-so's novels'.

20.5   Personal *a* after *tener, querer*

These verbs may acquire different meanings when used with personal *a*:

Tengo un hijo y una hija	I've got a son and a daughter
Tenemos una asistenta griega	we have a Greek maid

But:

Tiene a un hijo en casa y al otro en el ejército	she has one son at home and the other in the army
Tengo a mi tío como fiador	I've got my uncle to act as guarantor
La humedad de la noche . . . tiene a las veredas resbaladizas y brillosas (Vargas Llosa, Perú; *vereda* for Peninsular *acera* 'pavement'; *brillosas = brillantes*)	the dampness of the night . . . makes the pavements slippery and shiny
Quiere una secretaria	he wants a secretary
Quiere a una secretaria	he loves a secretary

20.6   Omission of personal *a* before numerals

Personal *a* may be optionally omitted before numerals:

Reclutaron (a) doscientos jóvenes	they recruited 200 young people
Vieron (a) media docena de soldados enemigos	they saw half a dozen enemy soldiers
Bayardo San Román {. . .} vio las dos mujeres vestidas de negro . . . (García Márquez, Colombia)	Bayardo San Román saw the two women dressed in black . . .
Sólo conozco un hombre capaz de componer esta emboscada maestra (García Márquez, Colombia; personal *a* omitted before *un* when it is a numeral rather than an article)	I only know one man capable of organizing this masterly ambush

Note   A particularized or identified personal noun will, however, take personal *a*: *yo conocía personalmente a sus tres hijas* 'I knew his three daughters personally'.

20.7   Personal *a* combined with dative *a*

Ambiguity may arise when two *a*s occur in the same sentence, e.g. ?*presenté a mi marido a mi jefe* 'I introduced my husband to my boss' or vice-versa. The common solution is to omit personal *a*:

Presenté Miguel a Antonia	I introduced Miguel to Antonia
Denuncié el ladrón al guardia	I denounced the thief to the policeman
Recomiende usted mi sobrino al señor director (from Esbozo, 3.4.6)	recommend my nephew to the director

Note   The problem of *preferir* is also solved in this way:
Yo prefiero Dickens a Balzac   I prefer Dickens to Balzac

20.8   Personal *a* before collective nouns

Personal *a* is normally used before collective nouns when these refer to human beings:

Sir Walter Raleigh enriqueció a la enclenque corte inglesa (*Cambio16*)	Sir Walter Raleigh enriched the feeble English court
No conocía al resto del grupo	he didn't know the rest of the group
Un paso que podría poner a Estados Unidos en una posición delicada (*La Prensa*, Arg.)	a step which could put the US in a delicate position
No has convencido al tribunal	you haven't convinced the court

A is obligatory in all these examples.

Compare the following sentences in which the nouns do not refer to inhabitants or members of a group, but to a place:

Los turistas inundan México	tourists are inundating Mexico
Hitler invadió la Unión Soviética	Hitler invaded the Soviet Union

Notes (i)   Before words like *país*, *nación*, *partido*, *movimiento*, when these words refer – or may refer – to people, *a* seems to be optional:

Criticó duramente al/el movimiento anarquista	he criticized the anarchist movement severely
Será imposible gobernar a Euskadi (*Cambio16*: omission possible)	it will be impossible to govern the Basque country
Son los sindicatos los que dirigen a esta nación (omission possible)	it's the unions which run this country
Un potente terremoto sacudió el/al país	a powerful earthquake shook the country
Luis García Meza, quien gobernó el país entre julio de 1980 y agosto de 1981 (*El País, al* possible)	L. Garcia Meza, who governed the country between July 1980 and August 1981

(ii)   Seeing, visiting, leaving or picturing a place does not call for personal *a* (this, at least, is established usage; the Academy's complaints are ignored):

Estamos deseando ver Lima	we're longing to see Lima
Se negó a visitar Rumania	he refused to visit Romania
Quería pintar Toledo	he wanted to paint Toledo
Abandonaron Madrid	they left Madrid

20.9   Personal *a* before inanimate objects

Personal *a* cannot appear before a noun denoting an inanimate object in straightforward sentences of the following kind:

He comprado un sacacorchos	I've bought a corkscrew
Escribe poesía	he writes poetry
Sus palabras delataban su derrotismo	his words betrayed his defeatism
Recuerdo aquel día	I remember that day

But, despite its name, personal *a* is used before inanimate nouns:

(a)   When there is likely to be ambiguity as to which is the subject and which the direct object of a verb. Such ambiguity is very common in relative clauses, where the verb often precedes the subject:

Es difícil saber en qué medida afectó esto a la economía cubana (Vargas Llosa, Peru)	it is difficult to know to what extent this affected the Cuban economy
Este producto es el que mejor impermeabiliza al algodón	this product is the one that best waterproofs cotton
La trama conceptual que subyace a esta obra	the network of concepts underlying this work
Una organización que protege a su coche	an organization which protects your car
Las fotografías que acompañan a estas líneas	the photographs accompanying these lines
A tres Autos y un Comercio quemaron (Spanish-American headline, strange to Peninsular speakers)	Three Cars and Store Burnt

This also sometimes happens when there is no real danger of ambiguity, when both subject and object are inanimate. It seems that this occurs only in those sentences in which the inanimate subject is also the true agent of the action. In a sentence like *la piedra rompió un cristal*, 'the stone broke a pane of glass' or *la novela causó una sensación* 'the novel caused a sensation', it can be argued that the agents of the action are the person who threw the stone or wrote the novel; *piedra* and *novela* are merely instruments. For this reason personal *a* is impossible. However, if the inanimate subject is the real agent of the action, personal *a* may appear, but it is not obligatory. It is as though the native speaker were not entirely confident that word order alone – loose in Spanish – sufficiently clarifies which is the subject and which the object. The issue is not in doubt if one of the nouns is a human being or is the instrument of a human being. But if both are of equal status, *a* makes absolutely clear which is the agent and which the object:

El cementerio de Santa Cruz, al que la vegetación devora inexorablemente (*Cambio16*)	the cemetery of Santa Cruz, which the vegetation is relentlessly devouring
Ambos creían que los astros regían a las pasiones (O. Paz, Mex.)	both believed the stars ruled the passions
Este morfema nominal concretiza al semantema (F. Abad Nebot)	this nominal morpheme makes the semanteme concrete
El suicidio de la muchacha . . . excitó a la opinión pública (Vargas Llosa, Peru)	the girl's suicide . . . stirred public opinion
Este clima caracteriza a la sierra andina	this climate characterizes the Andes range

A could be omitted in all these examples.

(b)　After impersonal *se* (see 24.2) so as to show that the *se* is indeed impersonal *se* and not a reflexive *se*:

En España se llamaba a la plata (Sp. *dinero*) *de los cohechos y sobornos "unto de México"*	in Spain they used to call the money from bribery and graft 'Mexican grease'

(O. Paz, Mex., cf. *la plata se llamaba* 'money was called . . .')

¿Se podía llamar a eso caridad? (Vargas Llosa, Peru)	could one call that charity?
En estos cuarenta años se protegía al coche español (*Cambio16*)	throughout these forty years Spanish cars were protected
Demasiado a menudo se comparó a esos órganos con filtros encargados de eliminar los desechos tóxicos acumulados en la sangre (*Ercilla*, Chile, in *Var.* 220)	too often these organs {the kidneys} were compared with filters charged with eliminating toxic wastes which had accumulated in the blood

20.10　*A* obligatory or preferred with certain verbs

(a)　Some verbs always take *a* whatever their object, e.g. *renunciar a* 'to renounce', *obedecer a*, 'to obey', *ayudar a*, *gustar*, *agradar*. However, this *a* may not always be personal *a* but some other manifestation of the preposition *a*:

Considera que la opción más sabia es renunciar gradualmente a la energía nuclear (*El País*: not personal *a*)	he considers that the wisest option is gradually to give up nuclear energy

Esto obedece a unas normas de comportamiento . . .	this obeys certain norms of behaviour
A los osos les gusta la miel	bears like honey
Este nuevo producto ayuda al cabello a recobrar su brillo natural (*a* normal)	this new product helps the hair recover its natural shine

It is worth recalling at this point that there is an important difference between personal *a* and dative *a*: the latter is usually reinforced by a redundant pronoun, whereas the former is not – at least in the Peninsula and in educated speech in much of Spanish America. Thus one says *le dije a tu padre* 'I said to your father . . .' (redundant *le*) but only *vi a tu padre* 'I saw your father' and not **le vi a tu padre*. Reinforcement with a redundant pronoun is only required when the object precedes the verb – *a tu padre le vi ayer . . .* 'I saw your father yesterday . . .': this word order device is explained at 31.3.

Sentences like *?lo vi a Miguel* are, however, common in the Southern Cone and are often heard in popular Spanish-American speech everywhere. See 11.14.4 for more details.

(b) *A* preferred after some verbs

Some verbs often take *a* before an inanimate object. These include *afectar a* 'to affect', *reemplazar a* 'to replace', *sustituir a* 'to substitute/replace', *superar a* 'to overcome/exceed', *acompañar a*, *criticar a*, *combatir a*, *llamar a* 'to name/call'. However, usage is uncertain with some of them, and native speakers sometimes disagree about the appropriateness of the use of *a* before an inanimate object:

Los historiadores británicos llaman "guerra peninsular" (a) lo que nosotros denominamos guerra de la independencia	British historians give the name 'Peninsular War' to what we call the War of Independence
Estas ventajas permiten al Volkswagen superar a sus rivales	these advantages allow the Volkswagen to beat its rivals
Las nuevas medidas también afectan (a) la deuda pública	the new measures also affect the public debt
Este nuevo tipo de transistor sustituye a los anteriores (*a* normal)	this new type of transistor replaces the former ones
El nuevo Ford ha reemplazado a la gama anterior	the new Ford has replaced the previous range

etc.

21 Negation

Spanish negative words discussed in this chapter are:

no	no, not	*nunca/jamás*	never/ever
nada	nothing	*en mi vida,*	never in my life
nadie	nobody	*tampoco*	not even/nor
ni	nor/not even		
ninguno	none/no		

For the construction *no . . . sino* 'not . . . but' see 27.1.

Matters requiring special attention are the stylistic consequences of use or non-use of the double.negative, e.g. *no lo he visto nunca/nunca lo he visto* 'I've never seen it/him'; the use of negative words in certain types of positive sentences, e.g. *¿quién ha dicho nunca eso?* 'who ever said that?', *más que nada* 'more than anything' etc., and use of redundant *no* e.g. *¡cuántas veces no te habré dicho!* 'how many times must I have told you!'.

21.1 *No*

21.1.1 Use and position

No normally precedes the word which it negates, but object pronouns are never separated from a verb: *no dije . . .* 'I didn't say', but *no se lo dije* 'I didn't say it to him/her/you/them'.

Mario no estaba	Mario wasn't there
No perdamos tiempo	let us not waste time
No todos son capaces de aprender idiomas	not everyone is capable of learning languages
Arguyen – y no sin razón –, que . . .	they argue – and not without reason – that . . .
Fumo puros, pero no siempre	I smoke cigars, but not always
No intentaba verla	I wasn't trying to see her
Intentaba no verla	I was trying not to see her

If a verb has been deleted, *no* retains its position: *bebe cerveza pero no bebe vino > bebe cerveza, pero no vino* 'he drinks beer but not wine'; *viene mañana, pero no esta tarde* 'he's coming tomorrow but not this afternoon/evening':

Se parece a mi hermano, pero no a mí	she resembles my brother, but not me
¿Sabéis nadar? Yo sí, pero él no	can you swim? I can, but he can't

In very emphatic denials, it may follow the noun:

¡Bases nucleares no!	no nuclear bases!
Aquí puede entrar todo el que quiera, pero borrachos no	anyone who wants to can come in here, but not drunkards
(or pero no borrachos)	
Ah no, eso no	oh no, not that

Notes (i) Compound tenses, i.e. the perfect tenses, do not allow participle deletion in Spanish: in answer to ¿lo has visto? 'have you seen him/it?' one says sí or sí, lo he visto, or no or no, no lo he visto, but not *no, no lo he . . . (compare English 'no, I haven't . . .'). This rule is apparently occasionally broken in the pluperfect: see 14.6 for an example.

¿Has sido tú? No, no he sido yo	was it you? No, it wasn't
¿Se lo has dado? No, no se lo he dado	did you give it to him/her/them? No, I didn't

But:

¿Estabas comiendo? No, no estaba	were you having lunch? No I wasn't
¿Quieres venir? No, no quiero	do you want to come? No I don't

(ii) If it means 'non-' or 'un-' no precedes the noun:

Yo estoy por la no violencia	I support non-violence
La política de la no intervención	the non-intervention policy
Es la única imagen no real en todo el libro (J. Marsé)	it's the only non-real image in the whole book

21.1.2   No as a question tag

¿No? at the end of a statement implies that the speaker already knows the answer, cf. 'isn't it?', 'do you?':

Usted habla inglés, ¿no?	you speak English, don't you?
Mejor tarde que nunca, ¿no?	better late than never don't you think?
Ustedes no aceptan cheques, ¿no?	you don't take cheques do you?

Note   A negative question is handled as in English: i.e. no confirms the negative. There is no Spanish equivalent of the contradicting 'yes' of French (si!) or German (doch).

¿No vienes? No	aren't you coming? No (I'm not)
¿No vas a enfadarte otra vez? Sí	you aren't going to get cross again? Yes I am
¿No cerraste con llave el armario? Sí	didn't you lock the cupboard? Yes. I did

21.1.3   'Redundant' no

An apparently superfluous no is inserted in certain types of sentence – a phenomenon common to other Romance languages (cf. l'affaire était plus compliquée que je ne pensais):

(a)   Colloquially, to avoid two ques side by side:

Prefiero que llueva que no que haga tanto calor	I'd rather it rained than that it should be so hot
(or . . . a que haga tanto calor)	
Más vale que vengas conmigo que no que te quedes solo aquí	better you come with me than that you stay here alone
(or . . . a que te quedes solo . . .)	

(b)   In informal language redundant no is often unnecessarily used in comparisons, especially before an infinitive:

Mejor gastar cien mil ahora que (no) tener que comprar un coche nuevo para el verano	better spend one hundred thousand now than have to buy a new car by summer
La obra de R. vale más para un conocimiento de la derecha que no para conocer la República (M. Tuñón de Lara)	R's work is more useful for gaining knowledge of the Right than of the Republic
Mejor que salgas con ellos que (no) con ella	better you go out with them rather than with her
. . . tensión más por problemas internos que no por preocupación por el país (Cambio16)	tension more over internal problems than from concern for the country

(c) Optionally, in interjections involving *cuánto* or *qué de*: use of *no* is rather literary nowadays:

¡Cuántas veces no lo había soñado en los últimos tiempos! (L. Goytisolo)	how often he had dreamt of it lately!
¡Qué de angustias (no) habrán pasado!	what anguish they must have suffered!
¡Cuántas veces (no) te lo habré dicho!	how many times must I have told you!

(d) Very frequently after *hasta* and *a menos que* in negative sentences:

No me iré de aquí hasta que (no) me diga la verdad	I won't leave here until he tells me the truth
No cobrarás hasta que (no) encuentre trabajo	you won't get the money until he finds work
No era noticia hasta que no la publicaba ABC (Cambio16)	it wasn't news until *ABC* published it

But *no* is not used if the sentence is positive:

Siguieron sin hacer nada hasta que llegó el capataz	they carried on doing nothing until the foreman arrived
Me quedaré aquí hasta que se ponga el sol	I'll stay here until the sun sets

(e) In literary usage, after expressions of fear. The *no* does not alter the sense. Note that *que* is used if the *no* is removed:

Temo no le haya sucedido/temo que le haya sucedido alguna desgracia	I'm worried he may have suffered some misfortune
Tenía miedo no le/que le vieran desde arriba	he was afraid that they would see him from above

21.1.4 *No más* (also written *nomás*)

In Spanish America this phrase has a variety of meanings which it does not have in Spain:

¿Donde está el hospital? En la esquina no más (Spain: *justo en la esquina*)	where's the hospital? Right on the corner
Lo vi ayer no más (Spain: *le vi ayer mismo*)	I saw him only yesterday
Pase no más (Spain: *pase, pase*, etc.)	but *do* come in
etc.	

Note On both continents, *no . . . más que* means 'only' and must be distinguished from *no . . . más de* 'not more than'. See 5.5.1.

21.2 Double negative

If a negative *follows* a verb, the verb must also be preceded by a negative. A negative sentence in Spanish requires that all the constituents of the sentence be negativized. Compare *nunca veía a nadie en ninguna de las habitaciones* 'I never saw anybody in any of the rooms':

No dice nada	he says nothing
Nadie dijo nada	no one said anything
Apenas come nada	he scarcely eats anything
Tampoco vino nadie	nor did anyone come
Nunca trae ninguno	she never brings a single one
No sabe ni latín ni francés	he knows neither Latin nor French
No la he visto nunca con nadie	I've never seen her with anyone

However, negatives may precede a verb, as in English:

Tampoco vino	he didn't come either
Apenas habla	he scarcely talks
Nadie cree eso	no one believes that
Ni en sueños hubiera pensado eso	not even in his dreams would he have thought that
Ninguna era más guapa que ella	no woman was more beautiful than her
Jamás/nunca la volvería a ver	(s)he was never to see her again

The difference between the constructions is sometimes merely stylistic, cf. *nadie vino/no vino nadie*. References under the individual items give guidance on this subject.

Note The double negative may occasionally be ambiguous, although intonation or context usually make the meaning clear:

Lo que dice no es nada		what he says is nothing (i.e. worthless)
	or	what he says isn't nothing (i.e. it isn't worthless)
Sonia no llora por nada		Sonia doesn't cry over nothing
	or	Sonia doesn't cry over anything
(cf. *Sonia llora por nada*		Sonia cries over nothing)

(Example from Kauffman (*Readings in Spanish–English Contrastive Linguistics*, 'Negation in English and Spanish', 156–73). *Sonia no llora sin motivo* expresses the first idea unambiguously.

21.3 *Nada, nadie, nunca, jamás, ninguno* in sentences which are positive in form or meaning

These words sometimes have the meaning of 'anything', 'anyone', 'ever', etc. in certain types of sentences.

  (a) After comparisons:

Más que nada, es taimado	more than anything, he's cunning
Más que a nadie, se parece a su padre	he's more like his father than anyone (else)
En España son muchos los que se precian de asar el cordero mejor que nadie (*Cambio16*)	there are many in Spain who pride themselves on roasting lamb better than anyone else
El mejor ejemplo que se haya visto nunca/jamás	the best example ever seen

Algo que {. . .} *les pareció más violento, más subversivo que nada que jamás oirían* (José Donoso, Chile)
something which seemed to them more violent, more subversive than anything they would ever hear

Habla más que nunca (*jamás* not possible)
he's talking more than ever

Este libro es más complicado que ninguno de los que yo he leído
this book is more complicated than any I've read

Ella es más inteligente que ninguna de las otras
she's more intelligent than any of the other girls/women

(b) In sentences which involve expressions of doubt, denial, abstention, impossibility, etc.:

Es dudoso que nadie pueda pasar por nativo en más de tres o cuatro idiomas
it's doubtful whether anyone can pass as a native in more than three or four languages

Dudo que encuentres a nadie con quien hablar
I doubt you'll find anyone to talk to

Durante todo aquel tiempo se abstuvo de todo contacto con nadie
during all that time he refrained from all contact with anyone

Se negó siquiera a hablar a nadie de la emisora (Cabrera Infante, Cuba)
he even refused to talk to anyone from the radio station

Es imposible ver nada de lo que está sucediendo
it's impossible to see anything of what's going on

Es horrible contar todo esto a nadie
it's horrible to tell all this to anyone

Es poco probable que ninguno haya sobrevivido
it's unlikely that any have survived

Me chocaría que jamás/nunca la encontrasen
I'd be amazed if they ever found her

(c) In questions or exclamations which expect a negative answer

¿A usted cuándo le han preguntado nada?
when did anyone ask you anything?

¿Quién ha visto a nadie que trabaje más que él?
who has ever seen anyone who works more than he does?

¿Quién hubiera pensado nunca/jamás que se casaría con Josefa?
who would ever have thought he'd have married Josefa?

¿Habráse visto nunca/jamás? . . .
did you ever see . . .!

¿Crees que ninguno de ellos te va a ayudar?
do you think any of them is going to help you? (or 'do you think none of them is going to help you?')

¿A qué culpar de nada a nadie? (Luis Cernuda)
Why blame anyone for anything?

(d) After *antes de, antes que*, and *sin*

He venido sin nada
I've come without anything

El campo, sin nadie ya, parecía triste y abandonado
the countryside, deserted by now (lit. 'without anyone now'), seemed sad and abandoned

Sin nadie que le cuidara
without anyone to look after him

Al otro día me levanté antes que nadie (Cortázar, Arg. dialogue)
the next day I got up before everybody else (lit. 'before anyone')

Esto hay que hacerlo antes de empezar nada
this must be done before starting anything (else)

Note   Statements of emotion involve a subtlety:

Me sorprendería que nadie me llamara/ que no me llamara nadie	I'd be surprised if nobody rang me
Me sorprendería que me llamara nadie	I'd be surprised if anyone rang me
Sentiría que nadie me viera así/que me viera así nadie	I'd be sorry if anyone sees me (looking) like this
Sentiría que nadie me viera así/ sentiría que no me viera así nadie	I'd be sorry if no one sees me (looking) like this

21.4   Further remarks on individual negative words

21.4.1   *Nada, nadie*

The rules for the position of these negative words in relation to the verb are as follows:

(a)   When *nada* or *nadie* are the complement of a verb, or follow a preposition, they normally appear in the double negative construction:

No sé nada	I know nothing
No conozco a nadie	I don't know anyone
No es nada/nadie	it's nothing/nobody
No hay nada/nadie	there's nothing/nobody
No lo haría por nada/nadie	I wouldn't do it for anything/anyone
No trabaja para nadie	he doesn't work for anyone
Porque la palabra 'felicidad' no era apropiada para nada que tuviera alguna vinculación con Alejandra (E. Sabato, Arg.)	because the word 'happiness' was not appropriate for anything which had any link with Alejandra

In literary styles they may precede the verb:

. . . nada prometen que luego traicionen	they promise nothing that they then betray
. . . nada hay menos concluyente en el terreno doctrinal que las respuestas dadas por los profesionales (*El País*)	nothing is less conclusive in the area of doctrine than the answers given by professionals
A nadie conozco más apto para esta labor literaria	I know no one more suited for this literary task
Por nada del mundo quisiera perderme eso	I wouldn't miss that for anything in the world
Como esos hombres silenciosos y solitarios que a nadie piden nada y con nadie hablan (E. Sabato, Arg.)	like those silent and solitary men who ask nothing from anyone and speak with no one

(b)   When *nada, nadie* are the subject of a verb, they normally precede it:

Nada parece cierto en todo esto	nothing seems sure in all this
Nada en la pieza es histórico (Vargas Llosa, Peru)	nothing in the play is historical
Nadie quiso creerle que era honrado . . . (Vargas Llosa, Peru, dialogue)	no one was willing to believe he was honest . . .
Nadie cree eso ya	no one believes that any more

But a double negative construction is used in questions:

¿No ha venido nadie?	has no one come?
¿No ha llegado nada?	hasn't anything arrived?

Note With some verbs, either construction may be used:

No me gusta nada/nada me gusta I don't like anything

Nada de lo que tú hagas me molesta/ nothing you do bothers me
no me molesta nada de lo que tú
hagas

21.4.2 *Nada* as intensifier

Nada may be used adverbially with the meaning 'not at all':

Manuel no trabaja nada Manuel does absolutely no work
No hemos dormido nada we haven't slept a wink
No ha sido nada cómoda la cárcel prison wasn't comfortable at all

21.4.3 Further remarks on *nadie*

Nadie takes personal *a* if it is the object of a verb:

Apenas conozco a nadie I hardly know anybody
No se veía a nadie en la playa there was no one to be seen on the beach

Note *Nadie de* should not be followed by a plural noun: *nadie de la clase* but *ninguno de los alumnos* 'none of the students', *ninguno de ellos* 'none of them', *ninguno de nosotros* 'none of us'.

21.4.4 *Ni*

'Nor, 'neither'. As with other negative words, if *ni* follows the verb to which it refers, the verb must itself be negated:

Ni tú ni yo lo sabemos neither you nor I know (it)

but:

No lo sabemos ni tú ni yo " "

Constructions like **ni tú ni yo no lo sabemos* are considered archaic or incorrect.

Unlike 'nor', *ni* is usually repeated before each member of a list: *no han llegado (ni) Antonio, ni Belchu, ni Ana, ni Mariluz* 'neither Antonio, Belchu, Ana nor Mariluz has arrived' (the first *ni* is optional).

Examples of the use of *ni*:

. . . ya que entonces no había en la since at that time there were neither
tierra ni sólidos ni líquidos ni gases solids nor liquids nor gases on the earth
(Borges, Arg.)

No tenemos ni coñac ni ron we have neither cognac nor rum
Ni fumo ni bebo/no fumo ni bebo I neither smoke nor drink
Ni los liberales ni los laboristas parecían neither Liberals nor Labour seemed
dispuestos a transigir inclined to compromise
No me interesa el tema ni lo que puedan I'm neither interested in the subject,
decir de mí en el pueblo nor in what they may say about me
(J. Marsé, dialogue) in the village
Ni con ella, ni con nadie, me puedo I can't communicate with her or with
comunicar (M. Puig, Arg. dialogue) anybody

Notes (i) *Ni* commonly translates 'not even'. It can often be reinforced by *siquiera*:

Ni (siquiera) en mis peores momentos not even in my worst moments did I dream
soñé que esto pudiera suceder this could happen

Pero ¡si no ha de tener ni (siquiera) diecisiete años!	but she can't even be 17!
Eres un inútil, no puedes ni (siquiera) freírte un huevo	you're useless, you can't even fry yourself an egg
Experiencia que no les sirvió ni para enfrentarse con un puñado de bandidos (Vargas Llosa, Peru, dialogue)	experience that didn't even help you take on a handful of bandits
No entiendo ni una palabra (siquiera)	I don't understand a word
¡Ni se te ocurra (siquiera) venir a verme!	don't even get the idea of coming to see me!

(ii)   Before a noun it may be an emphatic denial:

¿Sabes quién es? Ni idea	do you know who it is? No idea
¿Cuánto ganabas? Ni (siquiera) un céntimo	what were you earning? Not a cent

(iii)   *Ni* is required after *sin*: *vivía sin dinero ni ganas de tenerlo* 'he lived without money or the urge to have it'; *sin mujer ni hijos* 'without wife or children'; *el buque seguía aquellas vueltas y recodos sin vacilar ni equivocarse nunca* (from Ramsey & Spaulding, 11.45) 'the vessel followed those turns and bends without ever hesitating or making a mistake'.

21.4.5   *Ninguno*

'No', 'none', 'nobody' (cf. French *aucun*, German *kein*). The double negative rule applies: if *ninguno* follows the verb, the verb must itself be negated: *ninguno de ellos lo sabe/no lo sabe ninguno de ellos; nunca compra ninguno* 'she never buys a single one'. In certain types of sentences, it may be an equivalent of 'any': see 21.3 for examples.

It may be either adjectival or pronominal. As an adjective it loses its final -*o* before a masculine noun or noun phrase. It often loses its final -*a* before feminine nouns (but not adjectives) beginning with stressed *a-* or *ha-*: *ningún arma nuclear* 'no nuclear weapon'. (This, at least, is spoken usage, though the full form is properly written before such nouns). Examples:

En ningún momento pensé que . . .	at no point did I think that . . .
En ningún miserable pueblo costero	in no wretched coastal village
No aceptaremos ninguna solución parcial	we shall accept no partial (or 'biased') solution

The plural *ningunos/ningunas* is rare, presumably because there is scant need to mention more than one of something which does not exist. It may occur with nouns which are always plural: *ningunas vacaciones en Cataluña son completas sin una excursión al Pirineo* 'no holiday in Catalonia is complete without a trip to the Pyrenees'.
Examples:

(a)   Pronominal forms:

Ninguno de los que hablan un idioma está libre de dudas . . . (M. Seco)	none of those who speak a language is free of doubts
¿A cuál de los tres tomos se refiere usted? A ninguno	which of the three volumes are you referring to? To none
O se lleva todos, o ninguno	either you take them all, or none of them
Si he sido insincero con ninguno/alguno de vosotros, decídmelo (*ninguno* is more literary)	if I have been insincere with any of you, tell me so

(b) Adjectival forms:

El ministro no hizo ningún comentario/ no hizo comentario ninguno/alguno	the minister made no comment
Tampoco recibimos ninguna contestación/contestación alguna a nuestra carta anterior	neither did we receive any reply to our previous letter
Si es molestia, puedo esperar. Molestia ninguna/ninguna molestia	if it's a bother I can wait. No bother at all
No recuerdo que él haya dicho eso en ninguna ocasión	I don't remember him saying that on any occasion

Notes (i)　As the examples show, *alguno*, placed after the noun, may be used as an emphatic variant of *ninguno*: *en momento alguno* = *en ningún momento* 'at no moment at all'. See 9.4 for details.

　(ii)　When *ninguno* is the subject of a verb, person and number agreement seems to be optional when the pronoun appears: *ninguna de nosotras tiene/tenemos marido* 'none of us women has/have a husband', *ninguno de vosotros habéis/ha traído el libro* 'none of you has/have brought the book'. If the pronoun is omitted, the verb ending must make the meaning clear: *ninguno hemos dicho eso* 'none of us said that', *¿no salisteis ninguna anoche?* 'didn't any of you girls go out last night?'

　(iii)　If *ninguno* is a direct or indirect object and is placed before the verb, the redundant pronoun agrees with the accompanying noun or pronoun: *a ninguno de ellos los conozco* 'I know none of them', *a ninguno de nosotros nos quiere dar el dinero* 'he doesn't want to give the money to any of us'.

21.4.6　*Nunca* and *jamás*

Both mean 'never' or, in certain sentences, 'ever'. *Jamás* is somewhat stronger than *nunca*. It is usually, but not always a synonym of *nunca*: see note (i). The combination *nunca jamás* is strongly emphatic.

　Both require a double negative construction when they follow the verb phrase to which they refer: *nunca viene* = *no viene nunca* 'he never comes'; *nadie viene jamás* 'no one ever comes'.

Nunca/jamás conocí a nadie que hablase tan bien español	I've never met anyone who spoke Spanish so well
No sale nunca/jamás de casa	he never goes out of the house
Nadie nunca/jamás logró bailar con ella	no one ever managed to dance with her
No tiene dinero y tampoco siente nunca/ jamás su carencia	he has no money, nor does he ever feel the lack of it
Jamás/nunca oí que los Incas inventasen la rueda	I've never heard that the Incas invented the wheel
Eso no lo volveré a hacer nunca jamás	I'll never ever do that again
¡Habráse visto nunca/jamás! . . .	did you *ever* see . . .!
¿Has oído nunca/jamás que un elefante volase? (see note (ii))	have you ever heard of an elephant flying?
Cabe dudar si nunca/jamás existió un parentesco lingüístico entre el quechua y el aymara	there is room to doubt whether there ever existed a linguistic relationship between Quechua and Aymara

Notes (i)　*Jamás* cannot appear after comparisons: *ahora más que nunca* 'now more than ever . . .'; *trabaja menos que nunca* 'he's working less than ever'; *está más guapo que nunca* 'he's more handsome than ever'.

(ii)   In rhetorical questions inviting the answer 'no', *jamás/nunca* mean 'ever': *¿se vio jamás/nunca tal cosa?* 'was such a thing ever seen?', *¿se ha oído jamás/nunca que un hombre mordiera a un perro?* 'who ever heard' (lit. 'was it ever heard') that a man bit a dog?' Compare non-rhetorical question: *¿has estado alguna vez en Madrid?*.

21.4.7   *Apenas*
'Hardly', 'scarcely', 'barely', 'as soon as'. The variant *apenas si* is found in literary style for the meanings 'only' and 'scarcely'; it is not used in time statements or when *apenas* follows the verb.

The *pretérito anterior* (*hubo llegado*, etc.) may appear in conjunction with this adverb, especially in literary styles, though it is uncommon in speech. See 14.9 for discussion.

No te conozco apenas	I hardly know you
Apenas (si) te conozco	" "
En una semana apenas si cambió dos palabras con su tío (J. Marsé)	in the course of a week she barely exchanged two words with her uncle
Apenas llegamos/hubimos llegado cuando empezó a llover	we had scarcely arrived when it started raining
Hace apenas seis años	barely six years ago
Apenas tengo lo suficiente para pagar la cena	I've barely got enough to pay for supper

Notes (i)   *No bien* (in Argentina and perhaps elsewhere also *ni bien*) is an alternative: *no bien se hubo marchado cuando* . . . 'he'd barely left when . . .'.
   (ii)   *Nada más* is a colloquial alternative in time statements:

Nada más llegar, pasé por su despacho	as soon as I had arrived, I dropped in at his office
Lo haré nada más llegue	I'll do it as soon as I arrive

21.4.8   *En mi vida, en toda la noche*, etc.
The phrases *en mi vida/en la vida*, 'in my life', *en toda la noche* 'in the whole night', and one or two others, are occasionally used like negative particles, i.e. they may appear before a verb phrase with a negative meaning:

En mi vida le he visto	I've never seen him in my life
(or *no le he visto en mi vida*)	
En toda la noche he podido dormir	I've not been able to sleep the whole night.

With the exception of *en mi vida*, this construction is rather old-fashioned: *no he podido dormir en toda la noche* is more normal.

21.4.9   *Tampoco*
'Not . . . either', 'nor . . .', 'neither' (cf. French *non plus*). It is the opposite of *también* 'also'.

As with other negative particles, it requires a double negative construction if it follows a verb phrase: *tampoco creo en los ovnis = no creo en los ovnis tampoco* 'nor do I believe in UFOs'/'I don't believe in UFOs either':

¿Tienes la llave? No. Yo tampoco . . .	do you have the key? No. Nor do I . . .

Tampoco hay que olvidar que la inflación puede, en ciertas circunstancias, ser beneficiosa	nor should one forget that inflation can, in certain circumstances, be beneficial
Tampoco dice nada a nadie	nor does he say anything to anyone
Ellos tampoco hicieron ningún comentario	they didn't make any comment either

Ni or *y* can precede *tampoco*: *me dijo que no le gustaba el vino, y/ni tampoco la cerveza* 'he told me he didn't like wine or beer'. As this example shows, *ni* can only be combined with *tampoco* if a negative statement precedes.

22.5 *Cuánto*

Cuánto may function as a pronoun/adjective or as an adverb. In the former case it agrees in number and gender with the noun; in the latter case it is invariable.

(a) 'How much', 'how many':

¿Cuánto es?	how much is it?
¿Cuánta mantequilla queda?	how much butter is left?
¿Cuántos vienen?	how many are coming?
No ha dicho cuánta gasolina quería	he didn't say how much petrol he wanted
¿Cuánto han trabajado?	how much have they worked?

(b) In exclamations, 'how much!', 'what a lot!'

In exclamations, *cuánto* is shortened to *cuán* before adverbs or adjectives other than *más* and *menos* or before *mayor, menor, mejor, peor*. However, this shortened form is nowadays rarely found except in flowery journalese, and *qué*, or *lo* + adjective or adverb (discussed at 7.2.2) are more usual:

¡Cuántas veces (no) te lo habré dicho!	how many times have I told you!
¡Mira cuánta nieve!	look at all that snow!
¡Cuánta falta le hace a este niño alguien que le enderece!	how much this child needs someone to keep him on the straight path!
¡Cuánto pesa esta mochila!	is this rucksack heavy!
¡Cuán tarde ya para la dicha mía! (A. Machado, poetry c. 1905)	how late for my happiness!
Se iban dando cuenta de cuán difícil iba a ser su vida (i.e. *de lo difícil que iba a ser su vida*)	they were gradually realizing how difficult their life was going to be
¡Cuánto más trágico!	how much more tragic!
¡Cuánto mejor estarías así!	how much better you'd be like that!

Note In the comparative phrases *cuanto más/menos . . . más/menos* 'the more . . . the more' 'the less . . . the less', *cuanto* is not used exclamatorily and does not take an accent:

Cuantas más personas haya, mejor	the more people there are, the better
Cuantos menos hombres vengan, mejor lo vamos a pasar	the fewer men come, the better time we'll have
Cuanto más trabajes, más ganarás	the more you work, the more you'll earn

See 5.7 (Comparison) for more detailed discussion of this use of *cuanto*.

22.6 *Cómo*

'How' in direct and indirect questions and in exclamations: Sometimes it may mean 'why?'; it is less informal than the English 'how come?':

¿Cómo te llamas?	what's your name?
¿Cómo quieres que me peine?	how do you want me to do my hair?
No sé cómo hacerlo	I don't know how to do it
¡Cómo está el mundo!	what a state the world is in!
¡Cómo llueve!	look how it's raining!
¿Cómo no me llamaste ayer?	why didn't you ring me yesterday?
¿Cómo le dejas ir solo al cine a ese niño?	how can you let that child go to the cinema on his own?

23   Conditional sentences

Conditional sentences may be very varied in structure, but the commonest patterns are:

(1)   Open conditions:

Si viene me quedo/quedaré	if he comes I'll stay
Si han llegado, me quedaré	if they've arrived I'll stay

(2)   Remote conditions:

Si viniera/viniese, me quedaría/quedaba	if he were to come, I'd stay

(3)   Unfulfilled conditions:

Si hubiéramos/hubiésemos tenido más dinero, habríamos/hubiéramos comprado la casa	if we had had more money we'd have bought the house

(4)   Fulfilled conditions:

Si no salía/salió/había salido, era porque prefería quedarse en casa	if he didn't go/hadn't gone out, it was because he preferred to stay at home
Si llegaba temprano comíamos a las doce	if he arrived early we had lunch at twelve
Si dijo eso, comprendo que su hermana se haya enfadado	if he said *that*, I understand his sister getting cross

One point can hardly be overstressed: *si*, in the meaning of 'if', is never followed by the present subjunctive save in one rare construction. See 23.5.1 for details.

23.1   Open conditions

So called because fulfilment or non-fulfilment of the condition are equally possible. The subjunctive is not used in open conditions, and the tense pattern is the same as in English:

(a)   *Si* + present + present:

Si tenemos que pagar tanto no vale la pena	if we have to pay so much it's not worth it
. . . si (el elitismo) significa que selecciona sus miembros en razón de su aptitud, todas las universidades del mundo son elitistas (Vargas Llosa, Peru)	if elitism means that it selects its members according to their ability, every university in the world is elitist

(b)   *Si* + present + future (or present with future meaning):

Si el contrato no está mañana en Londres, no hay trato	if the contract isn't in London by tomorrow, the deal's off
Si llueve me quedo/quedaré en casa	if it rains I'll stay at home

(c)   *Si* + past tense + present or future (normally only possible when the subject of the verb in the main clause is not yet sure about the facts described in the if-clause):

Si han contestado ya, no les escribiré	if they've already answered, I won't write to them
Si terminaron la semana pasada nos queda poco por hacer	if they finished last week there isn't much left for us to do
Si llevaba minifalda su madre estará enfadadísima	if she was wearing a miniskirt her mother will be really cross

(d)   *Si* + present + imperative

Si queréis ver el desfile salid al balcón	if you want to see the parade go out on to the balcony

In reported speech referring to the past, the imperfect or pluperfect indicative appear in the if-clause, and the conditional (or colloquially the imperfect indicative) in the main clause:

(Me dijo que) me pagaría si había terminado	(he told me) he'd pay me if I'd finished
Dijo que la operarían si tenía algún hueso roto	she said that they'd operate on her if she had any broken bones

The prevalence of this type of construction in passages of indirect speech sometimes encourages students to believe that the pattern *si* + imperfect indicative + conditional is also the usual way of forming remote conditions in Spanish, as in French and English, e.g. 'if I had money'/*si j'avais de l'argent*..., Spanish *si tuviera/tuviese dinero*... The next section should correct any such misconception.

23.2   Remote conditions

In these 'remote' conditions the verb in the if-clause is in the imperfect subjunctive (*-ra* or *-se* form); the verb in the other clause is normally in the conditional.

There are two types, which correspond to the English sentences 'if you paid now it would cost less' and 'if I were rich I'd buy you a house'. The first is fulfillable, and is merely a slightly hypothetical variant of an equivalent open condition: there is little difference between *si pagaras ahora, costaría menos* 'if you paid now it would cost less' and *si pagas ahora, costará menos* 'if you pay now it will cost less'. In the second type, the condition is contrary to fact, and the subjunctive construction is the only possible one in Spanish: *si yo fuera/fuese rico, te compraría una casa.*

English and French-speaking students must avoid using the imperfect indicative in the if-clause (cf. *si j'étais riche*...):

Cambiarían su condición de extranjeros si pudiesen regresar a su tierra natal (*Cambio16*: or *pudieran*)	they would change their status as foreigners if they could return to their native country
Esto quiere decir que si usted realizase seis viajes con estas 15.000 ptas ahorraría más de 4.000 ptas (RENFE advert.: or *realizara*. Present indicative possible)	this means that if you made six journeys with these 15,000 ptas, you would save more than 4,000 ptas

Si supieras hacer el nudo como todos los chicos de tu edad, no te tendrías que quejar (Aldecoa, dialogue. *supieses* also possible, but indicative not possible)

if you knew how to make a knot like all the boys of your age, you wouldn't have to complain

Si por lo menos se pudiera limitar el contrabando de cocaína, se ahorrarían muchas muertes (Vargas Llosa, Peru, dialogue: or *pudiese*)

if one could at least limit cocaine smuggling, a lot of deaths would be avoided

Notes (i)   Use of the conditional in the if-clause is regional or substandard, but is common in Navarre, the Basque Provinces and neighbouring parts of Spain, in popular Argentine speech and no doubt elsewhere, e.g. **si no estaría preso, no lo habrían soltado* 'if he wasn't arrested they wouldn't have let him go' (M. Puig, Argentine dialogue, for *estuviera/ estuviese*). This should not be imitated.

(ii)   For use of the *-ra* subjunctive form as an alternative for the conditional, see 14.5.2 and 23.3.2.

(iii)   The imperfect indicative occurs in cases like *si sabía que sólo era por mi dinero, claro que no me casaría* 'if I knew that it was only for my money, obviously I wouldn't get married'. These can be thought of as open conditions in the past, or as a type of fulfilled condition, e.g. 'if I *already* knew that . . .' rather than 'if I were to find out that . . .'.

23.3   Unfulfilled conditions

These refer to a condition in the past which was not fulfilled. The verb in the if-clause is in the pluperfect subjunctive (*hubiera/hubiese hablado*, etc.) and the verb in the main clause is usually in the perfect conditional (*habría/hubiera hecho*, etc.):

Si él hubiera/hubiese tenido dinero, hubiera/habría saldado la cuenta

If he'd had money he'd have settled the bill

. . . si no hubiera sido por las contracciones del estómago, se habría sentido muy bien (Cortázar, Arg. dialogue)

had it not been for the stomach cramps, he'd have felt fine

Note   There are a number of simplified forms of this type of conditional sentences which are heard in spontaneous speech but are banned from writing or non-spontaneous language and are rather informal for foreign speakers, e.g.

Si me tocabas, te mataba con mi cuchillo (E. Sabato, Arg. dialogue)

if you'd touched me, I'd have killed you with my knife

Si lo llego a saber, te habría llamado

if I'd found out, I'd have rung you

Si sé que estás enfermo, no vengo

if I'd known you were ill, I wouldn't have come

23.3.1   Imperfect indicative for conditional

The imperfect indicative commonly replaces the conditional tense in spontaneous speech on both sides of the Atlantic (the subject is further discussed in 14.3.1d). This usage is perfectly acceptable in relaxed European Spanish but is not allowed in formal styles, and it may be less tolerated in some American republics than in others:

Si tuviese/tuviera dinero, me compraba un coche (for *compraría*)	if I had the money, I'd buy a car
Desde luego, si yo fuera hombre, no me casaba . . . (L. Goytisolo, dialogue)	obviously, if I were a man I wouldn't marry
Si de pronto tuviese/tuviera la certeza de que no voy a vivir más que dos días, de seguro me iba (for iría) a confesar (Unamuno, *Diario íntimo*)	if I suddenly found out for certain that I'd only two days to live, I'd certainly go to confession
Si no fuera por vosotros iba yo a aguantar a vuestro padre . . . (set expression: *iría* not used)	if it weren't for you, would I put up with your father?

23.3.2   *-ra* forms instead of the conditional

Imperfect subjunctive in *-ra* (but not, at least in careful language, the *-se* form) is a very common alternative for the conditional of the auxiliary verb *haber*, and is found with some other verbs. See 14.5.2 for discussion:

Si te hubieses quedado, lo hubieras/ habrías visto	had you stayed, you would have seen it
Con él o sin él, hubiera/habría sido igual	with him or without him, it would have been the same

23.4   Fulfilled conditions

These are not really conditions at all, but merely an elegant way of saying 'the reason why' 'just because', 'whenever' etc. The verb is never in the subjunctive.

Si me estaba contando todos aquellos proyectos era porque inexorablemente pensaba realizarlos (F. Umbral)	if he was telling me about all those plans it was because he was inevitably intending to carry them out
Si he tenido suerte, la culpa no es mía	it's not my fault if I've been lucky
Si llegaba pronto, comíamos antes	if he arrived early we had lunch sooner

23.5   Remarks on *si*

23.5.1   *Si* (= 'if'): general

Si is never followed by the present subjunctive (except occasionally, in formal literary style after *saber*: *no sé si sea cierto* 'I do not know whether it be true' for *no sé si es cierto*).

Ser cannot be deleted after *si*. Compare *si es urgente* 'if urgent', *ven antes si es posible* 'come earlier if possible'.

Si sometimes has a merely emphatic function: *pero, ¡si tiene más de cincuenta años!* 'but he's more than fifty years old!'.

In the phrase *apenas si* it has no function: *apenas (si) la conocía* 'I/he/she/you barely knew her'.

23.5.2   Replacement of *si* by *como*

In type 1 (open) conditions, in informal language, *como* with the present or imperfect subjunctive may replace *si*. This is usually confined to threats and warnings:

Como vuelvas a hablarme de mala   if you talk to me in a nasty way again,
   manera, me voy   I'm going
Como sea carne de cerdo, no lo como   if it's pork, I won't eat it
Me dijo que como fuera/fuese carne de   he told me that if it was pork, he wouldn't
   cerdo, no lo comería   eat it

Como with the indicative = 'since':

Como es carne de cerdo, no lo como   since it's pork, I won't eat it

23.5.3   Replacement of *si* by *de*

De plus an infinitive may replace *si* and a finite verb in an if-clause. This is apparently only possible if the verb in the if-clause and the verb in the subordinate clause are in the same person, i.e. one can say *de haberlo sabido, me hubiera quedado en casa* 'had I known, I'd have stayed at home' (both first-person), but not **de llover, me quedo en casa* 'if it rains I'm staying at home' (*si llueve me quedo/quedaré en casa*):

De seguir así acabarás haciéndote   if you carry on like that, you'll end by
   comunista   becoming a communist
De no haber sido nombrado director   had he not been appointed director general
   general de Radio y Televisión, habría   for Radio and Television, he would
   pasado a desempeñar el cargo de   have gone on to fill the post of
   embajador de España en Washington   ambassador of Spain in Washington
   (*Cambio16*)
De no estar allí la puerta condenada,   had the blocked door not been there,
   el llanto no hubiera vencido las fuertes   the crying would not have carried
   espaldas de la pared (Cortázar, Arg.)   through the tough facing on the wall

De thus used must have a hypothetical or future reference. One can say *de llover, lloverá mucho* 'if it rains it'll rain a lot', but not **de ser guapa, es mi novia* 'if she's beautiful, she's my girlfriend' (timeless statement). *De* cannot therefore be used in type 4 (fulfilled) conditional sentences (23.4).

23.6   Other ways of expressing conditions

(a)   The gerund may sometimes have a conditional force: *hablando de esa manera no consigues nada* 'you'll get nowhere by talking like that' = *si hablas de esa manera . . .* 'if you talk like that'. See 19.2.1b, note, for more examples.

(b)   A negative if-clause may be introduced by some phrase meaning 'unless', e.g. *a menos que, a no ser que*:

Debe estar en casa, a no ser que haya ido   he must be at home, unless he's gone to
   al bar con sus amigos   the bar with his friends

(c)   'If' may be expressed by some phrase meaning 'on condition that', e.g. *con tal (de) que, a condición de que*:

Compraré los riñones, con tal (de) que   I'll buy the kidneys provided they're fresh
   estén frescos

(d)   *Al* + infinitive properly means 'on . . . -ing', but is sometimes seen with a conditional meaning:

?Al ser verdad esta afirmación se tendrá que repensar todo	if this claim is true, everything will have to be re-thought

This is not acceptable in the Peninsula, and is probably an American regionalism. It is stylistically dubious.

(e) *A* + infinitive can have conditional force in a few cases:

A no ser por mí, le hubieran matado	had it not been for me, they'd have killed him
A juzgar por lo que dicen . . . *(= si se juzga por lo que dicen . . .)*	to judge by what they say . . .
A decir verdad, no me cae bien *(= si digo la verdad . . .)*	to tell the truth, I don't like it/him/her/ you

(f) *Por si . . .* forms conditionals of the sort translated by 'in case . . .' or some similar phrase:

Me asomé a la ventana por si venía	I looked out of the window in case he was coming
Compramos otra botella por si acaso	we'll buy another bottle just in case
Por si esto fuera poco, también me han robado el reloj	as if that weren't enough, they've stolen my watch too

23.7 Miscellaneous examples of conditional sentences

The following are translations of typical English conditionals (some taken from Quirk, Greenbaum *et al.* (1972), 11.32):

Had he known, he wouldn't have protested	*si lo hubiese/hubiera sabido no habría/ hubiera protestado* or *de haberlo sabido . . .*
Were that the only reason, there'd be no problem	*si ésa fuera/fuese la única razón, no habría problema*
If possible, come earlier	*si es posible, ven antes* (not **si posible . . .*)
I won't compromise, even if he offers/ were to offer me money	*no transijo, incluso/aun si me ofrece/ ofreciera/ofreciese dinero*
It'll be impossible unless you change your attitude	*será imposible, a menos que/salvo que/ a no ser que cambies de actitud*
Provided no objection is raised, the meeting will be held here	*con tal (de) que no haya ninguna objec- ción, la reunión se celebrará aquí*
Should it turn out to be true, things will be different	*si resulta ser verdad, las cosas serán distintas*

23.8 Translating 'if I were you . . .', etc.

If I were you, I'd keep quiet	*yo de usted/yo que usted/si yo fuera usted, me callaría/callaba*

Yo que usted is the older Peninsular formula; *yo de usted* seems to be a Catalanism which is spreading. *Yo en . . .* is heard in Argentina:

Yo en vos me iría a la enfermería (M. Puig, dialogue)	if I were you I'd go to the sick bay

24 Passive and impersonal sentences

Impersonal statements are those in which the identity of the agent of an action is irrelevant: 'they say carrots are good for the eyes', 'you get a bad deal in that shop', 'one ought to do it this way', 'Gaelic is spoken in Skye', 'tickets for sale', etc.

There are several types of impersonal construction in Spanish, of which the most important are 'impersonal *se*' and the passive with *ser*: *este puente se construyó en 1887/este puente fue construido en 1887* 'this bridge was built in 1887'. Used thus, the two constructions are usually more or less equivalent, but passive with *ser* may be used in sentences which include mention of the agent and are therefore no longer impersonal: *este puente fue construido por los militares* 'this bridge was built by the military'.

Other types of impersonal statement generally resemble English, e.g. *a veces uno se da cuenta de que no importa* 'sometimes one realizes it doesn't matter', *no vayas a ese restaurante – te dan poco* 'don't go to that restaurant – they don't give you much', etc.

24.1 Passive with *ser*

The passive with *ser* is formed from the appropriate tense and person of *ser* 'to be' and the past participle, which agrees in number and gender with the subject of *ser*:

Active	**Passive**
Manuel escribió la respuesta	*la respuesta fue escrita por Manuel*
Manuel wrote the reply	the reply was written by Manuel
Solucionaron los problemas	*los problemas fueron solucionados*
they solved the problems	the problems were solved

There are several points to be made about this construction:

   (a) English is unusual in allowing indirect objects to form a passive construction: 'he was given two pounds', 'they were told a tall story' – *se le dieron dos libras, se les contó un cuento chino. *Él fue mandado una carta* is a monstrous howler for *se le mandó una carta/le fue mandada una carta* 'he was sent a letter'.

   (b) Whereas 'impersonal *se*' constructions occur in ordinary speech, the passive with *ser* is more characteristic of written or non-spontaneous language. In informal speech the passive is usually replaced by impersonal 'they': *tres manifestantes fueron arrestados* = *arrestaron a tres mani-festantes* 'they arrested three demonstrators'; *fue entrevistado ayer* = *le entrevistaron ayer* 'they interviewed him yesterday'. In fact some grammarians assert that the passive with *ser* is not found in spontaneous speech, but this is not completely true:

Ese jardín es alemán, y la película se ve que fue hecha en Alemania (Puig, Arg. dialogue)	that garden's German, and you can see the film was made in Germany
. . . y es que traen un telegrama de Berlín que ella es invitada a filmar una gran película (*idem*)	and the thing is they bring a telegram from Berlin (saying) she's being invited to make a big movie
Se trata de los papeles de mi marido . . . Deben ser ordenados antes de que muera. Deben ser publicados (C. Fuentes, Mex. dialogue)	it's about my husband's papers. They have to be sorted before I die. They have to be published.
. . . yo no estoy siendo interrogado (*idem*)	I'm not being interrogated

However, such examples are noticeably more common in the dialogue of Spanish-American novels; the passive with *ser* is very rare in spontaneous Peninsular speech.

(c)   The passive with *ser* is, however, extremely common in written Spanish on both continents and probably more so in the Americas. Its increasing use is perhaps one of the most obvious developments in written and formal language in the last half century especially in newspapers, where it may reflect rushed translations of English-language agency wires. Sentences like . . . *la revolución cubana, cuyas realizaciones formidables para el pueblo son llevadas a cabo en condiciones verdaderamente heroicas* (Vargas Llosa, written declaration, June 1971: his political views have since changed) 'the Cuban revolution, whose formidable achievements for the Cuban people are being carried out in truly heroic circumstances' would almost certainly have been written . . . *se llevan a cabo en condiciones . . .* in the recent past, and still surprise Peninsular speakers. But the advance of this 'Anglicized' passive seems unstoppable, and it may eventually become a pervasive feature of Spanish. Until that day English speakers should beware of a tendency to overuse it, especially in speech.

(d)   If no agent is mentioned, the passive with *ser* is often identical in meaning with impersonal *se*: *encontraron dos cargas explosivas que fueron desactivadas* and *encontraron dos cargas explosivas que se desactivaron* both mean 'they found two explosive charges which were defused', although the first is unambiguous whereas the second might conceivably be read as '. . . which defused themselves'. But often there is a difference of nuance which may become crucial. The passive with *ser* is less impersonal than the *se* construction in the sense that the latter completely eliminates information about the agent from the message, whereas the former does not. Thus it is probably more usual to say *el reo fue sentenciado* 'the prisoner was sentenced' than *se sentenció al reo* since the agent (the judge) is obviously implicitly present in the message: *se sentenció* almost implies 'someone sentenced the accused'. But *en el siglo dos todavía se hablaba latín* 'Latin was still spoken in the second century' is more normal than . . . *el latín era hablado todavía* because the agent, in this case 'people', is too obvious or vague to be worthy of any mention.

Por cannot be used with impersonal *se*: **el latín se hablaba por los romanos* is bad Spanish for *los romanos hablaban latín*. This constraint reflects the impersonality of *se* and may partly explain the increasing popularity of the passive with *ser*.

(e) The passive is more common with verbs of perfective aspect (preterite, future, perfect, pluperfect) and with the infinitive than with imperfective (imperfect, present, continuous tenses): *ayer fue entrevistado* is normal, *ayer era entrevistado* is unusual or journalese. However, passive sentences in which the verb is timeless or habitual are nowadays increasingly common in writing and non-spontaneous speech, and more so in Spanish America than Spain:

El viajero es sorprendido por la ciudad de la Paz (J.M. Arguedas, Peru)	the traveller is surprised by the city of La Paz
Los mismos ascensores son usados para el trasporte de enfermos (*Cambio16*)	the same lifts are used for carrying patients
. . . *mientras Cabinda era defendida heroicamente por los combatientes del MPLA* (Fidel Castro, speech on Angola)	while Cabinda was being heroically defended by fighters of the MPLA
Basta saber que un hombre es buscado para que todos lo vean de manera distinta (C. Fuentes, Mex., dialogue)	it's enough to know a man's being sought for everyone to look at him in a different way

Most Peninsular informants found these sentences unnatural and preferred a *se* construction or, where the agent is mentioned, an active sentence, e.g. *los mismos ascensores se usan . . ., mientras los combatientes del MPLA defendían . . .*, etc.

(f) The difference between the true passive *la ciudad fue destruida* 'the city was destroyed' (action) and *la ciudad estaba destruida* 'the city was in a state of destruction' is discussed at 24.1.4.

Examples of the passive with *ser*:

Fue alcanzado por una bala	he was hit by a bullet
La conferencia será pronunciada por el decano	the lecture will be given by the dean
Han sido detenidos por la Guardia Civil	they've been arrested by the Civil Guard
Las muestras les serán devueltas (or *se le devolverán las muestras*)	the samples will be returned to you
Está siendo debatido en este momento (or *se está debatiendo . . .*)	it's being debated right now
El hijo de Pilar Ternera fue llevado a casa de sus abuelos (García Márquez, Colombia: *llevar* cannot be passivized with *ser* if it means 'wear')	Pilar Ternera's son was taken (i.e. carried) to his grandparents' house

24.1.1   Constraints on the passive

Many verbs, for no obvious reason, do not allow the passive with *ser*. These are more numerous than in English, which has similar constraints, e.g. 'the window was broken by Jill' but not *'the stairs were descended by Jill'. Only familiarity with the language will eliminate such malformations as *fueron esperados por sus padres* 'they were expected by their parents', *fue permitido a hacerlo* (but *le fue permitido hacerlo* is correct) 'he was allowed to do it', both of them sentences which should be expressed in active form or, in the second example, by impersonal *se*: *se le permitió hacerlo*.

The constraints on the Spanish passive often appear to be quite arbitrary: *fue abandonada por su marido* 'she was abandoned by her husband' is correct, but 'she was beaten by her husband' can only be *su marido le pegaba* although *fue golpeada por su marido* is possible. Likewise, one can say *la casa fue destruida por una bomba* 'the house was destroyed by a bomb', but not *la ventana fue rota por una piedra* 'the window was broken by a stone', which, curiously, is difficult to translate into Spanish: *esta ventana la han roto de una pedrada.*

Sometimes the passive is wrong with a personal pronoun, but acceptable with other types of agent: *él era admirado por todos* 'he was admired by everybody', but not ?*él era admirado por mí* 'he was admired by me' (*yo le admiraba*).

In the following sentences passive with *ser* is not used, for no very obvious reason:

Me besó una estrella de cine	a filmstar kissed me
Me arañó un gato	a cat scratched me
Me dio un periódico	he/she/you gave me a newspaper
La peina un peluquero muy conocido	a very famous hairdresser does her hair
A la niña la lavó la madre	the mother washed the little girl
Me irritó el humo	the smoke irritated me

etc.

It would be beyond the scope of this grammar to establish a comprehensive list of verbs which do not admit passivization with *ser*. As a general rule it seems that a sentence may be passivized with *ser* only when the subject of the verb in the simple sentence is also the true and active agent in the sentence. Passive with *ser* should also be used with caution when the action is accidental or involuntary – at least pending deeper familiarity with the language. It should be avoided with verbs which take an 'indirect' object pronoun, e.g. *le* instead of *lo/la* in Spanish America and *le* instead of *la* in Spain. Thus *pegar* 'to beat', *entender* 'to understand', *obedecer* 'to obey' cannot be passivized with *ser*.

24.1.2   Avoiding the passive

English speakers may be tempted to overuse the passive. It can be avoided by the following stratagems:

(a) Make the sentence active – the simplest solution, although stylistically tedious if overdone:

Los críticos le alabaron	the critics praised him
(fue alabado por los críticos)	
Suspendieron la sesión	the session was suspended
(la sesión fue suspendida)	

(b) Use *se* (discussed below)

The following typical piece of Anglicized journalese:

. . . *si el Gobierno mexicano es visto obedeciendo a los Estados Unidos* . . . *(Cambio16)*	if the Mexican government is seen to be obeying the USA

could be better expressed by:

. . . *si se ve que el Gobierno mexicano está obedeciendo a los Estados Unidos*

This device can only be used if the agent is not included in the sentence: *el fenómeno fue observado por un astrónomo japonés* 'the phenomenon was observed by a Japanese astronomer' cannot be recast using *se*.

(c) Since one function of the passive is to focus attention on the object of a verb – compare 'he preferred Jane' and 'Jane was preferred by him' – the effect of an English passive can often be produced by putting the object in focus position – i.e. before the verb. A 'redundant' object pronoun then usually becomes necessary:

Todo esto ya me lo había explicado mi amigo	all this had already been explained to me by my friend
La explicación hay que buscarla en otra parte	the explanation must be sought elsewhere
Las puertas las cierran los porteros a las diez	the doors are shut by the doormen at ten o'clock

This construction is discussed further at 11.14.1 and 31.3.

24.1.3 Passive meaning of the infinitive

The distinction between an active and passive verb is sometimes blurred in infinitive constructions. The following forms seem peculiar to English ears:

un partido heterogéneo y sin estructurar	a heterogeneous and unstructured political party
El edificio está a medio construir	the building is half built
Eso ya era de prever	that could be foreseen

24.1.4 Comparison between *fue convencido* and *estaba convencido*

(The subject is also raised at 18.1).

The passive with *ser* denotes an action; the participle with *estar* usually describes a state arising from an action – i.e. it is not dynamic. Compare *la puerta fue abierta* 'the door was opened' and *la puerta estaba abierta* 'the door was *open*'. The possibility of making this contrast is normally confined to verbs with a dynamic meaning. The participle of a non-dynamic verb will probably only denote a state and therefore may only admit *estar*, cf. *estoy acostumbrado* 'I'm used to', *estás deprimido* 'you're depressed' (*ser* impossible).

In some cases a special participle is used with *estar*: cf. *estaba despierto porque había sido despertado por una voz de hombre* 'he was awake because he had been woken by a man's voice'. See 18.1.2 for further discussion.

Examples (the translations are designed to emphasize the difference):

La ciudad fue destruida	the city was destroyed
La ciudad estaba destruida	the city was in ruins
Fui detenido	I was arrested
Yo estaba detenido	I was under arrest
La reunión fue aplazada por decisión del presidente (action)	the meeting was postponed by a decision of the president
Cuando llegué me encontré con que la reunión estaba aplazada (state)	when I arrived I found the meeting was postponed
Este sitio fue elegido porque abunda el agua, y estaba muy bien elegido porque había también una buena carretera	this place was chosen because there is abundant water and it was very well chosen because there was a good road as well
Vino aquí . . . convencido de que iba a ser el mandamás. Y se encontró con que todo estaba hecho y muy bien hecho (Vargas Llosa, Peru, dialogue)	he came here convinced he was going to run the show. And he found everything was done and done properly
. . . los hechos históricos no están gobernados por leyes (O. Paz, Mex. State)	historical facts are not governed by laws
La operación estaba ordenada por el Rey (witness, expressed as a state)	the operation was ordered by the King

24.2   Impersonal uses of *se*

Since it directs attention away from any outside agent, *se* with a third-person verb very often has an impersonal meaning. If the verb is transitive, the impersonal *se* construction is, in principle, no different from a reflexive construction. In other words, *se discutieron varios problemas* could mean 'several problems discussed themselves' as well as 'several problems were discussed': common sense invites the second interpretation. Spanish has, however, gone further than French in allowing impersonal *se* constructions with intransitive verbs, e.g. *se está bien aquí* 'one feels good here'/'it's nice here' (which obviously cannot be translated by the passive). Problems arise because native speakers perceive the construction in *se está bien* as in some way different from *se discutieron varios problemas*, and may reserve the description 'impersonal *se*' for the former, and '*se pasivo*' for the latter. Nevertheless, they are here treated as manifestations of a single underlying principle.

Examples of impersonal uses of *se*:

Los cangrejos se cuecen en vino blanco	(the) crabs are cooked in white wine
. . . nunca se oyeron y leyeron en el Perú tantas definiciones de la libertad de información (Vargas Llosa, Peru)	never were there heard and read in Peru so many definitions of freedom of information
Su primera novela se publicó en 1982	his first novel was published in 1982
No se han traído a la Tierra suelo y muestras de minerales del planeta Marte	soil and mineral samples from the planet Mars have not been brought to Earth
Se reparan relojes	watches mended
Se veían los árboles desde la ventana	the trees were visible from the window
Algunas otras deficiencias de nuestra obra podían deberse a la dificultad de interpretación de ciertas entradas del cuestionario mismo (J.M. Lope Blanch, Mex.)	some other defects in our work could be due to the difficulty of interpreting some entries in the questionnaire itself
Se acababan de promulgar varias leyes	several laws had just been published
O se va a referéndum, o habrá guerra civil	either a referendum is held, or there will be a civil war
Que se sepa	as far as is known
Se decidió no ir	it was decided not to go
En su círculo, o se es rico o no se entra	in his circle one's either rich or one doesn't get in
En España se lee poco	either 'people don't read much in Spain' or 'it isn't read much in Spain'
A las tres de la madrugada pareció llegarse a un acuerdo tácito para descansar (Cortázar, Arg.)	at three in the morning it appeared that a tacit agreement was reached to get some rest
Por la mañana se avanzó muy poco (*idem*)	very little progress was made in the morning
Véase la página siguiente	see following page

Notes (i)   For a comparison of this construction with the true passive (*el problema se solucionó/el problema fue solucionado*) see 24.1.

(ii)   Impersonal *se* may not be followed by *por* and the real agent of the verb: **la decisión se tomó por el presidente* is bad Spanish for *la decisión fue tomada por el presidente* 'the decision was taken by the President'. This rule is constantly broken in speech, and occasionally in writing, but this is considered incorrect:

*La decisión de irnos se tomó conjuntamente y por personas de la misma línea política (F. Ordóñez in *Cambio16*)	the decision to leave was taken jointly and by persons sharing the same political line
*El terrorismo no debe atacarse aisladamente por las naciones que lo padecen (Felipe González in *El País*)	terrorism must not be combated individually by those nations which suffer from it

These blunders could have been avoided either by use of passive with *ser*, or by a simple active construction.

(iii)   As the examples show, there is no objection to using *se* with 'intransitive' verbs like *ser/estar* 'to be', *dormir* 'to sleep', *vivir* 'to live', etc. With such verbs the usual English translation will be 'one' or 'people': *en España, por la tarde, se duerme* 'in Spain, in the afternoon, people sleep'.

Such sentences demonstrate the difficulty of deciding whether *se* is a subject or object pronoun. In this case *se* is best simply thought of as a sign denoting the absence of a known or relevant subject.

Sentences like *se es feliz* 'people are happy' were once condemned by purists as Gallicisms, cf. *on est heureux*, but are nowadays accepted.

(iv) *Se* may be used to form an impersonal imperative, useful for footnotes, written instructions and so on: *no se crea que* 'let it not be believed that', *téngase presente que* 'let it be borne in mind that . . .', *desarróllese en castellano el siguiente tema* 'develop the following topic in Spanish'.

24.2.1   Agreement of the verb with impersonal *se*

In theory, any verb used with *se* and a plural noun must be plural. This is true for all constructions with *se*, whether reflexive, reciprocal or impersonal. In other words, there is in theory no formal distinction between impersonal *se* and other kinds of *se*:

Los niños se están lavando (reflexive)	the children are washing
No se hablan (reciprocal)	they don't talk to one another
Las tuercas se quitan con llave, no con martillo (impersonal)	bolts are removed with a spanner, not with a hammer
Se mezclan en el turmix los tomates sin pepitas y sin piel (impersonal)	the tomatoes, with skins and pips removed, are mixed in the liquidizer
Se enviaron los hombres y las armas necesarios para concluirla (i.e. *la lucha*: Fidel Castro, speech)	the men and weapons necessary to finish it {the fight} were sent

Agreement rules are broken only if the noun is preceded by personal *a*, or if an object pronoun appears in place of a noun preceded by personal *a*:

Se acusó a tres personas	three persons were accused
Se les/las acusó	they were accused

This construction is explained at 24.2.2.

When *se* is used the rules of agreement are always respected when a plural noun precedes the verb: *los libros se vendían a cien pesetas* 'the books were sold at 100 ptas'.

When *se* is used impersonally and the verb precedes a plural noun, popular language sometimes breaks the rules of agreement: **se compra objetos usados* 'used articles bought'. Generally speaking, this should not be imitated and it may sound quite illiterate, but a singular verb is less shocking in spontaneous speech than in writing. This error is probably less common than is sometimes claimed.

The following forms may be unacceptable to many speakers:

?*Y nunca más se ha tenido noticias de su paradero* (*ABC*; for *se han tenido . . .*)	no further news has been received of his whereabouts
?*Se vende pisos* (for *se venden . . .*)	flats for sale
?*Se necesita agallas para hacer eso* (Spanish informant overheard: *se necesitan agallas*)	you need courage to do that
?*Se les dio varios premios* (for *se les dieron . . .*)	several prizes were given to them

But in the following sentences a singular verb is required:

(a)   Indirect questions involving *cuánto*, *qué*, *cuál*:

Se calculó cuántos kilos había	it was calculated how many kilos there were
Se averiguó qué existencias quedaban	a check was made of what stocks remained
Se ignora cuáles serán los medios que faciliten el acceso de los trabajdores a la propiedad de los medios de producción (Cambio16)	it is not known what measures will exist to provide workers access to ownership of the means of production

(b)   Whenever a verb is followed by *que* (*tener que* excepted):

Se cree que . . .	it's believed that . . .
Se calcula que . . .	it's calculated that . . .
Se dice que . . .	it's said that . . .

(c)   Usually when a verb is followed by an infinitive
But agreement is required after *poder, deber, tener que, haber de, querer, acabar de*:

Se trató de coger las uvas	an attempt was made to pick the grapes
Cuando se piensa en cosas pasadas y se trata de reconstruir oscuros recuerdos (E. Sabato, Arg.)	when one thinks of things in the past and one tries to reconstruct obscure memories
Se intentaba resolver estos problemas	an attempt was made to solve these problems

but:

Se tienen que resolver varios problemas	several problems must be solved
Se deben terminar hoy mismo	they must be finished today
Se pueden colocar aquí	they can be placed here
. . . cosas que no se quieren hacer	. . . things one doesn't want to do

With the verbs *ver, oír* there is some disagreement. *Se ve caer las hojas* 'one can see the leaves falling' seems the safest option, but some speakers may insist on *se ven caer . . .* The authorities disagree.

Note   Auxiliary verbs like *poder* or *deber* are often incorrectly left in the singular, e.g. **se puede imprimir textos con más rapidez con un procesador de textos* (Spanish weekly, for *se pueden . . .*) 'texts can be printed more rapidly with a word processor'. Compare the following correct examples:

En Londres por la calle se pueden observar los tipos de personas más extrañas (Cosmopolitan, Spanish ed.)	in London one can observe the strangest sorts of people in the streets
Se deben limpiar bien las verduras antes de cocerlas	the greens should be washed well before boiling

(d)   In advertisements or notices of the sort 'waiters required', non-agreement is very common even in carefully edited texts, and some grammarians accept it; but many speakers reject the singular:

Se busca(n) camareros	waiters required
Se necesita(n) pintores	painters needed

24.2.2   Overlap of impersonal and other types of *se*
'Impersonal *se*' is usually unambiguous if there is no other noun in the sentence which might be taken for the subject (e.g. *se creía que . . .* 'it was believed that') or if the noun is inanimate: *los platos se lavan* is unlikely to

mean 'the plates wash themselves' – which can always be said *los platos se lavan a sí mismos*. But the burden of ambiguity may be intolerable with animate nouns, particularly those referring to humans, since *se mataron dos ingleses* may mean 'two Englishmen killed themselves' as well as 'killed one another'. The language has developed a device for removing the ambiguity by marking the logical object noun in an impersonal statement by the preposition *a*. The verb is always singular:

Se mató a dos ingleses	two Englishmen were killed
Se criticó duramente al cineasta	the film-maker was severely criticized
Se incitaba a las muchachas a trabajar	the girls were encouraged to work harder
más que los muchachos	than the boys
Se les/los notaba cansados	one could see they were tired

Notes (i)   Some speakers prefer *le* to *lo* (in *loísta* dialects) or *la*, and *les* to *los* in sentences like *se les notaba cansados* 'one could see they were tired'. See 11.6.12 for discussion.

(ii)   If the logical object is inanimate, this construction is rarely used since clashes of meaning with the reflexive cannot normally arise: *se han dicho muchas tonterías* 'a lot of silly things have been said'. But one nevertheless finds sentences like *se ha comparado a los ordenadores con el cerebro humano* 'computers have been compared with the human brain' which are thus constructed so as to avoid all possibility of a reflexive meaning. Personal *a* is used in such sentences, despite the fact that the noun is inanimate. See 20.9b for further comments.

(iii)   A sentence like *se mató a dos ingleses* exemplifies the peculiarities of *se*. *Se* is traditionally thought of as an 'object' pronoun, but in the above example *a dos ingleses* is apparently clearly the 'object' of *matar*, in which case *se* is functioning as a subject. This theoretical problem has troubled many linguists, but need not concern the practical user of the language.

(iv)   The verb must be singular in this construction. **Se les notaban cansados* is not Spanish, although this mistake is sometimes heard in uneducated speech.

24.3   Other impersonal constructions

24.3.1   *Uno/una* as a pronoun

This is similar to the English 'one' in that it is often an oblique way of saying 'I' or 'we'. A woman uses *una* if the pronoun refers to herself, but *uno* if no self-reference is intended. Its object forms are *lo/la/le*.

como los pájaros que comen las migas que uno les tira (Cortázar, Arg. dialogue, woman speaking)	like birds eating the crumbs one throws to them
Bueno, si no le dicen a una como hay que hacerlo (woman speaking)	well, if they don't tell one how to do it . . .
Se puso a canturrear, ya que siempre olvidaba lo que uno le decía	he started humming, since he always forgot what one said to him
Uno no hace mal a la gente que le es indiferente (E. Sabato, Arg. dialogue, woman speaking)	one doesn't do harm to people one is indifferent to

Apagarse en Brahma es intuir que uno mismo es Brahma (Borges, Arg.)

to extinguish oneself in Brahma is to realize that one is oneself Brahma

Notes (i) *Uno* must be used to make an impersonal expression from a verb which already has *se* (since two *ses* cannot occur side by side):

En este pueblo se aburre uno mucho

in this village one gets bored a lot

Se empieza fumando unos cigarrillos y poco a poco se convierte uno en un fumador empedernido

one starts by smoking a few cigarettes and gradually one becomes a heavy smoker

(ii) Colloquially, *uno/una* may mean 'someone'. See 9.3 note (iv).

24.3.2 Miscellaneous impersonal constructions

The second-person singular and third-person plural can be used impersonally, much the same as in English, although *tú* is not used in formal circumstances (in which case *usted*, *uno* or *se* is preferred):

Dicen que es verdad
(se dice que . . .)

they say it's true

Yo nunca voy allí porque te cobran más que en otra parte (le cobran a uno más)

I never go there because they charge you more than elsewhere

Es increíble, si lo piensas (si uno lo piensa)

it's incredible if you think of it

25 *Ser* and *estar*

Ser and *estar* both translate the English 'to be', but the difference between the two Spanish words is fundamental and sometimes elusive.

Basically *ser* denotes nature or identity, while *estar* denotes condition, state or place: *soy español, pero estoy en Londres* 'I'm Spanish, but I'm in London'; *es callado* 'he's the quiet type', *está callado* 'he's silent/he's keeping silent', *puede que sea así* 'perhaps he is like that', *puede que esté así* 'perhaps that's the condition/situation he's in'.

It is misleading to imagine that *estar* always refers to temporary states, while *ser* indicates permanence. This is often true but is contradicted by sentences like *está muerto* 'he's dead', or the fact that one can say *soy calvo* or *estoy calvo* 'I'm bald'. Nor is a characteristic expressed by *ser* necessarily permanent. A brunette can change the colour of her hair and then say *antes era morena pero ahora soy rubia* 'I was a brunette before, but now I've become a blonde', the point being that both colours are nevertheless considered to be essential attributes of the woman, not 'states'.

Ser is used with a few adjectives which indicate states which are often transitory, e.g. *feliz, desgraciado, pobre, rico, consciente*, but these are probably best treated as exceptions, cf. *está deprimido* 'he's depressed', *está contento* 'he's happy/content', *está animado* 'he's full of life'.

Some adjectives, e.g. *calvo, gordo* may be used with either *ser* or *estar* with hardly any significant change of meaning. *Estar* before a noun phrase can only usually denote situation. Compare *¿es el jefe?* 'is he the boss?' with *¿está el jefe?* 'is the boss in?' It must be remembered that *ser* is used for location of events as opposed to people or things: *¿dónde es la fiesta?* 'where's the party?', but *¿dónde está el libro?* 'where's the book?'

Ser is used to form the passive: *fue criticado*, see 24.1. *Estar* is used to form the continuous aspect of verbs: *está hablando* 'he's talking'. See chapter 15.

25.1 Uses of *ser*

25.1.1 *Ser* to define identity or nature
(a) With adjectives or adjectival phrases referring to origin, identity or nature, i.e. physical, moral and mental characteristics:

309

¿Quién eres?	who are you?
¿Cómo eres?	what are you like?
¿De dónde eres?	where do you come from?
Soy Pepe, soy de Córdoba, soy abogado, alto, moreno, delgado y católico	I'm Pepe, I come from Cordoba, I'm a lawyer, I'm tall, dark, slim and a Catholic
¿De qué es la mesa? Es de madera	what's the table made of? Wood.
Es natural que le quiera	it's only natural she should love him
París es la capital de Francia	Paris is the French capital
Las mariposas son diferentes de las polillas	butterflies are different from moths
El marxismo es materialista	Marxism is materialist
El cobre es ideal para los cables	copper is ideal for cables
Es evidente que no piensa venir	it's obvious he's not intending to come
Siempre me ha sido fiel	he/she has always been loyal to me
Así es como hay que hacerlo	that's the way to do it
Esa chaqueta es bien bonita	that jacket is very nice
La situación era de risa	the situation was extremely funny
Esa chica es de miedo	that girl is tremendous
Era una película de guerra	it was a war film
Oye, que es de verdad	listen, it's true

For cleft sentences of the type *ella es la que lo dijo* 'she's the one who said it' see 30.2. For *calvo, gordo, delgado*, marital status and behaviour, see 25.3.1.

(b) *Ser* is normally used with *pobre/feliz/desgraciado/inocente/ culpable/consciente* 'poor/happy/unhappy/innocent/guilty/aware' despite the fact that they may be thought of as states or conditions:

Ahora que el precio del petróleo ha bajado, este país es pobre	now that the price of oil has gone down, this is a poor country
El acusado dijo que era inocente	the accused said he was innocent
Hay muchos que no se sienten culpables aunque lo sean	there are many people who don't feel guilty even when they are
Soy consciente de mis limitaciones	I'm conscious of my limitations
La gente así no suele ser feliz en la vida, señora (M. Vargas Llosa, Peru)	people like that are not usually happy in life, señora
Pocas veces fue tan feliz como en las horas que precedieron a la entrevista con Bordenave (E. Sabato, Arg.)	he was seldom so happy as during the hours before his interview with Bordenave
- Soy tan desgraciada - me dijo (G. Cabrera Infante, Cuba)	I'm so unhappy, she told me
Ella me dijo soy pobre, pero honrada, Tan sólo bailo para ganarme el pan (Argentine tango)	she told me, I'm poor but honest, I only dance to earn my living

Notes (i) Many native speakers reject ?*está feliz* but some – especially in Spanish America – accept it. *Estar pobre* as a transitory state is also sometimes possible: *estoy más pobre que una rata* 'I'm as poor as a church mouse' (lit. 'poorer than a rat').

(ii) Peninsular usage normally differentiates between *ser consciente* 'to be aware' and *estar consciente* 'to be conscious' (i.e. not asleep or knocked out). Spanish-American language seems to have retained the older usage:

Estamos conscientes de que el debate y la	we're aware that debate and argument in

discusión en la libertad son demandas de los jóvenes del país (*Unomásuno*, Mex.)	(an atmosphere of) freedom are demands of the young people of the country

(c) *Ser* is used before noun phrases:

es médico/abogado/bibliotecario	he's a doctor/lawyer/librarian
Es un estafador	he's a swindler
Es el jefe	he's the boss
Es mentira/verdad/una tontería	it's false/true/nonsense
Es la una/son las doce	it's one o'clock/twelve o'clock
Me contó que había sido payaso	he told me he had been a clown
Ha sido un año/verano frío	it's been a cold year/summer
Esto es lo que me fastidia	this is what I find annoying
Esto es harina de otro costal	this is a different matter (lit. 'this is flour from another sack')
Esto es decir las cosas como son	this is calling a spade a spade
Soy hombre que odia las medias tintas, el agua turbia, el café flojo (M. Vargas Llosa, Peru)	I'm a man who hates things which are not clearly defined, cloudy water, weak coffee
. . . rompieron en cierto modo la tradición de que sea un cristiano quien presida el Parlamento español (*Cambio16*)	. . . to some extent they broke with the tradition that the speaker in the Spanish Parliament should be a Christian

Note Exceptions to this rule are *está un día hermoso* 'it's a beautiful day' (colloquial) and *estar pez*, e.g. *estoy pez en matemáticas* 'I'm absolutely stupid in maths'.

25.1.2 *Ser* to denote reaction

Me es/resulta simpática	I find her likeable
Esto me es/resulta molesto	this is uncomfortable for me
Todo le era distinto (A. Carpentier, Cuba)	everything seemed different to her

25.1.3 *Ser* of events

If 'to be' means 'to be held' or 'to happen' it must be translated by *ser*:

La fiesta es/se celebra en su casa	the party is at his place
Hay un incendio en la casa pero no sé en qué piso es	there's a fire in the building but I don't know which floor it's on
¿Dónde es la manifestación?	where is the demonstration?
La guerra civil fue en 1939	the Civil War was in 1939

Use of *estar* may imply a physical object. Compare:

¿Dónde es la conferencia?	where's the lecture (being held)?
¿Dónde está la conferencia?	where's the lecture? (i.e. the lecture notes or typescript)

25.2 Uses of *estar*

25.2.1 *Estar* to describe state as opposed to identity or nature

(a) With adjectives which indicate mood, physical condition or non-characteristic features in general:

Está más bien triste	he's rather sad
Estuvo enfermo una temporada	he was ill for a time
Hoy no estoy muy católico	I don't feel very well today
Estoy segura de lo que te digo	I'm certain of what I'm telling you
Estaba rojo de vergüenza	he was red with shame
El agua que se añada tiene que estar caliente	the water to be added has to be hot
El televisor está estropeado	the television doesn't work
Está parado desde febrero	he's been out of work since February
Estuvo callado todo el tiempo	he was silent all the time

(b)   *Estar de +* adjective or noun to indicate mood, temporary employment or situation:

Está de buen/mal humor	he's in a good/bad mood
Está de camarero en Inglaterra	he's working as a waiter in England
Está de veraneo	he's taking his summer holidays
Está de viaje	he's travelling
Estamos de charla	we're having a chat
¿Estás de permiso?	are you on leave?
Están de broma	they're larking about

Colloquially:

Estás de un guapo subido	you look especially pretty/handsome
Estaba de un antipático . . .	he was in such a bad mood . . .

(c)   Followed by *con +* noun:

Está con gripe	he's got the flu
Estaba con una cara malísima	he looked terrible
Estaba con un traje rojo muy bonito	she was wearing a beautiful red dress

(d)   Followed by an adverb or an adjective used as an adverb:

¿Cómo estás? Estoy bien/mal	how are you? I'm well/not at all well
Estamos fatal	we're feeling rotten
El nombre está mal. Se llamaba Luis José (Cambio16)	the name is wrong. His name was Luis José

(e)   *Estar que:*

Está que muerde	he's in an exceedingly bad mood (lit. 'he's ready to bite')
Hoy estás que no hay quien te aguante	you're unbearable today

25.2.2   *Estar* to indicate location
(For *ser* used for the location of events see 25.1.3).

Segovia está en España	Segovia is in Spain
El cerezo está en el centro	the cherry tree is in the middle
No está (en casa)	he's not at home
Está encima de todo	it's on top of everything

But with nouns which are permanent fixtures or features there is a colloquial tendency to use *ser* in these cases:

¿Dónde es la casa de tu amigo?	where's your friend's house?
Aquí era la plaza de las Carretas	this is where Carretas Square used to be
(Borges, Arg. dialogue)	
Turku es en Finlandia, ¿no?	Turku's in Finland, isn't it?

Estar would be correct in all these three sentences.

25.2.3 *Estar* meaning 'to suit', or to indicate 'fit'

Este traje te está muy bien	this dress suits you
El abrigo te está corto	the coat is short for you
El puesto de ministro le está grande	the ministerial job is too big for him

25.2.4 *Estar por/para*

(See also 28.14.8).

Estoy por salir a dar una vuelta	I'm tempted to go for a walk
Estoy para salir a ver a mi madre	I'm ready to go out to see my mother
Eso está por hacer	this is still to be done
Esto está para hacerlo ahora	this is to be done now

25.2.5 Idioms

¿Estás en lo que te digo?	do you follow what I'm telling you?
Está claro que	it's obvious that

25.3 *Ser* or *estar?*

25.3.1 *Ser* and *estar* more or less interchangeable
(a) With words indicating marital status:

Sale con una chica que es/está divorciada	he's going out with a girl who's divorced
Tiene que mantener a su madre que es/ está viuda	he has to keep his widowed mother
Le pregunté si era/estaba casado	I asked him whether he was married

The tendency is to use *ser* for a stranger, although *estar* is not wrong. One would usually ask *¿es usted casado?* 'are you married?', but two friends meeting again would say *¿estás casado?* or *¿todavía estás soltero?* 'are you married?' or 'are you still single?'.

(b) With *calvo*, *gordo* and *delgado*, *estar* is always used when there has been a change of state. Elsewhere the two verbs are practically interchangeable except in generalizations, when *ser* is required:

¡Mujer, pero qué gorda estás!	good heavens, haven't you got fat!
Siempre ha sido calvo/delgado, pero ahora está más calvo/delgado que nunca	he's always been bald/thin but now he's balder/thinner than ever
Ayer conocí a la novia de mi primo. Parece simpática pero está/es muy gorda	yesterday I met my cousin's girlfriend. She seems nice but she's very fat
No le gustaba porque era/estaba gordo/ calvo/delgado	she didn't like him because he was fat/bald/thin
Las mujeres de esa tribu son muy gordas	the women of that tribe are very fat

(c) With adjectives describing social manner when 'to be' = 'to behave':

Estuvo/fue muy cortés conmigo	he/she behaved very courteously towards me
Siempre está/es cariñosa	she's always affectionate
Tienes que estar/ser más amable con él	you must be kinder to him

But

Hoy has sido bueno	you've behaved well today

because *estar bueno* means 'tasty', 'appetising'. Also

Hoy has estado bueno	you had a good day today (ironical)

Estar cannot be used for general statements: *antiguamente los ingleses eran muy corteses* (not *estaban*) 'formerly the English were very courteous'.

Note   When the adjective is used with an imperative, only *ser* can be used:
Sé más amable con él   be nicer to him

(d)   With adjectives applied to events and with *vida* and *situación*:

La conferencia fue/estuvo muy interesante	the lecture was very interesting
La situación es/está caótica	the situation is chaotic
La fiesta fue/estuvo muy animada	the party was very lively
La vida es/está cara hoy día	life is expensive nowadays

But *La vida es difícil/maravillosa/amarga* can only be general comments on life. *La vida está difícil* means 'life is difficult now'.

(e)   With adjectives referring to weather applied to *día* and *tiempo*:

El día es/está bueno	the weather is nice today
Es/está un tiempo soleado, agradable	the weather is sunny and pleasant

25.3.2   *Ser* and *estar* with dates

¿Qué es hoy/qué día es hoy?	which day of the week is it today?
¿A qué estamos/a qué día estamos?	which day of the week is it today?
Hoy es miércoles	today is Wednesday
¿A cuántos estamos?	what day of the month is it today?
Hoy es (el) 13 de diciembre	today is the 13th of December

25.3.3   *Ser* and *estar* with prices

¿Cuánto/a cuánto/a cómo/son las uvas?	how much are the grapes?
Son a cincuenta pesetas el kilo	fifty pesetas a kilo
¿Cuánto (es lo que) le debo?	how much do I owe you?

Also:

¿A cuánto están las uvas?	how much are the grapes (at this moment)?
¿A cuánto están esas acciones?	what's the price of those shares?

25.3.4   *Estar* implying impression or change of condition

When *estar* denotes impression, sensation or appearance, it often calls for translation by a special verb in English e.g. 'to look', 'to taste', 'to feel' or 'get'. Use of *estar* rather than *ser* often shows there has been a change of condition. Compare:

Es muy guapa	she's very good-looking
Está muy guapa	she's looking very attractive
Este niño es muy alto	this child is very tall
Este niño está muy alto	this child has grown very tall
Es muy joven/viejo	he's very young/old

Está muy joven/viejo	he looks very young/old
¡Qué fuerte eres!	how strong you are!
¡Qué fuerte estás!	how strong you are (today/these days)
Este sillón es ya viejo	this armchair is old
Este sillón está ya viejo	this armchair is getting old
†*El pollo es riquísimo*	[the] chicken is very good
El pollo está riquísimo	the chicken tastes delicious
†*El café es horrible*	(the) coffee is horrible
El café está horrible	the coffee tastes horrible
Tráelo como sea	bring it any way you can
Tráelo como esté	bring it as it is
Eres muy española	you're very Spanish
Estás muy española	you're looking very Spanish (or behaving like a typical Spanish woman)

The examples marked † are ambiguous: †*el pollo es riquísimo* is either a general statement about chicken, or it could mean 'the chicken (uncooked) is very good quality'. *Estar* could only mean 'to taste'.

25.3.5 *Ser* and *estar* involving change of meaning

There are some words whose meaning changes radically by choice of *ser* or *estar*. The following list is not exhaustive:

ser aburrido	boring	*estar aburrido*	to be bored
ser atento	courteous	*estar atento*	attentive
ser bueno	good	*estar bueno*	tasty
ser cansado	tiresome	*estar cansado*	tired
ser católico	catholic	*no estar católico*	unwell
ser decidido	resolute	*estar decidido*	decided
ser consciente	aware	*estar consciente*	conscious (not asleep or knocked out)
ser despierto	sharp/alert	*estar despierto*	awake
ser un enfermo	an invalid	*estar enfermo*	ill
ser interesado	self-seeking	*estar interesado*	interested
ser listo	clever	*estar listo*	to be ready
ser (un) loco	scatterbrained	*estar loco*	mad
ser malo	bad	*estar malo*	ill
ser negro	black	*estar negro*	very irritated
ser orgulloso	proud (pejorative)	*estar orgulloso*	proud of something/somebody
ser rico	rich	*estar rico*	delicious
ser seguro	safe	*estar seguro*	convinced
ser torpe	slow-witted	*estar torpe*	clumsy, moving with difficulty
ser verde	green/smutty	*estar verde*	unripe
ser violento	violent/embarrassing	*estar violento*	embarrassed
ser vivo	sharp/alert	*estar vivo*	alive
(*ser un vivo*	unscrupulous)		

26 Adverbs

Spanish adverbials (i.e. adverbs and adverb phrases) can be divided into two large classes: invariable words and phrases, and adverbs formed from adjectives by adding the suffix *-mente*. Examples of the first type are *mal* 'badly', *ayer* 'yesterday', *aposta* 'on purpose', *en serio* 'seriously' (i.e. not jokingly). Examples of the latter are *tranquilamente* 'tranquilly', *violentamente* 'violently', *naturalmente* 'naturally'. Although the suffix *-mente* is very productive, there are severe and apparently arbitrary constraints on its use.

A few adjectives also function as adverbs: *hablaban fuerte* 'they were talking loudly'.

More common in Spanish than in English, especially in writing, is the use of an adjective where English uses an adverb: *el rey los recibió agradecido* 'the king received them gratefully', *vivían felices* 'they lived happily'.

26.1 Adverbs in *-mente*

26.1.1 Formation
If the adjective has a separate feminine form, *-mente* is added to it. Otherwise it is added to the invariable singular form:

Masc. singular	Fem. singular	Adverbial form	
absoluto	*absoluta*	*absolutamente*	absolutely
cansado	*cansada*	*cansadamente*	in a tired way
evidente	*evidente*	*evidentemente*	evidently
leal	*leal*	*lealmente*	loyally
tenaz	*tenaz*	*tenazmente*	tenaciously

etc.

26.1.2 Accent rules for adverbs in *-mente*
The original stress should be preserved in pronunciation. As a result, many adverbs in *-mente* have two stress accents, one on the vowel which carries a written accent, another on the penultimate syllable: *crítico/críticamente* 'critical'/'critically', *electrónico/electrónicamente* 'electronic'/'electronically', *hábil/hábilmente* 'skilful'/'skilfully', *sarcástico/sarcásticamente* 'sarcastically'. Pronunciation of such words with a single penultimate stress should be avoided.

26.1.3   Consecutive adverbs in *-mente*

If more than one adverb in *-mente* is joined by a conjunction (e.g. *y*, *ni*, *pero*, etc.), *-mente* is dropped from all but the last:

Se lo dije sincera y llanamente	I told him sincerely and plainly
Trepaban lenta, segura y	they climbed slowly, surely and
determinadamente	determinedly
Esto presenta un problema político	this presents a major political problem,
mayor, y ni intelectual, ni política,	and neither intellectually, nor
ni económicamente se puede mantener	politically nor economically can such
tal postura (*El País*)	a position be sustained

This is an important rule of written Spanish, infrequently observed in spontaneous speech. But it is not normal when no conjunction is present: *y así, separados por el muro de vidrio, habíamos vivido ansiosamente, melancólicamente* (E. Sabato, Arg.), 'and thus, separated by the wall of glass, we had lived anxiously, melancholically'.

26.1.4   Limits on the use of the suffix *-mente*

-mente cannot be added to all adjectives, although there is no accounting for experiments, as when Cortázar coins *pelirrojamente* 'red-hairedly' in his novel *Rayuela*.

In general, though with important exceptions (cf. *difícil/difícilmente* 'difficult', *lleno* 'full', but 'fully' = *plenamente*), the set of Spanish adjectives which take *-mente* corresponds to the set of English adjectives which allow the adverbial suffix *-ly*. These are chiefly adverbs of manner.

The following do not take *-mente* (at least in normal styles):

(a)   Adjectives denoting physical appearance: *rojo* 'red', *negro* 'black', *calvo* 'bald', *gordo* 'fat', *cojo* 'lame', *viejo* 'old'/'aged', etc.

(b)   Adjectives denoting origin, nationality, religion: *cordobés* 'Cordoban', *argentino* 'Argentine', *protestante* 'Protestant', *musulmán* 'Muslim', etc. (Two exceptions are *católicamente* and *cristianamente*: *tienes que educar a tus hijos católicamente* 'you must bring up your children in the catholic manner'.)

(c)   Ordinal numbers, e.g. *segundo* 'second', *quinto* 'fifth', *vigésimo* 'twentieth'. (Exceptions: *primeramente* 'chiefly'/'firstly' and *últimamente* 'lately'/'lastly'.) *En segundo lugar* = 'secondly'.

(d)   Some adjectives, for no obvious reason, e.g. *vacío* 'empty' ('emptily' = *huecamente*), *lleno* 'full' (*plenamente* = 'fully'), *importante* 'important', and most adjectives in *-ón*, cf. *mandón* 'bossy', *peleón* 'aggressive'/'prone to start fights'.

(e)   Many verbal participles which cannot, by meaning, function as adverbs.

However, some Spanish participles take *-mente* while their English counterpart does not. The following are some of the many participle forms which may take *-mente*. They usually refer to behaviour, or to frequency, speed or some other idea which could have an adverbial application:

atrevido	*atrevidamente*	daring(ly)
abatido	*abatidamente*	downcast
acentuado	*acentuadamente*	marked(ly)
abierto	*abiertamente*	open(ly)
decidido	*decididamente*	decided(ly)
deliberado	*deliberadamente*	deliberate(ly)
debido	*debidamente*	due/duly
equivocado	*equivocadamente*	mistaken(ly)
exagerado	*exageradamente*	exaggerated(ly)
irritado	*irritadamente*	irritated(ly)
perdido ('lost')	*perdidamente*	hopeless(ly) (e.g. in love)
resuelto	*resueltamente*	resolute(ly)
reiterado	*reiteradamente*	repeated(ly)

etc.

26.1.5 Popular forms

Popular forms like *buenamente* and *malamente* are occasionally heard in familiar speech with specialized meanings:

Lo terminamos, pero malamente	we finished it, but it was rushed
Hazlo buenamente cuando puedas	do it in your own time when you can

The forms ?*mayormente* 'a great deal' 'especially' (common in Spanish America) and ?*mismamente*, cf. ?*mismamente el cura* 'the priest himself', are usually considered substandard or popular.

26.1.6 Meaning of adverbs in -*mente*

The existence of an adverb in -*mente* does not mean that the root adjective cannot itself function adverbially, with or without the same meaning. Constant reading and dictionary work are the only solution to this problem, e.g.:

en vano/vanamente	in vain/vainly
de inmediato/inmediatamente	immediately
directo/directamente	directly
Siempre obra locamente/a lo loco	he always acts wildly/in a mad fashion

but only:

Está locamente enamorado	he's madly in love

26.1.7 *Igual* or *igualmente*?

Igualmente means 'equally', but *igual* (as well as meaning 'equal') is an invariable adverb in its own right meaning 'the same':

otros problems igualmente difíciles	other equally difficult problems

but:

Una bata que le caía igual que hecha a medida (L. Goytisolo)	a housecoat which fitted her exactly as if it had been made to measure
Y ¿por qué no puedo yo hacerlo igual?	and why can't I do it the same way/as well?
En eso ustedes son igual a las mujeres (M. Puig, Arg. dialogue) (also *igual que . . .*)	you're the same as women in that respect
Es igual que tú (also *igual a ti*)	she's the same as you

Tú eres igualmente delgado   you're equally slim
Tú eres igual de delgado   "   "   "

26.1.8 Too many adverbs in *-mente*
It is bad style to include too many adverbs in *-mente* in a single paragraph:
the final syllables set off ugly rhymes. The barbarous sentence *Evidentemente, todas las lenguas evolucionan constantemente, y sería totalmente
absurdo pretender detener arbitrariamente su crecimiento* makes passable
English in literal translation – 'clearly, all languages evolve constantly, and
it would be totally absurd to attempt to arrest their growth arbitrarily' – but
must be recast in Spanish along the lines of *es evidente que todas las lenguas
están en constante evolución, y sería totalmente absurdo pretender detener
de manera arbitraria su crecimiento.*

   A form in *-mente* can usually be replaced by *con* + an abstract noun or
by some other adverbial phrase, e.g. *alegremente = con alegría* or *de un
modo (or manera) alegre, rabiosamente = con rabia* or *de un modo rabioso,
ferozmente = con ferocidad* or *de un modo feroz*. The sentence *vivían de un
modo tranquilo, feliz y libre* 'they lived quietly, happy and free' is much
better Spanish than *vivían tranquila, feliz y libremente.*

   For a selection of adverbial phrases, see 26.2.2.

26.1.9 *-ísimamente*
The suffix *-ísimo* (see 4.4) may be added (judiciously) to adverbs of manner
and time. The result is very emphatic:

claramente	*clarísimamente*	extremely clearly
intensamente	*intensísimamente*	extremely intensely
recientemente	*recientísimamente*	extremely recently
tiernamente	*tiernísimamente*	extremely tenderly
urgentemente	*urgentísimamente*	extremely urgently

etc.

   More common alternatives exist, e.g. *con gran claridad, con enorme
intensidad, con gran urgencia*, etc.

26.1.10 Adverbs in *-mente* to mean 'from a . . . point of view'
Adverbs in *-mente* are freely used to indicate point of view:

Económicamente, este país va a la ruina economically, this country is on the road
              to ruin
Personalmente, lo dudo   personally, I doubt it

26.2 Adverbs of manner

26.2.1 General
These include words like *bien* 'well', *mal* 'badly', *despacio* 'slowly',
aprisa/deprisa/pronto 'quickly', *adrede/aposta* 'on purpose', *igual* 'the

same', as well as most of the adverbs formed in *-mente*.

There are countless adverbial phrases: *a propósito* 'deliberately', *en balde* 'in vain', *a contrapelo* 'unwillingly', *en serio* 'seriously'. A selection appears at 26.2.2

Adverbs of manner can modify verbs, participles, adjectives or other adverbs:

Habla despacio	he talks slowly
Lo quieren así	they want it that way
Esto está mal hecho	this is badly made/this is the wrong thing to do
Está bien	it/he/she's okay
Estoy totalmente agotado	I'm totally exhausted
Está profundamente triste	he's profoundly sad
Me da igual	it's all the same to me
Aquí estamos mejor/peor	we're better/worse (off) here

A few can even modify nouns:

Hace mucho tiempo que una cosa así no ocurría en la ONU (*El País*)	it has been a long time since something like this happened in the UN
Cenamos algunas cosas que ella traía en su equipaje, latas y así (F. Umbral)	we had supper on a few things she was carrying in her luggage – tins and that sort of thing
una niña bien	a 'nice' girl (pejorative)
dos coñacs con hielo, y dos cafés igual	two cognacs with ice, and two coffees the same way

Bien and *así de* can intensify adjectives:

Es bien lista	she's pretty clever
Bien bueno que está, ¿eh?	great, isn't it (sarcastic)
¿Adónde vas así de guapa? or . . . *vas tan guapa* . . .	where are you off to looking so pretty?

26.2.2 Adverbial phrases of manner

These are innumerable, and often provide an elegant alternative to an unwieldy adverb in *-mente*. The following is a small sample:

a buen paso	at a smart pace
a ciegas	in the dark
a conciencia	conscientiously
El agua sale a chorros	the water is pouring out
a destiempo	inopportunely
entrar a empujones	to push one's way in
a escondidas	secretly/clandestinely
a fuego lento	on a low flame
a hurtadillas	by stealth
al alimón	together by turns/jointly (from *torear al alimón* – 'to take turns goading the bull')
a la carrera	at full speed
a la fuerza	by force/under obligation
a la ligera	hastily/without proper thought
a las claras	clearly (i.e. without beating about the bush)
(llorar) a lágrima viva	to shed floods of tears

a mano	by hand
a matacaballo	at break-neck speed
a medias	by halves
a oscuras	in the dark
a quemarropa	point-blank
a ratos perdidos	at odd moments (i.e. moments of free time)
a regañadientes	reluctantly/unwillingly
a sabiendas de que . . .	fully aware that . . .
a tiempo	in time (e.g. for the train)
a tientas	by touch/by feel
al raso	in the open/out of doors
al sereno	in the open/'under the stars'
bajo cuerda	on the sly/in an underhand way
con delirio/locura	madly/passionately
con frecuencia/a menudo	frequently
de balde	free (= without paying)
de continuo	continuously
de corrido	at one go/straight off
de costumbre	usually
de golpe	suddenly
de improviso	unexpectedly
(aprender) de memoria	(learn) by heart
de ordinario	normally/usually
de puntillas	on tiptoe
de rodillas	kneeling
de seguro	for certain/sure
de sobra	in excess/more than enough
(leer algo) de un tirón	to read something in one sitting/ straight through
en cambio	on the other hand
en confianza	confidentially
en cueros (vivos)/en pelota	stark naked
en el acto	on the spot
en lo sucesivo	from now on/hereafter
(hablar) por los codos	to talk too much (lit. 'through the elbows')
sin empacho	coolly/unconcernedly
sin reserva	unreservedly
sin ton ni son	willy-nilly/thoughtlessly

etc.

Not all of these are in use in Spanish America.

26.2.3 Adjectives as adverbs of manner

The masculine singulars of a few adjectives serve as adverbs, but only in certain phrases (e.g. *hablar claro* 'to speak clearly' but only *expresarse claramente/con claridad* 'to express oneself clearly'):

Hablan alto/bajo/claro	they talk loudly/softly/clearly
Lo hemos comprado barato/caro	we've bought it cheap/dear
El tren va directo a Tuy	the train goes direct to Tuy
Hay que tirar fuerte	you have to pull hard

Se me apiló firme (Cortázar, dialogue, Arg., Spain: *se me arrimó*)	he pushed himself tight up against me
Anda rápido que vamos a llegar tarde (see 26.2.6 for *rápido*)	walk fast or we'll arrive late
Respiraba hondo como si le costara trabajo	he was breathing deeply, as if with difficulty
Me sienta fatal	it doesn't suit me/agree with me at all
Él no juega limpio	he doesn't play fair

The following are typical of familiar speech, and are not to everyone's taste:

Lo hemos pasado estupendo/fantástico/ bárbaro	we had a tremendous/fantastic time
La chaqueta le sienta bárbaro a Mariluz	the jacket looks terrific on Mariluz
Tres mil pesetas te las presta fácil (from Beinhauer, 228)	he'll lend you 3,000 ptas, for sure

Note Colloquial Spanish-American provides numerous examples unacceptable in Spain but not without their charm, and some of them perhaps doubtful on their home ground:

Qué lindo canta	*doesn't he/she sing pretty
El maíz germina fácil (Arg.)	*maize germinates easy
Pero toca muy bonito (Peru)	*but he plays real nice
No, yo pensé distinto (Mex.)	*no, I figured different
(All examples from Kany, 53–5).	

26.2.4   Adjectives used to modify both subject and verb

Very common in Spanish is the use of an adjective in combination with a verb to produce an effect more easily created by an adverb in English. This is not a true adverbial use of the adjective, since the adjective agrees with the number and gender of the subject. The device is restricted in the spoken language to a limited range of verbs and adjectives.

The effect is to make the adjective act both as an adverb and an adjective, i.e. it modifies both the verb and the subject of the verb.

Sometimes the construction is obligatory: *las niñas cansadas dormían* 'the tired girls were sleeping' is not the same as *las niñas dormían cansadas* which is most nearly translated as 'the girls were tired and asleep' or 'sleeping in their tiredness', but one could hardly say ?*las niñas dormían cansadamente* 'the girls were sleeping tiredly' which modifies the verb but not the subject!

Obviously, this construction is confined to those adjectives which can equally well modify a noun or a verb, e.g. *inocente* 'innocent', *confuso* 'confused', *feliz* 'happy', but not adjectives like *harapiento* 'ragged' or *azul* 'blue' which can hardly modify a verb.

Se desvistió mientras se miraba distraído en el espejo del armario (Cortázar, Arg.: or *distraídamente*)	he got undressed as he gazed absently at himself in the wardrobe mirror
Las mujeres protestaban indignadas (or *indignadamente*)	the women were protesting indignantly

Las máquinas de escribir tecleteaban incansables	the typewriters were clattering tirelessly
Sonrió tranquila . . . (J. Marsé)	she smiled gently
Viven felices (normal style)	they live happily

26.2.5 Nouns used adverbially
For familiar constructions like *llover cantidad, divertirse horrores* see 26.3.6.

26.2.6 *Rápido*
Rápido is an adjective, and is correctly used in phrases like *tren rápido, comidas rápidas,* etc.

As an adverb it is, like 'quick', familiar; *aprisa, con prisa, deprisa, rápidamente, pronto* are 'correct' adverbial forms: *¡rápido (aprisa/pronto), que se va el tren!* 'quick, the train's going!'; *¡fuera! ¡Rápido!* 'get out! Quick!'. Forms like *lo he hecho rápido* are familiar.

26.2.7 *A la* and *a lo*
Both may form adverbial phrases of manner, but *a la* followed by a feminine adjective is much more common than *a lo,* which is probably nowadays confined to set phrases:

tortilla a la francesa	plain omelette
lenguado a la normanda	sole à la normande
despedirse a la francesa	to take French leave (i.e. not say good-bye)
divorcio a la italiana	divorce Italian-style
Viven todavía a la antigua	they still live in the old style
Siempre viste a la inglesa	he always dresses English-style
a lo loco	crazily

Note *En plan . . .* is rather colloquial, like '-style': *viajar en plan turista* 'to travel tourist-style', *hablar en plan Tarzan* 'to talk Tarzan-style'.

26.2.8 Note on position of adverbs of manner
For further remarks on the position of adverbs see 31.9.

An adverb of manner usually follows an intransitive verb:

Trabaja actualmente en una segunda novela	he is now working on a second novel
Este problema está íntimamente ligado al problema del paro	this problem is intimately linked to the problem of unemployment
Esa cara de asco que parece ser habitualmente la suya	that look of disgust which seems habitually to be his

In a transitive sentence, the adverb usually follows the object – *habla griego correctamente* – or the verb – *habla correctamente el griego* 'he speaks Greek perfectly/without making mistakes'. The former is more usual.

The difference is usually almost imperceptible, but strictly speaking an adverb which follows the object modifies the whole verb phrase, whereas an adverb which precedes the object modifies only the verb. Thus *robaba dinero con frecuencia* 'he frequently stole money', but *robaba con frecuencia dinero* 'frequently he stole money . . .' is the appropriate order if further items, e.g. jewellery, are to follow.

26.3 Intensifiers and moderators

Intensifiers and moderators intensify or weaken the force of a verb, adverb, adjective and, occasionally, noun. Typical intensifiers are *muy* 'very', *mucho/poco* 'much'/'little', *intensamente* 'intensely', *algo/más bien* 'rather', *increíblemente* 'incredibly', *sobremanera* (literary) 'exceedingly'. Many intensifiers have other functions, and are dealt with elsewhere, e.g. *algo* see 9.2, *demasiado* see 9.9, *mucho* see 9.11, *poco* see 9.11, *más bien* see 9.2.

26.3.1 *Muy*
Muy 'very' is originally an abbreviated form of *mucho*, and the full form must be used in isolation –

Es muy inteligente	he's very intelligent
¿Es inteligente? Sí, mucho	is he intelligent? Yes, very

26.3.2 Intensifiers in *-mente*
These cannot modify another adverb in *-mente*, i.e. 'he speaks English incredibly fluently' cannot be translated **habla inglés increíblemente corrientemente* but must be recast, e.g. *habla inglés con una soltura/facilidad increíble*:

Ha actuado con admirable honradez	he's acted admirably honestly/with admirable honestly
Lo hicieron con una prisa absurda	they did it absurdly quickly/with absurd haste
Le voy a hablar con una franqueza total	I'm going to talk to you totally frankly

etc.

26.3.3 *Más* and *menos*
For the use of *más* and *menos* in comparisons, see chapter 5.

Más is used as an intensifier in familiar speech, without any comparative meaning:

Es que eres más tonto . . .	heavens, are you stupid!
Está más borracho . . .	is he drunk!

26.3.4 *Lo* as an intensifier
For *lo* in sentences like *pobrecita, con lo enferma que está . . .*, *cuéntale lo bien que canta, camina lo más lentamente que puedas*, see 7.2.2.

26.3.5 *Qué* and *cuán* as intensifiers
Interrogative *¿qué?* is discussed at 22.3; *¿cuánto?* at 22.5.

Qué . . . is a very frequent intensifier; *cuán* is archaic, but is occasionally revived in certain styles:

¡Qué brutos somos!	aren't we stupid!
¡Qué listo eres!	aren't you clever!
¡Qué aburrido!	what a bore!
¡Qué tarde se me ha hecho!	how time's crept up on me!/my, I've made myself late!
¡Qué de veces te lo he dicho (usually *cuántas veces . . .*)	how many times I've told you!
Melania insistió tosiendo un poquito para demostrar cuán mal estaba (J. Donoso, usually *lo mal que estaba*)	Melania insisted, coughing slightly to demonstrate how ill she was

For *no recordaba lo guapa que eres* 'I didn't remember how attractive you are', etc., see 7.2.2.

26.3.6   Nouns used as intensifiers

Familiar speech uses some nouns as intensifiers – not to every taste, as the translation shows:

Lo pasamos bomba (already old-fashioned?)	we had a terrific time (lit. 'we had a bomb of a time')
Canta fenómeno	he's a smashing singer
Nos aburrimos cantidad	we were bored stiff
Nos hemos reído cantidad	did we have a laugh!

26.4   Adverbs of doubt

Words meaning 'perhaps', 'probably', 'possibly' may call for the subjunctive and are discussed under 16.7.3.

26.5   Adverbs of place

26.5.1   *Aquí, ahí, allí*

It is important to distinguish carefully between *ahí* and *allí*: to the untrained ear they tend to sound similar, at least in some varieties of Spanish. These adverbs are closely linked in meaning to the demonstratives and the personal pronouns:

yo (speaker)	*este* 'this near me'	*aquí* 'here near me'
tú (hearer)	*ese* 'that near you or me'	*ahí* 'there near you or me'
él (other)	*aquel* 'that near him'	*allí* 'there'

In other words, *ahí* points to space near the hearer. Misuse of *ahí* and *allí* produces a bizarre effect. Carnicer remarks that to ask a person from another country *¿qué tal se vive ahí?* instead of *allí* – 'what's it like living (just) there?' – prompts him to look under his chair.

Vente aquí a pasar unos días con nosotros	come here and spend a few days with us
Aquí construiremos la casa, ahí el garaje, y allí al final del jardín, la piscina	we'll build the house here, the garage there, and the swimming pool there at the bottom of the garden

Deja la linterna ahí a tu lado	leave the torch there next to you
Sería interesante visitar Groenlandia,	it would be interesting to visit Greenland,
pero no quisiera vivir allí	but I wouldn't like to live there

If the place referred to is out of sight, *ahí* is generally used if it is near by or in the same town, *allí* for more remote places:

Lo he comprado en esa tienda.	I bought it in that shop.
Ah, sí, yo compro siempre ahí	Oh yes, I always shop there
Ya están ahí monsieur Fréjus y	M. Fréjus and M. Bebé are here, and
monsieur Bebé, y quieren cocktails	they want cocktails
(Cortázar, dialogue: note *están ahí* = 'have arrived')	
Si vas a Cáceres, mándame una postal	if you go to Caceres send me a card
desde allí	from there
Me voy a Madrid. ¡Qué casualidad!	I'm going to Madrid. What a coincidence!
¡Yo también me voy allí mañana!	I'm going there tomorrow as well!
Mi hermana nació en Caracas, y yo	my sister was born in Caracas, and I
también nací allí	was born there too

But natives may use *ahí* for *allí* (but not vice-versa), if they feel emotionally close to the place they are talking about:

¿Conoces la iglesia a la entrada del	do you know the church on the way in to
pueblo? Pues ahí/allí se casaron mis	the village? Well, that's where my
padres	parents got married
Y al fin llegué a Manaos. De ahí era	and I eventually got to Manaos. From
fácil pasar a Iquitos.	there it was easy to cross to Iquitos.
–Y ¿ahí fue donde conociste al	'And that was where you met Sr
señor Julio Reátegui?	Julio Reategui?'
(Vargas Llosa, Peru, dialogue)	

Notes (i) Distance in time should be reflected in the appropriate use of *ahí* and *allí*, although the rule is applied loosely in speech:

Allí fue donde lo compré	that's where I bought it
Ahí es donde lo he comprado	that's where I bought it
(perfect tense denoting recency)	
Allí fue donde le atropellaron	that's where he was run over

(ii) Colloquially *ahí* is used to mean 'somewhere' when the speaker is indifferent or secretive about the exact location:

¿Dónde has estado? Por ahí	where have you been? Somewhere
¿Dónde está Julia? Por ahí	where's Julia? She's somewhere around

(iii) *Ahí* may encroach on *allí* in Spanish-American speech:

Ahí está, dijo, y ahí estaba porque	'there it is', he said, and there it was
él lo conocía . . .	because he was familiar with it
(García Márquez, Col., dialogue, pointing to a comet in the sky)	

26.5.2   *Acá, allá*

In the Southern Cone, and perhaps elsewhere in Spanish America, *acá* has more or less replaced *aquí*, even in good writing: *acá en la Argentina si querés una taza de té, tenés que beber mate* = in Peninsular Spanish *aquí en Argentina, si quieres una taza de té, tienes que beber mate* 'here in Argentina if you feel like a cup of tea you have to drink *mate*'.

In Spain, *acá* and *allá* are much less common than *aquí, ahí, allí,* and denote vague or non-specific location or, most commonly, movement (often with the preposition *para*):

Ven acá/aquí, que te voy a contar una cosa	come here, I'm going to tell you something
Íbamos allá/hacia allí cuando nos le encontramos	we were on the way there when we ran into him
Que se venga para acá en cuanto pueda	he must come here as soon as he can

Notes (i) *Allá* is optionally used of large distances, or to express vague yearnings. In time phrases it emphasizes remoteness and may be obligatory:

Allá/allí en Argentina tenemos mucha familia	we have a lot of family out there in Argentina
Allá/allí en la Luna, no hay agua	up there on the Moon there's no water
Nos casamos allá en los años veinte (not *allí*)	we got married way back in the twenties
El sur era y es acentuadamente indio; allá la cultura tradicional está todavía viva (O. Paz, Mex.)	the south was and is markedly Amerindian; (down) there traditional culture is still alive
Al otro lado de las lágrimas, allá arriba en lo alto de su rabia, más allá de las ramas del almendro y de las palmeras . . . (J. Marsé)	on the other side of her tears, up there high in her rage, beyond the branches of the almond trees and the palms . . .

(ii) *Acá* and *allá* can take an intensifier, unlike *aquí*, *ahí*, *allí*:

Más allá del sistema solar	beyond the solar system
Más acá de la frontera	on this side of the frontier
Muévelo un poco más acá/hacia aquí	move it this way a bit
¡un poquito más acá!	this way a bit!
lo más acá/allá posible	as far over here/there as possible

El más allá is 'the Beyond' of religion and science fiction.

(iii) *Allá* with a pronoun translates 'let him/her get on with it', 'it's your look-out', etc.

Allá él si hace tonterías	if he wants to fool about, that's his affair
Bueno, allá tú si no me haces caso	well, if you don't pay any attention to me, it's your problem

(iv) *Acá* is sometimes used in time expressions in informal language, though it sounds a little old-fashioned (at least in Spain):

¿De cuándo acá no se dice hola a los amigos? (*desde cuándo . . .*)	since when have people not been saying 'hullo' to their friends?
Desde las elecciones acá, este país ya no tiene remedio	since the elections, this country's been beyond hope
De un tiempo acá se le nota cansada (*desde un tiempo a esta parte*)	she's been looking tired for some time now

26.5.3 Use of adverbs of place as pronouns
One hears uneducated speakers use *aquí/ahí/allí* for *éste/ése/aquél*: *aquí me dice* = *éste me dice* (itself very familiar). The same phenomenon occurs in Spanish America, and also with *acá/allá*.

26.5.4 Adverbs of place with prepositions
All the adverbs of place can be preceded by *de, desde, hacia, hasta, por* and, less commonly, *para* (for which see *acá/allá*).

Los melocotones de aquí son mejores que los de Estados Unidos
the peaches (from) here are better than the ones from America

Mira el sombrero que lleva la señora de allí
look at the hat that lady over there is wearing

Hasta aquí hemos llegado y de aquí no paso
we've got this far and I'm going no further

Desde aquí se ve el mar
you can see the sea from here

Se sale por aquí
this is the way out

etc.

26.5.5 *Dentro/adentro, fuera/afuera*

'Inside' and 'outside' respectively.

In Spain *dentro* and *fuera* are preferred after prepositions (except perhaps *para*). *Afuera, adentro* strictly speaking denote motion towards and should be used only in this sense, although they are occasionally found in isolation with the meaning of *fuera, dentro*.

Peninsular usage:

Te esperamos fuera
we'll wait for you outside

Por dentro era negro, y por fuera blanco
on the inside it was black, on the outside white

El gas tiende a escaparse hacia fuera
gas tends to escape outwards

Dentro había flores en macetas
inside there were flowers in pots

Afuera quedaba el domingo de verano, despoblado y soso (F. Umbral)
outside was the summer Sunday, empty (lit. 'depopulated') and lifeless

(*fuera* is more normal)

Ven (a)dentro y te lo explicaré
come inside and I'll explain it to you

Vamos a cenar fuera
we're eating out (tonight)/we're having dinner outside

He estado fuera algunos días
I've been out of town a few days

Al acabar el discurso se oyeron gritos de ¡fuera! ¡fuera!
when the speech ended shouts of 'out! out!' were heard

¡Las manos fuera de Cuba!
hands off Cuba!

Es de fuera
he/she/it's from abroad

Vamos para (a)dentro, que hace frío
let's go inside, it's cold

Dentro de la caja había otra
inside the box was another

Te espero fuera del cine
I'll wait for you outside the cinema

Su ocurrencia ha estado fuera de lugar
his witty remark was out of place

Spanish-American usage (especially Argentina):

Adentro de and *afuera de* are also used as prepositional phrases. Spaniards usually prefer *dentro, fuera* in all the following examples:

Afuera hacía calor porque empezaba enero (Cortázar, Arg.)
outside it was hot because January was beginning

Adentro de Aqueronte hay lágrimas, tinieblas, crujir de dientes (Borges, Arg.)
within Acheron there are tears, darkness, gnashing of teeth

Afuera en el parque, y adentro, por la casa entera seguían los disparos (José Donoso, Chile)
outside in the park, and inside, throughout the house, the shooting continued

El perro se quedó afuera
the dog was left outside/stayed outside

Después que el viejo marino hubo mirado un momento hacia adentro de sí mismo
after the old sailor had gazed within himself for a moment

(Ibarzábal, Cuba, quoted Kany, 326.)

Notes (i) Only *adentro*, *afuera* should be intensified: *más adentro* 'further inside', *más afuera* or *más hacia fuera* 'more to the outside'.

(ii) Omission of *de* in the prepositional phrase, common in SA, heard in Spain, is considered incorrect: *dentro de mi corazón, fuera de la casa*.

(iii) *Fuera de* can mean *aparte de*, 'apart from' but is rather colloquial: *fuera de él no hay nadie en que yo pueda confiar* 'apart from him, there's no one I can trust' (not all grammarians accept this construction).

26.6 Adverbs of time

26.6.1 *Ya*

Ya has a wide variety of uses. In many common constructions its meaning is determined by the time of the verb which it modifies:

Vienen ya	they're coming right now
Ya llegarán	they'll arrive, for sure
Ya han llegado	they've already arrived
Ya llegaron (SA)	they already arrived (American)
Ya no vienen	they're not coming any more
Ya no llegarán	they won't arrive any more
(but only *aún/todavía no han llegado*	they haven't arrived yet)

Further examples:

Los autores que aportaron nuevos recursos estilísticos al ya idioma castellano (or *al que ya era idioma . . .*)	the authors who contributed new stylistic resources to what was already the Castilian language
Ya en la época romana existía un puente sobre el río	as far back as the Roman period there was a bridge over the river
Eres hombre ya	you're a man now
¿Quién se acuerda ya de lo que era el Charleston?	who can remember what the Charleston was any more?
Estaba perdido, extraviado en una casa ajena donde ya ni nada ni nadie le suscitaba el menor vestigio de afecto (García Márquez, Colombia)	he was lost, adrift in a strange house where nothing and nobody aroused the slightest trace of affection in him any more
Ya desde mucho antes, Amaranta había renunciado a toda tentativa de convertirla en una mujer útil (*idem*)	long before this (already), Amaranta had abandoned all attempts to change her into a useful woman

But *ya* has idiomatic uses, particularly with the non-past tenses. It can indicate impatience, accumulating frustration, fulfilled expectations, resignation, certainty about the future or, in negative sentences, denial of something expected:

Iros, iros a la playa, que ya me quedo yo aquí a lavar la ropa (Carmen Godoy in *Cambio16*; *iros* is familiar Peninsular usage for *idos*. See 17.5c for discussion)	go on, off you go to the beach while I stay here washing the clothes (martyred tone)
Lleva seis meses en la cama. Si eso no es grave, pues ya me dirás	he's been in bed six months. If that's not serious, then you tell me what is
Porque la tarea que tenemos planteada es casi una tarea de titanes. Pero el país puede resolverla. Ya verán. (*Cambio16*)	because the task confronting us is almost a task fit for Titans. But the country can solve it. You'll see.

Sirve ya la cena, que hemos esperado bastante	serve supper now, we've waited long enough
Por mí, que se vaya ya	he can go right now, as far as I'm concerned
El estudiante de nuestros días – ya no pensaré en el estudiante del año 2000 o 2500 – (Variedades, 174)	the student of our day – I shan't even consider the student of the year 2000 or 2500 –
Ya le pasaré la cuenta cuando gane el gallo (García Márquez, Colombia, dialogue: *ya* here postpones the blow)	I'll send you the bill when your cockerel wins
¡Basta ya! ¡calla ya!	that's enough! Not another word!
¡Ya está bien!	that's enough!
Bueno, eso es el colmo ya	well, that *is* the limit!
Ya puedes tener buen olfato con la nariz que tú tienes	you can well have a good sense of smell with the nose you've got
Ya puedes invitarnos con el dinero que tú tienes	I should think you *could* pay for us with the money you've got
Por mí, ya puede llover, que tenemos tienda de campaña	as far as I'm concerned, it can go ahead and rain – we've got a tent
Hitler habría sido todavía peor – y ya es decir – si a su criminal racismo hubiera juntado un fanatismo religioso (ABC)	Hitler would have been even worse – and that's saying something – if he had added religious fanaticism to his criminal racism
Cuando ya acabemos de limpiar la casa . . .	when we finally finish cleaning the house . . .
No, no, ya te digo que él no sabía nada de todo aquello	no, no, I'm *telling* you he knew nothing about all that
¡Ya tuviste que contarme el final!	you *would* have to tell me the ending!
Ya lo sé	I already know/I *know*
Ya empezamos . . .	(oh dear) here we go again . . .
Ya era hora	it's about time . . .

Notes (i)   *Ya . . . ya* is a literary alternative for *o . . . o* 'either . . . or':

Ya porque la idea del matrimonio acabara por asustarle, ya porque no pudiera olvidar a María, no apareció en la iglesia	either because the idea of marriage eventually frightened him, or because he could not forget Maria, he did not appear at the church

(ii)   *Ya* may be an abbreviation of *ya lo sé* 'I know', or *ya entiendo* 'I understand':

Cuando veas la luz verde pulsa el botón rojo. Ya	when you see the green light, push the red button. Right/understood

26.6.2   *Recién*

In Spain *recién* can only appear before participles, e.g. *recién pintado* 'newly painted', *recién casado* 'newly wed', *recién divorciado* 'recently divorced', *un chico recién salido del colegio* 'a boy who has recently left school'. Its use before other parts of speech is very rare.

The use of *recién* as a free-standing adverb of time is one hallmark of Latin-American Spanish almost everywhere. It is very common in speech and also appears even in quite formal written language.

It has two basic meanings:

(a) 'right now' or 'just now':

Recién lo vi	I've just seen him
(Spain *le acabo de ver*)	
¿Cuándo lo dijo? Recién	when did he say it? Just now
(Spain *ahora mismo*)	

(b) 'Only', as in 'only now', 'only this year':

Pero recién en los últimos siete años la desesperada ciencia se ha aferrado a una hipótesis: la del movimiento de placas o bloques (*Tiempo*, Chile, quoted *Var.* 39)	but only in the last seven years has science, in despair, seized hold of a hypothesis: the movement of (continental) plates or blocks
Recién entonces me di cuenta (Spain *sólo entonces*)	only then did I realize
Recién mañana llegará (Spain *no llegará hasta mañana*)	he won't be here till tomorrow
– *Y él recién entonces se da cuenta de que está herida porque las manos se le están manchando de la sangre de ella* (M. Puig, Arg. dialogue; Spain: . . . *sólo entonces se da cuenta . . .*)	and only then he realizes that she's injured because his hands are being stained with her blood

Used thus, *recién* precedes the word or phrase it modifies. There is a charming colloquial diminutive *reciencito*.

26.6.3   Other adverbs of time

Other adverbs of time, e.g. *ahora* 'now', *antes* 'before', *anteriormente* 'formerly', *después* 'later', *en seguida* 'straight away', *entonces* 'then', *luego* 'later on'/'then', *posteriormente* 'subsequently', should be sought in the index. Words and phrases that present no major problems of syntax or usage are not discussed in this grammar and should be sought in a good dictionary.

27 Conjunctions

Some of the words and phrases discussed in this chapter might be more accurately described as adverbs or particles. A large number of Spanish subordinating conjunctions, e.g. *cuando, sin que, después de que* are associated with the subjunctive and are discussed in the chapter on the subjunctive. Such conjunctions are merely listed in the appropriate section of the present chapter.

27.1 *Sino, pero, mas*

All of these translate 'but'. *Mas* (no accent!) is virtually extinct, but is occasionally found in flowery written language and in the bad Spanish of students contaminated by French and Portuguese.

The distinction between *pero* and *sino* is crucial.

Sino contradicts a preceding statement, which is itself usually, but not invariably, negative. Before a verb phrase *sino que* must be used:

No quiero pan, sino vino	I don't want bread, but wine
no tú, sino él	not you, but him
no éste, sino ése	not this one, but that
El pueblo mexicano {. . .} no cree ya sino en la Virgen de Guadalupe y en la Lotería Nacional (O. Paz, Mex.)	the Mexican people now only believe in the Virgin of Guadalupe and the National Lottery
¿Qué puedo decir sino que lo siento?	what can I say but that I'm sorry?

(N.b. interrogative sentence treated as negative)

Yo no dije que fuera mentira, sino que no lo creía	I didn't say it was a lie, but that I didn't believe it
No sólo van a misa todos los días, sino que rezan en sus cuartos también	they not only go to Mass daily but they pray in their rooms as well

Notes (i) *Sino* must not be confused (as it sometimes is in old texts) with *si no*, 'if not'.
    (ii) *No . . . sino* translates 'only':
Yo no podía sino dar gracias a Dios . . .   I could only thank God
    (iii) **Si que* for *sino que* is substandard: **se exhibieron no sólo productos de la América Central, si que también de Cuba y Panamá* (quoted Kany, 464).

Pero restricts the meaning of the first statement, but does not contradict it. In *no está enfermo, pero dice que está cansado* 'he isn't ill, but he says he's tired', *dice que* does not contradict *no está* . . . Compare *no está enfermo, sino que está muy cansado* 'he's not ill, but very tired'.

Habla francés, pero mal	he speaks French, but badly
No van a misa todos los días, pero rezan en sus cuartos	they don't go to Mass every day, but they do pray in their rooms
Pero ¿es posible?	but can it (really) be possible?

27.2 *O*

'Or'. It is written and pronounced *u* before a word beginning with *o* or *ho*: *hombres o mujeres* 'men or women', but *mujeres u hombres* 'women or men' (written Spanish). This change does not always take place if *o* is the first word in a sentence.

O . . . *o* translates 'either . . . or': *o lo sabe o no lo sabe* 'either he knows it or he doesn't'.

Os digo que u os apartáis, u os araño (From dialogue in a popular novel, although *o os apartáis* is more likely in speech)	I tell you, either you get out of my way, or I'll scratch you

Notes (i) This replacement of *o* by *u* is often neglected in the spoken language.

(ii) *O* should be written with an accent when it appears alongside a number to avoid confusion with zero: *6 ó 5* '6 or 5'.

27.3 *Y*

'And', and used much the same as its English equivalent. It is written and pronounced *e* before a word beginning with a pure *i* sound, e.g. *Miguel e Ignacio, padre e hijos*, but not before words beginning with a *y* sound: *carbón y hierro*, etc. and not always at the head of a sentence: *¿Y Ignacio?*.

Substitution of *e* for *y* is not always applied in informal speech, but should be made in writing.

27.4 *Que*

27.4.1 General
Que has three functions in Spanish:

(a) As a relative pronoun (*la mujer que vi, el año en que nací*, etc.) discussed in chapter 29;

(b) *Qué* with an accent means 'what' and is best thought of as an entirely different word: it is discussed at 22.3;

(c) As a subordinating conjunction: this function is discussed in this chapter.

Que introduces clauses in much the same way as the English conjunction 'that':

Dice que viene	he says that he's coming

Cree que no ha pagado	he thinks that he hasn't paid
Parece que va a llover	it seems that it's going to rain

However, the absence of a personal infinitive construction in Spanish makes this use of *que* much more common in Spanish than in English:

Te aconsejo que no lo hagas	I advise you not to do it
Quiero que vengas	I want you to come
Les pidió que no firmasen	he asked them not to sign
etc.	

27.4.2   *De* before *que*

In certain circumstances a subordinate clause must be introduced by *de que*. This is necessary:

(a)   After phrases including a noun:

Se dio cuenta de que ya no llovía	he realized that it was no longer raining
Cuando yo era chico y me. desesperaba ante la idea de que mi madre debía morirse un día . . . (E. Sabato, Arg.)	when I was a little boy and despaired at the idea that my mother would have to die one day . . .
Tenía miedo de que . . .	he was afraid that . . .
Soy partidario de que . . .	I'm in favour of . . .
el argumento de que . . .	the argument that . . .
la creencia de que . . .	the belief that . . .
la causa de que no llegara a tiempo	the cause of his not arriving on time

(b)   After a number of common verbs which require the preposition *de*:

Me acuerdo de que . . .	I remember that . . .
Me olvidaba de que . . .	I was forgetting that . . .
Me admiraba de que . . .	I was surprised that . . .
Me alegro de que . . .	I'm glad that . . .
Estoy convencido de que . . .	I'm convinced that . . .

and similarly after *persuadir de* 'to persuade', *extrañarse de* 'to be puzzled at', *maravillarse de* 'to be amazed', *entristecerse de* 'to be saddened', *enfadarse de* 'to get angry', *enterarse de* 'to find out', *molestarse de* 'to be annoyed', *satisfacer de* 'to satisfy', *quejarse de* 'to complain', etc.

(c)   After certain adjectives which are normally followed by *de*:

Estoy seguro de que . . .	I'm sure that . . .
Estamos contentos de que . . .	we're pleased that . . .
Estoy cansado/harto de que . . .	I'm tired/fed up with . . .
Soy consciente de que . . .	I'm aware that . . .

(d)   After subordinators which include *de*:

antes de que llegase	before he arrived
después de que se fueron	after they went
a condición de que . . .	on condition that . . .
a cambio de que . . .	in exchange for . . .
etc.	

There is however a colloquial tendency, stronger in Spanish America than in Spain, to drop the *de* in the more common of these constructions:

Wenceslao se había dado cuenta que la maniobra de Juvenal era extraviar a sus	Wenceslao had realized that Juvenal's maneouvre was (designed) to lead

primos en la fantasía utilizada como engañifa (José Donoso, Chile)	his cousins astray by fantasy used as a trick
. . . *pero estoy segura que es lo que haces* . . . (L. Goytisolo, dialogue)	but I'm sure that that is what you're doing
Para que te convenzas que la dignidad no se come (García Márquez, Colombian dialogue)	to convince you that (lit. so you convince yourself) that one can't eat dignity

Note   In general, omission of *de* in most of these examples may be rejected as substandard by Peninsular speakers.

However *antes que* seems to be in more or less free variation with *antes de que* everywhere, cf.

Venda ese gallo antes que sea demasiado tarde (García Márquez, Colombia, dialogue)	sell that cockerel before it's too late

Peninsular informants found *antes que* acceptable but less common than *antes de que*.

27.4.3   *Dequeísmo*

There is a growing tendency on both continents to insert a redundant *de* after verbs meaning 'say', 'think', 'believe', e.g. *decir*, *afirmar*, *creer*, *sostener*, *negar*, *pensar*, *confesar*, *argüir*, etc. Examples are occasionally found in sources which should know better: **Radio Bagdad informó de que la carretera que une la capital iraquí con Basora estaba expedita en todo su recorrido* (*Panorama Semanal de El País*, 27.2.84) 'Radio Baghdad announced that the road linking the Iraqi capital with Basra was open throughout its whole length'. Sentences like **dice de que no viene* for *dice que no viene* are vehemently rejected by educated speakers and should be avoided at all costs.

Hablar de que is, however, used colloquially for 'to talk about . . .' in such sentences as *habló de que Miguel estaba enfermo* 'he talked about M. being ill'.

27.4.4   *Que* **at the head of a phrase**

Que may appear at the head of a sentence, especially in speech. Its main functions are:

(a)   To reinforce the idea that the statement which follows either expresses something expected, or is being repeated. In this case some verb like *decir* or *preguntar* may have been omitted:

¿Que cómo se llama mi película?	(did you ask) what's my film called?
¿Que si me gustó?	(did you ask me) if I liked it?
¿Que por qué no van obreros al teatro?	(you're asking me) why workers don't go to the theatre?!
Que no quiero verla	(I said that) I don't want to see her/it
Oye, que aquí pone que no hay que abrirlo	listen, it says here that it mustn't be opened
¡Que sí! ¡Que no!	Yes! No! (impatient repetition)
¡Socorro! ¡Que me ahogo!	help! I'm drowning!

(b)   As a colloquial subordinator of cause. It is often inserted to connect one idea to another where English uses a pause represented in writing by a dash:

¡Aprisa! ¡Aprisa! ¡Que se va!	hurry! Hurry! It's going! (e.g. the train)
Eso dijo, que lo oí yo con mis propios oídos	that's what he said – I heard it with my own ears
Habla más bajo, que es mi jefe	talk softer – (s)he's my boss
No hagas ese ruido, que me está volviendo loco	don't make that noise – it's driving me mad
¡¿Dónde está mi marido que lo degüello?!	where's my husband – I'm going to slaughter him!
No me des la lata con lo que dicen los lectores, que tengo cosas más importantes de que ocuparme (Carmen Rico Godoy in *Cambio16*)	don't pester me with what the readers are saying – I've more important things to bother about

(c) Colloquially, to show that the truth has dawned after some doubt:

¡Ah! Que usted es el fontanero	ah – so you're the plumber then
Que tú eres entonces el que lo hizo	so you're the one who did it then
¿Que no quieres ir conmigo?	you mean you don't want to go with me?

(d)   With the subjunctive, in commands, exhortations and wishes, e.g. *que venga en seguida* 'tell him to come/have him come immediately'. See 16.7.2a for details.

27.4.5   *Que* in indirect questions

Decir que may mean 'to ask'. *Que* is also used optionally after *preguntar* 'to ask':

Me dijo que cuándo quería cenar	he asked me when I wanted dinner/supper
Yo me pregunto (que) dónde estará ella estudiando	I wonder where she's studying
Le pregunté (que) qué hacía allí	I asked him what he was doing there

27.4.6   Omission of conjunction *que*

Que is occasionally omitted, but much less so than the English 'that':

(a)   Particularly, after certain verbs, if the following verbs is in the subjunctive. But this construction is practically confined to business correspondence or rather affected journalism:

Les agradeceríamos comunicasen a su sucursal de Sevilla . . .	we would be obliged if you would inform your Seville branch . . .
Les rogamos nos comuniquen qué nuevas medidas hemos de tomar en el asunto	please let us know what further steps we should take in the matter
No importa le tilden de bufón (Popular press, Spain)	it doesn't matter if they dub him a clown

Such omission is best avoided by the foreign student.

(b)   In relative clauses introduced by *que*, so as to avoid too many *ques*. This is probably confined to written language:

Desde este punto de vista, que pienso comparten muchos españoles	from this point of view, which I think many Spaniards share
Me contestó con una serie de argumentos que supongo están de moda hoy día	she replied with a series of arguments which I suppose are fashionable nowadays

27.4.7 Replacement of subordinating *que* by an infinitive

For a discussion of sentences like *dice estar enferma* (for *dice que está enferma*) see 17.2.

27.4.8 Miscellaneous examples of *que*

The bracket indicates that the *que* is optional:

Qué bien (que) lo hemos pasado (two *que*s sound uneducated)	what a nice time we've had
. . . y él habla que habla (colloquial)	and he kept talking away . . .
Yo venga a pedirle el divorcio y él que no	I kept on asking him for a divorce and he wouldn't have it/kept saying no

27.5 Causal conjunctions

The most common are:

porque	because	*ya que*	since
como	since, as	*puesto que*	since
pues	for (= 'because')	*en vista de que*	in view of the fact that

27.5.1 *Porque*

Porque means 'because', *por qué*, spelt and pronounced differently, means 'why'. *El porqué* means 'the reason why'. *Porque* may also be found as an optional alternative to *para que* after those words which allow *por* (see the section on *por* and *para* 28.14):

Hemos hecho un esfuerzo enorme porque los demás tengan comida suficiente	we have made an enormous effort in order that the rest should have sufficient food

Porque may require the subjunctive. See 16.4.3b.

Note *Por* is intimately associated with the idea of cause, e.g. *te lo mereces, por tonto* 'serves you right for being stupid', *se perdieron por no haber comprado un mapa* 'they got lost as a result of not having bought a map'. See 28.14.4a for more examples.

27.5.2 *Como, ya que, puesto que, que, en vista de que*

All of these may translate 'since'. *Que* is discussed under 27.4.4b. When it means 'since', *como* can only appear at the head of the sentence, perhaps preceded by another conjunction: **no comía como no tenía apetito* 'he didn't eat since he had no appetite' is not Spanish; *como no tenía apetito, no comía* is.

Como/ya que quieres que me vaya me voy	since you want me to go, I'm going
Puesto que quieres que me vaya, me voy	" "
Pero, como yo no sabía qué hacer . . .	but since I didn't know what to do
Luego, como veía que no llegaban . . .	then, since he could see that they were not arriving . . .
La reunión se aplazó en vista de que no vino casi nadie	the meeting was postponed since almost nobody turned up

Note *Como* with the subjunctive translates 'if' in conditional sentences; see 23.5.2.

27.5.3   *Pues*

Pues has numerous uses, but its basic function is probably to show that the words that follow have been inspired by something said just previously, or that the speaker has reflected momentarily before continuing.

(a)   *Pues* meaning 'because'

It should be employed very sparingly as a causal conjunction since, as Gili y Gaya remarks, *caracteriza la redacción entre infantil y adolescente el hallazgo del pues causal como nota que presta al estilo cierto empaque literario y llega a barrer la conjunción porque. Esta fase suele durar poco . . .* (*Estudios de lenguaje infantil*, 15).

Pues may thus be an elegant written variation on *porque* in the hands of a stylist, but non-natives should stick to *porque*:

La voz no se sabe si es femenina o de hombre, pues es aguda, verdaderamente penetrante (Arguedas, Peru)	you can't tell whether the voice is a woman's or a man's, for it is high-pitched, truly piercing
. . . podría suceder que la especie humana fuese incapaz de soportar los catastróficos cambios del mundo contemporáneo. Pues estos cambios son tan terribles, tan profundos y sobre todo tan vertiginosos, que aquellos que provocaron la desaparición de los reptiles resultan insignificantes (E. Sabato, Arg.)	it could happen that the human species may be unable to stand the catastrophic changes in the modern world. For these changes are so terrible, so profound and, above all, so vertiginous, that those which brought about the disappearance of the reptiles appear insignificant

(b)   'In that case . . .'

No queremos comer ahora. Pues, cuando ustedes quieran . . .	we don't want to eat now. In that case, when you like . . .
No quiero estar aquí. Pues vete	I don't want to be here. Go away then.

(c)   Like the English 'well', it may downtone an answer to a question, adding a modest or tentative note, or perhaps showing that the speaker has reflected a moment before answering:

¿En qué situación se encuentran las negociaciones entre los dos gobiernos? Pues, el hecho es que no hay negociaciones	What is the state of the negotiations between the two governments? Well, the fact is there are no negotiations
¿Quiénes estaban? Pues . . . Manuel, Antonio, Mariluz . . .	Who was there? Er . . . Manuel, Antonio, Mariluz . . .

(d)   It may add emphasis or a note of contradiction:

Yo creía que estaba enfermo. Pues no	I thought he was ill. Well he isn't
No, si ya me figuro dónde está ¡Pues me va a oír! (Buero Vallejo, dialogue)	No, I can well imagine where she is. Well, she's going to hear what I've got to say!

Notes (i)   In some parts of Latin America and Northern Spain, conversation is sprinkled with *pues*: *oye pues, vámonos pues*, etc.

(ii)   Students of French should not confuse *pues* with *puis* which means *después, entonces* and *luego*.

27.5.4 *Luego* or *entonces?*
Both these words double as adverbs and conjunctions. They occasionally coincide in meaning, but foreigners confuse them.

(a) As time words, *entonces* means 'at that moment', whereas *luego* means 'later on'. *Luego* in this sense is stressed: *luego viene* 'he's coming later'. If the *luego* is not stressed here, it means 'so'/'in that case':

Abrí la puerta, y entonces me di cuenta de lo que había pasado (*luego* here = *después*)	I opened the door, and then realized what had happened
Entonces supe que Mario había mentido (*luego* = 'later on')	I realized then that Mario had lied
Desde entonces he sido feliz	from that time on I have been happy
Recuerdo que los cines de entonces siempre apestaban a agua de colonia	I remember that cinemas at that time always stank of Eau de Cologne
el entonces catedrático de griego	the professor of Greek at that time/ the then professor of Greek
Gary Hart derrotó al hasta entonces favorito demócrata Walter Mondale	Gary Hart defeated the until then democrat favourite Walter Mondale
¿Quién es? Te lo diré luego	who is it? I'll tell you later
Lo haré luego	I'll do it later
hasta luego	see you later
(cf. *hasta ahora*, 'see you in a minute')	
Según dice mamá, que luego estuvo seis años liada con Tey . . . (J. Marsé)	according to mother, who later on was involved with Tey for six years

Note Compare *luego de hacerlo* = *después de hacerlo* 'after doing it'.

(b) *Entonces* may mean 'in that case' and *luego* may mean 'therefore', and the two words may coincide in meaning in some contexts. In this meaning *luego* is not stressed:

En Madrid hace 40 grados, en Seville 38. Entonces hace más calor en Madrid que en Sevilla (or *Luego, hace . . .*)	in Madrid it's 40 degrees, in Seville 38. In that case it's hotter in Madrid than in Seville
Es . . . mi secreto. Entonces ya me lo contarás. Los secretos siempre se cuentan (Buero Vallejo, dialogue, *luego* not possible)	'It's my secret'. 'Then you'll soon tell me. Secrets always get told'
Pienso luego existo (set phrase)	I think therefore I am

27.5.5 Other way of expressing 'then' (adverb of time):
The following words also convey the idea of 'then':
   después, 'after', *acto seguido* 'next/immediately after', *a continuación* 'next/immediately after', *en seguida* 'immediately afterwards'.

27.6 Concession

The main ways of introducing a concession are:

aunque/bien que/y eso que/así/ aun cuando	although/even though/even in the event that

a pesar de que/pese a que*/por más	despite the fact that
que/a despecho de que*	
por mucho que	however much
no obstante que*/sin embargo de que*	notwithstanding the fact that

Asterisked forms are typical of literary language.

All of these, except *y eso que*, may appear with the subjunctive and are discussed at 16.4.8.

27.6.1   *Y eso que*

Y eso que is stylistically informal and does not take the subjunctive. It can only refer to events which are realities, i.e. it means 'despite the fact that': *no la reconocí, y eso que la había visto dos días antes* 'I didn't recognize her although I'd seen her two days before':

Lo primero que hice fue darme cuenta de *que el terrón no estaba a la vista y eso* *que lo había visto saltar hasta los* *zapatos* (Cortázar, Arg., dialogue)	the first thing I did was realize the sugar lump was out of sight, even though I'd seen it bounce down to my shoes
Y eso que devolvió de forma increíble *varias bolas* (*El País*)	despite the fact that he made some incredible returns (in tennis)

27.7   *Incluso, aun, hasta*

These all mean 'even'. *Aun*, in this sense, is written without an accent: *aún* means *todavía* 'still', and has a stressed *ú*.

Incluso/hasta/aun crudos me gustan	I like them (masc.) even (when they're) raw
Incluso si/aun si viene tarde, la *esperaré*	even if she comes late I'll wait for her

Note   Another construction occurs occasionally:

Cansado como estaba, ayudó a su madre *a hacerlo*	tired as he was, he helped his mother do it

Also, more colloquially, *incluso cansado como estaba* or *aun cansado como estaba*. Also *aun estando/incluso estando tan cansado como estaba . . .*

27.8   Condition and exception

The chief conjunctions of condition and exception are:

   (a)   Condition (all require the subjunctive and are discussed under 16.4.7):

con tal (de) que	as long as/provided that
a condición de que	on condition that
bajo (la) condición de que	under the condition that
siempre que	as long as
siempre y cuando	provided always that
mientras no	as long as
como	as long as

   (b)   Exception (all mean 'unless' and are discussed at 16.4.7b):

a menos que	*excepto que/salvo que*

a no ser que	*como no* . . .
fuera de que	*si no* (if not)

27.9 Subordinating conjunctions of purpose and aim

These are typically:

in order that	so that
para que	*de manera que***
porque	*de modo que***
a que	*de forma que***
a fin de que	*no sea/fuera/fuese que* (lest)
con el objeto de que	

All conjunctions of purpose require the subjunctive and are discussed under 16.4.2. Those which are asterisked may also indicate result, and are then followed by the indicative. See 16.4.4 for discussion.

27.10 Subordinating conjunctions of result

Subordinators which express manner can denote either a result or an aim. In the latter case they take the subjunctive. The most common of these are:

de modo que/de manera que/de forma que/así que	so that (i.e. 'in such a way that')
conque . . .	so . . .

These are discussed under 16.4.4, but it should be noted that the phrases *de **tal** modo que*, *de **tal** manera que*, *de **tal** forma que* can only express result:

Gritó de tal modo/manera/forma que todos los vecinos se asomaron a la ventana	he shouted in such a way that all the neighbours leaned out of their windows

27.11 Subordinating conjunctions of time

These include such words and phrases as:

cuando	when		
antes de que	before	*en tanto que*	as long as
apenas	scarcely	*mientras*	while/as long as
no bien	scarcely	*hasta que*	until
después de que	after	*al mismo tiempo que*	at the same time as
así que	as soon as		
en cuanto	as soon as	*a la vez que*	at the same time as
nada más que	as soon as	*a partir del momento en que*	from the moment that
tan pronto como	as soon as		
una vez que	once/as soon as	*cada vez que*	every time that
siempre que	whenever/as long as	*a poco de que*	shortly after
		al poco rato de que	shortly after

All of these require the subjunctive in certain circumstances and are discussed under 16.4.6.

28 Prepositions

The simple prepositions are usually held to be:

a	*de*	*hacia*	*según*
ante	*desde*	*hasta*	*sin*
bajo	*durante*	*mediante*	*sobre*
con	*en*	*para*	*tras*
contra	*entre*	*por*	

Most of these may combine with other words to form prepositional phrases such as *debajo de, frente a, con motivo de, a razón de,* etc., a class so numerous that they cannot be discussed here and must be sought in a good dictionary.

Prepositional usage is more subject than other areas of syntax to the vagaries of linguistic change, and the whole subject is plagued with quibbles and doubts. In this chapter prepositions are treated in alphabetical order and special emphasis has been given to aspects of prepositional usage which are likely to be unfamiliar to English speakers.

28.1 *A*

This ubiquitous preposition has many uses. Apart from problems with personal *a*, which is discussed in chapter 20, English speakers are prone to use it wrongly in translating phrases like 'at the dentist's' 'at Cambridge', 'at the station'. See **(c)** for discussion.

(a) Motion, TO, AT, UP, DOWN, etc.

Almost any verb of motion is likely to be followed by *a*. As a result its meaning includes 'on', 'into', 'onto', 'up', as well as 'to' and 'at'.

Por fin llegaron a Managua	they finally got to Managua
Fui a/para que me diera hora	I went to make an appointment
Bajó al sótano	he went down to the basement
Se acercó al buzón	he approached the letter box
Me subí al coche/al tren	I got in the car/on the train
El gato se subió a un árbol	the cat ran up a tree
Salté a un autobús	I jumped on a bus
Lanzaban piedras a/contra las ventanas	they were throwing stones at the windows
Arrojó la espada al aire	he hurled the sword into the air
Entró a/para saludarnos	he came in to say hullo to us
Salieron a/para dar batalla	they went out to do battle
Ha venido a/para/por hablar con usted	he's come to talk to you

Lo pegó al/en el sobre	she stuck it on the envelope
Cuélgaselo al cuello	hang it round his neck
(cf. *cuélgalo en la pared*	hang it on the wall)
Cayó al suelo/al mar	it fell to the ground, into the sea
Se tiró al vacío	he threw himself into the void
una expedición a Marte	an expedition to Mars
salida a la calle	way out to the street
tiro al blanco	target shooting

Notes (i)   *A* is omitted after verbs of motion before *aquí, acá, ahí, allí, allá*:

Ven aquí/ven acá	come here
Ven para acá	come here
Allá voy/voy para allá	I'm going there

(ii)   Cf. Spain *entrar en el cuarto*, SA *entró al cuarto* 'he entered the room', although *entrar a* is also heard in Spain. The noun everywhere takes *a*: *entrada a la galería* 'entrance to the gallery'.

Spain also prefers *en* with *penetrar*, *ingresar* 'to join (club, etc.)', *introducir* 'to insert', but the use of *a* is widespread in SA, even in writing, cf. *ingresa como adepto laico a la orden* (Borges) 'he entered (historic present) the order as a lay follower'.

(iii)   *Para* is also found colloquially after *ir*: *voy para Lugo* 'I'm making for Lugo'.

(b)   After verbs of giving, sending, informing, etc.

Dáselo a papá	give it to father
Le envió cien dólares a su hijo	he sent his son $100
Le dejó su finca a su yerno	he left his country estate to his son-in-law
Comunicaremos los datos a los aseguradores	we shall inform the insurers of the details

etc.

Note   For the use of the redundant pronoun in the first three of the foregoing examples, see 11.14.2.

(c)   Place (static)

The use of *a* to denote 'at' or 'in' a place is very limited in Spanish. English-speakers – particularly those who know French, German or Italian – must avoid the use of *a* in sentences like *estoy haciendo mis estudios en Cambridge* 'I'm studying *at* Cambridge', *te esperaré en la estación* 'I'll wait for you *at* the station (*à la gare, am Bahnhof*, etc.), *vive en Londres* = *il habite à Londres*, etc. Apart from set phrases like *al lado de* 'at the side of', *a la luz de* 'in the light of', *a* can only be used with a few nouns like *vuelta*, 'turn', *salida* 'exit', *entrada* 'entrance' which denote actions or moments in time rather than places. Thus *os esperaré a la salida* is best thought of as 'I'll wait for you on the way out' rather than 'at the exit', which is *en la salida*.

In phrases like *estaba asomado a la ventana* 'he was leaning in/out of the window', *asomar* is a verb of motion: *estaba en la ventana* is, however, safer than *estaba a la ventana* 'he was at the window'.

Similarly, *fue a estudiar a París* is only a variant of *fue a París a estudiar* 'he went to Paris to study': it does not mean 'he went to study *at* Paris' – . . . *en París*.

A is used to translate 'at' in a number of situations involving close proximity to an object, e.g. *a la barra* 'at the bar', *a la mesa* 'at table' (i.e. 'at mealtime'); but note *se sienta en una mesa de la calle y pide una cerveza* 'he sits down *at* a table in the street and asks for a beer' (Cortázar, Arg.).

Vivo a la vuelta	I live round the corner
a orillas del mar	on the sea shore
Oí pasos a mi espalda	I heard footsteps at my back
Nuestra anfitriona estaba sentada a mi lado	our hostess was sitting at my side
(cf. *la suerte estaba de mi lado*, 'luck was on my side')	
Se pasa horas sentado al ordenador	he spends hours sitting at the computer
Se arrodilló a los pies de la Virgen	he knelt at the feet of the Virgin
Está con el agua al cuello	he's up to his neck (in troubles: *hasta* implies real water)
a la izquierda/derecha de	to the left/right of
a lo lejos/en la distancia	in the distance
Se sentaron al sol/a la luz/al calor del fuego/a la sombra/al amparo de un roble	they sat in the sun/light/warmth of the fire/shade/in the shelter of an oak

Compare:

Espérame en la parada del autobús	wait for me at the bus stop
Estaba parado en un semáforo	he was waiting at a traffic light
Mario está en el banco	Mario is at/in the bank
Los niños están en el colegio	the children are in/at school
(cf. *mi hijo todavía no va al colegio*)	my son isn't at school yet (i.e. doesn't go yet)
La vi en la puerta de la iglesia	I saw her at the church door

Notes **(i)** *A la puerta* is good Spanish, but we found that some American informants preferred *en* – but cf. *Morelli habla del napolitano que se pasó años sentado a la puerta de su casa . . .* (Cortázar, Arg.) 'Morelli speaks of the Neapolitan who spent years sitting at the door of his house . . .'.

(ii) Spanish thus has no prepositions which can differentiate 'he's at the hospital' and 'he's in (the) hospital': verbs are used instead – *ha ido al hospital* and *está en el hospital*.

(d) Manner (adverbial phrases of manner with *a* are innumerable:)

a pie/a mano/a lápiz	on foot/by hand/in pencil
a golpes/a tiros/a patadas	with blows/by shooting/with kicks
Pedía socorro a gritos	he was shouting for help
un documento escrito a máquina	a typed document
El servicio es a voluntad del cliente	service charge at the customer's discretion
Las patatas están a punto	the potatoes are done
Le cortaron el pelo al rape	they cropped his hair short
Estoy a dieta	I'm on a diet
a la buena de Dios	any old how/willy-nilly
a oscuras/a la luz del día	in the dark/by daylight
La carpa se puede asar a la parrilla	carp may be grilled
Estaba vestido a la inglesa	he was dressed English-style

etc.

Note   The curious construction with *a* found in the phrase *sois dos a ganar* 'there are two of you earning' may perhaps be included under this heading.

(e)   In certain time phrases

A denotes arrival at a specific point in time: *al año siguiente* implies 'on the arrival of the following year', but *en 1946* implies 'during 1946'.

It is particularly common in the construction *al* + infinitive where it means 'on . . .-ing', e.g. *al ver* 'on seeing', *al volverse* 'as he turned round/back':

a las diez/a medianoche	at 10 o'clock/at midnight
Se cansa a los cinco minutos	he gets tired after five minutes
Al año de que le tocara la lotería se le había acabado el dinero (see 14.8.1)	a year after winning the lottery his money was finished
Se casaron a los veinte años	they got married at the age of twenty
(Se casaron con veinte años)	
al día siguiente/al otro día	on the following day
a la mañana siguiente	the following morning
a la caída de la noche/al alba	at nightfall/at dawn
al mismo tiempo	at the same time
A su recepción pagaré la cantidad estipulada	on receipt I shall pay the stipulated amount
a su regreso, a su llegada	on his return, on his arrival
Estamos a miércoles/a quince	it's Wednesday/the fifteenth
tres veces al/por día	three times a day
Se enfada a/por la menor provocación	he gets angry at the slightest provocation
Ten cuidado al doblar la esquina	be careful when you turn the corner
Al amanecer ya se habían marchado	they were gone by dawn
Procure inhalar menos al fumar	try to inhale less when smoking

Notes (i)   One can say *a su muerte dividió el reino en tres partes* 'at his death he divided the kingdom into three parts', but only *cuando nació* . . . 'at his birth . . .'.

   (ii)   Note *ya deben estar al llegar* 'they must be about to arrive'.

(f)   To translate 'of' or 'like' after verbs meaning 'smell', 'taste', 'sound', and also after the nouns derived from some of these:

Me suena a cuento chino	it sounds like a tall story to me
Esto sabe a pescado	this tastes of fish
En esta casa huele a quemado	there's a smell of burning in this house
La mantequilla apesta a ajo	the butter reeks of garlic
Había un leve olor a fritura y a crema bronceadora (F. Umbral)	there was a faint smell of frying and suntan cream
La ginebra tiene un sabor a agua de colonia	gin has a taste like Eau de Cologne

(g)   'Fitted with', 'propelled by':

Grammarians reject *a* as a Gallicism in the following constructions, but most of them are normal in ordinary language:

olla a presión	pressure cooker
caldera a/de gas-oil	oil-fired boiler
cocina a/de gas	gas stove

motor a/de dos tiempos	two-stroke motor
un suplemento a color	a colour supplement
(*El País*: also *en color*)	
un avión a/de dos motores	a twin-engined plane
un coche que va a/por metanol	a methanol-powered car

Note   The use of *a* to denote an ingredient is occasionally seen in advertising language, but should not be imitated: *crema bronceadora a lanolina* 'sun-tan cream with Lanoline' (better *con lanolina*).

(h)   Rate, measure, speed, amount, distance:

Se vende a mil pesos el metro	it's on sale at 1000 pesos a metre
¿A cómo están las peras?	how much are the pears?
Volaba a más de dos mil kilómetros por hora	it was flying at more than 2000 km per hour
Compraba tebeos de segunda mano que luego revendía o cambiaba a razón de dos por uno (L. Goytisolo)	he used to buy second-hand comics which he then resold or swapped at the rate of two for one
Está a cinco manzanas (SA *cuadras*) *de aquí*	it's five blocks from here
a montones	in heaps
frutas al por mayor	wholesale fruit
Trabaja a ratos/a veces	he works now and again/sometimes

(i)   It translates 'from' after a number of words with such meanings as 'steal', 'confiscate', 'buy', and after *oír* 'to hear':

Le robaron una sortija a mi tía	they stole a ring from my aunt
Una banda de traficantes de drogas, a los que aprehendieron trece kilos de cocaína (*La Vanguardia*)	a gang of drug peddlars, from whom thirteen kilos of cocaine were confiscated
Le compró un coche a su vecino	he bought a car from his neighbour
La policía se instaló en el piso ocupado al acusado	the police moved into the flat confiscated from the accused
Se lo oí decir a Amparo	I heard Amparo say it
Eso se lo has oído a tu padre	you've heard that from your father

Note also:

Le encontraron cien pesos a tu primo	they found a hundred pesos on your cousin

And similarly verbs such as *quitar* 'take away', *sustraer* 'steal', *confiscar* 'confiscate', *llevarse* 'take away', *sacar* 'to take out/remove', etc. However, *recibir, adquirir, aceptar* take *de*: *aceptar algo de alguien* 'to accept something from someone'.

(j)   Before certain types of direct object (the so-called 'personal *a*', e.g. *vi al gitano* 'I saw the gypsy'). See chapter 20 for detailed discussion.

(k)   After verbs meaning 'begin', 'start', 'get ready to . . .':

Rompió a llorar	he burst into tears
Echó a correr	he broke into a run
El cielo empezaba a despejarse	the sky was beginning to clear

and similarly after *comenzar, ponerse, prepararse, disponerse*. See the chapter on the infinitive for further discussion.

(l) After numerous verbs, adjectives and adverbs which must be learned separately:

Tendían emboscadas a las Ninfas (Borges, Arg.)	they laid ambushes for the Nymphs
Aspiraba a hacerse médico	he was aiming to become a doctor
Me iba acostumbrando al ruido	I was getting used to the noise
Tienes que hacerte al trabajo	you have to get used to the work
Prefiero una vida mediocre a ser héroe	I prefer a mediocre life to being a hero
Te ayudaré a apretar las tuercas	I'll help you tighten the nuts
El viejo argumento de que la religión sirve de freno a los instintos	the old argument that religion serves as a curb on the instincts
Se ha convertido al budismo	he's converted to Buddhism
jugar al fútbol/al hockey	to play football/hockey
tocar algo al acordeón/a la guitarra	to play something on the accordeon/guitar
Pudo salvarse agarrándose a/de un árbol	he managed to save himself by clinging to a tree
No hay otro igual a él	there is no other equal to him
Tenía el jersey liado en torno a la cintura	he had his jersey tied round his waist
Es muy parecido al de ayer	it's very much like the one from yesterday

etc.

Note *Acostumbrar a* + infinitive: *la hora en que la gente acostumbra a salir del trabajo* 'the time people usually leave work'.

(m) To link two nouns whenever ambiguity might arise from the use of *de*: *el amor de Dios* = 'God's love' and 'love for God', i.e. *el amor a Dios*. Often either preposition is possible.

A is also often used to link two nouns when a common verbal phrase exists which also requires *a*, e.g. *les tiene miedo a los toros* 'he's afraid of bulls', *su miedo a los toros* 'his fear of bulls':

el abrazo de un padre a su hijo	the embrace that a father gives to his son
el amor a la patria	love for one's home country
La Casa Blanca confirmó el boicot a los Juegos de Moscú (*Cambio16*)	the White House confirmed the boycott of the Moscow Games
el respeto a la autoridad	respect for authority
Lo denunciaron como traidor a/de su clase	they denounced him as a traitor to his class
Insinué algo en el prólogo al libro de Lafaye . . . (Octavio Paz: *del* possible)	I hinted something in the prologue to Lafaye's book . . .
Espero que no sea una referencia personal a mí	I hope it's not a personal reference to me
El culto al sol tendría sus ventajas	sun-worship would have its advantages
Es un insulto al/para/contra el buen nombre de nuestra compañía	it's a slur on our company's good name
Organizaron una manifestación para reivindicar su derecho al voto	they organized a demonstration to demand their right to vote
El departamento se encargará de la protección a/de la carretera	the department will take over responsibility for protecting roads
El ataque a la ciudad costó muchas vidas	the attack on the city cost many lives

28.2 *Ante*

'Before' (i.e. 'in front of') or 'in the presence of', and like its English equivalent it can, in literary usage, have a spatial meaning, 'facing'/'in front of'; *frente a* or *delante de* are used in ordinary language. *Delante de* makes clear that position rather than 'presence' is implied, cf. *justificarse ante Dios* 'to justify oneself before God', but *arrodillarse delante de la Virgen* 'to kneel before (a statue of) the Virgin'.

Ante is very common in the figurative meaning of 'faced with', 'in the face of'. It must not be confused with the entirely separate word *antes* 'before' (in time):

El taxi paró ante/frente a/delante de la casa	the taxi stopped in front of the house
Ante mí/frente a mí/delante de mí se elevaba una enorme torre	before me there rose an enormous tower
Se sentía nervioso al comparecer ante el tribunal	he felt nervous on appearing before the court
ante este dilema . . .	faced with this dilemma . . .
ante tamaño insulto . . .	in the face of such an insult . . .
Ante tantas posibilidades, no sabía cuál escoger	faced with so many possibilities, he didn't know which to choose
Ante todo, quisiera agradecer al organizador . . .	above all, I would like to thank the organizer . . .

Note   *Frente a* for *ante* in phrases like *frente a estos problemas* seems to be spreading, but for some it still sounds like 'in front of these problems'.

28.3 *Bajo*

'Beneath' or 'under'. It may be a literary alternative to *debajo de* 'underneath', but in this sense it is spatially less specific (cf. 'under' and 'underneath'): *se resguardaron bajo un haya* 'they sheltered under/beneath a beech tree' but *enterró el botín debajo de un roble* 'he buried the loot underneath (i.e. under the roots of) an oak tree'.

Carnicer notes that for those educated speakers who use *bajo*, the difference is that it implies 'a good distance under' or 'under but not close to or touching' – *bajo una masa de nubes* 'under a mass of clouds', *no me quedo ni un minuto más bajo este techo* 'I'm not staying one more minute under this roof' – whereas *debajo de* implies 'underneath and close to whatever is on top': *hay mucho polvo debajo de la alfombra* 'there's a lot of dust underneath the carpet'.

Thus ?*el perro está bajo la silla* 'the dog's beneath the chair' sounds affected in both languages: *debajo de la silla* 'under(neath) the chair'.

Bajo must be used in the figurative sense of 'under' in phrases like *bajo el gobierno de* 'under the government of', *bajo ciertas condiciones* 'under certain conditions', etc.

Yo prefiero sentarme bajo el (or *al*) *sol*	I prefer to sit in the sun

bajo las estrellas/la lluvia/un cielo azul, etc.	beneath the stars/in the rain/beneath a blue sky
bajo tierra	underground
(or *debajo de la tierra*)	
bajo la monarquía/la república/el socialismo	under the monarchy/republic/socialism, etc.
La temperatura alcanzó treinta bajo cero	the temperature reached thirty below zero
bajo tantos golpes . . .	under so many blows . . .
bajo los efectos de la anestesia	under the effects of the anaesthetic
bajo juramento	under oath
bajo pena de muerte	on pain of death
Actuaron bajo órdenes	they acted under orders

28.4 *Cabe*

An archaic or rustic equivalent of *junto a*, *cerca de* 'by/near' occasionally still found in Spanish-American authors.

28.5 *Con*

(a) In many contexts it coincides with the English 'with', but is used more widely than the latter.

Sentences like 'the boy with the blue Mercedes' require *de*: *el chico del Mercedes azul*. But if 'wearing' or 'carrying' are implied, *con* is usual, unless the article is habitually associated with the person: cf. *nunca te he visto con gafas* 'I've never seen you with glasses', but *¿te acuerdas del viejo del impermeable que venía todos los días?* 'do you remember the old man with/in the raincoat who used to come every day?'.

Fui a la reunión con Niso	I went to the meeting with Niso
Llegaron dos policías con perros	two policemen with dogs arrived
Yo sí te he visto con camisa de seda	*I* have seen you in a silk shirt
Está escrito con/a lápiz	it's written with a/in pencil
No podía quitarlo con una llave normal	I couldn't get it off with a normal spanner
Con lo enferma que está . . .	and with her being so ill . . .
Nos trató con mucha cortesía	he treated us with much courtesy
té con miel/café con leche	tea with honey/coffee with milk
Se produjeron varios enfrentamientos con la policía	there were several clashes with the police
Se levantó con el sol	he got up with the sun
con la llegada del otoño	with the arrival of autumn
etc.	

Notes (i) *Con* cannot be used in combination with the nominalizer *el*: Contrast *el chico con la americana blanca – el de la americana blanca* 'the boy with/in the white jacket' – 'the one with/in the white jacket'. Phrases like **el con gafas* are not Spanish.

(ii) *Con* differs from *a* in phrases like *con la llegada de la primavera* 'with the arrival of spring' in that *a la llegada* implies 'at the moment of the arrival of', which is too punctual for the onset of a season. Compare:

| Todos se marcharon a la llegada de la policía | they all left on the arrival of the police |
| Con la llegada de Pepe, todo empezó a cambiar | with Pepe's arrival, everything began to change |

(b)   After phrases meaning 'to show an attitude towards' *con* alternates with *para con*, much as 'with' alternates with 'towards':

| Es muy cariñoso (para) con su mujer | he's very affectionate towards his wife |
| Su amabilidad es igual (para) con todos (from Luque Durán (1973)) | his kindness is the same towards all |

But if the object of the attitude does not benefit by it, *para* is not used:

Es muy crítico con su hijo	he's very critical with/towards his son
Eres muy cruel con tu novia	you're very cruel to your girlfriend
Es poco confiado con sus colegas	he's not very sure with his colleagues

(c)   It may be used with expressions signifying meeting, encounter, collision, 'facing up to', 'struggle with', etc.

Me encontré/tropecé hoy con tu jefe	I ran into/met your boss today
Ha vuelto con su marido (*ha vuelto *a* is not used in this sense)	she's gone back to her husband (or 'she's come back with her husband')
Me tengo que ver con Carmen para hablar del contrato	I have to see Carmen to talk about the contract
Tengo que vérmelas con el vecino	I'll have to have it out with the neighbour (i.e. have a frank talk with)
Iba en la moto y se dio un golpe con/ contra un poste	he was on his motorbike and crashed into a post
Mi bicicleta rozó con un camión	my bicycle scraped against a lorry
Se enfrentaron con los guerrilleros	they clashed with the guerrillas
Tendremos que enfrentarnos con el problema/enfrentar el problema	we'll have to face up to the problem
Los ingleses suelen dudar con el subjuntivo	English people usually hesitate over the subjunctive
Estamos luchando con el problema del paro	we're struggling with the problem of unemployment
Está regañado con sus tíos	he's fallen out with his uncle and aunt

(d)   It may – strangely to Anglophones – mean 'containing':

un vaso con/de agua, un saco con/ de patatas (From Luque Durán)	a glass of water/sack of potatoes
Llevaba una cesta con pan, huevos, uvas y vino	he was carrying a basket of bread, eggs, grapes and wine
(*de* is not possible here)	
una jeringa con morfina	a syringe full of morphine

Note   This use eliminates any ambiguity caused by *de*, which either means 'full of' – *una cesta de huevos* is 'a basketful of eggs' and it cannot contain anything else – or may denote the container but not the contents, cf. *una botella de coñac* 'a bottle of cognac' or 'a cognac bottle'; but *una botella con coñac* 'a bottle with cognac in'. Compare *he visto un saco de patatas al entrar* 'I saw a sack of potatoes as I was coming in' and *he visto un saco con patatas al entrar* 'I saw a sack with potatoes in as I was coming in': the former could mean a potato sack.

(e) 'Despite' or some other concessive phrase (*a pesar de* is often equivalent):

Con/a pesar de todos sus esfuerzos, nunca llegó a coronel	despite/for all his efforts, he never made the rank of colonel
Con ser inteligente y rico nunca llegó a nada	despite being intelligent and rich, he never came to anything
Con todo, la vida no es tan terrible	despite everything, life isn't so awful
Con lo guapa que estarías con el pelo recogido . . .	to think how attractive you'd look if you had your hair up . . .

But *con* does not seem to be used in this sense with verbs which denote actions:

Incluso tomando seis aspirinas no se le quitaba el dolor	even despite his taking six aspirins, the pain didn't go away

(f) *Con* plus an infinitive may, like the gerund, have a conditional sense:

Con hacer (or Haciendo) lo que yo os digo, todo irá bien	provided you (pl.) do what I say everything will go well
Con tener un poco más de suerte me hubiera hecho rico	if I'd had a bit more luck I'd have got rich
Sólo con pulsar una tecla el ordenador almacena los datos	if you simply press a key the computer stores the data

(g) It may, like the gerund, mean 'as a result of':

Se nos ha ido la tarde con hablar/ hablando tanto	the afternoon's gone with all this talking
No conseguirás nada con tratarme/ tratándome de esa manera	you'll achieve nothing by treating me that way
Con cambiar/cambiando de empleo no resuelves nada	you'll solve nothing by changing jobs

(h) It may indicate the cause or origin of a condition:

Estamos muy entusiasmados/ilusionados con la perspectiva de un nuevo gobierno	we're very excited about the prospect of a new government
Está muy preocupado con sus negocios	he's very worried about his business affairs

Compare *me preocupo por ellos* 'I worry about them', and *me preocupo de hacer todo lo posible* 'I take care to do everything possible'.

Se puso enfermo con malaria (or *enfermó de malaria*)	he fell ill with/from malaria
Se mareó con el vaivén del tren	he felt sick because of the swaying of the train
Me contento con lo que tengo	I content myself with what I have
Se alegró con/de la noticia del nacimiento de su nieto	he cheered up at the news of his grandson's birth

(i) Miscellaneous examples of *con* used in ways unfamiliar to English speakers:

Hace años que él se escribe con ella	he and she have been writing to one another for years
Murió con más de setenta años	he died aged more than seventy
Usted fue el último que lo vio con vida	you were the last one to see him alive

Ha vuelto con su marido	she's gone back to her husband
Voy a verme con ella esta noche	I'm seeing her tonight

28.6   *Contra*

A close equivalent of 'against', but it may mean 'at' after verbs meaning firing, throwing, launching, etc.

En contra de is an equivalent of *contra* when the latter means 'in opposition to'. Use of a possessive instead of a prepositional pronoun is permitted with *en contra*: *se están organizando en contra tuya/en contra de ti* 'they're organizing themselves against you'.

El régimen ha organizado una campaña contra/en contra de la corrupción	the regime has organized a campaign against corruption
Contra lo que creen algunos, yo no soy pesimista	despite/to the contrary of what some believe, I am not a pessimist
Apoya tu pala contra el árbol	lean your spade against the tree
En ese caso optarían por lanzar un misil contra el enemigo	in that case they would opt for launching a missile at the enemy
Lanzó la piedra contra el árbol (from Luque Durán)	he threw the stone at the tree (intending to strike it)
(cf. *la lanzó al árbol*	he threw it up at the tree (e.g. a lasso or rope))
Me di cuenta de que tiraban contra nosotros	I realized they were firing on/at us
Conviene inyectarse contra la hepatitis antes de viajar a esas regiones	it's a good idea to get immunized against/ for hepatitis before travelling to those regions
(not *inyectarse *para . . .*)	
Navegábamos contra viento y marea	we were sailing against wind and tide
Hay que dejar un depósito contra el valor del coche (or *por el coche . . .*)	you have to leave a deposit against the value of the car

Note   The use of *contra* for *cuanto* in such phrases as *cuanto más trabajas, más te dan* 'the more you work, the more they give you', though heard in some Latin-American dialects, should be avoided. See 5.7 for details.

28.7   *De*

28.7.1   General uses

Section **(a)** covers those uses of *de* which correspond to the English 'of' or to the 'Saxon genitive', *'s*. These sentences should give English speakers no great trouble. French speakers must resist the temptation to replace *de* by *a*: *c'est à vous?* = *¿es de usted?* 'is it yours?'.

  (a)   'Of', 'belonging to':

el primer ministro de Tailandia	The prime minister of Thailand
los discos de mi primo	my cousin's records
la matrícula del coche	the car number-plate
las bisagras de la puerta	the hinges of/on the door
el primero/uno de mayo	the first of May

Ese attaché es del profesor	that briefcase is the teacher's
¿De quién es esto?	whose is this?

(b) Origin:

See 28.7.5 for the difference between *de* and *desde*.

Soy de México	I'm from Mexico
un ser de otro planeta	a being from another planet
un vino de solera	a vintage wine
Este manuscrito es de la Biblioteca Nacional	this manuscript is from the National Library
una oda del siglo quince	a fifteenth-century ode
un dolor de cabeza	a headache

etc.

Notes (i) English speakers tend to use the preposition *en* to denote belonging to or originating from a place: *los hombres de Grecia* 'the men **in** Greece' (= Greek men); *las flores de los Andes* 'the flowers **in** (= of) the Andes':

Las colinas de tierra adentro son más verdes	the hills inland are greener

The temptation is particularly strong after a superlative: *éste es el mejor restaurante de Madrid* 'this is the best restaurant in Madrid'; *el más antiguo monumento del Perú* 'the most ancient monument in Peru'; *el mejor momento de mi vida* 'the best moment in/of my life'.

(ii) *Viene de Toledo* normally only means 'he's coming from Toledo': *es de Toledo* = 'he's from Toledo'.

(c) 'Made of', 'consisting of':

una estatua de oro macizo	a solid gold statue
un manuscrito de pergamino	a parchment manuscript
una novela de ciencia-ficción	a science-fiction novel
Tiene una voluntad de hierro	she has an iron will
Este yogur es de leche de oveja	this is ewe's-milk yoghurt

etc.

(d) 'About' in the sense of 'concerning':

It is doubtful whether *de* often means 'concerning', except after certain verbs like *hablar, quejarse de, protestar* : *una carta de amor* 'a love letter' is very different from *una carta sobre amor* 'a letter about love'.

De, when it is used to mean 'about' implies something less formal than *sobre*, which is closer to 'on the subject of':

No quiero hablar de mis problemas personales	I don't want to talk about my personal problems
Esta noche va a hablar sobre problemas personales	tonight he's talking on/about 'personal problems'
Es que yo quería hablar con usted de mi salario (salario = 'salary' in SA)	actually I wanted to talk to you about my wages
No hace más que quejarse de que tiene demasiado trabajo	all he does is moan about having too much work
¿De qué va la cosa?	what's it all about?

(e) 'Costing':

Las naranjas de cien pesos son las mejores	the 100-peso oranges are the best
Han comprado una casa de un millón de libras	they've bought a million-pound house

(f)   Emotions arising from something:

Tengo miedo del agua	I'm afraid of the water
(see note)	
el respeto de/a los derechos humanos	respect for human rights
Me da pena de él	I'm sorry for him
Yo también experimenté la obsesión de/por la forma literaria	I also experienced the obsession for literary form

And similarly *el horror de/a/hacia una cosa* 'horror towards/about a thing'.

However, after *sentir, experimentar* and similar verbs the following words take *por* or *hacia*: *compasión* 'pity', *simpatía* 'affection'/'liking', *admiración* 'admiration', *desprecio* 'contempt', *odio* 'hatred', etc.

Note   Also *le tengo miedo al agua, tengo miedo de/le tengo miedo a todo.* See 28.1, item (m).

(g)   In certain adverbial phrases of manner:

Lo escribió de manera que nadie pudiera leerlo	she wrote it in such a way that no one would be able to read it
Me puse a pensar de qué modo podría ayudarlos	I set about thinking how I could help them
Le ha venido de perlas	it suited him just right
Sólo he estado en Sevilla de paso	I've only been in Seville on the way to somewhere else
Intentaron entrar de balde	they tried to get in for free
Sale todos los sábados de juerga	he goes out 'on the town' every Saturday
Estuvimos de bromas hasta las tres de la mañana	we were up until three telling jokes/larking about

etc.

(h)   Condition (English 'as', 'in'):
This construction is closely related to the previous one.

De pequeña yo era muy bajita	as a little girl I was very small
Trabajó dos meses de camarero	he worked as a waiter for two months
¿De qué vas al baile? De pastora	what are you going to the ball as? As a shepherdess
Tú aquí estás de más	you're not needed here
Yo de ti/de usted no lo haría (or *yo que tú . . .*)	if I were you I wouldn't do it
Vi a una criada de blanco paseando al niño	I saw a maid in white taking the child for a walk

(i)   To mean 'if'
For *de* plus the infinitive used for *si* in the 'if' clause of a conditional sentence, see 23.5.3.

(j)   Age, measurements:

un hombre de cuarenta años	a man aged forty
un pan de tres días	a three-day old loaf
Esta soga tiene tres metros de largo	this rope is three metres long
En algunos puntos el mar tiene más de seis kilómetros de profundo	in some places the sea is more than six km deep

(k)   *De* is used after certain adjectives before an infinitive – provided the infinitive is not itself followed by an object. Compare:

| *Su conducta es difícil de comprender* | his behaviour is difficult to understand |

and

| *Es difícil comprender su conducta* | it's difficult to understand his behaviour |

See 17.7 for further examples.

(l)   *De* is used after *más* and *menos* before numerals and quantities:

Ha comprado más de tres kilos	he's bought more than three kilos
Hace más de cuarenta grados	the temperature is over 40 degrees
Eran más de las cinco	it was past five o'clock
Los cojinetes necesitan menos de medio litro de aceite	the bearings need less than half a litre of oil

See 5.5.1 for further discussion.

(m)   *De* replaces *que* in comparisons involving a clause:

Todo ha sido mucho más fácil de lo que se temía	everything has been easier than was feared
Es más listo de lo que parece	he's cleverer than he seems
No uses más de los que necesites	don't use more than those you need

See 5.5.2 for discussion.

(n)   *De* alternates with *para* in sentences of the type 'his attitude is not to be copied', 'his stories aren't to be believed':

| *Sus excusas no son de/para creer* | his excuses aren't to be believed |
| *Su habilidad no es de/para subestimar* | his cleverness is not be underestimated |

(o)   After certain verbs meaning 'to take by', 'seize by', 'pull on', etc.

La cogió de la mano	he took her by the hand
Me tiraba de la manga	he was pulling on my sleeve
El profesor le asió de una oreja	the teacher took him by an ear

(p)   To denote the agent in some types of passive construction:

| *acompañado de su esposa* | accompanied by his wife |

See 28.14.4b for discussion.

(q)   In certain set time phrases:

| *de día/de noche* | by day/by night |
| *Se levantó muy de mañana* | he got up very early in the morning |

(r)   In construction of the type 'poor you', 'that fool John', etc.

Tendrás que habértelas con el gandul de Fulano	you'll have to tackle that lay-about so-and-so
¿Sabes lo que ha hecho la pobre de su mujer?	do you know what his poor wife has done?
pobre de ti . . .	poor you . . .

(s)   Partitive *de*

De is occasionally used before adjectives – particularly demonstrative adjectives – to mean 'some of', 'one of': *hay de todo* 'there is a bit of everything':

Puedes comprar de todo	you can buy a little of everything
Tráiganos de ese vino que nos sirvió ayer	bring us some of that wine you served us yesterday
Él todavía necesitaba de otras distracciones	he still needed other amusements
María era de esas personas que nunca se sabe cuándo están diciendo la verdad	Maria was one of those people who you never know when they are telling the truth (lit. translation)
Vive en una casa de ésas	he lives in a house like those

28.7.2   *Deber* or *deber de*?

The basic rule is that *deber* implies obligation, and *deber de* assumptions: *debes comer menos* 'you must eat less', *deben de ser las cinco* 'it must be five o'clock'.

In practice this distinction is nowadays blurred, and even the best writers use *deber* for assumptions: *debía ser una criatura de pocos años* (Cortázar, Arg.), 'it must have been a very young child', etc.

The best formulation at the present state of the language seems to be that *deber* is probably always right, but *deber de* should only be used for assumptions:

Debes hacerlo ahora mismo	you've got to do it right now
Debían (de) haber pensado que que estabas enfermo	they must have thought you were ill
En ese caso debe (de) ser verdad	in that case it must be true
etc.	

28.7.3   *De* before *que*

Some verbs, all verbal phrases involving a noun or adjective, and some adverbial phrases, must be followed by *de que* when they introduce a clause:

Se dio cuenta de que ya no llovía	he realized that it was no longer raining

See 27.4.2 for discussion.

28.7.4   *Dequeísmo*

For the popular and spreading tendency to use *de que* instead of *que* after verbs of belief and communication, e.g. **dice de que no viene* for *dice que no viene* 'she says she isn't coming', see 27.4.3. This construction is vehemently repudiated by educated speakers everywhere.

28.7.5   *Desde*, and *de* with the meaning of 'from'

The existence of two Spanish words which both mean 'from' is a source of confusion. Nor is the distinction always strictly observed by native speakers.

Desde stresses the idea of movement or distance more than *de*. It is therefore appropriate when motion 'from' a place requires some unusual effort, or when the point of origin is mentioned but not the destination, as in *os veo desde mi ventana* 'I can see you from my window'. (Formulation from Luque Durán, 1973).

It is freely used in time phrases.

Desde nuestro balcón se divisa la cima de Mulhacén	from our balcony one can make out the summit of Mulhacén
Desde aquí el camino es muy bueno	from here the road is very good
Avanzó desde la puerta con un cuchillo en la mano	he moved forward from the door with a knife in his hand
He venido andando desde el centro: el metro está en huelga	I've walked all the way from the centre: the Metro is on strike

Y entonces una soga lo atrapó desde atrás (Cortázar, Arg.)	then he was caught from behind by a rope
Desde hoy/a partir de hoy tienen que llegar a tiempo	from today you must arrive on time
Desde que ganó las quinielas ya no se habla con sus amigos	since he won the pools he doesn't talk to his friends any more
Los tenemos desde 50 centavos hasta cinco pesos	we have them from 50 centavos to 5 pesos

Notes (i) If *a, hasta* or some other preposition of destination appears, *desde* is often interchangeable with *de*:

De/desde aquí a/hasta el centro las calles son muy estrechas	from here to the centre the roads are very narrow
De/desde aquí a la cima mide diez mil metros	from here to the summit it measures 10,000 metres
Desde/de 1922 a 1942 estuve en Colombia	from 1922 to 1942 I was in Colombia
But	
He estado en Colombia desde 1922	I've been in Colombia since 1922

If no such prepositional phrase of destination occurs, *desde* is usually the safer option, though usage is fickle:

Las partículas subatómicas que llegan desde/de otras galaxias	subatomic particles which arrive from other galaxies
¿Desde dónde estás hablando?	where are you talking from? (e.g. by radio or phone)
Desde entonces no le he vuelto a ver	since then I haven't seen him

(ii) In the following types of sentence only *de* is possible:

Yo soy de Madrid	I'm from Madrid
Las hojas caen ya de los abedules	the leaves are already falling from the birches
Sacó tres diamantes de la bolsa	he took three diamonds from the bag
Pasó de secretario a jefe en tres meses	he went from secretary to boss in three months
Hizo un modelo de un trozo de madera	he made a model from a piece of wood
Del techo pendía una enorme araña de luces	from the ceiling hung an enormous chandelier
Se ha venido de España a vivir en Inglaterra	he's come from Spain to live in England
Sólo la veo de Pascuas a Ramos	I only see her once in a blue moon (lit. 'from Easter to Palm Sunday')

(iii) *Desde ya* is commonly found in the River Plate region with the meaning of 'right away'. *Desde luego* means 'of course' on both continents.

28.8 *Durante*

'During'; 'for' in phrases denoting duration of time. However, as its relation to the verb *durar* 'to last' suggests, it implies a certain length of time – five minutes, an hour, ten days, years, etc. For *un segundo, un instante* or whenever the brevity of a period is emphasized by some word like *sólo* or *solamente*, omission of *durante* or its replacement by *por* (see 28.14.5b) may be called for.

Examples of *durante* and of other phrases denoting duration:

durante aquel mes/año	during that month/year
Durante años no llovió	it didn't rain for years
Trabajó durante años en un supermercado	(s)he worked for years in a supermarket
Hace años que no te he visto	I haven't seen you for years
Hace años que no te veo	" "
Llevo años sin verte	" "
Llevo dos años en este cargo	I've been in this job for two years
He estado dos años en el cargo	" "
Llevaba dos meses en Chile	I'd been in Chile for two months
Había estado dos meses en Chile	" "
¿Cuánto tiempo lleva usted aquí?	how long have you been here?
¿Cuánto tiempo llevaban aquí?	how long had they been here?
Estuvo mirando un momento la puesta del sol	he watched the sunset for a moment
Sólo entraré (por) un segundo	I'll only come in for a minute
Sólo quiero la habitación por dos días	I only want the room for two days

Notes (i) Spanish Americans may use *por* where Peninsular speakers insist on *durante*: see 28.14.5b for discussion.

(ii) English speakers, especially if they are reinforced in the habit by the French *depuis*, often neglect the idiomatic use of *llevar* as the best translation for 'for' in time phrases which denote an action which is or was still in progress, e.g. in sentences like *llevo horas aquí* 'I've been here for hours', *llevábamos años diciéndolo* 'we'd been saying it for years'.

28.9 *En*

As a preposition of place *en* is disconcertingly vague since it combines the meanings of 'in' and 'on' (French *sur* and *dans*), as well as 'at', 'into', 'onto': *en la caja* 'in the box', *en la mesa* 'on/at the table', *está en la comisaría* 'he's in/at the police station'. For the relationship between *en* and 'at' in sentences like 'at the station', 'at Cambridge', see 28.1c.

When it means 'on a horizontal surface', it alternates with *sobre* and, sometimes, with *encima de*. Thus one can say *en/sobre/encima de la mesa* 'on the table', but *mi hijo duerme en mi cama* 'my son sleeps in my bed', since 'inside' is implied.

En may be replaced by *dentro de* 'inside' if clarity or emphasis are required.

(a) As an equivalent of 'in', 'on' or 'at':

Tus camisas están en el cajón	your shirts are in the drawer
Mi pipa estaba en/sobre/encima de la mesa	my pipe was on the table
Cuelga el cuadro en la pared	hang the picture on the wall
Dio unos golpes discretos en la puerta	he tapped discreetly on the door
La llave está en la puerta	the key's in the door
Gasta mucho dinero en juegos de azar	he spends a lot of money on gambling (lit. 'games of chance')
Los empleados estaban sentados en sus mesas (see note (i))	the clerks were sitting at their tables
El agua ha penetrado en las vigas	the water has soaked into the joists

Uno de mis pendientes se ha caído en el agua (see note (ii))	one of my earrings has fallen into the water
La bruja lo transformó en rana	the witch turned him into a frog
Propusieron convertirlo en sanatorio	they suggested turning it into a sanatorium
en otoño/primavera/1924	in autumn/spring/1924
Todavía está en proyecto	it's still at the planning stage
Te da ciento y raya en latín	he's miles better than you in Latin

Notes (i) Compare *se sentó a la mesa* 'he sat down at table' with *siempre se comporta mal en la mesa* 'he always misbehaves at table'. See 28.1c for discussion.

(ii) The example suggests the wearer was already in the water, e.g. swimming. If trajectory down to the water is meant, *a* is more usual: *se tiró al río* 'he jumped into the river', *el avión cayó al mar* 'the plane fell into the sea'.

(iii) *Entrar* and similar verbs take *en* (often *a* in Spanish America, and occasionally in Spain): *entró en el cuarto* 'he entered the room'.

(b) To express the thing by which something else is judged or estimated:

Los daños se han calculado en diez millones de dólares	the damage has been calculated at ten million dollars
El tipo oficial quedó fijado en 151,93 por dólar (*El País*)	the official rate was fixed at 151.93 to the dollar
Lo vendieron en un millón de pesetas	they sold it for a million pesetas
Te tenía en más	I thought higher of you
El progreso logrado en esta investigación es computable en cero	the progress achieved in this investigation can be reckoned as zero
Me lo presupuestaron en cien mil	they gave me an estimate of 100,000 for it
Se nota que es inglés en su manera de hablar	one can tell he's English by the way he talks
Le conocí en el andar	I knew him from the way he walked

(c) In a number of adverbial phrases:

Lo tomaron en serio	they took it seriously
en cueros/en broma/en balde	naked/as a joke/pointlessly
en fila/en seguida (or *enseguida*)	in a row/straight away
Estoy en contra	I'm against

etc.

(d) To mean 'as':

Como is much more usual nowadays in the following sentences:

Hablar de esa manera, en ser superior, es absurdo	to talk like that, as a superior being, is absurd
Os hablo en perito	I'm talking to you as an expert

(e) After a number of common verbs, and in several miscellaneous constructions:

Pensé mucho en usted	I thought of you a lot
Quedamos en vernos a las siete	we agreed to meet at seven
Tardaron cinco semanas en reparar el coche	they took five weeks to mend the car
Vaciló en contestarme	he hesitated before answering me
No dudó en devolvérmelo	he didn't hesitate over giving it back to me
No ayuda en nada	he/she/it's no help at all
La reina abdicó en su hijo	the queen abdicated in favour of her son
Se interesa mucho en la filatelia	he's very interested in stamp collecting
El fue el primero/último en hacerlo	he was the first/last to do it

See 17.1 for remarks on prepositional usage with verbs. (For *en* plus a gerund see 19.2.2).

28.10   *Entre*

Both 'between' and 'among'. *Entre* also has a number of uses unfamiliar to English speakers.

Prepositional pronoun forms are not, nowadays, used after *entre*: *entre Juan y tú recogeréis los papeles* 'you and John will pick up the pieces of paper between you' (not **entre Juan y ti*).

(a)   'Between':

Estábamos entre la espada y la pared	we were between the sword and the wall (i.e. 'we had our backs to the wall')
Cuestan entre mil y dos mil	they cost between one and two thousand
Entre tú/usted y yo . . .	between you and me . . .
Lo terminaron entre María y su hermana	Maria and her sister finished it between them

etc.

Note   The last example is typical of a construction unfamiliar to English speakers: *llenan el pantano entre cuatro ríos* (from Moliner, I, 1146) 'four rivers combine to fill the reservoir', *lo escribieron entre cuatro de ellos* 'four of them wrote it between them'.

(b)   'Among'

It is used with a wider range of nouns than its English equivalent, e.g. *entre la niebla* 'in the mist', *encontraron la sortija entre la arena* 'they found the ring in the sand'.

No pude encontrar el libro entre tantos tomos	I couldn't find the book among so many volumes
Vivió diez años entre los beduinos de Arabia	he lived for ten years among the Bedouins of Arabia
La perdí de vista entre la muchedumbre	I lost sight of her in the crowd
No podía decidir entre tantas posibilidades	I couldn't choose among so many possibilities

etc.

(c)   'Among themselves', 'one from the other'

In the second of these two meanings, *entre* is used in a way unfamiliar to English speakers. It is especially liable to appear with the pronoun *sí* (discussed in detail at 11.5.3):

En casa hablan castellano entre sí (or *ellos*)	at home they speak Spanish among themselves
Los dos hermanos siempre discutían entre sí/ellos por quién tenía que acostarse primero	the two brothers always argued among themselves over who had to go to bed first
Es más fácil que dos personas vivan en armonía cuando se respetan entre sí	it's easier for two people to live in harmony when they respect one another
Los idiomas que se hablan en la India son muy diferentes entre sí	the languages spoken in India differ widely one from another

(d)   It can translate the English phrase 'what with':

Entre los niños y el ruido que hacen los albañiles, me estoy volviendo loca
what with the children and the noise the builders make, I'm going mad

Entre el problema de la inflación y la deuda exterior este país va cuesta abajo
what with the problem of inflation and the foreign debt, this country is going downhill

(e)   In certain phrases, in a way strange to English speakers:

Van como ovejas al matadero, decía entre sí
they're going like lambs to the slaughter, he said to himself

Decía entre mí . . .
I said to myself . . .

El museo está abierto entre semana
the museum is open on weekdays

28.11   *Hacia*

(a)   A close equivalent of 'towards', but rather wider in application since it also translates the English suffix -*ward/-wards:*

El satélite viaja hacia Venus
the satellite is travelling towards Venus

La muchedumbre se dirigía hacia el palacio presidencial
the crowd was making for the presidential palace

Señaló hacia el este
he pointed to the east

Hacia el oeste no había más que dunas
towards the west there was nothing but dunes

La actitud de la EEC hacia tales problemas parece ambigua
the attitude of the EEC towards such problems seems ambiguous

El incidente ocurrió hacia las tres de la tarde
the incident occurred towards three in the afternoon

El coche rodaba hacia atrás
the car was rolling backwards

Se apoyaba hacia delante en un bastón
he was leaning forwards on a stick

In time phrases, *hacia* can usually be replaced by *sobre*, and with dates by *para*: *sobre las tres de la tarde*, 'around 3 p.m.', *para octubre* 'towards/around October'.

(b)   Emotions, attitudes 'towards':

Por, *con* and *para con* are also possible, but not always interchangeable. Deep emotions such as love or hatred prefer *hacia* or *por*; attitudes (e.g. kindness, severity, irritability) prefer *hacia* or *con*.

su profundo amor hacia/por/a todo lo andaluz
his deep love for everything Andalusian

Mostraba una indiferencia total hacia/por las críticas
he displayed total indifference towards criticisms

la simpatía de los insurgentes hacia el modelo cubano
the insurgents' sympathy for the Cuban model

For *para con* see 28.5b.

28.12   *Hasta*

(a)   'As far as', 'until', 'up to':

hasta ahora . . .
until now/up to now

Llegaron hasta el oasis, pero tuvieron que volverse
they got as far as the oasis, but had to turn back

No nos vamos hasta el día trece	we're not leaving until the thirteenth
Siguió leyendo hasta que no había luz	he kept reading until there was no light
Bailaron hasta no poder más	they danced until they were exhausted
Estoy de exámenes hasta la coronilla (or *hasta las narices*)	I've had enough of exams (I'm sick to death of exams)
hasta luego	goodbye/au revoir

(b) *Hasta que no*:

See 21.1.3d for this construction.

(c) As an equivalent of *incluso* 'even':

Hasta llegó a ofrecerles dinero	he even went as far as offering them money
Hasta en Inglaterra hace calor a veces	even in England it's hot sometimes

Note In Mexico, and in neighbouring countries, *hasta* has acquired the meaning of 'not until': *perdona que te llame hasta ahora* (Fuentes, dialogue), 'sorry for not ringing you before now'; *bajamos hasta la Plaza de la Independencia* 'we're not getting off until Independence Square'; *hasta entonces me di cuenta* 'I realized only then' or 'I didn't realize until then'.

28.13 *Mediante*

A close equivalent would be 'by means of' some instrument, argument or device:

Es inútil intentar abolir el abuso del alcohol mediante/por/con decreto	it is useless to try to abolish alcohol abuse by decree
Lograron abrir la caja mediante/con una antorcha de butano	they managed to open the safe by means of a butane torch

28.14 *Para* and *por*

28.14.1 The difference between them

The existence of two prepositions which both sometimes seem to mean 'for' or French *pour* is one of the stumbling blocks of the language. The difference is best learnt from examples and can hardly be stated clearly in the abstract. One basic distinction is that *para* expresses purpose or destination, and *por* cause or motive; the difference is perhaps most clearly visible in the two sentences *hago esto para ti* 'I'm making this for you (to give to you)' and *hago esto por ti* 'I'm doing this because of you/on your behalf'. But such contrasting sentences are rare. English speakers are usually confused by sentences like 'this fence is for the rabbits': since this really means 'because of the rabbits' one must say *esta valla es por los conejos*.

The Spanish Civil Guards' motto *todo por la Patria* 'everything for the home country' exemplifies *por* at its most confusing. It means 'everything (we do is done) for the home country', i.e. 'all our actions are inspired by the mother country', whereas *todo para la Patria* would mean 'everything (we have is) for the home country', i.e. 'we give all our belongings to the home country'.

It is useful to recall that if 'for' can be replaced by 'out of' or 'because' then *por* may be the correct translation, but not *para*: *lo hizo por amor* 'he did it for (out of) love'; *lo hago por el dinero* 'I do it for (because of) the money'.

Historically *para* descends from a combination of Latin *per* and *a* which combined the meanings of the two prepositions and thus superimposed the idea of destination or purpose on the meaning of 'for'. Further examples:

Llevo el abrigo por/a causa de mi madre	I'm wearing this coat because of my mother (she'll be cross/worried if I don't)
Llevo este abrigo para/a mi madre	I'm taking this coat for my mother
Han venido por ti	they've come to get you/come because of you/come instead of you
Han venido estos paquetes para ti	these parcels have come for you
Lo has conseguido por mí	you've got it as a result of me
Los has conseguido para mí	you've got it for me

Particularly troublesome is the fact that *por* and *para* can be almost identical in meaning in some sentences which states intention –

Ha venido por estar contigo	he's come to be with you
Ha venido para estar contigo	" "

whereas in others only *para* is possible –

El carpintero ha venido para reparar la puerta	the carpenter's come to mend the door

This problem is discussed at 28.14.7.

Note   The form *pa* is substandard for *para* and should be avoided. It is accepted in a few humorous familiar expressions used in Spain (and possibly elsewhere), e.g. *es muy echao p'alante* 'he's very forward', *estoy p'al arrastre* 'I'm all in/exhausted', *p'al gato* 'worthless' (literally 'for the cat').

28.14.2   Uses of *para*
Para is used:

(a)   To indicate purpose, object or destination, e.g. *¿para quién es esto?* 'who(m) is this for?', *trabaja para ganar dinero* 'he works to earn money', etc. –

Este dinero es para Oxfam	this money is for Oxfam
Todo mi cariño es para ti	all my affection is for you
Tomo pastillas para/con el fin de adelgazar	I take pills in order to slim
Una mesa para dos, por favor	a table for two, please
Se preparó para saltar	he got ready to jump
Lo hace para/con el fin de llamar la atención	he does it to attract attention
Estudia para médico	he's studying to become a doctor

Notes (i)   For the distinction between *he venido para verle* and *he venido por verle*, which both mean 'I've come to see him', see 28.14.7.

(ii)   *Para* can also express ironic purpose, like the English 'only to':
Se abstuvo durante años de fumar y   he refrained for years from smoking

beber, para luego morir en un accidente de coche	and drinking, only to die in a car accident
Corrió a casa para encontrar que ya se habían marchado	he hurried home only to find that they'd already left

(iii) The following construction may also be thought of as a expressing the object or purpose of something:

Sus historias no son para/de creer	his stories aren't to be believed (lit. 'aren't for believing')
No es para tanto	it's not that serious/it doesn't call for that much fuss

(b) Direction after verbs of motion:

Íbamos para casa cuando empezó a llover	we were on the way home when it started raining
La secretaria ya ha salido para Burgos	the secretary has already left for Burgos
Ya va para viejo	he's getting old now
Va para ministro	he's on the way to becoming a minister

(c) To indicate advantage, disadvantage, usefulness, need:

Fumar es malo para la salud	smoking is bad for the health
La paciencia es un requisito indispensable para los profesores	patience is an indispensable requirement for teachers
Con esto tenemos para todos	with this we've enough for everybody
Es mucho dinero para tres días de vacaciones	it's a lot of money for three days' holiday
Tú eres para él lo más importante	you're the most important thing to/for him

(d) Reaction, response, mood:

Para mí eso no es justo	that doesn't seem fair to me
Esto para mí huele a vinagre/esto a mí me huele a vinagre	this smells of vinegar to me
Para mí que hablas mejor que él	my impression is that you speak better than him
Para su padre es un genio	he's a genius in his father's eyes

Notes (i) For *para con* in sentences like *es muy atento para con los invitados* 'he's very courteous towards guests', see 28.5b.

(ii) *Para* can also translate 'not in the mood for': *no estoy para bromas* 'I'm not in the mood for jokes'.

(e) To translate 'for' when it means 'considering', 'in view of':

Está muy alto para su edad	he's very tall for his age
Estás muy viejo para esos trotes	you're very old for all that
Es poco dinero para tanto trabajo	it's not much money for so much work

(f) 'To' in certain reflexive expressions:

Me lo guardo para mí	I'm keeping it to/for myself
Esto acabará mal, me decía para mí/entre mí	this will end badly, I said to myself
Murmuraba para/entre sí	he was muttering to himself

(g) 'About' in the meaning of 'on the point of':

Ya deben estar para/al llegar	they must be about to arrive
La leche está para cocer	the milk's about to boil

28.14.3   *Para* in time phrases

(a)   To translate 'by':

Lo tendré preparado para las cinco	I'll have it ready by/for five o'clock
Estaremos de vuelta para la merienda	we'll be back by tea
Para entonces ya estaremos todos muertos	we'll all be dead by then

(b)   'For':

La boda está fijada para el día quince	the wedding's fixed for the fifteenth
Vamos a dejarlo para otro día	let's leave it for another day
Tenemos agua para tres días	we've enough water for three days
Vamos a tener lluvia para rato	we are going to have rain for some time
Una habitación individual para seis días	a single room for six days

(c)   'Around', 'towards':

El embalse estará terminado para finales de noviembre	the dam will be finished around the end of November
Volveremos para agosto	we'll return around August

Notes (i)   In the last example *para* is more precise than *hacia* and *por* and less precise than *en*.

(ii)   *Ir para* is a colloquial translation of 'for nearly . . .' in time phrases:

Va para cinco años que trabajo aquí	I've been working here for nearly five years

28.14.4   Main uses of *por*

(a)   *Por* often means simply 'because of', as in *¿por qué?* (two words!) 'why?' (i.e. 'because of what?') and *porque* 'because':

No pudimos salir por/a causa de la nieve	we couldn't go out because of the snow
No podíamos ver el bosque por/a causa de los árboles	we couldn't see the wood for the trees
el índice de muertes por/a causa de infecciones pulmonares	the death rate from lung infections
Lo hice por dinero	I did it for money
la razón por la que me voy	the reason for my leaving
muchas gracias por el regalo	many thanks for the present
Me pusieron una multa por aparcar en el centro	they fined me for parking in the centre
Te ha pasado por tonto	it happened to you because you're a fool
Las críticas de la izquierda vienen por/a causa de tres temas	criticism from the left arises from three topics

Por may thus indicate the origin or inspiration of an emotion or mental state:

No lo puedo ver por lo engreído que es	I can't stand him for his conceitedness
Me fastidia por lo mal que canta	he annoys me because of his bad singing
Le odio por su mal genio	I hate him for/because of his bad temper
su amor por/hacia/a sus hijos	his love for his children
Siento mucho cariño por/hacia ella	I feel great fondness for her
Su fascinación por los Estados Unidos	his fascination with the USA
El gobierno demuestra poco interés por los derechos de la mujer	the government shows little interest in women's rights
Siento una enorme curiosidad por saber si ésta es la única vida	I feel enormous curiosity to know whether this is the only life

Tuvo un recuerdo nostálgico por el Londres de su juventud	he had a nostalgic recollection of the London of his youth
La delató por despecho	he informed on her out of spite

(b) *Por* = 'by' in passive constructions:

Sus novelas fueron elogiadas por los críticos	his novels were praised by the critics
La catedral fue diseñada por Gaudi	the cathedral was designed by Gaudi
Los campos estaban devastados por la sequía	the fields were devastated by drought
El suelo estaba cubierto por/de un lecho de hierba	the ground was covered by a bed of grass
Sociedad y economía aztecas por M. León-Portilla	*Aztec Society and Economy* by M. León-Portilla

Note   *De* is not nowadays used in passive sentences, but it is used with certain verbs which are best learnt separately. Where there is a possibility of using either *por* or *de*, the former usually implies an active agent, the latter generally implies a state; thus *de* is common when *estar* is used: see 24.1.4.

Me sentía tentado de tomar el atajo	I felt tempted to take the short cut
Jesús fue tentado por el Diablo	Jesus was tempted by the Devil
María dijo algunas palabras en voz muy baja [. . .] *seguidas de un ruido de sillas* (E. Sabato, Arg.)	Maria said a few words in a very low voice, followed by a sound of chairs
En todas partes era seguido por una muchedumbre de admiradores (*le seguía una muchedumbre* is more *castizo*)	he was followed everywhere by a crowd of admirers
El formulario debe estar acompañado de dos fotos	the form must be accompanied by two photos
Llegó acompañado por dos agentes	he arrived escorted by two policemen
Yo nunca he estado persuadido de la verdad de su versión de los hechos	I've never been persuaded of the truth of his version of the facts
Fui persuadido por su versión de los hechos	I was persuaded by his version of the facts
Las zonas pantanosas suelen estar plagadas de mosquitos	marshy zones are usually plagued with mosquitoes
En verano las vacas están atormentadas por las moscas	in summer the cows are tormented by flies

(c)   'Runs *on*', 'works *by*'; 'by means of':

El sistema de alarma funciona por rayos infrarrojos	the alarm system works by infra-red rays
El tratamiento por/con rayos X ha producido resultados animadores	treatment by X-rays has produced encouraging results
Un coche que marcha por/con/a gas-oil	a car which runs on diesel oil
Se puede pagar por/con talón bancario	payment by cheque accepted
Abrieron la puerta por la fuerza	they opened the door by force
[*el Buda*] *enseñaba la aniquilación del dolor por la aniquilación del deseo* (Borges, Arg.)	the Buddha taught the extinction of suffering by the extinction of desire

(d)   'In support of'

This includes the idea of effort or activity on behalf of anything:

Yo voté por los liberales	I voted for the Liberals
una campaña por/en pro de/a favor de la libertad de la prensa	a campaign for press freedom
¿Estás tú por la violencia?	do you support violence?
Él es senador por Massachusetts	he's senator for Massachusetts
Aprendió a tocar el piano por sí misma/ella sola	she learnt to play the piano by herself

(e) Exchange *for*, substitute *for*, distribution *'per'*:

Llévelo al departamento de reclamaciones y se lo cambiarán por uno nuevo	take it to the complaints department and they'll change it for a new one
Yo no cambiaría mi vida por la suya	I wouldn't change my life for his
Te han dado gato por liebre	they've served you cat for hare (i.e. swindled you)
Te quieres hacer pasar por lo que no eres	you're trying to pass for other than what you are
¿Por quién me toma usted?	who do you take me for?
Lo doy por supuesto/sentado	I take it for granted
Él dará la clase por mí	he'll give the class instead of me
Come por tres	he eats three persons' share
tres raciones por persona	three helpings per person
cien kilómetros por hora	100 km an hour
40 horas a la/por semana (*a* is more usual)	40 hours a week
la media anual por español	the annual average per Spaniard
El dos por ciento es/son protestante(s)	two per cent are Protestants

(f) Prices, amounts of money:

un cheque por/de cien libras	a cheque for 100 pounds
Compró una casa por un millón de dólares	he bought a house for one million dollars

Note *Por* is used with *pagar* only when the verb has a following direct object:

He pagado mil libras por este ordenador	I paid £1000 for this computer
He pagado mucho por él	I paid a lot for it

But

Yo lo pagué la semana pasada	I paid for it last week

(g) 'To judge *by*':

por las señas que me ha dado . . .	from the description he's given me . . .
por lo que tú dices . . .	from what you say . . .
por lo visto	apparently

(h) 'In search *of*'

Informal Peninsular speech prefers *a por*, a construction grudgingly admitted by grammarians and rejected by Spanish Americans:

Ha ido (a) por agua	he's gone for water
Le enviaron (a) por el médico	they sent him for the doctor

(i) 'Through' (= 'by means of'):

Conseguí el empleo por/a través de mi tío	I got the job through my uncle
Me enteré por un amigo	I found out through/from a friend
Le reconocí por la descripción	I recognized him from the description

(j) *Por* in adverbial phrases of manner:

por correo/avión/mar	by mail/air/sea
(but *en tren, en coche, en bicicleta, a pie*)	
Los denuncio por igual	I denounce both/all sides equally
por lo general/generalmente	generally
por lo corriente/corrientemente	usually
Me lo tendrás que decir por las buenas	you'll have to tell me one way or another
o por las malas	

(k) 'However . . .' in concessions:

Por más inteligente que seas, no lo vas a resolver	however intelligent you may be, you won't solve it
Por mucho que protestes, te quedas aquí	however much you protest, you're staying here
Por fuerte que ustedes griten, el patrón no les sube el salario	however loud you shout, the boss won't raise your wages

(l) Miscellaneous examples:

Por mí haz lo que quieras	as far as I'm concerned, do what you like
¿Por quién pregunta?	who are you asking for?
Es agrimensor, o algo por el estilo	he's a surveyor, or something like that
Siéntese por Dios	but *do* sit down
(not curt)	
Cinco por tres son quince	$3 \times 5 = 15$
Mide 7 por 5	it measures 7 by 5

(m) With numerous verbs, e.g.:

apurarse por	get anxious about
decidirse por	to decide on
desvelarse por	to be very concerned about
disculparse por	to apologize for
interesarse por	to be interested in
jurar por	swear by/on
molestarse por	to bother about
optar por	to opt for
preocuparse por	to worry about
tomar por	to take for

28.14.5 *Por* in time phrases
(a) *Por* = 'in'

por la mañana/tarde/noche	in the morning/evening/night
Debió ser por mayo	it must have been in May
por aquellos días	in those days/during those days

(b) 'just for', 'only for' (often in conjunction with *sólo*):

Entraré sólo por un momento	I'll come in just for a moment
Me he matriculado sólo por un trimestre	I've signed on for only one term
Me ha prestado el coche sólo por tres días	he's lent me the car for 3 days

Por and *para* are interchangeable in time expressions fixing the time needed for something:

Sólo necesito la asistenta por/para unos días	I only need the cleaner (i.e. daily help) for a few days

Note Spanish-Americans may use *por* where Peninsulars use nothing or *durante*: *estuvimos hablando por más de tres horas* 'we were talking for more than three hours', *por cuatro o cinco años nos tuvieron acorralados* 'they had us cornered for four or five years'

(Vargas Llosa, Peruvian dialogue), . . . *la congelación de los salarios por seis meses* 'wage freeze for six months' (*idem*). See also *durante*, 28.8.

28.14.6 *Por* as a preposition of place
(a) 'All over', 'throughout':

He viajado por Latinoamérica	I've travelled around Latin America
Había muchos libros desparramados por el suelo	there were many books scattered over the floor

(b) 'In': less precise than *en* and often implying motion:

La vi por/en la calle	I saw her in the street
Debe estar por el jardín	it must be somewhere in the garden

(c) 'Up to':

El agua le llegaba por la cintura	the water was up to his waist
Me llegas por los hombros	you reach my shoulders (e.g. to a growing child)

(d) 'Through', 'out of', 'down':

Se tiró por la ventana	he threw himself out of the window
Entró por la puerta	he came through the door
Se cayó por la escalera	he fell down the stairs
Salía agua por el/del grifo	water was coming out of the tap

(e) In conjunction with adverbs of place, to denote direction or whereabouts:

por aquí	this way/around here
por allí	that way/around there
por delante	from the front/in front
por detrás	from behind/behind
por entre	in between

28.14.7 *He venido por hablarle* or *para hablarle*?
Both prepositions may translate 'to' or 'in order to' in sentences like 'I've come to talk to you'. In some cases they are virtually interchangeable:

¿Para qué has venido?	what have you come for?
¿Por qué has venido?	why have you come?
Estoy aquí para/por verle	I'm here to see him

A useful rule seems to be: if the English sentence can be rewritten using a phrase like 'out of a desire to' or 'from an urge to', then *por* can be used. If not, then *para* is indicated; i.e. *por* refers to the mental state of the subject, *para* to the goal of his action.

Thus, *me dijeron que estabas en Madrid y he venido por verte de nuevo* 'I heard you were in Madrid and I've come to (out of an urge to) see you again' is possible. But **el fontanero ha venido por reparar el grifo* is as absurd as 'the plumber has come out of an urge to mend the tap':

Estuve toda la noche sin dormir por/ para no perderme el eclipse	I spent the whole night without sleeping so as not to miss the eclipse
Llegó a las cinco de la mañana por/ para cogerlos en la cama	he arrived at five in the morning so as to catch them in bed
No lo haces más que por/para fastidiar	you only do it to annoy
Me quedo en casa por/para no dejar sola a la abuela	I stay at home so as not to leave grandmother alone

Dame una aspirina para calmar el dolor	give me an aspirin to ease the pain
Incluso contrataron a un detective privado para buscarle	they even hired a private detective to look for him

etc.

28.14.8   Some vital differences between *por* and *para*

Tengo muchas cosas por/sin hacer	I have a lot of things still to do
Tengo muchas cosas para hacer	I have many things to do
Estoy por hacerlo	I feel inclined to do it
Estoy (aquí) para hacerlo	I'm here in order to do it
Estaba para hacerlo	I was about to do it
Está por/sin acabar	it isn't finished yet
Está para acabar	this has to be finished
Está para acabar de un momento a otro	it's about to finish at any moment

28.14.9   'For' not translated by *por* or *para*

La razón de mi queja	the reason for my complaining
Bebía porque no tenía otra cosa que hacer	she drank for want of something else to do
Los días eran cortos pues era ahora noviembre	the days were short, for it was now November
El deseo de fama	the desire for fame
Lloró de alegría	she wept for joy
Es una buena esposa a pesar de lo que gruñe	she's a good wife for all her grumbling
No dijo una palabra durante dos horas	he didn't say a word for two hours
No le he visto desde hace meses	I haven't seen him for months
Llevamos tres semanas sin que recojan la basura	they haven't collected our rubbish for three weeks
Estuvimos horas esperando	we waited for hours
Se podía ver muy lejos	you could see for miles
ir a dar un paseo	to go for a walk
irse de vacaciones	to go for a holiday
Me voy a Madrid unos días	I'm going to Madrid for a few days

28.15   *Según*

'According to', 'depending on'. As with *entre*, a following pronoun appears in the subject form: *según tú* 'according to you':

Según el parte meteorológico	according to the weather report
Según tú, se debería abolir la televisión	according to you, television should be abolished
Iremos modificando el programa de estudios según el tipo de estudiante que se matricule	we'll modify the syllabus according to the type of student who signs on
Los precios varían según a qué dentista vayas	the prices vary according to which dentist you go to
(or *según el dentista al que vayas*)	
Me decidiré luego, según cómo salgan las cosas	I'll decide later, depending on how things turn out

Notes (i)   As the examples show, *según* often functions as an adverbial:

¿Vas tú también? Según	are you going too? It depends
La policía detenía a los manifestantes	the police were arresting the demonstrators
según iban saliendo del edificio	as they came out of the building
Lo haremos según llegue papá	we'll do it as soon as father arrives
(*en cuanto llegue* is more usual)	

   (ii)   The following are colloquial or dialect:

Dirías que es un millonario según habla	you'd think he was a millionaire from the
(*por la manera en que habla*)	way he talks
A mí, según qué cosas, no me gusta	there are certain kinds of thing I don't
hacerlas	like doing
(regional for *ciertas cosas . . .*)	

The last example is typical of eastern Spain.

28.16   *Sin*

'Without'. *Sin* raises few problems for the English speaker, except when it appears before an infinitive, in which case it sometimes cannot be translated by the English verb form in -ing: cf. *dos Coca-Colas sin abrir* 'two Coca-Colas, unopened' (or 'not opened'). See 17.3.1.

No subas al tren sin billete	don't get on the train without a ticket
Como vuelva a verte por aquí te echo sin	if I see you around here again I'll throw
contemplaciones	you out on the spot (lit. 'without
	consideration for you')
Fumaba sin cesar	he was smoking ceaselessly
Estoy sin blanca	I haven't got a penny
¡Cuántos hay sin comer!	how many there are who have nothing
	to eat!
Está más guapa sin peinar	she's more attractive without her hair done

28.17   *Sobre*

This preposition combines some of the meanings of the English words 'on', 'over', 'on top of' and 'above'.

   (a)   As a preposition of place

It is an equivalent of *en* in the sense of 'on': *en/sobre la mesa* 'on the table', *en/sobre la pared* 'on the wall'. *Encima de* is also used of horizontal surfaces: *encima de la mesa* 'on (top of) the table'.

   However, where 'on top of' is impossible in English, *encima de* is impossible in Spanish: *los hinchas se encuentran todavía en/sobre el terreno* 'the fans are still on the pitch'.

Querían edificar sobre estos terrenos un	they wanted to build a new hotel on this
hotel nuevo	land
Este neumático tiene poco agarre sobre	this tyre has poor grip on wet surfaces
mojado	
Los rebeldes marcharon sobre la capital	the rebels marched on the capital
El castillo está edificado sobre un	the castle is built over a picturesque
pintoresco valle	valley

Dios vigila sobre sus hijos	God watches over his children
Una mujer habla con un chico y un árbol agita unas hojas secas sobre sus cabezas (Cortázar, Arg.)	a woman is talking to a boy and a tree is waving a few dry leaves over their heads
Un sol de fuego caía sobre los campos	a fiery sun fell on the plains

Note   Compare *sobre, encima de* and *por encima de* in the following examples:

El rey está por encima de/sobre todos (rest, not motion)	the King is above everyone
Mi jefe siempre está encima de mí	my boss is always breathing down my neck
La bala pasó por encima de su cabeza, rozándole el pelo (motion)	the bullet passed over his head, just touching his hair·
El avión voló por encima de/sobre la ciudad (motion: *sobre* implies height and is often more literary than *encima de*)	the plane flew over the city

(b)   Approximation (more usually with time):

Llegaremos sobre las cinco de la tarde	we'll arrive around 5 p.m.
Tenía sobre cuarenta años (. . . *unos 40 años* is more usual)	he was around forty years old
Costó sobre cien mil (*unos 100.000* . . . is more usual)	it cost around 100,000

(c)   'About' (= 'on the subject of'; see 28.7.1d):

Pronunció una conferencia sobre los problemas del Oriente Próximo	he delivered a lecture on the problems of the Near East
La OMS advierte sobre el peligro del uso de tranquilizantes sin receta médica	WHO (World Health Organization) warns on use of tranquillizers without medical prescription

(d)   Centre of rotation:

El mundo gira sobre su eje polar	the world spins about its polar axis
Las puertas se mueven sobre bisagras (From Luque Durán, 1973)	doors turn on hinges
Dio media vuelta sobre el pie izquierdo (*ibid.*)	he did a half-turn on his left foot

(e)   Superiority or precedence 'over':

El triunfo de los conservadores sobre la izquierda	the victory of the conservatives over the left
No tiene derecho a reclamar su superioridad sobre los demás	he has no right to claim superiority over others
Sobre todo, quisiera agradecer a mi mujer . . .	above all, I would like to thank my wife . . .
El crecimiento, en términos reales, de las exportaciones en el primer mes de 1984 supera el 50% sobre enero de 1983 (*El País*)	in real terms, the growth in exports in the first month of 1984 is 50% higher than January 1983
impuestos sobre la renta	taxes on income

28.18   *Tras*

'Behind', 'after'. It is a close equivalent of *detrás de* 'behind', and *después de* 'after', and is very rare in everyday speech. Its brevity makes it popular with journalists.

Tras de is an equally literary variant.

Dos siluetas deformes se destacaron tras el vidrio esmerilado (L. Goytisolo)	two distorted outlines loomed through/ behind the frosted glass (i.e. semi-opaque ground glass)
¿Quién sabe qué cosas pasan tras las cortinas de aquella casa?	who knows what things happen behind the curtains of that house?
Un generoso proyecto tras el cual se esconden intenciones menos altruistas	a generous project behind which less generous intentions lurk
Una banda de gaviotas venía tras el barco	a flock of gulls was following the boat

Detrás de could be used in all the above examples.

Así, tras de los duros años de 1936 a 1939 . . . (popular press)	so, after the hard years between 1936–39
Tras una rueda de prensa que duró más de dos horas, el presidente . . .	after a press-conference lasting more than two hours, the president . . .

Notes (i) In both the previous examples *después de* is possible. Occasionally *tras* is unavoidable:

Siguieron el mismo ritmo de trabajo, año tras año/día tras día	the followed the same work-pace, year after year/day after day
Tras de sus ojos se fue como imantado (Unamuno)	he went off after her, drawn by her eyes, as though magnetized
Han puesto un detective tras sus pasos	they've put a detective after him/on his trail

   (ii) Note also the following construction:

Tras de tener él la culpa, se enfada (or *encima de tener él . . .*)	not only is it his fault; he has the nerve to get angry

29 Relative clauses

29.1 Relative pronouns

There are four relative pronouns in Spanish, *que, quien(es), el que, el cual*. *El que* and *el cual* agree in number and gender with the antecedent (i.e. *el que, la que, los que, las que; el cual, la cual, los cuales, las cuales*). *Quien* has a plural form *quienes*. Foreign students tend to overuse *el cual* which nowadays tends to be confined to formal styles.

Cuando, donde and *como* may also introduce relative clauses: *fue allí donde la vi*, etc.

29.1.1 Choice of relative pronoun

Choice between these pronouns is determined by whether the pronoun is the subject or object of the relative clause, whether it follows a preposition, and by numerous elusive factors of style and rhythm.

Choice of pronoun is also sometimes determined by whether a clause is restrictive or non-restrictive:

(1) Restrictive clauses limit the scope of their antecedent, e.g.

Las chicas que eran suizas se callaron   the girls who were Swiss stopped talking

This refers only to those girls who were Swiss.

(2) Non-restrictive clauses or appositive clauses do not limit the scope of their antecedent, e.g.

Las chicas, que/las cuales eran suizas, se   the girls, who were Swiss, stopped talking
   callaron

This sentence clearly claims that the girls are all Swiss. In writing, non-restrictive clauses are typically marked by a comma and in speech by a pause. Spanish usually allows the option of using a different relative pronoun (in this case *el cual*) to make clear that the clause is non-restrictive, but in this sentence English relies only on a comma and pause before the relative pronoun.

A relative clause which refers to the whole of a unique entity is bound to be non-restrictive (note that English does not allow 'that' for 'which' in the following sentence):

La abadía de Westminster, que/la cual   Westminster Abbey, which is one of the
   es uno de los monumentos más   monuments most visited by tourists
   visitados por los turistas

29.1.2 The position of relative pronouns: general remarks

It need hardly be said that no Romance language allows prepositions to be separated from a relative pronoun: 'the path (which) we were walking along' = *el camino por el que caminábamos*. Nor can an object relative pronoun be omitted: 'the plane I saw' = *el avión que (yo) vi*.

Less obvious is the fact that Spanish does not allow the relative pronoun to be separated from its antecedent by a verb phrase, unless the phrase is in apposition. Thus the following is correct:

Las flores, algunas amarillas y otras azules, que crecían en los arriates	the flowers, some yellow and others blue, (which were) growing in the borders

But the type of sentence sporadically heard in English ?'those women were Japanese (whom) we saw yesterday' (for 'those women (whom) we saw yesterday were Japanese') must not be translated by **esas mujeres eran japonesas que vimos ayer*. The correct forms are *esas mujeres que vimos ayer eran japonesas* or *eran japonesas esas mujeres que vimos ayer*.

Further examples:

Acudieron corriendo los vecinos, que/ quienes/los cuales no pudieron hacer nada	the neighbours came running, but could do nothing (literally, 'who could . . .')

Not **los vecinos acudieron corriendo, que . . .*

Han vuelto las cigüeñas que hicieron su nido en el campanario el año pasado	the storks that made their nest in the belfry last year have returned

Not **las cigüeñas han vuelto que . . .*

29.2 Relative subject pronouns

29.2.1 In restrictive clauses

When the relative pronoun is the subject of the relative clause, e.g. 'the man who arrived yesterday', and the clause is restrictive, *que* is the normal relative pronoun for all types of antecedent:

Los inversionistas que se quemaron los dedos	the investors who burnt their fingers
El tren que llega . . .	the train (which is) arriving . . .
Contemplaba las hojas que caían de las ramas	she watched the leaves (which were) falling from the branches

Some of these clauses can be expressed by a participle in English, but not in Spanish:

El hombre que vende las entradas	the man selling tickets
La señora que estaba/está sentada en el coche	the lady sitting in the car

Note Pronouns such as *alguien, alguno, nadie, ninguno, mucho, poco, varios*, may appear before the relative particle *que*, but *todo* requires *el que*:

No conozco a nadie que tenga carnet de piloto	I don't know anyone with a pilot's licence
No hay ninguno que me guste	there's none that I like
Muchos que piensan como yo	many who think like me

Contrataron a varios que sabían taquigrafía	they hired several people who knew shorthand
Procura evitar a todos los que hablen mal de los demás	try to avoid all those who speak ill of others

29.2.2   In non-restrictive clauses

The following options are available:

que

quien/quienes (usually people only)

el cual (emphatic and less common; see 29.5)

Que is usual, unless the relative pronoun is separated from its antecedent or the relative pronoun is emphasized, when *el cual* is possible. *Que* is obligatory after personal pronouns. *Quien* is commonly used, especially in written language, for persons. *El que* is not normally used (but see note ii):

La tradición, que es obra del olvido y de la memoria (Borges)	tradition, which is the work of forgetting and remembering
Me refiero sólo a México, que es mi patria	I'm referring only to Mexico, which is my home country
Fueron a hablar con José, que/quien/ el cual estaba de mal humor	they went to talk to José, who was in a bad mood
Yo que siempre me preocupo por ti y tú que no me haces ni caso . . .	I who am always worrying about you and you who take no notice of me at all . . .
. . . y ahora hablando con ella, que tenía el sol de la tarde en el rostro (F. Umbral)	and talking to her now, with the evening sun on her face

Notes (i)   In 'cleft' sentences (discussed at 30.2) a nominalizer (e.g. *el que*, *quien*) must be used:

Fue María quien/la que dijo la verdad	it was Maria who told the truth
Soy consciente de que tengo que ser yo mismo el que/quien resuelva el problema	I'm aware that I must be the one to solve the problem myself

(ii)   *El que* translates 'the one who/which' and is discussed under nominalizers (30.1):

Aquella chica es Charo – la que lleva el chandal rojo	that girl over there is Charo – the one wearing the red tracksuit.

El que is rare as a subject relative pronoun, though the preceding construction is similar to a non-restrictive clause, cf.

Hacia el final de los debates, comenzó a perfilarse una cuarta opción, la que reclamaba un 'nuevo concepto de un nacionalismo pluralista' (El País)	towards the end of the discussions a fourth option began to take shape, one which demanded a 'new concept of a pluralist nationalism'

29.3   Relative object pronouns

29.3.1   In restrictive clauses

Non-human antecedent: *que*

   (occasionally *al que*, see note (v))

Human antecedent: *que* if personal *a* is omitted

   al que or *a quien* after personal *a*

Quien is slightly more formal than *el que*.
For omission of the personal *a*, see note (iii).

Volvió a hundirse el barco que habían intentado reflotar	the boat (which) they had tried to reflo.. sank again
Las sucursales que hemos tenido que cerrar	the branches (which) we have had to close
La actriz que/a la que/a quien vi ayer	the actress (whom) I saw yesterday
El profesor que/al que/a quien yo más admiro	the teacher I admire most
El chico que te presenté ayer	the boy I introduced to you yesterday

al que/a quien changes the sense here, since the *a* would be interpreted as a dative preposition: 'the boy to whom I introduced you yesterday . . .' In general, if personal *a* clashes with dative *a*, the former is dropped. (See 20.7 for discussion.)

Los militares que/a los que/a quienes han ascendido	the military men (whom) they have promoted

In this example *a los que/a quienes* are preferred since *que* alone may be taken as a subject pronoun.

Notes (i) There is a colloquial tendency, which may sound uneducated, to insert a redundant pronoun in this type of clause:

Los gramáticos aconsejan muchas cosas que nadie (las) dice	grammarians recommend many things which no one says

(ii) Object relative pronouns in restrictive clauses can be omitted in English, but not in Spanish:

El fontanero que/al que/a quien había despedido tres días antes	the plumber he'd sacked three days earlier
(*fontanero* = *plomero* in Spanish America)	
Lo mejor que le puedes comprar es un perfume	the best thing you can buy her is a perfume

However, the following construction is found in journalism, official documents or business letters:

Un libro y una tesis a tomar muy en serio por estudiosos y ciudadanos en general (Cambio16)	a book and a thesis to be taken very seriously by students and citizens in general
La reunión a celebrarse en diciembre	the meeting to be held in December

The usual construction is *la reunión que se celebrará*, etc.

(iii) Personal *a* is usually omitted when the clause is clearly restrictive. But if it is non-restrictive, it must be retained – though the difference is occasionally elusive. Peninsular informants generally insisted on *a* in the following examples:

Tengo un profesor al que/a quien han nombrado miembro de la Academia	I have a teacher whom they've appointed as a member of the Academy
Es el único al que la ley no ha condenado	he's the only one the law hasn't condemned
Hace unos días, en el puerto, me dijiste que yo era la primera persona a la que habías querido (Sabato, Arg., dialogue)	a few days ago, at the harbour, you told me I was the first person you had loved

Único generates disagreement. One hears *tú eres el único que quiero* 'you're the only one I love', some prefer *al que quiero*, but others accept both.

(iv) *El que* or *quien* are obligatory in all types of clause if *que* alone creates ambiguities, as in *ése es el autor que siempre ataca* 'that's the author who (or 'whom he') always attacks'. *Al que* or *a quien* . . . show clearly that 'whom he always attacks' is meant.

(v)   Personal *a* is rare with non-human objects, but if it occurs *el que* is the preferred relative pronoun:

Hemos encontrado enormes listas de coches a los que tenían controlados (Cambio16)	we have found enormous lists of cars which they had under surveillance

29.3.2   In non-restrictive clauses

Non-human antecedent: *que*

(*al que*, *al cual* if personal *a* is used)

Human antecedent: *al que*
                    a quien
                    al cual

Personal *a* is obligatory if the antecedent is human.

El cual, always commoner in non-restrictive clauses, may be preferred after a pause, for emphasis, when the antecedent is separated from the relative or when the relative is separated from the verb of which it is the object. See 29.5 for further details:

Los anillos de Saturno, que un satélite artificial fotografió de cerca	the rings of Saturn, which an artificial satellite photographed close up
Los cocodrilos del Nilo, que los antiguous tenían por sagrados	the Nile crocodiles, which the ancients held sacred
Tres cajas de ropa, que/las que, no pudiendo olvidar a su difunto marido, se negaba a vender	three chests of clothes which, being unable to forget her late husband, she refused to sell
Plutón, esposo de Proserpina, a la que/ a quien/a la cual robó	Pluto, the husband of Proserpine, whom he carried off

(*a la que* or *a la cual* shows clearly that it was Proserpine who was carried off)

Me encontré ayer a tu suegra, a quien/ a la que hacía mucho tiempo que yo no veía	I met your mother-in-law yesterday, whom I hadn't seen for some time

In all these examples *el cual* could replace *que* if emphasis or formality are called for.

29.4   Relative pronoun after prepositions

29.4.1   Restrictive clauses

(a)   Non-human antecedents: *el que*.
(In some circumstances *que* alone is preferred: see 29.6.)

For details of *donde*, *cuando* and *como* as relative particles, see 29.8–10.

(b)   Human antecedents: *el que* or *quien* are the usual solutions. The fact that *quien* is not marked for gender is sometimes useful. With either type of antecedent, *el cual* may be preferred in the circumstances described at 29.5.

El perro con el que cazo	the dog I hunt with

Tuvo una discusión de la que salió malparado	he had an argument which he came out of badly
Resguardar el tesoro de la insana codicia de los humanos es la misión a la que ha dedicado su vida (Borges, Arg.)	safeguarding the treasure of the insane greed of humankind is the mission to which he has dedicated his life
La amenaza de guerra bajo la que vivimos	the threat of war we're living under
La puerta tras la que se escondió	the door behind which she hid
la maniobra en virtud de la que consiguió un éxito inmerecido	the manoeuvre whereby he gained an undeserved success
. . . han emitido comunicados en los que se recuerda la ilegalidad de las acciones propuestas (*ABC*)	. . . have published communiqués in which attention is called to the illegality of the proposed actions
El café al que/adonde voy todos los días	the café I go to every day
La calle desde la que/donde he venido andando	the street I've walked from
Hay chequetrenes con los que usted puede viajar por un valor de 15.000 a 20.000 pesetas, pero por los cuales usted sólo paga 12.750 y 17.000 ptas respectivamente (Advertisement: *el cual* separated from its antecedent)	there are 'Traincheques' with which you can travel to a value of 15-20,000 pesetas, but for which you only pay 12,750 and 17,000 pesetas respectively
Los amigos a causa de los que/quienes llegamos tarde	the friends on whose account we arrived late
¡Una gentuza a la que no tiene Vd. derecho a hablar! (Buero Vallejo, dialogue)	a rabble that you've no right to talk to!
¿. . . y todas . . . ésas con quien has paseado y . . . que has besado? (Buero Vallejo, dialogue) (*quien* for *quienes* is colloquial)	and what about all those . . . women you've walked out with and . . . kissed?
Yo era para ella {. . .} el ser supremo con el que se dialoga, el dios callado con quien creemos conversar (F. Umbral)	I was for her {. . .} the supreme being one talks with, the silent god we imagine we are conversing with
Nos ha sorprendido que este programa le guste a un tipo de gente para la que no estaba pensado (interview, *Cambio16*)	it surprised us that this programme is liked by a type of person it wasn't intended for

Notes (i)   If the gender of a human antecedent is not marked, *el que* cannot be used:

No hay nadie con quien hablar	there's no one to talk to
Busca a alguien de quien te puedas fiar	look for someone you can trust

(ii)   After 'neuter' antecedents like *algo* or *nada*, *lo que* or *que* are used:

No hay nada con (lo) que puedas sacarle punta	there's nothing you can sharpen it with
Iba a morir allí, no por algo en lo que creía, sino por respeto a su hermano mayor (Vargas Llosa, Peru)	he was going to die there, not for something he believed, in, but out of respect for his elder brother

(iii)   Popular and rapid informal speech often avoids combining prepositions and relative pronouns by a type of construction banned from writing:

?*En casa de una mujer que yo vivía con ella . . . (con la que yo vivía)*	in the house of a woman I was living with
?*Te acuerdas del hotel que estuvimos el año pasado (. . . en el que estuvimos . . .)*	d'you remember the hotel we stayed in last year?
*Soy un emigrante que siempre me han preocupado los problemas de la emigración	I am an emigrant who has always been concerned with the problems of emigration
(*. . . al que siempre han preocupado los problemas*) (Reader's letter in *El País*)	

This construction is not uncommon in Golden-Age texts.

29.4.2   Non-restrictive clauses

El que is normal for non-human antecedents, *quien* for persons, but *el cual* is more frequent than in restrictive clauses, especially after the longer prepositions or after prepositional phrases. See 29.5 for details on *el cual*:

La curiosa fontanería de algunos hoteles, con la que/la cual hay que tener mucha paciencia	the curious plumbing in some hotels, with which one must be very patient
La fidelidad al mito cristiano viejo tras el cual, a partir del siglo XVI, los españoles nos guarecemos y enmascaramos (J. Goytisolo)	fidelity to the old Christian myth behind which we Spaniards have been sheltering and disguising ourselves since the 16th century
Razona a la manera de un Wittgenstein, a quien/al que/al cual admiro mucho	he reasons in the same way as a Wittgenstein, whom I admire a great deal
Y sin llegar al extremo de un Lezama Lima, para quien todo es metáfora de todo . . . (Vargas Llosa, Peru)	and without going to the extreme of a Lezama Lima, for whom everything is a metaphor for everything

Note   There is a colloquial tendency to insert a redundant pronoun in this type of clause:

Sólo por ti dejaría para siempre a don Memo, a quien tanto le debo (Fuentes, Mex. dialogue)	only for you would I leave Don Memo for ever. I owe him so much (literally '. . . Don Memo for ever, whom I owe so much)

29.5   *El cual*: further discussion

In general, *el cual* is more formal than *el que* or *quien*, and is yielding to them; foreigners spoil much good Spanish by overusing it. It may be preferred or obligatory in the following contexts:

   (a)   It seems always to be used after *según* except when this means 'depending'/'it depends' as in *¿qué precio tienen? Según los que quiera* 'what's their price? It depends on which ones you want'.

Los postulados marxista-leninistas según los cuales todos los males del planeta vienen de los países industrializados (*Cambio16*)	Marxist-Leninist arguments according to which every evil on the planet comes from the industralized countries
José Carlos Mariátegui, según el cual 'el marxismo leninismo es el sendero luminoso de la revolución' (Vargas Llosa, Peru)	J. C. Mariátegui, according to whom 'Marxist Leninism is the shining path to revolution'

(b) It is often preferred after long prepositions (i.e. more than one syllable), e.g. *para*, *contra*, *entre*, *mediante*, or after prepositional phrases, e.g. *a pesar de*, *debajo de*, *delante de*, *frente a*, *en virtud de* etc., although *el que* is increasingly common in these contexts. *El cual* is common when the antecedent is separated from the relative pronoun by intervening words, or when the relative is separated from its verb:

una formación profesional mediante la cual los funcionarios de grado medio estén capacitados para . . . (*Cambio16*)	professional training whereby middle-grade civil servants will be equipped to . . .
Hay cuerpos, seres, con atmósfera propia, dentro de la cual es bueno vivir (F. Umbral)	there are bodies, beings, with their own atmosphere, within which it is good to live
El viaje duró cinco días, en el transcurso de los cuales vimos muchas maravillas	the journey lasted five days in the course of which we saw many marvels
Una maniobra en virtud de la cual consiguió un éxito inmerecido	a manoeuvre by virtue of which he gained an undeserved success
YAACABÓ. Pájaro insectívoro de la América del Sur, cuyo canto suena como su nombre, al cual tienen los indios de por mal agüero (Entry in Moliner, II, 1562)	YAACABÓ. An insect-eating bird of South America, whose song sounds like its name, (and) which the Indians regard as ill-omened

But compare:

El otro fue alcanzado por ocho balazos, a consecuencia de los que moriría minutos más tarde . . . (*El País*)	the other one received eight bullet wounds, as a consequence of which he was to die a few minutes later
. . . la localización de la abadía, sobre la que Adso evita toda referencia concreta (U. Eco, translated by R. Pochtar)	. . . the location of the abbey, about which Adso avoids all specific reference

(c) *El cual* is used after *algunos de . . . todos . . ., la mayoría de . . ., parte de* and similar phrases:

Los jóvenes españoles, la mayoría de los cuales son partidarios del divorcio	young Spaniards, the majority of whom are in favour of divorce
. . . árboles, pocos de los cuales tenían hojas	trees, few of which had leaves
. . . defender la revolución social, parte integrante de la cual era la emancipación de la mujer	to defend the social revolution, of which an integral part was the emancipation of woman
Corren por Madrid muchos rumores, algunos de los cuales vamos a recoger aquí	many rumours are circulating in Madrid, some of which we shall report here

(d) As the subject of a verb, *el cual* seems to be obligatory after a heavy pause such as a sentence break – a construction not easily imitated in English:

Fueron a hablar con su tío, un setentón de bigote blanco y acento andaluz, que hacía alarde de ideas muy avanzadas. El cual, tras un largo silencio, contestó . . .	they went to talk with his uncle, a seventy-year old with a white moustache and Andalusian accent who boasted very advanced ideas. Who, after a long silence, replied . . .

e que *after a preposition*

nay be preferred for rhythmic or stylistic reasons, and some writers, e.g.
r (Cuba), use it more than others.

..ative *que* after a preposition

Que alone is preferred as a relative pronoun after prepositions in certain circumstances difficult to define:

(a) After *a* (when it is not personal *a*), *con* and *de* (unless it means 'from'), especially after abstract or generic nouns.

La película a que me refiero	the film I'm referring to
La discriminación a que están sometidas nuestras frutas y hortalizas . . . (*El País*)	the discrimination which our fruits and vegetables are subject to
La calurosa hospitalidad con que he sido recibido (*Cambio16*)	the warm hospitality with which I have been received
La notoria buena fe con que Collazos expone sus dudas y sus convicciones (Vargas Llosa, Peru)	the well-known good faith with which Collazos expounds his doubts and convictions
La única pista con que contaba en el caso	the only clue he had in the case
Ese conjunto de sutiles atributos con que el alma se revela a través de la carne (E. Sabato, Arg.)	that set of subtle attributes by which the soul reveals itself through the flesh
Las especies de escarabajo de que estoy hablando	the species of beetle I am talking about
Con toda la riqueza, alegría y creatividad de que es capaz	with all the richness, joy and creativity of which he is capable

El que would be possible, though less elegant, in the foregoing examples.

(b) Frequently after *en* when precise spatial location is not intended. Compare *la caja en la que encontré la llave* 'the box in(side) which I found the key', but *la casa en que vivo* 'the house I live in', not *'the house inside which I live'.

En que is also preferred when the preceding noun is a period of time. After *día, semana, mes, año, momento* the *en* is also often omitted:

El desierto humano en que ella estaba perdida (F. Umbral)	the human desert she was lost in
Me gustaría vivir en un sitio en que/ donde no hubiera coches	I'd like to live in a place where there were no cars
Las formas racionales en que se basa la vida social (Vargas Llosa, Peru)	the rational forms on which social life is based
La época en que todavía se hablaba latín	the period in which Latin was still spoken
El momento político en que salía (Vargas Llosa, Peru)	the political moment at which it appeared

(In all the examples so far *el que* is also possible, but not in the following:)

Una noche en que iba a buscarla (F. Umbral)	one night I went to fetch her
El día que te vi	the day I saw you

El único día que se produjeron diferencias de importancia fue el jueves (*La Nación*, Arg., in *Var.* 124)	the only day on which any important differences were recorded was Thursday
El año que nos casamos	the year we got married
El mes que llovió tanto	the month it rained so much
En los meses que estuvo Edwards en Cuba (Vargas Llosa, Peru)	during the months Edwards spent in Cuba
Durante el año y medio que he estado en el cargo	in the year and a half I've been in the job

Note If the antecedent is precise as to the number of units of time, *el que* is used:

Aquellos millones de años en los que el hombre aprendió a cazar y a servirse de sus herramientas	those millions of years in which man learned to hunt and use his tools
Un tipo de genocidio que estará consumado dentro de treinta años, en los que las buenas intenciones de ciertas instituciones . . . (A. Carpentier)	a type of genocide which will be complete within thirty years in which the good intentions of certain institutions . . .

29.7 *Cuyo*

This translates 'whose', and is often an elegant alternative for an otherwise tortuous relative clause. It agrees in number and gender with the following noun. If there is more than one noun, it agrees only with the first: *una mujer cuyas manos y pies estaban quemados por el sol* 'a woman whose hands and feet had been burnt by the sun'.

Aquellos verbos cuyo subjuntivo es irregular	those verbs whose subjunctive is irregular
Un hombre de cuya honradez no dudo	a man whose honesty I don't doubt
Una medida cuyos efectos son imprevisibles	a measure whose effects are unforeseeable

Notes (i) Grammarians condemn such commonly heard sentences like **se alojó en el Imperial, en cuyo hotel había conocido a su primera mujer* '. . . in which hotel he had met his first wife', better *. . . el Imperial, hotel donde había conocido a su primera mujer*. But this construction is allowed with *caso*:

Nos han alertado acerca de la posibilidad de que todos los hoteles estén completos, en cuyo caso la reunión será aplazada	they have warned us of the possibility that all the hotels may be full, in which case the meeting will be postponed

(ii) *Del que/de quien* occasionally replace *cuyo*:

Un torero, de quien alabó el tesón y el valor a toda prueba	a bullfighter, whose indefatigable steadfastness and courage he praised

(iii) Familiar speech often avoids *cuyo* by a construction banned from careful language:

?Los alumnos que sus notas no están en la lista	the students whose marks aren't on the list

(*cuyas notas no están . . .*)

Occasionally this invades written language:

*a diferencia de los proyectos de ley	unlike the draft bills sent by the

enviados por el Gobierno, de los que	Government, whose approval by the two
cabe presumir su aprobación por las	Chambers, without too many
dos Cámaras sin demasiadas	modifications, may be assumed . . .
modificaciones (*El País*)	

(iv)   *Cuyo* is not used in questions (except in some local Spanish-American dialects): ¿*De quién es esa mochila?* 'whose rucksack is that?', not *¿cuya mochila es ésa?*.

29.8   *Donde, adonde, en donde* as relatives

Donde is commonly used as a relative, especially after *hacia*, *a* (in the meaning of 'towards'), *desde*, *de* meaning 'from', *por* meaning 'along'/'through', *en* meaning 'place in', etc.

As a relative its use is rather wider than the English 'where':

Lo recogí en la calle donde te vi	I picked it up in the street where I saw you
Añoraba las playas donde se había	he longed for the beaches where he had
paseado durante aquel verano	strolled that summer
Ése es el baúl de donde sacó los	that's the trunk from which he took the
papeles	papers
Decidieron fortificar la ciudad hacia	they decided to fortify the city towards
donde avanzaban las tropas enemigas	which enemy troops were advancing
Un balcón desde donde se podía ver	a balcony from which/where one could
el desfile	see the parade

In all the above examples, *el que* or *el cual* could be used with the appropriate preposition, instead of *donde*.

Volvieron a encontrarse en París, donde	they met again in Paris where they had
se habían conocido veinte años	met for the first time twenty years
antes	before

Notes (i)   *Adonde* is not the same as *a dónde*; the former is a relative, the latter is found in indirect questions:

El pueblo adonde yo iba	the village I was going to
No quería decirle a dónde yo iba	I didn't want to tell him where I was
	going (to)

(ii)   *En donde* is spatially more specific than *donde*, and is rather literary:

El niño hizo sus primeros estudios en	the child received his elementary education
la casa de los señores Olivares, en	in the Olivares' house where children
donde {. . .} *se congregaban*	from well-to-do catholic families
los hijos de las familias católicamente	congregated
acomodadas (C. Fuentes, Mex.)	

Donde alone would have come to the same thing.

29.9   *Como* as a relative

Como is officially recommended after *la manera* and *el modo*, although *en que* is used after *forma*, and usually after the other two:

La manera como un país se fortalece y	the way a country strengthens and
desarrolla su cultura es abriendo sus	develops its culture is by opening
puertas y ventanas (Vargas Llosa, Peru)	its doors and windows
Me gusta la manera como/en que lo hace	I like the way he does it
Me gusta la forma en que lo hace	" "

Notes (i) *En que* is more usual in informal language.

(ii) *Mismo* plus a noun requires *que*:

Lo dijo del mismo modo que lo dijo antes	he said it the same way as he said it before
Llevas la misma falda que yo	you're wearing the same skirt as me

29.10 *Cuando* as a relative

Cuando occurs only in non-restrictive clauses:

En agosto, cuando les den las vacaciones a los niños, nos iremos al campo	in August, when the children have their holidays, we'll go to the countryside
Incluso en nuestros días, cuando nadie cree ya en las hadas	even in our day, when no one believes in fairies any more

But

Sólo puedo salir los días (en) que no trabajo (restrictive)	I can only go out on the days I'm not working

Notes (i) *Cuando* is used with *apenas, aún, entonces, justo, no, no bien*:

Apenas había aparcado el coche cuando se acercó un policía	he had hardly parked the car when a policeman came up
Aún/todavía no había empezado a estudiar cuando le dieron un empleo	he hadn't yet started studying when they gave him a job
Empezó entonces, cuando los demás todavía no habían llegado	he began then, when the others hadn't yet arrived
justo cuando . . .	just when . . .
etc.	

Compare the following restrictive clauses:

en un momento en que . . .	at a moment when . . .
en una época en que . . .	in a period when . . .
en un año (en) que . . .	in a year when . . .
etc.	

(ii) *Que* is used in the following phrases:

Ahora que usted sabe la verdad	now (that) you know the truth
Luego que haya terminado	as soon as he's finished
Siempre que haya bastante	as long as there's enough
Cada vez que me mira	whenever he looks at me
De modo que/de manera que	so that
etc.	

In cleft sentences *donde, como* or *cuando* may be obligatory: *es así como hay que hacerlo* 'this is how it must be done', *fue entonces cuando lo notó* 'it was then that he noticed it'. See 30.2.

29.11 *Lo cual* and *lo que*

These are used when the antecedent is not a noun but a whole sentence or an idea. Since the clause is always non-restrictive, *lo cual* is common, especially in writing. Compare:

Trajo una lista de cifras que explicaba su inquietud	he brought a list of figures which (i.e. the list) explained his anxiety

and

Trajo una lista de cifras, lo cual/lo que explicaba su inquietud	he brought us a list of figures, which (i.e. the fact he brought it) explained his anxiety

Further examples:

En un primer momento se anunció que los misiles eran americanos, lo cual fue desmentido en Washington (El País)	initially it was stated that the missiles were American, which was denied in Washington
Fue su mujer quien hizo pintar de amarillo las paredes, lo que/lo cual le irritó enormemente	it was his wife who had the walls painted yellow, which irritated him enormously
Llegué tarde, por lo que/lo cual no pude asistir a la reunión	I arrived late, for which reason I couldn't attend the meeting
El año siguiente fue la exaltación de Amadeo de Saboya al trono de España, lo cual le tuvo vagando por Madrid hasta altas horas de la madrugada (J.M. Guelbenzu)	the following year there occurred the elevation of Amadeo of Savoy to the Spanish throne, which had him wandering round Madrid until the small hours

29.12 Relative clauses after a nominalizer

A nominalizer (e.g. *el que* meaning 'the one who/which') cannot be followed by the relatives *el que* or *el cual*. The noun must be repeated or, in written language, *aquel* is used:

Se imagina un nuevo don Julián, una versión moderna de aquel al que rinde homenaje el título del libro (Vargas Llosa, Peru not *el al que . . .)	he imagines a new Don Julian, a modern version of the one to whom the book's title pays homage
Mi casa es más grande que la casa (or que aquella) en la que vives tú	my house is bigger than the one you live in
Traiga otro plato – no me gusta comer en los platos en los que otros han comido	bring another plate – I don't like eating off those others have eaten off

29.13 Miscellaneous examples of relative clauses

Falta saber las condiciones en que está	we have yet to know what conditions he is in
Falta saber en qué condiciones está	" "
Falta saber en las condiciones que está	" "
Según el cine a que vayas	depending on what cinema you go to
Según al cine que vayas (All examples from Moliner.)	" "
Era la habitación más pequeña en (la) que jamás he estado	it was the smallest room I've ever been in
Era la habitación más pequeña de todas las que he estado (familiar spoken language)	" "
¿Cómo se explica el fenómeno singular que fue la victoria de los liberales?	how does one explain the singular phenomenon of the liberals' victory?
El espectáculo conmovedor que son las ruinas de Machu Picchu	the moving spectacle of the Machu Picchu ruins

30 Nominalizers and cleft sentences

30.1 Nominalizers

30.1.1 Introductory

A marked feature of Spanish is the use of the article to create noun phrases from words which are not themselves nouns: *rojo* 'red', *el rojo* 'the red one'; *explotado* 'exploited', *las explotadas* 'exploited women', etc.

This device may be applied to possessive adjective/pronouns – *mío* 'mine', *el mío* 'my one'/'the one belonging to me': see 8.5 for discussion.

This chapter discusses an important type of nominalizer, *el de, lo de, el que, lo que* and *quien* used as pronouns with such values as 'the one from', 'the one belonging to . . .', 'the one who/that . . .', 'the person who . . .', etc., cf. French *celui de, celui qui, celle qui, ceux qui, ce qui*, etc. Some grammars treat these under relative pronouns, but they are in fact devices for turning a verbal or prepositional phrase into a noun phrase: *los que interrogan* is close in meaning to *los interrogadores, los de antes* to *los anteriores, el que/quien habla catalán* to *el hablante de catalán*, etc.

For the use of *el que* and *quien* as relative pronouns, (*el hombre con el que/con quien hablaba, la mesa en la que escribo*) see chapter 29.

For *quién* in questions, see 22.4.

30.1.2 *El de*

'The one(s) belonging to', 'that/those of', 'the one(s) from', etc. It agrees in number and gender with the noun it replaces:

Entre los problemas de España y los de Estados Unidos, creo que los de los EE.UU son más graves	between the problems of Spain and (those of) the USA, I think the USA's are more serious
Los de Buenos Aires son mejores	the ones from B.A. are better
los de siempre	the same ones as always

Note Translation by a Saxon genitive or compound noun is sometimes appropriate:

Quita los de ayer y pon los de la semana pasada	take away yesterday's and put last week's
Tenía los ojos saltones como los de una rana	he had bulging eyes like a frog's
La industria del petróleo y la del carbón	the oil and coal industries

387

30.1.3   *Lo de*

The neuter version of the above phrases. Like all neuter pronouns, its use is obligatory if there is no noun to which the pronoun can refer. *Lo de* has limited applications.

(a)   It is a common equivalent of 'the . . . business/affair' in such phrases as *lo del dinero perdido* 'the affair of the lost money':

Se puso enferma por lo de su hijo	she fell ill because of the business of her son
Siempre está a vueltas con lo de que cuándo nos vamos a casar	(s)he's always coming back with the issue of when we're going to get married
Lo de que perdió el dinero no me convence	that story about his losing the money doesn't convince me

(b)   It is common in Argentina and other parts of Spanish America in the meaning *en casa de* 'at . . .'s house': *en lo de Ángel* 'at Ángel's place'.

30.1.4   *El que*

This translates 'the one(s) who/which', 'that/those which', etc., (Fr. *celui/ celle/celles/ceux qui*). It agrees in number and gender with the noun it replaces:

La que está fuera	the one (fem.) who/which is outside
El que llegó ayer	the one that arrived yesterday
Los que dicen eso	the ones/those who say that
Vivo en la que está pintada de blanco	I live in the one (which is) painted white
Con la que tienes que hablar es con ella	the one you have to talk to is her

Notes (i)   *El de* and *el que* can be combined:

La libertad de la televisión debería ser siempre la del que la contempla . . . no la del que la programa (*El País*)	freedom in television should always belong to the person watching it . . . not to the person programming it

(ii)   *El que* (invariable) + subjunctive translates 'the fact that' (*el hecho de que*), see 16.3:

El que España no tenga petróleo explica el efecto que tuvo la recesión de los años ochenta	the fact that Spain has no oil explains the effect the recession in the eighties had

30.1.5   *Lo que*

The neuter version of the above: it refers to no specific noun. It can normally be translated by the phrase 'the thing that . . .' or by the pronoun 'what' (cf. Fr. *ce qui/ce que*):

Lo que más me irrita es . . .	what most irritates me is that . . .
Se asombró de lo que dijo el portavoz	he was amazed at what the spokesman said
La valla se prolonga todo lo que da de sí la vista	the fence stretches as far as the eye can see
Le pasa lo que a ti	the same thing happens to him as to you

Compare:

Por Rosario fue por la que se pelearon	Rosario was the woman they fought over

and

Por Rosario fue por lo que se pelearon	Rosario was what they fought over

Note   *La que* is often used in warnings as a humorous equivalent of *lo que*: *no sabes la que te espera* 'you don't know what's waiting for you . . .'; *¡la que te tienen preparada!* . . 'what they've got in store for you! . .'

30.1.6   *Quien* as an equivalent of 'the one who'

Quien/quienes can optionally replace *el que* in many contexts provided it refers to a human being. Since *quien* is not marked for gender, it is not an exact equivalent of *el que*, and must be used when reference to a specific gender is to be avoided. Only *quien* is possible in the meaning of 'no one':

El que diga eso es un cobarde	the person who says that is a coward
Quien diga eso es un cobarde	(same, but rather literary)
Quienes/los que no estén de acuerdo, *que se vayan*	anyone not in agreement should go
Que se lo diga al que/a quien quiera	let him tell whomever he likes
Quien no es mala persona es el sargento	someone who's not a bad fellow is the sergeant

El coronel no tiene quien le escriba
   (García Márquez, title, *el que* impossible
   here)
	the colonel has no one to write to him

Tú no eres quien para decirme eso (colloquial, *el que* impossible)	you're no one to tell me that
Como quien espera heredar una fortuna	like someone hoping to inherit a fortune

Note   Since it is indeterminate, *quien/quienes* cannot be used when the identity or sex of the person referred to is known and stressed:

Le vimos con la que vive al lado	we saw him with the girl who lives next door

(**le vimos con quien vive al lado* =
   *'we saw him with whoever lives next
   door'.)	

30.2   'Cleft' sentences

30.2.1   Introductory

A number of the examples under 30.1 are 'cleft' sentences (the term is from Quirk, Greenbaum *et al.*, 1972). These are those in which an object, predicate or adverbial phrase in a sentence is isolated and focused by using 'to be' (*ser*). This can be done in one of two ways:

Simple sentence	*Cleft sentence*
the fire started here	it was here that the fire started
	here was where the fire started
John said it	it was John who said it
	John was the one who said it
I cut it with this knife	it was this knife I cut it with
	this knife is the one I cut it with

The structure of such sentences differs in Spanish from its French and English counterparts, and there are important differences between Peninsular and American usage with regard to cleft sentences containing a preposition.

30.2.2 'She is the one who . . .', etc.

English speakers, especially those who know French, are tempted to join this type of cleft sentences in Spanish by the particle *que*, but only a nominalizer (*el que* or *quien*) can be used:

Es este coche el que compré	it's this car I bought
Este coche es el que compré	this car's the one I bought
(NOT **es este coche que compré*)	
Es esa chica la que/quien lo hizo	it's that girl who did it
Esa chica es la que/quien lo hizo	that girl is the one who did it
Fue usted el que/quien lo dijo	it was you (masc.) who said it
Usted fue el que/quien lo dijo	you were the one who said it
Esto es lo que más rabia me da	this is what makes me most furious
Lo que más rabia me da es esto	" "
Porque doña Pilar nunca es ella la que aporta el dinero (interview in *Cambio16*)	because it's never Doña Pilar who brings in the money
El pelaje overo es el que prefieren los ángeles (Borges)	lamb's fleeces are the ones which angels prefer
Para entonces será la guerra mundial la que haya solucionado todo (*Cambio16*)	by then it'll be world war that will have solved everything

30.2.3 Cleft sentences involving prepositions

If the first half of the cleft sentences contains a preposition, the preposition must normally be repeated in the second half, i.e. Spanish says 'it's with her *with whom* you must speak' (*es con ella con la que/con quien tienes que hablar*).

A major difference exists here between Peninsular and American Spanish. American Spanish, especially spoken but also written, regularly uses *que* alone, in a way similar to French or English 'that'. This 'gallicism' is vehemently rejected by many native Spaniards (though heard increasingly among younger generations of Spaniards):

Sp. *Es desde esta ventana desde donde se ve el mar*	it's from this window that you can see the sea
SA. *Es desde esta ventana que se ve el mar*	
Desde esta ventana es desde donde se ve el mar (avoided in Span. America?)	this balcony is where you can see the sea from
Sp. *Era por este motivo por el que decidió cambiar de empleo*	it was for this reason that he decided to change jobs
SA. *Era por este motivo que decidió . . .*	
. . . pero es con la Maga que hablo (Cortázar, Arg. dialogue. Spain *. . . con la que/quien hablo*)	but it's Maga I'm talking to
No fue por Pepita sino por Teresa por la que/quien se pelearon (Spain)	it wasn't Pepita but Teresa they fought over
Es quizá por ello por lo que los electores han elegido el cambio (*Cambio16*)	perhaps this is why voters have opted for change
Es por eso que en el lenguaje deportivo abundan las hipérboles (*El Litoral*, Arg., Sp. *por lo que . . .*)	that's why hyperboles abound in sporting language

Clauses of time, place or manner require *cuando*, *donde* and *como* respectively, although Spanish Americans may use *que*, especially in informal speech:

Sp. *Fue aquí donde ocurrió*	it was here that it happened
SA. *Fue aquí que ocurrió*	
Aquí fue donde ocurrió	
Es en esta última novela donde se enfrentan los más verídicos tipos clericales trazados por Galdós (*Ínsula*, Spain)	it is in this last novel where the most lifelike clerical figures drawn by Galdós confront one another
Fue en Pueblo Nuevo que supimos que el novio de Petra no había vuelto más al pueblo (Cabrera Infante, Cuban dialogue, Sp. *donde*)	it was in Pueblo Nuevo that we found out that Petra's boyfriend had never returned to the village
La chica se acuerda de que es ahí que está la guarida del brujo (M. Puig, Arg. dialogue, Sp. *donde*)	the girl remembers that there's where the wizard's lair is
Fue en casa de ella [. . .] que tuvo lugar aquel encuentro con Vallejos (Vargas Llosa, Peru)	it was in her house that this meeting with Vallejos took place
Sp. *Es así como hay que hacerlo*	it's this way you have to do it
SA. *Es así que hay que hacerlo*	" "
Así es como hay que hacerlo	" "
Fue entonces cuando, podríamos decir, comenzó la historia del automóvil (*El País*, Spain)	it was then, we might say, that the story of the car began
Naturalmente tenía que ser en ese momento . . . que sonara el timbre (Cortázar, Arg., Sp. *cuando*)	of course it had to be at that moment . . . that the bell rang

Notes (i) Care is required with cleft sentences involving *lo que*. The neuter pronoun must be retained, cf. *lo que me sorprende es su timidez/es su timidez lo que me sorprende*.

Es la inseguridad lo que le hace reaccionar de esa forma	it's insecurity that makes him react like that (i.e. 'what makes him react thus is insecurity')
Ha hecho cine, teatro, televisión, pero es con la canción con lo que le gustaría triunfar (*Cambio16*)	he has worked in cinema, theatre and TV, but it is in singing that he would like to make a hit
Era un traje negro lo que llevaba	it was a black suit that he was wearing (answers question 'what was he wearing?')

but –

El que llevaba era el traje negro	the one he was wearing was the black suit (answer to 'which suit was he wearing?')

(ii) English makes the verb 'to be' singular when it is shifted to the head of a cleft sentence: 'the mosquitoes are what annoys him'/'it's the mosquitoes which annoy him'. *Ser* normally remains plural in such cleft sentences:

Tenían que ser los partidos socialistas quienes/los que implementaran esta política de austeridad	it had to be the socialist parties which implemented this austerity policy
Son los mosquitos lo que me irrita	the mosquitoes are what annoys me
Lo que me irrita son los mosquitos	what annoys me is the mosquitoes

but not universally –

En la terrible escasez que vive el país, *lo único que no falta es cigarrillos* (Vargas Llosa, Peru)	Amidst the terrible shortages the country is living through, the only thing which isn't lacking is cigarettes

(iii) Cleft sentences involving lengthy prepositional phrases may be connected by *que* in Spanish-American usage, but are likely to be avoided by careful Peninsular speakers:

?*Fue bajo esta impresión que continuamos* *con el programa*	it was under this impression that we carried on with the programme
(*Fue así, bajo esta impresión, como* *continuamos con el programa*)	
Teniendo en cuenta que es gracias al *número de parados que podemos* *mantener la inflación a nivel europeo* (*Triunfo*, Spain, Arg. writer)	bearing in mind that it is thanks to the number of unemployed that we are able to keep inflation at European levels
Fue a causa de eso que lo hizo (Spanish- American)	it was because of that that he did it

or

Lo hizo a causa de eso

or

Fue a causa de eso por lo que lo hizo

(iv) The complexities of cleft sentences can often be avoided by not using *ser*:

Por eso te digo

Desde esta ventana se ve el mar

Se pelearon por Pepita, no por Teresa

(v) The use of *quien* for things was once normal in Spanish, and still survives although it should not be imitated:

No fueron las máquinas quienes *desencadenaron el poder capitalista,* *sino el capitalismo financiero quien* *sometió la industria a su poderío* (E. Sabato, Arg.)	it was not machines which unleashed capitalist power, but finance capitalism which subjected industry to their domination

30.2.4 Translating 'that's why'

Porque means 'because', and cannot be used to translate sentences like 'she's got the flu, that's why she didn't come to work'. A cleft construction with *por* is called for: *está con gripe, por eso (es por lo que) no ha venido al trabajo*:

Por eso lo hice	that's why I did it
Fue por eso por lo que no te llamé antes	that's why I didn't ring before
Fue por eso que no te llamé antes	" "
(Spanish-American equivalent)	" "
Ésa es la razón por la que no lo *compré*	that's the reason why I didn't buy it

30.2.5 Agreement in cleft sentences

The view of María Moliner, confirmed by native informants, is that in the singular either *tú fuiste el que le mataste* or *tú fuiste el que le mató* 'you're the one who killed him' is correct, but strict agreement seems to be the only possible construction in the plural: *vosotros fuisteis los que le matasteis* 'you were the ones who killed him'. Further examples:

Yo fui la que me lo bebí	I was the woman who drank it

Yo fui la que se lo bebió
El que lo sé soy yo   I'm the one (masc.) who knows
El que lo sabe soy yo
Somos los únicos que no tenemos ni   we're the only ones who haven't got a
   un centavo para apostar   *centavo* to bet
   (García Márquez, Colombia, dialogue)
Vosotros sois los que lo sabéis   you're the ones who know it
Ellos son los que trabajan más   they're the ones who work hardest
– *Vos sos el que no me aguanta. Vos sos*   you're the one who can't stand me. You're
   el que no aguantás a Rocamadour   the one who can't stand Rocamadour
   (Cortázar, Arg. dialogue; Spain *tú*
   eres for *vos sos*, *aguantas* for
   aguantás.)

31 Word order

31.1 General

Word order, specifically the position of the subject in relation to its verb, is much more flexible in Spanish than in English or French: *dice María que . . .* is as common as *María dice que . . .* 'Maria says that . . .', and the difference is not, as is sometimes said, merely 'stylistic'. However, in plain prose style and ordinary conversation, word order seems nowadays to be a good deal more rigid than fifty years ago: literary Spanish of a by-gone age tended to imitate the word order of Classical Latin prose and poetry.

The subject of Spanish word order requires a separate book: unquantifiable factors like rhythm, context, register and psychology affect the ordering of the main constituents of a Spanish sentence. In general, word order has more or less the same function in Spanish as stress and intonation in English, and in this chapter, italicized words in the English translations must be read with emphasis.

31.2 *Viene Antonio* or *Antonio viene*?

If a sentence consists only of a subject and a verb, the rule is: unfocused element comes first. Thus, to the question *¿quién viene?*, 'who's coming?', we must reply *viene Antonio* '*Antonio's* coming'. *Antonio viene* is as strange here as 'Antonio's *coming*'. But *Antonio está durmiendo* 'Antonio's *sleeping*' is the only possible order in reply to the question *¿qué está haciendo Antonio?* 'what's Antonio doing?'.

    (a) Subject focused:

¿Qué pasa? Se ha caído un libro	what happened? *A book* fell down
Ha muerto Franco	*Franco* is dead
Han vuelto a España ya muchos	*many* have returned to Spain already
Se abrió la puerta y entró Juan	*the door* opened and *John* came in
Faltan diez minutos	there are *ten minutes* to go
Siempre sucede algo extraño	*something strange* always happens
Quizá se ha interrumpido el servicio de autobuses	perhaps the *bus-service* has been interrupted

Note Undefined nouns (i.e. not preceded by definite article or a demonstrative) almost always follow the verb in such sentences. See 31.8, item b.

(b)   Verb focused:

¿Qué hace Miguel? Miguel está leyendo	what's Miguel doing? Miguel's *reading*
Turner se volvió. Tenía una pistola en la mano	Turner *turned round*. He had a gun in his hand
De repente, Horacio aulló	suddenly Horace *howled*

etc.

Notes (i)   Interrogative sentences obey special rules. See 31.6.

(ii)   Subject personal pronouns are usually emphatic by nature, cf. *escribo* 'I'm writing, *yo escribo* '*I*'m writing'. As a result there are three types of pattern of emphasis: no emphasis, pronoun emphasized, and whole verb phrase emphasized:

(a) *si vienes conmigo en vez de quedarte aquí . . .*	if you come with me instead of staying here . . .
(b) *si vienes tú conmigo en su lugar . . .*	if *you* come with me instead of *him* . . .
(c) *si tú vienes conmigo en vez de irte con él . . .*	if *you come with me* instead of *going with him* . . .

In **(a)** the subject is not emphasized. In **(b)** *tú* is emphasized by contrast with *él*. In **(c)** the verb phrase *tú vienes* is stressed by way of contrast with the verb phrase *irte con él*.

31.3   Word order in sentences which include verbal objects

A sentence consisting of a subject verb and object (direct or indirect) can theoretically appear in Spanish in the following forms:

1	*Inés leyó el libro*	SVO
2	*El libro lo leyó Inés*	O (redundant pronoun) VS
3	*El libro Inés lo leyó*	OS (redundant pronoun) V
4	*(Inés el libro leyó*	SOV)
5	*Leyó Inés el libro*	VSO
6	*Leyó el libro Inés*	VOS

Of these possibilities only the first three are at all common in everyday language. (4) might occur in songs or comic verse, and (5) and (6) are typical of flowery literary style.

(1) is a neutral word order corresponding to an English sentence spoken with equal stress on 'Inés' and 'book'. (2) makes the object into the topic of the sentence, and introduces the subject as new information, e.g. in answer to the question *¿quién leyó el libro?* '*who* read the book?'. (3) also makes the object into the topic, but focuses on the verb and not on the subject: e.g. *la moto mi marido la compró el año pasado y el coche hace una semana* '(as for the) motor cycle, my husband bought it last year, and the car (he bought) last week'.

Examples:

Mi secretaria ha escrito una carta	my secretary's written a letter
¿Quién escribió esta carta?	who wrote this letter?
Esta carta la escribió mi secretaria	*my secretary* wrote this letter
Las cartas mi secretaria no las escribe, sino que las corrige	my secretary doesn't *write* the letters but *corrects* them
Si me toca la lotería, me iré de aquí	if I win *the lottery*, I'll leave here

El negocio lo había empezado Pedro Vicario (García Márquez, Colombia)	as for the business, *Pedro Vicario* had started it (better: 'the business had been started by P.V.')
Che Guevara escribía versos. Y también los escribían otros luchadores por la revolución latinoamericana (C. Barral in *Cambio16*)	Che Guevara wrote poetry. And *other fighters* for the Latin-American revolution wrote poetry too

Notes (i)   OVS order focuses the object of the verb, and therefore often has the same effect as passive with *ser*, for which it is often a less formal substitute:

El médico intenta averiguar si la reacción la provocó una alergia o una enfermedad (instead of . . . *fue provocada por una alergia* . . ., etc.)	the doctor tries to find out if the reaction was produced by an allergy or an illness

(ii)   In 2 and 3 the object must normally be 'echoed' by an object pronoun which agrees with it in number and gender: *éstos los dejo aquí, los demás me los llevo* 'I'll leave these here, I'll take the others with me'. This rule is not applied to nouns which are not preceded by an article or demonstrative adjective. Compare *este paquete lo dejo aquí* 'I'll leave *this parcel* here' and *demasiada prisa se ha dado el Gobierno en este caso* 'the Government has been too hasty in this case', *aviones tenemos aquí que han costado más de treinta millones* . . . 'we've got planes here that cost more than 30 million . . .':

31.4   VS order in relative clauses

Verb-Subject order is strongly preferred in sentences containing a relative clause in order to keep the antecedent close to the relative pronoun and to avoid throwing the verb to the end of the sentence. This neat device could usefully be adopted in English, as the clumsy translations show:

No existe todavía el coche que yo quiera comprar (**El coche no existe todavía que yo quiera comprar* is not Spanish)	the car that I want to buy doesn't exist yet
Estas acciones han rendido más que las que compró tu madre	these shares have yielded more than the ones your mother bought
Todo está dispuesto para que el sábado próximo se inicie aquí el carnaval de invierno que organiza el Departamento de Turismo (*El Mercurio*, Chile, in *Var.* p. 182)	everything is ready for the opening here next Saturday of the Winter Carnival organized by the Department of Tourism
Gana la partida aquel que más fichas posee de su color cuando el tablero esté completo (instructions in *El Ordenador Personal*)	the game is won by the person holding most counters of his own colour when the board is full
Así dice la carta que nos envió tu padre	that's what's in the letter your father sent (lit. 'thus says the letter which your father sent')
Son innumerables las dificultades que plantea la lucha contra el terrorismo (*La Vanguardia*)	the difficulties posed by the struggle against terrorism are innumerable

But verb phrases are not divided unnaturally:

Solía detenerse a hablar con ella en la aldea abrasada por la sal del Caribe donde su madre había tratado de enterrarla en vida (García Márquez, Colombia, rather than *donde había tratado su madre de enterrarla en vida*)	he used to stop to talk to her in the village, parched by the salt from the Caribbean, where her mother had tried to bury her alive
[*Las maestras*] *no tienen la culpa: si no existiera la maldita instrucción primaria que ellas tienen que aplicar . . .*	[The school mistresses] aren't to blame: if the wretched primary education they have to administer didn't exist . . .

31.5 Word order with impersonal *se*

See 12.11 for discussion.

31.6 Word order in questions

VS or VSO order is usual in questions:

¿Ha comprado mamá leche?	has mother bought any milk?
¿Qué pensaría tu mujer de todo esto?	what would your wife think of all this?
¿Tienen Juanita y María la sensación de aportar una ayuda efectiva viviendo en la barriada? (Vargas Llosa, Peru, dialogue)	do Juanita and Maria get the feeling that they're helping effectively by living in the *barriada* (quarter)
¿Cuándo va a incluir su revista programas y artículos dedicados a ordenadores tales como los ya citados? (Reader's letter in *El Ordenador Personal*)	when is your magazine going to include programs and articles devoted to computers like the ones mentioned above?

Note In speech, intonation alone may indicate a question, without change of word order.

31.7 Sentence-initial position of highlighted items

Any item may be focused (topicalized) by placing it at the head of an utterance. This often has the same effect of introducing the item with some formula like *en cuanto a . . .* 'as for', *con respeto a . . .* 'as regards', etc.

De dinero no quiero volver a oír ni una palabra	about *money* I don't want to hear another word
Al verano inglés debían llamarlo estación de las lluvias	the English summer ought to be called the rainy season
Por no haber llegado a tiempo habéis perdido lo mejor	you've missed the best part by arriving late
Como en la foto de la boda no creo que yo vuelva a estar	I don't think I'll be like I was in the wedding photo again
Lo que yo digo es que la culpa quien la tiene es el Gobierno	what I say is that the one to blame is the Government

Americano vino uno solamente (Cuban TV interview)	as for Americans, only one came
– *Lléveme adentro de una de esas casas* . . .	'Take me inside one of those houses . . .'
– *Casas fueron antes, ahora son oficinas* (M. Puig, Arg. dialogue: Peninsular usage requires *dentro de* . . .)	'They used to be houses, now they're offices.'
Muchas cosas he leído, pocas he vivido (Borges, Arg.)	I've read many things but lived few

etc.

Spanish-American headlines and classified advertisements (especially in Colombia and nearby) favour bold inversions of word order in order to sensationalize the focal point of a sentence:

Signada por muchos altibajos estuvo la actividad bursátil (*La Nación*, Arg., in *Var.* 124 *signada = caracterizada* in Spain)	Stock Exchange Activity marked by many rises and falls
Causa de deslizamiento verán expertos (*El Comercio*, Peru)	Experts to Investigate Cause of Landslide
A tres coches quemaron	Three Cars Burnt
Ingeniero buscamos (advert.)	engineer required

Such language sounds strange to Spaniards.

31.8 Seven miscellaneous word order rules

(a)   In general, only *no* should separate a preposition from its infinitive (in which respect Spanish differs from French):

Su nombramiento se demoró por estar siempre la vacante ocupada	his appointment (to the post) was delayed because the vacant position was always occupied
La promesa de una vida de ocio fue frustrada al negarse el Fisco a devolverle el dinero	the promise of a life of leisure was frustrated when the Inland Revenue Department refused to return the money to him
Se equivocó por no haber pensado antes	he went wrong as a result of not thinking beforehand

(b)   The order VS is almost always found if the subject is an undefined noun (i.e. not preceded by the definite article or by a demonstrative adjective):

Sonó un tiro	a shot rang out
Pasa un coche	a car passes by
Viene un autobús	a bus is coming
Se declara estado de urgencia	state of emergency declared

But SV order may appear with such nouns (a) if they are qualified in some way (e.g. by an adjective), or (b) if more than one indefinite noun is the subject of the verb:

Una ley histórica prueba que pueblo que no gana su libertad . . . *con sus propios esfuerzos, no es libre* (*Cambio16*)	a historical law proves that a people which does not win its freedom by its own efforts is not free

Difícil historia espera a África si . . .
    cae bajo el colonialismo soviético (*ibid.*)
	a difficult history is in store for
	    Africa if it falls under Soviet colonialism

Señoras preponderantemente obesas se
    diseminaban en la platea
    (Cortázar, Arg.)
	ladies, mainly overweight, were occupying
	    the orchestra pit

Sociólogos, economistas y antropólogos
    aseguran que, por asombroso que
    parezca, es así (Vargas Llosa, Peru)
	sociologists, economists and
	    anthropologists claim that, however
	    surprising it may seem, this is the
	    case

All four examples are literary in style.

Note A noun with the indefinite article can sometimes be the topic of a sentence (i.e. represent given or background information), in which case SV order is normal:

Un ordenador Philips MSX hará que
    muchas de las gestiones cotidianas sean
    más llevaderas (advert., Spain)
	a Philips ˈMSX computer will make many
	    everyday business activities more
	    bearable

(c) Set verb phrases should not be broken up by the insertion of other words:

Probablemente las obras se llevarán a
    cabo para febrero (not **se llevarán*
    probablemente a cabo . . .)
	the work will probably be carried out by
	    February

(d) In this connection, words should not be inserted between an auxiliary and a participle, e.g. *siempre he dicho* or *he dicho siempre* but not **he siempre dicho* (students of French take note: *j'ai presque toujours pensé que* is *casi siempre he pensado que* or *he pensado casi siempre que*). This rule is sometimes broken: see 14.6.1 for discussion.

(e) Unstressed object pronouns (*me, te, se, la, lo, le, nos, os, los, las, les*) are never separated from their verb: *te lo diré luego* 'I'll tell you later', *sólo te quiero a ti* 'I only love you'/'I love only you', etc.

(f) Adjectival phrases are kept close to the noun they modify:

Regresó como a las seis y media con un
    ejemplar arrugado y manchado de
    huevo de las Últimas Noticias del
    mediodía
    (C. Fuentes, Mex.)
	he returned around 6.30 with a crumpled
	    and egg-stained copy of the mid-day
	    Últimas Noticias

However, compound nouns formed with *de* are not broken up: one says *un coche de alquiler japonés* 'a Japanese hire car', not **un coche japonés de alquiler*. There is no infallible way in this case of determining whether a noun is a compound or not.

(g) VS order is commonly used to avoid verbs or verb phrases left dangling at the end of a subordinate clause:

Cuando llegó esa noticia nosotros, los
    convencidos, empezamos a dudar
	when that news arrived, we, the
	    convinced, began to doubt

El tratamiento debe repetirse durante
    toda la vida, salvo que se realice con
    éxito un trasplante de riñón
    (*Ercilla*, Chile, in *Var.* 220)
	the treatment must be repeated throughout
	    {the patient's} life, unless a
	    successful kidney transplant is
	    performed

And a predicate is not separated from its immediate subject:

El "bárbaro" que aniquila al romano   the 'barbarian' annihilating the decadent
   decadente era menos sabio que éste,   Roman was less learned than the latter,
   y, sin embargo, no es dudosa la   and yet the former's superior historical
   superior calidad histórica de aquél   quality is not in doubt
   (Ortega y Gasset, instead of the less
   elegant *la superior calidad histórica*
   de aquél no es dudosa)
Tu inglés es tan bueno como pueda serlo   your English is as good as could be in
   el de una persona que siempre ha vivido   a person who's always lived in Mexico
   en México

31.9   Positioning of adverbials

Generally speaking, adverbials (i.e. adverbs, adverbial phrases and adverbial clauses) are placed either immediately before or immediately after the word(s) which they modify. This produces the common 'unEnglish' order Verb–Adverbial–Object (cf. *besó fervorosamente la mano de su anfitriona* 'he kissed his hostess's hand fervently').

Adverbials of time are very often put before adverbials of place: 'we went to grandma's house yesterday' = *fuimos ayer a casa de la abuela*.

Note particularly the position of the adverbials underlined in the following sentences:

Fue inútil que los párrocos advirtieran   it was no use the parish priests in the
   <u>*en los pueblos*</u> *a las mujeres que sus*   villages warning women that their
   maridos las abandonarían si llegaba   husbands would leave them if the
   la ley del divorcio (*Cambio16*)   divorce law was introduced
Parece que la habilidad más importante   it seems the most important skill is
   es la de memorizar información para   memorizing information in order to
   <u>*luego*</u> *escupirla en un examen*   churn (lit. 'spit') it out later in an
   (Spanish popular press)   examination
Alguien dijo que uno de esos   someone said that one of those
   desventurados había huido a Mysore,   unfortunates had fled to Mysore, where
   donde había pintado <u>*en un palacio*</u>   he had painted the figure of the tiger
   la figura del tigre (Borges, Arg.)   in a palace
Me di cuenta de que había estado <u>*antes*</u>   I realized I'd been in that place
   en aquel sitio   before
¿Sabes que el presidente Romeo Lucas   do you know someone made an attempt
   sufrió <u>*ayer*</u> *un atentado? Estaba en su*   on President Romeo Lucas's life
   coche parado en un semáforo cuando   yesterday? He was waiting in his car
   <u>*desde una bicicleta*</u> *le arrojaron un*   at some traffic lights when someone
   diccionario   on a bicycle threw a dictionary at him
   (Joke quoted in *Cambio16*, about a
   Guatemalan dictator who spoke an
   Amerindian language better than
   Spanish)
Siempre has creído que <u>*en el viejo centro*</u>   you've always believed that no one lives
   <u>*de la ciudad*</u> *no vive nadie*   in the old city centre
   (C. Fuentes, Mex.)

For further remarks about the position of adverbs see 26.2.8.

32 Diminutive, augmentative and pejorative suffixes

32.1 General

There are numerous suffixes which may add an emotional tone to a word, e.g. *-ito*, *illo*, *-ón*, *-ote*, *-azo*, *-aco*, *-ejo*, etc.

The effect of these suffixes is very unpredictable. Sometimes they simply create new words without any emotional colouring at all: compare *ventana* 'window', *ventanilla* 'window of a vehicle'; *la caja* 'box', *el cajón* 'drawer' (in furniture). These words are standard lexical items and must be learnt separately.

Very often they add an emotional tone to a word or phrase, e.g. affection, endearment, contempt, irony, repugnance, and they may sound affected, effeminate, childish or too familiar if used inappropriately. Consequently foreign learners are advised not to experiment with these suffixes since inexpert use may produce unfortunate effects. *Estarías mejor con el pelo recogido* means 'you'd look better with your hair up'; *estarías mejor con el pelo recogidito* means the same, but sounds either painfully condescending or like an adult talking to a little girl; ?*estarías mejor con el pelito recogidito* is ludicrous and would be said by no one.

In view of this and the fact that the forms and frequency of the suffixes differ widely from continent to continent and region to region, the following account is very summary. For a detailed picture of Peninsular use of these suffixes, see A. Gooch's *Diminutive, Augmentative and Pejorative Suffixes in Modern Spanish* (Oxford 1970), from which a number of the following examples are taken.

32.2. Diminutive suffixes

32.2.1 Formation
The following are found, *-ito* and *-illo* being the most common in Central Spain, and very frequent elsewhere. *-ico* and *-iño* have a regional flavour.

Usual form	Variants		
-ito	-cito	-ecito	-ececito
-illo	-cillo	-ecillo	-ececillo
-ico	-cico	-ecico	-ececico
-uelo	-zuelo	-ezuelo	-ecezuelo

Usual form	Variants	
-ete	-cete	-ecete
-ín		
-iño		

All are marked for gender in the usual way: a final vowel is replaced by *-a*; *-ín* makes its feminine *-ina*.

The following remarks apply to typical educated usage in Central Spain and probably to educated usage in many places, but they should be checked against the speech habits of Spanish Americans.

Words of more than one syllable ending in *-n*, *-l* or *-r*, and words ending in *-e* usually take the form in *-c-*. The following formations were generated spontaneously by Peninsular informants, but not all are guaranteed to be in common use. It must be emphasized that diminutive suffixes are theoretically very productive and could conceivably be added to almost any noun:

girasol	sunflower	*girasolcito*
surtidor	spout/fountain	*surtidorcito*
mujer	woman	*mujercita*
mejor	better	*mejorcito*
mayor	bigger	*mayorcito*
charlatán	talkative	*charlatancito*
cajón	drawer	*cajoncito*
montón	pile	*montoncito*
madre	mother	*madrecita*
padre	father	*padrecito*
cofre	case/box	*cofrecito*
puente	bridge	*puentecito*

(But note *café* > *cafetito*, less commonly *cafecito*).

Words of one syllable commonly take forms in *-ec-*:

flor	flower	*florecita*
pan	bread	*panecillo* (i.e. 'bread roll')
pez	fish	*pececito/pececillo*
tos	cough	*tosecita/tosecilla*
pie	foot	*piececito* (?*piececillo* – if it is ever used)
voz	voice	*vocecita*
sol	sun	*solecito/solito*

The suffix *-illo* is often faintly pejorative or denotes lack of importance, cf. *catarrillo* 'bit of a cold'/'touch of a cold', *mundillo* 'petty little world'/ 'clique', but generalization is hazardous and many formations are merely diminutive, e.g. *mesilla de noche* 'bedside table', *arbolillo* 'small tree', *infernillo* 'spirit lamp', etc.

The other suffixes are best studied in context, e.g. *río* > *riachuelo* 'river/rivulet'.

32.2.2 Uses of the diminutive

The main effects of these suffixes are:

(a) To give a friendly tone to a statement:

This very common use of the diminutive may simply give a warm tone to a remark. In a bakery one might say *deme una barrita de pan* 'give me a loaf of bread' which is merely a cheery equivalent of *deme una barra de pan*. This use of the diminutive does not imply smallness but merely signals the speaker's attitude to the hearer:

Falta una pesetilla	you're just one peseta short
(Compare *falta una peseta*	you're a peseta short)
Dame un paquetito por ahora	give me just one packet for now
Ahora sólo queda el jaleíllo de las entradas	all that's left is the business of the entrance tickets
(*jaleo* = row, fuss)	
Me tiras el vaso con el codo. A ver si tenemos más cuidadito . . .	you're knocking my glass over with your elbow. Let's see if we can't have a little bit more care . . .
Voy a echar una siestecita	I'm going to have forty winks
Un momentito, por favor	just a moment, please
Me lo contó un pajarito	a little birdy told me
¿Alguna cosita más?	if you'd like something else . . .
(*¿Alguna cosa más?*	anything else?)

(b) To modify the meaning of adjectives and adverbs by adding a warm tone or, sometimes, by making them more precise – e.g. *ahora* 'now', *ahorita* (colloquial) 'right now':

cerquita de la catedral	just by the cathedral
Las empanadas están calentitas	the meat pies are lovely and hot
Ya eres mayorcito	you're a big boy now
(*mayor* = grown up, older)	
Está gordito	he's put on a bit
(*Está gordo*	he's fat)
¡tontito!	silly!
(*¡tonto!*	stupid!)
mentirosillo	'fibber'
mentiroso	liar

(c) To denote endearment or affection:

Luisito, mamita (SA), *abuelita*	Luis, mummy, granny
Vamos, m'hijito	come on son
(Spanish-American)	

(d) To denote smallness:

The diminutive form may have a specialized meaning, cf. English 'book'/ 'booklet':

el gato/gatito	cat/kitten
el perro/perrito	dog/little dog, doggy
(*el cachorro* = puppy)	
el conejo/conejito	rabbit/baby rabbit
la cocina/cocinita	kitchen/kitchenette
el palo/palillo	stick/toothpick
la caja/cajita	box/box for matches, etc.
la vara/varilla	rod/thin stick, spoke, wand
la guerra/guerrilla	war/guerrilla warfare

etc.

Note Occasionally the diminutive form is of different gender:

la maleta suitcase	*el maletín* small hand case
la botella bottle	*el botellín* (typically small bottle of beer)

el avión aircraft	*la avioneta* light aircraft
el camión truck	*la camioneta* van/light truck

(e)   To create a new noun:
In such cases, the diminutive ending has no diminutive function:

el coche/el cochecito	car/pram
la mariposa/la mariposilla	butterfly/(clothes) moth
la manzana/la manzanilla	apple/camomile
la masa/la masilla	dough/mass, putty
la ventana/la ventanilla	window/vehicle window
la bomba/la bombilla	bomb/light bulb
la tesis/la tesina	thesis/dissertation
el ajo/el ajillo	garlic/chopped garlic
el bolso/el bolsillo	bag/pocket
el caballo/el caballete	horse/easel

etc.

(f)   To denote a combination of diminutive and pejorative:
In Spain *-illo*, *-ejo*, *-uelo* are particularly likely to have this function:

la cultura/culturilla	culture/'smattering of culture'
la calle/calleja/callejuela	street/alley/narrow little alley
el arroyo/arroyuelo	stream/trickle, rivulet
el rey/reyezuelo	king/petty king, princeling

etc.

32.2.3   Diminutive forms in Spanish America
In many areas of Spanish America, diminutive forms pervade popular speech to an extent which amuses Spaniards, but the following examples may be rustic or quaint even on their own territory:

Viene ya merito (Mex.)	he's coming right now
(i.e. *ahora mismo*)	
Merito ayer no más (Mex.)	only yesterday
(i.e. *ayer mismo*)	
Ahorita lo voy a hacer	I'll do it straight away
(i.e. *ahora mismo*)	
Clarito la recuerdo	I remember her vividly
Apártate tantito, que voy a saltar	get out of the way a bit, I'm going to jump
(Guatemalan, from Kany, 385)	
Reciencito llegó . . . (see 26.6.2 for *recién*)	he's just this minute arrived

32.3   'Augmentative' suffixes

Typical, in order of frequency, are *-ón, -azo, -ote, -udo*.

(a)   These are mainly used to denote intensity or large size, almost always with some associated pejorative idea of clumsiness, unpleasantness, awkwardness, excess, etc.:

rico/ricachón	rich/stinking rich/'loaded'
pedante/pedantón	pedant/insufferable pedant
el soltero/solterón	bachelor/confirmed bachelor

contestón	tending to answer back
preguntón	constantly asking questions
cursi/cursilón	affected/incredibly affected
fácil/facilón	easy/facile
la broma/el bromazo	joke/joke pushed too far
el coche/cochazo	car/'heck of a car'
el libro/librazo	book/tome
la ginebra/un ginebrazo	gin/an enormous shot of gin
el gringo/gringote	gringo/bloody gringo
la palabra/la palabrota	word/swearword
el favor/favorzote	favour/'heck of a favour'

etc.

(b) To form an entirely new word. The suffix then has no connotations of size or awkwardness and may even imply smallness:

la rata/el ratón	rat/mouse
la caja/el cajón	box/drawer
la cintura/el cinturón	waist/belt
el fuego/el fogón	fire/stove
la tela/el telón	cloth/theatre curtain
la cuerda/el cordón	string/shoe-lace
la leche/el lechazo	milk/sucking lamb

etc.

Note (i) *-azo* is much used to form nouns which denote a blow or flourish with some object:

el aldabón/aldabonazo	knocker/thump with a door knocker, blow on door
el codo/codazo	elbow/dig with elbow
la bayoneta/el bayonetazo	bayonet/bayonet thrust

etc.

32.4 Pejorative suffixes

These are not particularly frequent, especially now that graphic insults are often expressed by language once thought shocking. The words formed by them should be learnt as separate lexical items. Typical suffixes are *-aco, -arraco, -acho, -ajo, -astro, -uco, -ucho, -ejo* and a few others.

They variously denote ugliness, wretchedness, squalor, meanness, etc.

el pájaro/pajarraco	bird/sinister bird
el poeta/poetastro	poet/rhymer, poetaster
el pueblo/poblacho	village/'dump', squalid village
el latín/latinajo	Latin/Latin jargon, dog Latin
la casa/casuca	house/pathetic little house
la palabra/palabreja	word/horrible word
el hotel/hotelucho	hotel/dingy hotel

etc.

33 Spelling, accent rules, punctuation and word division

33.1 Spelling

33.1.1 The *Nuevas normas* and the alphabet

For rules of pronunciation, see the Appendix. The spelling rules are those laid down by the Academy in the *Nuevas normas* which came into official use in 1959 and are now, with reservations, generally adopted by editors everywhere. But even thirty years later the old spelling is still commonly used by persons who are not connected with the world of publishing and editing. The spelling – particularly the use of the accent – of works published before that date will therefore differ in detail from this account. Among the more striking innovations were the removal of the accent from the words *fui*, *fue*, *dio*, *vio*, and its adoption in words like *búho*, *rehúso*, *reúne*, *ahínca*, *prohíbe*, *ahíto*, etc.

The Spanish alphabet consists of the following letters:

a	*a*	g	*ge*	m	*eme*	s	*ese*	z	*zeta/zeda*
b	*be*	h	*hache*	n	*ene*	t	*te*		
c	*ce*	i	*i*	ñ	*eñe*	u	*u*		
ch	*che*	j	*jota*	o	*o*	v	*uve*		
d	*de*	k	*ka*	p	*pe*	w	*uve doble*		
e	*e*	l	*ele*	q	*cu*	x	*equis*		
f	*efe*	ll	*elle*	r	*erre/ ere*	y	*i griega*		

Double *r* (*erre doble*) is a separate sound but is not treated as a separate letter of the alphabet. *Ch* and *ll* are traditionally treated as separate letters so that in alphabetical lists words beginning with *ch* or *ll* follow words beginning with *c* or *l*, *mancha* follows *mancornas* and *collado* follows *colza*, etc. This is very inconvenient for computerized sorting and out of line with other languages that use Latin letters, and a number of authorities, including Manuel Seco, now advocate standard alphabetical order.

The Academy rules that accents should be written on capital letters, a convention that is also problematic for computers and wordprocessors and is often ignored.

Note Letters of the alphabet are all feminine – *la cu*, *la uve* – and one says *la/una a*, *la/una hache*, despite the rule that singular feminine words beginning with a stressed *a* sound require the masculine article, cf. *el hacha* (fem.) 'the axe'.

33.1.2   Relationship between sounds and letters

Spanish spelling is not entirely rational, but it is much more logical than French or English. Basically one sound corresponds to one letter, so one merely needs to hear words like *colocar, chaleco, calenturiento* to be able to spell them correctly. However, the rule of one sound for one letter is broken in the following cases:

(1)   *H* is always silent (except in some rural dialects), but is common in writing, where it is merely a burden on the memory: *hacha, hombre, Huesca, Honduras, ahíto*, etc.

The sound /w/, when it is not preceded by a consonant, is spelt *hu*: *huele, ahuecar, Náhuatl*, etc.

(2)   *Z* does not appear before *i* or *e*, where it is written *c*: *cebra* 'zebra', *hacer, nación* etc. There are a handful of exceptions, e.g. *zeta, zéjel, Nueva Zelandia* (in Spain *Nueva Zelanda*), *zigzag* (plural *zigzags*).

Spelling in Spanish America and Andalusia is much more irrational than in central Spain since *z, c(e), c(i)* and *s* are pronounced identically, so that words like *caza* and *casa, ves* and *vez, Sena* and *cena* sound the same in these areas.

(3)   The sound of *c* in *cama* is written *qu* before *e* and *i*: *querer, quiso, saque*, etc.

The letter *k* is consequently not needed in Spanish, and is found only in foreign words like measurements preceded by *kilo-*, or in *kantiano, krausismo*, etc.

The sound /kw/ is always written *cu*, e.g. *cuestión, cuáquero* 'Quaker' (students of Portuguese and Italian take note!).

(4)   The sound /x/ (like *ch* in 'loch') is always written *j* before *a, o* and *u*, and is usually written *g* before *e* and *i*: *rige, general, Gibraltar*, etc.

There are numerous exceptions to the latter generalization, e.g. the preterite of all verbs whose infinitive ends in *ducir* (*produje, produjiste, produjimos, produjisteis, produjeron*, etc.) and many other words, e.g. *jeringa, Jesús, jesuita, jeta, Jiménez, jirafa, jersey*, etc.

(5)   The sound of *g* in *hago* is written *gu* before *e* and *i*: *ruegue, guirnalda*.

The sounds /gwe/ and /gwi/ (both quite rare in Spanish) are written *güe* and *güi*, e.g. *lingüista, desagüe, averigüe, nicaragüense*. This is the only use of the dieresis in the modern language.

(6)   *B* and *v* sound exactly the same, and are usually pronounced as a voiced bilabial fricative /β/, although they both sound like the English *b* after *n* or *m* or after a pause. The English sound /v/ does not exist in Spanish and English speakers of Spanish often make a false distinction between the pronunciation of the Spanish written signs *b* and *v*, so they usually do not confuse these letters in writing. Native speakers who are poor spellers make blunders like **uba* for *uva*, **Premio Novel* for *Premio Nobel*, etc. – mistakes which are at least the sign of a correct pronunciation.

(7)   *X* is often like *s* before a consonant: *extender, extracto, extremo,*

etc. In one common case, *México/mexicano*, (older Peninsular form *Méjico/mejicano*), and in one or two Mexican place names (e.g. *Oaxaca*) it is pronounced /x/ (like the Spanish *j*).

(8) *N* is pronounced *m* before *b*, *v*, *p*: *en Barcelona, invitar, en París*.

(9) *R* and *rr* represent a flapped and a rolled *r* respectively. But *r* is pronounced like *rr* when it is the first letter in a word – *Roma, rueda* – or when it occurs within a word after *l*, *n* or *s*: *Israel, sonrisa, alrededor*.

When a prefix ending in a vowel is added to a word beginning with *r*, the *r* is written double: *infra + rojo = infrarrojo* 'infra-red', *contra + revolucionario = contrarrevolucionario*.

(10) *Ll* is properly a palatalized *l* – /ʎ/ – but is nowadays pronounced like the letter *y* by many (but not all) speakers, to the dismay of purists. Poor spellers sometimes make mistakes like **cullo* for *cuyo*, **balloneta* for *bayoneta*. It is much better to pronounce it *y* than to pronounce it like the *lli* of 'million' (which is written *li* in Spanish).

(11) *M* is often pronounced *n* at the end of words: *álbum, referéndum, ultimátum*.

(12) The three initial groups of consonants *ps*, *mn* and *gn* are pronounced *s*, *n* and *n* respectively and may now officially be spelt thus; but some cannot bring themselves to write *sicología* for *psicología* or *siquiatría* for *psiquiatría*, so some uncertainty prevails.

(13) The *p* in *septiembre, séptimo* is sometimes silent and may now be dropped, but many find the forms *setiembre, sétimo* repugnant.

(14) If the prefix *re-* is added to a word beginning with *e* one of the *es* may be dropped in writing: *remplazo, rembolso*, although this option is not usually taken up.

33.1.3   *Trans-* or *-tras-*

Some uncertainty surrounds the spelling of words which begin with the prefix *trans-* or *tras-*. Educated usage seems to be:

Normally *trans-*	Usually *tras-*	Always *tras-*
transalpino	trascendencia	trasfondo
transatlántico	trascendental	trashumancia
transbordar	trascendente	trashumante
transbordo	trascender	trasladar
transcribir	trasponer	traslado
transcripción	trasvasar	trasnochar
transcurrir		traspapelar
transcurso		traspasar
transferencia		traspaso
transferir		traspié
transformación		trasplantar
transfusión		trasplante
transgredir		traspunte
transgresión		trasquilar
transgresor		trastienda
transmigración		trastocar
transmisión		trastornar

Normally *trans-*
transmitir
transparencia
transparentar
transparente
transpirenaico
transportar
transporte
transposición
transversal

Always *tras-*
trastorno
trastrocar
trastrueque

Source: Manuel Seco, *Diccionario de dudas y dificultades de la lengua española*, 9th ed., 361–2. Seco notes that in the case of the first two columns the alternative spellings in *tras-* and *trans-* respectively are tolerated by the Academy but are not in general use.

33.2 The written accent

33.2.1 General rules
Native Spanish speakers are rather cavalier about the use of the written accent in handwriting, but in printing and formal writing the rules must be observed.

The basic rule is that if a word has predictable stress, no written accent is required. If the stress in a word falls unpredictably, its position must be shown by an acute accent.

Stress falls predictably:
(a) On the last syllable, if the word ends in a consonant not *n* or *s*;
(b) On the penultimate syllable, if the word ends in a vowel or *n* or *s*.

If the stress in a word does not conform to either of these two patterns, it must be indicated by a written accent.

The following words therefore require no written accent: *cama, calle, denle, quinqui, redondo, tribu, virgen, sacacorchos, atlas, jueves, Madrid, Paraguay, coñac, volver, cabaret* (pronounced *cabaré*), *natural, reloj* (usually pronounced *reló*), *contestad*.

The following are stressed unpredictably and must have a written accent:
fácil, difícil, quórum, álbum, nación, récord, rehén, dirán, vírgenes, líquenes, revés, síntesis, química, decídmelo, alérgicamente, contéstenles, etc.

Note Words ending in two consonants of which the second is *s* (all of them foreign words) are normally stressed on the last syllable: *Orleans, complots, cabarets. Fórceps, bíceps, récords* are exceptions.

33.2.2 Diphthongs and the position of the stress accent
Spanish vowels are divided into strong (*a, e, o*), and weak, (*i, u*).

These may appear in combinations of two or three, e.g. *eai, au, uai, iai,* etc. An intervening *h* is disregarded, so that *au* and *ahu, eu* and *ehu, ai* and *ahi*, etc. are treated the same way (at least since the publication of the *Nuevas normas*).

A strong vowel plus an unstressed weak vowel is counted as a single vowel for the purpose of determining the position of the written accent. Therefore the following words are stressed predictably: *arduo, continuo, lengua, Francia, historia, produjisteis, amabais*, etc., and the following words have unpredictable stress and require a written accent: *amáis, debéis, volvió, continúo* (first-person present of *continuar*), *hacía, respondía*.

Note Students of Portuguese should note that this rule is the exact opposite of the one applied in Portuguese, which writes *colónia, história*, but *temia* (stressed like the Spanish *temía*).

33.2.3 Written accent on diphthongs and combined vowels
If one of a group of combined vowels is stressed, the written accent may or may not appear on it. There are four possibilities:

(a) If the combination is strong + weak, the stress falls predictably on the first vowel, so the following require no written accent: *deis, vais, aire, Laura, causa, Palau, Berneu, alcaloide*, etc., and the following are exceptions: *país, baúl, aún* (pronounced differently from *aun*), *reír, reís, reúne, reímos, rehúsa, ahíto, ahínca, prohíbe, egoísta, arcaísmo, embaír, ahí, oís*, etc.

(b) If the combination is weak + strong, the stress falls predictably on the second vowel, so the following require no accent; but see note (i): *tiene, luego, cuenta, tiara, piojo, cuanto, acuoso, respetuoso, fue, vio, dio, pie*, and the following are exceptions: *dúo, búho, fío, ríe, lía*, etc.

(c) If the combination is weak + weak the stress also falls predictably on the second vowel, so the following require no accent; but see note (i): *fui, fuimos, beduino, fluido, construido, destruir, Piura, viuda*. For this reason *huido, construido* are written without an accent and *creído, reído* with.

(d) If the combination is strong + strong, then the two are counted as separate syllables, so the following are stressed predictably: *jacarandaes, bajaes, caed, noes, caos, ahonda, crea, atea, ateo, creo, leen, loa, loo*, etc., and the following are exceptions: *aéreo, león, deán, rehén, Mahón*, etc.

Notes (i) The forms *rió, lió, fió, lié, huís, huí*, etc. are apparent exceptions to the rule that the second vowel is predictably stressed in the combination weak + strong and weak + weak: compare *fui, fue, vio, dio*. They are given a written accent to show that the vowels are pronounced separately, whereas *vio, dio, fui* and *fue* are pronounced /bjo/, /djo/, /fwi/, /fwe/. Compare the pronunciation of *pie* 'foot' (/pje/) with *pié* /pi-é/, from *piar*.

(ii) A combination of a strong vowel with two weak vowels is treated like a single vowel for the purpose of determining the written accent, so that *continuáis* is in fact an exception and must be written with the accent.

(iii) When an object pronoun is added to a finite verb form (nowadays rare) the original written accent is retained: *acabó + se = acabóse* for *se acabó*.

(iv) If a word bearing a written accent is joined to another to form a compound, the original written accent is discarded: *tío + vivo = tiovivo* 'merry-go-round', *balón + cesto = baloncesto* basketball, etc.

33.2.4 Written accent: some common doubtful cases
The following forms are recommended

acrobacia	*exégesis*	*paradisiaco*
afrodisiaco	*fríjol*	*parásito*
amoniaco	*fútbol*[2]	*pediatra*
austriaco	*géiser*	*periodo*
cardiaco	*hipocondriaco*	*policiaco*
chófer[1]	*ibero*	*polígloto*
cóctel	*láser*	*psiquiatra*
demoniaco	*maniaco*	*quiromancia*[3]
or *demoníaco*	*metempsicosis*	*rádar*
dinamo	*meteoro*	*reptil*
dispónte,	*misil*	*reuma* (us. *reúma*)
compónte,	*olimpiada*	*sánscrito*
deténte, etc.	*orgía*	*termostato*
electrodo	*ósmosis*	*tortícolis*
elegiaco	or *osmosis*	*utopía*
etíope	*pabilo*	*zodiaco*

Some 'mispronunciations' are usual in speech: *soviet, oceano* (written and correctly pronounced *océano*), *aeródromo*.

[1]but in much of Spanish America written and pronounced *chofer*
[2]although *futbol* is heard in some American countries.
[3]and so all words ending in -*mancia* with the meaning 'divination'

33.2.5 Accent on interrogative forms
In the case of some words, the interrogative form carries an accent. This indicates a fact of pronunciation: the interrogative form is stressed, as can be seen by contrasting *dice que* . . . 'he says that . . .' and *dice qué* . . . 'he says what . . .' or *cuando llega* 'when he arrives' and *¿cuándo llega?* 'when is he arriving?'.
These words are:

cómo	*dónde*
cuál	*qué*
cuándo	(also *por qué*)
cuánto	*quién*

Consult the index for further details.

33.2.6 Accent used to distinguish homonyms
In the case of some two dozen common words, the written accent merely eliminates ambiguities:

	without accent	**with accent**
de/dé	of	subjunctive of *dar*
el/él	the (def. article)	he/it
este/éste *ese/ése* *aquel/aquél*	} see 6.3	
mas/más	but (rare)	more
mi/mí	my	me (after prepositions)
se/sé	reflexive pronoun	(i) I know, (ii) imperative of *ser*
si/sí	if	(i) yes, (ii) prepositional form of *se*
solo/sólo (see 9.14)	alone	only (*solamente*)
te/té	object form of *tú*	tea
tu/tú	your	you

Notes (i)   *Dé* loses its accent if a pronoun is attached and the stress is regular: *denos*, 'give us', *deme* 'give me', etc.

(ii)   *O* ('or') takes an accent when it appears between two numerals so as to avoid confusion with zero: *9 ó 5* '9 or 5'.

(iii)   The following words do NOT have a written accent: *da, di, fe, ti, ve*.

(iv)   *Aun* 'even' and *aún* 'still/yet' are in fact pronounced differently in good Spanish.

33.3   Capital letters

These are used much more sparingly than in English.

(a)   Capital letters are used:

(1) After a full stop.

(2) With proper nouns, but not with the adjectives derived from them: *Madrid, la vida madrileña* 'Madrid life'; *Colombia, la cocina colombiana* 'Colombian cooking'; *Shakespeare, el lenguaje shakespeariano* 'Shakespearean (or Shakespeare's) language'; *Ministerio de Justicia* 'Ministry of Justice', *Partido Conservador* 'Conservative Party', *Las Naciones Unidas* 'The United Nations', etc.

Occasionally adjectives may be capitalized to show that they are part of a name, e.g. *Nueva Zeland(i)a* 'New Zealand', *el Reino Unido* 'the United Kingdom', *la Unión Soviética* 'the Soviet Union', etc.

(b)   Lower case letters are used for:

(1) Months, seasons and days of the week: *julio* 'July', *agosto* 'August', *verano* 'summer', *invierno* 'winter', *jueves* 'Thursday', *viernes* 'Friday', *martes* 'Tuesday', etc.

(2) Names of religions and their followers: *el cristianismo* 'Christianity', *el catolicismo* 'Catholicism', *el protestantismo* 'Protestantism', *el islam* 'Islam', *un testigo de Jehová* 'a Jehovah's witness', *los musulmanes* 'the Muslims', etc.

(3) Official titles, e.g. *el presidente de la República*, 'the President of the Republic', *la reina de Gran Bretaña* 'the Queen of Great Britain', *el papa Juan XXIII* 'Pope John XXIII', *los reyes de España* 'the King and Queen

of Spain', *el ministro de Obras Públicas* 'the Minister for Public Works', etc.

(4) Book and film titles: only the first letter is in upper case, as well as the first letter of any proper name which appears in the title: *Cien años de soledad*, *El otoño del patriarca*, *El espía que surgió del frío* ('The Spy who came in from the Cold'), *Vida de Manuel Rosas*, *La guerra de las galaxias* ('Star Wars'), etc.

(5) For points of the compass: *norte* 'North', *sur* 'South', *este* 'East', *oeste* 'West'. They may be capitalized if they are part of a name: *América del Norte*, 'North America', etc.

33.4 Punctuation

33.4.1 Main features
The point, comma, colon, semicolon and brackets are used much the same as in English, except that in much, but not all, of the Hispanic world, and certainly in Spain and the Southern Cone, the point is used like the English comma in numbers, and vice-versa: 1.567.789 = 1,567,789 and 1,005 = 1.005.

The chief difference between Spanish and English is in the use of inverted commas (*comillas*).

The signs « and » are used (at least in Spain) like our single inverted commas for quotations within sentences, to indicate slang, dialect or other unusual forms, and occasionally to indicate dialogue within a paragraph:

> *Un inspector de bigotillo con acento «pied noir», acompañado de un gendarme de uniforme, va recorriendo las mesas pidiendo documentación: «No pasa nada, es sólo una operación de rutina». Sin embargo, todo este impresionante montaje sorprende a todos. (Cambio16)*

A further quotation within «» is indicated by ' '.

In the representation of continuous dialogue, inverted commas are not used, the words spoken being introduced by a dash. They are terminated by another dash only if unspoken words follow, e.g. *– Ahora váyase – dijo – y no vuelva más hasta que yo le avise.*

Punctuation in direct speech is often disconcertingly placed after the dash: *– Aprovecha ahora que eres joven para sufrir todo lo que puedas – le decía –, que estas cosas no duran toda la vida.* (García Márquez, *El amor en los tiempos del cólera*).
Example:

> —¿Te parece que hablo de él con cierto rencor, con resentimiento? —Juanita hace un curioso mohín y veo que no pregunta por preguntar; es algo que debe preocuparla hace mucho tiempo.
> —No noté nada de eso —le digo—. He notado, sí, que evitas llamar a Mayta por

su nombre. Siempre das un rodeo en vez de decir Mayta. ¿Es por lo de Jauja, porque estás segura que fue él quien empujó a Vallejos?

—No estoy segura —niega Juanita—. Es posible que mi hermano tuviera también su parte de responsabilidad. Pero pese a que no quiero, me doy cuenta que le guardo un poco de rencor. No por lo de Jauja. Porque lo hizo dudar. Esa última vez que estuvimos juntos le pregunté: «¿Te vas a volver un ateo como tu amigo Mayta, también te va a dar por eso?» No me respondió lo que yo esperaba. Encogió los hombros y dijo:

—A lo mejor, hermana, porque la revolución es lo primero.

—También el Padre Ernesto Cardenal decía que la revolución era lo primero —recuerda María. Añade que, no sabe por qué, ese Padre pelirrojo de la historia de Mayta le ha traído a la cabeza lo que fue para ella la venida al Perú de Ivan Illich, primero, y, luego, de Ernesto Cardenal. (M. Vargas Llosa, *Historia de Mayta*, Seix Barral)

33.4.2 Question and exclamation marks

Spanish is unique among the world's languages in that a question or exclamation must be introduced by an upside-down question or exclamation mark, and followed by normal question and exclamation marks. The logic behind this rule is that it enables readers to start the intonation for a question or exclamation at the right point, so words which are not included in the interrogatory or exclamatory intonation pattern lie outside the signs:

Oye, ¿quieres una cerveza?	hey, d'you want a beer?
Hace calor, ¿verdad?	it's hot, isn't it?
–Si te digo que no he gastado más que dos mil pesetas, ¿me vas a creer?	if I tell you I've only spent 2000 ptas, will you believe me?
Pero, ¡qué estupidez!	but what stupidity!
¡Lo voy a hacer! ¿Me oyes?	I'm going to do it! D'you hear me?
etc.	

33.5 Division of words at end of line

A thorough knowledge of the structure of Spanish syllables is necessary for a good pronunciation, and students should consult manuals of phonology and phonetics for precise details. As far as word division at the end of a line is concerned, the following rules apply:

(a) The following combinations of written consonants are not divided: *ch, ll, rr*, and combinations of stops and liquids, i.e.

br	*cr*	*fr*	*gɾ*	*pr*	*dr*	*tr*
bl	*cl*	*fl*	*gl*	*pl*		

(b) Bearing in mind that the combinations listed under (a) count as one consonant, a single consonant is always grouped with the following vowel:

ha-ba	*ro-ca*	*nu-do*	*a-gua*	*Ma-hón*	*pe-lo*	*ra-za*
ha-cha	*ca-lle*	*pe-rro*	*ca-bra*	*co-fre*	*o-tro*	*co-pla*

and no syllable begins with more than one consonant:

cal-do	*cos-ta*	*cuan-do*	*par-te*	*can-cha*
as-ma	*hem-bra*	*em-ble-ma*	*com-bi-nar*	*in-na-to*
ex-cla-mar	*con-lle-var*	*cons-truc-ción*		
al-co-hol	*re-hén*	*pa-guen*	*se-quí-a*	*blan-den-gue*
re-zon-gar				

(c) Any two adjacent strong vowels (*a*, *e*, *o*) may be split:
A-te-ne-o co-ar-ta-da le-a ca-os a-é-re-o
But in practice it is considered inelegant to begin a line with a single vowel,
so *Ate-neo*, *a-é-reo* are preferred.

(d) Combinations of weak vowels (*i*, *u*) with another weak vowel or
with a strong vowel (*a*, *e*, *o*) may only be split if an accent is written on a
weak vowel. Thus
*viu-do cié-na-ga fiel-tro can-táis a-ma-bais bue-no
ha-cia re-cien-te*
but –
pa-ís re-ís hu-ís pí-o ha-cí-amos

Notes (i) The above rules are always valid and reflect the pronunciation; but the Academy
rules that when a word is clearly divisible on etymological grounds it may be split
accordingly, and some may prefer an etymological division:
de-sa-gra-da-ble or *des-a-gra-da-ble*
in-ter-re-la-cio-na-do (words in *interr-* are properly divided thus)
vos-o-tros or *vo-so-tros*
sud-a-me-ri-ca-no or *su-da-me-ri-ca-no*
etc.

(ii) Any of these rules is overridden to avoid a comic or shocking result. One does not
write *sa-cerdote*, *cal-culo*, *al ser-vicio del gobierno*, etc. (examples from Martínez de Sousa).

(iii) There is confusion over the combination *tl*. The rule is that it is optionally separable,
except in the words *a-tlas*, *a-tle-ta* and any of their derivatives.

(iv) Foreign words should be divided according to the rules prevailing in the language of
origin.
(Sources: I.R. Macpherson (1975), *Nuevas normas* (1959), J. Martínez de Sousa (1974)).

Appendix: Notes on pronunciation

The following minimal account of Spanish pronunciation must be supplemented by study of native speech habits. Phonetic transcriptions are based on the International Phonetic Alphabet modified for the sake of clarity.[1]

Vowels

The Spanish vowel system is very simple, but no Spanish vowel corresponds exactly to anything in southern British or standard American English. There is relatively little variation in the pronunciation of vowels throughout the Hispanic world.

There are five vowels:

a /a/ as in French *sa*. Shorter than father: *cama* /káma/, *las* /las/.

e /e/ in open syllables (ones ending in a vowel), as in French *ses* /se/. Much shorter than English *day*, and with no trace of a final *y* sound: *pero* /péro/, *debe* /déβe/, *te* /te/. In most closed syllables (i.e. ones ending in a consonant), before /x/ and before and after /rr/ it is somewhat closer to English ten: *puerta* /pwérta/, *ven* /ben/, *dejo* /déxo/, *tierra* /tjérra/, *reto* /rréto/.

i · /i/ like French *vite*; shorter than seat and with no trace of a final *y* sound: *si* /si/, *Lima* /líma/.

[1]The unfamiliar signs are
β *b* in Spanish *lobo*; not found in English.
ð *th* in English *that*.
γ *g* in Spanish *lago*; not found in English.
θ *th* in English *think*.
j *y* in English *yacht*.
rr *rr* in Spanish *perro*; not found in English.
tʃ *ch* in English *church*, but not aspirated.
x *ch* in Scottish *loch* or *j* in Spanish *ajo*.
ʎ *ll* in Spanish *calle*; not found in English.
ñ *ñ* in Spanish *caña*; not found in English.
ŋ *ng* in American or Southern British *sing*.
ʒ *j* in French *jour* or *g* in *beige*.
An acute accent marks the stressed vowel.
The table of consonants contains further details on the pronunciation of these unfamiliar signs.

416

o   /o/   in open syllables (ending in a vowel) like shortened French trop; much shorter than close and with no trace of a final *w* sound: *cosa* /kósa/, *lodo* /lóðo/. In closed syllables (ones ending in a consonant), before /x/ and before or after /rr/ somewhat closer to English not: *corte* /kórte/, *tonto* /tonto/, *corre* /kórre/, *roto* /rróto/.

u   /u/   like French coup. Shorter and more rounded than soon and with no trace of final *w* sound: *uso* /úso/, *cuyo* /kújo/. Silent in the combinations *gue/gui*, *que/qui*, pronounced /ge/, /gi/, /ke/, /ki/. A dieresis preserves the *u*: *güe* = /gwe/, *güi* = /gwi/, cf. *nicaragüense* /nikaraɣwénse/, *lingüista* /liŋgwísta/.

Diphthongs (not exhaustive)

ai, ay	/aj/	like English sigh: *dais* /dajs/
au	/aw/	like English cow: *causa* /káwsa/
eu	/ew/	*e* (as in bed) + *w*: *Europa* /ewrópa/
ei, ey	/ej/	like say: *deis* /dejs/, *ley* /lej/
ia, ya	/ja/	*y* + Spanish *a*: *cambia* /kámbja/, *ya* /ja/
ie, hie, ye	/je/	like yes: *tiene* /tjéne/, *hierro* /jérro/, *yermo* /jérmo/
io, yo	/jo/	*y* + Spanish *o*: *pasión* /pasjón/, *yo* /jo/
iu	/ju/	*y* + *u*: *viuda* /bjúða/
oi, oy	/oj/	like *oy* : *sois* /sojs/, *voy* /boj/
ua, hua	/wa/	like *w* + Spanish *a*: *cuando* /kwándo/, *Chihuahua* /tʃiwáwa/
ue, hue	/we/	like *w* + Spanish *e*: *cuenta* /kwénta/, *hueco* /wéko/
ui	/wi/	like *w* + Spanish *i*: *fui* /fwi/, *ruin* /rrwin/
uo	/wo/	like *w* + Spanish *o*: *asiduo* /asíðwo/

The following triphthongs are also common:

iai as in	/jajs/	like 'yice': *cambiáis* /kambjájs/
iei	/jejs/	like 'yace': *cambiéis* /kambjéjs/
uai	/wajs/	like 'wice': *conceptuáis* /konθeptwájs/ (SA /konseptwájs/)
uei	/wejs/	like 'wace': *conceptuéis* /konθeptwéjs/ (SA /konseptwéjs/)

If the above combinations of vowels are not pronounced as diphthongs or triphthongs, i.e. if an *i* or *u* is stressed, this is indicated by writing the accent on the stressed vowel: *pa-ís* /país/ *huí* /u-í/ (not */wi/), *lío* /lí-o/, *haríais* /arí-ajs/, *continúo* /kontinú-o/ (compare *continuo* /kontínwo/).

Vowel length plays no part in determining the meaning of Spanish words, and all vowels tend to be uniformly short and of the same quality, whether stressed or not: all the *a*s of *la alabará* sound about the same, /lalaβará/. Compare the *a*s in the English 'Panama Canal'.

Identical vowels are pronounced as a single vowel, somewhat lengthened in careful diction: *le enviamos* /lembjámos/, *a Ana* /ána/, *la armonía* /larmonía/, *dio órdenes* /djórðenes/.

Diphthongs, i.e. combinations of weak vowels (*i* and *u*) with strong vowels (*a*, *e* and *o*), are pronounced as described earlier. Adjacent dissimilar strong vowels, i.e. combinations of *a*, *e*, *o*, do not form diphthongs but are nevertheless run together in rapid speech to form a single syllable while retaining their separate values. In other words *la encuesta* is pronounced /laeŋ-kwés-ta/ (three syllables) even in rapid speech, not */leŋ-kwés-ta/, and *yo he observado* is pronounced /joeoβserβáðo/ (four syllables). English speakers find it difficult to avoid inserting a glottal stop, *y* or *w* between such vowels.

Consonants

Spanish consonants are more subject to regional variations, especially *c/z*, *s*, *ll*, and *y*.

b & v   These two consonants are pronounced the same, and the following pairs are identical in Spanish: *novel/Nobel* /noβél/, *rebela/revela* /rreβéla/, *Ribas/Rivas* /rríβas/, *la base/lavase* /laβáse/, *boto/voto* /bóto/, etc.

   b/v has two pronunciations. The less frequent is as English **b**ed, found only after *m* or *n* or at the head of a breathgroup:[2] *gamba* /gámba/, *en verano* /emberáno/, *¿Dónde vives? Valencia* 'Where do you live? Valencia' where the reply is the first word in a breathgroup and is pronounced /balénθja/ (SA /balénsja/).

   In all other contexts *b* and *v* are pronounced as a voiced bilabial fricative /β/, a sound which does not exist in English. It is produced by murmuring through barely opened lips: *uva* /úβa/, *labio* /láβjo/, *lo ve* /loβé/, *de Buenos Aires* /deβwenosájres/.

   The sound /v/ as in English 'vat' does not exist in Spanish.

c   (1) before *a*, *o*, *u* as /k/, i.e. like *c* in French **c**ar or as in English **c**ar but without the following aspiration: *cama* /káma/, *cosa* /kósa/, *cuanto* /kwánto/.

   (2) before *e*, *i*: in Central Spain, including Madrid, as /θ/, i.e. like English **th**ink; in Southern Spain and everywhere in Spanish America like English **s**ink: *cero* /θéro/ or /séro/, *hice* /íθe/ or /íse/, *nación* /naθjón/ or /nasjón/.

ch   /tʃ/ i.e. as in English **ch**urch but without the following aspiration: *mucho* /mútʃo/, *chaqueta* /tʃakéta/.

---

[2]By breathgroup is meant a string of sounds pronounced with an uninterrupted flow of breath. 'Words' are not separated within a breathgroup, cf. *¿Dónde está Miguel? No sé . . . A lo mejor está en la otra habitación.* 'Where's Miguel? I don't know . . . Perhaps he's in the other room', which consists of three breathgroups in uninterrupted speech: /dondestámiɣél nosé alomexórestáenlaotraβ itaθjón/.

d   (1) /d/ as in French *dire*. This sound is heard only after *n* and *l* or at the head of a breathgroup: *en Dinamarca* /endinamárka/, *falda*, /fálda/, *el día* /eldía/, *¿Dónde?* /dónde/. English *d* is alveolar, i.e. pronounced against the ridge of gum behind the upper teeth; French and Spanish /d/ is dental, i.e. pronounced by pressing the tongue against the upper teeth. The difference is audible to Spanish speakers.

(2) /ð/ approximately as in English **th**is. This is the pronunciation of Spanish *d* in other contexts. Between vowels (especially in the ending -*ado*) and at the end of words it is pronounced very softly or sometimes not at all. It is better pronounced too faintly in these contexts than too hard, but foreigners are not expected to drop it altogether. Natives have a fine ear for the difference between *lado* pronounced /laðo/ with the faintest of /ð/s, which is standard educated pronunciation, *lao* with no consonant, i.e. /lao/, which is familiar and informal, and the diphthongized form /lau/ which is considered vulgar or dialect. Examples: *Madrid* /maðrí(ð)/, *rueda* /rrwéða/, *le da dos* /leðaðós/, *hablado* /aβláðo/, *tenido* /teníðo/.

f   /f/, i.e. as in English **f**at.

g   (1) before *e* and *i* as /x/, i.e. the same as Spanish *j*, like the *ch* in German la**ch**en, a**ch**: *general* /xenerál/, *auge* /áwxe/, *Gibraltar* /xiβraltár/. Most Spanish Americans soften it to almost an English *h*.

(2) before *a*, *o*, *u* it has two pronunciations:

(a) /g/ as in English **g**et. This is the less frequent sound and occurs only after *n* and at the head of a breathgroup: *tango* /táŋgo/, *en Grecia* /eŋgréθja⁻ (SA /eŋgrésja/), *¡Gabriel!* /gaβrjél/.

(b) /γ/, i.e. a voiced velar fricative, not found in English. The tongue and throat are in the same position as for the hard /g/ but no closure takes place: *lago* /láγo/, *la gama* /laγáma/, *la bodega* /laβoðéγa/, *tu garaje* /tuγaráxe/.

    The combinations *gue* and *gui* are pronounced /ge/ and /gi/. *Güe* and *güi* are pronounced /gwe/ and /gwi/, cf. *pague* /páγe/ and *desagüe* /desáγwe/.

h   always silent, except in some rural dialects. A few words are distinguished by spelling alone, e.g. *ha/a* /a/, *hasta/asta* /ásta/, *hierro/yerro*, /jérro/ *hecho/echo* /étʃo/, etc.

j   /x/, i.e. a voiceless velar fricative like the *ch* in lo**ch** or German la**ch**en: *Méjico* /méxiko/ (Mexicans spell the word *México* but pronounce it the same), *ojo* /óxo/, *jirafa* /xiráfa/. *G* is pronounced exactly the same as *j* before *e* and *i*, so *jira* and *gira* are both pronounced /xíra/. Most Spanish-Americans pronounce it softer, like the *h* in **h**at.

k   like French *k* in kilo. Same as **k**ill but without aspiration. Found only in foreign words, e.g. *kilogramo* /kiloγrámo/, *kilómetro* /kilómetro/.

l   /l/, i.e. like *l* in British English leaf and not like the 'dark *l*' of fold or of American English live, leaf: *falda* /fálda/, *lirio* /lírjo/, *cal* /kal/.

ll   (1) /ʎ/, a palatalized /l/, i.e. *l* pronounced with the tongue flat against the roof of the mouth: *calle* /káʎe/, *llamar* /ʎamár/. This sound does not exist in English and English speakers often replace it by the *lli* of million, which is in fact spelt *li* in Spanish as in *alianza* /aljánθa/ (SA /aljánsa/). Students who have difficulty with /ʎ/ should adopt the following pronunciation:
(2) /j/, i.e. like *y* in *y*acht. This is the pronunciation of the majority of speakers on both continents. Purists complain, but the battle against *yeísmo* is probably a lost cause.
   In Argentina it is normally pronounced /ʒ/, i.e. like the *j* in French *jour*.

m   /m/ as in English. At the end of a word it is usually pronounced like *n*: *mero* /méro/, *remueve*, /rremwéβe/, *álbum* /álβun/.

n   Pronunciation depends on the following sound:
(1) before /g/, /k/, /x/ as /ŋ/, i.e. *ng* in si*ng*er: *cinco* /θíŋko/ (SA /siŋko/), *en Grecia* /eŋgréθja/ (SA /eŋgrésja/), *en Jamaica* /eŋxamájka/. Some people pronounce it thus at the end of a word.
(2) before /m/, /p/, /b/ like *m*: *en Madrid* /emmaðrí(ð)/, *con Pedro* /kompéðro/, *en balde* /embálde/, *enviar* /embjár/, *en verano* /emberáno/.
(3) elsewhere like English *n*: *duende* /dwénde/, *kontestan* /kontéstan/, *nadan* /náðan/.

ñ   /ñ/, i.e. a palatalized /n/. This sound does not exist in English. It is found in French oignon, but the *ni* of onion is spelt *ni* in Spanish and pronounced /nj/: *Tania* /tánja/ is quite different from *taña*. Pronounce *ñ* with the tongue flat against the roof of the mouth: *sueño* /swéño/, *España* /espáña/.

p   /p/ i.e. as in French *p*ar. Same as English s*p*ot but not as in *p*ot where it is aspirated: *pata* /páta/ *el pie* /elpjé/.

q   This occurs only in the combinations *qui* and *que* which are pronounced /ki/, /ke/: *química* /kímika/, *saque* /sáke/.

r   (1) /r/ a flapped *r*, pronounced with a single tap of the tongue: *ahora* /aóra/, *cara* /kára, *el bar* /elβár/.
(2) at the beginning of a word and after *l, n* or *s* the same as *rr* below: *la rueda* /larrwéða/, *una rata* /unarráta/, *alrededor* /alrreðeðór/, *sonrisa* /sonrrísa/, *israelí* /irraelí/ (it is correct to drop *s* before /rr/, but not all speakers do).

rr   /r/ A trilled *r* with several taps of the tongue: *perro* /pérro/, *arriba* /arríβa/, *corre* /kórre/. In some American regions it is pronounced as a fricative somewhat similar to Castilian Spanish *s*.

s   There are two pronunciations, but *s* as in snow will suffice for most purposes.

(1) In standard Castilian, i.e. the Spanish of Castile and Central Spain, a 'cacuminal' *s*, pronounced with the tip of the tongue against the alveolar ridge. The effect on Spanish-American ears is rather like *sh*.

(2) Elsewhere, including Spanish America, like *s* in snow: *rosa* /rrósa/, *los hermanos* /losermános/, *hasta* /ásta/.

Before voiced consonants it is voiced, though less than the *s* of English rose, and this pronunciation must be avoided in other contexts: *desde* /dézðe/, *más grande* /mazɣránde/, *tres vinos* /trezβínos/.

In Andalusia, the Southern Cone, Venezuela, Central America and Cuba, but not in most of Mexico, Peru and Colombia, it is pronounced like English *h* in **h**at at the end of a syllable, and in some dialects is dropped altogether in this position: *las puertas* /lahpwértah/, *los cascabeles* /lohkahkaβéleh/, *mismo* /míhmo/.

t	/t/, i.e. a voiceless dental stop as in French **t**on. English *t* is not pronounced against the teeth but against the alveolar ridge, and is often aspirated: *toro* /tóro, *tres* /tres/, *hasta* /ásta/.
(v)	pronounced the same as Spanish *b*, q.v.
w	in foreign words only, as Spanish *b/v*, e.g. *el wáter* /elβáter/, or more or less as English *w*, e.g. *whisk(e)y* /wíski/ or /gwíski/.
x	Usually as /ks/ or /ɣz/, but very often /s/ before consonants: *taxi* /táksi/, *extra* /ékstra/, /éstra/, *examen* /eɣzámen/.
y	most commonly as /j/, i.e. *y* in *y*acht, but often preceded by a faint *d* sound at the beginning of a word: *yo* /jo/, /djo/, *mayo* /májo/, *reyes* /rréjes/. In some parts it sounds like the *j* of jam. In Argentina and Uruguay it is usually pronounced /ʒ/, i.e. like the *j* of French jour or the *g* of beige.
	Many speakers make no distinction between *y* and *ll*.
z	(1) In Castilian (i.e. Madrid, Central Spain) as /θ/, i.e. *th* in English **th**ink: *lazo* /láθo/, *precoz* /prekóθ/.
	(2) In Southern Spain and throughout Spanish America the same as Spanish *s*. For Spanish Americans the following pairs sound the same: *casa/caza* /kása/, *mazada/masada* /masáða/, *tasa/taza*, /tasa/, *loza/losa* /lósa/, etc. *C* before *e* and *i* (see above under *c*) is pronounced the same as *z*.

Stress

In all polysyllabic words one syllable is always stressed. The position of the stressed syllable is not strictly speaking predictable, but it can always be deduced from the (correctly) written form of the word by the following rules:

(a) A vowel marked by an acute accent is always stressed:
nación /naθjón/ (SA /nasjón/), *dámelo* /dámelo/, *pregúntenselo*

/preɣúntenselo/, *volví* /bolβí/, etc.

(b) If no written accent appears then:

(i) if the word ends in a vowel or *n* or *s* it is stressed on the penultimate syllable: *admite* /aðmíte/, *izquierdista* /iθkjerðísta/ (SA /iskjerðísta/), *hacen* /áθen/ (SA /ásen/), *origen* /oríxen/, *respondes* /rrespóndes/ *paraguas* /paráɣwas/;

(ii) if the word ends in any consonant other than *n* or *s* it is stressed on the last syllable: *Madrid* /maðrí(ð)/, *natural* /naturál/, *feroz* /feróθ/ (SA /ferós/), *prever* /preβér/, *Paraguay* /paraɣwáj/.

It is worth repeating that stressed and unstressed vowels in Spanish sound more or less the same. There is no 'Italian' lengthening or drawling of stressed vowels (the Spanish of some parts of the Southern Cone excepted), and no significant tendency to reduce unstressed vowels as there is in English, French and Portuguese.[3]

---

[3]Omission of unstressed vowels is often heard in Mexico, including the capital, and in parts of the Andes, e.g. /tresjénts/ for *trescientos*, /ofsína/ for *oficina*.

Index

Forms preceded by an asterisk are rejected by educated speakers.

Forms preceded by ? are not universally accepted.

For irregular verbs not listed in this index see Table of Irregular Verbs 13.4, pp. 177–183.

English alphabetical order is used.

1 'Cleft sentences': sentences of the type 'it's here that I saw it', 'it was then that it happened', 'it's her I want to talk to', etc.